Educating Children with Diverse Abilities

editors
Adrian Ashman & John Elkins

Pearson Education Australia
Unit 4, Level 2
14 Aquatic Drive
Frenchs Forest NSW 2086

First published 2002

Publisher: Catherine Godfrey
Project Editor: Kathryn Fairfax
Copy Editor: Ross Gilham
Indexer: Russell Brooks
Cover and internal design: Green Words and Images
Typeset by Midland Typesetters, Maryborough, Victoria
Printed in Malaysia

1 2 3 4 5 06 05 04 03 02

ISBN 1 74009 632 0

National Library of Australia
Cataloguing-in-Publication Data

Educating children with diverse abilities.

[1st ed.].
Bibliography.
Includes index.
ISBN 1 74009 632 0.

1. Special education. 2. Inclusive education. I. Ashman, Adrian F. (Adrian Frederick). II. Elkins, John, 1940– .

371.9

An imprint of Pearson Education Australia

Contents

3 The school context 73

JOHN ELKINS

4 Early schooling for infants and children with diverse abilities 114

ANNE JOBLING AND SUSANA GAVIDIA-PAYNE

SECTION 2 THE RESPONSIVE SCHOOL COMMUNITY 167

5 Behaviour in and out of the classroom 172

ROBERT CONWAY

About this book

Since the first edition of *Educating children with special needs* was released more than ten years ago, the educational systems in our region have undergone major changes. These have not been as monumental as the collapse of the Soviet Union or the disintegration of the country we knew as Yugoslavia, or as catastrophic as the spread of the HIV/AIDS virus around our world. Nevertheless, the changes in educational systems have affected millions of people.

In all states and territories in Australia and in New Zealand, education departments have endured review and restructuring and, in most cases, more than once. Major areas or sections within departments have been blended with others and some have been abolished altogether. In the process, the devolution of administrative and financial responsibilities via school-based management has given school principals and senior staff a greater say in how funds are spent at the local level than ever before.

For the purpose of this book, one of the major changes has been the demise of a field called "special education". Ten years ago in all educational authorities, the special education department or directorate was a potent administrative body. Staff in these offices supported teachers across their states or jurisdictions, developed and ran inservice programs, prepared and distributed resource materials, and liaised with others responsible for the curriculum at the primary-school and secondary-school levels. Although special education was an important sector of education, teaching in this field was not necessarily an attractive career path, and special education students were not an altogether popular group of children with whom a teacher might wish to work.

In general terms, special education no longer exists. The emphasis is upon the provision of opportunities for all students in regular schools and classes regardless of their skills and abilities, gender and ethnic origin, disability, or impairment. A small group of educators remains responsible for supporting teachers who work with students who have very high support needs, or for whom the regular curriculum is unlikely to be suitable. In short, most students who once were termed "special" now receive all—or a major part—of their education in regular classes.

The concept of inclusion—providing relevant and appropriate learning opportunities in regular classes and regular schools—is a fundamental administrative policy. It refers to the active participation of students in regular education settings in a way

that is consistent with their skills, abilities or talents and the educational demands of the curriculum.

These changes, and the acceptance of inclusive policies and practices, have not been without costs. They have brought not only some satisfaction, but also frustration, to the students and their parents or advocates and to teachers—as a consequence of the demands placed upon public and private education systems alike.

Despite the general adherence to non-categorical models of education (i.e., placing emphasis upon the student's needs rather than upon the sensory, physical, psychological, or intellectual conditions that afflict them), there remains a need for a "source book" or "first reader" for those who are about to embark on a career in education. If you peruse the first edition of *Educating children with special needs* you will find it vastly different from this edition of *Educating children with diverse abilities*. However, this edition is still intended for students who are largely unfamiliar with the educational system (other than having been a product of it). It is designed to give you a broad understanding of the principles of inclusive education and the ways in which teachers deal with students with very diverse learning needs.

Readers of this book might be undergraduate students who are training to become teachers, those in other disciplines such as speech pathology, physiotherapy, occupational therapy, nursing, psychology, or those in adult and disability services. All benefit from knowing how to expand the learning opportunities for all children and how educators and supporting professionals can best serve the diverse needs and interests of these children. The book might also be relevant to postgraduate students who are intending to work in the area of learning support, or to those interested in familiarising themselves with that body of knowledge.

The primary purpose of a source book is to provide the reader with basic information. It is a starting-point in a search for knowledge. In this volume you will find guides to other resources that are now available on the World Wide Web and other major databases located in most comprehensive libraries. These are the virtual information repositories of knowledge that are part of our realities in this new century and millennium. So, as a source book, *Educating children with diverse abilities* is intended to stimulate your search for knowledge and to provide a mental map to guide your further research.

Using this book

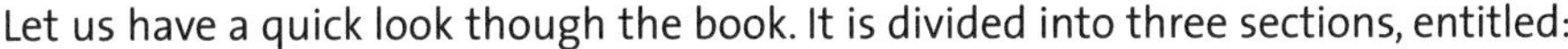

Let us have a quick look though the book. It is divided into three sections, entitled:

- Section 1 Setting the context for teaching and learning;
- Section 2 The responsive school community; and
- Section 3 Adapting curriculum and instruction.

Section 1 deals with a number of general issues related to the education of all students. This section introduces some important terms and concepts. It deals with our society and cultures, and highlights the significant impact of the family on the educational process for all children. It looks at the nature of schooling and, importantly, emphasises the crucial learning that occurs in the early years of life, and the value of play (see Chapter 4).

Section 2 introduces the educational provisions that have been developed largely for students in regular classes. The difficulties faced by many students in the past were often associated with an inflexible learning environment. In other words, students might succeed if the instructional setting—the school community—could accommodate the way in which children learn effectively. And, of importance to newly trained teachers in particular, student success would be enhanced if the school community could better accommodate the management of student behaviour and the creation of a classroom that facilitates learning.

In this section are chapters that deal with students' behaviour and with teaching methods that foster cooperation and collaboration. There are also creative ways of supporting students who have rare talents and skills, and others who are limited only by a sensory impairment. Most of the ideas and teaching strategies in the first two sections apply to all students, not just to those who have some learning restriction.

Section 3 deals with changes to the curriculum and instructional methods that might be necessary to support students for whom the regular class is not always appropriate. For some young people, only modest changes are required. For others, substantial adaptations are needed within the teaching–learning setting to enable them to achieve success at school, and in later life. We are not so much concerned about the problem condition as such, but about the limitations it places on the student, and how it can be overcome for each individual. Throughout this book, the authors have been keen to stress the importance of the individual. Each person is

unique and, hence, the way in which teaching and learning occurs is, by necessity, different for everyone.

Having considered the general structure of the book, let us look now at the structure of the chapters. In Section 1, the configurations of the chapters vary because of the information being presented. You can see what we mean by looking at the four outlines for Chapters 1, 2, 3 and 4 (pages 5, 41, 73, and 114 respectively).

In Sections 2 and 3, the chapters have a more consistent structure, but there are some idiosyncratic aspects. Turn to the beginning of Chapter 5 (page 172), which we can use as an example. In the first part of each chapter, the authors provide orientation and background information about the students and the area of study in general. These are considered under section headings about *definition of terms*, *prevalence*, the *areas of concern*, and *identification*. In the second part of each chapter, the contributing authors discuss the range of educational strategies that have been, and are, used to assist students to learn as effectively and efficiently as possible. This includes guidelines for the inclusion of the students in regular school settings, and some of the continuing challenges that are still to be addressed and overcome.

As this is a source book, at the end of each chapter you can find a section entitled "Suggested reading". The books, journals, and websites listed can guide you to important sources of information on the topic. We have included World Wide Web sites where you might locate reliable data. We are always tentative to do this for two reasons. First, website addresses (URLs) can change without notice and there are few things more frustrating than being unable to locate a resource where you have been told to look. Second, we prefer you to do your own searches because the Web is an exciting labyrinth where you can discover information that has particular appeal or interest to you, rather than be directed to look at only a limited number of sites. Our only reservation is that you be very sceptical about the information you might find on personal URLs. There is no intellectual or professional censorship imposed on websites. Websites of professional bodies and associations are likely to be accurate, but this might not be the case elsewhere. Let the user beware.

In every learning situation, the outcome is always dependent upon personal effort. So, you can also find a further section at the end of each chapter entitled "Practical activities". The intent of this section should be self-evident, but it is important to make two comments.

First, understanding the needs of any students and about how best to facilitate their learning does not come only from reading. Teaching and learning are personal experiences and you can gain immeasurably from your course of study if you make personal contact with students who have a wide range of learning needs, and with those assisting them (e.g., parents, teachers, specialist consultants, therapists, and

counsellors). The practical activities urge you to learn about these individuals and to synthesise your ideas.

Second, be willing to share your discoveries with your fellow students, workmates, and family members. The underlying agenda of this book is the need to understand and appreciate the lives of people who are struggling with the problems and challenges of an ever-changing world, just as you are.

We hope that reading this book proves to be as stimulating for you as the preparation of it has been for us. We wish you success in your endeavours.

Adrian Ashman and John Elkins

About the contributors

Dr Michael Arthur, Lecturer, Special Education Centre, Faculty of Education, The University of Newcastle.

Professor Adrian F. Ashman, Schonell Special Education Research Centre, The University of Queensland.

Emeritus Professor Eddie Braggett, Charles Sturt University, Wagga Wagga.

Associate Professor Robert Conway, Special Education Centre, Faculty of Education, The University of Newcastle.

Joanna Curzon, Senior Advisor Special Education, Ministry of Education, New Zealand.

Professor John Elkins, Schonell Special Education Research Centre, The University of Queensland.

Dr Susana Gavidia-Payne, Research Coordinator, Victorian Parenting Centre.

Dr Robyn M. Gillies, Schonell Special Education Research Centre, The University of Queensland.

Dr Anne Jobling, Senior Lecturer, Schonell Special Education Research Centre, The University of Queensland.

Dr Christina E. van Kraayenoord, Senior Lecturer, Schonell Special Education Research Centre, The University of Queensland.

Dr Paul Pagliano, Senior Lecturer, Department of Special Education, James Cook University.

Associate Professor Ken Ryba, Coordinator, College of Education, Massey University.

Dr Linda Selby, Director of Professional Studies, Auckland College of Education.

Dr Jeff Sigafoos, Department of Special Education, University of Texas, Austin. Formerly Professor of Education, The University of Sydney.

Section 1

Setting the context for teaching and learning

From the beginning of the 20th century, it was taken for granted that primary and secondary schools were designed for students of average ability, when teaching and learning was based solely upon "the curriculum". In practical terms, this meant that students who were not average could attend if they did not place a strain on the regular class program or typical teaching practices. But who is average?

Students without clearly identifiable disabilities, but who had problems with learning, were sometimes held back to repeat a grade, or they left school if they were continuing to have difficulty when they reached 15 years of age. Those who were known to be very bright or talented had to survive as best they could in an environment that did not offer opportunities to excel. Any students who persistently exhibited unacceptable behaviour—despite their intellectual ability—could find themselves punished, suspended from school, or expelled.

To accommodate students who had a problem dealing with the regular curriculum, alternative educational experiences were developed, often outside the regular school system. Once these were established, usually to serve students with a specific diagnosis (e.g., intellectual disability, or a sense impairment), teachers and the public came to regard it as natural that there should be two systems of education, often with separate funding bases. By the 1970s in Australia and New Zealand it was clear that conditions in regular schools had become sufficiently flexible to enable them to serve students with learning and/or behaviour difficulties. Initially, these services were provided on a part-time basis, although sometimes full-time specialist tuition was provided to students outside the regular classroom, i.e., by withdrawing students and providing them with a special program.

Providing personalised learning support (e.g., teachers' aides, or therapists) was costly. Such support was available to a very small group of students in centralised locations, and was organised rationally, at least from the perspective of education administrators. Some special schools drew students from an entire state whereas

others required them to travel long distances by special buses or taxis so that they could receive their education in special schools or special classes within regular primary or secondary schools.

Education reform in the United States in the early 1970s led to a reconceptualisation of appropriate experiences and opportunities for students who attended special schools and classes. The terms *integration* and *inclusion* quickly became accepted as policies and practices that focused attention on what *could* be provided in regular school and regular classes, rather than what could *not* be provided. This reform had an effect on countries such as the United Kingdom, Australia, New Zealand, and many others. As examples of successful integration were publicised, parents, regular school staff, and guidance personnel became more favourably disposed toward the enrolment of students with disability or impairment in regular classes than they had been before. School systems adopted policies that espoused the transfer of students from special education sites, provided there were no adverse effects on regular students, and on the assumption that the cost of integrating students would be substantially less than maintaining them in a separate educational setting.

A hierarchy of special services was developed in Australia based on the concept of *least restrictive environment*—a term that had become widely accepted in the United States following the passage of the *Education of All Handicapped Children Act* in 1975. Until that time, professionals had typically made decisions about school placement and support services in Australia and New Zealand. However, the American innovation of case conferences to determine eligibility for services and to prescribe specific programs (called individualised education programs or IEPs) became accepted, and families were given some choice and allowed to contribute to the decision-making procedures. It should be noted that IEPs are called individual education programs or plans in various countries. In this book, however, the term individual education plan is used as it is commonly known in Australia.

As the number of support services expanded for children in the birth to preschool years and beyond the compulsory education age, parents became progressively more involved in decision-making. Similarly, as curricula expanded to include less academic elective subjects, parents and caregivers were accepted as partners in the process of educating students with special needs. Family centred services were common for infants and toddlers with disabilities, and for students with exceptional talents. In addition, parent advocacy and support groups grew strongly and constituted an important voice in promoting integration (i.e., bringing special students into regular classes and schools). Full inclusion of children in regular education settings with suitable support was the goal to which they strived. In other words, many parents actively sought the opportunity for their children to attend the

same schools as their brothers and sisters, but with support commensurate with their skills and abilities.

Debate about the education of students with diverse abilities has occurred in other places in the world. Perhaps the best national examples of full inclusion of students with learning difficulties are Italy and some parts of the United States and Canada where the term, inclusion, reflects the student's involvement in the class group. In other words, the student is not simply provided with the opportunity to participate fully in activities, but is assisted to do so. Relatively little evaluation of inclusion has been carried out, despite the fact that it has been advocated for many years. There are some reports of significant social gains through contact with peers but modest academic gains for students with high support needs. In many parts of the world, there are numerous individual examples of the success of including students with high support needs. These examples show that full inclusion *can* be successful, but it is also evident that there are many ways in which a regular class placement can prove challenging and unsatisfactory.

Although there has been some research comparing the effectiveness of integration and segregation, particularly for students with mild intellectual disability, in most cases the issue of inclusion is not amenable to contrast research. Emerging issues include teacher and student attitudes toward inclusion, the establishment of a supportive school climate, the availability of supportive resources, flexible classroom teaching–learning practices, and parental involvement in school activities. Thus, instead of asking *whether* inclusion is better than placement in a special education setting, we find participants asking *how* inclusion can be made a successful experience for all concerned. Not if, but how.

This leads to the issue of curriculum. The concept of the individual education plan (IEP) is fundamental to realistic programming for students with high support needs. The IEP process takes little account of the traditional mainstream curriculum but focuses on what is essential for a satisfying life both in the present, and when a child reaches adulthood. This is a clear example of fitting education to the student, rather than the reverse. So, if the IEP is to be successful in regular classrooms, there must be considerable flexibility in its curriculum content and in the pedagogical processes necessary to achieve the program goals.

There are two accepted curriculum contexts in regular classrooms. In the first, the student with special learning needs can participate with peers although attainments might not be as high as the ideal. In essence, this is little different from the situation that exists in many regular classrooms in which all students are expected to achieve but with varying degrees of success. For some students, the touchstone is access to the curriculum by providing sign interpreting or brailled texts. For others, cooperative learning activities can be used to stretch and challenge students with limited

intellectual abilities while, concurrently, they receive considerable support and encouragement from their peers.

The second circumstance occurs when a mainstream curriculum activity provides an opportunity for a student to learn something different while still participating in classroom activities with their peers. This provides the context in which all students can work on the same subject (e.g., mathematics, science) and even on the same general topic (e.g., the environment), but have different goals and realistic expectations, and use different materials.

Another perspective on inclusion comes from the belief that regular schools must change if they are to meet the needs of all students. This puts the concern to educate all students alongside other challenges in areas such as ethnicity, gender equity, and poverty. By developing a curriculum that is relevant to the diverse needs of students (sometimes called an inclusive curriculum), teachers can look at the educational needs rather than pay heed to labels that provide little information about how to provide an appropriate education that maximises academic and social development. Hence, schools need to display concern for the outcomes of schooling, particularly the quality of life enjoyed throughout at least the young adult years, if not beyond.

In this first section, we consider some of the fundamental issues concerning the education of all students. In Chapter 1, Ashman deals with the global context that includes the social and cultural aspects of education. In Chapter 2, Ashman and Elkins focus on issues of human rights and discrimination, and provide an historical overview of the way in which special education services have been provided internationally. In Chapter 3, Elkins focuses upon the challenges faced by education authorities, systems, schools, and individual teachers in providing effective and efficient teaching–learning experiences for all students. In Chapter 4, Jobling and Gavidia-Payne draw attention to the importance of the early years of life as the significant foundation for later learning.

1

Society, culture, and education

ADRIAN ASHMAN

Case studies

As you read the two brief case studies below, think about the range of problems that each of the teachers might encounter and how they could resolve them. Are there issues to do with culture, student behaviour, contact between the school and the parents, or the appropriateness of the curricula that they are required to present? Are there attitudes and beliefs that each of the teachers might project to facilitate the teaching–learning process?

Julie Andersen, Year 8

Her friends and colleagues told Julie Andersen that it could not get much worse. And sometimes she agreed with them. She had not been this cold since she had lain, with a broken ankle, in the snow on a windswept mountainside waiting for the arrival of the ski patrol. But this was not Colorado. It was a Melbourne classroom in the middle of winter. It was raining and she was wearing the equivalent of four layers of clothing and was still frozen to the core of her existence. The students were too.

The students. Well, it was Year 8. There were 29 in her English class. Twelve nationalities. Her students spoke nine languages other than English. There were three boys who understood about half of what she said, if that, having been relatively new arrivals to Australia. There were two boys whom she suspected of dealing drugs, and a girl who Julie knew came to school each morning affected by her drug of choice.

And there was George, a meek Australian who seemed to be unhappy most of the time. She knew a little about George. He told her a few secrets when she shared her lunch with him one day when his hunger was as obvious as his curly brown hair. His stepfather was physically abusive and it was only a matter of weeks—or days—before George would no longer be sitting in the third row in her classroom but homeless: a street kid.

But there were so many things about her motley group that she adored. The curriculum Julie was supposed to follow had been thrown out of the window in early March, and it was never recovered. Okay, she had not completely trashed the principles but the specifics were as unrecoverable as the contents of a virus-ridden computer.

Twelve nationalities. Opportunities for 13 cultural experiences. And she milked the kids for all she could get. The craziest thing was that they saw Julie Andersen as the leader of their pack. They would walk over red-hot coals for her. Take revenge against anyone who might challenge or threaten her.

Julie did everything she could to have her students understand and appreciate the diversity of culture. Instead of the usual English books that students in the other Year 8 classes were trying to avoid reading, her students brought in books in their own languages (even English) and parents were invited to the school to tell the stories. Even Con (yes, he was a green grocer), who worked 14 hours a day, came to tell his version of the book his son had brought along as his contribution to the study of Language in Culture. The class ate sweetmeats from 13 cultures, vegetarian dishes

from 13 cultures, and recited prayers from the same 13. Julie was amazed that six deities could have caused so much havoc over the centuries, but pleased that, in her class, the same gods were all benign.

Meadow Park, Northern Territory—Year 3

Jim Samson was born in central Australia. His people are traditional owners of the land that includes the most awe-inspiring geological features on the Australian continent, the rock known as Uluru.

When he was 20, Jim went to Adelaide and was trained as a teacher. Now he lives in Darwin with his wife Jenny and their two children. Then there are his other children, 31 independent thinkers in his Year 3 class.

Each year for the past five, Jim's class has been split about 50:50 indigenous children to Caucasians. It has not been easy to deal with two prominent cultures. The Aboriginal parents expect Jim to teach and uphold traditional values. The White Australians (a term Jim prefers to avoid when he can) expect him to teach in the same way as Murphy O'Rourke in the adjacent Year 3 class.

Being Aboriginal has created some problems for Jim as he has attempted to accommodate two societies and, to quote him, "There are times when I've been stunningly successful, but it's a bit like doing magic tricks on a tightrope."

Jim's classroom is a predictable environment in which everyone understands and adheres to clearly articulated classroom rules. They make the rules on the first day every year. There are courtesies established that respect each culture and very few communication and behavioural irregularities. Jim is tough and kind. He has always been an advocate of small group work and all of his students are quite familiar with the expectations that accompany cooperative learning and problem-solving activities.

"Sometimes I'm just amazed at how well the kids work together. I think things have changed over the past ten years or so. Cultural differences just don't seem to have the same effects on my kids as they did on their parents."

It has taken a few years for Jim to establish the right blend of individual and group work, the right blend of traditional Aboriginal and White values and beliefs, and the right mix of myths and legends and contemporary technologies and issues. Jim admits that being a teacher is stressful.

"One of the things I try to do as often as I can is to draw out each student's strengths, which means providing as many opportunities as I can for them to contribute and feel appreciated. I don't see my class in terms of colour. It's not a matter of black and white. I want every one of them to grow up to be a good citizen who respects the rights, customs, laws, and beliefs of others while appreciating the values of their own culture at the same time. It's not been easy and I've got a long way to go. Maybe I'll achieve it one year before I retire."

What you will learn in this chapter

This chapter provides a general orientation to the context in which teaching and learning occurs. All students are subject to the same general influences of society and the dominant culture that prevails. Of course, there are huge individual differences among children and adolescents that make the process of education a stunningly individual one. In this chapter you will learn:

- how society and culture are defined;
- about the influence of the family on educational opportunities;
- about the different types of families and the effect these have on children's education;
- about prejudice;
- about learning that occurs inside and outside the classroom;
- how school communities can accommodate cultural and social diversity; and
- how school professionals and parents can collaborate to enhance the effectiveness of the school community.

Diversity and variation

Diversity and variation are as fundamental to human existence as the air we breathe. Even twins who develop from the same fertilised ovum express individuality, experience private events, and react to the world and others in ways peculiar to each of them alone. If this is true, then the process of learning—of being educated—is also an intensely personal experience despite the reality of classrooms containing 10, 20, 100, or 1,000 warm bodies and textbooks, lessons, and lectures that are designed for the mythical average student.

What is to be learnt over the course of a person's life, and how that knowledge is to be transmitted, is dictated by society and its culture. Hence, education is concerned not only with socialisation but also with the preservation of social order. Schools are venues for learning, but they are also agencies of social control. Children and teenagers are required to attend school from the age of six to 15 years (16 years in Tasmania) despite their willingness or otherwise to do so. Parents must ensure that their children attend and penalties can be imposed if parents do not comply or have not put into place an appropriate alternative educational program, such as homeschooling. Some writers have also drawn attention to the clustering of school buildings that isolate students from the outside world in a prison-like manner. Still others refer to the imposition of discipline and management policies that are aimed at maintaining control, such as wearing school uniforms, and observing school routines, bells, and timetables. In some places, physical punishment for misdemeanours is still tolerated and practised (see Foster & Harmen, 1992).

Whether these forms of social control are necessary will remain debatable for the foreseeable future. What is important here, however, is how educational outcomes are intimately linked to society and culture.

The fabric of society

The evolution of any society—the collection of persons living together in a more-or-less-ordered community—occurs concurrently with the development of its culture. Culture has been defined in many ways. The modern understanding is of a storehouse of essentially human or national values, but it also has a social-historical sense to do with meaning-bearing activities of all forms (Mulhern, 2000). To bring this into focus, culture can be viewed as the collection of norms, values, beliefs, traditions, activities, language, achievements, and possessions that characterise a group of people. In Australia, the dominant English-speaking culture emphasises the role of the nuclear family unit, Christian religious beliefs and practices, work and recreation/leisure ethics, and the valuing of material possessions (see Bennett, Emmison, & Frow, 1999). In New Zealand, Maoritanga (the concepts of Maori culture and perspectives) operates alongside the English-speaking culture to sustain the values, beliefs, and teachings of the indigenous peoples.

In Australia, as in many other Western societies (such as the United States, France, Canada, and the United Kingdom), there has been a broadening of the cultural mosaic as those who have immigrated to make a new life in their adopted country maintain their own traditions while embracing the dominant culture to a greater or lesser extent. As a consequence of this, multiculturalism is part of the political rhetoric and a sometimes-stunning reality in many communities. Consider, for example, that around 24% of Australians were born in other countries and nearly half of the population has direct links with relatives born overseas. About 2.5 million people speak a language other than English at home (Australian Bureau of Statistics, 1997, 2000b).

Hence, while the primarily British–North American culture remains dominant, there is a continuing diversification of influences and an acceptance or aspects of other traditions that enrich our community. One only has to walk the aisles of any supermarket to appreciate the impact of Asian, Indian, and Middle Eastern eating habits.

Families and education

The family is generally considered to be the foundation of society. Indeed, satisfying the needs of the family might have been the only consideration when such groups banded together to form the earliest communities. But changes have occurred over the millennia and, in society today, one might argue that the permanence of the collective is more important than the survival of any part of it. Nevertheless, the family unit remains crucial for guiding the growth and development of children. Its influence

extends beyond the reproduction and nurturing of offspring into the physical and economic, emotional, and psychological domains that affect the provision of a loving, caring, and secure environment. The family also plays an often-underestimated role in the education of children. In the early years of life, for example, children learn to manipulate the physical surroundings and those within them: an apprehensive whimper in the middle of the night will often lead to a period of comfort provided by an ever-attendant parent. In later years, children learn to take their place in society and to conform to conventions of right and wrong in a vast range of situations.

The first years of the child's life are arguably the most important, for it is during this period that the basic intellectual and emotional (affective) aspects of learning are established (e.g., meaning-making, curiosity, and persistence). Schools use this constellation of behaviours to extend the child's social and cultural knowledge and, in certain situations, to replace some of the child's expressed attitudes and beliefs that might not correspond to those held by society in general. The knowledge gained by the child during these early years is dependent to a large degree on the organisation of the family and the dynamics that occur within it. This, in turn, becomes the foundation on which teaching and learning is based during the decade—or more—of formal schooling.

Indigenous peoples

It is impossible to write about society, culture, and education without dealing, albeit briefly, with the first inhabitants, because their cultures are those of our land. As Jennifer Isaacs said in the introduction to *Australian Dreaming*:

> Aboriginal history is Australian history. The history of mankind on the Australian continent did not commence when Captain Cook landed on the Eastern coast but 40,000 years before that when the ancient predecessors of the Aboriginal people began their sea voyages south. (Isaacs, 1980, p. 9)

So, education in Australia did not begin with the first school set up in New South Wales following the English settlement, but many thousands of years before when the first Australians taught their young about the ways of life, their laws, social organisation, and customs. These were transmitted through legends and song-cycles providing accounts of geological changes that occurred over the years of their habitation of the land and the social events that have significantly influenced their culture. Not the least of these, one might now suggest with 20/20 hindsight, was the coming of the Europeans to *Terra Australis*.

English-speaking society has largely ignored Aboriginal culture and excluded Aboriginal people. It was only in the 1870s that Aboriginal children were enrolled in state schools, sometimes on reserves to avoid any adverse influence on White children. And it was not until the early 1970s that school principals in New South Wales lost

the right to refuse or defer the enrolment of an Aborigine if there was community opposition to the presence of that child in the school (see Lovat, 1992). There have been substantial changes over the past 20 years and the cultural deficiencies that Aboriginal people were thought to have are now recognised as cultural differences, although these are still a challenge to many communities.

Most educational practice is based upon the principle of building on earlier learning, moving from the child's existing knowledge base to the unknown. For many Aboriginal children, a curriculum based in the Western—largely British–North American—culture provides little connection to their languages, traditions, and values. Consequently, their persistence with formal schooling and their level of success, when judged by Western standards, is seriously compromised.

There are some important differences between the dominant Australian and Aboriginal cultures. The notion of not challenging the teacher's views, for example, is one that is shared with some Asian countries. For Aboriginal children, questioning an elder (e.g., a teacher) is considered rude, and such a demand—common practice among White Australians—might offend traditional practices and require new, perhaps situation specific, communication skills (see Heitmeyer, 1998). There are times, for example, when students might pause before replying, while they work out what to say. The words and body language they generally use at home might not have the same meaning in standard English. Such a delay can lead to a teacher pressing for an answer, or passing to another student for the answer. This can communicate a depreciation of the Aboriginal student's contribution, and can be humiliating.

Aboriginal students who excel, or who have a learning problem which is independent of cultural influence (e.g., a sense impairment or a developmental disability) might require special attention. In the first case, it is important to reassure such students that they can maintain their places within the indigenous community and achieve excellence at school at the same time. In the second case, it is essential to prevent the failure spiral that the nonperforming students can enter through loss of confidence and self-esteem and which, in turn, exacerbates further low achievement and avoidance behaviour.

Indigenous students confront a number of schooling challenges associated with the mismatch of cultures and traditions but these are not altogether different from those faced by other students with diverse abilities and backgrounds. Indeed, the threats to achievement are much the same for all students. These include:

- the identification of any physical or medical problems that might affect learning efficiency;
- the development of English-language skills;
- encouragement that can elevate self-concept and learning independence over time;

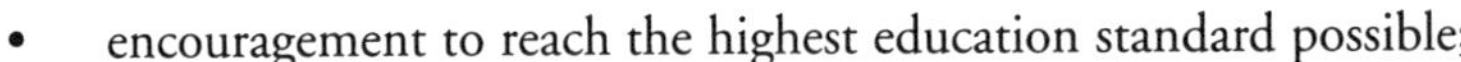

- encouragement to reach the highest education standard possible;

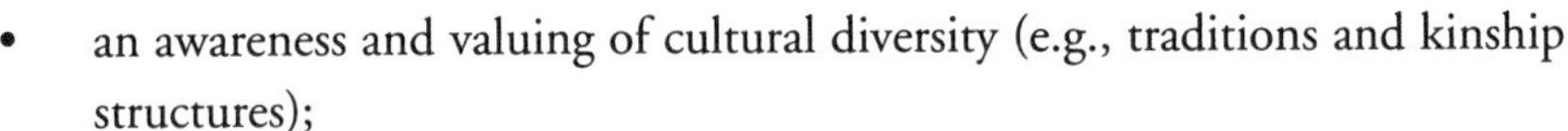

- an awareness and valuing of cultural diversity (e.g., traditions and kinship structures);
- career or vocational guidance; and
- the development of partnerships between school and the community (e.g., establishing two-way exchanges between the school and parents about culture, expectations, and scholastic objectives).

These matters can become important when there are stresses imposed upon the child and the family by cultural, language, interpersonal, or financial circumstances. There are also children who, because of their extremely advanced abilities and talents, find themselves under great pressure to succeed and to blend into their peer group at the same time.

Disrupted families

The nuclear family remains the dominant unit in most countries. Despite this, the traditional family of mother, father, and one or more children is becoming less common over time. According to the 1996 Australian Census of Population and Housing, 49% of the population aged 15 years and over was in a registered marriage, and an additional 5% was in a de facto relationship. An estimated 28% of men and 23% of women will never marry and 46% of marriages are likely to end in divorce. The number of children involved in divorces was 1.13 per hundred children and, in nearly two-thirds of the divorces that involved children, the youngest was under 10 years of age (Australian Bureau of Statistics, 2000a).

The figures above suggest that more and more children are being raised in non-traditional family units. Several researchers have reported how children respond to these living patterns, and it has been argued that special attention or consideration should be given to them in school. Certainly, when there is a marriage breakdown, the effect is more harmful for adolescents than for younger children. The risk of dropping out of school almost doubles from 15% for children in two-parent households to 30% for children with one parent only, with the consequential outcomes on educational attainment being about equal for boys and girls (McLenahan & Sandefur, 1994).

The effect of parents remarrying after divorce also has an impact on the children. As with the breakdown of marriage, the impact on adolescents is greater than that on younger children. These young people are likely to resent the intrusion of the step-parent—girls being more resentful than boys—and many choose to disengage from the family, spending little time at home involved in family activities, with a consequent risk of delinquent, antisocial, and self-destructive behaviour.

The influence of family life, however, goes well beyond the divorced or single parent household and includes step families, adoptive families, intergenerational

and multi-racial families, and families that are headed by lesbian or gay parents, or by a parent who has never been married. In the same way that special attention—or simply a watchful eye—is given to children whose families are in crisis, consideration might also be given to children who experience child-rearing practices that are not the norm of society. In some cases the extra attention is warranted: in others, it is not.

Adoptive and multi-racial families

Parents who adopt children face a range of problems. There is a small body of literature about families in which the adopted children are from other racial backgrounds, have a physical impairment, or have an intellectual disability. There is no consensus about the level of disruption to families when the children have any of these characteristics. Some researchers report problems due to children's behaviour difficulties, whereas others have found no significant disturbance because the parents derive considerable satisfaction from these adoptions. Little support outside the family is available to parents who adopt children born in other countries but there are financial and other provisions available for families in which there is a child with a disability (e.g., respite care and support groups; see Rosenthal & Groze, 1992).

As they grow up, children in multi-racial families are confronted with the issue of identity because society needs to define them in some simple way and this is difficult to determine if a child does not fit neatly into one racial category. If a child is to be defined on the basis of colour or facial characteristics the child needs to know about identity and how to exist safely with it. At school, there might be pressure on a multi-racial child to have a mono-racial identity—for instance, to identify as Chinese or Vietnamese despite the fact that the child and the parents, and perhaps the grandparents, were born in Australia. In Box 1.1 (page 15) is one mother's view about some of the problems experienced by multi-racial families.

Families with limited financial means

The term *poverty* is based upon an index of per capita household disposable income. For some people, living on a very meagre income might be inconvenient but not a terrible burden. For others (e.g., those with several dependent children), the likelihood of a Centrelink pension income lasting for two weeks is simply ridiculous.

Poverty lines are income levels designated for various types of income units (i.e., family groups, which also include single persons). For a single person without any dependents the poverty line is about $218 per week. For a family of two adults and two children it is about $506 per week (Melbourne Institute of Applied Economic and Social Research, 2000).

Trying to determine how many Australians live at or below the poverty line is fraught with danger. The 1996 Australian census suggested that approximately a million households (families and persons who live alone) are living near or below the poverty

Box 1.1 Living with Nathan

My name is Jennifer and I live in Adelaide. When I got married it took a few years for my husband, Aaron, and I to work our way around to starting a family. We both thought it was important to get established financially before we took on the responsibility of another mouth or two to feed, and we worked pretty hard in both of our jobs to save as much as we could.

I was 27 and Aaron was 30 when we finally decided it was time. Well, boy did we try! The problem was that nothing happened and, after about 18 months, I went to see my GP and had some tests done. It turned out that I was ovulating quite normally but Aaron was all but completely sterile. I'd like to say that he took that revelation pretty well but, being a typical man, he thought his masculinity was compromised and it took a while to get over that. Both of us wanted to have kids and he wasn't keen on any of the surrogate parent ideas and we finally decided to adopt.

This is going to sound funny but we wanted to adopt a baby that was Asian. We'd heard about all the kids up for adoption and we jumped through all the administrative hoops and, after almost 18 months, we went to Korea to collect Nathan. He was so beautiful. I can't hope to explain what it felt like when I carried him into our home for the first time. He was only 12 months old, but I took him into each room and explained what it was—my explanation of the toilet was hilarious—and then I showed him his bedroom. I remember crying with joy in bed that night and lying awake waiting for him to make a noise so I could rush into his bedroom and cuddle him.

Well, life was pretty good and Nathan, his dad and I did so many things together. Going to work was a huge inconvenience but I was lucky that I had a job I could do mostly from home. Almost before I knew it, Nathan was heading off to school and, like most mums I suppose, I wondered how he was going to fit in and how the school was going to react to him.

One afternoon when he was in Year 3 he came home from school with his uniform all messed up. He told me that he'd got into a fight because one of the kids called him a slant-eye. No doubt about it, Nathan does not have Caucasian eyes and, even though I was absolutely furious, I thought the education system had at least succeeded in teaching visual discrimination skills to some of the children, and racial discrimination as well! (Is this what my taxes are paying for?)

I sat him down and we talked for an hour about what it was like to be different. I told him that some people couldn't see the person below what was on the outside and that was their problem. Nathan already knew he was adopted and had no concerns with that at all. Then we role-played how he could interact with kids if it ever happened again.

Nat is fifteen now, and the most wonderful son. He's had some prejudice to contend with over the years and has been in a couple of fights. He's proud of his Korean heritage—and we are too—and we're planning a family holiday there in the next couple of years.

You ask me if life would have been different if Nat had been an all-Australian kid? Of course it would. I remember pushing him through the supermarket when he was really young and this woman poked her head into the carriage and reeled back in horror when she realised the baby was Asian. I remember one of our friend's youngest children asking why Nat had a funny looking face. Oh, then there was a Year 6 teacher who had some problem with cultural differences. I'm not naïve enough to think that prejudice and discrimination is going to stop when he leaves school but, by then, he'll know how to fight his own battles.

Just one last thing. I wouldn't swap my Nathan for any other boy in the world.

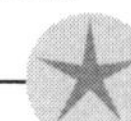

line, but the census measure of income is recognised as being very crude. If we are sufficiently bold to extrapolate, assuming an average of 2.7 persons per household, we arrive at a figure of between 2.1 and 2.6 million people, or a broad order of magnitude of 12–15% of the population. Of course, many of these are older people receiving a pension only, but the impact on children living in poverty must still be staggering. In addition, there are thousands of homeless youth who receive no government support at all. They live in a range of locations from shelters to squats under bridges, derelict buildings, caves, and countless other locations around our cities. These homeless young people might not—for one reason or another—be included in census data.

Living in a low-income family has a substantial effect on children and adolescents. There are some discrepancies in research findings reported in the literature due to the use of different methodologies employed by various investigators, but there are some consistent results (see Brooks-Gunn, Britto, & Brady, 1999). Overall, these children have a higher incidence of health problems, and intellectual, emotional, and behaviour disorders (including school expulsions and grade repetition) than those living in more favourable circumstances. In general, the effect of poverty on school achievement is greater than the effect of poverty on emotional or behaviour problems, although the influence declines during adolescence. Of concern is the co-occurrence of poverty with other factors that affect performance at school, such as family structure and parenting behaviour, race or ethnicity, or violence or abuse within the home.

Families with gay or lesbian parents

There is a growing literature on families in which the sole parent is lesbian or gay, or in which both parents are of the same sex. An issue often raised is the extent to which

growing up in a gay or lesbian family influences a child's development. The issue is raised because it is assumed that the parents exert influences on the children that are significantly different from those provided by heterosexual parents.

Research dealing with these matters has revealed no substantive differences in child-rearing practices among such parents. Their children grow up being no different to their peers in their expression of recreation or career interests, mental health, future employment decisions, job stability, social relationships, or sexual identity (Patterson & Chan, 1999).

In Box 1.2 (below) is a short account written by a father about some of the issues he has had to face raising his daughter.

Box 1.2 Living with Catherine

My name is Sean. I married Tracy when I was 20, a year before I started my first real job as a high school science teacher. Our daughter, Catherine, was born two years later.

I don't want to explain everything about what it's like to be gay but, when Catherine was two, I came to a point in my life where I had to accept that I wasn't heterosexual. It wasn't easy to abandon my wife and child, but I did, and found myself an apartment in the city and began my new life. I didn't actually abandon Tracy and Catherine. I contributed as much money as I could to their welfare and, over a period, Tracy accepted who I was and allowed me to visit Catherine whenever I wanted.

Anyway, I met Peter about a year after I moved to the city and we've been together for 19 years now. That's longer than most marriages I know.

A couple of years after that, Tracy remarried, and she and Catherine moved in with her new husband and his two girls. It didn't work out all that well. In fact, from what I can gather, that's an understatement. Catherine hated the new husband and the stepsisters and the only option was to move her in with me and Peter.

Because I'm her father and also a teacher, I had a lot to do with Catherine and her schooling. I went to the parent–teacher nights, I even went to working bees at the school and sometimes Peter would come along to help as well. He was terrific about Catherine although there were times—early on in our relationship—when he thought he was being ignored because I was giving all of my attention to her. He was probably right. We talked about it and worked out how I could share my time and affection equally between the two of them. It took some effort but we got there.

I can't remember that anything about Catherine's education was unusual. She was an average student—maybe a bit above average—and she had lots of

friends. I remember the night she came into my study when I was marking assignments and asked me about my relationship with Peter.

"One of my friends says you're a faggot. I know what that means. Are you?"

I'm sure I blushed. I sat her down, told her that I didn't especially like the word faggot but, yes, I was gay and Uncle Peter was my boyfriend. I explained that I loved him and I loved her but in a different way. Then—this blew me off the planet—she said:

"Okay, I can understand that. Good night, Dad."

She kissed me and skipped off to bed. And that was it.

Over the years, Catherine's brought her friends home and we've had lots of good times. We have birthday parties and Tracy comes to everything that's important—like for meals at Christmas and Easter and birthdays—and we've talked for hours on the phone about how Catherine's doing at school and who her friends are.

I know people get worried that kids who live with gay and lesbian parents will turn out weird, but I want to declare that Catherine is as normal as any young lady could be. We had a father and daughter talk about sex and she's always been very open with me. I'm sure she confides in me about things she wouldn't dream of telling her mother.

As far as I can see, Catherine is a well-adjusted young lady. She's been with the same boy now for two years. I don't especially like him but that's what fathers are supposed to say, isn't it? I don't know that she'll marry him. If she does, I guess I'll cope.

What does Peter think? I don't think he expected to inherit a family when we met, but he's been great. Sometimes we argue about what Catherine's doing. He thinks I'm too permissive. I think it's been good for him, though. He's never had a girlfriend and it's added a different dimension to his life. In many ways, it's brought us closer together than if we'd been just two guys living together in the 'burbs.

Difference and prejudice

Being different from others is something that many of us cherish as adults. We might express our individuality through the clothes we wear, by the way in which we have our hair cut and dyed, through body piercings and tattoos, the colour or style of our motor vehicle, or even the type of food we prefer to eat. Being unconventional by choice has substantially different implications from being different by accident.

Difference is based on society's conventions of normalcy. Perhaps not unreasonably, there is a focus on people and events that advance the aims of a society, or enhance a society's reputation among its competitors. For example, we glorify our top athletes and feel a sense of pride when our nation's anthem is played after victory. How many

of us have not secretly wished that we were on the Olympic dais awaiting our gold medal, and flashing a smile that would stop traffic? There are also members of our society who display differences that might be perceived as being at variance with other people's expectations or interests. These might include leather-clad adults who have a fascination with a particular brand of motor cycle, those who choose to live without the possessions that others believe are essential, and people from minority ethnic and social groups (such as those introduced earlier in this chapter). It is important not to forget another heterogeneous group, such as people who live with a vast range of sense, physical, intellectual, or learning disabilities.

Some writers have expressed concern at the effect that perceptions of difference can have on the community's response and, in particular, the development and maintenance of prejudice. Davidson and Davidson (1994), for example, drew attention to the commonly accepted roots of prejudice,including economic competition, sexual apprehensions, cultural styles, the social history of racism, and family characteristics—although they emphasised that parents have less influence on the development of prejudice in their children than had been previously thought. Nevertheless, the basic proposition is that in-group versus out-group differences constitute the foundations of prejudice (see, e.g., Gaertner & Dovidio, 2000; Leyens et al., 2000).

The roots of prejudice lie deep with the developing child and can persist through the entire adult life. Box 1.3 (below) provides a brief description of such an occurrence.

Box 1.3 The persistence of prejudice

About a year ago I went to a nursing home not far from where I live to interview some older adults. There was nothing remarkable about the nursing home. It was a set of two-storey brick buildings with wide covered verandahs on the ground level with deck chairs scattered about. The lawns and gardens were well kept and the facilities seemed to be well above the government standards.

As usual, I asked the Director of Nursing to show me around the premises and she was more than happy to oblige. As we toured I took note of the activities in which the residents were engaged and the extent to which they interacted with each other. We were heading back to the ward to begin the interview with four women and a man who had volunteered to participate in my study. That was when I saw Betty.

Betty looked different from the others and I guessed that she had an intellectual disability. As I watched, she shuffled toward a group of women who had gathered around a trolley where one of the housekeeping staff was serving afternoon tea. Betty had obviously learnt some social graces because she stood back from the group and waited patiently until there was a space at the trolley before moving in. Then I couldn't believe what I saw. One of the

other residents took a step toward Betty and pushed her out of the group. Betty didn't change her expression but simply backed away a couple of paces and waited until her fellow residents had their tea and biscuits and moved off.

I asked Terri—my guide—about Betty.

"She's mentally retarded."

"How long has she been here?" I asked.

"Oh, seven or eight years I guess. She came with her mother—they were admitted together—and when her mother died a couple of years ago, Betty stayed on. There wasn't really anywhere for her to go."

"How does she fit in?"

"Not very well. The other residents don't like her. They know she's retarded and they don't like her being around. Even though some of the others are pretty far-gone with dementia, something keeps telling them that Betty's different and they exclude her. I don't think there's anyone—except the staff, of course—who have anything to do with her. It's a bit sad, really."

As it happened, the woman who had pushed Betty away from the tea trolley was one of my participants and, when I'd asked all the questions I had to for my study, I asked how she got along with the other residents.

"Just fine, dear. They're all lovely."

"There's a woman called Betty here somewhere, isn't there? How do you get along with her?"

Doris's face changed from the benign smile she had worn during the interview to a frown.

"She doesn't belong here," she said tersely.

I asked naïvely, "Why not?"

"She handicapped."

"Is she not a nice person?"

"She's handicapped. She doesn't belong here. This is for normal people, not like them. They have their own places."

It took a couple of minutes to establish that Doris had harboured a prejudice against people with an intellectual disability for as long as she could remember. She told me about a couple of children with learning problems whom she had known when she was going to school.

"They don't change, you know? They have their own places to go to. I don't know why we have to put up with her."

She wanted to make sure I remembered.

As part of the learning process, children attempt to blend new experiences and knowledge with existing assumptions and beliefs about the world in which they live. As their ideas of human nature prove inadequate, the assumptions they hold are

modified by new perceptions and a developing tendency to view the world in an overly simplified way. Stereotyping is an ideal way to reduce the mental overload of keeping the constellation of each individual's characteristics separate. Grouping by similarities and difference is, perhaps, an automatic cognitive (thinking) process. However, stereotyping inevitably leads to negative judgments, prejudice, and stigmatisation based upon how much a person deviates from the characteristics of the in-group. Disability, age, size, appearance, or membership of an ethnic or sexual minority group are common reasons for discrimination (Heatherton, Kleck, Hebl, & Hull, 2000)

One way of attacking prejudice is to provide children with an alternative way of viewing their relationships with others. The idea is to exclude the foundation of difference (such as race, age, or impairment) and substitute one inclusive identity (such as nationality, neighbours, student of Parramatta North Primary School, or members of Mrs Kirby's Year 2 class). Doing this focuses attention on in-group favouritism and subtly redirects the child's attention away from difference toward inclusion. Gaertner and Dovidio (2000) called this the Common Ingroup Identity Model. It has several advantages in that it: (a) produces more positive intergroup attitudes; (b) promotes inclusion; (c) encourages standards of justice and fairness; and (d) leads to positive and trusting intergroup behaviours, such as helping and personal disclosure.

Certainly, children learn about prejudice from comments made in the family home but they also learn from their social interactions outside the home. Of course, children learn much more than in-group versus out-group differences. At this point, it is valuable to consider where education occurs in contemporary society. This leads to some thoughts about how best we can construct educational settings that take into account—and value—variation and diversity.

Education in contemporary society

Learning can be a solitary experience, but education—the systematic transfer of the knowledge and ways of society—involves partnerships between the learner and others in the teaching–learning process. These might include other children, parents, teachers, tertiary instructors, a training officer at work, supervisor, or the boss. Alternative teaching–learning partners might include the authors of a book like this, or the creator of a website or instructional compact disk.

Teaching and learning occurs in almost every situation. In the early years of life, the context is primarily the family and the neighborhood and these experiences are hugely influential on the young person. Family characteristics and the attitudes and beliefs of parents determine, to a reasonable extent, how the child reacts and responds to educational experiences during the years of schooling.

In the first five years of life, a child gains much through the bonding process (through touch, warmth, and the responsiveness of parents) that facilitates language development and cognitive and emotional growth. The routines of the household demonstrate regularity, planning, and problem-solving. Discipline that is sensible and reasoned is also important for establishing boundaries, the nature of relationships, a sense of what is right and wrong, and the rudiments of the identity that allows a child to position himself or herself in relation to others. Interactions with parents, siblings, and peers assist by exposing the youngster to experiences that can facilitate positive attitudes toward reading, numeracy, and a range of values about the importance of learning and discovery.

Later, the teaching–learning ecology expands to include the school, community and, indeed, the rest of the world through television, the Internet, and the World Wide Web. As the child becomes older, the neighbourhood becomes an increasingly significant contributor to education. Social contacts expand beyond the immediate (or extended) family to encompass many other children and adults. Access to libraries, museums, art galleries, shopping centres, parks, and recreation and leisure facilities further expands the learning and socialisation process. If parents work in the neighborhood where they live, the child might grow up having experienced role models for work and employment routines. Conversely, if the child lives in a situation in which there are few opportunities to learn about the world and interact with it successfully, or is not exposed to positive models of learning, the childhood and adolescent years might be characterised by intellectual, social, or emotional isolation (see e.g., Brooks-Gunn, Denner, & Klebanov, 1995).

Throughout life, experience is the essential prerequisite for effective problem-solving because it is the primary source of an individual's knowledge base. Even a modest level of rebellion can have positive outcomes. For example, children play with matches, skip school, mix with undesirable companions, take things that are not theirs, and defy a range of limitations and rules imposed by parents, schools, and society. Although these activities might be distressing and infuriating for parents and others, valuable life experiences are acquired, most often without long-term physical or emotional damage, and without involvement with law enforcement agencies. Even those who engage in delinquent behaviour often survive. Carroll (1995), for example, reported that 85% of youths admit to engaging in some law-breaking activity but only 1 to 2% ever appear before a magistrate and, of these, only 3% repeat their court appearance.

Although challenges to law and order cannot be ignored, experiences that enable children and youth to test their independence and the consequences of their actions are essential to the development of problem-solving skills, initiative-taking, and self-determination. For young people with a disability, the opportunities to risk-take are fewer than those available to their non-disabled peers because they often encounter unintended constraints from parents and other caregivers. For example, because of

limited mobility, they might not have the opportunity to post a letter, use the telephone, or operate common household appliances. Because of modest intellectual capabilities, they might have meals or snacks prepared for them, travel with a chaperon, and have few opportunities to deal with money and exchange goods. Other skills that are important to day-to-day living include short- and long-term life planning of personal care, health, and recreation, even including personal safety and self-defence.

Maximising learning opportunities for all young people is the dictum of most contemporary educators and guided (or mediated) experiences ensure that students acquire the relevant learning and problem-solving skills. The British tradition of education that has been most influential in Australia has placed emphasis on learning that occurs within the formal instructional settings—the school and the tertiary institution. There has been an implicit conviction that what a student learns in the classroom or from prescribed textbooks is the most important information to be gained. Certainly, there are times when a didactic form of instruction might be the most efficient way of transmitting specialist knowledge (e.g., learning physical laws and equations, the basics of algebra or calculus, and philosophical propositions). However, there is much that children learn from others outside the classroom and much that a young and older adult can (and must) learn on the job, and even during recreation and leisure activities. Consider, for example, that a child spends approximately 30 hours at school each week but 40 outside school during the week and another 26 in recreation and leisure activities on the weekend. It seems odd to think that these 66 waking hours are spent without any learning taking place. In reality, much occurs beyond the school precinct.

It is interesting to compare the nature of learning that occurs in formal and informal settings. The characteristics of the learner's behaviour in each are shown in Table 1.1 (page 24).

The distinction between the characteristics of formal and informal learning situations is not new. Others have presented similar views when advocating changes in education systems or when promoting a preferred brand of intervention that exhorts teachers to become more democratic, to be more student-oriented, to use collaborative and peer tutoring methods in their classrooms, adopt new educational technologies, or allow for discovery and exploration. Sometimes these exhortations to teachers to "change their evil ways" are met with glazed eyes and whispers. "This is all very well for her," the teacher might say, "but she doesn't have 29 kids in a class all dedicated to making my life miserable." Or, "When does he think we're going to have time to do all this?"

These comments reflect attitudes and constraints about what can and cannot be achieved, and can be completely justified. These days, many education systems are under pressure to be more cost efficient, to do more with less, and to be more accountable to parents and to the law makers at the same time. It is rare to hear comments

Table 1.1 How learning occurs inside and outside the classroom

Characteristics of the learning

Formal setting

Students participate because of curriculum and instructional requirements

Teacher initiates learning and monitors progress

Students are most often involved in independent learning or competitive situations

The student is expected to persist regardless of motivation, attitude, physical circumstances, or interest in the task

Learning time is constrained by a timetable

The learning challenge is often linked to conceptual and book-based learning

The learning outcome is formally assessed and affects the student's school progress

Learning products are often emphasised and linked to assessment

Learning may occur through didactic teaching and books with minimal peer interaction

The language of instruction is often adult and middle class

Informal setting

The learner is involved because of personal interest

The learner self-initiates and self-monitors progress

The learners are involved in activities that are collaborative or competitive, personal or group based

When the learner gets tired or bored the activity stops

There is generally time to explore and discover

There is usually personal challenge, repetition to consolidate skills, and problem-solving in practical activity

Learning outcomes are not formally tested or assessed but sometimes displayed

The process is generally more important than a product

Learning might occur by interacting with or watching more competent others

There is generally mediation by peers who use the same language and who often have similar attitudes and beliefs

about being accountable to the consumers of education—the students—and especially to those who have specific learning support needs for whom the relevance of what they are being asked, or required, to learn is of paramount importance.

Spears-Burton (1992) reported a classroom anecdote that supports the intrinsic desire to learn that seems characteristic of young people's experiences outside formal

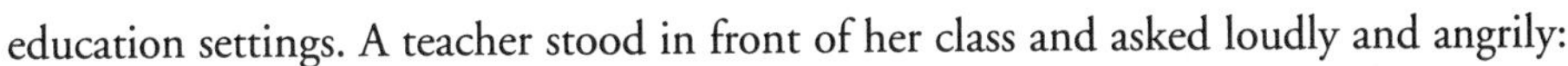

education settings. A teacher stood in front of her class and asked loudly and angrily:

"What do I have to do to get you people to read?"

From the back of the class in a very soft voice came the reply:

"Give me a book I like and I'll read it."

From time to time, many of us wonder why we are being asked to study some topic. When I was young, for example, I learnt that the area of a circle is calculated using the formula $A = \pi r^2$. I cannot recall a single occasion in my adult life when I have had cause to use this formula. I can also still recite parts of Shakespeare's Henry V, such as the king's rousing speech to the troops before the battle of Agincourt. But I have never had any need to recite this rote learnt prose now, nor even when I memorised it many years ago.

When the purpose of learning is lost or obscure, it is not unreasonable that the student's motivation and effort wanes, and this is especially so for students who have a history of learning problems. These students are often far from intellectually inferior creatures. Some can strip and rebuild a car engine over the weekend (without having pieces left over), are accomplished surfers of the Web, correspond with keyboard pals around the world through the Internet, know where to find the local platypus colony in the river, and have a storehouse of information so fantastic that it could never have been acquired in a classroom under the conditions that prevail in many schools. The goal for teachers—and the education system in general—is to create links between the student's imagination and existing skills and the content of the school curriculum.

Cultural and social influences at school

In the pursuit of learning, the student is helped or hindered by a range of personal and family characteristics that includes motivation, attitudes, personality, gender, ethnic or racial background, family circumstances, and location. Those who live in advantageous circumstances can enhance their opportunities for success through schooling whereas those who are less fortunate can be supported in their attempts to overcome the adverse effects of their life circumstances. However, a school's ability to support all students is likely to be limited because it is part of the wider community. Teachers are generally members of the dominant cultural group and are influenced by the norms, rules, and imperatives of society.

Although it is easy to be critical of school and teachers, it is important that they not be blamed for all social ills. There might be some justification for holding the education system responsible for the lack of opportunities that some students experience because of the breadth of diverse backgrounds and abilities represented in a school community. In some countries, schools are held accountable for not

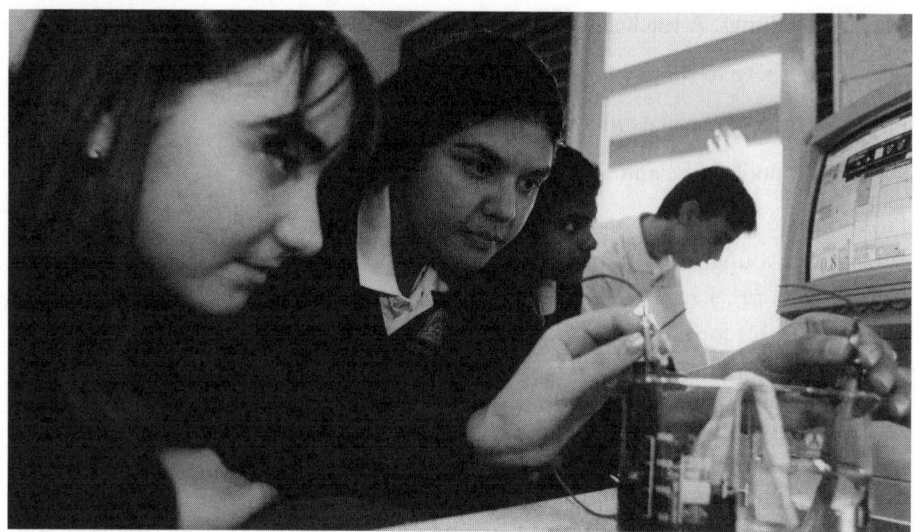

Opportunities abound in every educational setting for students to work together for their mutual benefit.

overcoming all the pre-existing differences among students, and teachers—individually and collectively—are blamed for students' failure to meet minimum education standards. Certainly, some students fall through the service cracks to the considerable consternation of concerned parents. For example, while I was preparing this chapter I took a phone call in my office from a mother who described herself as being "not very well off". Her speech tone and choice of words reflected exasperation. When in Year 2, her son had been assessed as being about 12 months behind in reading and numeracy. Over the past two years, she had tried unsuccessfully to have the school react to his apparent needs by providing additional support in these curriculum areas, with only a modest degree of success. She had hired a tutor to provide private coaching at home, adding to the family's financial hardship, but this did not seem to be enough. Where could she go to get the help she thought her son needed? To what extent was the school avoiding its responsibility?

Mortimore (1997) argued that the school is one of the few social mechanisms available to students that can redress disadvantaged circumstances and provide a compensating boost. The more effective the school is, the higher is the proportion of students who:

> . . . will get to the starting line in the competition for favourable life-chances. How well such students will perform in the subsequent race will depend on their talents, motivation, and luck; but at least they will have a chance to compete. (p. 483)

As we know, the rhetoric does not always reflect reality. Schools should be places where equality is paramount, where difference is minimised, and where diversity and

variation are accepted as fundamental aspects of society, but they appear not to be. Some writers (e.g., Preston & Symes, 1992) have suggested that school actually promotes social stratification and inequality and that the needs of the least advantaged are infrequently high on the agenda of educational priorities in schools. In a sense, school systems do not appear to take into consideration that there are the haves and have-nots in our community: there are families in which the presence of a computer (or more than one) is as familiar as the television, and there are others in which a telephone call requires a walk up the street to where the phone might or might not work, depending upon the level of vandalism that week. There are other families in which there is a person with an intellectual, sense, or physical handicap, or a person who displays behaviour that is socially unacceptable. Such diversity should not be beyond the capacity of the school to provide an appropriate level of support and education opportunities.

Cultural diversity and awareness

Some educational sociologists have argued that there has been a hybridisation of culture and that the time has passed when each cultural minority is a distinct entity—the idea is one of a cultural mosaic (McCarthy, 1998). Nowadays, the notion of a conversation between cultures might be apt, in which cultures are interdependent and interwoven, and in which the definition of one culture depends upon its interaction with another. In Australia, for example, being an Aboriginal person has meaning because of the social dialogues that have occurred between Aborigines and the those who began to populate the country at the end of the 1700s.

Multiculturalism and education within a multicultural context aim to address the conversation between cultures rather than focus on any culture in isolation. The challenge for educators is to deal with situations in which those from one culture might perceive the traditions, values, and beliefs of someone from another as being the antithesis of their own.

Cultural values and attitudes

Identification with a culture or ethnic background often is a stimulus for intolerance and discrimination. We forget that the standards we accept as our cultural norm might be distasteful or insulting to people who have grown up in other countries. We might find it abhorrent that capital punishment is still practised elsewhere, and that there are still places where governments condone physical mutilation for minor crimes. In Australia, some people frequent unclad bathing beaches oblivious to the fact that exposing oneself at a beach could lead to imprisonment in some neighbouring countries. There are even matters of etiquette that reflect cultural differences. For example, I remember visiting friends in America for dinner and noticing them look

askance at my knife-and-fork skills, the epitome of the very best of English manners instilled deeply into my psyche by my mother when I was a child. And I recall an American visitor eating at my parents' dining table and my father leaning over with a wicked grin on his face and announcing loudly, "Why don't you eat like everyone else?"

When travelling overseas, most people practise tolerance and respect the prevailing customs. We expect that others do likewise when they are here. In addition, we are sensitive to our own cultural norms. There is a social distance when talking to others, we remove a hat when inside (although the advent of the peaked baseball cap has done much to undermine that genteel etiquette), and we say "please" and "thank you" as courtesies when purchasing an item in a shop.

In education, there is an imperative to recognise cultural influences and to be as inclusive of these as possible while, at the same time, providing the acculturation and socialisation that conforms to the values and standards of the dominant group. In Australia, multiculturalism in education was introduced in the late 1970s through federal government initiatives with a view to making all levels in the formal education system responsive to the significance and contribution of the various cultures represented within the Australian population. The emphasis on multicultural education came as a result of research that supported the view that children from ethnic minorities did not achieve the educational standards of mainstream children. Efforts were therefore made to remove language barriers and facilitate access to community and education support services (such as interpreters for parents).

In the 1990s, an era began in which a national agenda was established for a multicultural Australia. This agenda emphasised:

- a commitment to Australia and its national interests;
- equality of rights to freedom from discrimination, and an equitable sharing of resources (discussed further in Chapter 2);
- the opportunity to participate fully in society to advance the country's economic and social development;
- the development of cross-cultural understanding;
- sharing in the cultural heritage; and
- respect for, and response to, Australia's cultural diversity.

Cultural diversity might be seen as a contributor to school failure but it is far from a simple cause-effect relationship. Table 1.2 (page 29) shows a number of factors that interact with culture to affect a student's success at school. As might be expected, when factors combine, the effect can be even more significant.

Of course, overcoming cultural differences is not the primary obligation of the school but an integral part of the process of education. Similarly, achievement is not solely

Table 1.2: Factors that contribute to success or failure in school

Factor	**Effect on school achievement**
Age	Research evidence has shown that children who immigrate before age 10 years, or who were born in Australia, have more success at school than those who immigrate at a later age.
Gender	In some cultures there is more emphasis placed on the male children achieving a good education than their sisters. This can be offset to some extent by the greater academic achievement of girls than boys.
Intelligence	Intelligence is a determining factor only when what is thought intelligent in one culture is not in another, or when one culture emphasises different aspects of intelligence. Several researchers, for example, have reported extraordinary spatial skills among Australian Aborigines (see Klish & Davidson, 1984). This becomes an issue if most instruction is through the verbal/linguistic modality.
Disability and impairment	Having a disability or impairment can increase a person's vulnerability when other factors are influening school performance. The need for additional support to redress physical, health, sense, and developmental conditions can conflict with family and society attitudes and responsibilties.
Language	Acquiring the language of the dominant culture is imperative for school success. Adolescents have greater difficulty than younger children and find school difficult until they can assimilate themselves. For most students, however, the imperative to learn English is powerful.
Emotions and attitudes	These factors are distributed across all students and become an issue only if an individual encounters prejudice or experiences continuous failure due to other issues (e.g., low language proficiency, very high family expectation). The emotional reaction can lead to reduced motivation and/or low self-esteem with commensurate negative attitudes to school.
Culture	This is a factor in success because there is a pervasive attitude within schools to dismiss alternative cultures. This might cause some children to avoid school although adolescents seem able to embrace two cultures and can move readily between them, accepting the dominant culture while at school but following the values and practices of their original culture in the home.
Social class	This is a major influence on school success. Students from families in which middle class values prevail are more successful than those in which working class values and attitudes exist. Children from an ethnic minority tend to be viewed by the community as being on the lower social strata.

Factor	**Effect on school achievement**
Interracial tensions	In some communities, interracial conflicts might lead to verbal or physical bullying, and this can have a major impact upon individuals and the school community as a whole. It might encourage some students to skip school because of fear of victimisation.

the responsibility of the teacher or the school. These days there is movement toward the development of partnerships and collaborations to achieve educational outcomes for students who have specific learning support needs. At this point it is useful to consider how these collaborations can be created.

Collaboration and consultation

Collaboration and *consultation* are commonplace terms in the education literature. Collaboration is a process based upon:

- an equal relationship in which mutual trust and open communication exist;
- joint approaches to problem identification;
- the pooling of resources to identify and select strategies to solve an identified problem; and
- a shared responsibility in the implementation and evaluation of the program or strategy put into place.

Establishing a workable collaboration between stakeholders is an essential component within classrooms (among students and teachers), within schools (among students, staff, and families), and within the education system (among schools, administrators, and professional colleagues).

The role of the stakeholders

The notion of collaboration has become more important in recent years with the evolution of school-based management. Nowadays, within a core budget provided by the education departments, the school administrators are responsible for all management aspects—including the hiring and firing of teachers, and the distribution of funds to maintain property and equipment and to support teaching–learning programs (see Cranston, Dwyer, & Limerick, 2000). Professional collaborations occur frequently as part of an interdisciplinary team approach when used to assist in the teaching of students, both those who are experiencing learning difficulties, and those of high ability (Ogletree, Fischer, & Schulz, 1999; Thyer & Kropf, 1995; Taradash, 1994; Warren & Payne, 1997).

The role of school professionals

Much has been written about the role of the teacher because there has been a gradual movement away from the didactic chalk-and-talk approach to instruction, toward one that involves facilitation, negotiation, and guidance. We now talk of the teacher facilitating and guiding learning experiences, negotiating the curriculum with the learner, and working in partnership with students.

The changing policies and practices of education systems—especially those relating to the inclusion of students with diverse learning needs—have increased the demands and expectations on teachers and other professionals (such as guidance officers, counsellors, school psychologists, and curriculum consultants). Many children who once would have attended special classes or schools are now gaining their education in mainstream settings, and teachers are required to operate across ability groups and age groups. They also have to deal with students with widely differing backgrounds, multi-teacher classrooms, with pastoral care groups, and with other classroom organisation patterns. Working in these situations requires a broadening of the role and expertise of teachers and more frequent contact with other specialist teachers and consultants than ever before.

Some teachers respond to the demands of the contemporary classroom challenge in novel and creative ways to meet the needs of their students. At the same time, the challenge prompts others to look for solutions that involve the line of least resistance.

Non-teaching professionals—such as counsellors, consultants, and specialist teachers—enjoy a position that varies between staff member and visitor, depending upon their location and the supervisory practices that operate within individual schools. Whereas years ago, many dealt with students on a one-to-one basis, they are now providing a range of consultancy services and the primary *modus operandi* is support to the teacher in the classroom. Even school counsellors are more concerned with teaching practices than a decade ago. Therefore, collaboration is increasing in importance as the needs and expectations of the school community change, especially in relation to the inclusion of those students who previously were accommodated in special schools and classes.

Several writers have emphasised the damaging effects of administrative practices that are not conducive to collaboration (Harris & Zetlin, 1993). They have advocated changing practices so that the school's hierarchy is not an obstacle to collaboration: when the position of teacher is not highly regarded, when there is minimal collegial support, and when decisions are made unilaterally by a senior administrator. This is often the case in high schools in which the social order is explicit, running from principals, through deputies, to subject heads, and so on down through the ranks. A similar division can be obvious in some primary schools, especially when they are large.

The role of parents

All children can benefit from parental involvement in their informal and formal education. Visits to museums, art galleries, national parks, special exhibitions, and innumerable recreation and vacation destinations provide all children with a richness of experiences that further their knowledge and interests, and expose them to what some writers have called cultural capital (Bourdieu & Coleman, 1991).

Parents always played some role in education but their involvement in their children's schooling is not always as an active participant. For some, their investment might be in a monitoring role only in respect of their children's accomplishment ("What nice things happened to you at school today?"; "Have you started your homework?"; "I want to talk to you about your report card.") and the only direct contact with the school—other than the occasional parent–teacher night—might come after a summons to the principal's office where the wrongdoings of their child are elaborated in indignant detail and they are asked to sustain an argument against a verdict of expulsion. In other cases, the school and the family have worked cooperatively to provide the child with the widest range of educational opportunities possible, regardless of the child's abilities and skills. The crucial factor appears to be the parents' perceptions of school.

There is a body of evidence that suggests that middle-class families form relationships with schools that are different from those formed by families who are less socially advantaged. There is a tendency, for example, for wealthy parents to send their children to private schools or, at least, to state schools with reputations for high-quality programs and teachers. For many of these students, the pathway from school to tertiary education to full-time employment of choice is largely unimpeded, unless problems are encountered along the way. For students from less fortunate backgrounds there might be many pitfalls that need negotiation at all levels of education. Henry (2000), for example, argued that many working class students do not have an appropriate education offered to them. They find textbook work difficult, the curriculum and assessment demands foreign, teachers unhelpful, and they often encounter conflicts inside and outside the family that impede steady progress. Certainly, students who experience learning difficulties for a range of reasons, who have medical, sense, or physical complications, or who fall beyond the boundaries of the dominant culture are in jeopardy of having a less than optimal education.

The need for parents to be involved in their children's education has always been a matter for debate. I do not recall my own parents being overly concerned with my day-to-day schooling, although there were always moans and gnashing of teeth when my end-of-term reports appeared and my truly mediocre performance was exposed. I cannot remember any of my friends' parents taking much more interest in their education either. These days, when the structure of many homes does not

conform to the traditional nuclear family (e.g., when both parents work or when there is only a single parent in the home), it is perhaps more difficult for parents to be closely involved in children's education and virtually impossible to maintain daily contact with the education program. Hence, most parents do not participate in school life once their children have completed preschool, and many have little understanding of the curriculum, how their children are taught, and even their rights as parents.

Parents can play a variety of roles in the school community. Some become involved in the daily life of the school through parent auxiliaries, parents and citizens associations, parent tutoring or other volunteer programs, and a range of occasional visits for school fetes, sporting events, open days, and sex education programs for young adolescents. The overwhelming majority of parents, however, limit their involvement to attendance at parent–teacher evenings or when children are experiencing behaviour or learning difficulties. In most of these situations, the parental role is passive, if not deferential.

Parents who adopt a position of subordination do so for a variety of reasons. At least some have abdicated the role of educator to the school, and seem indifferent to their children's behaviour or learning. Many carry into their adult lives the teacher–student, dominance–submissive role assignment that was learnt during their own school days. Others believe that the modern process of education has exceeded their competence and they feel uncomfortable because they have no expertise in the education process. Some also choose a passive role because they believe that an aggressive or assertive attitude to school administrators or teaching staff might affect the quality of instruction that their child will receive.

Although there are many schools in which parent involvement is actively sought, there are others in which parents are not encouraged to participate and information about children is withheld. In addition, many parents do not know how to respond to difficult situations and reluctantly accept the notion that schools, rather than parents, are responsible for education. Of course, deference is not universal. Some parents actively seek involvement in their child's education, especially when the child has a particular learning need (e.g., if the child is gifted or talented, or has a serious learning problem). In many cases, collaboration among parent, teacher, and specialist has proven to be very successful but there is a general recognition by all stakeholders that there is a lack of communication between home and school.

Building the bridges of collaboration

The foundation for collaboration must come from a belief in relationships of openness, trust, and support within the school community; parental involvement in the school decision-making processes, a belief in the need for personal development, and the evolution of the curriculum to serve the needs of all students. These points

constitute a definition of the collaborative ethic and can hardly be challenged as being inappropriate, although they are not always present in primary or secondary schools.

The goal for education systems these days is the establishment of heterogeneous schools that:

- accommodate the unique educational needs of all students through responsive and varied instructional options;
- include all school personnel and members of the wider community in the decision-making process, depending upon who is affected and who has skills and expertise to aid the decision-making process; and
- have academic achievement and the mastery of social and life skills as program objectives.

At the heart of the collaboration ethic is the concept of equality. Each partner must play an active role in accepting responsibility for the problem and moving the team toward resolution. However, emphasising equality is misleading because there are few partnerships in which true equality exists. One member of a team is generally the more dominant, skilful, or knowledgeable. However, this expert status should not imply a right to control. It is more productive to allocate coordination based upon the activities or the problems being confronted. The ability to move backwards and forwards between partners without sustaining a hierarchy is an important prerequisite to equity in partnerships. I prefer the terms *equity*, *reciprocity*, and *interdependency* to *equality* in this context as they imply an evenhandedness rather than a balanced relationship.

Not all problems require collaboration but there is a tendency among those professionals who believe in it to seek mutual resolutions to all problems. In a school in which the collaborative ethic is not completely accepted, it is counter-productive to assert collaborative solutions. Perhaps it is better to ask, "Is collaboration a realistic approach to problem solving in the present context?" as many teachers, parents, and students do not understand what collaborative problem-solving involves, and might not wish to participate.

The key to successful collaborations is communication. However, few of us are skilled communicators, regardless of our backgrounds and professional credentials. Pre-service teacher training programs rarely include specific subjects, units, or modules in communication skills and processes that characterise collaborative activities (such as how to talk to a parent during a parent–teacher interview). Some teacher educators might talk about team-teaching, and some student teachers might observe or participate in cooperative teaching lessons or classrooms in which two teachers work together. Counselling trainees and school psychology trainees fare somewhat better as their training programs generally provide sessions (although not necessarily practical experience) in consultation or collaborative consultation.

Most parents do not know how to communicate effectively with school personnel and this is likely to be a result of their lack of contact with the school and lead to unhelpful perceptions on both sides. For example, in a very early study, Leitch and Tangri (1988) reported that teachers perceived that only 1% of parents ever initiate contact with the school, and that only 5% will make contact after they receive a notice concerning their child's poor academic performance. Although some teachers assert that it is the parents themselves who avoid visiting the school, many parents perceive that they are unwelcome visitors and do not have the opportunity to learn about the school and its operation. How can this be changed?

One answer is through parent education, and the school can be a useful venue for this activity. Encouraging parents to use the school as a resource can lead to greater involvement in the school community and can enhance the collaboration ethic within the school. At the most basic level, any interaction between parents and school personnel must include a briefing about the role of the school, the teachers, specialist staff, and a synopsis of how the interaction and/or problem-solving process can proceed. If the process is to be collaborative, parents must understand that there is joint responsibility and accountability for the problems and the process of solving them.

A more systematic form of parent education can occur through parent-effectiveness training, which might be offered by a school counsellor, a psychologist, or a teacher or parent who is interested or qualified in this area. A criticism of such a proposal might very well include arguments that:

- most parents do not attend;
- those who need it most are the least likely to be involved;
- the resources needed are too costly;
- parents do not have the time to attend the school for such activities; and
- it is not the role of the school to educate parents.

Many of these points are valid, but the purpose of the exercise is to increase the effectiveness of the relationship between parents and the school. Schools must take the lead in involving parents as this is a fundamental aspect of the collaborative ethic. Parents can also be consulted about school policy-making, curriculum and resource development, and can be invited as guest speakers or student mentors in classroom or community-based teaching programs.

Collaboration is not the silver bullet that will solve all of the problems confronting students with vast individual differences, education professionals, schools, and school systems. If there is a solution, it might come as a result of understanding the needs of each student, not simply the way in which a student does or does not learn, but being aware of, and accepting, family and cultural backgrounds, taking steps to redress

inequity, and providing support and services if they are needed. Bruner (1996) argued that culture lies at the core of education. He stated that education can not simply be reduced to a description of how students process information, learn, and solve problems—because education relates to the more general notion of meaning-making, which encompasses ways of perceiving, thinking, feeling, and carrying out discourse. To be truly educated young people need to know about their culture because it shapes the intellect and provides the material that enables us to construct our world and understand our place in it.

Postscript

There are many hurdles to overcome if we are truly to embrace the view that all children can be accommodated in regular classes in regular schools. Each of the stakeholders in the education community is an important contributor to the schooling process and to changes that provide an appropriate level of support and encouragement to all students. There are many potential hindrances to collaboration that are hidden deep in the human subconscious and are linked to our own experiences as children, students, and adults. Some of these are related directly to our belief structures and values, whereas others are encountered at the level of the system.

Many years ago, the existentialist Rollo May commented that the most important goal is establishing a bridge between the system and the individual. He wrote:

> How can we be certain that our system, admirable and beautifully wrought as it may be in principle, has anything whatsoever to do with this specific Mr. Jones, a living, immediate reality sitting opposite us . . . May not just this particular person require another system, another quite different frame of reference? And does not this [person], or any person for that matter, evade our investigation, slip through our scientific fingers like seafoam, precisely to the extent that we rely on the logical consistency of our own system? (May, 1958, p. 3)

This quotation encapsulates the change in frame of reference that is needed if we are to establish an education system that embraces diversity and variability. It challenges us—novices and experts alike—to examine our attitudes and beliefs so that we can encourage change. We need to communicate to students, families, and our professional colleagues that we are willing to look for alternative ways of assisting all children, regardless of their strengths and weaknesses, regardless of the cultures from which they have come, and regardless of their aspirations for the following day, or week, or the rest of their lives. School administrators must value the contributions of others rather than simply evaluate these contributions. Parents must recognise that the school is part of their community and that the education of their children is their responsibility, rather than viewing the school as a surrogate parent that minds (and thankfully educates) them between 9 am and 3 pm.

SUMMARY

Education is a process concerned with socialisation and the preservation of social order. Schools are venues for learning but are also agencies of social control. As such they are the facilitators of culture: that is, the collection of norms, values, beliefs, traditions, activities, language, achievements, and possessions that characterise a group of people.

The culture that pervades modern societies has changed as a consequence of immigration. In Australia, for example, around 24% of Australians were born in other countries and nearly half of the population has direct links with relatives born overseas. About 2.5 million people speak a language other than English at home.

Culture is transmitted by all social agencies but perhaps the first and most important of these is the family. The nature of the family unit also has changed over the past few decades. There are now more children than ever living in circumstances not defined by the traditional family of father, mother, and one or two children. Children live in households with a divorced or single parent, and in stepfamilies, adoptive families, intergenerational and multi-racial families, families headed by lesbian or gay parents, or families with a parent who has never been married. The stresses within these families might be accentuated by conflict and abuse.

Living in these non-traditional circumstances can define difference, defined according to society's conventions and notions of normalcy. Being different can be a positive or negative attribute. The worst scenarios are those that prompt prejudice and discrimination. Discrimination can stem from disability, age, size, appearance, ethnicity, or sexual identity. Children learn about prejudice from comments made in the family home, and also from the social interactions they experience outside the home that have to do with being in the in-group or out-group.

The school and the schooling experience provide students with the knowledge and guidance that they need to become contributors to the community and society in which they live. The challenge that we face is how to provide these experiences in the most effective way that recognises individuality. Learning can be a solitary experience but it can also involve partnerships between the learner and others in the teaching–learning process. These might include other children, parents, teachers, tertiary instructors, a training officer at work, a supervisor, or the boss. And the most important learning experiences are not necessarily those that occur in the classroom.

Collaboration is an important element of the schooling process. It relates to relationships that promote openness, trust, and support within the school community (the physical site and the various stakeholders). These days, many schools attempt to bring the community into the school and seek partnerships with partnerships with parents and other resource persons who can contribute to the education of all students.

Suggested reading

Bruner, J. S. (1996). *The culture of education*. Cambridge, MA: Harvard University Press.

Lamb, M. E. (Ed.). (1999). *Parenting and child development in "nontraditional" families* (pp. 27–304). Mahwah, NJ: Erlbaum.

Leicester, M. (2000). *Systems of education: Theories, policies, and implicit values*. London: Falmer.

Ogletree, B. T., Fischer, M. A., & Schulz, J. B. (Eds). (1999). *Bridging the family-professional gap: Facilitating interdisciplinary services for children with disabilities*. Springfield, IL, US: Charles C. Thomas, Publisher.

See also the March issue of the journal *Unicorn* (Volume 27, No. 1), a special issue entitled "Reconciliation through education and training: Building bridges, confidence and capacity".

Practical activities

1. Make contact with two people of different ethnic backgrounds—people who were born and educated outside Australia. Ask them to tell you about their school days and childhood and adolescent experiences. Compare these with your own experiences and those of your friends.
2. When you next visit a school, interview teachers who have children from diverse cultural backgrounds in their classes. Ask specifically about the influence of the students' cultures on peers and the teachers' classroom experiences, and about any changes that are made to accommodate cultural diversity.
3. Get together with your study friends and make a list of all the characteristics that represent the society in which you live. This could include, for example, driving on the left hand side of the road, having the garbage collected, being able to read, being able to keep perishable products in a refrigerator, having an ambulance service, and so on. (Your list should be huge.) Consider the circumstances of people who live in an African or South American country in respect of your list. How does education fare?

References

ABS, *see* Australian Bureau of Statistics (ABS).

Australian Bureau of Statistics (ABS) (1997). *Basic community profile* (ABS Catalogue No. 2901.0). Canberra, ACT: Author.

Australian Bureau of Statistics (2000a). *Marriages and Divorces, Australia, 1999* (ABS Catalogue No. 3310.0). Canberra, ACT: Author.

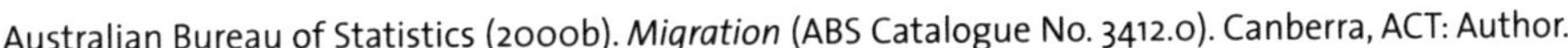

Australian Bureau of Statistics (2000b). *Migration* (ABS Catalogue No. 3412.0). Canberra, ACT: Author.

Bennett, T., Frow, J., & Emmison, M. (1999). *Accounting for tastes: Australian everyday cultures.* New York: Cambridge University Press.

Bourdieu, P. & Coleman, J. S. (Eds) (1991). *Social theory for a changing society.* New York: Russell Sage Foundation.

Brooks-Gunn, J., Britto, P. R., & Brady, C. (1999). Struggling to make ends meet. In M. E. Lamb (Ed.). *Parenting and child development in "nontraditional" families* (pp. 27–304). Mahwah, NJ: Erlbaum.

Brooks-Gunn, J., Denner, J., & Klebanov, P. (1995). Families and neighborhoods as contexts for education. In E. Flaxman & A. H. Passow (Eds). *Changing populations, changing schools* (pp. 233–252). Chicago: NSSE distributed by the University of Chicago Press.

Bruner, J. S. (1996). *The culture of education.* Cambridge, MA: Harvard University Press.

Carroll, A. (1995). *The development of delinquency: Integrating reputation enhancement theory and goal-setting theory.* Unpublished doctoral dissertation, University of Western Australia, Nedlands, WA.

Cranston, N., Dwyer, J., & Limerick, B. (2000). Making a difference? School and community practices. In D. Meadmore (Ed.). *Education: Culture, economy, and society* (pp. 99–113). Oxford: Oxford University Press.

Davidson, F. H. & Davidson, M. (1994). *Changing childhood prejudice: The caring work of the schools.* Westpoint, CN: Bergin & Garvey.

Foster, L. E. & Harman, K. (1992). *Australian education: A sociological perspective* (3rd ed.). Sydney: Prentice Hall.

Gaertner, S. L. & Dovidio, J. F. (2000). *Reducing intergroup bias: The common ingroup identity model.* Philadelphia, PA: Psychology Press/Taylor & Francis.

Harris, K. C. & Zetlin, A. G. (1993). Exploring the collaborative ethic in an urban school: A case study. *Journal of Educational and Psychological Consultation*, 4, 305–317.

Heatherton, T. F., Kleck, R. E., Hebl, M. R., & Hull, J. G. (Eds.) (2000). *The social psychology of stigma.* New York: The Guilford Press.

Heitmeyer, D. (1998). The issue is not Black and White: Aboriginality and education. In J. Allen (Ed.), *Sociology of education: Possibilities and practices* (pp. 195–216). Katoomba, NSW Social Science Press.

Henry, M. (2000). It's all up the individual . . . isn't it? Meritocratic practices. In D. Meadmore, B. Burnett, & G. Tait (Eds). *Practising education: Social and cultural perspectives* (pp. 47–58). Frenchs Forest: Prentice Hall-Sprint Print.

Isaacs, J. (1980). *Australian dreaming: 40,000 years of Aboriginal history.* Sydney: Lansdowne.

Klish, L. & Davidson, G. R. (1984). Indigenous games and the development of memory strategies in children. In J. R. Kirby (Ed.). *Cognitive strategies and educational performance* (pp. 203–213). Orlando, FL: Academic Press.

Leitch, M. L. & Tangri, S. S. (1988). Barriers to home–school collaboration. *Educational Horizons*, 66, 70–4.

Leyens, J. P., Paladino, P. M., Rodriguez Torres, R., Vaes, J., Demoulin, S., Rodriguez Perez, A., & Gaunt, R. (2000). The emotional side of prejudice: The attribution of secondary emotions to ingroups and outgroups. *Personality and Social Psychology Review*, 4(2), 186–197.

Lovet, T. J. (1992). *Sociology for teachers*. Wentworth Falls, NSW: Social Science Press.

May, R. (1958). *Existence: A new dimension in psychiatry and psychology*. New York: Simon & Schuster.

McCarthy, C. (1998). *The uses of culture: Education and the limits of ethnic affiliation*. New York: Routledge.

McLenahan, D. & Sandafur, G. (1994). *Growing up with a single parent: What hurts and what helps?* Cambridge, MA: Harvard University Pess.

Melbourne Institute of Applied Economic and Social Research (2000). *Poverty lines, Australia, June Quarter, 2000*. Melbourne: Author.

Mortimore, P. (1997). Can effective schools compensate for society? In A. H. Halsey (Ed.), *Education: Culture, economy, and society* (pp. 476–487). Oxford: Oxford University Press.

Mulhern, F. (2000). *Culture/metaculture*. London: Routledge.

Ogletree, B. T., Fischer, M. A., & Schulz, J. B. (Eds) (1999). *Bridging the family–professional gap: Facilitating interdisciplinary services for children with disabilities*. Springfield, IL: Charles C Thomas.

Patterson, C. J. & Chan, R. W. (1999). Families headed by lesbian and gay parents. In M. E. Lamb (Ed.), *Parenting and child development in "nontraditional families"* (pp. 191–219). Mahwah, NJ: Erlbaum.

Preston, N. & Symes, C. (1992). *Schools and classrooms: A cultural studies analysis of education*. Melbourne: Longman Cheshire.

Rosenthal, J. A. & Groze, V. (1992). *Special needs adoption: A study of intact families*. New York: Praeger.

Spears-Burton, L. (1992). Literature, literacy, and resistance to cultural domination. In C. K. Kinzer & D. J. Leu (Eds), *Literacy research, theory, and practice: Views from many perspectives* (pp. 393–401). Chicago: The National Reading Conference.

Taradash, G. (1994). Extending Educational Opportunities for Middle School Gifted Students. *Gifted Child Quarterly*, 38, 89–94.

Thyer, B. A. & Kropf, N. P. (Eds) (1995). *Developmental disabilities: A handbook for interdisciplinary practice*. Cambridge, MA: Brookline Books.

Warren, L. L. & Payne, B. D. (1997). Impact of middle grades' organization on teacher efficacy and environmental perceptions. *Journal of Educational Research*, 90(5), pp. 301–308.

2

Rights and learning opportunities

ADRIAN ASHMAN AND JOHN ELKINS

Case studies

Look around the playground of any school during recess or lunch. You can see hundreds of students. No matter how hard you look it is difficult to pick, by their looks alone, those who might be having learning problems. You will appreciate, however, that each student can benefit from some individual attention. But how would you provide that individual instruction?

When you read the two case studies below, think about the range of duties that any teacher has. These include in-front-of-the-class instruction with large and small groups, individual time with certain students, assessing students' performance, managing students' time, developing resources, teaching social and interpersonal skills, modelling good study and learning behaviours, consulting with colleagues, parents, and other support personnel. Think about how the teachers in the case studies structure their work time to achieve maximum coverage.

Brendan

Brendan's title is Special Education Consultant and he is employed by a large private school in a regional city. He has been a teacher for 23 years. Brendan trained as a primary teacher but took up his first special education position about 14 years ago when he was working in the state education system.

Working with "the kids" (as he refers to them) is Brendan's reason for living. He is enthusiastic about everything he does and follows the philosophy that you can get through to all children regardless of their idiosyncrasies or the problems they are experiencing. He completed a master's degree focusing on special needs education and is a regular attender at weekend courses and inservice programs.

Brendan has a room the size of a normal classroom that is full of resources. It is simply called The Resource Room. He has enrichment materials for a gifted and talented group that he sees on a weekly basis, special reading and mathematics materials that range from Year 1 to senior high school, and boxes of handouts, worksheets, books, magazines, and even comics. He has two computers that hold a collection of self-learning programs including typing skills, arithmetic probes, and a speech-writing program for children who have difficulty writing but who can speak stories into the microphone and watch as the computer writes them onto the screen. Brendan has dictionaries and encyclopaedias on CD, and even a collection of brain games.

Brendan is a teacher and consultant. He has sessions with individual children in withdrawal-from-class sessions, such as 10-year-old Jake who has Fragile X syndrome and 15-year-old Tim who has a serious behaviour problem. They come along twice a week for a class period each time. He works with Jake on language skills, and is doing a combination of social-skill training and counselling with Tim (that is linked to the mathematics lesson the boy would otherwise be missing).

For about 12 periods each week, Brendan team-teaches with colleagues. However, it is not exactly team-teaching. The class teacher presents the lesson to the whole class and Brendan works with a small group toward the back of the classroom. He is adamant that he does not work only with the students who have learning problems.

"If I only spend time with the slower kids, they'll learn really quickly that I'm there because they're dumb and no one will want to be with me. If I work with the bright kids, and the average kids, and the kids who need me most, no one gets stigmatised."

There is no doubt that Brendan spends more time with the students with learning difficulties but you would know this only if you were counting the minutes that he is with each student. Importantly, he never singles out any students to work in class on a regular basis. Over the course of a year, he will have worked with all the students several times in each of his team-teaching classrooms.

Work does not finish when the final bell goes in the afternoon. Then it is time for a quick consultation with a teacher or two to check on students' progress, or time to have a formal session with a parent. The last thing he does most days is stroll around the playing fields where he chats with the students. Of all the teachers in the school, Brendan is by far the best known to virtually all of the students.

Janine

Janine has been teaching for three years. She began at a primary school in a new outer-metropolitan suburb that was undergoing very rapid development. Janine admits that she was terrified the day she met her first group of students—a Year 3 class. She remembers the sinking feeling in her stomach when the principal told her that she would have Susan in her class—a girl with an intellectual disability. She went to the university library on the following afternoon to find anything that might allay her fear of impending failure.

She spent the first few days getting to know the children, memorising their names and making the lessons as much fun as she could. She spent each night preparing her materials for the following day and trying to think of ways of including Susan in the lessons, because it was clear that most of the content that Janine was expected to teach was beyond Susan's capabilities.

After two weeks, Janine was starting to fall into a routine that involved teaching the lesson (arithmetic, spelling, or English) as quickly as she could. Then she would hand out prepared worksheets to the other students and spend most of the remaining time teaching Susan the basic skills. When the students were working on a project in small groups, the lessons were much easier, because Susan could work alongside the others, and all that Janine had to do was ensure that the children knew how to interact positively with each other, and that Susan contributed.

Two months later, Janine was exhausted, but she was getting help from a visiting learning-support teacher, Glenda, who helped her adapt major chunks of the

curriculum so that Susan could do much the same type of activities as the other children. Janine usually prepared two sets of materials: one for the class as a whole, and another just for Susan. She also encouraged those children who finished their work quickly to assist Susan, and it was not too long before there were more than enough willing helpers. In fact, Janine had to make up a helpers' roster.

"It was a lot of hard work," she said, "especially for a first-year-out teacher, but I learnt a terrific lot about group work and adapting the curriculum. Glenda was fabulous and I don't think I would have survived if she hadn't come in every couple of weeks to see how I was going. I saved up all of the problems—I used to write them in a notebook—and got Glenda to help me find solutions. The biggest problem was Susan's behaviour. Because she wasn't keeping up she used to annoy the other children, and we had to find ways to keeping her on-task."

The learning-support teacher encouraged Janine to sit with the students and, communally, to work out how they should respond when Susan interrupted their work.

"It didn't work immediately, but we soon got the hang of telling Susan that it was important we got our work done. Then we would role-play a better way of dealing with her. She was, in fact, a pretty good kid and the others were great."

Janine had the same group of children in the following year when they progressed into Year 4.

What you will learn in this chapter

This chapter deals more specifically with the areas of disability and learning problems than Chapter 1. You will read about:

- terms that have been used to describe those who have problems at school and the effects of labelling;
- human rights and the right to education;
- the wide range of students who can be assisted by additional teaching–learning support;
- the development of special provisions for students who need additional support to succeed at school;
- least restrictive alternatives and individual education programs; and
- gaining some insight into the number of people who might need special support at some time in their lives.

When parents wave goodbye to their children or drop them at the school gate, they believe that what happens to them during the day will lead—in the long term—to their children's happiness and a fulfilling adult life. For most, this expectation will be met, to a greater or lesser extent. Their children will establish friendships, enjoy team

and individual sports, come to accept (if not necessarily value) their classroom experiences, homework, assignments, and tests, and eventually finish secondary school with careers in mind and a sense of the future.

For some parents and children, however, negotiating the unpredictability and sometimes frustrations of schooling can make the years of formal education considerably less than a positive experience for all concerned. There are many reasons for this. For example, there are children whose early experiences have not encouraged discovery and curiosity, those who have aggressive or antisocial behaviour, and still others who, by chance alone, have been born with, or acquired, a disabling condition.

We usually think of a disabling condition as a sense, physical, learning, or intellectual impairment that was present at birth or acquired during childhood or adolescence. However, now that you have read Chapter 1, you will appreciate that there are also life circumstances, and even special gifts and talents, that can precipitate problems at school.

Until a few years ago, special provisions for students who could not take full advantage of the school curriculum were mostly available in special schools or special classes. There were schools and classes for those with hearing, vision, and intellectual disabilities, and for those with behaviour disorders, in which opportunities and experiences were designed to help students learn and develop to the fullest possible extent. In North American literature there are still references to the term *special education* used to describe a range of additional services available to students who have special learning needs. This term is no longer common in Australia as all states and territories have adopted a policy that encourages the education of all students in regular classes. As you will discover as you progress through this book, there are still circumstances and conditions that warrant special provisions for certain students, but the ideal is to educate all students in a supportive regular class environment in which their learning needs are met.

It is useful at this point to review several concepts and issues that have guided the development of contemporary education policies and practices. First, let us deal with the issue of labelling.

Terms and labels

Over centuries, human beings have developed a language to describe those who are different. Often the most obvious differences within a culture are those associated with physical and intellectual capabilities. In the past, terms such as exceptional, disabled, impaired, and handicapped served the purpose of describing individuals who had a condition that affected progress in school, in their careers or vocations, or in their abilities to deal with the routines of daily life. These terms were often used carelessly and interchangeably although each had a specific meaning.

The term *exceptional* refers both to people who perform below some accepted average standard and also to others who have superior skills and abilities. Just because people are gifted or talented in some (or many) ways does not mean that they experience no difficulties in their learning or working environments, or in the ways in which they are expected to learn or act. In other words, extremely bright children might not be able to perform in class as teachers expect because these children are asked to do tasks that might have been mastered several years before or might be ludicrously simple for them.

The term *disability* is often used to refer to bodily functions or processes that are not working correctly, but not the *individual* as a totality. For example, a person might have restricted use—or no use—of a particular sense (vision or hearing), or might have paralysis that reduces the use of a limb and, hence, mobility. In all other bodily functions, the person might have no problems whatsoever. An analogy might clarify this point. If a tyre on a motor vehicle has a puncture, or the chip that regulates the flow of fuel is faulty, it is only that part of the car that is disabled. Sometimes the vehicle might not operate but the breakdown is due to the *one part* only that is non-operational. In the same way, a child who has very poor eyesight (called a vision impairment) might not be able to read but, when provided with corrective lenses, the development of reading skills might progress at a normal rate. The problem that the person faces as a result of a disability is called the *handicap*.

Here are two examples that will help to clarify the distinction between a disability and a handicap. A child who is newly arrived from a country where English is not the mother tongue will have difficulty keeping up with classmates and might be handicapped in terms of promotion from one grade to the next because the child cannot master curriculum content. A child with impaired vision can be handicapped when playing cricket if the opposition team members are sighted. However, handicap is situation specific: that is, a disability can be a handicap in one aspect of life but not in another. Students with a language difficulty might not be hindered at all when playing soccer, and the child with a vision impairment might function normally in many social interactions.

Hence, handicap refers to the restriction resulting from a disability. In many cases the restriction is not an inevitable consequence, but socially imposed. If building codes did not stipulate the provision of ramps and if architects persisted in designing buildings with steps only, wheelchair users would not be able to gain ready access. When there is community acceptance that ramps, lifts, and wheelchair-accessible toilet facilities are to be standard inclusions in all public buildings, then people with mobility restrictions will no longer be handicapped in their daily activities.

There is an interesting anomaly. The term *handicap* is not typically used to describe students who have above average ability (the terms we normally use are *gifted* or *talented*). However, there are many instances of gifted or talented children who are handicapped by their inability to mix with their less able peers, or because they decide not to show just how bright they really are in class or in their schoolwork.

The World Health Organization (WHO) established definitions for the terms *disability*, *handicap*, and *impairment,* although usage is inconsistent within the general public, among professionals, and in different countries. Nevertheless, the WHO definitions provide useful reference points for thinking about the implications of an impairment or a disability (see Box 2.1 below).

One way in which educators have dealt with the exceptional circumstances of children and adults is to define them according to the apparent cause of the problem. For example, a student with very limited eyesight has a vision impairment. A student who has difficulty reading is said to have a learning difficulty. By describing individuals in this way, it is easy to conclude that all who are affected by the same condition are totally different to others who are not exceptional in their physical or intellectual characteristics. By doing so, we also highlight the differences between groups rather than the similarities. In other words, we assume—incorrectly—that each individual is affected in the same way and to the same extent. As is made abundantly clear in the following chapters, diversity is the key to understanding and meeting the needs of each learner. To avoid this trap (of assuming all to be the same), we must think *individual* rather than group.

The label trap

Next time you are in a crowd, notice the amazing physical differences that exist among members of our species, and then look for similarities. You will see that similarity goes hand-in-hand with variety. Our tendency, however, is to classify people according to our expectation of what they should be like. Pick up a copy of a magazine such as *Surfing World* or *House and Garden* and look for the characteristics of those about whom the stories were written. Do they wear certain types of clothes or have hairstyles that conform to a certain fashion? If they do, are their choices also original? What

Box 2.1 World Health Organization definitions

Impairment—loss or abnormality of psychological, physiological, or anatomical structure or functions.

Disability—any restriction or lack of ability (resulting from impairment) to perform an activity in the manner or within the range considered normal for a human being.

Handicap—a disadvantage for an individual resulting from impairment or disability that limits or prevents fulfillment of a role that is normal for that individual.

might you assume about those mentioned in the stories? Do you think that they hold values similar to, or different from, your own?

Classification can be useful because it helps us to reduce the complexity of our world by putting like things together: by labelling items according to general and specific attributes. We do it with animals, forms of transport, cities, fun things to do, and people whom we like and dislike. Dividing people into groups can have advantages, but it is also fraught with danger. Labels can be positive (like Olympian), or negative (like criminal). But when you think about it, it is hard to come up with a label that is truly neutral. Male has certain social connotations, as does homeowner. And there are sure to be some who would assign negative value to a person who was called normal. In reality, the primary purpose of a label is the separation of one group from others—predator versus prey, homeowner versus home renter, gold medallist versus silver medallist, worker versus welfare recipient, normal versus funky (or whatever the "in" term might be).

The tendency, in the past, to classify children for educational services led to the same attitudinal divisions of in-group versus out-group and led to the segregation of children with certain characteristics from their peers attending regular classes. Historically, the purpose of labelling was for exclusion: that is, taking the individual away from the services or facilities that were available to the general population, although the corollary was placing this student in an education program designed specifically for him or her. However, the end result was a collection of labels that had clearly negative connotations.

These days we have rejected pejorative terms (e.g., retardate, spastic, or subnormal) and those terms that emphasise the disability are used much less frequently (e.g., slow learner, retarded, learning-disabled, or disturbed). Now, if there is a need to specify a complicating condition, we highlight the person and not the disability (this is called person-first language). For example, we refer to a person with a sense impairment or a child with a learning difficulty. The one notable exception seems to be those with very high ability or extraordinary talents, to whom we still refer as gifted and talented.

There are five main disadvantages to labelling.

1. Labels focus on the negative aspects, thereby leading people to think only of the inadequacies or deficiencies rather than think of the person's strengths.
2. Labels perpetuate misconceptions of homogeneity. In education settings, this is especially disadvantageous because the same medical or physical condition can be expressed in many ways. Children with an intellectual disability, for example, display the same range of personality and other human characteristics as do those in the wider population.
3. Labels sustain myths and half-truths based upon assumptions that purportedly explain an individual's status or behaviour. For instance, it might be said that,

"Students from Asian countries are all brilliant at mathematics but they aren't inventive". Some Asian individuals might have a propensity for mathematical reasoning, but not all.

4. Labels imply permanence. Once assigned a label, people carry the label with them throughout their lives. This can lead to a lowering of expectations, resulting in a self-fulfilling prophecy. For instance, it might be said: "He has an attention deficit disorder, so he's always going to be impulsive".
5. Labels lead to stigma and inappropriate social responses such as pity, teasing, ridicule, rejection, hostility, or prejudice.

Human rights

A discussion of learning opportunities for all students raises the issue of human rights. We might ask, for example, whether a student who is physically aggressive has the right to an education with other students, who are in danger of attack. Must a student who has very severe intellectual disabilities and little chance of living independently have a right to educational resources when others who have no impairment have insufficient resources to meet their needs? To what extent should a school community accommodate cultures that are inconsistent with the dominant culture within society?

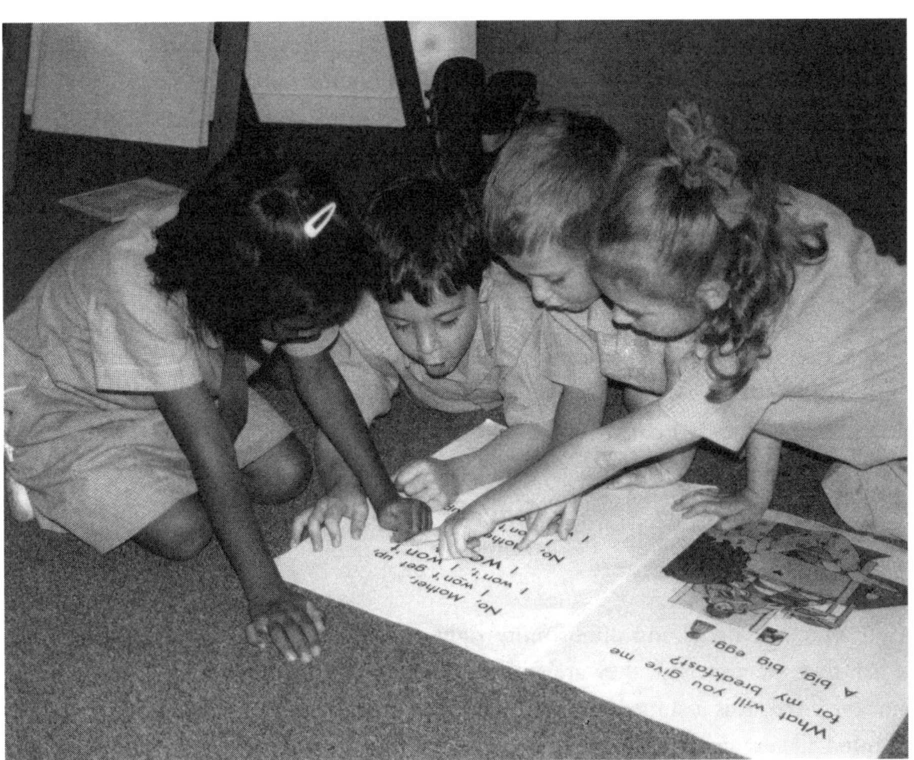

Is the right to primary education an opportunity or outcome right?

Are there limits to the right to life, the right to shelter, the right to education, or the right to a career?

Although at least some of these questions might seem to be rhetorical, they do bring forward debate that takes us into the realm of speculation and conjecture. In the philosophical domain, such questions are far from straightforward and the answers are often far from conclusive or convincing.

Philosophers tell us that a *legal right* is an equitable or moral claim to possessions, privileges, or immunities. *Human rights* are those that all (or almost all) people have regardless of their behaviour or position in society. Hence, those opposed to capital punishment argue that, despite the nature of the offence, a criminal has a right to life that cannot be denied, even by a court. Human rights are different from legal or social rights that must be recognised by the courts or by society in general. So, an individual does not have to show that human rights have been earned. They are inalienable, in that they cannot be lost or sold, but they do not always override other considerations. Two of the key issues relate to *equality* and *opportunity*.

Equality and opportunity

Some groups of people receive preferential treatment because we believe that there is a need to compensate them for past discrimination or a need to remove an inequity. In the United States, the cause of African–Americans is one example that comes immediately to mind. In Australia, perhaps two prominent examples are those relating to equal employment opportunities for women, and the provision of places for Aboriginal students in the tertiary education sector. However, treating one group in the community advantageously can mean the denial of the same rights to others. For example, if we provide special enrichment activities for students considered to be gifted or creative, we might deny other students the opportunity to be enriched in the same way.

Philosophers have dealt with concerns about equal opportunities by dividing rights into *outcome rights* and *opportunity rights*. An individual has an *outcome right* to a desirable (or essential) condition or state of affairs, and an *opportunity right* to bring about a desired state of affairs. For example, we have an outcome right to adequate housing and an opportunity right to own a Lear jet. An opportunity right applies only to *the chance* to bring about the desirable state; it is not a guarantee of the favoured outcome.

Both outcome rights and opportunity rights can be exercised or waived. However, when they are exercised, they are still different. Rights also exist even when they are not exercised. It is assumed, for example, that the right not to be physically struck is continually exercised unless explicitly waived by consenting to be touched when vigorously playing a contact sport.

In education, equal rights might imply that students with a special support need cannot be denied education in regular classrooms simply because they have a disability. However, for some of these students it can be argued that regular class placement might not be to their advantage and the question can be posed: "Does the assertion of equal rights justify the provision of special services, such as infant stimulation programs for young children with an intellectual disability?" The answer depends on whether education is an outcome right or an opportunity right.

The United Nations (UN) Universal Declaration of Human Rights makes the right to higher education an opportunity right dependent upon ability. Hence, if a person achieves the appropriate standard at the end of secondary school that person may enter a degree program commensurate with his or her achievement. However, the UN declaration does not clarify the position on primary education. If the right to primary education is an opportunity right, then providing additional resources to some students cannot be justified on the basis of equal rights. If that right is an outcome right, then the outcome must be specified carefully. If the right is to the full development of a person's intellectual capacities, gifted students would have as much right to special programs as those with very serious learning difficulties. If the right is to a certain level of achievement, the latter children have an argument for access to support that gifted students do not have.

Having said all of this, the right to education, training, habilitation, and guidance as set out in the UN declaration is not binding on governments. In Australia, the near-universal provision of education is due to the will of government, although the principle of equal access to education was set out in the National Strategy for Equity in Schooling (Ministerial Council on Education, Employment, Training and Youth Affairs, 1994). This strategy was based upon the belief that all Australian children—regardless of their sex, culture, linguistic background, race, location, socio-economic background, or disability—should participate fully in the education system and become active and informed citizens.

The strategy identified six priority categories of students whose participation and educational outcomes were lower than for other groups. These were students:

- with a disability;
- with difficulties in learning and/or emotional or behavioural disorder;
- at risk of dropping out of school;
- from low socioeconomic backgrounds;
- from Aboriginal and Torres Strait Islander backgrounds;
- from non-English speaking backgrounds; and
- who are geographically isolated.

The philosophical arguments about rights are readily dismantled when subjected to the rigours of reality, as some writers have done. One of the strongest statements on the availability of special needs education in Australia was presented many years ago by Hayes and Macalpine (1986). They claimed that most of the rights relating to education do not have obligations associated with them. They are human rights in the sense of an international convention, but when abuses take place, the victims have no recourse. Fortunately, this situation changed somewhat with the passage of the *Disability Discrimination Act* (Commonwealth of Australia, 1992) and complementary state Acts which, in general, make it illegal for an education authority to discriminate against a student because of disability. Individual state Acts have been tested a number of times and it is likely that legal precedent will provide some guidance on matters related to the placement of students with special support needs in appropriate education settings and the provision of services.

To a large extent, support for students with diverse teaching–learning needs has been the result of individual initiatives by teachers and advocates. In general, however, it is only those students with the most obvious needs and those who cause disruption and disturbance at school who attract a system response.

The breadth of need and support

The most obvious individuals who require special education support are those with an intellectual disability. These children are sometimes perceived to have such modest skills and potential that they might never attain the competencies necessary to live satisfying adult lives in the community. This view is generally false, as the results from a recent study conducted by a research team at the Schonell Centre at the University of Queensland has shown. Young, et al. (2001) reported that even people who have lived for up to 50 years (most of their lives) in an institution for persons with intellectual disability can manage reasonably well in the community with an appropriate level of support, some more independently than others.

Of course, many students with intellectual disabilities need extra support in schools. However, as discussed in Chapter 1, there are others who need a range of services, equipment, alternative instructional strategies and curricula to assist them to learn quickly and efficiently. There are also others who, although not needing special support, can be advantaged by having the teacher pay a little extra attention to obviate any developing problems. A list of these is given in Table 2.1 (page 53).

Legislating for additional education support

A very brief history

In terms of culture, learning, and attitude, the period known as the Renaissance was the harbinger of reform and change. During this time, new educational experiences

Table 2.1 Children who need special care or attention

Those who require adapted teaching methods or curriculum

Children with intellectual abilities or acquired brain injury

Children from newly immigrated families where English is not the first language

Children with serious academic learning problems (e.g., in literacy or numeracy)

Children who are exceptionally gifted or talented

Children from traditional indigenous families

Children with behaviour disorders (e.g., attention deficits)

Those who require additional material or personnel resources

Children with sense impairments (e.g., vision or hearing)

Children with physical impairments (e.g., cerebral palsy)

Children requiring ongoing medical support (e.g., epilepsy, diabetes, or muscular dystrophy)

Children with multiple physical/sensory/intellectual impairments

Children who are subject to neglect or abuse within their families

Children living outside a family group (e.g., homeless, or in detention)

Children with a serious psychiatric disorder (e.g., depression)

Those who require understanding, not necessarily intervention

Children generally

Children living in non-traditional family units

Children living in poverty-stricken families

Children living with a family member who has a serious medical or psychiatric illness

Children living with foster families

Children with backgrounds different from the dominant culture (e.g., ethnic or religious)

became available to those who had previously been excluded from schooling, those with hearing and vision impairments. The earliest attempts to overcome vision impairment began in the 16th century and involved the use of raised type. A Spaniard, Francisco Lucal of Saragossa, carved letters on wooden tablets to assist blind people to read, and an Italian, Girolamo Cardano, developed a device to assist reading and writing through the sense of touch using a method similar to modern braille.

The 17th and 18th centuries witnessed changes in attitudes and morality. With the rising awareness of enlightened child-rearing practices came the introduction of

primary schools in Europe and America, and several special schools were also opened for deaf and blind children. In the second half of the 18th century came the establishment of de l'Epée's School for the Deaf, Valentin Haüy's Institution for Blind Children in Paris. It was there that the blind Louis Braille later invented the 6-dot system of reading and writing which bears his name. The first school for the deaf in Old Kent Road, London, was established at around the same time.

One series of events in the closing years of the 18th century is often considered to be the starting point in the history of special education. It brought the name of Jean-Marc Itard from what might have been obscurity to common knowledge in the field of intellectual disability. At that time, it must have been difficult to imagine why an 11- or 12-year-old boy was wandering the desolate countryside in the French department of Aveyron (about midway between Marseilles and Bordeaux). However, it is not surprising that scientific minds, ripe with enthusiasm for discovery, accepted that a young human could have been raised in the wild. Indeed, 14 such cases of feral children had been reported up to that time, some living among wolves, bears, wild sheep, and oxen.

Victor, as the boy was known, was taken by civil authorities to Paris in 1801, where Philippe Pinel (the reformer of the notorious asylums of Bicêtre and Salpêtrière) examined him. Pinel was far from convinced that Victor was a noble savage, as he had been described. He pronounced him comparable to other children and adults whose damaged intellectual abilities rendered them incapable of providing for their own needs, or of developing through systematic instruction.

In contrast to Pinel's nativist view that learning and knowledge were solely dependent upon heredity, Itard was a *sensationalist.* He believed that all knowledge was derived from sensation and he was supremely confident that Victor could be transformed into a civilised human being through appropriate instruction. Victor had many animal-like behaviours. He selected food by smell but was indifferent to both fragrant and foul odours. He drank while lying flat on the ground, immersing his mouth in the water. He often walked on all fours or fell into a running gait. He fought with his teeth, tore off his garments, and seemed unresponsive to sounds, even when a pistol was fired directly behind him.

Itard began intensive work with Victor which was to extend over nearly a decade but, regardless of his intensive work, he was far from successful. He was unable to restore Victor to normality and, although frustrated by his apparent failure, Itard had achieved some notable successes. Humphreys—the first translator of Itard's book dealing with Victor's education—claimed that the boy's social and emotional development had been impressive. At the end of his training, Victor was clean, affectionate, able to read a few words and capable of understanding much of what was said to him. Sadly, the story of the wild boy did not have a happy ending in the style

of George Bernard Shaw's *Pygmalion*. Victor disappeared into obscurity and lived out his life in custodial care (Kenner, 1964).

From an education point of view, Itard had been the first teacher to observe and study the intellectual development of his pupils in a clinical manner. He had been the first special educator to prescribe and document teaching methods based upon psychological principles and the human characteristics of persistence, patience, and respect. Sarason and Doris (1979, p. 69) concluded that "If Itard failed, it was a magnificent failure."

When Itard finished, his student Edouard Séguin began a new era. He opened a school for children with intellectual disabilities in the mid-1830s and documented his teaching theory and practice in *The moral treatment, hygiene and education of idiots and other backward children*. The book was received in France with great enthusiasm, epitomising an educational science by providing philosophical premises, an enabling theory, a description of instructional methods, the collection of data, and evidence of results.

Political unrest in France in the mid-1800s prompted Séguin to emigrate to the United States where he settled in Ohio and recommenced his general medical practice. Several schools based upon his teaching model were already operating in the United States and he soon became involved in their management.

Special education in Australia

In the early years of colonial Australia people with a disability or impairment were housed in insane asylums, hospitals and depots for invalids. They were collected in these places mostly for convenience with little—or no—concern for type of disability or prospect of treatment or cure. Residential establishments for children and adults with mental disorders appeared in most of the colonies along the east coast of the mainland and in Van Diemen's Land, notably in Sydney, Melbourne, and Hobart. Many of these early institutions followed the overseas tradition of accommodating psychiatric patients and those with an intellectual disability in the same facility, often in the same wards. In 1811 the first public institution for people with an intellectual disability was established in New Norfolk (outside Hobart) in a precinct that became part of the Royal Derwent Hospital.

It was not long before other institutions came into existence. The Castle Hill Mental Hospital was founded to the west of Sydney and, in 1813, the Society for the Promotion of Christian Knowledge and Benevolence was formed which later became the Benevolent Society of New South Wales. In 1820, the Benevolent Asylum first admitted abandoned children.

During the early years of the colony, education was available to the privileged few but, surprisingly, the first systematic attempt at schooling occurred at Port Puer near

Hobart in Van Diemen's Land (now Tasmania). About 10% of all convicts sent to New South Wales were boys. Some were as young as nine years of age. In 1837, the sailing vessel *Frances Charlotte* left England for the penal colony. Before this voyage, children had been included in the manifest of adult convicts and handled in the same way as adults. Those on the *Frances Charlotte* were treated—and allowed to act—as children (within predetermined boundaries) and given school work onboard ship. At Point Puer, they continued their education under the Lancastrian peer tutoring system that was popular in England at that time, in which older boys were given responsibility for teaching their younger peers.

Most of the boys at Point Puer had few scholastic skills. This was not surprising since 41% of the English population at the time were illiterate. Their education consisted of reading, writing, learning the simple rules of spelling, arithmetic, tables, and ciphering. Despite these attempts, the boys made very little academic progress except in reading. In 1837, of the 99 illiterate boys in the colony, only 58 were being taught to read. In 1848, 114 of the 160 illiterates had mastered basic reading skills (Hooper, 1967).

From these humble beginnings, a major disability and special education industry emerged in much the same way as in other Western countries. The Gold Rush days of the mid-1800s brought new pressures on a community swelling with immigrants and schooling was available through both national and denominational systems that followed guidelines provided in the *National Education Act* of 1848. Although some education (perhaps not in a conventional form) was provided in institutions for delinquent and destitute children from early in the 1800s, it was not until the second half of the 1800s that attention was given to children with an intellectual disability and mental illness. Records of the Watt Street Hospital (now part of the Royal Newcastle Hospital) from 1872, Kew Cottages (in Melbourne) from 1889, and the Minda Home (in Adelaide) from 1898 refer to the employment of a teacher who, doubtless, developed and implemented some educational programs (Andrews, Elkins, Berry, & Burge, 1979).

Following international trends, the first special schools for students with sensory impairments were founded in 1880. Schools for students with a hearing impairment were opened around that time in Sydney and Melbourne (Sweetman, Long, & Smyth, 1922).

Compulsory education was legislated near the turn of the 20th century and education became a state responsibility. In Victoria, the *Education Act* of 1890 empowered the government to found special schools, although Children's Cottages had already been established in 1887 at the Kew Cottages institution, which accommodated persons with intellectual disability. The first special school was opened in the Melbourne suburb of Moonee Ponds in 1897 and, in 1911, a committee of the Victorian

Education Department began an inquiry into the education of subnormal children. It was thought that a careful study of their characteristics would lead to more effective programs than existed at the time. As a result of the committee's deliberations, the Bell Street School for Subnormal Children was opened in Fitzroy in July 1913 under the administrative direction of Stanley Porteus. Some time later Porteus developed the Porteus Maze Test and became the director of the renowned Vineland Training School for Feebleminded Girls and Boys in New Jersey in the United States.

The Bell Street School was established for children described as educable (i.e., those with IQ scores between 50 and 70) provided that they did not live in an institution. A second school for those termed "educable mentally defective children" was opened in 1915 in Port Melbourne and, in February 1923, the Victorian *Education Gazette* described another form of special education arrangement called Opportunity Grades. Unlike the schools at Fitzroy and Port Melbourne, Opportunity Grades were designed for children who were educationally backward (i.e., IQ 71–85) and were conducted in classrooms within regular schools where students received individual tuition in reading, writing, and arithmetic. By 1929, a program for training teachers to work in these Opportunity Grades was available and similar programs were developed to train teachers for work in the growing number of special schools.

Thus, by the second decade of the 20th century, initiatives were being taken to improve the education of students with learning and intellectual disabilities, with an increasing number of students being served. By the 1930s, two types of educational support had been developed. These were the special classrooms (e.g., Opportunity Grades) for children with mild disabilities (referred to as the educationally backward), and separate special schools for those children with intellectual disability who were deemed educable. Children with intellectual disabilities considered to be "trainable" only (with an IQ less than 50) were often excluded from these schools and classes although some received instruction at private schools established by various parent and voluntary organisations (such as the Endeavour Foundation in Queensland).

One of the factors contributing to the growth of special education in the years after World War II was the passage of various state Education Acts. The *Education Act* in Western Australia, for example, required the Minister to provide suitable instruction for all school-aged children (McCall, 1954). Under this Act, the distinction between educable and ineducable was dropped, but this did not mean that programs for the latter group were quick to develop. These various Education Acts parallelled developments in England in 1944 and were designed to ensure that every child received an instruction appropriate to his or her age, ability, and aptitude (Lumsden, 1954).

Although state governments in Australia had, by the 1950s, assumed formal responsibility for educating children with intellectual disability, children with a more severe intellectual disability were still generally excluded from the educational system. This

situation prevailed in some regions well into the 1970s. In the meantime, however, voluntary organisations increased their commitment to the many school-aged children with a severe intellectual disability. Before the involvement of predominantly parent groups, young people often were confined to institutions in which there were few attempts to provide education or training, or they were kept at home by parents who were convinced that they could provide better care and training than was available in an institution. The involvement of parent groups in the 1940s and 1950s thus came in response to long-term neglect.

The developments described above appear to be substantial, although the education of students with special support needs was still a minor feature of the education landscape. Many students who would qualify for school-based support today, completed their formal education without having received any compensatory or remedial education. Most students with a mild sense or motor disorder received prosthetics (e.g., spectacles or hearing aid) and were then left to cope with regular class activities. Moreover, teachers who were generally accustomed to controlled and quiet classes were often less than enthusiastic about the disruption caused by the students and their sometimes-noisy equipment—such as a brailler being used by blind students.

Class placement under the streaming system accumulated the bright students in the top classes and the less capable ones in the bottom classes. Those in the top group headed for tertiary education via an academically rigorous program, whereas those in the bottom were often subjected to a much diluted program which, in many cases, meant a major in manual or industrial arts regardless of individual needs or talents in nonacademic areas.

In the mid-1960s a negative reaction to special classes began in the United States. School administrators, policy-makers, and researchers gradually began to concede that special education was becoming a dumping ground for students who did not work well in a regular class. Arguments were mounted for reintegration of students with special needs into regular classes in which they could benefit from contact with non-disabled peers.

There have been several Australian state government legislative initiatives aimed at changing educational practice. One attempt to deal with the provision of special services for children with a handicap occurred in Victoria through the passage of the *Handicapped Children Act* in 1973. This Act defined a child with a handicap as one whose educational progress would be adversely affected unless special provisions were made at a special centre, special unit or class, or service directed toward overcoming a specific impediment.

A further development came with the Victorian state government's *White Paper on Strategies and Structures for Education* (1980). In this document, it was argued that school staff should use teaching methods and procedures that endeavoured to link

sound educational theory with practice and evaluation. The document also claimed that parents have a right to ask for, and receive, information about the educational arrangements suggested or provided for their children. Other education authorities in Australia have issued policy statements that outline the rationale, principles, types of provision available, and ways in which the curriculum can be achieved (see, as examples, Department of Education, Queensland, 1993; Northern Territory Board of Studies, 1994).

The impact of North American legislation

Perhaps the most significant international event to change the nature of education and special education was the passage of the *Education of All Handicapped Children Act* through the United States Congress in 1975. The law, known as PL 94–142 (the 142nd public law passed by the 94th Congress), enabled access to public school classrooms for thousands of children who previously had been ineligible for a public school education because of the severity of their physical disabilities or learning difficulties. This law was reauthorised in 1990 as the *Individuals with Disabilities Education Act* (IDEA) and a report was published in 2000 on the implementation of the IDEA Act (see US Department of Education, 2000).

The cornerstone of the legislation—and the supplementary PL 99-457—was the link between federal funding to school systems and the provision of an appropriate, free public education for all students between three and 21 years of age, regardless of type or severity of the individual's handicapping condition. The Act legislated assistance for school systems to meet the costs of educating students with special needs. State and local school districts were required to allocate funds up to the amount normally assigned to a non-handicapped student, and the federal government provided additional resources needed to support the specialist services and essential resources.

To receive financial assistance from the US government, each state was to ensure that school systems within its borders complied with the law. The major provisions included:

- the identification and assessment of a student with disabilities;
- the provision of an appropriate public education at no cost to the parents or guardians;
- consultation with parents or guardians, and provision of information related to the identification, assessment, and placement of their children;
- the placement of the child in the least restrictive educational environment consistent with the child's needs;
- the preparation and submission of an education plan for each student with a disability;

- the use of non-discriminatory testing and evaluation procedures and confidentiality of records; and
- training for teachers and other personnel to allow them to meet the needs of students with disabilities.

The Public Law stimulated widespread comment in the US popular press and in scholarly journals and drew attention to the need for fundamental changes in educational services for students who needed additional support beyond that being offered to other students. The US legislation had little effect on education systems in Australia and New Zealand. However, the principles on which the legislation was written did have an effect, and it was not long before Australasian educators and researchers began to advocate the introduction of inclusive education policies, albeit at a less urgent rate than being pursued in the US.

Two important concepts associated with the US legislation were seen to be of special attention. The notions of *least restrictive environment* and *individual education plan* (IEP) were soon advocated as fundamental concepts to facilitate the integration and eventual inclusion of students with special needs in regular classes and schools.

The least restrictive environment

The general principle of services for students with special support needs is the provision of instruction in an environment that is as near to normal as possible, consistent with the student's ability and the limitations imposed by any handicapping condition. In general, the regular classroom is accepted as the most suitable location for all students as it provides age-appropriate role models and interactions with peers, together with a setting that is conducive to learning. In addition to the usual instruction provided to all students, additional support services might be needed to ensure that the student's learning needs are being met.

However, it is also conceded the regular classroom might not always be the most appropriate setting for every child and that alternatives might need to be considered from time to time. One solution involves the division of student time between the regular classroom and another situation (e.g., special class or school, or unit).

There have been numerous attempts to describe the combinations of services and/or educational settings that are suitable for students with specific education needs and that ensure placement in the least restrictive environment. Perhaps the most common representation is the cascade of services described by Reynolds (1962) and later by Deno (1970). We have made some amendments to the original description to make it more relevant to contemporary education in Australia and New Zealand (see Figure 2.1, page 61), and Conway has further adapted this in Chapter 5 (see page 195).

The model in Figure 2.1 is not hierarchical. There is a basic assumption that students with a special learning need can be accommodated in regular classrooms. In other words, the model supposes that students are placed in a setting that provides learning and social experiences that are as close as possible to the normal classroom. However, at times specialist support or a specialist learning environment might be needed to achieve certain teaching and learning objectives. In other words, when it is necessary to provide additional support, these intensive educational experiences should be as brief as possible.

The various options shown in Figure 2.1 (below) are described as follows:

- *The regular classroom* is the accepted model with its social and intellectual requirements and opportunities and as a place where there are recognisable peer role models and standards of behaviour. Typically one teacher aims to accommodate the needs of all students. In some cases, additional equipment and resources are provided for students with special support needs, such as large print books or braille machines for students with a vision impairment.
- *Regular class plus consultative assistance* enables children with special needs to remain as full-time members of the regular classes. Help is provided to teachers (rather than directly to the child) by specialist consultants (e.g., consultants in reading, mathematics, art, primary or secondary special education, or behaviour) to overcome difficulties that the teacher might experience when working with students with special needs.
- *Regular class plus itinerant specialist assistance* is a common approach used to provide assistance on an irregular or infrequent basis (e.g., once a term) to an individual or a small group of students who have specific and common needs. The most frequent use of this option is with students who have a hearing or vision impairment.

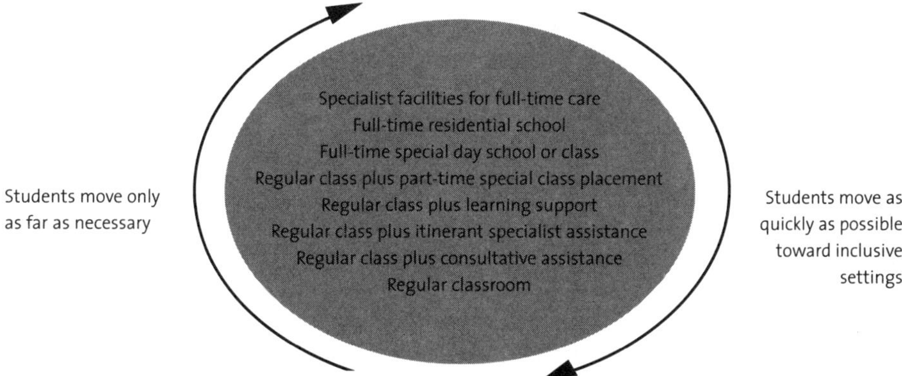

Figure 2.1 An educational services model.
Source: Deno, E. (1970).

- *Regular class plus learning support* is an efficient way of reducing the time that a student might spend out of the regular classroom receiving special instruction. Typically, a support (i.e., remedial) or resource teacher withdraws students for a number of periods per week for an intensive program in an area of academic weakness. The program called Reading Recovery was introduced using this model (Clay, 1993). Another option becoming more common in Australian schools is the use of parents and other volunteers to help students experiencing reading or other learning difficulties who are in the regular classroom on a full-time basis. In some schools, learning support teachers withdraw regular and gifted students for special mini-programs to reduce the negative connotation of withdrawal.
- *Regular class plus part-time special class placement* can be arranged for students who might benefit from additional help in a curriculum area (such as reading), or when some special training would lead to improved social or academic performance. The ratio between regular class work and special class work varies according to the availability of resources.
- *Full-time special day school or class* placement might be recommended if children are in need of specialist services that are not readily available in a regular school. These can include intensive physical therapy or similar services provided by personnel not usually located in primary or secondary schools.
- *Full-time residential schools* are isolated learning situations and are used only for children who are in need of both structured and intensive training or care (e.g., those who are hospital in-patients). Two groups of children for whom this environment might be chosen are students who have a profound intellectual disability and those who have a serious emotional disorder.
- *Specialist facilities for full-time care* include a wide range of residential facilities, such as disability wards in hospitals (although these are now rare). They might be long-term treatment centres—for example, for young people with extremely serious intellectual or multiple disabilities, or for children who are in need of continuous medical supervision (e.g., in a hospital ward). These facilities might also be designed for relatively short-term placement of children (such as those awaiting court appearances), or for the treatment of critical incidents (such as a severe emotional disturbance). Although education and training can occur at many (if not all) of these sites, the extent of instruction provided depends largely upon the purpose of the facility.

Individual education plans (IEPs)

An IEP is a mandatory inclusion under the requirements of the US Public Law 94-142 and the subsequent *Individuals with Disabilities Education Act*. Notwithstanding the legal requirements, the reality of IEPs in the United States appears not to match the ideal. Many teachers and administrators fail to accept the IEPs as part of a total process for educating students with special needs. They view the IEPs as isolated products to be used as evidence of legal compliance. Sometimes, the focus is upon how the forms are completed, rather than on how to plan and implement effective programs. In some schools, teachers evade the obligation—and contravene the spirit of the Act—by copying an IEP written for one student and applying it to another (or several others) without amendment.

Australian and New Zealand teachers and education authorities have not been confronted with a legal—and economic—prescription of the type associated with the the United States legislation. Although there has been an obvious movement toward the inclusion of students with special needs into regular classes, and although there might be an administrative policy directive that IEPs be prepared for students, teachers are not *legally* compelled to develop programs to suit children's specific needs.

In Australia, IEPs are typically written only for students who have been authenticated as needing the highest level of support. In most cases, these are prepared with care and diligence. In New Zealand, IEPs (and individual development plans—IDPs—at the early childhood level) are an administrative requirement. To facilitate the introduction and use of IEPs, the New Zealand Ministry of Education, in conjunction with Massey University and the Central District Branch of the Special Education Service, prepared inservice material to be used as part of school staff development processes (Thomson et al., 1991). This program dealt with, among other matters, school organisation, the development of educational goals and objectives for the child, program adaptations, and communication skills needed to facilitate an effective IEP team.

Briefly, the IEP serves as a written commitment of resources and relevant services. It records the participants' responsibilities, a management device that states goals and objectives and ensures the availability of resources and services, a statement of agreement by the stakeholders (e.g., parents and school staff), and an ongoing evaluation device for measuring student progress.

An IEP must contain:

- a statement of the student's current educational achievement levels;
- the annual educational goals, including short-term instructional objectives;
- a statement detailing educational services to be provided and the extent to which each child participates in regular programs;
- the anticipated date for the start of these services and the expected duration of the services; and
- the appropriate objective criteria and evaluation procedures, with a review at least annually to determine whether the instructional objectives have been met.

IEPs in New Zealand typically accompany requests from a school for assistance from outside the school's operating grants—for example, directly from the Ministry of Education. This being the case, IEPs tend to relate to students with low incidence conditions—such as multiple disabilities—as schools are primarily responsible for children who have less severe learning problems.

However, in Australia, parents, teachers, educational administrators, and researchers were concerned with the long-term effects of segregating students from their non-disabled peers. Indeed, in 1975, the federal Schools Commission began to urge the state education departments to move away from special classes and school placement to integration. Integration is now an established part of the education process in Australia and New Zealand, although there are still many educators who question the wisdom of integration and dispute whether students with special needs can achieve full inclusion within regular classrooms. In Chapter 3, issues relating to both term (integration and inclusion) are considered, together with contemporary trends in the provision of appropriate education for students with special needs.

Contemplating statistics

With modern technology and databases, it would seem to be a relatively modest task for policy-makers and service-providers to predict future resource needs in the fields of human services and education. The incidences of most debilitating conditions have been known for decades. For example, sensorineural hearing loss occurs in about two children in every 1,000. To take another example, about 30% of school-age children have a vision impairment, but in only about two cases in every thousand is the impairment sufficient to warrant special educational adaptations beyond the correction provided by spectacles.

Some medical conditions are gender specific. For example, about 1% of the population have an intellectual disability; one in every 10,000–15,000 girls are affected by Rett syndrome; and on average one in 3,500 boys is affected by Duchenne muscular dystrophy. The incidence of some conditions—such as Down syndrome—increases with the age of the mother.

Statistics on incidence are available at the level of state services but national figures on physical, medical, psychological, and intellectual conditions are not as accessible from sources such as the Australian Bureau of Statistics (ABS) as one might like.

The document entitled "Disability and Disabling Conditions" (Australian Bureau of Statistics, 2001a) provided information based upon 1998 data across the human lifespan. The ABS uses definitions drawn from the World Health Organization and refers to *disability* as a restriction or lack of ability—resulting from an impairment—to perform an activity in the manner or within the range considered normal. A long-term health condition is one that has lasted, or is likely to last, for six months

or more. Not all long-term health conditions restrict people in their everyday activities and result in a disability.

Population statistics

According to the ABS document quoted above, of a population of approximately 18.6 million people in 1998, there were 3.61 million Australians with a disability (about 19%) and a further 3.16 million with a long-term condition or impairment that is not disabling (17%). Males and females were equally represented. The likelihood of having a disability rises with age, with boys having higher rates of disability (from 5% at birth to 12% during adolescence) than girls (3% to 7%). These data reflect the higher incidence of birth disorders in boys and their higher prevalence of childhood complications.

The likelihood of having a restricting impairment (one that limits easy movement around the community or performance of basic self-care activities) also increases with age. For those aged 85 years and over, 75% of women and 68% of men have a physical impairment compared with 3% each of boys and girls aged to 14 years. However, some impairments are more common at particular ages. For example, of those with an intellectual impairment, 42% are aged under 25 years and 30% of those with a psychological impairment are aged between 35 and 54 years.

The severity of restriction varies according to the type of impairment a person has. People with head injury, stroke or brain damage and those with a psychological or intellectual impairment are the most likely to have a profound or severe restriction. Generally, women have higher levels of restriction than men because of their higher numbers in the older age groups. Of the 199,800 women with an intellectual impairment, 70% had a profound or severe restriction, compared with 53% of the 293,300 men with this type of impairment. Similarly, of those with a sense or speech impairment, 48% of women and 34% of men had a profound or severe restriction.

Disability is commonly associated with older people, but children are at risk because of conditions present at birth and as a consequence of environmental factors such as accidents. A number of conditions occur more frequently or are of particular interest for other reasons. These include asthma, attention deficit disorder/attention deficit and hyperactivity disorder (ADD/ADHD), intellectual and developmental disorders, and hearing or speech loss. Of the 3.9 million children aged to 14 years in 1998, fewer than one in 12 had a disability (296,300 or 8%). Boys are more likely to be affected (10%) than girls (5%). In addition, there were more boys with one or more of the selected conditions than girls (291,700 and 181,200 respectively).

Asthma is the most common persistent health condition for young people, affecting about 312,000 children. However, unlike other conditions, there is a lower level of restriction associated with this condition. For example, about 74% of those with asthma live normal or near-normal lives.

While the overall incidence of these selected conditions is greater for boys than for girls, the difference between the sexes is particularly pronounced in the case of ADD/ADHD. Of children with a disability, nearly one in five boys (19%) had this condition, compared with one in 14 girls (7%). Although ADD/ADHD represents only a small number of children overall, it is a condition that has been diagnosed more frequently during the past ten years or so.

School statistics

Determining the number of children who require special support in schools has become a more and more difficult task. The first edition of this textbook in 1989 included a section listing the number of students who were receiving support because of various educational needs. With each edition of the book, the data became less secure as state education authorities gradually changed the way in which they collected and recorded data about special needs services. Today, it is not possible to provide comparative data.

Some data can be gained from ABS reports. The 1999 *Child Care Survey* provided information about the children who attended preschool from about the age of three years. In that year, there were 231,600 attending preschool. From the age of five, children are expected to attend school.

In each Australian state and territory, there is a different emphasis upon the various types of educational services available for students with special support needs. In many instances, identification is based upon a subjective evaluation or on assessment data (in a process called ascertainment) that can lead to the identification of a student as being in need of support at a specific time or in a certain situation, but fail to do so in the case of a similar student in another place at another time. Hence, it is now quite difficult to compile figures that reflect the number of children (or adults) who have a particular educational need. Although such figures might be informative, they give no indication of the level or extent of support needed, or given.

The ABS compiles a school census report each year that includes information on children in government and non-government schools. Some indication of the size of the education community can be gained from Table 2.2.

The ABS document entitled *Schools Australia: Preliminary* (Australian Bureau of Statistics, 2001b) reported that, in August 2000, there were 9,595 schools in Australia. Of these, state Departments of Education ran 6,961 (73%). Schools catered for 3,247,456 full-time students and, of these, about 69% were in government schools. There were 150,610 full-time equivalent teachers in government schools and 67 449 in non-government schools. There had been a gradual increase in the number of students attending school over the preceding decade: from 3,031,400 in 1989 to the figure given above in 1999.

Table 2.2 Students attending school by gender

LOCATION	MALE	FEMALE	TOTAL
	Primary		
New South Wales	322,767	306,197	628,964
Victoria	232,092	219,613	451,705
Queensland	187,965	178,192	366,157
South Australia	82,116	77,256	159,372
Western Australia	98,665	93,376	192,041
Tasmania	24,182	23,038	47,220
Northern Territory	13,370	12,733	26,103
Australian Capital Territory	16,539	15,735	32,274
Total	**977,696**	**926,140**	**1,903,836**
	Secondary		
New South Wales	233,118	232,234	465,352
Victoria	174,766	175,252	350,018
Queensland	119,229	117,525	236,754
South Australia	44,984	45,029	90,013
Western Australia	63,244	62,478	125,722
Tasmania	18,112	18,205	36,317
Northern Territory	5,651	5,627	11,278
Australian Capital Territory	14,245	13,921	28,166
Total	**673,349**	**670,271**	**1,343,620**

Source: Australian Bureau of Statistics (2001b).

Table 2.2 (above), shows data relating to school attendance based on 2000 data. For additional information, you are referred to the ABS website where you can find a warehouse of interesting material <www.abs.gov.au/Ausstats>.

Providing programs and resources for students with diverse education needs has been a continuing challenge for governments and non-government education authorities. It might seem appropriate simply to provide educational opportunities for all children as required. However, sound financial planning and resource management demands that at least some consideration be given to estimating the number of students who might require additional support inside or outside school (e.g., students who are termed gifted or talented, or students with serious mobility problems). For some children—such as those with vision or hearing impairments—the known extent of

the impairment can be used as a basis for such an estimation. For others, in whom the disability is less overt or very rare (e.g., Rett syndrome, muscular dystrophy, or serious multiple impairments such as vision and hearing impairments) prevalence statistics are also known, but the provision of appropriate supports for these children might be based solely on when and where such disabilities occur.

The ABS (2001b) document provided some detail about children who need special attention. Its data revealed 185,800 children aged to 14 (5% of all children) who have some form of schooling restriction. Consistent with the higher disability rate for boys, they were twice as likely as girls to have this type of restriction (6% and 3% respectively). As might be expected, schooling restrictions were reported more often for children who had ADD/ADHD or for those with an intellectual or developmental disorder (84% and 88% respectively). Various problems arise as a result of these restrictions, but the most common problems reported were learning and intellectual problems, which affected 73,300 boys and 24,200 girls.

There is a range of supports available to children with a schooling restriction. For example, 77,400 children attended a special class or school, and 89,200 received special assistance or tuition. However, not all children received as much support as they needed, but approximately 85% received some form of support.

Meeting educational needs

Traditionally, education has been provided in class size groups. In the 1950s, these groups often contained 40, 50, or even 60 students, all of whom were competing for limited resources and teacher attention. Assignment to a class was made on the basis of age and, sometimes, on the basis of achievement. In other words, the top students were assigned to the "A" class, the average students to the "B" class, and the low ability students were relegated to the "C" class. However, this form of segregation did not remove all variations in ability. "A", "B", and "C" classes still contained students with a range of abilities, although the variability was somewhat reduced.

Over the years, class sizes have shrunk and teachers and parents have taken some solace in the belief that smaller classes provide greater learning opportunities for students. However, the question of how to provide the *most* appropriate instruction has remained largely unanswered. In many classrooms, instruction might still be aimed at the average student (whether through expediency or design). This means that brighter students survive (or are held back), and that lower ability students have to catch up through increased personal effort or additional assistance, or fall farther behind.

Educators in Australia and overseas have tried, through personal and school-based initiatives, to solve the dilemma of how to manage mixed ability classes. They have focused upon the assessment of individual student needs, the evaluation of the most

appropriate instructional settings, and consideration of the most appropriate teaching strategies. The use of the word *appropriate* is the weak element in this approach because what might be appropriate for one child might be inappropriate for another. The adaptation of a curriculum in a certain way might assist one child but it might be detrimental to another who has the same medical condition. How teachers and school systems have addressed these issues differs from place to place and, in some countries, meeting children's needs *appropriately* has a political and legislative connotation.

SUMMARY

Students with special needs have traditionally been provided with services from within the educational domain known as special education. Such students have been supported by teachers who have special training to work with them and, in many situations, have been presented with a curriculum that has been modified to take into account their special circumstances. Over the past few years, an ever increasing number of students with physical and intellectual disabilities has been included in regular classrooms and served by classroom teachers, with or without assistance from specialist teachers or consultants.

The World Health Organization has established definitions for several terms that have been used widely, but not universally, in special education. "Impairment" refers to the loss or abnormality of psychological, physiological or anatomical structure or functions. "Disability" refers to any restriction or lack of ability (resulting from impairment) to perform an activity in the manner or within the range considered normal for a human being. "Handicap" refers to the disadvantage for an individual that results from impairment or disability that limits or prevents fulfilment of a role that is normal for that individual.

Labelling is a controversial issue in education. Without a label, the provision of special education services to some students is difficult to justify. Although there might be some advantages in classifying children according to some predetermined characteristics, problems with labelling and classification have been more compelling than has the attraction of convenience. There are five main disadvantages to the use of labels. Labels focus on the negative aspects of the disability, divide people into mutually exclusive categories, lead to stigma and inappropriate social response, foster myths and half-truths, and can lead to lower expectations of achievement in a variety of academic and non-academic areas.

A commonly used representation of available settings is that of a hierarchy of support services that is based on the assumption that students are placed in an educational setting that provides learning and social experiences that are as close as possible to those of a normal classroom. The various options include: specialist facilities for full-time care; full-time residential school; full-time special day school; full-time special

class within a regular school; regular class plus part-time special class placement; regular class plus resource teacher or support services assistance; regular class plus consultant assistance; and the regular classroom.

The written history of special education began in the first few years of the 1800s through the work of Itard and Séguin. In Australia and New Zealand, as elsewhere, special provisions for children with special needs began in the mid-1800s with the establishment of schools and classes for students with a visual or hearing impairment. During the second half of the 1800s, special programs for children with intellectual disabilities and mental illness were inaugurated. The beginning of the 20th century saw the introduction of compulsory education and the consequent establishment of special schools for students with an intellectual disability.

The reaction against the segregation of students with special needs into special schools and classes came from parents, teachers, educational administrators, and researchers who were concerned with the long-term effects of segregating students from their non-disabled peers. In 1975 the Schools Commission in Australia promoted the movement toward integration. Today, integration is considered the appropriate model for the education of students with special needs, particularly for those who have a mild intellectual disability or physical impairment.

Determining the number of students who need support and the form of support needed has become increasingly difficult over the past ten years or so. The best estimate comes from an extrapolation of results from various surveys and suggests that approximately 5% of school-aged children have a condition for which special services are necessary.

Two issues have emerged as important concepts in special education. *Individual education plan* refers to the development of special education programs that meet the specific needs of individual students. *Least restrictive environment* refers to the placement of individual students in the most suitable education setting.

Suggested reading

Here are three important websites you can visit:

- the website of the Human Rights and Equal Opportunities Commission at <www.hreoc.gov.au>;
- the Australian Privacy Commissioner's website at <www.privacy.gov.au>; and
- the Salamanca statement on principles, policy, and practice in special needs education that reaffirms the right to education of every individual, as enshrined in the 1948 Universal Declaration of Human Rights; it was made by the world community at the 1990 World Conference on Education for All in Salamanca, Spain; the URL is <www.unesco.org/education/educprog/sne/salamanc>.

Also peruse the following journals:

- *Disability and Society*;
- *Mental Retardation*; and
- *The International Journal of Disability, Development and Education*.

Practical activities

1. Take a stroll around your town or city. Make a list of the sites or buildings that might restrict the access of people who have a disability or impairment, and those that make access easy. You might limit your study to restaurants, schools, and state or council buildings and services. How many of these disability access spaces are inadvertently discriminating (e.g., ramps at the back of buildings only)? Have a wander around your own home and make the same evaluation. How easy would it be to get around your home if you were blind or restricted to a wheelchair?
2. Make contact with one or more advocacy groups in your area, region, or state (e.g., Epilepsy Foundation, Autistic Association, self-advocacy groups for people with an intellectual disability, associations or societies for the blind, Association for Gifted and Talented Children). Ask for literature on the rights of people generally, and on the right to an appropriate education. When you have a collection of this literature, look for common concerns or for overlap of material.
3. Make contact with your local education authority and collect literature on the forms of special education support that are available.
4. Refer to Figure 2.1 (page 61). What circumstances do you think would require children to be placed in a full-time special day school? How might this learning environment be changed to allow for greater integration of children with special needs into a less restrictive situation?
5. Collect information relating to the history of special education in your region (e.g., number and location of special schools). What were some of the significant factors that led to changes in support services?

References

Andrews, R. J., Elkins, J., Berry, P. B., & Burge, J. A. (1979). *A survey of special education in Australia: Provisions, needs and priorities in the education of children with handicaps and learning difficulties*. St Lucia, Qld: Fred and Eleanor Schonell Educational Research Centre.

Australian Bureau of Statistics. (2001a). *Disability and Disabling Conditions* (ABS Catalogue No. 4433.0). Canberra, ACT: Author.

Australian Bureau of Statistics. (2001b). *Schools Australia, Preliminary* (ABS Catalogue No. 4220.0). Canberra, ACT: Author.

Clay, M. (1993). *Reading Recovery: A guide book for teachers in training*. Portsmouth, NH: Heinemann.

Commonwealth of Australia. (1992). *Disability Discrimination Act 1992*. Canberra: Australian Government Publishing Service.

Deno, E. (1970). Special education as developmental capital. *Exceptional Children*, 37, 229 – 237.

Department of Education Queensland. (1993). *Educational provisions for students with disabilities: Policy statement and development plan*. Brisbane, Qld: Author.

Hayes, R., & Macalpine, S. (1986). A lawyer's views of special education: Past, present and future. *Australian Journal of Special Education*, 10, 33–9.

Hooper, F. C. (1967). *Prison boys of Port Arthur: A study of the Point Puer Boys' establishment, Van Diemen's Land, 1834 to 1850*. Melbourne: Cheshire.

Kenner, L. (1964). *A history of the care and study of the mentally retarded*. Springfield, IL: Charles C. Thomas.

Lumsden, J. (1954). Developments in the provision for handicapped children in England. *The Slow Learning Child*, 1, 33–36.

McCall, J. (1954). Developments in the provision for handicapped children in Western Australia. *The Slow Learning Child*, 1, 22–26.

Ministerial Council on Education, Employment, Training and Youth Affairs. (1994). *National strategy for equity in schooling*. Carlton, Vic: Curriculum Corporation.

Northern Territory Board of Studies. (1994). *Special education policy: Provision for students with disabilities in Northern Territory schools*. Darwin: Northern Territory Department of Education.

Sarason, S. B., & Doris, J. (1979). *Educational handicap, public policy and social history*. New York: The Free Press.

Sweetman, E., Long, C. R., & Smyth, J. (1922). *A history of state education in Victoria*. Melbourne: Education Department of Victoria/Critchley Parker.

Thomson, C., Brown, D., Chapman, J., Benson, A., & Pine, T. (1991). *Individualised Educational Planning: A guide for meeting learners' needs*. Wellington, NZ: Ministry of Education.

US Department of Education. (2000). *To assure the free appropriate public education of all children with disabilities: Twenty-second Annual Report to Congress on the Implementation of the Individuals with disabilities Education Act* (Available at http://www.ed.gov/offices/OSERS/OSEP). Jessup, MD: Author.

Victorian State Government. (1980). *White paper on the strategies and structures of education*. Melbourne: Government Printer.

Young, L., Ashman, A., Sigafoos, J., & Grevell, P. (2001). Closure of the Challinor Centre II: An extended report on 95 individuals after 12 months of community living. *Journal of Intellectual and Developmental Disability*, 26, 51–66.

3

The school context

JOHN ELKINS

Case studies

Marcelle

Marcelle is 17 years of age and attends a high school near her home. Her education used to differ markedly from that of other young women in her neighbourhood. Until last year she had an education program based in a special class loosely attached to another high school several suburbs distant. She had been taught to use public transport and no longer needed to be brought to school by taxi. There she learnt functional daily-living skills including personal hygiene and some basic cooking. She also learnt to recognise survival words such as "drink" and "toilet".

Specialist teachers and other professionals provided hands-on services with Marcelle on a one-on-one or two-on-one basis whenever there were sufficient staff. She never had homework, had few friends outside her special class, and none from her own suburb. But when the results of pioneering research on the inclusion of students in high school classes became known, educators cautiously accepted a request from Marcelle's parents that she attend her local high school and participate in a range of classes—all of which contained mostly students who did not have major disabilities.

Although teachers were somewhat apprehensive about the change, with guidance from a special educator they soon learnt how to involve Marcelle in one of two ways. Sometimes she achieved progress toward a reduced set of learning outcomes that were consistent with those of the class when they were working on mathematics or English activities. At other times, she learnt how to perform cognitive, motor, or social tasks unique to her needs while participating in small group activities pertinent to the class lesson. For example, if there was a science lesson, Marcelle was included in the small work groups and, with support and considerable patience from her classmates, was able to participate in the experiments.

Overall Marcelle, her family, and the school community have grown through the experience of her inclusion. According to her parents, she has become a new person. She looks forward to school each day, is much easier to manage at home, has significantly improved her vocabulary, and is paying much more attention to her personal care.

Constance McGregor

Now that community attitudes are much more accepting than in past decades—think back to the 2000 Paralympic Games in Sydney—it is likely that the principal of a primary school is likely to be the first person who is approached to discuss school enrolment with the parents of a child with a disability. This is what happened to Constance McGregor toward the end of the school year.

Mrs Edakis, the mother of a Year 2 student called Tony, had phoned to discuss her son's attending Endeavour School in the new year. She brought Tony to the appointment

and he seemed interested in the school environment. Mrs Edakis explained that Tony had been seriously ill as a toddler and that his previously normal development had been compromised, with delayed language, mild autistic tendencies, and fascination with electric torches and ladders. Tony had received weekly speech therapy for the past two years, and had attended both a regular kindergarten and an early-intervention program each week.

Ms McGregor was aware of the many factors that would need consideration. Mrs Edakis did not reject the option of a special class or school for Tony. She simply wanted him to have the best school experience, academically and socially. Of course, having Tony attend the same school as his sister was desirable but she knew how valuable the specialist input had been to Tony's development since his illness. Mrs Edakis asked Constance whether Tony could receive ongoing speech therapy. Fortunately this was a possibility, but the length of the waiting list would need to be checked. At the same time Constance would enquire about some teacher's aide time. These services, she knew, would be contingent upon an assessment and the preparation of an individual education plan (IEP).

The review team would face the challenge of developing a feasible plan that would work in a regular classroom. Constance knew that experienced special educators often constructed IEPs as if the student were in a special setting. It would be imperative to involve the class teacher right from the start. But did she have a teacher in the reception classes who could take on the challenge of providing an excellent education for Tony? Yes, there was at least one experienced early-childhood teacher who could handle the challenge and several others who would be willing to do so in future years if Tony's inclusion was successful.

Constance knew that provision of resources would be essential if the Teachers' Union representative on the school staff were not to oppose Tony's placement, but she knew also that entanglement in anti-discrimination legislation was something to be avoided. An overarching consideration was the belief that inclusion should be attempted. As principal, it was her responsibility to set up the attitudinal and resource context for Tony's enrolment to be successful.

What you will learn in this chapter

This chapter deals predominantly with students who have high support needs because of a disability or impairment. It focuses attention on changes to schools and education practices as a consequence of the adoption of a policy of inclusion in states and territories in Australia and in New Zealand. In this chapter you will learn about:

- the difference between the terms *integration* and *inclusion*;
- the development of special education services, and their effectiveness;
- the feasibility of including all students in regular schools and classes; and

- the need to consider how changes might occur in the curriculum to assist the inclusion of students with diverse abilities in regular classes.

From integration toward inclusion

Students with a disability have developmental needs that must be addressed not only by their parents but also by schools and school systems. These students have not traditionally been served in regular schools and classes but by a special education system although, in recent years, much debate has occurred about the most appropriate ways of educating them. Many terms have been used to describe the notion of educating students with disabilities in regular classrooms. These include integration, mainstreaming, and inclusion. However, the terms have not been used consistently and it is important to make distinctions among these terms at the commencement of this chapter.

I avoid the term mainstreaming because it was predominantly used in the United States, and has fallen from common use. Inclusion is an often-preferred word because it implies the complete acceptance of a student with a disability in a regular class, with appropriate changes being made to ensure that the student is included in all activities of the class. Following Loreman (1999), I use integration to mean the education of students with disabilities in regular schools *without significant change* in the nature of the host school.

Integration often occurs when students who have been in a special school or class are educated for some or all of the day in regular classrooms. In many cases additional support is provided, although some students manage without formal assistance. There is usually a limit to the available support and, for this or other less tangible reasons, some students are deemed unsuitable for integration. Another characteristic of integration is its frequent occurrence at a school that is not the school the students would have attended if they did not have a disability. In many situations, specialist teachers and supports for students with disabilities are available at specified schools, often as a result of education systems trying to provide resources economically. Thus, inclusion is characterised by the design of regular schools, both physically and in curriculum, to provide for the full education of all students who seek to attend. This mission to provide appropriately for all students applies not only to public schools, but also to those operated by religious organisations and independent schools. It is clear that although inclusion might exist for particular students in a small number of schools, it is not the usual policy or practice in Australia. The circumstances for inclusion appear to be more positive in New Zealand.

There are variations among the standard categories of disability. Most students with vision impairments, and those with hearing impairments who do not use sign languages, are well supported in regular classes. However, any necessary support staff and resources will have been provided by sources outside the school's regular budget.

This can tend to reduce the extent to which students with disabilities are thought to belong to the school community. Students whose disabilities do not require a high level of resources are also commonly enrolled in regular classes but, under current circumstances in which schools are competing for students and for high academic achievement, such students might not be highly valued by schools. However, although the situation of many students with disabilities attending regular schools is best described as integration, there has been a remarkable trend over the past three decades toward the only students who attend special schools being those with very high support needs and often multiple impairments. It appears that few educators or members of the public see this situation as inappropriate. Parents themselves are somewhat polarised, with some groups being ardent advocates for inclusion, whereas others prefer to support traditional segregated special education services. It is understandable that some parents might wish to have a choice, allowing them to change the school placement if there are problems at their child's existing school.

The situation in the Australian states and territories and in New Zealand is complicated by political and structural changes that have had profound effects upon education bureaucracies. Thus, in some cases special education is no longer used to describe any administrative unit within an education department. Although most types of service provision for students with special needs have remained, there have been changes in the proportion of students served in special schools, in special classes, and in regular classes, and much variability exists across education systems and sectors.

Another facet of change has been the increased prominence within education of the political concept of *social justice*. Social justice seeks to maximise educational outcomes for all students. This has been supported by the advent of anti-discrimination legislation in the area of disability. Thus, there has been considerable discussion about providing education *fairly* to all students, including those with disabilities. In addition, the likelihood of parents rejecting segregated settings as being discriminatory has increased. Various North American advocates of the inclusion of children with severe disabilities in regular classes have visited the antipodes to challenge parents and school staff to be more assertive in dealing with educational bureaucracies. These have included Michael Giangreco, Bruce Strulley, Doug Biklen, Marsha Forrest, and Jack Pearpoint. In New Zealand and, to varying extents in some Australian states, parents and local communities have considerable control over schools, and some of the advocacy role has shifted from central bureaucracies to local school councils or boards. Cases determined in the Australian Human Rights and Equal Opportunity Commission have, in some instances, resulted in the defendant school or education system having its discriminatory practices allowed under the clause that allows discrimination on the grounds of unreasonable hardship. Other actions brought by parents have resulted in schools being required to pay damages (van Kraayenoord,

2000). Unfortunately, when parents' claims of discrimination have been upheld, it has usually resulted in the child's enrolling elsewhere. This has occurred because of the time taken for the tribunal to reach a decision, and the likelihood that the confrontation has soured relationships between the school and the student and family.

Even if schools have provided an appropriate program, an understanding of the full meaning of inclusion can be lacking. Recent cases have highlighted events such as holding a high school prom at an inaccessible venue, and selecting a school excursion that was inaccessible to students using wheelchairs. Judging by newspaper columns and letters to the editor, the general public remains unappreciative of what such practices indicate.

It is important to recognise that regular schools already provide varied educational experiences for students, and that meeting the needs of those who have disabilities or other special education needs is often a simple extension of this practice. In secondary schools, the curriculum is highly differentiated in response to student choice and need (Hart, 1996). In primary schools, curriculum differentiation occurs mostly through classroom teachers' use of informal grouping and assignment setting. Within the constraints of, for example, tertiary entrance requirements, such approaches are also common in secondary schools.

Schooling for students with special needs must be considered in a family context. This means that schools need to work in partnership with parents. In most cases, parents are those best placed to know how school can tailor its services to the needs of an individual child. By using procedures such as individual education plans (IEPs), mutual information flow can be improved. Parents are also increasingly involved in school governance and this might result in a parent of a child with disabilities being in a position to influence policy and practices in the school.

Background issues

As we saw in Chapter 2, in the early decades of the 20th century special education services in Australia tended to be provided in special schools outside the regular state education systems. Such special schools were mostly for children with sensory disabilities. Later, special schools for children with physical disabilities were established and, later still, special provisions were made for students with an intellectual disability.

This last group of children, who today we would regard as having moderate to very high support needs, were usually not expected to attend school, in part because society often expressed disapproval of their participation in community life. Thus, it was not until around the 1950s that there was a general move to provide education for such children and this initiative came not from state education departments but from organisations (often called subnormal children's welfare associations) that had been formed by parents and concerned citizens. Again, these children were placed in special

schools—in those days often called training centres, since the staff were not always required to be trained teachers.

As IQ tests became more widely available, students who had displayed very poor school progress were assessed to see if low intelligence was indeed the cause. When low IQ was found, usually in the range from 50 to 70 points, it was often concluded that an alternative and separate form of schooling would be beneficial. Thus, in New South Wales the Opportunity (OA) classes were developed and in Queensland both special classes and separate special schools were set up, again with the label "opportunity". It is a matter of debate how much these segregated provisions were an attempt to give failing students a new opportunity by freeing them from the demands of the rigid state school curriculum. Another interpretation of the support given to the establishment of special schools and classes is that regular teachers were freed from the need to provide appropriately for these students with apparently low ability. In considering this issue it is worth remembering that, until the 1960s, schools often had class sizes of more than 40, that teachers often had only one or two years of preservice education, and that guidance or consultancy services were very rarely available.

The effectiveness of special education services

One way of analysing alternative patterns of organisation of special education services is to compare their *effectiveness*. In the United States, Epps and Tindal (1987) noted that studies comparing regular and special class placement—particularly for children with mild intellectual disabilities—were common in the 1950s and 1960s, prior to the ideological ferment that gave birth to PL 94–142. It was usually concluded that there was no advantage in special class placement for these students. This view had been popularised by Dunn's (1968) classic article "Special education for the mildly retarded: Is much of it justifiable?". Later reviewers commented on the poor quality of the efficacy research, particularly because of bias in subject selection. For example, Carlberg and Kavale (1980) found that only 50 of 860 studies were sufficiently free of design flaws to warrant inclusion in their review. Their results indicated some disadvantages accruing from special class placement for children with IQs in the 50–90 range. Wang and Baker (1985–86) also conducted a review of more recent efficacy studies and found support for mainstreaming rather than for placement in separate classes.

One of the problems associated with the comparison of special versus regular class placement is the implication that placement equals treatment type. Until the 1990s, these efficacy studies were not successful (Epps & Tindal, 1987). Indeed, it is probably true to say that the provision of special educational services to children in any particular state or nation has little to do with research evidence as to the best way to teach children with particular disabilities. Therefore, we need to examine other evidence about integration versus segregation to determine if either is of benefit to students educationally or socially.

It is apparent that evidence of the efficacy of integrated or segregated placement of children with mild educational problems is unlikely to be crucial in deciding what type of education is best. Another perspective has emerged from sociological literature in England, the United States and, more recently, Australia. In brief, it is argued that once they are established, separate special education services act to perpetuate the need for their existence. As such, there was a pronounced bias of opinion favouring segregated special education. Tomlinson (1982), Barton (1986), and Swann (1988) are early British researchers who have put forward such sociological explanations. More recently, Jenkinson (1996) and Slee (1996) have offered some ideas based on recent Australian experiences, whereas Slee and Weiner (1998) discuss the tension between school effectiveness and social justice.

In the United Kingdom, the term special educational needs has been used, and it has been the accepted view that up to 20% of children need some form of additional educational support during their school experience. Clearly, if this were an accurate estimate, and if support were to be provided to one-fifth of children at some stage of their schooling, we would be forced to ask whether the huge resources going into supplementary programs would not be better applied to the reform of regular education. If we accept that special education is a relative concept (being needed only to the extent of regular school provision), there is a risk that strengthening this special education will weaken regular schools, thereby increasing the need for special provisions. And so the cycle continues. At times education systems in some countries have developed so many types of schools that it has seemed difficult to find a regular school!

When we look back 20 years, we note that a distinction was made between normative categories that relate to a known cause (such as impaired vision, hearing, or physical disability) and the other non-normative forms of special educational need (particularly learning disability, behaviour problems, and mild intellectual disability). Sociological arguments are more compelling when applied to non-normative varieties of educational support. British sociologists have made a valuable contribution by countering the rosy, philanthropic view of special education with one that alleges that it serves "prevailing dominant social and economic and professional vested interests" (Tomlinson, 1982, p. 2). They have also criticised guidance and school psychology staff for the way in which they have professionalised and mystified the identification and placement of children with special needs. It is important to note that guidance officers and advisory staff have played, and in some places still play, an important role in placement of children in special programs and facilities through a process of identification and diagnosis that is sometimes called ascertainment of special needs. In practical terms, it is difficult to judge to what extent criticisms of English practices can

be transferred to Australia or New Zealand. However, unless there is strong parent advocacy in schools, there is a risk of professional domination of policy and practice. It would be valuable for you to read about the London borough of Newham's documentation of how parents brought about change from special schools to inclusion over a 12-year period (Alderson, 1999; Rogers, 1996).

Given current moves in several Australian states and territories toward widespread achievement testing in regular schools, it is interesting to note that Swann (1988) considered that mainstream developments in the United Kingdom—such as a national curriculum and achievement testing—were more likely to influence special education than was government policy itself. Socio-political influences on the segregation-versus-integration question have been noted by Henderson (1988) and Tarr (1988) in Victoria where, despite the landmark pro-integration policy adopted in the Ministerial Review (Integration in Victorian Education, 1984), the place of special schools has remained largely unchanged.

Normalisation in education

The word "mainstreaming" was used in the United States to refer to the integration of special education students in regular (or mainstream) classes. The term implies placement in the mainstream. Sometimes hasty or inappropriate student transfers have been criticised as "maindumping" (Chapman, 1988) and there was some early evidence that relatively few children with special needs were truly mainstreamed in American public schools (Danielson & Bellamy, 1989). However, vigorous advocacy for the inclusion of virtually all students with a disability has been increasing as evidence has accumulated on numerous successful programs for students with substantial disabilities (Giangreco, 1989, 1992, 1993, 1996). Here the evidence was not about the possible merits of comparative effectiveness but that inclusion actually worked to provide the academic and social benefits desired.

The concept of the *least restrictive environment* that had been developed in PL 94–142 (now IDEA) was, in a sense, an amalgam of the *cascade* model of service described in Chapter 2 (see page 59) and the concept of *normalisation* that arose in the Scandinavian countries. Bank-Mikkelsen (1969) was one of the early writers to argue against a too protective approach to services for children and adults with disabilities, and to advocate that they should enjoy a lifestyle as close as possible to that of society in general. Nirje (1985) added that the achievement of such outcomes needed to be based upon methods that were culturally normative. These ideas were also adopted by Wolfensberger (1972) who became prominent in America and elsewhere for his views that emphasised the *valuing* of people. Later preferring the term *social role valorisation*, Wolfensberger has taken emphasis away from mechanical application of rules, and has reasserted that valuing of people in society is paramount (Wolfensberger, 1984; 1988). This suggests that it is inappropriate to expect administrative action alone

to produce successful outcomes. If children with disabilities are to be educated successfully, much effort might need to be expended on preparing other children, teachers and the wider community to understand and accept the philosophy of inclusion (Thomas, 2001).

Enacting policy for students with disabilities

Early Australian criticisms of special schools for students with a disability were raised more than two decades ago by Berry, Andrews, and Elkins (1977). They found that, from the perspective of normalisation, special schools were substantially better than other types of disability services such as sheltered workshops and residences, although special schools were usually sited away from neighbourhood facilities, thereby restricting the social integration of the students. Following the transfer of most voluntary organisation training centres (as special schools were once called) to state education departments, neighbourhood location of special schools became more common.

Examples of improvements in special schools can be seen in the study of transition programs conducted by Elkins and Atkinson (1985) who identified a number of strategies used by special schools to provide high-quality programs that secured effective transition to adult life, including work. These strategies included links with technical and further education (TAFE), mobilising the school community to increase the receptivity of employers to accepting special students in their workforce, careful prevocational programming such as the operation of enclaves in local factories, and maintaining interest in, and support for, students for up to a year after graduation.

What can these studies of special schools tell us about inclusion? If students in special schools are happy and learn to adapt to their social environment, their parents might well prefer the certainty of special schooling for their children to the uncertainty of inclusion. Another question about which we know little is what happens after schooling is completed? If special schools were successful in preparing students with physical or intellectual disabilities to participate fully in the community, arguments for inclusion during the school years would be less convincing. An extreme example of this view can be seen in the Hungarian approach called conductive education, which involves educating children with physical disabilities in a residential special school and denying them regular school placement until they can deal with obstacles such as stairs (Sigafoos et al. 1991). Although the goal is normalisation as adults, it is argued that Conductive Education might require a special setting in order to help the student achieve independence in mobility, eating and dressing, as well as success in academic learning.

As noted earlier, we have relatively little data from the follow-up of special school students. Conversely, if students who have been educated in the mainstream are not able to pursue adult activities in the community and, instead, find themselves working

in supported environments or living relatively unproductive lives in protective residential facilities, then arguments favouring inclusion lose some force. Christie (1981), for example, noted that some students with cerebral palsy who had enjoyed apparently successful regular secondary education had not made successful transitions to work in the community. In these cases one might suspect that the problem was a deficiency in transition programs compounded by a lack of vocational support in the community, rather than placement in regular schools. Unfortunately, employment for young adults with disabilities is too often unattained, even for those who complete secondary schooling or tertiary studies.

Can all students be included?

An answer to the question of whether all students can be included depends on what we take inclusion to mean. Some evidence on inclusion for all students comes from settings in which segregation is not possible. For example, in isolated rural areas, children with disabilities perforce must be educated along with their peers. Although this does not always produce successful outcomes, it does suggest that if expertise and resources can be provided, the local community might well be accepting and supportive of a child with disabilities (Armstrong, Armstrong, & Barton, 2000; Ashman & Elkins, 1996).

In contrast, provincial towns and, especially, cities are environments in which community cohesion is often minimal, and it is easy for teachers and parents to expect that others (i.e., specialists) should provide services for those who have special needs. So, in some contexts there are strong influences against regular school placement for at least some students with severe disabilities. Nevertheless, it has been asked whether it is possible to eliminate all segregated special education (Brown et al., 1991).

Some groups, especially organisations such as Queensland Parents of People with a Disability, have claimed that this is both possible and desirable. In the United States, organisations such as The Association for Severe Handicap, now known as TASH, advocate inclusion more strongly than the Council for Exceptional Children, which reflects the needs of teachers already working mostly in special education service delivery.

School systems continue to wrestle with the pattern of services for students with disabilities. For example, in New South Wales a report by McRae (1996) on the feasibility of inclusion was considered and some of its recommendations were adopted. However, a 2001 report conducted for the National Council on Intellectual Disability rates the standard of inclusion for students with intellectual disabilities in Australia as being below average (Wills & Jackson, 2001), although this study can be criticised for relying on a biased sample of informants. Also, inclusion has been fairly widely adopted for students with sensory and physical disabilities. The proportion of the total student population currently educated in segregated facilities is at an all-time low, but

this situation conceals two important issues. The first is the probable underfunding of services to students in regular school classrooms. This results in increased stress and a growing anxiety among teachers that inclusion might be favoured by government for financial reasons. The second is the continuing high support needs of those students still in segregated facilities. Thus, a better mechanism for providing these students with support is needed if they are to be included in regular classrooms.

Factors that influence regular class placement

Although contexts differ in their receptivity to students with special needs, there is also variability in the extent to which parents and their children with disabilities seek regular education settings. In the first place, if parents have initially obtained a regular school placement—often at preschool level—there is a natural tendency to expect the school to maintain appropriate education for the child. Thus, a move to a special school occurs only if the regular school proves unsatisfactory, or if the school rejects the child's continued enrolment. Of importance here are the criteria which might determine continuing enrolment or exclusion. From the parents' perspective, the most important issue is likely to be the child's happiness and general social development. Failure to make academic gains can also feature, particularly if this has a negative influence on the child's self-concept and behaviour.

In a regular primary school class, motivation can be readily stimulated and maintained.

It is evident that three issues constitute the main points of resistance from regular schools to the inclusion of students with disabilities. The first is the provision of physical access for students who use wheelchairs or have other constraints on their mobility. Although new buildings generally conform to standards set down in building codes, the majority of older schools present access problems, and most education authorities resist making expensive modifications to permit one student to attend the school of their choice.

Second, a student's behaviour must not cause undue stress for a teacher. Problems typically cited are toileting, aggression to others, lack of intelligible speech, or making uncontrolled noises that disturb other students. If an aide is provided to relieve the teacher of some of the stress, inclusion is more likely to occur. From the teacher's perspective, aggressive or non-compliant behaviour is the major reason for seeking to exclude or transfer a child. Failure to learn is important only when the gap between the child's needs and the main class curriculum becomes too great. It seems likely that teachers who use more flexible teaching methods might find it easier to manage a child with major learning problems (see Gillies, Chapter 8, this volume). Thus, the major dimensions of concern for teachers are behaviour and learning. If children have physical or sensory disabilities, a relatively modest investment of consultant time, and the provision of appropriate aids, can often enable a regular class teacher to manage without undue strain (Department of Education, Queensland, 1995; Ward, Bochner, Center, Outhred, & Pieterse, 1987).

The third cause of concern to many teachers occurs when the student's achievement level is substantially below that of low-achieving students in the class. This requires the teacher to either program separately (mostly impractical) or find ways to include the student with a disability in common activities in ways that provide valuable learning opportunities.

There is yet another perspective that has influenced Australian education policy and practice: the rights of children with disabilities to be educated in regular schools (as you will recall from Chapter 2). Until recently, human rights have not figured high in general community awareness in Australia. Thus, in most states, if a parent chooses to enrol a child with a severe disability in a regular school, the principal and teacher are likely to respond in terms of the *practicality* of accepting the child, rather than immediately recognising the *right* of the child to be educated in the regular school. In recent years, policy statements have strengthened parental rights to choose educational placements, but there is still likely to be some variability among education systems and schools in the approach taken to enrolment of students with serious disabilities. (You might seek current state policy documents from education authorities in your state or territory.)

In the United States, there is a history of vigorous advocates for full inclusion. For example, Brown and his colleagues (1991) claimed that a mainstream placement is

not simply a right but is beneficial, since children with severe disabilities need to be placed in an environment in which they can learn from their non-disabled classmates. Stainback and Stainback (1982), Certo, Haring, and York (1984) and Biklen (1985) also provided strong statements in support of regular class placement of children with severe disabilities. In Australia there has been a number of case studies of such placement (e.g., Cope, 1987). However, there have been cautionary statements regarding problems with regular class placements that have not automatically engendered positive peer attitudes, increased social interaction or improved learning.

At present, it is probably true to say that both regular teachers and special educators mostly affirm the right to regular class placement. However, few would expect inclusion to be successful without careful planning and preparation and there is some strident opposition (e.g., Kauffman & Hallahan, 1995). An attempt at moving this rancorous debate forward productively has been made by Andrews et al. (2000). This group of 15 scholars noted that early detection and intervention might be an area in which the special versus regular dichotomy need not exist. Then regular schools can work to include young children who have been served in an exemplary manner prior to enrolment in the first grade. Thus, doing special education better and including students in regular classes need not be contradictory aims.

Because there has been a number of cases of alleged discrimination in the Human Rights and Equal Opportunities Commission, it has been suggested that a set of disability standards be created. Transport, building access, insurance, and employment are areas in which standards have been established or are being negotiated (see <www.hreoc.gov.au> and follow the links to disability standards). For education, draft standards have been released for consultation. It appears as if the Disability Standards in Education—if they are agreed upon—will assist the interpretation of the notion of unjustifiable hardship in anti-discrimination legislation.

Naturalistic research

There is a small but growing body of naturalistic, observational research on the classroom life of children with special needs. In early research, Zetlin (1987) for example, found four subgroups differing in social acceptance:

- High-status students were usually in full-time special education classes and had no interest in academic achievement. They often truanted and infracted school or community rules. They were regarded as hopeless cases by teachers, and often were verbally abusive of low-status special education students. Their placement in segregated classes was not indicative of lower IQ but was a reflection of their acting-out behaviours.
- Middle-status students were not overtly anti-academic, although their achievement was low. Typically they were in resource programs. Two subgroups

were noted according to whether their friendships were predominantly among: (a) special education students or (b) regular students.

- Low-status students tended to have a visible disability or to be behaviourally atypical. Some were loners and others had friends of similar low status. They were passive and conforming, and were often harassed by other students. Out of school, they had few peer contacts and their families provided most of their social activities.

Zetlin indicated that students who display attitudes and behaviours that conform to school norms are the most easily assimilated. The converse also applies. It is interesting that it was not those with the lowest IQ who were difficult to integrate, but those whose IQ was in the normal range. Teachers also behaved differently with students in each subgroup, being more personal and encouraging with low-status students. However, Zetlin considered that teachers' reluctance to interact supportively with high-status students was due to their wish to avoid confrontations. Zetlin's study shows the complexity of the social dynamics among adolescents with low academic achievement.

In a very early Australian study, Henry (1981) provided a rich account of the school lives of children with mild intellectual disabilities. She used constructs of teachers' warmth and demandingness to examine the observational data collected in the classroom and playground. An example of the observational records collected by Henry is given in Box 3.1 (page 90).

Positive child–child interactions appear to be characteristic of regular classrooms in which there is an integrated low achiever, although the retention of such children in the regular classroom (in contrast to their placement in a special class or school) might result from teachers and peers regarding their behaviour as acceptable. Children with a mild intellectual disability who are integrated receive much more help from their peers than they give. However, occasionally during these interactions, patronising or derogatory remarks can be made by the helpers, indicating their perception of the inferiority of the target child's work.

Examples of regular placement

It is helpful to consider examples of integration or inclusion policy and practices followed in a number of countries and to note similarities and differences with our own education systems. Several interesting accounts can be found in issues of the *International Journal of Disability, Development and Education*. There is an excellent account of inclusion in several countries published by the OECD (1999). Here, I consider only two examples outside Australia and New Zealand.

United Kingdom

Although most of our thinking about integration has been influenced by American writers, the United Kingdom (UK) Warnock Report (1978) was a major milestone because a distinguished committee made a comprehensive review of special education in that country. In 1981, the government enacted legislation that incorporated some of the Warnock recommendations.

By the mid-1980s, it was common for children under five years of age to make use of a variety of nursery schools and classes, day centres and playgroups in which children with special needs were accepted. Some attended special education facilities such as nursery classes in special schools.

In the UK, the major policy emphasis is on ensuring that all students receive appropriate education. Although inclusion is supported, it is expected that special schools will have an important role for some time yet. However, there has been considerable activity over recent years in the reintegration of children who have been removed from regular schools, often for reasons of unacceptable behaviour. This appears to have been successful only because of very detailed preparation by teachers from both the special school and the receiving school. Involvement of schools, parents, psychologist, and the student is seen as being crucial to success. A report by the Centre for Studies on Inclusive Education (Jordan & Goodey, 1996) gives advice for establishing inclusive school policies that has much of value for the Australian and New Zealand contexts. Its website has much worthwhile information, including the Index for Inclusion. See <http://inclusion.uwe.ac.uk/csie/csiehome.htm>.

> The Index is a set of materials to support schools in a process of inclusive school development, drawing on the views of staff, governors, school students, parents/carers and other community members. It is concerned with improving educational attainments through inclusive practice, and thus provides an attempt to redress a balance in those schools which have concentrated on raising student attainment at the expense of the development of a supportive school community for staff and students.
>
> <http://inclusion.uwe.ac.uk/csie/index–inclusion–summary.htm>

Concerns in the UK have been with mainstream issues such as a national curriculum and achievement testing, statementing (i.e., identifying needs), and financing support to meet needs and local management of schools (Elias, 1994). There are signs that similar issues will emerge in Australia in the near future, and complications for integration might arise as schools try to respond to calls for excellence in teaching and accountability.

Box 3.1 A description of classroom interactions with a girl with a mild intellectual disability

Marie-Anne's interactional profile shows that she was the recipient of few teacher questions in the whole-class setting. Question-and-answer sessions in fact were not common, taking place mainly in the context of competitive games, which Marie-Anne tended to avoid.

Three or four children at a time are competing to work sums on board. The teacher has now asked most children: "Who hasn't had a go?" She calls out Thomas, Terry, Mary, and Timothy who haven't. Marie-Anne doesn't put her hand up. Todd looks at her accusingly, and calls: "Mrs. Hastings!" Marie-Anne and a couple of others put hands up this time. T does not ask them. Time to go.

Occasionally Marie-Anne was asked a question and was able to respond, though the following incident underlines the difficulty she had in keeping up with the class.

T: "Sum pads out quickly. Write down the answer. I want you to add up these numbers in your head." She starts. Marie-Anne is still getting paper out. People are working it out, but some have hands up already. T gives answer quickly.

T: "Who had it?" Children put hands up and call: "Me!"

Marie-Anne, a minute later, has worked it out: "Me!" T gets her to work it out aloud. Correct. "Good girl." Marie-Anne smiles. Next one. Marie-Anne has it right. Bill is asked. He's correct. Marie-Anne smiles because she got it right too. Next one. Marie-Anne didn't write; says to herself: "I didn't do that one." Next one. Marie-Anne writes quickly and puts hands up madly. T: "Who got it right?" Chorus, including Marie-Anne: "Me!" Next one. "Who got it right?" Marie-Anne just sits, but not disconsolate or upset. Similarly with next. Three harder ones. Chorus: "That's hard," and "Easy" from others. Marie-Anne rocks on chair; has not done it.

She asks: "What was it again, Mrs. Hastings?" T repeats, but Marie-Anne, although obviously trying to work it out, can't keep up.

By far the greatest proportion of Marie-Anne's contact with the teacher came from directives concerned with school work: "Get your work book out now, Marie-Anne"; "Go on with the next exercise"; "Bring it back to me when you've finished."

She received, too, a considerable proportion of individual information, often given in response to an initiative taken by herself. As the incident given above shows, she was not at all backward in initiating such approaches, and indeed they form the second largest category of her contacts with the teacher.

Marie-Anne's work was corrected frequently by the teacher in the individual work sessions that always occupied the major part of the mornings; often, too, her work was corrected by a neighbour with whom she changed books following spelling or mathematics tests:

Bill is correcting her spelling; calls out: "Mrs. Hastings, Marie-Anne's only got one wrong."

T: "That's good, Marie-Anne." Marie-Anne looks thrilled.

Sometimes, however, the teacher's correction of work was accompanied merely by a nod of acceptance or by no feedback at all:

Marie-Anne brings out completed work. T just looks.

"Go and do the next." Marie-Anne sits and goes on with it. Brings out new work, reads it out to the teacher. With one prompting question from the teacher (to eliminate a wrong answer) she gets it. T ticks it (no comment).

Source: Henry (1981), pp. 222–223.

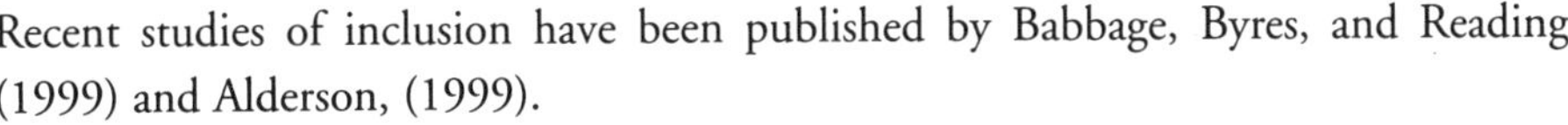

Recent studies of inclusion have been published by Babbage, Byres, and Reading (1999) and Alderson, (1999).

United States

The United States (US) constitution contains a Bill of Rights that enables citizens to seek redress against the government through the courts if they believe that discrimination has occurred. The extensive civil rights campaigns for ethnic minorities during the 1960s provided a model for advocacy on behalf of children with disabilities.

However, inclusion might reflect the wealth of local districts, since federal funding is insufficient to provide all the extra costs of special education. Exemplary practices can certainly be found. Almost 20 years ago, I witnessed a secondary school in Mesa, Arizona, in which a high school student with cerebral palsy was provided with a full-time aide since the student used a wheelchair, and could not write or speak intelligibly. With such a personal assistant, she could participate fully in the academic and social life of the school.

However, although such examples of inclusion are relatively common now, they are certainly not universal. Indeed, as has been the case in Australia, special schools and classes have continued, although principals of special schools now enrol children with more severe disabilities who previously might have been excluded from school.

A decade ago, placement of children with disabilities in American schools showed that there had been little change in the use of separate facilities for students with handicaps (Danielson & Bellamy, 1989). Around 8% of children receive special education support in regular classes, resource rooms or special classes, whereas about 0.5% are in public or private special schools. These figures have remained virtually unchanged since before the introduction of PL 94–142. In addition, a quarter of those in regular schools were in full-time special classes and almost half were in resource rooms.

However, substantial variation among states suggests that some have been more successful in upholding the spirit of the least restrictive environment, and it is clear that many school districts have moved to an inclusive model. Furthermore, the individual education plan itself has not guaranteed that students are more likely to be helped in the mainstream. Overall, it is still doubtful whether inclusion is the dominant service option for students with special needs in the US. Vermont includes more students with disabilities than any other state in the US. Box 3.2 (page 93) contains an analysis by Giangreco based on US government data.

New Zealand

The education system in New Zealand has undergone many changes in the last 10 years (Mitchell, 1996). Schools now have greater autonomy and responsibility than before, within guidelines set by Ministry of Education approval of each school charter.

There are various types of day and residential schools for students with disabilities, as well as units in regular schools and itinerant support services for students in regular classes. One feature of New Zealand education is the particular place of Maori, and efforts are continuing to ensure that support services are appropriate to Maori students and that there is adequate Maori representation in service delivery and management (see Fraser, Moltzen, & Ryba, 2000). Of particular importance is increased recruitment of Maori into the various professions that deliver special education and related services.

New Zealand education administrators have attempted to provide systematic inservice training in mainstreaming, and many schools have had staff skills increased through inservice courses and programs. The Department of Special Education at Auckland Teachers' College has sponsored workshops by Marsha Forrest and Jack Pearpoint that have enabled teachers to gain practical skills for enabling the inclusion of students with quite high support needs in regular classrooms.

Special education in New Zealand has seen many changes over the years, although it is unclear whether further decentralisation or privatisation of education will occur, and whether contestability will change the central support role for the Special Education Service. It is inevitable that further changes in the pattern of education services will continue to occur. One good way to keep up to date is to try the home page of Professor David Mitchell which has many relevant articles and links to special education issues. One of particular interest describes inclusion in eight South-Eastern Asian and Pacific countries (Mitchell, 2001). The website can be accessed at <www.waikato.ac.nz/education/edstudies/mitchell/facemenu.html>.

One example from Australia

Victoria was the first Australian state to renew its approach following the Ministerial Review of Educational Services for the Disabled. Its report *Integration in Victorian*

Box 3.2 Michael Giangreco comments about inclusion in the United States

Across the US in all 13 disability categories in IDEA, only 24 states report [that] more than 50% of their students with disabilities are included in the regular class as their primary placement. Only four states include more than 70%. Vermont leads the nation with 84% included in regular class overall. The remainder of these students are in a variety of placements.

There are no public special education schools or centers in Vermont. There is no state institution for children or adults with developmental disabilities either; they are all served in community-based facilities. Vermont is the only state in the USA to have voluntarily closed its institution (in the 1980s), and I believe [it] may be the only state without such an institution. Some, probably most, of the students who do not have regular class as their primary placement are served in a resource room. There are also a few special classes sprinkled around the state and a few students in residential placements. Some are homebound. More and more, homebound is a choice that families are making (regardless of whether their children have disabilities or not).

Vermont is first within all or most of the IDEA subcategories. Here is a sampling.

Over 90% of students classified as having a learning disability are included (only 20 states include more than 50%).

About 95% of students classified as having a vision impairment are included (only 26 states include more than 50%).

About 75% of students classified as having mental retardation are included (only five states include more than 30%).

About 70% of students classified as having an emotional disorder are included (only three states include more than 50%).

About 60% of students with multiple disabilities are included (only four states include more than 30%).

About 83% of students with autism are included (only three states include more than 50%).

As you can see, not all students with disabilities are included in Vermont, but the vast majority are. Relative to most of the US, Vermont is far ahead in regular class placement. That said, quality still has a long way to go.

Source: M. Giangreco (personal communication, 1 March 2000).

education, published in 1984, signalled the intention of the Victorian Education Department to increase the participation of children with special needs in the education programs and social life of regular schools, and to maintain the participation of all children in those contexts. Although recognising that segregated settings would

continue for a time, the review suggested that resources should be directed to support integration.

The Victorian review argued for changing the nature of schools so that they better supported students with disabilities, thus reducing or eliminating the handicapping consequences of disabilities. The improved coordination of services was seen as a high priority, with the Education Department assuming responsibility for many services previously provided by other agencies. Importantly, coordination was seen as important at regional and school levels also. Each school council was to develop policy for integration and to overview its operation. Furthermore, special attention was given to increasing the awareness of integration within the school community.

An enrolment support group (ESG)—including parents, student (if appropriate), a parent advocate, teacher, and principal—was recommended to oversee the enrolment of children with special needs. Of importance was the participation of professionals, such as guidance or special education consultants, only by invitation. The ESG was to assess what was needed to provide an appropriate regular class placement, to identify any extra resources needed, and to reconvene at the behest of parent or teacher.

Although the classroom teacher is clearly the key person in integration, it was proposed that *integration teachers* be appointed to schools on a full-time or part-time basis. *Integration aides* were to be appointed to reduce the handicap associated with certain disabilities, and therapy services were to be provided in schools as required.

Changes were certainly made following the Victorian review. These included:

- the establishment of an Integration Unit by in the Ministry of Education;
- the employment of integration teachers and integration aides (many part-time);
- $20 million devoted to supporting students in over 1,000 regular schools;
- parents and schools devoting energy to securing resources; and
- the deprofessionalisation of the Enrolment Support Group which meant that many people with experience and expertise were excluded from contributing to the planning of integration for particular children.

A change in state government late in 1992 and a review of the integration program by the state Auditor-General brought about some changes to the pattern of education services in Victoria during the 1990s.

A critical report, *Integrated education for students with disabilities* (Auditor-General of Victoria, 1992), concluded that policies such as non-categorisation meant that little was known about students receiving integration support and that it was "not possible to judge whether resource allocations were being made on an equitable basis between departmental regions and individual schools, [and whether] students were benefitting significantly—socially and educationally—from resources provided" (p. 78).

Both the Auditor-General's report and Pickering (1991) noted that failure to attend to the career needs of special education staff had, among other factors, resulted in their not transferring to regular schools in roles such as integration teachers. Moreover, that many students did not move from special to regular schools might well have been affected by the attitude of special school staff. Almost immediately upon release of the Auditor-General's report, Cullen and Brown (1992) were asked to conduct a program effectiveness review. Some of their recommendations are described below.

- Balanced and comprehensive information should be given to parents to aid their decision-making.
- Programs for children with disabilities should be monitored and evaluated annually.
- The creation of a resource index would make funding equitable and more certain.
- Exchange of staff expertise between regular and special schools needs to occur more readily than at present.
- All schools enrolling children with disabilities should have access to professional advice.
- Integration teachers and aides to be given training.
- Inservice training for teachers should be provided about students with disabilities.

Since integration has been a particular focus of attention in Victoria over the past decade, it might be helpful to contrast practices in Victoria with those in the United States under IDEA. Although the history of special education and the integration-versus-segregation debate have been similar in both jurisdictions, the legal basis is different because, constitutionally, the American position on civil rights is much stronger. Another difference is funding which, in Australia, is more egalitarian, being less dependent on local taxation. But the central control that gives this benefit also takes control away from local communities, and support at the local level might be important in ensuring successful inclusion.

Inclusion and the curriculum

If continued progress toward greater inclusion in Australia is to be made, several issues need to be addressed by education authorities. These include the modification of the curriculum to include the needs of children with disabilities, the development of positive attitudes to disability, the role of school integration policies, and the possibility of having regular classroom teachers assume major responsibility for educating children with special needs.

It is vital, as we consider the curriculum for students with special needs, that we first invert our thinking to recognise that these students all have capabilities, and it is these capabilities that are the starting point for learning. To put it in another way, we should describe a glass as being half-full, and not as half-empty.

Another fundamental orientation is to regard teaching as assisting learners to perform some physical or mental action that lies just beyond their present capabilities.

Both of these ideas saturate the concept of curriculum for students who do not fit well into traditional classrooms.

What is curriculum?

There are many facets to curriculum, which in its broadest sense has to do with teaching and learning activities across many domains (knowledge, skills, values, and attitudes), and especially with the scope and nature of student experiences as set out generally by society and specifically by educational authorities, principals, and teachers. The dominant form of curriculum is that which is devised by educational authorities with reference to the age of students (or the number of years they have attended school), often with no regard to the diversity of student achievements at any particular age or grade level. In some cases the curriculum is formulated as little more than a syllabus (or list of topics to be taught) whereas, in others, the curriculum takes the form of broad guidelines that are meant to be interpreted by teachers in the light of local circumstances and the characteristics of particular students.

Over the past three decades or so there has been a move away from syllabus statements toward guidelines for content and process in which teacher autonomy is accepted. However, there has been some move back to central control either through national or state prescription, or as a response to industry demands for vocational relevance and competency in the curriculum.

Whatever the level of specificity and central control, there are some things that children learn in school that lie outside most formal curriculum documents. If students attend schools in which no students with disabilities are enrolled, nondisabled students might well lack values, knowledge and skills that would assist them to interact successfully with persons with disabilities. They might also learn, through the absence of students with disabilities, that it is natural to treat others differently (or that discrimination is acceptable).

Current Australian curricula have been influenced at the upper age levels by governments seeking to have schooling better prepare youth for a complex, changing, and multiskilled workplace. Various reports have recommended that curricula be structured around a limited set of key learning areas. A book edited by Cherry Collins (1995) offered a useful overview of curriculum change in Australia. Collins claimed that, after a period of vigorous debate and considerable change in curricula, a period

of some stability seems likely. Influences from business and manufacturing have brought attempts to unify curriculum across Australia and to introduce competencies thought to be relevant by industry. Although some attention has been given to these changes by special educators, relatively little consideration has been given by those centrally involved in curriculum reform as to what changes might mean for students who have special learning needs.

Little attention has been given to the appropriateness of newer competency-based curricula and of the accompanying profile assessments for students with disabilities. However, special education has developed its own competency-based approach in the individual education plan (IEP). Thus, we might expect teachers to try to bring the IEP and competency approaches into rough alignment. This might not be easy, since the mainstream curriculum has not been designed for students with diverse learning needs. Obviously, there are many assumptions made about student competencies in terms of knowledge, skills, and attitude. Yet, these assumptions probably do not apply well to students with disabilities, forcing teachers to design activities that enable participation.

There are two basic models of classroom activity for included students. In one, the goals are similar for all students, with an expectation that outcomes differ in degree. In the other, participation has different goals for the students with very different learning needs. In practice, both models might apply in different areas of the curriculum. These models can be called multilevel instruction, and curriculum overlapping.

In *multilevel instruction*, students have different expectations for breadth and sophistication of outcomes in the same content area, and heterogeneous groups are frequently used so that support is extended to the less proficient learners. In contrast, *curriculum overlapping* has qualitatively different goals for a student with certain support needs (e.g., social skills) although they might participate in lessons with their peers who have advanced cognitive learning goals. In a science class, relevant activities—such as fetching equipment, or counting events or objects—might be integral to the lesson in which others are learning about scientific principles through experimentation.

Matching the curriculum to students with special needs has not been easy as evidence from Australia, New Zealand, and other countries has shown. Attempts have been made to standardise curriculum in different countries, but few of these have taken the needs of all students into account. Where this has been done, as with the National Curriculum in the UK, many significant problems have been encountered. Such standard curricula often constrain teachers and make it difficult to meet individual needs. A different idea is contained in the concept of *inclusive curriculum*. This has been interpreted as sensitivity to such matters as gender, race, and poverty in deciding

both content and method. Gordon and Rosenblum (2001) discuss the shared construction of race, sex, and sexual orientation. However, theoreticians who have had considerable influence on education in these three areas have usually neglected to include disability in their work. For disability, there are two aspects—the obvious one is the creation of curriculum relevant to the needs of the students, and the other being a recognition that knowledge about, and attitudes to, disability are necessary prerequisites for working with students with special needs. It is an indictment on past curriculum that disability was never mentioned, so much so that widespread ignorance and prejudice have hampered the efforts of people with a disability to participate fully in society. There are many examples in literature, science, history, art, citizenship, and physical education in which knowledge, values, and attitudes can include the topic of disability. Refashioning curricula to include the needs of all students cannot proceed on the assumption that mainstream content and teaching methods are ideal. Thus, there are increasing calls for the inclusion of all students to become the reformation of regular education.

Interestingly, calls for inclusion are strongest from parents of students with major support needs, whereas parents of those with mild educational problems might argue for at least part-time, segregated instruction. This suggests that the school reform issue is, indeed, the heart of the matter. The common conception of regular schooling is of relatively common instructional methods and content in any classroom, even though the range of student achievement is quite large, perhaps equivalent to several Year levels. If regular schools can offer greater flexibility of curriculum content for all students, then the concerns of both groups might be met. Some schools achieve this through flexible grouping, through the use of collaborative teaching situations, cooperative learning, and by ensuring that all students are valued and their achievements recognised. Primary schools probably find that the biggest challenge is to break down the isolation experienced by the teacher working alone in a single classroom—requiring the entire staff to help solve problems faced by individual teachers. In contrast, secondary schools have plenty of flexibility, but often large enrolments and a mix of teachers present other challenges in delivering effective curriculum to all students.

Another factor influencing the ability of schools to respond to the challenge of full inclusion is the presence of other stressors, including increasing accountability measures (such as reporting of student achievement), socioeconomic disadvantage, increased prevalence of behaviour problems, and increased class sizes. Clearly there is no justification for inclusion that is inadequately resourced, either in material terms or, probably more importantly, in inservice support.

Teachers can modify some aspects of their teaching to meet the needs of some students. Examples include having a choice of textbooks with different difficulty (i.e., different readability levels), and setting assignments with graduated tasks

enabling more able students to be challenged whereas the less able can accomplish the easier tasks. However, caution should be observed when adjusting readability by shortening sentences or substituting vocabulary. Often the coherence of text is damaged through such changes. It might be better to annotate the text with brief explanations of difficult vocabulary, to underline major ideas, to ask preliminary questions, or to use alternate (non-text) media with limited reading or writing demands (e.g., video or computer) to engage in higher level thinking about content. Another approach is to use group introduced methods that encourage students to help each other, as in Reciprocal Teaching (Palincsar & Klench, 1992).

The Commonwealth government has placed increasing emphasis on all students meeting benchmarks for literacy and numeracy. Although schools do not expect many students with intellectual disabilities to reach the benchmarks for specific ages, there is a general recognition that literacy and numeracy achievements are important goals for all students regardless of their varying education and personal histories.

Technology

Many aspects of curriculum are amenable to support and extension through technology. As you will see in Section 3, curriculum access for students with sense or physical impairments can be markedly improved by mechanical, electrical, or electronic devices, often with sophisticated microprocessors to add a measure of artificial intelligence to their operation. Here I simply want to draw attention to the range of technologies available so that you can consider these as you work your way through the following chapters.

With the advent of the Internet, World Wide Web, and CD-ROMs there are enormous opportunities for the use of multimedia in education in ways that enhance the content and learning modes available to all students, including those with special needs.

Some of the most sophisticated examples of technology-supported learning environments have been developed at Vanderbilt University in Nashville, Tennessee, by Bransford and others (1996). Using the acronym MOST (Multimedia Environments that Organize and Support Text), they have developed dynamic visual support for comprehension that can accelerate linguistic and conceptual development that is primarily language-based. Highly motivating video presentations provide structure and enable participation, for example, by the student recording a verbal soundtrack to go with the video. Print books can be produced with stills from the video and transcription of the student-supplied soundtrack. Thus, students can learn to identify text structures (e.g., story grammars and contextual schemata) that enable them to comprehend written text.

Hence, technology provides opportunities to support learning of students who experience difficulties, regardless of the cause of the disability. Basic curriculum

areas—such as reading, writing, mathematics, and spelling—and generic information-gathering have received attention. Although some applications of technology have been transitory, particularly early use of software for personal computers, word processors have become invaluable tools for increasing the volume and quality of created writing. The availability of word processors at home and at school is unlikely to increase the amount of revision students do but, if teachers and parents plan carefully, students can improve their writing at every level from overall cohesion, to spelling and punctuation. However, standard word processing software is much more powerful and complicated than most students need and, for the early stages of proficiency, a program designed specifically for student use might be more appropriate. Intelligent word processors can ease the burden of typing and spelling by suggesting complete words from the initial few letters. These programs are described in more detail in Chapter 11.

A key feature of successful integration is the relevance of the regular school curriculum for all students. Indeed, in recent years the term *inclusive curriculum* has been used to emphasise the point that schools need to be sufficiently flexible to fit the characteristics of all students who are enrolled. There are several aspects that must be considered. For some students, particularly those with physical or sense impairment, the major issue is their access to the curriculum provided for other students. Ramps, toilets, aids, brailled and taped text materials, and FM transmitters and receivers might be necessary to enable them to gain physical access to the curriculum. For other students, although ultimately sharing the same curricular goals as their peers, additional opportunities to learn are required because they have not developed the knowledge base that is required of students at a particular grade level. They need to be taught material that school staff members assume is learnt incidentally outside school. For other students, existing skills are well above their peers.

Figure 3.1 (page 101) indicates how the special education curriculum explicitly addresses such issues. If the school day and year are not lengthened, it is almost inevitable either that education for some students must be continued for several extra years, or that some of the content of the regular curriculum must be eliminated. Both of these options have been used in special schools and classes, where students sometimes stay until they are 18 or, in rare case, even 21 years old, and where curricula are planned with student needs in mind. However, for students integrated in regular classrooms, there might be more difficulties associated with the provision of suitable curriculum experiences, especially during adolescence.

Anti-discrimination

Up to this point in the chapter I have dealt with the relevance and practicalities of inclusion for students with special needs. There are many other factors, however, that impinge upon the practice of inclusion and constitute elements of the school context.

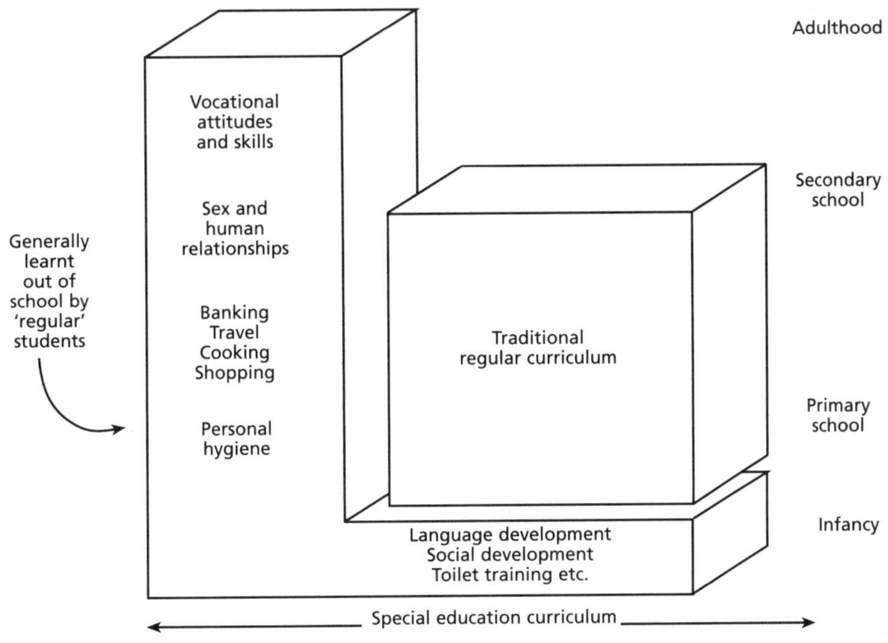

Figure 3.1 A model of special education curriculum

In Chapter 2 we raised the issue of anti-discrimination legislation as a topic relevant to the integration of students with disabilities and the provision of programs and services to them. The fundamental issue is what we commonly call a fair go, although usually the term equity is used. Helping all students acquire an understanding of disability discrimination can contribute to their overall appreciation of what is equitable, and it is recommended that all Australian teachers become familiar with the Disability Discrimination Acts as well as other human rights legislation. Valuable resources are available from the Human Rights and Equal Opportunity Commission.

Equity is not equality, and different treatment that was commonplace in special education is not necessarily equitable. Conversely, treating everyone the same can be discriminatory. The situation becomes complex when unfair treatment might not be discriminatory, and fair treatment might be. For example, many things happen to people that are unfair but not (legally) discriminatory. The Disability Discrimination Acts seek to eliminate discrimination on the grounds of disability in the areas of work, accommodation, education, access to premises, clubs and sports; in the provision of goods, facilities, services and land; and in existing laws and the administration of Commonwealth laws and programs.

Let us briefly focus on discrimination in education. Educational authorities must not discriminate against a student with a disability by refusing to accept an application for

enrolment, or in the terms and conditions of admission of the student. They must not discriminate by denying or limiting access to an educational benefit provided by educational authorities. However, discrimination would be lawful if to do otherwise would constitute unjustifiable hardship on educational authorities. Determining what constitutes such hardship might require a hearing by a tribunal.

Thus far in Australia, many examples can be seen of education being provided for students with disabilities that has been accepted by the students and their parents as fair and reasonable accommodations. However, several disputes have arisen that have not been solved by conciliation, and hearings have been held by anti-discrimination commissioners. One outcome of these cases has been a recognition that fewer disputes might occur if nationally accepted standards for education were developed similar to those which apply in, for example, building design. It remains to be seen whether this endeavour to establish standards for non-discriminatory education will be successful.

Universities have been among the most successful educational institutions at eliminating discriminatory practices. Students with very high support needs, such as those with dual sense impairments, and those with quadriplegia, have been successful in gaining both bachelor degrees and higher degrees. However, the range of courses undertaken by these students has been quite restricted, with most selecting humanities, law, music, and the social sciences.

There are additional issues faced by schools if excluding a student with disability is considered by school administrators and teaching staff who believe that they cannot cope. Unlike most other areas in which disputes arise, the first step is conciliation rather than resolution by tribunal. Williams (1996) provided a comprehensive analysis of legal aspects of education for students with learning difficulties. In the case, *L v Minister for Education*, for example, the Tribunal took the view that direct discrimination (i.e., exclusion from school) was lawful because the education authority would suffer unjustifiable hardship, particularly the human costs involved. These included the demands on the teacher and disruptions to other students.

Another area of dispute can be whether a complainant actually has a disability. This will arise with regard to the area of educational problems called learning difficulties, since it might not be possible to show the existence of an impairment. A case in England in 1995 established that such claims could be pursued in court. In Australia, however, there has not been a test case involving students with learning difficulties, although Williams (1996) suggested that it is probable that such cases will arise in the future. In 1997 the National Children's and Youth Law Centre commenced a study of disability discrimination in education. See Flynn (1997) for complete details.

The website for the Human Rights and Equal Opportunities Commission is a useful resource for current practices about exclusion from regular schools. See <www.hreoc.gov.au/disability_rights/index.html>.

Policies for integration

Since the beginning of the 1990s, national and state governments have provided explicit policy statements about the education of students with special needs, and about integration. In Queensland, the ascertainment policy specifies a process to determine students' special educational needs—that is, what support, programs, and placements are appropriate. The participation of parents in the process is a key element in the policy, as is regular review (at least every three years).

A Policy Statement and Management Plan adopted by the Department of Education, Queensland (1993) placed the education of students with disabilities—in a social justice context as it affects curriculum organisation, content and teaching methods, student assessment, and resource allocation. The plan also reflects legislative changes, not only the *Education Act* but also anti-discrimination and disability services legislation. In addition to specifying the policy for educating students with disabilities, Education Queensland (as it is now called) has developed a management plan in which goals and strategies are set out for schools, school support centres, and various administrative entities. Developments such as these indicate that students with disabilities will be a responsibility shared across all stakeholders in the education system. It is useful to search the website of your state or national education system to learn about policies and practices of greatest relevance to you.

A vital part of the success of integration is the development of school policy. Australian integration efforts have tended either to have been imposed from the state level or to have resulted from the enthusiasm of a few teachers. Yet, if all the staff members of a school have been involved in formulating an integration policy, effective integration is likely to be the result. Most policy documents include statements that reflect the following elements:

- principles of organisation of support;
- attitudes toward students with special needs;
- roles of designated staff;
- links with feeder schools;
- identification and diagnosis;
- arrangements for support and its cessation;
- ways of making students independent learners;
- organising resource materials;
- record-keeping;
- involvement of external support specialists;
- staff development for integration; and
- parent links.

Box 3.3 Extract from a high school staff handbook

G uses the little hearing she has very well, but she also relies heavily on lipreading and she needs to be able to see her teacher's face clearly. She has considerable support from a support teacher in lessons, but she still needs encouragement to speak for herself, which she *can* do quite clearly. She is a very willing and hardworking girl who tries very hard to follow the lesson.

J has muscular dystrophy and, although his movements are very limited, he is able to get around in his electric wheelchair. He is unable to participate in some practical subjects because his arms are very weak. Academically he is of average ability. He is shy and lacking in confidence but should be encouraged to socialise more and sit in close proximity to others in class. He needs help with toileting, which might sometimes make him late for lessons. His is a progressive illness and he will need increasing help.

M has spina bifida and is semi-paralysed from the waist downwards. She walks with two sticks and can manage stairs only slowly (e.g., for fire drill). She uses a wheelchair for long distances, (e.g., on outings). She has hydrocephalus with a valve inserted, to drain excess cerebral fluid from her brain. Inevitable learning difficulties arise from hydrocephalus. Beneath an apparent sociable self-confidence is considerable basic insecurity and lack of confidence, with heavy reliance on teachers when at school. The educational psychologist has suggested that she needs much encouragement. She scored an IQ of 103 (revised Stanford Binet Test) but her achievement level is about one year below her chronological age.

Instructions were also given on general topics such as hearing aids, physical disabilities and classroom management.

A whole school approach can be encouraged if staff members are informed about the students in the school who have a disability and how they might be helped in a range of situations and activities. In one high school four pages of information are included in its staff handbook to help teachers involved with students who have hearing or physical disabilities. This statement ensures that teachers are aware of student needs, and know how to deal with situations that might arise. For example, in the section on fire drill, there are clear instructions for the evacuation of those students who need help. In addition, there is a short but detailed pen sketch of each of the students with disabilities, including suggestions for management (see Box 3.3, above).

A final word on inclusion

In recent years the notion of inclusive curriculum has highlighted similarities among several groups of students. Using the notion of social justice, participation in education should not involve discrimination against females, ethnic minorities, indigenous groups, and those with diverse learning needs. This has made integration an issue of equity.

A second aspect of inclusive curriculum is the need for schools to be organised *ab initio* with individual differences among students in mind. In other words, it is not adequate for schools to be structured as if all students of a given age were similar, and with all departures from a hypothetical average student being a nuisance. Thus, schools must differentiate among students in order to give them equal access to common educational goals.

A third feature is the incorporation into the curriculum of knowledge and values that are pertinent to each of these groups of students. Gender, ethnicity, and disability are topics that occur in the language, social studies, and science curricula. If all students have a more informed basis for attitudes and actions, instead of stereotypes derived from ignorance, a short-term benefit of this approach should be a more cooperative school climate than might currently exist. A long-term benefit should be an adult community that is less likely to perpetuate discrimination against those with disabilities and sees equity in including people with disabilities in employment and community living. Much work is needed to develop fully the concept of inclusive curriculum and there is a danger that the potential of the concept of inclusive curriculum might be lost if inclusion becomes merely a synonym for integration or mainstreaming.

Given the rather revolutionary nature of proposals to educate all children within regular classes, it is not surprising that there have been several expressions of caution and even outright opposition. Kauffman and Hallahan (1995) have edited a volume of criticisms of full inclusion.

The issues in Box 3.4 are representative of the current debate in Australia about how best to educate students with disabilities. It is likely that further debate will ensue.

SUMMARY

Integration can be considered from a number of perspectives: human rights, legislation, efficiency, and history. In Australia and New Zealand, the nature of the constitutions does not make it easy to establish mainstream placement for children with disabilities as a basic right. Also, legislation tends to be framed in ways that do not bind governments to *do* certain things, only to *permit* them to do so.

Special education grew to be a major component of education systems. Its influence stabilised, then declined as there was a movement toward the transfer of responsibility for students with special needs back to the regular classroom teacher. Thus, integration has been intimately connected to the past pattern of segregated special education.

Box 3.4 Some issues about full inclusion

- Students with severe behaviour problems cannot be managed by most regular classroom teachers and require at least temporary special placement with expert staff.
- Inclusion has more support from advocates than from empirical research studies.
- There are two lines of debate about inclusion. One concerns enrolment of students with high support needs in regular classes. The other concerns how students with mild learning or behaviour problems should be assisted by full- or part-time withdrawal.
- Deaf (sign-using) persons choose to place themselves outside disability, regard themselves as a cultural and linguistic minority, and resist inclusion in mainstream classes.
- Professionals in the field of special education fear that inclusion will result in loss of specialist knowledge.
- Special education professionals might dislike the need to work with regular teachers rather than directly with students who have disabilities.
- Any form of special education has the potential to be very stressful for teachers, yet the high costs of resourcing their education are difficult to secure. To teach under the constraints of laws and regulations adds to the pressure.
- Is the reality that neither inclusion nor separate special education is—or ever will be—very effective if the measure of success is comparison with students who do not have disabilities?
- Is separate special education the easy way out, rather than tackling the reform of regular education?
- Inclusion is favoured as a cost-cutting exercise, particularly by conservative governments.
- Accepting separate special education reduces the incentive for regular teachers to learn how to teach students who are more difficult to teach. That is, it de-skills teachers.
- Advocates for full inclusion do mean all—they are committed to "all" because otherwise they would be discriminating on the basis of disability. Others feel that there is a minority of students who cannot be included in regular classrooms.
- The place of education has a particular strength in middle America where, in the past, everyone has attended his or her neighbourhood school. With the fragmentation of schooling into many systems, an increasing number of independent schools, and the trend toward decentralisation of government schools, going to the nearest school is not likely to have the same meaning as in the past.

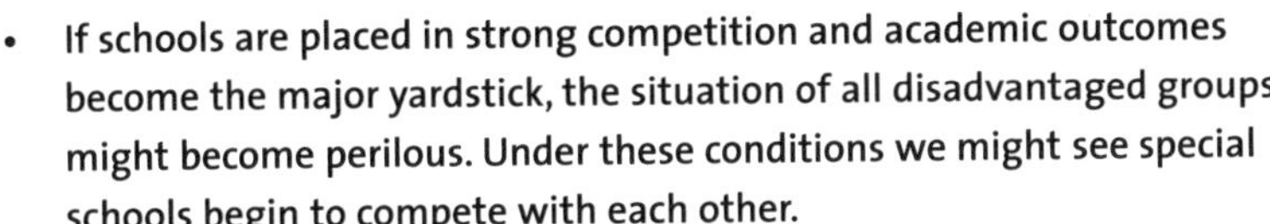

- If schools are placed in strong competition and academic outcomes become the major yardstick, the situation of all disadvantaged groups might become perilous. Under these conditions we might see special schools begin to compete with each other.

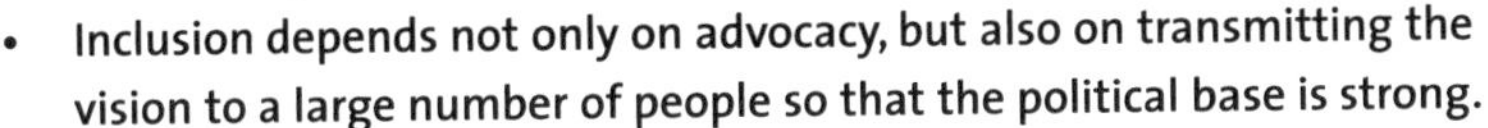

- Inclusion depends not only on advocacy, but also on transmitting the vision to a large number of people so that the political base is strong.
- Adopting a stance based on empirical evidence requires that people be convinced. Many political decisions run counter to evidence and, instead, respond to popular opinion.
- Inclusion in education is the mission of some parents and educators of children with very high support needs. Researchers who were willing and able to implement inclusive education have demonstrated that it can be done, but not by those who do not wish it to be done.
- Inclusion in education is the corollary of non-discriminatory practices for the work, leisure, and residential situations of adults with disabilities.
- Delivery of needed support in regular classrooms often presents insoluble bureaucratic problems. Money allocated to provide support is locked into identifiable units—such as special schools—and cannot easily be "attached" to a child and shifted with him or her from school to school.
- Some ability to choose other than full-time regular class placement is needed. Deaf students who use signing need others with whom to communicate, and there might be other situations in which a unit within a large school is appropriate.

Despite many studies having been conducted to see whether students with a mild educational handicap learn better in regular or special classes, it has not been possible to obtain a definitive answer. One implication of this failure is the importance of monitoring the implementation of integration policies and practices to ensure that they actually are beneficial. Integration has, therefore, been more an ideological commitment than an empirically validated solution to educating students with special needs.

Indeed, integration is based on the philosophy of normalisation which affirms the value of children with disabilities, highlights the discriminatory nature of segregated education settings, and requires education to be provided in as normal a fashion as possible.

Claims have been made that all children can be educated in regular schools, and it seems that success depends upon the commitment of schools and community. Thus, international comparisons need to take into account the social, educational, and political context in which integration occurs.

Although the rhetoric of integration is powerful, it might not be sufficient for successful implementation. In determining what practical considerations might be important,

evidence from qualitative studies illustrates the complexity of the interactions among students with disabilities, peers, regular and support teachers, parents and the community.

Contrasts and similarities can be seen in the special education systems of different countries and states. Furthermore, integration policy and practices are dynamic, and it seems likely that further changes will be witnessed in future. As programs of teacher education become more comprehensive, it is likely that regular teachers will be better prepared for managing students with special needs. Inservice programs are needed for the many regular teachers who feel under-prepared for their vital role in integration. School policies are needed to ensure that everyone in the school community is involved, and that integration is not simply left to the "experts".

A final and unsolved issue is how to transfer, to regular education teachers and regular education settings, the commitment to students with problems that is characteristic of special education and special educators. In some respects, special educators in the past overplayed the special nature of special education, and implicitly told mainstream education that it was not competent to meet the needs of special children. Much work needs to be done to reverse such attitudes so that integration becomes a goal of regular education and not something imposed upon it.

Suggested reading

Allan, J. (1999). *Actively seeking inclusion: Pupils with special needs in mainstream schools.* London: Falmer Press.

Capper, C. A., Frattura, E., & Keyes, M. W. (2000). *Meeting the needs of students of all abilities: How leaders go beyond inclusion.* Thousand Oaks, CA: Corwin Press.

Friend, M. & Bursuck, W. D. (1996). *Including students with special needs.* Boston: Allyn & Bacon.

Janney, R. & Snell, M. E. (2000). *Behavioral support.* Baltimore, MD: Paul H. Brookes.

Lang, G. & Berberich, C. (1995). *All children are special: Creating an inclusive classroom.* Armadale, Vic: Eleanor Curtain Publishing.

Mittler, P. (2000). *Working toward inclusive education: Social contexts.* London: David Fulton.

Shapiro Bernard, S., Tashie, C., Martin, J., Malloy, J., Schuh, M., Piet, J., Nisbet, J., Lichtenstein, S. (1996). *Petroglyphs: The writing on the wall.* Concord, NH: Institute on Disability/UAP, University of New Hampshire.

Practical activities

1. Check to see if your library has a videotape or film dealing with integration. View this with some friends and discuss issues that seem important.
2. Obtain a copy of your national, state, or regional policies on special education. Consider these policies from the perspectives of students with disabilities, their parents, teachers, and system administrators.
3. Go to a regular school and obtain a copy of documents such as prospectus, school policy, staff handbook, annual report, and cooperative school review. Identify the nature and extent of references to students with disabilities in these documents. If necessary, draft amendments to the documents so that a parent contemplating enrolling a child with a disability would find them informative.
4. With some of your study friends, consider the following two issues: What would be the impact upon students, parents, and teachers if all special schools were to be closed? Should Australia and New Zealand introduce laws like PL94–142 to ensure the best education for students with disabilities? Why or why not?

References

Alderson, P. (Ed.) (1999). *Learning and inclusion: The Cleves School experience*. London: David Fulton.

Andrews, J. E. , Carnine, D. W., Coutinho, M. J., Edgar, E. B., Forness, S. R., Fuchs, L. S., Jordan, D., Kauffman, J. M., Patton, J. M., Paul, J., Rosell, J., Rueda, R., Schiller, E., Skrtic, T. M. & Wong, J. (2000). Bridging the special education divide. *Remedial and Special Education*, 21, 258–260, 267.

Armstrong, F., Armstrong, D. & Barton, D. (Eds) (2000). *Inclusive education: Policy, contexts and comparative perspectives*. London: David Fulton.

Ashman, A. F. & Elkins, J. (1996). School and integration. In B. Stratford & P. Gunn (Eds), *New approaches to Down syndrome* (pp. 341–357). London: Cassell.

Auditor-General of Victoria. (1992). *Integrated education for children with disabilities*. Special Report No. 17. Melbourne: Government Printer.

Babbage, R., Byers, R. & Redding, H. (1999). *Approaches to teaching and learning: Including pupils with learning difficulties*. London: David Fulton.

Bank-Mikkelsen, N. (1969). A metropolitan area in Denmark: Copenhagen. In R. Kugel & W. Wolfensberger (Eds), *Changing patterns in residential services for the mentally retarded* (pp. 227–254). Washington, DC: President's Committee on Mental Retardation.

Barton, L. (1986). The politics of special educational need. *Disability, Handicap and Society*, 1, 273–290.

Berry, P. B., Andrews, R. J., & Elkins, J. (1977). *An evaluative study of educational, vocational and residential programs for the moderately to severely mentally handicapped in three states*. St Lucia: Fred and Eleanor Schonell Educational Research Centre.

Biklen, D. (1985). *Achieving the complete school*. New York: Teachers College Press.

Bransford, J. D., Miller Sharp, D., Vye, N. J., Goldman, S. R., Hasselbring, T. S., Goin, L., O'Banion, K., Livernois, J., Saul, E., & the Cognition and Technology Group at Vanderbuilt (1996). MOST environments for accelerating literacy development. In S. Vosniadou, E. de Coste, R. Glaser, & H. Mandl (Eds), *International perspectives on the design of technology-supported learning environments* (pp. 223–255). Mahwah, NJ: Lawrence Erlbaum Associates.

Brown, L., Long, E., Udvari-Solner, A., Davis, L., Vandeventer, P., Ahlgren, C., Johnson, F., Gruenewald, L., & Jorgensen, J. (1991). How much time should students with severe intellectual disabilities spend in regular education classrooms and elsewhere? *Journal of the Association for Persons with Severe Handicaps*, 16, 39–47.

Carlberg, C. & Kavale, K. (1980). The efficacy of special versus regular class placement for exceptional children: A meta-analysis. *Journal of Special Education*, 14, 295–309.

Certo, N., Haring, N. G., & York, R. (Eds) (1984). *Public school integration of severely handicapped students*. Baltimore: Paul H. Brookes.

Chapman, J. W. (1988). Special education in the least restrictive environment: Mainstreaming or maindumping? *Australia and New Zealand Journal of Developmental Disabilities*, 14, 123–134.

Christie, R. F. (1981). Integration of cerebral palsied persons in Queensland regular schools. Unpublished master's thesis, University of Queensland.

Collins, C. (Ed.) (1995). *Curriculum stocktake: Evaluating school curriculum change*. Canberra: Australian College of Education.

Cope, L. (1987, October). Integration: A parent-teacher's viewpoint. Paper presented at the 12th National Conference of the Australian Association of Special Education, Melbourne.

Cullen, R. & Brown, N. (1992). *Integration and special education in Victorian schools: A program effectiveness review*. Melbourne: Department of School Education.

Danielson, L. C. & Bellamy, G. T. (1989). State variation in placement of children with handicaps in segregated environments. *Exceptional Children*, 55, 448–455.

Deno, E. (1970). Special education as developmental capital. *Exceptional Children*, 37, 229–237.

Department of Education, Queensland. (1993). *Educational provision for students with disabilities: Policy statement and management plan*. Brisbane: Author.

Department of Education, Queensland. (1995). *Policy into practice: Inclusive curriculum for students with disabilities Case studies and resources*. Brisbane: Author.

Dunn, L. M. (1968). Special education for the mildly retarded: Is much of it justifiable? *Exceptional Children*, 35, 5–22.

Elias, G. C. (1994). Provision for pupils with special educational needs in England, with some implications for the Queensland context. In K. Wilshire (Chair), *Shaping the future: Review of the Queensland school curriculum* (Vol. 3, pp. 135–158). Brisbane: Government Printer.

Elkins, J. & Atkinson, J. K. (1985). *Comparative study of three school programs: OECD/CERI Project on the Transition of Handicapped Youth*. St Lucia: Fred and Eleanor Schonell Educational Research Centre.

Epps, S. & Tindal, G. (1987). The effectiveness of differential programming in serving students with mild handicaps: Placement options and instructional programming. In M. C. Wang, M. C. Reynolds & H. J. Walberg (Eds), *Handbook of special education: Research and practice* (Vol. 1, pp. 213–248). Oxford: Pergamon.

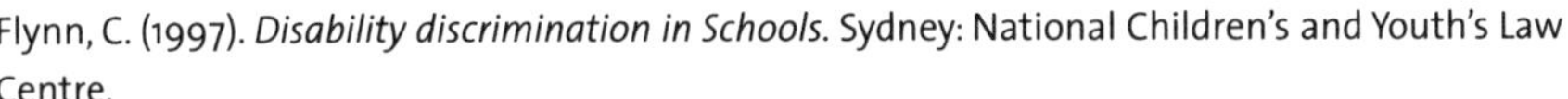

Flynn, C. (1997). *Disability discrimination in Schools.* Sydney: National Children's and Youth's Law Centre.

Fraser, D., Moltzen, R., & Ryba, K. (2000). *Learners with special needs in Aotearoa New Zealand* (2nd ed.). Palmerston North, NZ: Dunmore.

Giangreco, M. F. (1989). Facilitating integration of students with severe disabilities: Implication of "planned change" for teacher preparation programs. *Teacher Education and Special Education*, 12, 139–147.

Giangreco, M. F. (1992). Curriculum in inclusion-oriented schools: Trends, issues, challenges, and potential solutions. In S. Stainback & W. Stainback (Eds), *Curriculum considerations in inclusive classrooms: Facilitating learning for all students.* Baltimore, MD: Paul H. Brookes Publishing Co.

Giangreco, M. F. (1993). Using creative problem-solving methods to include students with severe disabilities in general education classroom activities. *Journal of Educational and Psychological Consultations*, 6, 113–135.

Giangreco, M. F. (1996). What do I do now? A teacher's guide to including students with disabilities. *Educational Leadership*, 53, 56–59.

Gordon, B. O. & Rosenblum, K. E. (2001) Bringing disability into the sociological frame: A comparison of disability with race, sex, and sexual orientation statuses. *Disability and Society*, 16, 5–20.

Hart, S. (Ed.) (1996). *Differentiation and the secondary curriculum: Debates and dilemmas.* London: Routledge.

Henderson, R. A. (1988). Integration: Similarities and differences—Australia and the United States. In A. F. Ashman (Ed.), *Integration 25 years on* (Exceptional Child Monograph No. 1, pp. 29–40). St Lucia: Fred and Eleanor Schonell Special Education Research Centre.

Henry, M. (1981). *Toward achievement and acceptance.* St Lucia: University of Queensland Press.

Integration in Victorian education. (1984). Report of the Ministerial Review of Education Services for the Disabled. Melbourne: Government Printer.

Jenkinson, J. C. (1996). *Mainstream or special: Educating students with disabilities.* London: Routledge.

Jordan, L. & Goodey, C. (1996). *Human rights and school change: The Newham story.* Bristol, UK: Centre for Studies on Inclusive Education.

Kauffman, J. & Hallahan, D. (Eds) (1995). *The illusion of full inclusion.* Austin, TX: PRO–ED.

Loreman, T. (1999). Integration: Coming from the outside. *Interaction*, 13(1), 21–23.

McRae, D. (1996). *The integration/inclusion feasibility study.* Report for the Minister for Education and Training New South Wales. Sydney: Ministry of Education and Training.

Mitchell, D. R. (1991). *Special education in New Zealand: Perspectives on the coming decade.* Country Report prepared for the 11th APEID Regional Seminar on Special Education (August), Yokosaka, Kanagawa, Japan.

Mitchell, D. R. (1996). The rules keep changing: Special education in a reforming education system. *International Journal of Disability, Development and Education*, 43, 55–74.

Mitchell, D. R. (2001). *Challenges and Successes in Implementing Inclusive Education in Eight Developing Countries in Asia and the Pacific.* Paper presented as part of a joint DISES Showcase Session with Dr Todd Fletcher, University of Arizona, at the Annual Convention of the Council for Exceptional Children, Kansas City, USA, 18–21 April 2001.

Nirje, B. (1985). Setting the record straight: A critique of some frequent misconceptions of the normalisation principle. *Australia and New Zealand Journal of Developmental Disabilities*, 11, 69–74.

Organisation for Economic Co-operation and Development. (1999). *Inclusive education at work: Students with disabilities in mainstream schools*. Paris: Author.

Palinesar, A. S. T. & Klenk, L. (1992). Entering literacy learning in supportive contexts. *Journal of hearing disabilities*, 25, 211 – 225, 229.

Pickering, D. (1991). A failure to meet special needs. The *Age*, 2 December, p. 9.

Rogers, R. (1996). *Developing an inclusive policy for your school*. Bristol, UK: Centre for Studies on Inclusive Education.

Sigafoos, J., Elkins, J., Hayes, A., Gunn, S., Couzens, D., & Roberts, D. (1991). *A review of programs for young children with severe disabilities: Final project report*. St Lucia: Fred and Eleanor Schonell Special Educational Research Centre.

Slee, R. (1996). Inclusive schooling in Australia? Not yet! *Cambridge Journal of Education*, 26, 19–32.

Slee, R. & Weiner, G. with Tomlinson, S. (Eds). (1998). *School effectiveness for whom?: Challenges to the school effectiveness and school improvement movements*. London: Falmer Press.

Stainback, W. & Stainback S. (1982). The need for research on training nonhandicapped students to interact with severely retarded students. *Education and Training of the Mentally Retarded*, 17, 12–16.

Swann, W. (1988). Trends in special school placement to 1986: Measuring, assessing and explaining segregation. *Oxford Review of Education*, 14, 139–161.

Tarr, P. (1988). Integration policy and practice in Victoria: An examination of the Victorian Government's educational provision for students with impairments, disabilities and problems in schooling since 1984. In A. F. Ashman (Ed.). *Integration 25 years on* (Exceptional Child Monograph No. 1, (pp. 63–67). St Lucia: Fred and Eleanor Schonell Special Education Research Centre.

Thomas, G. (2001). *Deconstructing special education and constructing inclusion*. Philadelphia, PA.: Open University, 2001.

Tomlinson, S. (1982). *A sociology of special education*. London: Routledge & Kegan Paul.

van Kraayenoord, C. (2000). Editorial. Victory for Scarlett. *International Journal of Disability, Development and Education*, 47, 221–224.

Wang, M. C. & Baker, E. T. (1985–86). Mainstreaming programs: Design features and effects. *Journal of Special Education*, 19, 503–525.

Ward, J., Bochner, S., Center, Y., Outhred, L., & Pieterse, M. (Eds) (1987). *Educating children with special needs in regular classrooms: An Australian perspective*. North Ryde, NSW: Macquarie University Special Education Centre.

Warnock, M. (1978). *Special education needs*. The Report of the Committee of Enquiry into the Education of Handicapped Children and Young People. London: HMSO.

Williams, P. (1996). *The law and students with learning difficulties: Some recent developments*. Perth, WA: Curtin Business School Working Papers 96.01.

Wills, D. & Jackson, R. (2001). *Education for All: UNESCO Report Card on Inclusive Education*. Fyshwick, ACT: National Council on Intellectual Disability.

Wolfensberger, W. (1972). *The principle of normalization in human services*. Toronto: National Institute on Mental Retardation.

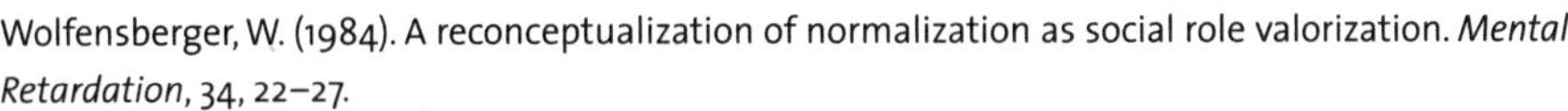

Wolfensberger, W. (1984). A reconceptualization of normalization as social role valorization. *Mental Retardation*, 34, 22–27.

Wolfensberger, W. (1988). Common assets of mentally retarded people that are commonly not acknowledged. *Mental Retardation*, 26, 63–70.

Zetlin, A. (1987). The social status of mildly learning handicapped high school students. *Journal of School Psychology*, 24, 165–173.

4

Early schooling for infants and children with diverse abilities

ANNE JOBLING AND SUSANA GAVIDIA-PAYNE

Case studies

Paul

Paul is a 4-year-old child who has mild developmental delays in language, and in fine-motor and gross-motor areas. Paul's delays, especially in motor areas, were identified soon after birth, as it was known that his mother was a carrier of the fragile X condition. Both of Paul's parents, Tracy and Michael, had received genetic counselling before Tracy became pregnant, and they had decided that they really wanted to have this child.

Before Paul's birth, Tracy and Michael had resources and supports in place, both formal and informal, to cater for his needs. Paul received physiotherapy and speech therapy from a very early age.

At four years of age, Paul is a delightful little boy, who fully participates in an early intervention program in which he has an individual plan that is reviewed every few months. Furthermore, Paul attends his local kindergarten two mornings a week, and takes full advantage of social interactions with other children. The kindergarten teachers work in a coordinated manner with Paul's early intervention teachers in a common curriculum, and with the assistance of speech therapy and physiotherapy which are incorporated in Paul's program. The plan is for Paul to attend his local school full-time.

Tracy and Michael could not be happier with Paul's program and with the progress he is making. They both feel that they are active participants in Paul's program as they attend all planning meetings, and have ongoing contact with the early intervention program.Those involved with the program work very hard at listening to any concerns they might have. In addition, Tracy attends a support group for parents of young children with diverse abilities that meets once a month at the early intervention centre. Tracy and Michael feel that these meetings have been very useful in helping them to deal positively with Paul's needs as he grows up.

Sarah

Sarah is a 2-year-old child who, for approximately six months, has presented unusual behaviours. She cries for no apparent reason, and runs around the house making unintelligible noises. Sarah's parents, Jason and Maria, are puzzled and very worried by Sarah's behaviour. She has even stopped saying the few words that she had learnt when she was about two years old. They have talked with their general practitioner, who has indicated that Sarah is probably going through the "terrible twos" and will soon grow out of it.

Although Maria and Jason accepted this explanation, they think that Sarah is getting worse rather than better. Sarah has two siblings, one older and one younger. Jason is very busy with the farm, and Maria is the primary carer for their children. Maria

indicates that she is not coping with Sarah's behaviour, especially while attempting to do all the things that need to be done at home at the same time. Maria often feels exhausted and unhappy.

A close friend of Maria has suggested that it might be a good idea to take Sarah to a paediatrician located approximately one hour away. When they visit the doctor, they feel he is vague about Sarah's problems, and that he does not offer any explanations for her behaviour. Instead, he suggests that perhaps they should be stricter in their discipline and recommends a couple of parenting books for them to read.

Following Jason and Maria's insistence, the paediatrician also refers them to the local hospital speech therapist. After seeing Sarah two months later (there is a long waiting list for his services), the speech therapist tells Jason and Maria that he has not ever seen a child like Sarah, and that he is not prepared to make a diagnosis. However, he feels that a full developmental assessment should be made at a hospital in the big city, approximately five hours away from Sarah's home.

At this time, Jason and Maria are confused by the information given to them, by the uncertainty of Sarah's problems, and by the long wait ahead of them before anything definite can be said. For them, the future looks grim.

What you will learn in this chapter

As you work your way through this chapter, you will learn about:

- prominent theoretical approaches used in the field of early childhood intervention;
- developments in programming for the delivery of early childhood schooling and services;
- play and its role in early schooling;
- program evaluation;
- characteristics of programs that work; and
- recent policy and systems issues facing the field of early childhood intervention.

Early interest in young children

During the 20th century, societal attitudes toward children changed dramatically. Education authors and social scientists contributed to these changes by writing about childhood as a critical period of development and by advocating programs for children prior to school entry. Educational experiences available to children were considered to be essential aspects in the care and socialisation of children within a modern society, and training colleges to educate teachers for these programs were established in Australia from the end of the 19th century. This renaissance in early childhood education

(Shane, 1971) became driven by a combination of events and circumstances. Social consciences had been aroused, the importance of early schooling had been established, and research work by notable developmental psychologists—such as Arnold Gesell (1940) and Jean Piaget (1936)—had raised the awareness of the education community about the concept of intelligence. Childhood was seen to have a purpose and a special place in a humane society and governments began to take responsibility for the provision of programs. These changes created the impetus for the major developments in education in the 1960s and 1970s that influenced schooling through the second half of the 20th century.

During the late 1900s attention also began to focus on children who were having difficulty coping with school. First, there was a growing recognition of the importance of people as individuals and as members of society. This took its impetus from the rights movements of the 1960s when legislation was passed to protect and enhance individuals and recognise the rights of minority groups including children and those with special learning needs. Before 1970, most children with a severe specific impairment or disability were institutionalised. Parents were encouraged to give up their children as many professionals considered this to be in the interests of the child and the family. However, by 1970 parents were starting to advocate on behalf of their children and they have remained in the forefront of many of the subsequent educational changes (Gunn, 1998).

Second, the study of child development became a rapidly growing interest in the psychology and education. This interest was encouraged by an early experiment of Skeel and Dye (1939) who placed orphans with women with disabilities in an institution and found that there was an increase in the children's IQ. Later McVicker-Hunt (1961) used the Piagetian stage theory to promote the effects of the environment and this spawned a number of nature or nurture debates, with various models of child development being proposed to account for the progress of children toward maturity. Human development was explained in terms of stability and change (Bloom, 1964), and Sameroff and colleagues (Sameroff & Chandler, 1975; Sameroff & Fiese, 2000) proposed a transactional model. The transactional model suggested the interdependence of developmental domains; that there is a dynamic interrelationship among child, caregiver, and the environment. This model has been offered as a framework for the examination of child development when risk might not be the only factor considered.

Given that the biological makeup of a child cannot be changed, what is the optimal environment? With such debates continuing today among child development professionals, the field has become better informed about the complexity of the interaction between nature (the child's biological makeup) and nurture (child-rearing that promotes intellectual and emotional growth).

Third, there has been an increased awareness of the benefits of education, with early schooling being viewed as an antidote for later school failure. Initially, attention was directed toward young children in low socioeconomic communities, the Head Start programs in the United States being the most prominent (Tjossem, 1976). But there has been a growing opinion that an impairment or handicap is an insufficient reason to deny educational opportunities (Bricker, 1970).

Children in early schooling

The infancy and toddler periods (from birth to three years of age) and the preschool period (from three to six years) are the years for early schooling. During this time children usually attend a variety of day care, kindergarten, and preschool programs. In Australia, some of these are provided by state government education or family day care services, whereas others are privately managed with some government support. From early in the 20th century, kindergartens have been one of the largest private providers of services for children in these age groups, such as those established by the Creche and Kindergarten Association in Queensland in 1907 (Fazldeen, 1997). To understand the needs of all children it is important to develop an awareness of the effect of diversity on the child's growth and development. Some aspects of diversity will affect the child's milestone development (a child's first words or when a child can stand unsupported), others will affect the child's interactions with their environment (how a child knows others are speaking or looking at them), while still others will affect their feelings and aspiration (the child success or failure at tasks they wish to pursue).

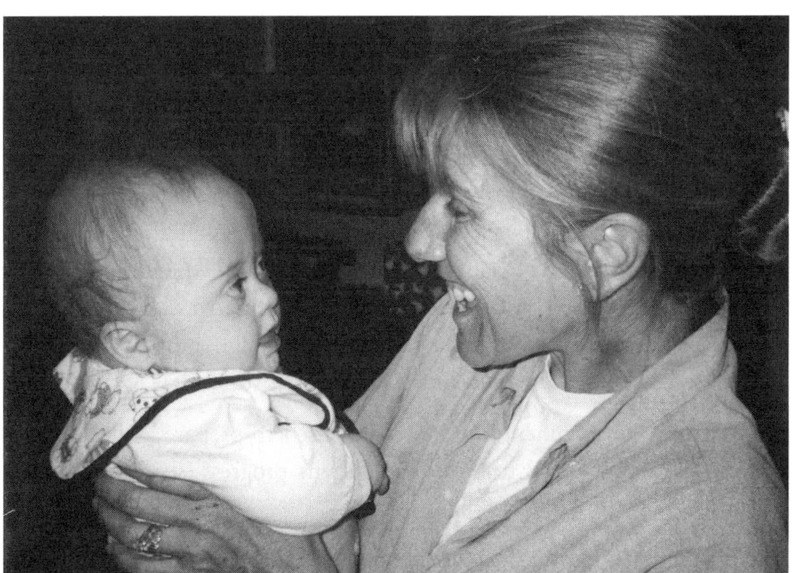

A mother and child can have excellent experiences in early childhood education settings.

Developmental domains

At this point it is useful to consider the several domains of human development: cognition, motor, communication, social and emotional. Early childhood development has been divided not only by age but also into domains that are marked by milestones and tasks that a child achieves in sequence. Many theorists have influenced the formulation of developmental domains. We have already mentioned Gesell and Piaget but there was also landmark work undertaken by Erikson (1963) and Vygotsky (1978). Perhaps the most influential for an understanding of early childhood were Piaget and Erikson.

Piaget divided the growth of intelligence into four main stages, two of which (sensorimotor and preoperational) occur within early childhood years. Behaviour patterns are elicited by specific stimuli such as blinking, sucking and grasping (called reflexes), followed by primary reactions (hand to mouth), secondary reactions (reaches for toy, moves it, watches and moves it again), and tertiary reactions (invents new ways to prolong events such as the ones above). These are followed by means–end combination (continued existence of an unseen object) and mental combination (invents new ways by imitating, pretending, and insightful problem-solving). These are all stages in the sensorimotor phase. The pre-operational stage (at approximately three and a half years of age) is represented by the preconceptual stage, followed by the intuitive stage (see Box 4.1, page 121). Piaget was interested in *how* children reach each stage, rather than *when* they reach each stage, although educators often forget this.

Erikson (1963) proposed stages for psychosocial development across the lifespan and, in doing so, drew attention to the interaction between the individual and the environment. Within the early childhood years, the stages of trust, autonomy, initiative and imagination are portrayed by presenting a number of problems that require resolution by the child. Trust is articulated as consistent loving care that provides trust-promoting experiences from which children can develop autonomy, by which they take on doing things themselves (such as going to the toilet and tying shoelaces). The stages of initiative and imagination follow, as children begin to explore their world, physically moving about it, and cognitively questioning everything. Hence, they begin to create and invent from these initiatives. Progression through these stages takes place in an orderly sequence, although problems might not be completely resolved before the child moves to the next stage.

The work of these developmental theorists was used to prepare a checklist for skills across developmental domains to measure children's progress (see Tables 4.1 and 4.2, page 122).

The Portage Guide to Early Education developed by Bluma, Shearer, Frohman, and Hilliard (1976) is a notable example and has been used to identify developmental delays.

Box 4.1 Piagetian and Eriksonian stages

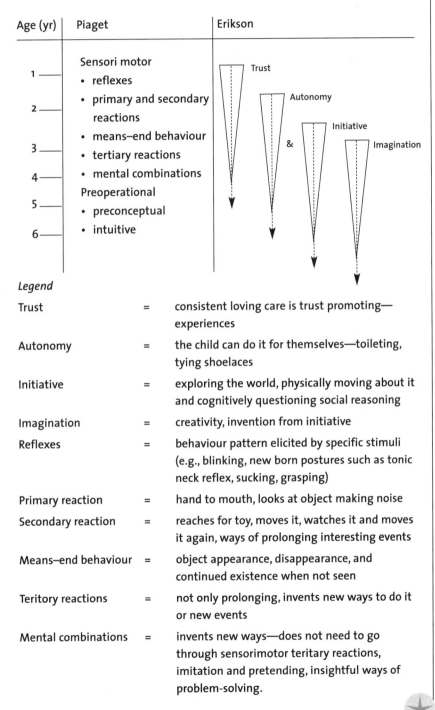

Age (yr)	Piaget	Erikson
1 2 3 4 5 6	Sensori motor • reflexes • primary and secondary reactions • means–end behaviour • tertiary reactions • mental combinations Preoperational • preconceptual • intuitive	Trust Autonomy & Initiative Imagination

Legend

Trust	=	consistent loving care is trust promoting—experiences
Autonomy	=	the child can do it for themselves—toileting, tying shoelaces
Initiative	=	exploring the world, physically moving about it and cognitively questioning social reasoning
Imagination	=	creativity, invention from initiative
Reflexes	=	behaviour pattern elicited by specific stimuli (e.g., blinking, new born postures such as tonic neck reflex, sucking, grasping)
Primary reaction	=	hand to mouth, looks at object making noise
Secondary reaction	=	reaches for toy, moves it, watches it and moves it again, ways of prolonging interesting events
Means–end behaviour	=	object appearance, disappearance, and continued existence when not seen
Teritory reactions	=	not only prolonging, invents new ways to do it or new events
Mental combinations	=	invents new ways—does not need to go through sensorimotor teritary reactions, imitation and pretending, insightful ways of problem-solving.

Table 4.1 The Portage (1976) checklist

DOMAIN	AGE	SKILLS/TASKS
Cognitive	2–3	names four common pictures matches textures
	3–4	names big and little objects repeats finger plays with words and actions
Motor	2–3	walks backwards unwraps small object
	3–4	walks tip-toe catches ball two hands
Communication	2–3	combines two words to express possessive answers "where" questions
	3–4	tells full name on request answers "how" questions
Social-emotional	2–3	cooperates with parent request 50% of time attends to music or story for 5–10 minutes
	3–4	cooperates with adult request 75% of time will take turns

Table 4.2 The Linder (1990) framework

DOMAIN	AGE	SKILLS/TASKS
Cognitive framework—sequencing skills	2–3	understands big and little
	3–4	understands tallest, largest, shortest
Motor framework—mobility in standing	2–3	runs whole foot, contacts, stops, and starts
	3–4	walks with heel to toe pattern
Communication framework—language comprehension	2–3	understands possessives "mine", "yours"
	3–4	follows multistep commands
Social-emotional framework—social relations with peers	2–3	child imitates peer
	3–4	begins to play with 2–3 peers cooperatively

More recently, Linder (1990; 1993) has provided a series of frameworks for observing a particular domain (e.g., cognitive, communication) in children during a play sessions.

These frameworks can be used to differentiate play behaviours and help the teacher to understand the level of functioning achieved by the child at the time of the observation. Observations should occur across settings (e.g., home, playgroup, preschool) and on different days, to gain a more complete picture of the child's competence.

Both checklists and frameworks have a series of sequenced skills and/or tasks that match ages or stages and measure a child's progress across the four developmental domains. These four domains of development (cognitive, motor, communication, and social-emotional) will now be discussed with regard to children with diverse abilities.

Cognitive development

The cognitive domain involves a wide range of complex skills that can take years beyond the early childhood period to develop. Piaget's stages in the growth of intelligence have shaped much of our thinking related to this domain. During infancy (sensorimotor stage, from birth to two years) the cognitive framework is *object permanency*, which relates to the control of body parts, the imitation of language or sounds, and the making of internal representations of reality. At the preschool age (preoperational stage from two to seven years) these cognitive skills expand to become more perceptive and flexible and children are able to use past experiences, consider more than one event at a time, and make and use symbolic and imitative representations. Young children with intellectual impairments generally have difficulties acquiring many of these basic cognitive skills within the age guidelines of the stage.

Children with sensory impairments are handicapped in the perceptual aspects of development (e.g., looking, listening, feeling), whereas those with physical handicaps have problems moving about their environment and manipulating objects. Time spent interacting and engaging in play during the early school years provides a location for these aspects of cognitive development (Bricker & Wood-Cripe, 1992; Lerner, Mardell-Czudnowski, & Goldenberg, 1987). Play activities assist the child with task attention, persistence, problem-solving, and the development of memory. Teachers can promote the domain by doing puzzle boards, sorting and matching shapes, building blocks and sandcastles, attending to colours and relationships, and classifying and sequencing objects or toys playfully (see e.g., Greenberg, 1994).

Motor development

Motor development is divided into gross and fine movements. The development of these skills has also been sequenced (see e.g., Gallahue, 1989) and qualitative stages

of specific skills (e.g., running and jumping) have been developed (Robertson & Halverson, 1984). Box 4.2 (below) outlines three developmental stages of jumping.

The gross motor milestone of *walking* is the milestone most eagerly awaited by parents. The fine motor skills associated with tool use (e.g., using cutlery and pencils) are also considered highly desirable. Walking expands the child's environment and learning opportunities, whereas tool use enables the manipulation of objects such as spoons, puzzle pieces, and balls.

For some children with an impairment or disability, achievement of proficiency in motor tasks can be slow and frustrating. But achievement should not be the only goal. The quality of the movements attained is also important. Children who have movement patterns that are awkward and/or immature may lack not only a sound basis for further skill development but also adequate movement knowledge, from kinaesthetic feedback, to make moving relevant and purposeful.

Box 4.2 Developmental stages of two-foot jumping

Stage 1 (approx. 18 to 30 months)

At this stage the child is really just stepping down with the body held in an upright position. The arms are held in opposition to leg movements, as in walking. As the child takes off, the legs are extended together, and landing is in an innate pattern (into a deep squat). The arms are somewhat retracted in a bird-like position, and are brought to the side again when landing. There is little involvement of the head in the action.

Stage 2 (approx. 21/2 to 31/2 years)

At this stage the child is in a squat position for take-off, with the trunk forward. The child leans forward to enable higher trajectory into the air. The legs are straightened quickly as the body moves into the air. In the flight phase, the legs are bent again to prepare for a squat landing. The arms are swung backwards and sideways (like bird wings), and come forward only when landing. The head is tilted backward in flight, but there are few other adjustments.

Stage 3 (approx. 4 to 51/2 years)

At this stage, during the take-off phase there is a greater lean forward of the trunk, but the child still has difficulty in coordinating arm and leg movements. The legs are well coordinated, with a straight-leg take-off, followed by the legs being held backward for flight, and then being swung forward to land in a squat position. If trying for distance, the child sometimes fails to coordinate a two-foot landing. The arms are not as well coordinated. They are swung forward for take-off, but take up various positions during flight before coming forwards in landing. The tilt of the head is now used to balance the body position throughout the jump.

In most early childhood programs for children with problems in this domain, physical and occupational therapists are usually included in the educational team to help children to achieve the motor development milestones. This is essential because, as motor patterns mature, children learn to engage in new and exciting motor experiences (such as climbing, dancing, games, writing, and drawing). Pellegrini and Smith (1998) outlined the importance of physically active play. In their analysis, motor activity in this type of play provides three developmental functions. In infancy, rhythmic stereotypical movements establish motor patterns and skills (e.g., kicking); in preschoolers, exercise play provides strength and endurance (e.g., running and jumping); and in middle childhood, rough and tumble play benefits social role negotiation (e.g., chasing and ball games with rules).

Communication and language

The domain of communication and language involves early interactions such as smiling and babbling, followed by the first words, and finally the attainment of speech with the development of expressive and receptive language skills. Communication involves exchanging ideas, information, and feelings and children progress through a number of developmental stages before maturity is reached. Children with sense impairments, intellectual impairments, and specific disabilities, such as autism or fragile X syndrome, frequently have problems reaching these developmental stages. Speech and language problems might also be experienced by some children who have physical impairments, or by those who have a home language other than English.

Because a certain level of communication proficiency is vital to learning and to interactions with others, assistance in overcoming problems is essential. Some children might have such severe communication problems that they are unable to convey their needs and choices to others. This may lead to behaviours that are inappropriate or aggressive. Intervention in these cases should involve the teaching of more appropriate communication strategies (Butterfield, Arthur, & Sigafoos, 1995). Speech pathologists frequently offer assistance with communication, but it is important that the emphasis is on the total communicative acts of the child. These include dealing with the content of communication, as well as methods, attitudes, and emotions, gestures, body posture and movement, physical distance, and the overall quality, quantity, and effectiveness of communication. In Box 4.3 (page 126), the activity of mask-making demonstrates some of these aspects of communication. Many programs have been designed with these in mind (see, for example, Berkell-Zager, 1999; Bricker & Woods Cripe, 1992).

Excellent opportunities for children to initiate and practise communication skills are provided by everyday discourses in play, by make-believe games, by the use of oral language (as in show-and-tell times), and by the development of independence in writing and reading activities.

Box 4.3 Making a mask

Children can make masks from many materials that can be explored for texture, colour and strength, but paper plates are frequently favoured.

Discussion about various types of faces, emotions, and story characters faces should precede such an activity. Stories can be read, or television characters discussed.

Various methods for making the mask can be suggested to the children—cut holes for eyes, draw and colour hair, cut and stick ears, and so on. To fasten the mask to the children's faces, suggest alternatives such as string, ribbons, and wool.

Let the children decide about their masks. Wait, and help only when necessary.

Children might wish to talk about the characters they have created, or the emotions represented by their masks. Extension and cooperative activities can include plays, story re-enactments, sock or paperbag puppets, or costume-making to add to the character of the masks.

Ear infections (especially otitis media, which is a frequent condition in young children and in Aboriginal and Torres Strait Islander children) can cause hearing loss if left unchecked. Children with ear infections can become restless and inattentive, which can affect their language learning.

Social-emotional development

Learning is a profoundly social process. As children grow they interact with their environment and develop interactional styles that enable them to be a part of their environment. Children with sensory impairments (such as hearing loss) might need an alternative communication system (such as a signing system) to facilitate interactions. Children with physical impairments might learn to use adaptive equipment, or have environments designed that enable them to interact with other children and adults. Maintaining eye contact and activities that encourage joint attention to the play, can also be useful.

Children with autism have particularly enduring problems in interacting with their environment. In their early years, a lack of consistent eye contact, so that joint attention to a task can be facilitated, plays a major role in the ongoing problems they display in social situations (Berkell-Zager, Shamow, & Schneider, 1999). Therefore, early introduction of support mechanisms and the teaching of specific strategies to the educators and parents to assist the child's development are considered essential. Odom et al. (1999), for example, reported that a peer-mediated strategy led to a significant number of peer interaction contacts and encouraged later initiations.

Teachers also rated highly the quality and competency of the interactions. Strategies such as using socially competent peers can be consistently used to engage and teach children who have delays in the social-emotional domain to initiate and maintain social interactions with other children and adults. Peer mediation is one effective strategy to encourage all children to interact with others.

In summary, for some children development in any of the domains might proceed at a slower pace than in others (Goodman, 1992), and the interaction of these children with the environment can be a frustrating challenge. For a small number of other children, communication of their needs and choice-making can be an almost impossible task. However, it has been shown that even for children with a significant developmental delay (such as Down syndrome), the sequence of progress is similar to that of their typically developing peers. Some of the differences among children might stem from different patterns of development, others originate from a permanent impairment, and still others come from a lack of opportunities and experiences.

The role of play in development

Play is a universal and dominant behaviour in childhood. It is spontaneous, energetic, organised, and mischievous and children show excitement in being actively involved and in control. The value of play in the development of the child was clear to the early pioneers who promoted the importance of childhood. Froebels, who pioneered the importance of early schooling, considered play to be the highest phase in child development, for it was the self-active representation of the inner self (see Hughes, 1924).

Definitions of play have been as varied as the nature of play itself and many experts have tried to define it. It has been defined as a sequence of social outcomes related to the child's intellectual progress and, variously, as an experimental dialogue with the environment, as a feeling and expression of joy and mastery, and even as the fool that might be king. In a classic publication that encompasses play and associated topics across a range of contexts, Bruner, Jolly, and Sylva (1976) stated that the phenomena of play cannot be framed into a single operational definition perfectly, and Schechner (1988) agreed, declaring that scholars should stop trying to define play, because it is undefinable!

Regardless of whether we need to define it or not, there can be no doubt about the importance of play in development, and observations of children at play produce knowledge that can be used to promote its importance (Pellegrini & Smith, 1998).

Young children learn best when they are actively involved in play and exploration and when they choose and initiate their own activities (Cavallaro & Haney, 1999). Playtime must be unstructured and free and, to achieve this, the environment for play should be sensitive to the child's needs and provide both indoor and outdoor

experiences with the self-selected equipment designed at the child's skill level (Thompson, Hudson & Mack, 1999). This type of environmental planning was initiated by Montessori in the slums of Milan (Montessori, 1946) and modified equipment (child-sized) has now become standard in early childhood settings. The outdoor play environment should be rich, challenging, and graduated, and should offer opportunities for children to manipulate. This is exemplified in the Hays Paddock Adventure Playground, Boroondara, Victoria. This is the first community playground in Australia designed so that all children, regardless of their ability, can play on an equal basis. The need for the playground was brought to the attention of the local council by two parents who identified a need for the playground to cater for all children—including those with hearing, sight, mobility, muscular-control, and behavioural difficulties.

Henniger (1994) considered that many play spaces for young children were developmentally sterile and presented a range of characteristics for the development of creative outdoor play spaces. Barbour (1999) discussed the interrelationships among playground design, different levels of physical competence, and peer relationships. Play outdoors stimulates a child's development and supports growth. Effective designs are therefore important. At play, children should choose spontaneously, devise their own activities, seek challenges that match their individual needs and interact with peers. Not only is design of playspace important, but also teachers need to develop incidental teaching responses to assist children to use the environment. This is especially so for children who have moderate to severe impairments.

In early schooling, the play of children is frequently associated with objects or toys. The importance of toys to human development has been outlined by Newson and Newson (1979), and they considered that there was no one toy that was best for a child. The market in educational toys is ever expanding, but the term educational usually indicates the quality of the product rather than its developmental significance. Toys are the tools of play and have no particular value of their own, and when toys are used to train a particular function the play becomes training, not play (Brodin 1999).

Play partners

Mothers

Mothers are often the first and most frequent early play partners of children, and much has been written about mothers' play. A lack of responsivity and the presence of attention problems in children can be frustrating for parents, especially for mothers. Early interactions are important for the child and the mother because communication needs to be developed whereby the child takes more and more responsibility and control over the interactions. Importantly, there must be a clear distinction between teaching and playing during any interaction so that the child can develop a sense of

Hays Paddock Adventure Playground, Boroondara, Victoria.

competence and control. When the opposite occurs, the child can develop a lack of interest in taking initiative in playing, and can feel helpless (Jobling, 1996).

Researchers have examined the interactional patterns of mothers as they play with their young children, and have concluded that some mothers require training. Consequently, various training programs have been developed (see Braithwaite, 1983; Leach, Swerissen, & Leach, 1988). However, if in the play interaction the mother's play became too directive, the role of a mother is changed. For example:

> . . . expecting mothers of disabled children to assume a major teaching role for their child may be counterproductive. It may make playing with the disabled child for "playing" sake difficult . . . mother becoming teacher . . . inherently changes the mother-child relationship which may be fragile anyway (Sloper, Cunningham, & Arnljotsdottir, 1983, p. 360).

Parents and children looking at books or reading stories together can benefit child–parent interaction, especially when the child has a disability (see the International Reading Association's *Babies need books* program in all Australian states). These activities have been promoted for children with diverse abilities (Dale, Crain-Thoreson, Notari-Syverson, & Cole, 1996; Farrell & Gunn, 2000) although this is not a common practice. For example, in a survey of 168 parents and caregivers of children in early childhood special education programs, fewer than half participated in daily story reading, or even weekly reading and writing activities (Marvin, 1994). In the group of caregivers whose children had multiple impairments only a few read to their young children or encouraged reading. This study highlights the effect of the can't-do expectations that are often expressed by researchers and educators.

Siblings and peers

Brothers and sisters are also important play partners because they can have a significant effect on a young child's socialisation. The nature of the interaction in terms of balance and control can be significant to the progress of play, and the feeling of competence gained from the activity. Of course, sibling interactions can create situations of dominance and control and these situations can disadvantage siblings with an impairment, but this outcome appears to be relatively uncommon. Parents can be anxious about playtimes, but Cuskelly and Gunn (1993) considered that this anxiety is not inevitable for dyads in which one sibling had Down syndrome.

Outside the family, peers are often play partners and the interactions are valuable for the establishment of interpersonal skills, cooperation, modelling, and the development of trust. The role of peers for young children has been emphasised in the classical research on the development of friendships. For example, Howes (1983; 1988) showed that peer friendships commence as young as 12 months and have a significant effect on a child's future development. There has been considerable research about the interaction with peers, especially when accommodating a peer with varying levels of

competence (Arthur, Bochner, & Butterfield, 1999). In some situations non-disabled peers might require instruction and need to learn how to meet the needs of their play partner and how to play with them (Choi, Jobling, & Carroll, 2000; Guralnick, 1993). For example, nondisabled peers can be taught non-verbal signing systems or frequently used gestures of their play partner. A program developed in Australia by Teitzel and Terkelson (1997) provides five workshop sessions to assist peer social interactions in inclusive settings. The involvement of socially competent peers with children who have disabilities is considered to be critical for the development of the social skills and acceptance of disabled children in education programs in regular schools and classes (Odom et al.,1999).

Teachers

The teacher's role is to enhance the natural growth processes by providing students with learning opportunities within an environment that is enriching, encouraging, and nurturing. Teachers can be play partners in a variety of situations, which range from teacher-directed to child-directed, that are operating in early schooling environments (Malone & Langone, 1999). Research is equivocal about the benefits of these differing styles of play interaction. For some children, therapists are partners in play, and occupational therapists can also develop interactions through play-based programs (Rodgers & Ziviani,1999).

In summary, play is critical to cognitive, emotional and social development. For children with impairments and disabilities, play might not occur spontaneously. For many it might need to be prompted and, for a few, even targeted for training. When this is the case play partners are very important in a variety of settings. These might include therapy sessions in the program at preschool or play group and in the home where parents and siblings can contribute significantly. Play needs consideration by all those who are involved in the various environments the child experiences.

Children with diverse abilities at play

The role of play in the lives of all children can hardly be overstated, but it is of special importance for the intellectual and social development of children with learning or developmental problems. Several studies in which children with impairments and disabilities have been observed playing have led to assertions that these children do not play, and that when they do interact, their playing is asocial with a random low level of activity and little spontaneity. For the educator, this style of play requires attention. All children need to play to develop so it became the role of early programs to teach the children who were considered trainable to play by providing interventions to remedy their play deficiencies. Consequently, play and development in children became inextricably linked, as play became a variable for both predicting and measuring development.

It might seem a little unusual for researchers to explore the notion of training play. However, teaching some children how to play has been seen as an important aspect of their education. Their cognitive, social, motor, and language deficits have been systematically assessed and addressed with specific developmentally sequenced play activities. The first curriculum devoted especially to play was developed by Fewell and Vadasy in 1983. They sequenced play milestones into 192 activities, such as building blocks, story listening and reading, make-believe games, and play on outdoor equipment. With this structure, deficits observed in children with disabilities could be remedied. For some children with severe impairments, intensive therapy programs went well beyond playing and incorporated physical manipulation and drug therapy.

Other styles of intervention, such as conductive education, focused on the development of independence in functional areas such as walking, dressing, and eating. Australian educators of children with specific learning needs followed these styles and developed a range of initiatives. These were reviewed by Watts et al. (1981) and Pietese et al. (1988), and later programs for children with severe disability were specifically reviewed by Sigafoos et al. (1991).

History of early intervention programs

In contrast to the play-based approach of early childhood educators, early childhood special educators acted as interventionists who focused on functional goals for the child (Udell, Peters, & Templeman, 1998). The premise was that positive educational outcomes would not occur for young children without intervention. The history of the development of this approach to programming is recent but interesting.

Systematic programs designed to alleviate disadvantage during the early childhood years began with Head Start in the United States. These were introduced in 1965 to address the impact of poverty and had a range of comprehensive intervention goals (Day & Parker, 1977; Tjossem,1976). In Box 4.4 (page 133) are the goals of two such programs.

Zigler and Styfco (2000) stated that the original aim of Head Start was to enhance social competence among children and their families by providing health care, nutrition, and social support services. Head Start was a national intervention program funded by the federal government to help the poor break the poverty cycle so that their children could enter school with similar skills to their more affluent peers, and share in the nation's resources. Many programs were established to address social inequities (Day & Parker, 1977; Gallagher, 2000; Tjossem,1976). These included:

- visiting toy libraries;
- television programs such as Sesame Street;
- the Portage Madison home visiting program;
- the University of Washington Down Syndrome Project;

Box 4.4 Goals of two early intervention programs

Goals of Florida Parent Education Infant and Toddler Program—established 1966:

Parents—to increase the amount of verbal instruction in the home as the early years are the optimal time to establish parental behaviours.

Child—to develop a higher level of intellectual performance through enhanced language development.

Goals of Parent and Child Toy Library—established 1969:

To stimulate intellectual development of young children.

To increase the effectiveness of parents so they can provide an environment that supports the cognitive development of their children and nurtures the development of a healthy concept.

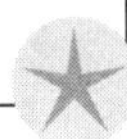

- the Florida Parent Education Infant and Toddler Program;
- the Ski-Hi Utah State University Program for hearing-impaired children in rural areas; and
- the Infant, Toddler and Preschool Research and Intervention Project initiated in 1970 at Peabody College.

The early results of these programs were very optimistic with reported increases of up to 10 IQ points and this led to exaggerated claims for early intervention programs generally. Not surprisingly, such programs expanded rapidly. Although many had highly unrealistic goals that could not be maintained (e.g., the eradication of school failure and the maintenance of IQ gains), the enthusiasm of these initial gains generalised to other programs for young children at risk due to an impairment or disability (Gallagher, 2000). As children who were at risk from causes other than poverty were also lagging behind their normally developing peers, intervention programs seemed to be an attractive alternative. So, from 1968 early intervention for children with disabilities became a part of the early schooling program with 10 to 15% of Head Start enrolments being children with disabilities. The typical preschooler with a disability received between 10 to 25 hours of support per week and the number of programs expanded rapidly in the 1990s (Bailey, 2000). These programs were either home-based or centre-based, and focused on improving the child's developmental outcomes with structured, carefully chosen activities that were directed and sequenced by adults (Bailey, 2000; Day & Parker, 1977; Tjossem, 1976). An example is shown in Box 4.5 (page 134).

This focus on the children's development meant that early attention to the social benefits (health, family support, and preparation for schooling) were overlooked, and the prodigious growth of programs meant that there were difficulties in monitoring

Box 4.5 An example of developmental activities

Purpose: This activity is to help the infant learn to use objects as tools for getting what he/she wants.

Position: The infant is shown propped on the mother's lap with a flat surface (tabletop or bench) in front of him/her.

Aim: for infant's hand to close over the string.

Action: place shoelace on flat surface in front of infant; if infant does not try to hold it, place over palm of his/her hand.

Aim: infant pulls the toy to him/her.

Action: while infant is watching, tie string to favourite toy and place out of reach in front of infant and say "Get the toy".

Aim: infant chooses string with toy attached.

Action: place toy with string attached out of reach again. Place two more strings alongside the string with toy attached.

Repeat the above but have the baby sitting alone on the floor. Mother might be behind or nearby. Have the three strings hanging over the flat surface to the floor within infant's reach.

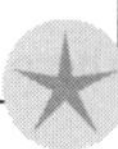

their quality (Bailey, 2000). Reports concerning the effectiveness of these early schooling programs were mixed, with various researchers suggesting that the key issue was simply the duration of involvement in a program.

One early study by Fewell and Oelwin (1991) considered time in the program important and reported that a substantial group of children made useful gains in self-help and development of social skills, but that there were no significant differences in the motor and language domains. The role of the parent as a teacher of his or her child and the quality of the parent–child interaction were also considered key variables in the child's developmental progress (Mahoney, Robinson, & Powell, 1992; Marfo & Kysela, 1988; Shonkoff & Meisels, 2000).

In 1992 Fisher examined 46 play-training studies and, like others (Goodman, 1992), reported that the results were inconsistent and diverse. It was suggested that intensive adult contrived play be replaced with play that is valued for fun and enjoyment, in conjunction with formal teaching of skills. Following a wide range of field observations, Goodman (1992) agreed with this mixed approach and criticised an adherence to developmental domain checklists that made both the environment and the program objectives too narrow, which often lacked in interest for the child.

The debate about the efficacy of programs has lasted for more than 30 years and remains unresolved (Bailey, 2000). Despite this, these programs have become the benchmark worldwide for effective interventions and have led to the new discipline of early childhood special education (Zigler & Styfco, 2000). Now the challenge is to foster as much passion about the quality of programs as there is about the access (Smith, 2000).

In Australia, the progress of the development of early childhood interventions programs followed the patterns of the American scene. Watts, et al. (1981) published an Australia-wide report on early schooling for young children with disabilities. This report, together with others about Australian toy libraries (Elkins, Calder, Conrads, Shepherd, & Coulston, 1980), a pilot project for special preschools in Queensland (Hayes et al.,1981) and a book by Braithwaite (1983), provided significant information about the initial development of early childhood services for children with special needs in the all states and territories. Braithwaite provided information on a project undertaken at Mt Druitt (New South Wales) in a new low-cost public housing area. The objective of the preschool programs was to develop and implement programs that would be educationally worthwhile for all children enrolled.

Table 4.3 (page 136) shows the programs offered by various services associated with early intervention across Australia (Watts et al., 1981).

Program approaches to early intervention had either a medical or educational focus. Prevention, diagnosis, treatment, care, and habilitation were the major concerns, with educational programs stressing assessment and development in the area

Table 4.3 Australian early intervention programs

STATE	EDUCATION DEPT	HEALTH DEPT/ COMMISSION	HOSPITAL	COMMUNITY SERVICES/ WELFARE	VOLUNTARY AGENCY*	TOY LIBRARY	UNIVERSITY PROGRAM	OTHER
NSW	4	12	—	1	18	—	5	—
Vic.	7	2	—	—	29	1	3	—
Qld	13	1	1	—	10	—	—	—
SA	5	4	8	5	9	3	1	5
WA	7	6	1	—	4	—	1	3
Tas.	6	3	—	—	3	—	—	—
NT	2	1	1	—	5	1	—	—
ACT	9	—	—	—	3	—	2	—

*Some voluntary agencies were partly supported with governmental funds.

of cognition, language, motor skills, self-concept, and social skills. The delivery of the program tended to reflect this focus and Watts et al. (1981) identified four orientations: remedial versus developmental; early intervention versus life span emphasis; segregated program delivery versus integrated program delivery; and/or child-centered emphasis versus family-based emphasis. During the 1970s, toy libraries had been established in Australia with the aim of making toys more accessible to families. Noah's Ark toy library started its services in Melbourne in 1971.Now, around the world, toy libraries provide advice on toys and games, and adapt toys for young children with diverse abilities. However, as in the USA, one of the most notable features of these programs was the absence of evaluation.

By 1988 these early intervention programs were well established, and Pieterse, Bochner, and Bettison (1988) comprehensively revisited a range of programs reporting that there was still no Australia-wide programming, even though governments strongly supported this fast-growing section of educational services for children. Therapy services and adaptive equipment (e.g., specially designed seating and computer technology) were becoming a more frequent part of early intervention programs, but there were still policy constraints on services and a shortage of therapists trained to work in early intervention programs. The training of early childhood special educators was receiving belated attention and the issue of how to blend early childhood and special education content and the collaboration of professionals working within the existing programs was progressing. The growth of a range of alternative and some controversial therapies was reported by Foreman (1988), who concluded that parents are likely to seek alternative sources of advice and services (even though data on success

of such treatments are scant), while optimal lifelong and quality services are difficult for them to obtain.

Challenges and changes to the interventionalist approach

The interventionalist approach to the education of young children with diverse needs did not go unchallenged (Jobling, 1988, 1996; Schwartzman,1991) with critics being particularly concerned about the role of play in these programs. Early childhood special education practices were becoming extremely effective at turning special preschools into places where play was tightly adult-controlled, more like work, and akin to drudgery. Special educators seemed to consider play some form of addiction for children and children became victims of their own need to play. Schwartzman, for example, considered that the seriousness with which educators had programmed play for children had transformed it and play for the players had evaporated. Also the outcome of several studies began to suggest that researchers might have misrepresented the play of children with disabilities. Linn, Goodman, and Lender (2000) noted, when observing passivity during a 47-minute session of unstructured play, that the passivity might indeed serve as a rest time for some children. They provided an anecdote:

> Elaine has been playing independently for 30 minutes. Most recently, animating the figures. She gathers the toys into a pile, attempts to gain her mother's attention and when told "mommy's busy" sits passively against the wall, staring into space. After 2½ minutes of passive behaviour, Elaine looks at her mother, briefly pushes a truck and then becomes engaged in a 4½ minute sequence of diapering the doll. Had Elaine's passive behaviour been interrupted, she would not have been given time to refuel and generate a new play scheme (Linn, Goodman, & Lender, 2000, pp. 23–24).

Nevertheless, the interventionalist approach seemed to persist in programs, and numerous discussions (about the contextual factors of play-based planning) developed between early childhood educators and early childhood special educators (Malone, 1999). Previous practices contributed to these discussions because many of the professionals involved in the early programs had a background in special education or therapy, whereas generally programs for young children had been the responsibility of early childhood educators. Also for professionals in USA, a comprehensive set of guidelines that stressed developmentally appropriate practice for all early childhood programs was not developed until the late 1990s (Bedekamp & Copple, 1997).

However, Fox, and Hanline (1993), with others, had begun to report a revised direction for early childhood special education. This approach involved a more naturalistic approach to play and the use of less intrusive teaching methods, with the importance of child-initiated play becoming more widely acknowledged in association with advocacy for play-based curricula (Hanline, 1999). The outcome of this has been the promotion of programming for continuing progress based around play activities, with

the child's interest being important for cognitive, motor, communication and social–emotional child development. In Australia, most early schooling settings follow this approach, with the Education Department of New South Wales recently introducing a program in which preschoolers actively construct their own learning. Intervention programs too are changing, with support rather than control being the focus of strategies for the new millennium (Early Childhood Intervention, Australia, 2000).

Delivering early schooling programs

Early childhood programs have not always been based on sound theoretical approaches. Many early intervention approaches aimed at addressing the needs of young children with learning or developmental disabilities have also lacked a theoretical basis, and have been conceptualised and implemented in an atheoretical manner. Nonetheless, it is evident that certain theories have provided a rationale for early intervention, establishing the basis for future conceptual and empirical work. It is useful at this point to summarise several of these in early childhood intervention.

Theoretical frameworks

The following is a description of those contemporary theoretical models that have been most influential in the development of early childhood intervention approaches. These theories have provided the necessary definitions and principles that have guided practice in the field.

Transactional regulation model

The transactional regulation model focuses on the variety of environmental and family factors that have a direct or indirect impact on the child. Early childhood intervention practices that follow this approach take into account the multi-directionality of change and the regulatory mechanisms that mediate change. A recent review of the model by Sameroff and Fiese (2000) further described the notion of transaction used to explain the mutual effects of context (i.e., family and social environment) on child (i.e., developmental characteristics) and child on context. At the same time, transactions between children and their contexts are embedded in a regulatory system that is characteristic of all developmental processes. At an intervention level, this translates into the examination of the strengths and weaknesses of the regulatory system that, in turn, allows the identification of targets of intervention. Such targets might be the child's behaviour, parents' perceptions of the child, or improvements in the parents' ability to take care of the child. Programs influenced by the transactional regulation model include those for failure to thrive and for infants of low birth weight.

Developmental psychoanalytic perspective

The developmental psychoanalytic approach to early childhood intervention proposes that development is the result of the mutual influences of biology and culture (Emde

& Robinson, 2000). It includes the consideration of notions such as affiliation and control and the role they play in development.

Proponents of the developmental psychoanalytic perspective also note that no knowledge is definite because uncertainty exists about human behaviour and the methods used to obtain knowledge. A notable contribution of the approach is its focus on *motivations* in early development, including *activity* (i.e., the child's need for exploration), *self-regulation* (i.e., the child's inborn propensity for regulation of behaviour); *social-fittedness* (i.e., the extent to which the child initiates, maintains, and terminates interactions with others); *affective monitoring* (i.e., the child's propensity to monitor experience according to what is pleasurable or unpleasurable); and *cognitive assimilation* (i.e., the child's tendency to explore the newness of the environment to make it more familiar).

The use of these motivations is crucial in early childhood intervention, along with the notions of morality, emotions, and caring relationships. A major practical implication of such concepts is the emphasis on programs that not only strengthen developmental pathways, but also prevent developmental and adaptation problems.

Behavioural perspective

The behavioural perspective uses the principles of applied behaviour analysis which maintains that behaviour is a result of one's physiology, learning history, and current situation. It primarily concerns itself with the relationships between the child's behaviour and environmental stimuli to explain how behaviours are established and maintained.

According to the behavioural approach, there are *antecedents* (i.e., context, situation, or trigger) to the child's behaviour that are immediately followed by *consequences* (i.e., results) that determine the likelihood of the behaviour occurring in the future. In practice, much of the work conducted using the behavioural approach has contributed to the development of assessment and packages containing carefully designed educational sequences, as well as learning and instructional strategies (Wolery, 2000). Similarly, based on the principles of behaviour, several strategies have been devised to deal with problem behaviours, and specific guidelines have been written about how interventions can be designed to change these behaviours when necessary.

Neurological approach

The neurological approach proposes that the impact of interventions is determined by the capacity of the nervous system to be modified by experience (Nelson, 2000). This process is commonly termed *neural plasticity* which, along with the notion of *critical periods* (defined as the period of time that offers a window of opportunity for development), is at the heart of the neurological approach. In this sense, the development of brain functions, starting as early as the 18th day of gestation, and continuing

postnatally, is of particular importance in the neurological approach. During the course of prenatal and early postnatal brain development, a number of environmental factors can have either a deleterious effect (as is the case with maternal malnutrition, drug use, and stress) or a beneficial effect (such as enriched environments). Proponents of the neurological approach contend that these facts clearly form the basis for early childhood intervention, and that any successful intervention eventually relies, to a degree, on the plasticity of the human brain.

Although the theoretical approaches mentioned above have provided a solid foundation for early childhood intervention in the last 20 years, a cogent set of theoretical premises guiding actual intervention has been lacking. It was not until the mid-1980s when Uri Bronfenbrenner, a prominent American developmental psychologist, proposed an ecological model for human development, that a clear link between theory and practice could be formulated for early childhood intervention (Dunst, 1985; Dunst, Trivette, & Deal, 1988).

Bronfenbrenner's (1979) ecological framework involves the scientific study of the progressive, mutual accommodation between an active, growing human being and the changing properties of the immediate settings in which the individual lives. Following the initial formulation of his model in the late 1970s, Bronfenbrenner has further pointed out the importance of the family as a context for human development, and the influence of external environments on family functioning. He contended that there are series of external influences that affect the capacity of families to foster the healthy development of their children. In his discussions of external influences, Bronfenbrenner explained that there are three different environmental systems that can serve as sources of external influence on the family. First, there are mesosystems, which are used to describe different setting influences such as hospitals, child care, school, and the peer group. Second, there are exosystems, which denote influences such as work, paternal, and maternal employment, parental social networks, and the community. Third, there are chronosystems, which describe the cumulative impact of developmental transitions over time. Bronfenbrenner cited numerous research studies to support his propositions about the context for child development.

Dunst and his colleagues formulated an approach to early intervention using Bronfenbrenner's ecological model, that produces broad-based family system changes (Dunst et al., 1994). That is, early childhood intervention focuses on the family as the unit of intervention through the provision of networks of supports that directly or indirectly influence child, parent, and family functioning. A considerable body of research has been generated by these authors, providing support for the premise that the needs and behaviours of children and their families are shaped by a series of immediate and distant family circumstances. In this sense, the conditions that determine family needs become the central point of intervention. Thus, service systems that provide early childhood intervention support must seek those informal

Part of a family group.

and formal supports that promote child and family competence through family-centred assessment and intervention.

In revisiting his approach to early intervention, Dunst (2000) proposed a third generation model. This included:

(a) provision of children's learning opportunities (i.e., opportunites that are engaging, interesting, and competency producing);

(b) parenting supports (i.e., information, advice, and guidance that that both strenghten existing parenting knowledge and skills); and

(c) family/community supports (i.e., any type of informal, community, and formal resources needed by parents).

Dunst argued that a comprehensive early intervention system that encompasses the above features strengthens the capabilities of the child, the parents, and the family. Unlike many of the other theoretical approaches addressed earlier, Dunst's model offers an opportunity to operationalise clearly defined elements of interventions on the basis of theoretical underpinnings which are constantly field-tested.

Recent research: outcomes and challenges

Research based upon the several theoretical approaches discussed above has not been as systematic as one might hope. In discussing the early intervention field, McWilliam (1999) succinctly stated that educational approaches designed to help families now include more and more practices that have little research basis, provoke intense debate among professionals, and usually require a disruption of the family's life. McWillliam's

comments are noteworthy considering that research in the 1980s and early 1990s clearly lacked a careful description of program features and focused, for the most part, on cognitive aspects of child development. In addition, earlier research was also criticised by the numerous conceptual, methodological, and statistical problems that plagued studies.

Nevertheless, findings of research over the last 20 years or so have accumulated to the point that some assertions can be made about the characteristics of early childhood intervention. Indeed, the pervading theme in the literature has been one of drawing empirical support to legitimise the existence of early childhood intervention efforts and to demonstrate their effectiveness by assessing global effects of programs on child development. Recently, renewed research efforts have yielded a much clearer picture of early childhood intervention, which, in addition to earlier descriptions of intervention efforts, can be characterised by the following principles:

- earlier intervention is better than later intervention (e.g., prevention of developmental delay);
- effects of specific program characteristics (e.g., child age at start of intervention);
- outcomes for families are as important as outcomes for children (e.g., intervention on parental stress); and
- programs must include naturally occurring life experiences and opportunities (e.g., inclusion of children with diverse abilities in mainstream classrooms).

Although it is recognised that contemporary research in early childhood intervention has established a strong theoretical and empirical base for practice, it has been also evident that a number of key program implementation issues must be addressed (Guralnick, 1997; Hanson & Bruder, 2001). In this regard, Hanson and Bruder (2001) have discussed four main challenges in the current US context and legislation that are equally relevant to the Australian special early childhood service system.

Complexity of the service delivery system

There are numerous agencies involved with many types of professionals who deliver services in their own idiosyncratic ways. In addition, there are multiple paths for referral to, and entry into, the service system, not to mention the diversity of treatment of approaches used in early intervention.

Addressing the complex range of needs of all families

The complex range of needs of families must be addressed at a time when they are facing particularly vulnerable times, such as the birth of a child with disabilities, or the initial diagnosis of developmental delay. As indicated earlier, families' circumstances

also vary enormously, determining a variety of needs in the life of a family, aside from those of their child with a disability.

Provision of services in natural environments

Natural environments include the home, child-care settings, or kindergarten situations that offer an optimal learning environment. Children with diverse abilities benefit from interactions with children of typical ability, learning throughout the day and in places where families spend time or where families would like to spend time.

Staff preparation and service delivery models

These present another challenge to the service system as the needs of families vary greatly. This requires the development of service-delivery models that minimise disruption, yet provide a comprehensive array of collaborative transdisciplinary expertise (i.e., flexible boundaries among discipline-specific interventions).

Discussion of the challenges in the practice of early childhood intervention inevitably raises the question of the effects of programs on children and families and what works best for whom, how it works, and in what context. Numerous attempts have been made to answer these questions from a research perspective, beginning with Casto and Mastropieri's controversial work in the mid-1980s (Casto & Mastropieri, 1986) to more recent work performed by Shonkoff, Hauser-Cram, Krauss, and Upshur (1992), Dunst (2000), and others. In this regard, Guralnick's work (1991, 1997) has been particularly salient in organising and integrating recent research findings so that the issue of program effectiveness is addressed in the practice of early childhood special education.

Program effectiveness

Guralnick (1997) contended that, from a first generation research perspective (i.e., initial research conducted during the 1970s and 1980s), early intervention programs have been effective as they have produced ". . . average effect sizes falling within the range of one half to three quarters of a standard deviation" (p. 11). As the field has evolved, however, especially in America with recent legislation and subsequent inclusion of new philosophies and variables, several questions remain to be answered by the current research and practice communities: Have programs been able to prevent or minimise developmental problems for those children at risk? For children with established disabilities, have early childhood intervention programs had a positive influence on child and family outcomes? What are the specific elements of early childhood intervention efforts?

Guralnick (1997) suggested that an early intervention system attempting to answer these questions should integrate programmatic features as a response to child and family characteristics that will influence child development outcomes, and that these

should eventually form the basis of any early childhood intervention service. As depicted in Figure 4.1 (below), stressors (i.e., in relation to a child with a disability or other family circumstances) are key determinants of the early intervention approach used for a particular child. Furthermore, recent evidence has suggested that the match between family characteristics and program characteristics is critical to the attainment of early intervention program effectiveness (Dunst, 2000).

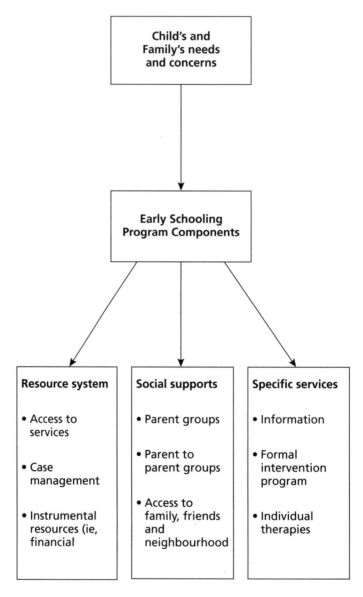

Figure 4.1 Components of Early Schooling programs. Adapted from Guralnick, M. J. (1997).

As indicated in Figure 4.1, early intervention components include a variety of supports ranging from less typical features (e.g., financial assistance, respite care) to the more visible elements (e.g., formal intervention program and other individual therapies. Guralnick's (1997) model can be considered at the core of early childhood intervention service provision. It is acknowledged, however, that not all programs can encompass all components.

For the purposes of this chapter, a number of questions still remain to be answered: What are the features of an ideal early intervention program? What can programs reasonably offer? What can they do to be more comprehensive while recognising current limitations and resources? The following section describes in more detail the characteristics of programs that work.

Characteristics of programs that work

There are certain features of early intervention programs that are givens—that is, basic characteristics without which programs are not operational. Some time ago Peterson (1987) neatly summarised these basic, yet essential, elements of an early intervention program, namely:

(a) service targets;

(b) beginning point of intervention;

(b) specific services to be provided;

(d) intervention setting;

(e) primary intervention agent;

(f) social context of services; and

(g) agencies providing services.

Peterson's assertions still remain current as they cater for the diversity of programs that can be found in the field.

However, if service providers are to embrace recent philosophies, principles, and model practices they need to take into consideration critical elements that are considered to be universal for effective service provision in early childhood intervention. The theoretical models outlined earlier provide the basis for the elements of what Peterson (1987) termed a "model program"—that is, ". . . a program for children in which its content and operational strategies are clearly conceptualised and defined in a manner that assures internal consistency and coherence" (p. 371). The various aspects of a program hang together, represent a particular theoretical and operational base, have the same goals and objectives, and provide evidence that they work. The components of model programs in the context of recent empirical findings are outlined below.

Assessment

An essential element of early childhood intervention programs is the existence of clear assessment procedures. These procedures are critical in identifying the child's unique needs; the family's resources, priorities, and concerns about the development of the child and the nature and extent of early intervention services required by the child and the family. Current assessment strategies focus on finding children with disabilities as early as possible, and on establishing intervention goals. The following are some guidelines for screening and assessment:

- Assessment processes, procedures, and instruments should be used only for their specified purposes.
- Assessment should include multiple sources of information.
- Assessment procedures should be reliable and valid.
- Family members should be an integral part of the assessment process.
- Assessment procedures should be culturally sensitive.
- Assessments should be conducted by staff who have extensive and comprehensive training.

Typically, different developmental domains (i.e., cognitive, communication, motor) are assessed by a battery of assessment instruments. Given the diversity of child and family outcomes sought in early childhood intervention programs and given the variety of theoretical frameworks used, a multidimensional approach to assessment has been emphasised (Neisworth & Bagnato, 1988). This has meant that several instruments have been developed including: curriculum-based; adaptive-to-handicap; process; norm-based; judgment-based; ecological; interactive; and systematic observation (see Neisworth & Bagnato, 1988, for a comprehensive list of assessment tools).

In addition, the literature has stressed the importance of the variety of assessment processes that come into play in early childhood intervention, that fit different purposes, and that answer a variety of questions (Peterson, 1987). Peterson indicated that there are six basic assessment processes:

- casefinding (i.e, accessing the population of 0–5 year olds and seeking referrals);
- screening (i.e., verifying if further evaluation is needed);
- diagnosis (i.e., analysing the nature and degree of the problem);
- educational assessment (i.e., pinpointing a child's skills and learning needs);
- performance monitoring (i.e., tracking ongoing child progress); and
- program evaluation (i.e., documenting program effectiveness).

Evidently, Peterson's observations fall short of including other assessment processes that have been more recently termed "family assessment procedures", which examine family

characteristics and priorities. In this regard, a number of strategies have been proposed, ranging from informal approaches (that identify family's goals through interview) to more formal methods (such as the use of standardised instruments that measure various aspects of family functioning). It is recommended that both informal and formal methods be used in conjunction to obtain a balanced picture of families.

In recent years it has been accepted that at least three major themes should mark early childhood special education assessment:

- intensified assessment of progress and growth for individuals and groups;
- methods typically associated with ecobehavioural research that need to be translated for practitioners to directly assess a variety of environmental conditions that affect child performance and development; and
- continued integration of assessment and intervention practices that will render decision-making program models about when and how to intervene.

In summary, assessment procedures are essential aspects of early childhood special education. Although assessment processes noted above remain current in the present climate of service provision, the *content* of assessment practices need to be expanded to incorporate aspects related to family needs and priorities. Similarly, the use and outcomes of assessment procedures must focus on helping practitioners understand their interventions and plan for improved services and supports for children and families.

Program planning

As a result of the implementation of assessment procedures, program planning constitutes a second essential part of the provision of early childhood intervention service. Presently, it is assumed that all program-planning activities are highly individualised and respond to the unique needs and assets of children and their families (Simeonsson, 2000). Typically, efforts include the goals and objectives, the services or specific programs that children and families will receive, and the specific curriculum that will be used, including the use of specific instructional strategies.

With the advent of US legislation in the last decade or so, a planning mechanism, the *Individualised Family Service Plan* (IFSP), has become the vehicle through which programs have been put in place. Variations of this mechanism have also been adopted in various Australian states (notably the Family Support Plan in Victoria). According to Beckman, Robinson, Rosenberg, and Filer (1994), the IFSP is a flexible, ongoing decision-making process that needs to be implemented in a systematic manner that allows families to consider various service alternatives. Usually a meeting is held to discuss these alternatives and strategies are designed to overcome possible obstacles in the achievement of the program goals. Much of the literature in this area emphasises the need for interventionists to establish partnerships with families so the

program-planning process is an enabling experience rather than a professional-directed exercise (Andrews & Andrews, 1993; Dunst et al., 1994).

At a more specific level, program planning involves the consideration of a *curriculum* that will enable the child to acquire various skills as stipulated in his or her program plan. As Wolery (2000) noted, most curricula include:

(a) the content to be learnt;

(b) the instructional methods or experiences for learning this content;

(c) means of identifying those parts of the content that are important for given learners; and

(d) a theoretical perspective for organising these elements.

The last aspect of the curriculum has been amply debated in the literature in terms of the merits of either the developmental approach or the behavioural approach.

More recently, the Division of Early Childhood (DEC) has proposed indicators to guide curriculum and intervention efforts. The DEC recommends curriculum and intervention practices that result in:

- no harm to infants, children, and families, or to their relationships;
- active engagement of infants and children with objects, people, and events;
- increased initiative, independence, and autonomy by infants and children across domains;
- increased ability to function or participate in diverse and less restrictive environments;
- independent (unprompted) performance of age-appropriate, pro-social behaviours, skills, and interaction patterns;
- supported or partial participation in routines and activities when independent performance is not possible;
- acquisition (initial learning) of important values, behaviours, skills, and interaction patterns across domains;
- generalisation, adaptability, application, and utilisation of important behaviours, skills, and interaction patterns across relevant contexts; and
- efficient learning (most rapid acquisition) of important goals (behaviours, skills, patterns of interaction).

Wolery (2000) called for the consideration of both developmental and behavioural frameworks in the design of curriculum in early childhood intervention. He argued that developmental theory provides the necessary framework for assessments and curriculum content, whereas the behavioural approach provides the instructional technology needed in early childhood intervention. The author also contended that

Thurman's (1997) ecological congruence model—which is both concerned with the development of the child and the fit between the characteristics of the child and the environment—should be considered in the design of curriculum. In summary, the range of theoretical models proposed seem to cater broadly for the development of sound curricula, taking into consideration the important steps proposed by Wolery.

The use of *instructional strategies* is another aspect of program planning in early childhood intervention. Generally, behavioural approaches hold the empirical evidence that provide support for the use of certain instructional strategies. Instructional strategies play a significant role in the teaching, maintenance, and generalisation of skills in young children, and in meeting a full range of their needs. Wolery (1994) proposed four different instructional procedures that vary along a continuum of control in child-environment interactions, and the amount of specific child-initiated behaviour. Most commonly known procedures include:

(a) positive reinforcement;

(b) naturalistic (milieu) strategies;

(c) peer mediated strategies; and

(d) prompting strategies.

Positive reinforcement is one of the most powerful strategies in changing human behaviour, despite the fact that " . . . the concept has been misunderstood, misused, and abused by many educators" (p. 120). Technically, positive reinforcement is the contingent presentation of a stimulus following a response that results in an increase in the future occurrence of the response. In a typical classroom situation, reinforcement can be used in shaping a particular behaviour, which might, in turn, produce positive benefits for children (e.g., learning appropriate social behaviour). It is important to note that there is a number of rules around the identification and use of reinforcers (see Wolery, 1994, for more details). *Naturalistic instructional strategies*, on the other hand, have been mainly used in the promotion of language and communication development. Wolery noted that naturalistic strategies have the following characteristics:

- they are used during ongoing activities and interactions;
- they involve repeated use of brief interactions between children and adults;
- they are responsive to children's behaviour;
- they involve giving children feedback and naturally occurring consequences; and
- they require purposeful planning on the part of adults.

Peer-mediated strategies have been used to promote social interaction learning, especially in inclusive settings. They also share some common characteristics:

- typically developing peers are taught ways of interacting with their peers with diverse abilities;
- the peers are taught to persist with interactions;
- both sets of peers are given consistent opportunities for using social and language skills; and
- the adult (teacher) provides positive reinforcement for use of target behaviours (Wolery, 1994).

Finally, *prompting strategies* involve the use of prompts (i.e., help given to someone to assist in the performance of a skill). Prompting strategies share a number of characteristics. They are used to help children learn a skill; prompts are systematically faded; and positive reinforcement is used. As with the use of positive reinforcement, a number of rules exists around the use of prompts. The reader is referred to Wolery (1994) for more details.

In conclusion, program planning is an indispensable element of early childhood special education, including the choice and implementation of curriculum, the use of instructional strategies, and their inclusion in the IFSP in the form of specific program goals across a number of developmental domains. Program goals reflect the concerns and aspirations of families who are considered key decision-makers in the process. Behavioural strategies have been the most effective in terms of skill acquisition, maintenance, and generalisation. The use of a diverse set of strategies is, however, encouraged on the basis of the specific characteristics of the child, the skill(s) to be taught, and the features of his or her environment.

Service coordination

A comprehensive early childhood special education service requires the delivery of programs in a coordinated and integrated manner. This is particularly critical given the diversity of needs in young children and the potential involvement of a multitude of agencies to address these needs effectively. Ideally, this means that within the parameters of the service plan, the program-planning tool, a service coordinator is nominated with the aim of forging collaborative links among the various agencies involved, and to focus on the establishment of shared goals with the family and joint service delivery.

The early intervention field has seen an evolution in the types of service coordination and collaborative arrangements, which for the most part, have used teams of professionals for the delivery of services. At the traditional end of the scale, the multidisciplinary team requires minimal integration of disciplines. Professionals represent their own disciplines and provide isolated services. Little input is required from families, who play the role of recipients of information. At the other end of the scale, a transdisciplinary team model is ideally the most suited to early childhood

intervention service delivery. In a transdisciplinary team, members share roles and cross discipline boundaries. Assessment and intervention tasks are all implemented jointly by team members, and families play an important role as equal partners in service delivery. Evidently, policies and interagency agreements are required for this level of collaboration to occur successfully.

To summarise, the process of collaboration requires that a number of competing demands be resolved for the key agencies involved. It also requires extreme levels of good communication and problem solving, leadership, and availability of resources. In a coordinated system, all parties actively participate in a productive and constructive process. Finally, it is also important to note that the successful implementation of a collaborative service delivery also needs the adoption of a framework of group process, which involves the establishment of a common goal and vision, the development of joint strategies, and an ongoing system of collaborative activities.

Family involvement

Family involvement is a central tenet of the effective provision of early childhood intervention service. The notion of family involvement has been used to denote the variety of roles played by families in the delivery of programs, from early identification to skill teaching and recipient of supports. Over the years, family involvement in early childhood intervention has evolved such that families are no longer mere recipients of information but are active partners in program implementation. In practice, this has meant the introduction of more active roles for family members, although there is great variability from service to service. Nevertheless, any discussion about service priorities in the field of early intervention must include families as key stakeholders.

Currently, much of the discussion about family involvement is placed within a context of family-centredness, and its importance in best practice in early childhood intervention service delivery. This construct has often been used as a philosophical and practical principle to underlie interventions. The concept has not been easily defined, although McWilliam, Tocci, and Sideris (1997) identified the following characteristics:

- investment in the child and competence in working with the child;
- respect for families' values and investment in diverse families;
- connection with families based on something in common;
- provision of informational and emotional support to the family; and
- the service provider's style (i.e., positive, responsive, friendly, and sensitive).

In addition, Beckman, Robinson, Rosenberg, and Filer (1994) noted that family-centred services are those that take into consideration the complex characteristics and variables that influence families. This, in turn, has an effect on how decisions are made about service delivery. In this process families' views and concerns are central to the design and delivery of interventions.

Recently, calls have been made to renew the focus of practices that can be typically considered family-centred, but which, because of historical connotations, have been greatly de-emphasised in the current climate. One example is the practice of parent education, which some would argue is an integral part of early-intervention practices in terms of the active participation of parents in their children's education. In conclusion, it would appear that although the philosophy and practice of family-centredness has been widely accepted in the field of early childhood intervention, its operationalisation in terms of actual services and programs continues to be debated.

Inclusion

Inclusion is an accepted and desirable practice in early childhood intervention. It means the placement of a child with diverse abilities in a community program that the child might otherwise have attended had he or she not had special needs. These programs vary greatly, from family support to child-care and recreational programs. The inclusion of children with diverse abilities has been amply debated, and for families, in particular, it has posed several dilemmas in terms of the educational and psychological implications for their own children with diverse abilities.

Box 4.6 The characteristics of effective early childhood special education within community early childhood programs

- **A program philosophy for inclusive early childhood services.**
- **A consistent and ongoing system for family involvement.**
- **A system of team planning and program implementation.**
- **A system of collaboration and communication with other agencies that provide services to young children with disabilities and their families.**
- **A well-constructed individualised family support program.**
- **Integrated delivery of educational and related services.**
- **A consistent and ongoing system for training and staff development.**
- **A comprehensive system for evaluating the effectiveness of the program.**

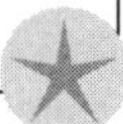

Source: Bruder, M. B. (1993).

It has been suggested that it might be more appropriate to discuss inclusion in the context of parental choices when confronted with placement options for their children and the realities that go with them. Although professionals have readily adopted the philosophy underlying inclusion, they need to consider the complexities associated with successful inclusion, such as the need for specific instructional strategies and curriculum, trained staff, resources, and all the other factors that can affect the success

of inclusion. In addition, a clear delineation of the desired goals and outcomes for children who have experiences in inclusive environments is also critical.

Transition

As early childhood intervention services and policies have evolved, transition has become a significant change in, and indispensable feature of, good practice. Transition processes have different meanings in different settings, and these vary according to the sociocultural and legal makeup of the service system. This is particularly true of the US and Australian systems. In the former, there are several transition points in line with the different legal requirements for services for young children with diverse abilities. In Australia, where such requirements do no exist, transition is typically discussed when children move out of an early childhood setting or service into a more formal school environment.

Nevertheless, the underlying principle behind the implementation of good transition practices is the idea of planning a seamless service systemthat is characterised by minimal disruption and trauma to both the child and his or her family. According to Atwater et al. (1994), transition is not a single event but an ongoing process that starts 6 to 12 months before a child leaves a program and continues throughout the child's period of adjustment to a new program. Furthermore, Wolery (1994) suggested that the characteristics of a good transition process require the following:

- development of a comprehensive transition plan that is based on strong collaboration among those services involved;
- inclusion of parents as active participants in planning;
- assessment of the family's needs for education and support related to the transition;
- administrative support for the receiving agency; and
- follow up to ascertain success of transition plan.

Other essential considerations in planning transitions include the need for carefully chosen skills (i.e., functional skills in the classroom setting) and introduction of teaching strategies that can be incorporated into ongoing activities.

Exemplary early childhood intervention programs

Reviews of early childhood intervention programs for children aged from birth to 5 years of age, have shown that positive outcomes for children are so contradictory that is difficult to make any definite conclusions. Nevertheless, some of the programs reviewed by Farran have shown successful outcomes. These have included those that have been typically cited in the literature such as Abecedarian/Project Care, parent–child development centres (e.g., AVANCE), High Scope, and Head Start. These programs have generally catered for children and families considered to be dis-

advantaged or at risk of developmental delay.

Some overall assertions can be made about the characteristics of examplary early intervention programs for children identified with specific developmental delays. For instance, programs for children who have milder delays have been found to be more effective than programs for children with more severe delays. Successful interventions for 3- to 5-year-old children who have speech and language impairments are also associated with participation in inclusive school environments. In addition, interventions during the sensorimotor period of development seem less effective than global infant interventions focused on positive family interventions.

An exhaustive review of the published literature in Australia reveals no documentation of early childhood intervention programs. Pieterse, Bochner, and Bettison (1988) provided the only published overview programs to date, which suggests that there are no known examplary programs. This is probably a reflection of the difficulties encountered by program operators or providers in documenting outcomes, and a lack of research in the area, rather than suggesting the non-existence of such exemplary programs.

Policy issues in the delivery of early childhood intervention programs

Although the characteristics of early childhood intervention programs that work are widely discussed at both research and practice levels, policies and systems sustaining them are less debated in the literature. Evidently, the discussion earlier highlights broad directions that have generally been dictated by the current state of affairs of the US service system and the considerable importance given to the early years at the practical, policy, legal, and research levels. As Thurman (1997) noted in his discussion of systems, ecologies, and the context of early childhood intervention in the US, policy and system development is shaped by myriad interacting socio-political factors that operate at many levels of influence. What these factors are and how they exactly shape the provision of early childhood services remains to be seen, despite the fact that there are numerous early childhood intervention programs already in operation.

The situation in Australia is vastly different from that in America. Despite several isolated program efforts, statewide and nationwide policy development in early childhood intervention has been scattered and haphazard. The establishment of services has been uncoordinated, seriously under-resourced, and often lacking in direction. This situation, coupled with the minimal support provided to research endeavours in the field, has resulted in a rather grim picture for the current early childhood intervention system for children with diverse abilities. If one were to apply Thurman's conceptualisation (Thurman, 1997) of systems and ecologies in early childhood service provision to the Australian context, it would become apparent that

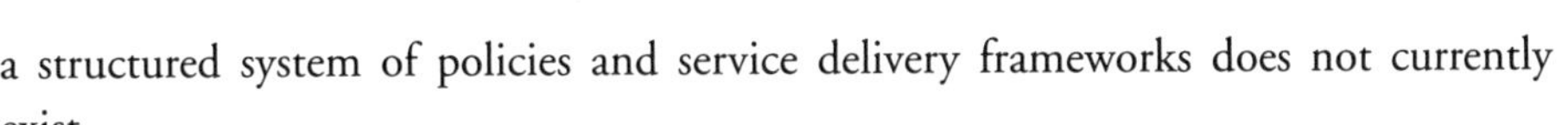

a structured system of policies and service delivery frameworks does not currently exist.

Recently, a proposal for the creation of a National Research Partnership for Human Development has been made in an attempt to develop a national research agenda for population studies in early human development. Similarly, the National Investment for the Early Years (NIFTEY), which is a cross-sectoral, interprofessional advocacy and knowledge-broking, non-government organisation, has brought together professional groups, academics, practitioners and policymakers to advance the case for early childhood development. It is expected that important social policies and research will emanate from these Australian initiatives.

At a state level, work is being undertaken in Victoria toward the development of a framework for an integrated early childhood intervention system. This is likely to be the first attempt made by a government to address the development of policies that will sustain a comprehensive early childhood system of services. Major features of these policies include several issues addressed above in the characteristics of services that work.

- Programs will ensure that children with diverse abilities will be provided with experiences that enhance their development.
- Programs will ensure that families have the necessary information to enhance their parenting role and make informed decisions about their child's needs.
- Programs will develop and strengthen collaborative partnerships among service providers.
- Programs will provide quality supports for children and their families.
- Programs will deliver measurable outcomes and promote best practice models.
- Programs will promote recruitment of trained staff.

In the absence of a unifying set of policies in early childhood intervention, a number of issues remain critical in the provision of programs and services. Much of the research literature indicates that although these issues are at the heart of a comprehensive system of early intervention service delivery, they still continue to be debated in terms of putting them into practice. The following section briefly outlines issues that are of particular relevance to the Australian context.

The preventative nature of early childhood intervention

Prevention is almost a synonym of early intervention if programs are designed to prevent or minimise developmental problems for those children at risk and with established disabilities. Gulranick (1997) stressed that at a policy level, early childhood programs have been accepted as practices that do make a difference. From an empirical perspective, however, the merits of early childhood intervention continue to

be discussed, as the preventative effects of specific program components are yet to be demonstrated. Clearly, progress in the right direction will require research to move beyond the analyses of the global effects of early childhood intervention efforts, which indeed support the premise that early childhood intervention is preventative in nature.

Parental supports

Parental support is undeniably another important aspect of early childhood intervention that has taken particular force due to the family-centred nature of contemporary service provision, which promotes overall family involvement in children's intervention from assessment to the provision of therapeutic services. More specifically, parental support in its various forms includes parent information, education, parental training, respite care, counselling, training in coping skills, and other forms of instrumental support such as the provision of specific resources (i.e., access to transport and housing). According to Sloper (1999), the needs and concerns of parents have been amply documented. However, they continue to be unmet. Sloper's findings indicate that despite the existence of promising models of parental support, the knowledge generated has not been put into practice, and has not influenced service development and policy. It appears that much needs to be done to test the effectiveness of current parental support efforts, and to translate the outcomes into policy and ongoing practice in early childhood intervention.

Staff training and support

Staff competencies are critical in the effective provision of early childhood intervention programs. Bruder (2000), in particular, has described the skills required in training for early childhood intervention professionals (see Box 4.7, page 157) at both preservice and inservice training levels. However, the knowledge generated through research has again not been translated into practice and policies, resulting in limited and outdated early childhood intervention efforts (e.g., along traditional discipline-specific competencies only). Without specific efforts such as the development of learning communities, the vision of effective service provision in early childhood intervention might be limited at both policy and practice levels. Within such learning communities, training promotes collaboration among multiple partners at multiple levels, attends to diversity issues, and promotes family involvement in staff training. A commitment to community-level efforts seems to be at the cornerstone of an effective system of training and support for practitioners in early childhood intervention.

Box 4.7 General training recommendations for skill training for early childhood intervention professionals

- Discipline-specific skills in infancy, early childhood development, and family-centred practices.
- Interdisciplinary and interagency skills.
- Working in teams.

Strategies for staff training models:

- Use of adult learning principles.
- Team-based training.
- Supervision, mentoring, and coaching.
- Case-study methodology.
- Provision of ongoing follow-up support.

Source: Bruder, M. B. (2000).

Evaluation of program quality

Evaluation of early childhood intervention programs has been a relatively neglected area of investigation despite the need to demonstrate the effectiveness and accountability of programs. At the heart of evaluation is the notion of quality and the various ways to measure it in service delivery. The literature in this area is inconclusive, having focused on global evaluation of program quality, which has generally assessed generic aspects of typical early childhood programs. It has been suggested that the multiplicity of variables in program delivery is such that it is difficult to identify the various aspects of quality programs.

The following appear to be important:

- efficacy (i.e, did the program have the desired effects?);
- acceptability (i.e., were the interventions in line with parents' and practitioners' beliefs and expectations?); and
- practicality (i.e., did all concerned find the interventions easy to use and maintain?).

Furthermore, the authors suggested that the basic building blocks of evaluation are evidence of treatment integrity in the interventions, and measures of child outcomes. Although these assertions account for the methodology used in evaluation, debate continues regarding the most appropriate aspects of program delivery to assess. It appears that the characteristics of programs that work, as discussed above, constitute a reasonable basis on which to build evaluation of program quality.

SUMMARY

The 20th century saw a growing interest in early childhood as a critical period of development and learning, which resulted in the establishment of early schooling programs for typically developing children. Subsequently, these programs were made available to infants and preschool children who experienced difficulties in learning, with the aim of promoting gains across a range of developmental domains. The importance of the early years (from birth to the entry into formal schooling) has been clearly demonstrated in the widespread development of early childhood intervention services for young children with diverse abilities.

The critical role of play in the provision of optimal developmental opportunities for young children has been widely recognised in these early childhood programs.

The history of the establishment of such programs has involved the adoption of various theoretical approaches. Although empirical evidence to support the use of such approaches in practice is yet to be demonstrated, evidence from numerous studies suggests that a combination of developmental and behavioural frameworks with an ecological basis might be best suited to the achievement of program goals for children and their families. In this context, family-centred principles, which focus on the individual needs and concerns of families and those of their children with diverse abilities, have been more recently advocated in the delivery of early intervention. In addition, a number of specific characteristics of programs that work have been identified, including assessment practices, program planning, service coordination, family involvement, inclusion, and transition practices.

Numerous program models have adopted these characteristics. However, a series of policy and system issues remains to be addressed in order to provide a coherent early childhood intervention service to young children with diverse abilities and their families.

Suggested reading

Bedekamp, S. & Copple, C. (Eds) (1997). *Developmentally appropriate practices in early childhood programs* (Rev. ed.). Washington, D.C.: National Association for Education of Young Children.

Cavallaro, C. C. & Haney, M. (1999). *Preschool inclusion*. Baltimore: Paul H. Brookes.

Guralnick, M. J. (Ed.) (1997). *The effectiveness of early intervention*. Baltimore: Paul Brookes.

Linder, T. W. (Ed.) (1993). *Transdisciplinary play-based assessment: A functional approach to*

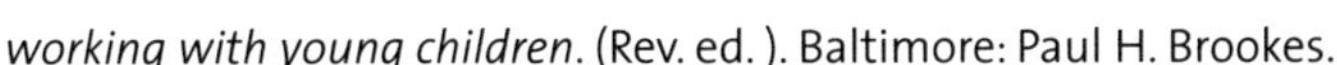
working with young children. (Rev. ed.). Baltimore: Paul H. Brookes.

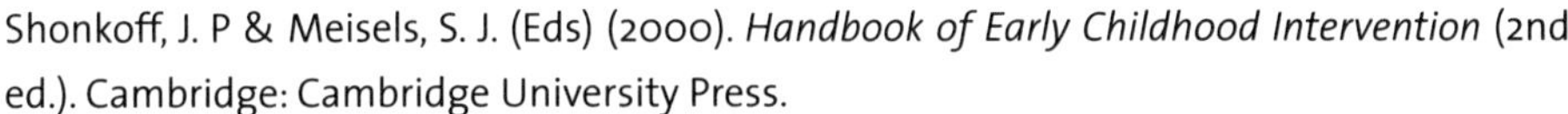
Shonkoff, J. P & Meisels, S. J. (Eds) (2000). *Handbook of Early Childhood Intervention* (2nd ed.). Cambridge: Cambridge University Press.

Thurman, S. K., Cornwell, J. R., & Gottwald, S. R. (Eds) (1997). *Contexts of early intervention: Systems and settings*. Baltimore: Paul H. Brookes.

Wolery, M. & Wilbers, J. (Eds) (1994). *Including children with special needs in early childhood programs*. Washington: National Association for the Education of Young Children.

Practical activities

1. Visit an early intervention program. Observe and record how the children play. What types of activities are offered? Are they adult or child directed?
2. Interview two kindergarten teachers regarding the theoretical approaches they use in teaching young children. Develop your interview questions around the various theories discussed in this chapter. Can you identify the approaches they use? Do they use one approach only or a combination of approaches.
3. Interview a parent of a child with a disability about the type of early childhood services that the child receives. Do they support the family and the child? Does the child have an IFSP? Does it include an inclusive environment? What therapy services does the child receive and how are they delivered?
4. Based on the discussion on assessment of developmental milestones, develop your own assessment tool based on your observations of a 3-year-old in a preschool setting. Use Linder's framework to help you.
5. After activity 4 above, design a number of indoor and outdoor activities that would assist the child's play and development across the developmental domains. Make sure activities can enable the child to initiate and take some control of the play.

References

Andrews, M. A. & Andrews, J. R. (1993). Family-centered techniques: Integrating enablement into the IFSP process. *Journal of Childhood Communication Disorders*, *15*, 41–46.

Arthur, M., Bochner, S., & Butterfield, N. (1999). Enhancing peer interactions within the context of play. *International Journal of Disability, Development and Education*, *46*, 367–382.

Atwater, J. B., Orth-Lopes, L., Elliot, M., Carta, J. J., & Schwartz, I. S. (1994). Completing the circle: Planning and implementing transitions to other programs. In M. Wolery & J. Wilbers (Eds), *Including children with special needs in early childhood programs* (pp.167–188). Washington, D.C.: National Association for the Education of Young Children.

Bailey, D. B. Jr (2000). The federal role in early intervention: Prospects for the future. *Topics in Early Childhood Special Education, 20*, 71–78.

Barbour, A. C. (1999). The impact of playground design on play behaviours of children with differing levels of physical competence. *Research Quarterly, 14*(1), 75–98.

Beckman, P. J., Robinson, C. C., Rosenberg, S., & Filer, J. (1994). Family involvement in early intervention: The evolution of family-centered service. In L. J. Johnson, R. J. Gallagher, & M. J. LaMontagne (Eds), *Meeting early intervention challenges: Issues from birth through three* (2nd ed., pp. 13–31). Baltimore: Paul H. Brookes.

Bedekamp, S. & Copple, C. (Eds) (1997). *Developmentally appropriate practices in early childhood programs* (Rev. ed.). Washington, DC: National Association for Education of Young Children.

Berkell-Zager, D. (Ed.) (1999). *Autism: Identification, education and treatment.* Mahwah, NJ: Erlbaum.

Berkell-Zager, D., Shamow, N. A., Schneider, H. C. (1999). Teaching students with autism. In D. Berkell-Zager (Ed.) *Autism: Identification, education and treatment* (pp. 111–139). Mahwah, NJ: Erlbaum.

Bloom, B. S. (1964). *Stability and change in human characteristics.* New York: Wiley.

Bluma, S., Shearer, M., Frohman, A., & Hilliard, J. (1976). *Portage guide to early education.* PLACE, WI: Cooperative Educational Service Agency.

Braithwaite, J. (1983). *Explorations in early childhood education.* Melbourne: Australian Council for Educational Research.

Bricker, W. (1970). Identifying and modifying behavioral deficits. *American Journal of Mental Deficiency, 75*, 16–21.

Bricker, D., & Woods Cripe, J. (1992). *An activity-based approach to early intervention.* Baltimore: Paul H. Brookes.

Brodin, J. (1999). Play in children with severe multiple disabilities: Play with toys—A review. *International Journal of Disability, Development and Education, 46*, 25–34.

Bronfenbrenner, U. (1979). *The ecology of human development.* Cambridge, MA: Harvard University.

Bruder, M. B. (1993). The provision of early intervention and early childhood special education within community early childhood programs: Characteristics of effective service delivery. *Topics in Early Childhood Special Education, 13*, 19–37.

Bruder, M. B. (2000). Family-centred early intervention: Clarifying our values for the new millennium. *Topics in Early Childhood Special Education, 20*, 105–115.

Bruner, J. S., Jolly, A., & Sylvia, K. (Eds). (1976). *Play: Its role in development and evolution.* New York: Penguin Books.

Butterfield, N., Arthur, M., & Sigafoos, J. (Eds) (1995). *Partners in everyday communicative exchanges: A guide to promoting interaction opportunities for people with severe intellectual disability.* Sydney: MacLennan and Petty.

Casto, G. & Mastropieri, M. A. (1986). The efficacy of early intervention programs: A meta-analysis. *Exceptional Children, 52*, 417–424.

Cavallaro, C. C. & Haney, M. (1999). *Preschool inclusion.* Baltimore: Paul H Brookes.

Choi, H-J., Jobling, A., & Carroll, A. (2000). Let's play: Development of peer training for children with autism. In *Supporting not controlling: Strategies for the new millennium—National Conference Proceedings* (pp. 91–98). Brisbane: Early Childhood Intervention Australia Inc.

Cuskelly, M. & Gunn, P. (1992). Maternal reports of behavior of siblings of children with Down syndrome. *American Journal on Mental Retardation, 97*, 521–529.

Dale, P. S., Crain-Thoreson, C., Notari-Syverson, A., & Cole, K. (1996). Parent–child book reading as an intervention technique for young children with language delays. *Topics in Early Childhood Special Education, 16*, 213–235.

Day, M. C. & Parker, R. K. (Eds). (1977). *The preschool in action: Exploring early childhood programs* (2nd ed.). Boston: Allyn & Bacon.

Dunst, C. J. (1985). Rethinking early intervention. *Analysis and Intervention in Developmental Disabilities, 5*, 165–201.

Dunst, C. J. (2000). Revisiting "Rethinking early intervention". *Topics in Early Childhood Special Education, 20*(2), 95–104.

Dunst, C. J. & Snyder, S. W. (1986). A critique of the Utah State University Early Intervention meta-analysis research. *Exceptional Children, 53*, 269–276.

Dunst, C. J., Trivette, C. M., & Deal, A. G. (1988). *Enabling and empowering families: Principles and guidelines for practice.* Cambridge, MA: Brookline Books.

Dunst, C. J., Trivette, C. M., & Deal, A. G. (Eds) (1994). *Supporting and strengthening families: Methods, strategies and practices.* Cambridge, MA: Brookline Books.

Early Childhood Intervention Australia Inc. (2000). *Supporting not controlling: Strategies for the new millennium—National Conference Proceedings.* Brisbane: Author.

Elkins, J., Calder, J., Conrad, L., Shepherd, J., & Coulston, A. (1980). *Toy libraries in Australia: A report with special attention to their role in services for young handicapped children and their families.* St. Lucia, Qld: Fred and Eleanor Schonell Educational Research Centre.

Emde, R. N. & Robinson, J. (2000). Guiding principles for a theory of early intervention: A developmental psycho-analytic perspective. In J. P. Shonkoff & S. J. Meisels (Eds), *Handbook of early childhood intervention* (2nd ed., pp. 160–178). Cambridge, UK: Cambridge University Press.

Erikson, E. H. (1963). *Childhood and society.* New York: W. W. Norton.

Farrell, M. & Gunn, P. (2000). *Literacy for children with Down syndrome: Early days.* Flaxton, Qld: Post Pressed.

Fazldeen, A. D. (1997). *Creche and Kindergarten Association of Queensland: A brief history, 1907–1997.* Newmarket, Qld: Creche and Kindergarten Association of Queensland.

Fewell, R. R. & Oelwin, P. L. (1991). The relationship between time in integrated environments and developmental gains in young children with special needs. *Topics in Early Childhood Special Education, 10*(2), 104–116.

Fewell, R. R. & Vadasy, P. F. (1983). *Learning through play.* Allen, TX: Developmental Learning Materials.

Fisher, E. P. (1992). The impact of play on development: A meta-analysis. *Play and Culture, 5*, 159–181.

Foreman, P. (1988). Alternative therapies. In M. Pieterse, S. Bochner, & S. Bettison (Eds), *Early intervention for children with disabilities* (pp. 335–350). Sydney: Macquarie University, Special Education Centre.

Fox, L. & Hanline, M. F. (1993). A preliminary evaluation of learning within developmentally appropriate early childhood settings. *Topics in Early Childhood Special Education, 13*, 308–327.

Gallagher, J. J. (2000). The beginnings of federal help for young children with disabilities. *Topics in Early Childhood Special Education, 20*, 3–6.

Gallahue, D. L. (1989). *Understanding motor development: Infants, children and adults.* Indianapolis, IN: Benchmark Press.

Gesell, A. (1940). *The first 5 years: A guide to the study of the preschool child.* New York: Harper.

Goodman, J. (1992). *When slow is fast enough!* London: Guildford Press.

Greenberg, P (1994) Ideas that work with young children. *Young Children, 49*(2), 12–18, 88.

Gunn, P. (1998). In retrospect. *International Journal of Disability, Development and Education, 45*, 249–252.

Guralnick, M. J. (1991). The next decade of research on the effectiveness of early intervention. *Exceptional Children, 58*, 174–183.

Guralnick, M. J. (1993). Developmentally appropriate practice in the assessment and intervention of children's peer relations. *Topics in Early Childhood Special Education, 13*, 344–371.

Guralnick, M. J. (1997). Second generation research in the field of early intervention. In M. J. Guralnick (Ed.), *The effectiveness of early intervention* (p. 9). Baltimore: Paul H. Brookes.

Guralnick, M. J. (1998). Effectiveness of early intervention for vulnerable children: A developmental perspective. *American Journal on Mental Retardation, 102*, 319–345.

Hanline, M. F. (1999). Developing a preschool play-based curriculum. *International Journal of Disability, Development and Education, 46*, 289–306.

Hanson, M. J., & Bruder, M. B. (2001). Early intervention: Promises to keep. *Infants and Young Children, 13*(3), 47–58.

Hayes, A., Steinberg, M., Cookley, E., Jobling, A., Best, D., & Coulston, A. (1981). *Special preschools: Monitoring a pilot project.* St. Lucia, Qld: Fred and Eleanor Schonell Educational Research Centre.

Henniger, M. L. (1994). Planning for outdoor play. *Young Children, 49*(4), 10–14.

Howes, C. (1983). Patterns of friendship. *Child Development, 54*, 1041–1053.

Howes, C. (1988). Peer interactions of young children. *Monographs of the Society for Research in Child Development, 53* (1, Serial No. 217).

Hughes, J. L. (Ed.) (1924). *Froebel's educational laws for all teachers* (Vol. XLI). New York: D. Appleton and Company.

Jobling, A. (1988). The 'play' focus in early intervention: Children with intellectual disabilities. *The Exceptional Child, 35*, 119–124.

Jobling, A. (1996). Play. In B. Stratford & P. Gunn (Eds), *New approaches to Down syndrome* (pp. 226–248). London: Cassell.

Leach, D. J. Swerissen, H., & Leach, P. D. (1988). Teaching parents to be direct instructors and child advocates: The parents as educational partners (PEPS) course for parents of intellectually handicapped preschool children. In M. Pieterse, S. Bochner, & S. Bettison (Eds), *Early intervention for children with disabilities* (pp. 283–304). Sydney: Macquarie University, Special Education Centre.

Lerner, J., Mardell-Czudnowski, C., & Goldenberg, D. (1987). *Special education for early childhood years.* Englewood Cliffs, NJ: Prentice Hall.

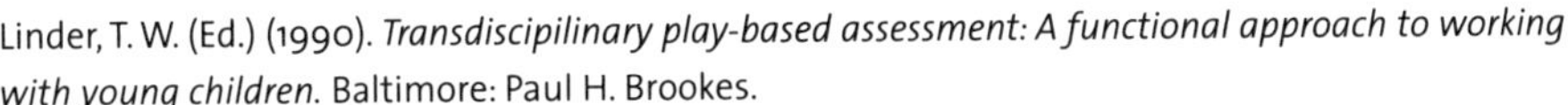

Linder, T. W. (Ed.) (1990). *Transdiscipilinary play-based assessment: A functional approach to working with young children.* Baltimore: Paul H. Brookes.

Linder, T. W. (Ed.) (1993). *Transdiscipilinary play-based assessment: A functional approach to working with young children* (Rev. ed.). Baltimore: Paul H. Brookes.

Linn, M. L., Goodman, J. F., & Lender, W. L. (2000). Played out? Passive behaviour by children with Down syndrome during unstructured play. *Journal of Early Intervention, 23,* 19–28.

Mahoney, G., Robinson, C., & Powell, A. (1992). Focusing on parent–child interaction: The bridge to developmentally appropriate practices. *Topics in Early Childhood Special Education, 12,* 105–120.

Malone, D. M. (1999). Contextual factors informing play-based program planning. *International Journal of Disability, Development and Education, 46,* 307–324.

Malone, D. M. & Langone, J. (1999). Teaching object-related play skills to preschool children with developmental concerns. *International Journal of Disability, Development and Education, 46,* 325–336.

Marfo, K. & Kysela, G. M. (1988). Frequency and sequential patterns in mothers' interactions with mentally handicapped and non-handicapped children. In K. Marfo (Ed.), *Parent–child interaction and developmental disabilities* (pp. 64–89). New York: Praeger.

Marvin, C. (1994). Home literacy experiences of preschool children with single and multiple disabilities. *Topics in Early Childhood Special Education, 14,* 436–454.

McVicker-Hunt, J. (1961). *Intelligence and experience.* New York: Ronald Press.

McWilliam, R. A. (1999). Controversial practices: The need for a reacculturation of early intervention fields. *Topics in Early Childhood Special Education, 19,* 177–188.

Montessori, M. (1946). *Education for a new world.* Madras, India: Kalakshetra.

Neisworth, J. T. & Bagnato, S. (1988). Assessment in early childhood special education: A typology of dependent measures. In S. L. Odom & M. B. Karnes (Eds), *Early intervention for infants and children with handicaps: An empirical base* (pp. 23–49). Baltimore: Paul H. Brookes.

Nelson, C. A. (2000). The neurobiological bases of early intervention. In J. P. Shonkoff & S. J. Meisels (Eds), *Handbook of early childhood intervention* (2nd ed., pp. 204–227). Cambridge, UK: Cambridge University Press.

Newson, J. & Newson, E. (1979). *Toys and playthings in development and remediation.* Harmondsworth, UK: Penguin.

Odom, S. L., McConnell, S. R., McEvoy, M. A., Peterson, C., Ostrosky, M., Chandler, L. K., Spicuzza, R. J., Skellenger, A., Creighton, M., & Favazza, P. C. (1999). Relative effects of interventions supporting the social competence of young children with disabilities. *Topics in Early Childhood Special Education, 19,* 75–91.

Pellegrini, A. D. & Smith, P. K. (1998). Physical activity play: The nature & function of a neglected aspect of play. *Child Development, 69,* 577–598.

Piaget, J. (1952). *The origins of intelligence in children* (M. Cook, Trans.). New York: International University Press. (Original work published 1936).

Peterson, N. L. (1987). *Early intervention for handicapped and at-risk children: An introduction to early childhood special education.* Denver, CO: Love.

Pieterse, M., Bochner, S., & Bettison, S. (Eds) (1988). *Early intervention for children with disabilities.* Sydney: Macquarie University, Special Education Centre.

Robertson, M. A. & Halverson, L. E. (1984). *Developing children: Their changing movement.* Philadelphia: Lea & Febiger.

Rodgers, S. & Ziviani, J. (1999). Play-based occupational therapy. *International Journal of Disability, Development and Education, 46*, 337–366.

Sameroff, A. & Chandler, M. (1975). Reproductive risk and the continuum of caretaking causality. In F. Horowitz (Ed.), *Review of child development research* (Vol. 4, pp. 187–245). Chicago: University of Chicago Press.

Sameroff, A. J. & Fiese, B H. (2000). Transactional regulation: The developmental ecology of early intervention. In J. P. Shonkoff & S. J. Meisels (Eds.), *Handbook of early childhood intervention* (2nd ed., pp. 135–159). Cambridge, UK: Cambridge University Press.

Schechner, R. (1988). Playing. *Play and Culture, 1*, 3–19.

Schwartzman, H. B. (1991). Imaging play. *Play and Culture, 4*, 214–222.

Shane, H. G. (1971). The renaissance of early childhood education. In R. H. Anderson, R. & H. G. Shane (Eds), *As the twig is bent: Readings in early childhood education* (pp. 3–11). Boston: Houghton Mifflin.

Shonkoff, J. P., Hauser-Cram, P., Krauss, M. W., & Upshur, C. C. (1992). Development of infants with disabilities and their families. *Monographs of the Society for Research in Child Development, 57* (6, Serial No. 230).

Shonkoff, J. P. & Meisels, S. J. (Eds) (2000). *Handbook of early childhood intervention.* Cambridge, UK: Cambridge University Press.

Sigafoos, J., Elkins, J., Hayes, A., Gunn, S., Couzens, D., & Roberts, D. (1991). *A review of programs for young children with severe disabilities: Final project report.* Brisbane: University of Queensland, Fred and Eleanor Schonell Special Education Research Centre.

Simeonsson, R. J. (2000). Early childhood intervention: Toward a universal manifesto. *Infants and Young Children, 12*(3), 4–9.

Skeel, H. M. & Dye, H.,B. (1939). A study of the effects of differential stimulation on mentally retarded children. *Convention Proceedings, American Association on Mental Retardation, 44*, 114–136.

Sloper, P. (1999). Models of service support for parents of disabled children. What do we know? What do we need to know? *Child: Care, Health and Development, 25*, 85–99.

Sloper, P., Cunningham, C. C., & Arnljotsdottir, M. (1983). Parental reactions to early intervention with their Down's syndrome infants. *Child: Care, Health and Development, 9*, 357–376.

Sloper, P., Turner, S., Knussen, C., & Cunningham, C. (1990). Social life of school children with Down's syndrome. *Child: Care, Health and Development, 16*, 235–251.

Smith B. J. (2000). The federal role in early childhood special education policy in the next century: The responsibility of the individual. *Topics in Early Childhood Special Education, 20*, 7–13.

Teitzel, T. & Terkelsen, J. (1997). *A peer in.* Tweed Heads, NSW: Tweed District Early Intervention Centre.

Thompson, D., Hudson, S. D., & Mack, M. G. (1999). Matching children and play equipment: A developmental approach. *Early Childhood News, 11*(2), 18–20, 22–23.

Thurman, S. K. (1997). Systems, ecologies, and the context of early intervention. In S. K. Thurman, J. R. Cornwell, & S. R. Gottwald (Eds), *Contexts of early intervention: Systems and settings* (pp. 3–17). Baltimore: Paul H. Brookes.

Tjossem, T. (Ed.) (1976). *Intervention strategies for high risk infants and young children.* Baltimore: University Park Press

Udell, T., Peters, J., & Templeman, T. P. (1998). From philosophy to practice in inclusive early childhood programs. *Teaching Exceptional Children, 30*(3), 44–49.

Vygotsky, L. S. (1978). *Mind in society* (M. Cole, V. John-Steiner, S. Scribner, & E. Souberman, Trans.). Cambridge, MA: Harvard University Press.

Watts, B. H., Elkins, J., Conrad, L. M., Andrews, R. J., Apelt, W. C. Hayes, A., Calder, J., Coulston, A. J., & Willis, M. (1981). *Early intervention programs for young handicapped children in Australia 1979–1980.* St. Lucia, Qld: Fred and Eleanor Schonell Educational Research Centre.

Wolery, M. (1994). Instructional strategies for teaching young children with special needs. In M. Wolery & J. Wilbers (Eds), *Including children with special needs in early childhood programs* (pp. 119–150). Washington, DC: National Association for the Education of Young Children.

Wolery, M. (2000). Behavioural and educational approaches to early intervention. In J. P. Shonkoff & S. J. Meisels (Eds), *Handbook of early childhood intervention* (2nd ed., pp. 179–227). Cambridge, UK: Cambridge University Press.

Yoder, P. J., Kaiser, A. P., & Alpert, C. L. (1991). An exploratory study of the interaction between language teaching methods and child characteristics. *Journal of Speech and Hearing Research, 34,* 155–167.

Zigler, E. & Styfco, S. J. (2000). Pioneering steps (and fumbles) in developing a federal preschool intervention. *Topics in Early Childhood Special Education, 2,* 67–70.

Section 2

The responsive school community

Regular schools have always enrolled students whose learning gives rise to concern. In most cases, teachers have coped with the diversity of skills and abilities reflected in their classroom, although not always in a manner that promoted their students' passion for learning. In the first half of the 20th century students with very serious intellectual disability, sense impairment, or other medical needs did not receive their education in regular schools or classes. Therefore, classroom teachers worked within the context of a relatively narrow definition of diversity.

Those students who, for a variety of reasons, could not accommodate the demands and constraints of the curriculum, and those whose interest in school approached zero, were often screened out after completing the minimum years of schooling. Many took up an apprenticeship or found employment in a job that required modest skills. Some of these are our parents and grandparents who have clearly demonstrated that success in their chosen career or vocation—and in adult life generally—was not predicated on conformity to school rules and teacher expectations.

Since the middle of the 20th century, when access to employment has required higher educational standards—particularly in literacy and numeracy—there has been a growing concern that removing students from the education system will do little other than promote high youth unemployment and juvenile crime. Consequently, special attention was given to identifying those children who required support as early as possible and to providing support for these children through special services or programs.

Much of the early interest in low achievement came from the medical profession, which regarded the difficulties experienced by many students as consequences of subtle constitutional impairment, often expressed as "minimal neurological dysfunction". In the United States, this was crystallised by the adoption of learning disabilities as a category within the *Education for All Handicapped Children Act* (see Chapters 1 and 2, this volume). Despite growing concern about the definitions used

to describe students with learning problems and about many of the practices associated with learning disability, students in this category became the largest and fastest growing group in US special education. In Australia, a different approach to learning problems was adopted, although it was still widely recognised that approximately 10% of students exhibit learning difficulties that cause concern to themselves, their parents, and the school community. Many teachers recognise that these two or three students in each class need help, but they also accept that they, as teachers, also need assistance to provide the level of support required of them. Let us deal with this group briefly.

Various models of support have been employed to assist students with learning difficulties. Initially, remedial teachers withdrew these students from their regular classes for individual or small group tuition, often in reading and mathematics. However, education systems have not been able to meet the growing demand for such services and various limitations of the withdrawal model have emerged. First, because the extra tuition was provided during school hours, students missed learning opportunities occurring concurrently in the regular classroom. Second, to the extent that remedial teachers were drawn from the more experienced and effective teaching staff, the average skill level of regular teachers was lowered somewhat. Another form of deskilling occurred as regular teachers transferred responsibility for the instruction of students with learning problems to the remedial teachers, thus obviating the need for their own professional development in relation to meeting the diverse needs of students in regular classrooms. This situation still occurs today.

In the latter years of the 20th century, the emphasis moved to assisting both teacher and targeted children in the regular classroom. This entailed different skills for the specialist—often called a learning support teacher—and a cooperative attitude on the part of regular teachers. Thus, collaborative consultation models were introduced at various levels within education systems, although relatively little research has been conducted to demonstrate their effectiveness.

A further complication was experienced. Students with learning difficulties are by no means the only, or indeed the major, concern of regular teachers. Recent surveys have shown that more than half of all students with major disabilities were being integrated into regular schools. Those whose support needs involve access to the regular curriculum are served periodically by itinerant specialists. Thus, students needing vision aids, braille machines, hearing amplification, or special seating or adaptation of the physical environment were to be managed by regular teachers on a day-to-day basis because itinerant specialist contact was infrequent.

With some notable exceptions—for example, in New Zealand—most teachers were not involved in extensive professional development programs that would assist them to manage classrooms containing students with disabilities. When this was the case, and where a learning support teacher was present in a school, this individual was

likely to be involved not only with students who experience modest learning difficulties, but also students with higher support needs. This would result in the support teacher being asked to do much more than was reasonable. For example, we know one support teacher had the following responsibilities:

- provide instruction—using a withdrawal approach—to students with learning problems;
- work collaboratively with classroom teachers to provide instruction to students with special needs within the regular classroom;
- liaise with the guidance officer and other specialist staff;
- prepare submissions for special funding for students with high support needs;
- undertake standardised educational testing for students in the school, and also for preschool children at risk;
- run the school special program for gifted and talented students;
- liaise with parents and run parent-training programs;
- refer students to outside agencies that provide special services;
- conduct training for volunteers who assist classroom teachers;
- coordinate the volunteer groups;
- liaise with preschools about the transition of at-risk students to the primary school; and
- facilitate the transition of students with special needs entering secondary school.

What is most concerning is that the support teacher's working week was divided among three schools! A carefully negotiated whole school plan is required to ensure that available expertise is allocated and shared so that all members of the school community, including volunteers and students, can support the learning of those in need of help. The responsibility should not rest with one person.

Students who exhibit inappropriate behaviour usually gain their education in regular classes, with classroom teachers doing whatever is possible to direct the students' energies appropriately and to minimise disturbances to other class members. Because these children are fewer in number than those identified as having a learning problem, once the behaviour is socially appropriate, the student should not demand much attention from teachers. It has, therefore, been uncommon for behaviour management specialists to supplement school staff in the manner of learning support teachers. Rather, it has often been school administrators and guidance or psychology staff who have done most crisis intervention in the area of behaviour management. However, as with learning support and the effective

integration of students with disabilities, a school policy needs to be negotiated so that all teachers implement a consistent management style.

Having said that whole school policies and collaboration among all members of the school community are essential elements in addressing the needs of students with learning difficulties and/or behaviour problems, it must also be said that the same applies to gifted and talented students. Because only a small proportion of students exhibit unusually high ability in some specific field, it is difficult to provide support within the school, unless these children receive assistance from a specialist teacher. In metropolitan areas, students with outstanding abilities might gather at one site (or a number of sites) to participate in programs that can include golf, the creative and performing arts, advanced mathematics, and physics.

In core academic curriculum areas, cooperative arrangements between levels of the education system have existed for many years to provide advanced curriculum experiences for especially gifted students. In schools with multi-age grouping (in which, for example, a class might contain children aged 6 to 10 years of age) or in schools with vertical timetabling (with various levels and subjects being taught concurrently) it might be possible for gifted students to advance more rapidly than most of their peers. However, organisational solutions are often difficult to arrange. One fundamental issue in providing for gifted students is the way in which time is managed to allow them to cover content more quickly, or to gain access to extra-curricular components. Another issue is the provision of specialised tuition beyond that usually available among school staff. These issues can be addressed by establishing contacts with experts face-to-face, or by using the resources of the Internet and the World Wide Web.

It is evident that the problems of providing education for students with various educational needs are similar, irrespective of whether we are discussing giftedness, learning difficulties, or behaviour problems. However, providing for all students in a regular classroom challenges the traditional age-level or grade-level curriculum, with its whole-class instruction and emphasis on core content. Flexible time allocations, relevant curriculum content, and dynamic pedagogy can go a long way toward meeting individual needs. The potential to overcome many existing obstacles using collaboration as the core principle and communication technology has yet to be fully explored, although interest in this area has grown exponentially.

Our perspective on the four chapters in Section 2 is to view them as the bases for whole-school reform, with emphasis being given to *educational* solutions to *educational* problems using social groups as the basis for learning. Although we always focus on individual needs, it is clear that various forms of group teaching–learning strategies (e.g., cooperative learning, collaborative teaching, and whole-school policy development) are keys to addressing the needs of individual students, including those with high support needs.

In Chapter 5, Conway documents the cascade of services available to students with behavioural and emotional problems emphasising the importance of keeping students out of regular schools and classroom for the least time possible. In Chapter 6, Pagliano discusses the way in which a responsive school community can support students with sense impairments (i.e., vision, hearing) and, in Chapter 7, Braggett writes of the way in which the skills and abilities demonstrated by gifted and talented students can be enhanced by resources and programs available inside and outside the regular class and school. Finally, in Chapter 8, Gillies provides a briefing on collaborative classroom methods that have been shown to increase the social and academic skills of all students.

5

Behaviour in and out of the classroom

Robert Conway

Case studies

These two case studies represent two classroom approaches, different family and school backgrounds, and different outcomes. The students attended similar schools, both of which had access to specialist behaviour support teachers. We refer to these students and their classroom situations throughout the chapter.

As you read on, you will notice different outcomes for Jaden and Chantelle. Think how the classroom conditions might have contributed to the outcomes, how the classroom and specialist behaviour support teachers assessed the situations, and the reasons for the approaches used in each case. Were the outcomes what you would have expected? Would there have been different results if the behaviour support teachers had not been involved?

Jaden, Year 1

Jaden is from a cultural minority group in his school. He had no formal assessments of his behaviour prior to his referral to the specialist behaviour support teachers, although both Community Services and the school were very concerned about his challenging behaviours and about other welfare issues. Specific behaviours noted by the specialist teacher included yelling and screaming, failure to remain in his seat, obscene language to teachers and students, oppositional behaviour, and stealing.

The program developed by the support teacher, with the reluctant support of the teacher, was a behaviour management plan to support Jaden in the classroom using a teacher's aide, plus a withdrawal program on social skills. In addition, the specialist behaviour teacher also worked to support Jaden's mother who had very poor literacy skills and a very poor relationship with the school.

Parents of other students in Jaden's class wrote to the principal expressing concern that he had a special behaviour management program and that he was allowed to get away with behaviours they considered unacceptable. Both Jaden and his mother were benefiting from the program when he disappeared from the school, apparently because she feared that her son would be taken from her by Community Services. The specialist behaviour teacher was disappointed that she was not able to continue working with Jaden and his mother as it appeared that real progress has been made.

Chantelle, Year 5

A medical specialist diagnosed Chantelle as having Attention Deficit Hyperactive Disorder (ADHD) combined with Oppositional Defiant Disorder (ODD)—a powerful combination of behavioural needs. Her main difficulties were an inability to build and maintain friendships with other students and frequent verbal clashes with the teacher and other students.

The program, implemented with strong support from her mother and indifference from her father, was one of peer reading to teach Chantelle to work with other students, in addition to joining a friendship group taught by the specialist behaviour

teacher in a small group withdrawal setting. During the program Chantelle moved to another school in the area and the same behaviour support teacher introduced friendship sessions and a whole class program on social skills training. Although Chantelle is still no angel in her new school, there have been small advances in social skills and her anxiety levels have decreased, allowing her to participate more successfully in the lessons.

What you will learn in this chapter

In this chapter, you will discover:

- what factors influence behaviour problems in classroom, schools, and the wider community;
- how students with special behavioural needs are identified and assessed;
- strategies that can be implemented within the classroom and more generally to assist students with behavioural problems and to assist their teachers;
- preventative and remedial strategies for students with specific behavioural needs;
- alternative placement options for students with severe behavioural problems; and
- problems that a student might face.

Classroom behaviours

Almost all children exhibit aggressive or antisocial behaviour at one time or another. When these are persistent and extreme they become a problem, and students who are seriously disruptive are the least acceptable group of students with special learning needs in regular classrooms. They are also the group most likely to be identified by mainstream teachers as needing specialist, segregated placement.

Over the past 20 years or so there has been a rapid expansion in the number and range of specialist services available for students with behaviour problems. In some cases this has resulted from political attempts to impose law and order campaigns in various states and territories, and these affect education and juvenile justice department services. The aim is to send a message that political parties and, presumably, the community at large, do not accept inappropriate behaviour.

The two case studies above highlight the key issues in terms of what the teacher might observe in the classroom, as well as the specific learning needs that students have. In Jaden's case, the inappropriate classroom behaviour was quite clear. Other behaviours noted in various children across school settings include physical aggression (including throwing things at other children, punching and kicking), stealing food by aggressive means, inappropriate touching and sexual behaviour toward girls, and difficulties in following directions. Most of these behaviours are very visible and are easily identified

because they are directed at the teacher and/or students, and are designed to attract maximum attention.

Other behaviours can be difficult to detect, particularly if they occur outside the teacher's view, such as stealing and inappropriate sexual behaviour toward girls. Stealing with aggression is a type of bullying that often occurs in unseen areas of the playground, or on the way to and from school. Bullying is considered later in the chapter.

Academic and learning deficits

The students in both case studies had serious learning needs that were reflected in the programs developed by the specialist behaviour teachers in conjunction with the class teachers. It is important to understand that, in the case of students with behaviour problems, there are nearly always associated learning difficulties. In the case of Chantelle, the learning difficulties included poor listening skills, inability to follow instructions, not recognising and making corrections, and poor reading skills. Jaden completed little or no work in any subject. Like Chantelle, he could neither follow directions nor complete any task without one-to-one assistance.

These deficits fall into two main categories, those that are specifically academic (e.g., reading and mathematics) and those that relate to thinking skills (such as following directions), or those that are metacognitive (such as recognising errors and correcting them) (see Ashman & Conway, 1997). The difficulty experienced by the teacher is the correction of the academic skills while the student is behaving in socially inappropriate ways such as being out of his or her seat. It is also difficult to adjust a student's social behaviour pattern (e.g., participating in a small group) while the individual is not engaged in an academic activity.

It is difficult to change a behaviour in isolation. Behaviour change needs to take place in the regular classroom with the regular teacher although, in the case of students with persistent behaviour problems, the teacher might require assistance.

Defining terms

Defining behaviour disorders is difficult. The Tasmanian Department of Education and the Arts (1992) stated this in their statement on behaviours of serious concern. They suggested that behaviour of serious concern is notoriously difficult to describe because it can occur in many forms and can only be identified as being serious when someone makes a social judgment about its occurrence in a specific context.

Unlike intellectual disability and sense impairment, for which there are generally accepted definitions, behaviour disorders have no such agreed definition. Terms in common use in Australia include: behaviour of serious concern; disruptive, disturbed, and alienated behaviours; emotional disturbance; emotional problems; behaviour

problems; social/emotional handicaps; behavioural disability; and socially unacceptable behaviours. Such a range of terms and associated definitions makes it hard to reach consensus.

The problem of definition is further exacerbated by the lack of distinction between students with mild behaviour problems in regular classes and those attending special settings for more severe behaviour disorders. In some states and territories there is a distinction made between behaviour disorders or behaviour problems, and emotional disturbance. Students displaying the latter have a specific diagnosis and generally attend a specific educational setting in which they receive services jointly from education and health professionals. However, students with emotional disturbance might also be supported in regular classes through outreach services and not be confined to special schools on a full-time basis.

For a student to be defined as severely emotionally disturbed, one or more of the following characteristics must be exhibited to a marked extent and occur over time:

- an inability to learn that cannot be explained by intellectual, sensory, or health factors;
- an inability to build or maintain satisfactory interpersonal relationships with peers and teachers;
- inappropriate behaviours or feelings under normal conditions;
- a general pervasive mood of unhappiness or depression; or
- a tendency to develop physical symptoms, pains, or fears associated with personal or school problems.

This definition provides guidance on the behaviours that might be present and indicates that a behaviour must be a persistent problem to be considered disturbed. The definition also alerts us to some constraints of defining behaviour disorders. These include: rate, duration, topography, and magnitude of behaviour occurrence; range and variability of behaviour; and relationship to other disabling conditions. The definition is the basis of identification and classification of students with behaviour problems in many Australian states and territories.

In the United States (US) there have been moves to broaden the definition of behaviour disorder to reflect the reasons for the behaviour pattern, particularly allowing for cultural and ethnic issues to be excluded before the definition is applied (Council for Children with Behavior Disorders, 1995). The current terminology includes the following points:

1. The term emotional or behavioral disorder means a disability characterised by behavioral or emotional responses in school programs so different from appropriate age, cultural, or ethnic norms that they adversely affect educational performance. This includes an academic, social, vocational, or personal skill that:

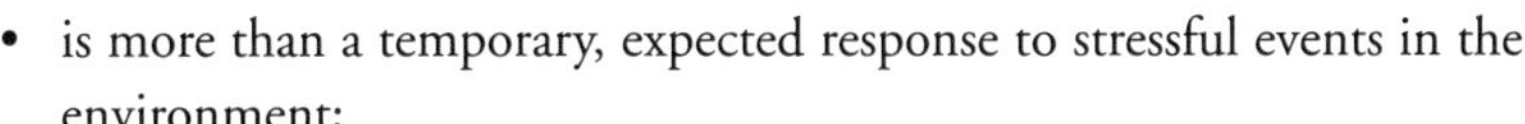

- is more than a temporary, expected response to stressful events in the environment;

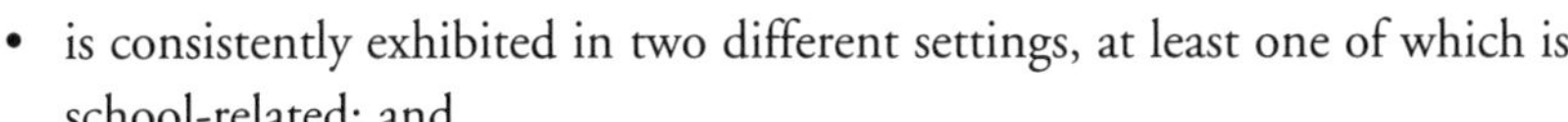

- is consistently exhibited in two different settings, at least one of which is school-related; and
- persists despite individualised interventions within the education program unless the child's or youth's history indicates that such interventions would not be effective.

2. Emotional or behaviour disorders can co-exist with other disabilities.
3. This category may include children or youth with schizophrenic disorders, affective disorders, or other sustained disturbances of conduct or adjustment when they adversely affect educational performance in accordance with section 1.

This definition has some very important advantages over earlier definitions in that it addresses the issue of the behaviour needing to occur in more than one setting and despite educational intervention.

The important issues in developing a definition are to account for as broad a range of behaviour variables as possible and to communicate succinctly a framework within which professionals can provide service. Wood (1979) proposed that a good definition should address the following questions:

- What or who is perceived as the focus of the problem? The disturber.
- How is the problem behaviour described? The problem behaviour.
- Where did the behaviour occur? The setting.
- Who regards the behaviour as disturbed? The disturbed.

What makes a behaviour disordered is its appearance in the wrong place, at the wrong time, in the presence of the wrong people, and to an inappropriate extent.

When does behaviour become unacceptable?

Certainly we all display behaviours at times that can be disordered or unacceptable, depending on location, frequency, intensity, duration, socioeconomic, and cultural influences, and age appropriateness of the behaviour.

Location is important because a drama or PE teacher, for example, might see active behaviour as being appropriate whereas another teacher (e.g., a mathematics teacher) might see the same behaviour as inappropriate. On a basketball court, aggressive outgoing team behaviour is valued whereas, in a mathematics class withdrawn silent working on individual tasks is expected. The difficulty for some students is making the distinctions between acceptable behaviour patterns in different locations.

The *frequency* of the behaviour is also important, because a behaviour that occurs once is unlikely to be a behaviour problem whereas behaviour that continues can be a

behaviour problem. If the *intensity* of the behaviour is such that a teacher takes offence immediately (e.g., swearing), the behaviour might be seen as a problem based on one event. If behaviour is of extended duration, each teacher has a different tolerance level. This is most common with attention seekers who initially might entertain both other students and the teacher, but who eventually wear out teachers' patience. The behaviour then becomes a problem.

Cultural factors are reflected in the different emphases that cultural groups place on behaviour. There is considerable debate in the US on assessment practices for students from cultural minority groups (Obiakor & Schwenn, 1996), as well as on the over-representation of students from cultural minorities in behaviour disorder settings (Ishii-Jordan, 2000), particularly in juvenile justice facilities. Whereas teachers might have certain expectations of students, families from different cultural backgrounds might not share these expectations, or expect their children to share them either.

The *socioeconomic status* of the family is another consideration because many students with specific behaviour problems come from socially disadvantaged backgrounds. Students from low socioeconomic situations and single-parent family background have been overrepresented in Australian studies of students with conduct disorders (Hemphill, 1996) and in studies of truancy (House of Representatives Standing Committee on Employment, Education and Training, 1996). Earlier Australian studies indicate that significantly more students attending schools in lower socioeconomic areas were identified as having a disorder. These studies suggested that resource allocations and preventative programs might need to be targeted to meet these needs.

Australian Aboriginal children can also be at risk because of the concurrence of a cultural minority status and a socioeconomic disadvantage. Participation by Aboriginal children in education is very low at all levels of the educational system, and is worst in rural and remote communities (Aboriginal and Torres Strait Islander Commission, 1999; Russell, 1999). Many Aboriginal children have low literacy levels, many display major behavioural problems at school, and many leave early to become the most arrested, most imprisoned, and most convicted group in Australian society (Carroll, Hattie, Houghton, & Durkin, 2001; Cunneen, 1999; Munns, 1998; Stewart, 1999). Although Aboriginal students present a major challenge for our educational system, the same is true for children from some other cultural minority groups. However, the supporting evidence about these groups is more anecdotal than published.

Incidence and prevalence

Although many of the early studies reported that around 4% of students have behaviour problems, Bor, Presland, Lavery, Christie, and Watson (1991) noted perception difficulties in the accurate assessment of regular classroom students by their

teachers, and difficulties in accurately assessing the perceived level of severity. Although the overall level of adjustment difficulty was 17% (which would be considered high), of these the teachers identified only 3.7% as having severe adjustment difficulties, 7% as having moderate difficulty, and 6.3% as having mild adjustment difficulties. The authors noted that their study did not seek prevalence figures and that they did not use a definition of adjustment problems. Rather they provided a list of ten behaviours that teachers could tick for each student as indicators of behavioural adjustment difficulties, including anxiety, social withdrawal, depression, and inattentiveness.

In a Western Australian study, Sugai and Evans (1997) examined teachers' perceptions of students with behaviour problems. They found that 2% of students were significantly different from their peers in self-management and social interaction. Although the results varied across schools, they were relatively stable across grades from P1 to Year 7.

In some cases, political or interest groups can inflate prevalence figures by arguing for the inclusion of students with labels such as Attention Deficit Hyperactivity Disorder. In addition, children with other primary disabilities (e.g., severe intellectual disability or autism) often exhibit behaviour disorders but are not included in behaviour disorders figures. One diagnostic label that is becoming increasingly common in schools is Asperger's Syndrome—considered to be a higher functioning type of autism. Given the behavioural and learning difficulties of students with ADHD or Asperger's Syndrome, a section of the classroom strategies later in this chapter focuses on these disorders.

Prevalence figures are based on widely differing samples and terminology. In addition, they reflect a snapshot rather than the changing patterns of prevalence in the population. Hence, they should be used as a guide only. In comparison to overseas figures, Australian prevalence rates are at the lower end of the range, varying from 1% to an amazing 30% depending on the criteria used for diagnosis.

Boys are more frequently labelled as having a behaviour disorder than girls. The ratio often quoted in the literature is 4:1 (Ryan & Lindgren, 1999) although in Australia it is closer to 2.1 boys to 1 girl. This is consistent with figures reported in Queensland schools for students identified by teachers as having adjustment difficulties and by teachers of primary-aged students in Sydney where the ratio was 2.5 boys to 1 girl (Bor et al., 1991; Stephenson, Linfoot, & Martin, 2000). The far greater number of boys in behavioural programs has a direct influence on programs developed mainly for boys, and some of these are unsuccessful with girls (Ryan & Lindgren, 1999).

As indicated by enrolment grade, age generally does not appear to be a major influence on the prevalence of behaviour disorders. Earlier studies in Queensland and Victoria suggest that primary and secondary levels are relatively consistent. In Queensland, the

figures were 3.6% for primary levels and 4.4% for secondary; in Victoria, the corresponding figures were 4.2% and 3.1%. A study in Western Australia (Sugai & Evans, 1997) found a consistency across early education and primary grades of 2%.

Identifying behaviour problems

A model is a way of describing the relationship between the causes of a condition and the nature of that condition. A model defines the condition and prescribes how to treat it. Two categories of models have been used to identify behaviour problems: medical models and conceptual models. Each is discussed below

Medical models

Before the emergence of a framework of educational services for children with behaviour disorders, medical diagnosis provided the classification system for all of these from the mildest to the most severe. The emphasis on medical or mental health models was primarily on severe or abnormal behaviours and on identifying collections of symptoms (syndromes), rather than on classifying behaviour based on classroom factors.

The Diagnostic and Statistical Manual for Mental Disorders (DSM-IV) developed by the American Psychiatric Association (1994) is the primary medical classification system, providing categories of disorders from infancy to adulthood, yet it does not enjoy universal support in terms of its application to students, particularly in educational settings. It does, however, provide clinical diagnoses for specific behaviour problems such as ADHD (see Box 5.3, page 219), Conduct Disorder, and Oppositional Defiant Disorder, all of which are used by medical staff to identify the need for medication. The presence of medical treatment can influence the choice of educational intervention. Which causal factors are used to explain behaviour disorders is largely influenced by professional training.

Conceptual models

Early models of behaviour disorders based the causes *within* the student—describing the causes as being genetic or biomedical (biological model) or as being imbalances in the personality structure of the student (psychodynamic model). In neither case was educational environment seen as a causal factor. Later models emphasised the role of the student's environment, including the school, as a causal factor in behavioural disorder. Some writers argued that the cause lay partially within the child and partially within the student's personality and emotional reactions to the school environment (psychoeducational model). Others saw the cause lying in faulty reinforcement of behaviours (behavioural model), or in poor interaction between the student and the ecosystem (ecological model).

Of these, the behavioural model has been the most relevant to educational settings and the model most widely accepted by teachers. The relatively simple emphasis on observable behaviours, rather than on underlying physiological or psychological causes, can be related to the classroom and does not necessarily require input from other professions to identify, assess, or remediate specific disordered behaviours. Although many studies have been reported on the effectiveness of behavioural approaches, concern has been expressed that these studies have often been conducted in rigorous conditions not normally replicable in the average classroom (see Alberto & Troutman, 1999; Porter, 2000).

Gordon, Arthur, and Butterfield (1996) used the concept of the *ecology of the classroom* as a basis for explaining classroom management. They emphasised the need to consider the personal ecology of each student as well as the nature of the classroom and the school. The idea of personal ecology—including personality, family variables, previous experiences, belief about self, and needs satisfaction—provides a clear transition between the individual and the classroom context. The classroom ecosystem reflects interactions among the physical environment, teacher characteristics, the curriculum (and how it is taught), and a multitude of student variables (Ashman & Conway, 1997). For example, research has shown that the seating arrangements in class affect the interactions of students and, hence, the management of the class (Gordon et al., 1996). If desks are in rows, disruptions are decreased as the opportunities for interactions are decreased. If students work at group desks, interactions are increased and this encourages cooperative learning.

More recent models have reflected an eclectic approach, moving away from an emphasis on behaviour alone in diagnosis and treatment to an awareness of the importance of cognitive and metacognitive skills (Ashman & Conway, 1997). The cognitive behavioural model places the cause of behaviour disorders in observable behaviours of the student and, in the absence of metacognitive skills, as self-monitoring, planning, and decision-making. This approach has the added attraction of encouraging students to take responsibility for their behaviours rather than relying on an external control (the teacher) for assessing the appropriateness of the behaviour. However, there are potential weaknesses in the emphasis on the student's motivation to be involved in self-management, and on the higher-level language skills that are required to work through the program (Porter, 2000).

Family factors

You will recall from Chapter 1 that the nuclear family of two parents and children no longer reflects the average family in many areas of Australia and New Zealand. There is an increasing incidence of single-parent families and blended families as a result of remarriage, and a shift in values held by the community about what is appropriate

behaviour for young people. These factors have ramifications for the role of the family as an agent of socialisation.

Three main types of family characteristics are considered risk factors in developing behaviour problems in children:

1. maladaptive family interaction and communication patterns;
2. excessive family stressors; and
3. socioeconomic disadvantage (Hemphill, 1996).

The same factors were addressed in the House of Representatives Standing Committee on Education, Employment and Training (1996). Table 5.1 (below) shows the aspects of a person's personal and family experience that were identified by the Standing Committee as affecting attendance at school and, hence, the likelihood of becoming involved in behaviour problems. Notice the similarity to the three broad categories identified by Hemphill (1996), as well as the link to school factors such as learning difficulties, boredom, lack of motivation to learn, and illiteracy. These school factors are discussed later.

Table 5.1 Aspects of personal and family experience that can lead to non-attendance at school

Transience and mobility
Lack of parental interest, support, and recognition of the value of education
Low socioeconomic status
Culture and cultural expectations
Unemployment
Family dysfunction
Substance abuse
Abuse of or by individual family members
Learning difficulties and underachievement (particularly illiteracy)
Boredom and lack of motivation for learning
Homelessness
Disadvantage
Isolation and inability to make friends
Low self-esteem and inappropriate anger responses

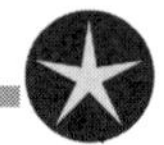

Adapted from House of Representatives Standing Committee on Employment, Education and Training (1996), p. 25.

There appears to be little direct evidence to confirm that any single family factor causes behaviour disorders or emotional disturbance. However, single-parent homes, marital discord, low socioeconomic status, and disturbed child–parent relationships might

increase the likelihood of disturbed and/or delinquent behaviours in children (Carroll et al., 2001; Williams & Carmichael, 1991). Submissions from across Australia to the House of Representatives Standing Committee on Education, Employment and Training (1996) identified a number of key elements as recurrent themes in truancy. These were: family conflict; poverty; single parent; blended families; neglect of physical and psychological wellbeing; lack of supportive care and concern; lack of communication; alcohol and substance abuse; emotional, physical and sexual abuse; stress; and damaged relationships. Students from dysfunctional family environments develop low self-esteem and fail to develop appropriate strategies to deal with anger and other personal problems. When several factors occur together, the probability that a child will develop a behaviour disorder is not additive, but multiplicative.

Family dysfunction might be either a result of the behaviour of the child with behaviour problems or the cause of the behaviour problems. The studies highlight the common desperation, despair, and guilt of parents who seek specialist behavioural placements for their child.

Although schools cannot be responsible for events that occur within the home, there is a need for school personnel to be sensitive to the difficulties that some students face within dysfunctional families. Educators and educational administrators need to be aware that any solution to behaviour problems in schools depends upon addressing the whole problem, not just one aspect of it. In the case of suspected abuse of students, teachers must report abuse to the appropriate authority.

School factors

Most researchers and educational administrators have suggested the importance of school factors in school-located behaviour disorders, although we cannot avoid the reality that behaviours are across settings.

Kauffman (1997) suggested seven ways in which school can contribute to behaviour disorders in children:

- insensitivity to students' individuality;
- inappropriate expectations of students;
- inconsistent management of behaviour;
- instruction in nonfunctional and irrelevant skills;
- ineffective instruction in critical skills;
- destructive contingencies of reinforcement; and
- undesirable models of school conduct.

This list of contributing factors highlights the interrelatedness of factors—particularly between academic failure and behaviour problems. The failure trap that commences with inability to succeed on an academic task can lead to an avoidance of schoolwork,

which can then lead to behaviour problems, with a cycle of failure being established. An associated factor is the level of academic task presented by the teacher. Many students with a behaviour disorder are unable to cope with regular curriculum topics, particularly in secondary schools. The combination of low student ability, grade level and high teacher expectations provides an environment for classroom disruption (Kauffman, 1997).

We shall return to these issues when we examine the ways in which educational assistance is provided.

Teacher attitude and tolerance

Teacher attitude and tolerance are important contributing school factors and are critical in the identification and/or labelling of students as having a behaviour disorder. This is seen most clearly in secondary schools where some teachers can have considerable difficulty with a particular student whereas others have no difficulty at all. The teachers experiencing difficulties are more likely to see the behaviour disorder as lying within the student, and more likely to ignore the reality that it is the outcome of interactions between teachers and students, and that this behaviour cannot be dismissed as the responsibility of the student alone (Houghton & Carroll, 1996). A study by Meadows, Neel, Scott, and Parker (1994) found that 79% of teachers deliberately used the same management techniques for students with behaviour problems as they used for regular students. As teachers, we need to examine our approaches to teaching and our responses to individual students.

The curriculum and teaching approaches

A critical school issue in both the cause of behaviour problems and their solutions is what we teach and how we teach it. The link between behaviour problems and learning difficulties has been clearly established. Among the features of schooling identified in the Burdekin Report (Human Rights and Equal Opportunity Commission, 1989) were irrelevant curricula, inflexible and alienating instructional structures, and rejection or neglect of under-achievers. As a principal who has worked with students at risk, Thompson (1992) identified curriculum irrelevancy as a major risk factor in adolescent behaviour problems, and Conway (2001) showed that a mismatch between students' reading abilities and the readability of textbooks contributes to behaviour problems.

Boredom has also been identified by secondary students in Victoria as being a reason for leaving school early (Holden & Dwyer, 1992). They also expressed a need to relate the curriculum to their own circumstances and their future as citizens. Bradley (1994) found that if learning was activity-based and imaginative, students were likely to become engaged in learning, and that once students were engaged in learning, the opportunities for behaviour problems were reduced.

Common assessment procedures and practices

Assessing the reasons and causes of behaviour problems in the classroom is an important start to understanding the behaviours and in setting up appropriate behavioural interventions. As can be seen from earlier sections of this chapter, there has been a tendency in the past to attribute behavioural difficulties either to particular theories about behaviour or to specific persons or places (e.g., the student or the home).

Today, assessment has become a far more systematic process, brought on to a large extent by the legal requirements of the 1997 amendments to the American *Individuals with Disabilities Education Act* (IDEA) (PL 105–17) that requires all students to have access to schools that are safe and conducive to learning. Under that legislation any student with a disability who interferes with his or her own learning or that of others is required—within 10 days of a disciplinary action by the school—to have a functional behavioural assessment plan developed to collect information to address the behaviours. Assessment is also influenced by the US Federal Department of Education's safe schools requirements (Dwyer, Osher, & Warger, 1998) based on a presidential direction, in response to a massacre in a high school in Oregon, that adults reach out to troubled children quickly and effectively.

Functional behaviour assessment

Functional assessment has its roots in analysing the challenging behaviours of students with severe intellectual disability in order to understand the function of the behaviour. With the advent of IDEA and greater inclusion of students with disabilities in regular classrooms, the approach is now being used far more widely in regular education, particularly with students with emotional and behaviour problems. In many cases, it is referred to as Functional Behavioral Assessment (FBA) to identify its application to students for whom the prime cause of concern is their behaviour. (Note here that the terms "behaviour assessment" and "behavioural assessment" are used in the North American literature.) For most students, the regular classroom, school rules and standard management practices are sufficient to maintain acceptable behaviour. If the student's behaviour is seriously interfering with his or her learning, and that of others, functional assessment might be appropriate.

As the rapidly expanding literature on FBA is almost entirely American, the references in the following sections are US-based rather than Australasian. A thorough overview and training program—both for FBA and for the development of behavioural intervention plans—has been developed by the Center for Effective Collaboration and Practice (CECP) <www.air.org/cecp>. The three-part training manual *Addressing student problem behavior* (CECP, 1998a, 1998b, 2000) will be supplemented by a fourth on train the trainer. Videos are also available to supplement the manual. There

are also numerous other CD, audio, video, text-based, and mixed-format training guides available commercially.

FBA is the process of gathering data to understand the student's behaviour and to determine a likely explanation of the purposes this behaviour serves (Schmid & Evans, 1998). There are two principles that underlie student behaviour. First, almost all behaviour serves a purpose—to get something that is desired, to avoid something undesirable, or to communicate a message or need. Second, behaviour occurs in a context—under certain conditions and not at other times.

A key feature is the identification of the relationship between the problem behaviours and the events before and after that make the behaviours more likely to occur again (Schmid & Evans, 1998). In addition, the environmental conditions or the ecological factors are also examined. The three factors are:

- what happens before the behaviour—predictors;
- what happens after the behaviour—maintaining consequences; and
- what environmental conditions affect the behaviour—setting events.

A reason for adopting an FBA approach is that it provides an objective method of identifying behaviours to target for intervention. If the teacher manipulates events after the behaviour has occurred, there is no opportunity to understand why the behaviour occurred in the first place. In an FBA approach, students can be taught to replace problem behaviours with more socially acceptable behaviours that still meet their needs.

> Students will change their behavior only when it is clear that a different response will more effectively and efficiently result in the same outcome. Identifying the purpose of problem behaviors, or more specifically, what the student gets or avoids through those behaviors can provide information that is essential to developing instructional strategies and supports to reduce or eliminate behaviors that interfere with successful classroom performance or participation (CECP, 1998, pp. 2–3).

Before describing the process of functional behaviour assessment, it should be remembered that the American model is based on the assessment being conducted by a team rather than by an individual staff member. The Individual Education Team in the US model is responsible for a student's Individual Education Program (the American IEP). If a student in an Australian school has a designated special need—particularly a student who has come from a special education setting—it is likely that he or she has an Individual Education Plan (the Australian IEP) that sets out the learning goals and how these learning goals will be taught and learnt.

Hence, the complete FBA process is used only when there are specific behavioural problems that warrant such a detailed approach. In Australian schools, the process is assisted by the learning support team in the school or by individual specialist teachers, including behaviour support teachers and teachers' aides.

The six basic steps in conducting an FBA (CECP, 1998b) are described below.

The seriousness of the problem

Through discussion with a specialist behaviour teacher or a colleague, the class teacher determines as accurately as possible the exact behaviour of concern (e.g., Tom is punching other students in the classroom). A colleague then observes the classroom to verify the behaviours and see whether the behaviours are demonstrated by other students as well, which might mean that the classroom procedures need to be changed rather than a specific program be set up for one student only. Such classroom observation is also an opportunity to see whether the behaviours are being triggered by any other factors in the classroom setting, such as teacher behaviour or expectations. If the teacher can adapt unrealistic academic or social expectations, there might be no need for a behavioural intervention for the student.

If, after discussing the outcomes of the observations and considering any cultural issues, the teacher and colleague believe that a full functional behavioural assessment is appropriate, they proceed through the subsequent steps.

The definition of the problem behaviour

A succinct definition of each behaviour is essential before data are collected. Hence, an appropriate definition is "closed fist hitting other students to the body and head", rather than a non-specific description of "being aggressive". It is also important to collect data in all possible settings. The information required is:

- when the behaviour occurs;
- the location of the behaviour;
- conditions in which the behaviour occurs and does not occur;
- who is present when the behaviour occurs;
- events or conditions that typically occur before the behaviour;
- events or conditions that typically occur after the behaviour;
- common environmental (setting) events; and
- any other behaviours that are associated with the behaviour.

As a result of collecting this information, some behaviours might be grouped together (e.g., in-seat and on-task) although there is always the option to return to specific behaviours later if the grouped-behaviour approach does not work.

Possible functions of the problem behaviour

It is important to collect information from a range of sources. This might include the completion of a checklist and rating scales by classroom teachers, parents, and the student (if appropriate), as well as interviews with teachers, parents, and psychologists, and, most importantly, direct observation in multiple settings on multiple occasions. Often these approaches to data collection are divided into direct assessment (observation) and indirect assessment (checklists, rating scales, and interviews).

Direct assessment

Direct observations in the classroom provide a clearer indication of the student's behaviour than do teacher rating scales and checklists, which are open to teacher bias and tolerance. Observation can provide valuable assessment and program information for that setting. Direct observation might include any of the following dimensions:

- rate (how often per unit of time it occurs);
- duration (how long it lasts);
- force (how intense it is);
- topography (what it looks like);
- locus (where it occurs); and
- latency (how long until the behaviour occurs).

Scatterplots, graphs, and Antecedent–Behaviour–Consequences (ABC) charts, or combinations of these, are commonly used to collect data. Although direct observation is subject to observer bias or inappropriate sampling, the extensive literature on the application of the technique across education settings demonstrates its appropriateness in assessing and identifying behaviour disorders (see Alberto & Troutman, 1999; CECP, 1998b; Rosenberg, Wilson, Mahaedy, & Sindelar, 1997b, for specific methods and charting).

Checklists and rating scales

Several authors have provided detailed analyses of teacher and parent rating scales, together with discussions of issues involved in their use (e.g., Karr & Wright, 1995; Rosenberg et al., 1997b). The authors point to the variability of checklists and rating scales in terms of quality, validity, reliability, and uncertainty regarding the purposes for which they are best suited. Of the rating scales, the Achenbach Child Behaviour Checklist (Achenbach, 1991) is the most widely used in schools as it has the advantage of using both parent and teacher ratings together with computer marking and analysis. The teacher report form also provides the opportunity to gather data on academic performance. There is also a youth-self report form for children and adolescents aged between 11 and 18 years.

Interviews

Interviews can assist in verifying information gathered through rating scales, checklists, or direct observations. However, there is no suitable substitute for direct observation of behaviour, particularly in the area of attention deficit dsorders in which medical diagnosis is often based on isolated clinical interviews with the child and parents, with no input from educators.

One of the key issues is ensuring that there is triangulation of gathering data for assessment so that as many opportunities and methods of gathering data are used as possible, and as many relevant players are involved as possible.

In the case studies about Jaden and Chantelle (pages 175–176), data gathering included multiple direct observations in the classroom and playground, teacher ratings, and interviews with the teachers and parents.

An example of gathering data from multiple sources is the use of a collaborative management approach that includes input from all relevant professionals—as proposed in the New South Wales Department of Education and Training's *Talk time teamwork* publication (NSW Department of School Education, 1995a). In this model, using blank forms provided in the document, documentation, and observational data are gathered from schools and medical practitioners at initial referral and throughout the monitoring of intervention approaches. This becomes useful both in the functional behavioural assessment and in developing the behavioural intervention plan.

Triangulation and/or problem pathway analysis

Having collected data, it is time to analyse the range of information to determine which specific social, affective, and environmental conditions are associated with the problem behaviours. Triangulation of data is very important, and a triangulation chart listing the data from each source can assist in visually comparing the data.

The aim is to identify possible patterns of behaviour, triggering events, consequences that trigger or maintain the behaviour, and the likely functions of the behaviour. It is also possible to develop pathways for the behaviour—from the setting events, to the antecedents, to the behaviour, to the consequences that maintain the behaviour.

The probable function of the problem behaviour

The statement is a concise summary of the information collected during the assessment phase so that the behavioural intervention plan can be written. It allows the person or team writing the plan to know that when *X* occurs, the student does *Y* in order to achieve *Z*.

For example, in the case of Chantelle, who did not relate to other students, the hypothesis statement was: "When Chantelle wants her peers to notice her, she swears

at the teacher to gain their attention." The strategy planned as a result of this hypothesis creates a power struggle with the teacher but does not increase student attention.

The hypothesis statement

It is important that the intervention plan not be developed until the hypothesis statement is tested. If there are any environmental changes that can be made—such as changing the curriculum content or its presentation, such that the behaviour changes—there is no need to proceed with developing a behavioural plan. For example, if the student was annoying others during a worksheet activity and the teacher produced worksheets that the student could complete unassisted and without disruption, then a behavioural plan for the student to work unassisted would not be needed.

CECP (1998b) recommends that up to five to seven lessons be used to test the hypothesis statement and to assess whether changes can be made without a formal plan. In other cases, such as aggressive behaviour or other serious behaviours, it might be appropriate to proceed with the behavioural plan.

The most important outcome of the functional behavioural assessment process is behavioural change. This can either be in the form of manipulation of environmental events (e.g., curriculum, teaching and learning strategies, or the layout of the classroom or playground), or the development of a behaviour intervention plan.

Ways of supporting learning

Behaviour problems that exist in the regular classroom

Before considering the types of behaviour problems that occur in the classroom, it is useful to remember that:

- children with a label of behaviour disorder or behaviour problem do not have a monopoly on problem behaviours;
- problem behaviours considered indicative of behaviour disorders are common among most normal children; and
- the problem behaviours manifested by children who are not thought to have a persisting behaviour problem are not generally different in kind from those shown by disturbed children but are different in frequency of occurrence, degree of severity, duration, and clustering.

Students who are referred for behaviour support might present a variety of behaviours. These include:

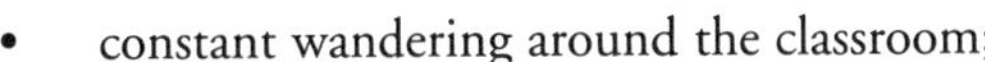

- constant wandering around the classroom;
- leaving the classroom or school without permission;
- frequent shouting in class;
- fighting with peers;
- teasing;
- frequent swearing;
- throwing equipment or furniture in a rage;
- threatening students and teachers;
- vandalism;
- non-compliance intended to disrupt;
- withdrawal, total silence, or no eye contact;
- persistent compulsive lying;
- stealing; and
- self-mutilation.

Common associated characteristics of students with mild to moderate behaviour problems reported in the literature include poor academic achievement, poor interpersonal relations, and poor self-esteem. A recent review of school violence and disruption in American schools provides a further insight on behaviour patterns in schools (Leone, Mayer, Malmgren, & Meisel, 2000).

Most teachers believe that there is a connection between learning difficulties and adjustment difficulties in the classroom. At first, the lack of interpersonal skills in students with behaviour disorders might be tolerated, or their acting-out behaviours might be reinforced by peers (Carroll et al., 1999). However, as their behaviours continue, they often become disliked or rejected by teachers and peers and, behind their apparent lack of concern, is a serious lack self-confidence.

Australian studies have identified a number of characteristics of students who have behaviour disorders or who are discipline problems in regular schools (e.g., Conway, Schofield, & Tierney, 1991; Oswald, 1995). Differences emerge among preschools, primary schools, and secondary schools. In primary schools, distractible—rather than acting-out—students pose the greatest difficulty to teachers. The behaviour difficulties of preschoolers have emerged only recently as a major concern. The number of referrals of students from early education settings to special education services has increased markedly. In the case of the service in which the author works, referrals for behaviour problems now constitute the largest group of referrals. In an epidemiological study of children in New Zealand preschool centres, Pavuluri and Luk (1996) found that the most commonly rated moderate-to-severe behaviour problems were

dependency, temper tantrums, and management difficulties. There were no major differences in the patterns for boys and girls.

A study of teachers of children from five to eight years of age in western Sydney found that teachers were most concerned about such behaviours as distraction, problems with listening, physical aggression, demands for teacher attention, inability to remain on-task, and disruption of others (Stephenson, Linfoot, & Martin, 2000). Teachers also identified the need for support and assistance in dealing with these problems. It is of interest that the study found that 7% of the students in the class had behaviours that were severe enough to warrant additional behavioural support. This is in contrast to a study of primary teachers in inner Sydney schools in which 15% of the students were reported by Beaman and Wheldall (1997) as needing support.

Finally, as part of a study of 58 randomly sampled New South Wales high schools, Conway, Tierney, and Schofield (1990) asked teachers to record the main discipline problem that they encountered each day, together with related statistical data such as lesson characteristics and student characteristics. The researchers found that the main discipline problems could be grouped into ten categories: lack of interest; noise; poor manners; disobedience; disruption; self-abuse; property abuse; verbal aggression; physical aggression; and physical danger. In each case the categories were subdivided into minor and major problems. Similarly, the teacher discipline action categories were divided into minor and major actions. From a teacher's perspective, it was important that the discipline actions taken by teachers were minor (e.g., reprimand or move seats) whether the discipline problem was major or not.

Where do we provide services to students with behavioural problems?

The cascade of services model can be used to describe the provisions for students with behavioural and emotional disorders in Australia. It represents a range of services, from students in the regular class to those with severe emotional disturbances in residential health setting or youth-training centres. Figure 5.1 (page 195) summarises the potential range of services across Australia and New Zealand, although they are not provided at all levels by all states and territories.

Note that in Levels 1 to 4, the student with behaviour problems is located in the regular classroom. Even at Level 5 the student might still be partially integrated in the mainstream and, following placement at Level 6, there is an expectation that students will return to the regular classroom if appropriate. Hence, most services, except for some students with severe emotional disturbance or those placed in juvenile detention, occur in the regular school with differing levels of teacher and student support.

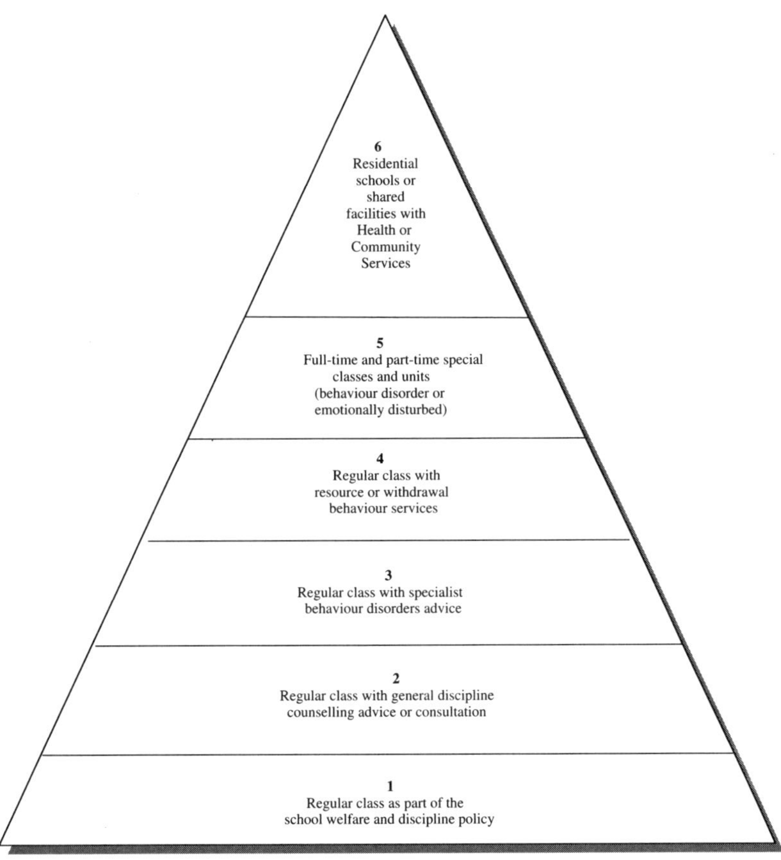

Figure 5.1 A model of education services for students with behaviour disorders.

Changing the way we teach in the regular school environment

The minimum requirement for managing all students is a total and consistent commitment to a positive school environment in which agreed behavioural expectations are developed, known, applied consistently and fairly, and supported at all levels within the school community and by higher educational authorities. In this section we look at ways in which this can be achieved, both at the total school level and in the individual classroom.

Before looking at these approaches, a statement in a Tasmanian document highlights the issues succinctly.

> It is contended here that schools and systems that attend only to the correction of misbehaviour will find that they have more and more misbehaviour to correct and that they will be less effective in actually correcting it. Conversely, effort and attention spent in increasing the productive learning and positive

> social behaviour of all students will prevent most misbehaviours from ever occurring, and will also provide the sort of setting in which problem-solving, corrective and rehabilitative procedures will be most effective on the few occasions when they are needed (Tasmanian Department of Education and the Arts, 1992, p. 10).

Maintaining a positive, well disciplined class in a supportive school community relies on the cooperation of all staff, who work to ensure that they are all involved in developing a consistent discipline and welfare policy and in applying that policy persistently.

The importance of early intervention

Early intervention is essential for students with behaviour problems. Today, many students are identified in early childhood settings, and interventions are put in place at that stage. Within school-aged placements there is, again, strong emphasis on early intervention. Although some behaviour problems do not appear in early years, the vast majority do and, without early attention, students and teachers can expect a worsening of the behaviour patterns, particularly in cases of conduct disorder (Hemphill, 1996). Walker, Colvin, & Ramsey (1995) bluntly stated the need for intervention in early school years.

> If antisocial behavior is not changed by the end of grade 3, it should be treated as a chronic condition much like diabetes. That is, it cannot be cured, but managed with the appropriate supports and continuing intervention (Walker, Colvin, & Ramsey, 1995, p. 6).

A model for schoolwide behaviour support

Most students with behaviour problems are part of the regular school and need their behaviour managed by teachers as part of the regular educational process. As noted above, students at the first four levels in the cascade model remain in the regular school with assistance and do not experience placement in a specialist setting. Within the regular school setting, the number of students receiving assistance has been described as a continuum of positive behaviour support in the effective behaviour support model of Lewis and Sugai (1999) (see Figure 5.2, page 197). The model proposes three levels of implementation that are consistent with the approach used in many Australasian schools.

At the *first level*, the school develops universal schoolwide management strategies to meet the needs of all students. They are based on the involvement of the whole school community: teachers, students, parents, and community. The strategies should be implemented consistently and efficiently across all school settings, with specific strategies dealing with areas such as corridors and playgrounds, as well as with classrooms.

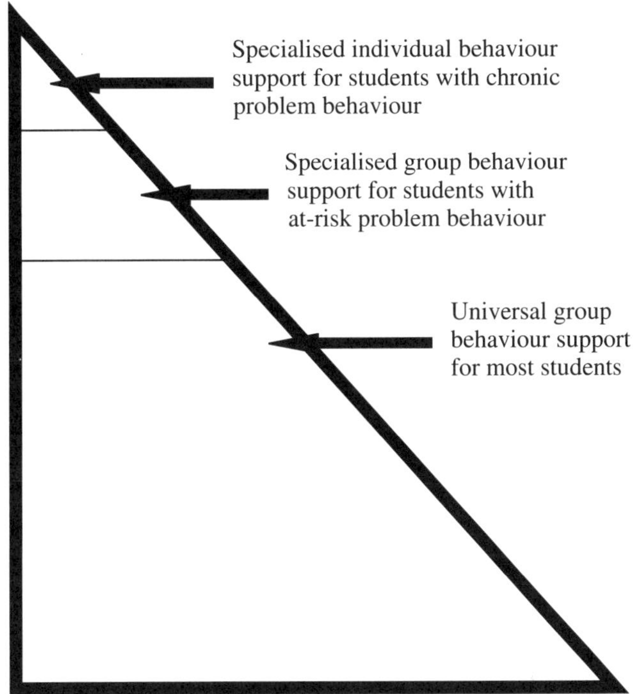

Figure 5.2 Effective behaviour support model.

At the *second level* are secondary support interventions to assist targeted individuals and groups who are at risk and who require repeated practice and environmental modifications to increase academic and social success.

At the *third* (or *tertiary*) *level* of support are targeted and highly specialised strategies for those few students (1–7%) who engage in serious challenging behaviours and who do not respond to the first or second levels of support. It is important to note that only this small percentage of students in the average school requires specialised individual behaviour support as a result of chronic behaviour. The remainder either conform to the behaviour (discipline) system (first level) or are managed within the discipline procedures of the school (second level).

Although the approach is very similar to some previous and existing approaches to managing behaviours in schools, the key difference is the development and implementation of a process that comes from *within* the school rather than from the principal or an external source. Real behaviour change comes from within and cannot be imposed. Hence, in reading the following total school approach, note that the school community develops the approach and, as a team (principal, staff, students, and parents), implements and monitors it.

Effective behaviour support is based on six key elements or stages, as shown in Box 5.1 (below). These six elements are:

- statement of purpose;
- schoolwide behavioural rules or expectations;
- procedures for teaching schoolwide expectations;
- continuum of procedures for encouraging schoolwide expectations;
- continuum of procedures for discouraging problem behaviours; and
- procedures for monitoring the impact of the schoolwide EBS program.

Box 5.1 Effective behaviour support elements

Statement of purpose

One of the important parts of the process is the development of a statement of purpose that is brief and positive and that, in a series of points, outlines what the school stands for (e.g., *places value on academic and social success*).

Schoolwide behavioural rules or expectations

A list of behaviour expectations is based on common problem behaviours from across the school. Positive statements replace problem behaviours. These are then grouped to form a set of school rules. Lewis and Sugai (1999) cited the example of a primary school team that developed five rules: *be respectful, be cooperative, be safe, be kind*, and *be peaceful*. The rules have specific examples for specific settings—such as the playground or the classroom. Hence, in this particular school, the rule, *be respectful in the playground*, had the following examples:

- keep game rules the same during the game;
- use appropriate language (no put-downs); and
- line up when the whistle blows.

The same school rule in assemblies had the example:

- keep hands and feet to self.

Procedures for teaching schoolwide expectations

At a minimum, schools should *tell* students what is expected, *show* them what the skill looks like, and *practise* the skill through role play and real-life situations across all school settings.

Continuum of procedures for encouraging schoolwide expectations

Positive reinforcement to encourage pro-social skills is needed to ensure that rules are followed. Reinforcement does not work in some cases because it is tokenistic. It should be a true acknowledgment of the student's involvement. State the rule that has been kept when providing the reward. In general, positive reinforcement should be shifted from tangible to social, from external to internal, from frequent to infrequent, and from predictable to unpredictable.

Continuum of procedures for discouraging problem behaviours

The school must develop clear examples of each rule-violating behaviour, and specific rules for the consequences of each problem behaviour. The goal is to develop a policy that:

- is implemented consistently schoolwide;
- clearly differentiates between behaviours that should be managed in the classroom and behaviours that should cause the student to be sent to the office; and
- provides a proactive strategy to identify and address the needs of students who have chronic problem behaviour.

The levels of rule-violating behaviour are:

Level 1—minor problem behaviour handled by individual teachers;

Level 2—major behaviour problems require the involvement of school executive staff;

Level 3—illegal acts require the involvement of district or higher level staff or agencies (such as the police).

Procedures for monitoring the impact of the schoolwide EBS program

Any behavioural system requires maintenance of records. A benefit of a good record system is the provision of information such as the most common referral time (during the day, week, or school term), and the rule violations that occur. Data might validate procedures or initiate revisions.

Source: Based on Lewis and Sugai (1999).

The success of the effective behaviour support approach is dependent on all staff, students, and parents being committed to the process, and on ensuring that all parties support the implementation of both behaviour rules and consequences. In many schools behaviour expectations are not maintained and there is little expectation that the school executive will enforce consequences for infringements of these behavioural expectations. Often this is because the school executive, in turn, feels unsupported by senior administrators at district and higher levels.

The successful management of students with emotional and behavioural problems relies very much on the management of the whole school discipline and management policy. If teachers know that they are supported, individual management is much easier. Nevertheless, management within the class still presents a major challenge to individual teachers.

In Australian schools, all teachers and students are involved in the school welfare and discipline policy. Hence, the aspirations of school administrators, as expressed in

school and class rules, are expected to be followed. The critical difference between Effective Behaviour Support and many other programs, is the focus on positive alternatives in contrast to school rules that might result in the use of time-out areas within classrooms, in-school suspension programs, and punishments (such as loss of privileges and, for serious offences, suspension and expulsion). In an American study on mainstreaming of students with behaviour disorders, Meadows et al. (1994) found that 95% of teachers maintained the same set of rules for all students; 79% used the same management techniques regardless of the individual student's behavioural needs, and only 21% created opportunities for an integrated student with behaviour problems to work with peers. The outcomes suggest that most teachers are unwilling to change their management practices to accommodate integrated students with behaviour problems.

A disturbing trend is the increase in teacher-perceived prevalence of behaviour disorders in schools. This has lead schools to adopt more structured and teacher-controlled models of management such as Canter's *assertive discipline* model and the use of the *levels approach. Assertive discipline* (Canter & Canter, 1992) reflects not the professed preventative approach but rather a punitive approach, and is at the authoritarian end of the discipline continuum (Porter, 2000). The major concern is the use of the term discipline synonymously with the term punishment in school discipline policies, and an acceptance that teacher-imposed punitive sanctions follow deviant behaviour as acceptable discipline. A shift in emphasis is needed to ensure that discipline becomes an education issue rather than a management issue. In addition, there is a need to provide an opportunity for analysis of curriculum and teaching strategies in the classroom to address the school factors that contribute to the occurrence of behaviour disorders, such as inappropriate lesson content, poor preparation, poor teaching, and poor student motivation.

The *levels approach* commonly includes six levels through which the students progress as a result of continuing unacceptable behaviour until, at Level 5, they might be expelled. The approach has no comprehensive conceptual basis and is not described in any text on discipline models. However, it has been widely used in some areas, such as in New South Wales, where it was documented as a useful strategy in the School Discipline Policy (NSW Department of School Education, 1996). However, the current policy provides a number of cautions in terms of its use—for example, that levels systems "can emphasise punishment at the expense of rewards . . . [and that] . . . Quality Assurance School Reviews indicate considerable parent concern about the use of levels systems" (p. 26).

Although whole school approaches might discourage students with mild disruptive behaviour, for those with serious behaviour disorders who reach suspension and expulsion, such approaches can end their access to both regular and special education programs. This issue was highlighted in the Commonwealth House of Representatives

inquiry into truancy and exclusion from school (House of Representatives Standing Committee on Education, Employment and Training, 1996). The Committee heard extensive evidence that discipline policies in all states and territories were being used to remove difficult students and to encourage them to move on. The concern was that initial suspension might be the beginning of long-term absence from education, with no attempt being made to provide alternative educational services.

The need for discipline policies in schools and the attraction of teacher-managed options (such as those discussed above), has led schools to adopt unchanged approaches, such as the levels approach, without due consideration of the needs of their own school. As a result, schools implement a discipline policy that has no staff or student involvement in its development, and hence no ownership or commitment. The most effective discipline policies found in schools are those that have been developed by teachers and students to meet their needs, and which have minimal operational requirements (Conway et al., 1991). However, for many schools, discipline and control for all is seen as the solution to controlling the unacceptable behaviour of the few. A possible positive solution might lie in approaches such as the effective behaviour support model, which aims at securing and maintaining student and teacher confidence in cooperatively developing teaching and learning strategies, and in which discipline becomes an educational issue rather than a teacher-imposed management issue.

Regular class management within the whole school approach

The individual classroom is where most teachers have greatest difficulty with students with behaviour problems. And, of course, there is a great variety of behaviours that threaten classroom learning.

A positive classroom environment

A key feature of regular classrooms for any student, particularly those classrooms that include students with behaviour problems, is the presence of a positive classroom environment (Guetzloe, 2000). She defined a positive classroom as a setting that meets the physical, psychological, social, and educational needs of all students. There are three dimensions in a positive classroom: conditions, curricula, and consequences.

Conditions in a positive classroom include:

- physical and psychological safety for teachers and students—no ridicule or humiliation by any person;
- knowledgeable, skilled, charismatic, and courageous staff with a strong background in behaviour management, a positive self-concept and a clear understanding of the educational needs of students with behaviour problems;

- attainable goals and objectives—for each student with a behaviour problem these need to be individualised, developmental, measurable and obtainable;
- relevant curriculum—providing a variety of experiences related to the lives, problems and needs of the students;
- positive instructional techniques—providing instruction that ensures success according to the student's individual goals and objectives;
- opportunities for socialisation—students with behavioural problems need to learn to communicate in a natural (group) setting under supervision;
- instruction in social skills—including peer instruction and cooperative learning;
- links to and among the student's worlds—school, peers, family's linkages through socialising, communicating and collaborating, and community participation;
- classroom structure—highly structured in terms of expectations, routines, rules and schedules and, as an essential, an explicit behaviour management system;
- classroom rules—few, fair, clearly displayed, taught, and consistently enforced with no loopholes for challenges; and
- violence and abuse not allowed—there must be non-physical aversive consequences for any acts of aggression, abusive language, or put-downs (otherwise the student might see these behaviours as being acceptable).

Curriculum in a positive classroom is a critical issue for students with behaviour problems as they may have missed many of the experiences that occur naturally in families, both before and during school, due to their non-acceptance by families, peers, and community members. Hence, curriculum needs to include the following:

- effective, motivating, and therapeutic curriculum—to meet often the most basic of learning needs, and hence become therapeutic as it ameliorates the problems that have contributed to the student being identified as having behavioural problems;
- thematic units—provide an integrated learning experience and have been shown to be very effective both in regular and special education;
- careful selection of instructional materials—relevant to the student's life, related to what he or she knows, and relevant to the student's neighbourhood and community.
- concrete, manipulable materials;
- age-appropriate materials to teach basic skills;

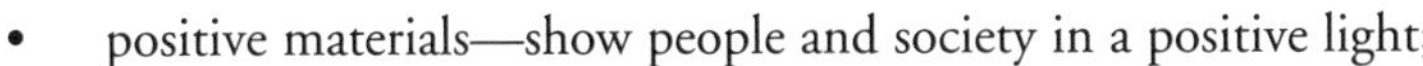

- positive materials—show people and society in a positive light;

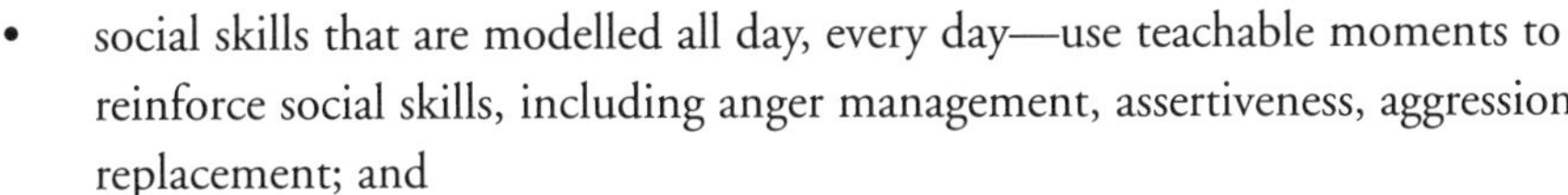

- social skills that are modelled all day, every day—use teachable moments to reinforce social skills, including anger management, assertiveness, aggression replacement; and
- materials that encourage interactions—students need to learn (under supervision) to communicate without arguments, fights, and put-downs.

Guetzloe (2000) proposed an "if . . . then" approach to curriculum for students with behaviour problems, as shown in Table 5.2.

Table 5.2 The "If . . . then" approach to curriculum for students with behaviour problems

IF THE PROBLEM IS:	THEN INCLUDE IN THE CURRICULUM:
unrealistic expectations	goal-setting and self-monitoring
social isolation	assertiveness, communication, and social skills
stress	self-control, coping, time management, relaxation exercises
preparation for the future	career and vocational education, government and law, home skills, relationships, marriage and family living, use of leisure time
self-esteem	art, music, dance, hygiene, clothing selection, weight-training, individual sports

Source: Guetzloe (2000).

Consequences in the positive classroom include:

- those that are positive, natural and logical;
- those that are primary or concrete rewards in conjunction with social rewards;
- token rewards that can not be counterfeited;
- the most desirable reinforcer—particularly for adolescents—is work avoidance; and
- the achievement of less desired activities before more desirable activities (called the Premack Principle).

The final words by Guetzloe (2000) give some hope to teachers working with students with behaviour problems in their class.

The relationship between and among conditions, curriculum and consequences in the educational setting [is a useful model]. If the conditions happen to be less desirable on any given day, the curriculum must be better than usual and the consequences more desirable. If the conditions are good and the curriculum is interesting and enjoyable,

the consequences may not be as important. If all of these are appropriate for the group at the same time, wonderful things can happen. (Guetzloe, 2000, p. 4)

Individual classroom management strategies

Reference was made earlier (page 196) to the use of the effective behaviour support model within the whole school approach (Lewis & Sugai, 1999). At the classroom level it is expected that there will be specific examples designed to meet individual needs. Based on the literature of specific management techniques, Lewis and Sugai identified a number of important recommendations, as follows.

Provide advance organisers or precorrections

To promote the positive behaviours that have been learnt, students must be reminded beforehand of the correct behaviour to increase the likelihood of its occurring in that setting. For example, "Before going into the classroom, remember to have your books and pens on the desk ready to start." Teachers can also model the desired behaviours.

Keep students engaged

The best way to keep students on-task is to ensure that the lesson content and presentation, and the reinforcement given, keep students motivated, and that alternative inappropriate sources of reinforcement or attention are not available. Keeping students engaged can occur by using short monitored tasks and by varying the lesson style through activities (such as informal lesson breaks).

Provide a positive focus

One of the most commonly identified difficulties for classroom teachers is keeping a positive focus with students who are seen as a constant threat to the teachers' classroom management. Commonly, teacher interactions are frequent, short, and negative. One strategy is to have at least four positive interactions to each negative one. The teacher should also ensure that a positive classroom climate exists, rather than one of confrontation.

Consistently enforce school and class rules

Stated simply, if it is worth having classroom rules it is worth ensuring that they are respected and followed by all students. Similarly, reinforcing school rules is an important part of ensuring a positive school behaviour plan.

Correct rule violations and social behaviour errors proactively

Correction needs to be consistently applied and, if possible, without drawing attention to the student and the problem behaviour. There is also a need to ensure that the teacher does not become involved in a power struggle with the student. If the behaviour persists, consideration should be given to moving to a specific behaviour intervention plan.

Changing academic instruction to reduce behaviour problems

A critical aspect of maintaining students with behaviour problems in an inclusive classroom is the recognition of the learning difficulties that students with behaviour problems face. This requires that adaptations be made to the teaching–learning environment. Social behaviours cannot exist in isolation; there must be a context to the behaviours and this is provided by the environment. Hence, to provide a successful learning experience in the inclusive classroom, the teacher must consider adapting the teaching content and its presentation, and the learning outcomes, so that all students learn (Houghton & Carroll, 1996). In a similar outcome to the findings of Meadows et al. (1994), researchers have shown that many teachers are unwilling to make curriculum adaptations.

The failure of teachers to adapt teaching styles and curriculum means failure of students to learn which, in turn, results in behavioural problems, and then failure to cope in the regular classroom. At this point, the process of seeking specialist placement or suspension commences. The challenge for students and teachers alike is to make changes such that classrooms work effectively.

The relevance of the curriculum to students with a behaviour disorder is a major issue, particularly at the secondary level. In a study of Queensland teachers, Bradley (1992) identified the need for curriculum to be more practical, for the teaching to include more activity-based and experiential work, and for assessment to be more related to the learning approaches used.

To maintain a student with behaviour problems within the classroom, changes need to be made to the teaching approach (Conway, 2001). This might involve reducing content to the core concepts that are the must-know learning outcomes from the curriculum topic, reducing vocabulary to remove unnecessarily complex terms, and focusing on the use of essential vocabulary in oral and written work. The combination of modified content and reduced vocabulary (in appropriate worksheets and oral work) with the use of small group practical activities assists students with behaviour problems to work in an environment that is more conducive to learning. Reduction of learning pressure (on both the students with behaviour problems and other students with learning difficulties) assists in creating a more positive learning environment.

Kauffman, Hallahan, Mostert, Trent, and Nuttycombe (1993) provided a list of eight questions for teachers to reflect upon in determining ways to change curriculum presentation and to reduce behaviour problems.

- How relevant to, or functional in, the student's life is the curriculum?
- Do I have the option of teaching something more relevant and functional?

- To what extent could I individualise instruction?
- How successfully is this student or group performing in the curriculum?
- Am I using an approach to teaching that provides too little structure, too much direction, too little positive feedback, or too much criticism?
- How frequently do my students have an opportunity to respond to academic tasks?
- What percentage of time are students actually actively engaged in learning?
- How, and how much, could I change the teaching strategies I use?

Although Kauffman et al. (1993) acknowledged that not all behaviour problems can be solved by changing the teaching–learning environment, such changes might avoid the need to embark on specific management programs.

In summary, the most useful strategies include:

- being well prepared;
- giving short-term tasks;
- providing clear academic and behaviour expectations;
- monitoring activities frequently; and
- encouraging cooperative learning.

Teaching social skills

Social skills are complex and include overt, observable behaviours as well as problem-solving behaviours. They often occur in difficult social situations. Elksnin and Elksnin (1998) identified a change in the responsibility for teaching social skills from a parental role to a school role, based on the realisation that academic success depends to a considerable extent on the social skills of students. They identified six types of social skills.

- *Interpersonal behaviours*—friendship-making skills, such as introducing yourself, joining in, asking a favour, offering to help, giving and accepting compliments, and apologising.
- *Peer-related social skills*—skills valued by peers and associated with peer acceptance: examples include working cooperatively, asking for and receiving information, and correctly assessing another's emotional state.
- *Teacher-pleasing social skills*—skills associated with school success, including following directions, doing your best work, and listening to the teacher.
- *Self-related behaviours*—skills that allow a student to assess a social situation, select an appropriate skill, and determine its effectiveness; other self-related behaviours include following through, dealing with stress, understanding feelings, and controlling anger.

- *Assertiveness skills*—skills that allow students to express their needs without resorting to aggression.
- *Communication skills*— skills that include listener responsiveness, turn-taking, maintaining conversational attention, and giving the speaker feedback.

Social skills training programs have been used to teach a wide variety of skills (see, Carroll, Bain, & Houghton, 1994; Taffe & Smith, 1994). Programs range from the teaching of specific behaviours (such as eye contact and facial expressions) to broader, more complex social skills (such as making friends). Although social skills were once taught in isolation, and then generalised to social settings in the classroom, more recently there has been a move to teach clusters of social skills, as well as incorporating cognitive and environmental influences in programs.

Many teachers prefer not to use packaged programs for social skills training, often because of the somewhat artificial form and American approach of such packaged programs. An excellent series of Australian resources are those by McGrath (see McGrath, 1997; McGrath & Edwards, 2000; McGrath & Francey, 1991; McGrath & Noble, 1993). As a result, teachers use ideas from a variety of sources and develop a program that meets their own needs. Kauffman et al. (1995) suggested that any teacher-developed program should be scrutinised using the following questions:

- What are the skills that need to be learnt?
- Am I actually teaching social competence through requiring students to interact?
- Am I teaching skills explicitly?
- Can I generalise the skills to other classroom settings?
- Is the approach that I am using meeting the needs of all the students, including those with special needs in the class?

In a review of the literature on social skills training, Knight, Graham, and Hughes (1995), suggest that the mnemonic ACCEPTANCE best describes the emphasis required in a social skills competence program:

- accepting a realistic view of self and others;
- communication and compromise;
- changing negative attitudes—academic and social; teacher and peer;
- emotions and their appropriate expression;
- promoting pro-social behaviours and strategies for learning;
- talking about problems and successes;
- acceptance of individual differences;
- nurturing social competence;

- cooperative learning; and
- encouraging positive interaction between all students.

Self-efficacy

Self-efficacy is the belief we have that we can do a task successfully. As many students with behaviour problems have had negative social experiences in classrooms, their self-efficacy might be lowered and they are therefore unwilling to persevere if obstacles or rejection occur. Taffe and Smith (1994) suggest that incorporating self-efficacy within social skills training programs has the possibility of enhancing positive peer relations.

Self-management skills

The move toward teaching students self-management skills has been a major step in educating students with behaviour problems. Self-management skills include monitoring, recording, and reinforcing performance. More importantly self-management skills incorporate the use of cognitive strategies such as taking responsibility for initiating learning through the acquisition of problem-solving skills. Ashman and Conway (1997) reviewed the problem-solving literature and emphasised the need to teach students how to formulate a strategy for attempting a task, enacting the strategy, and monitoring performance until the task is solved.

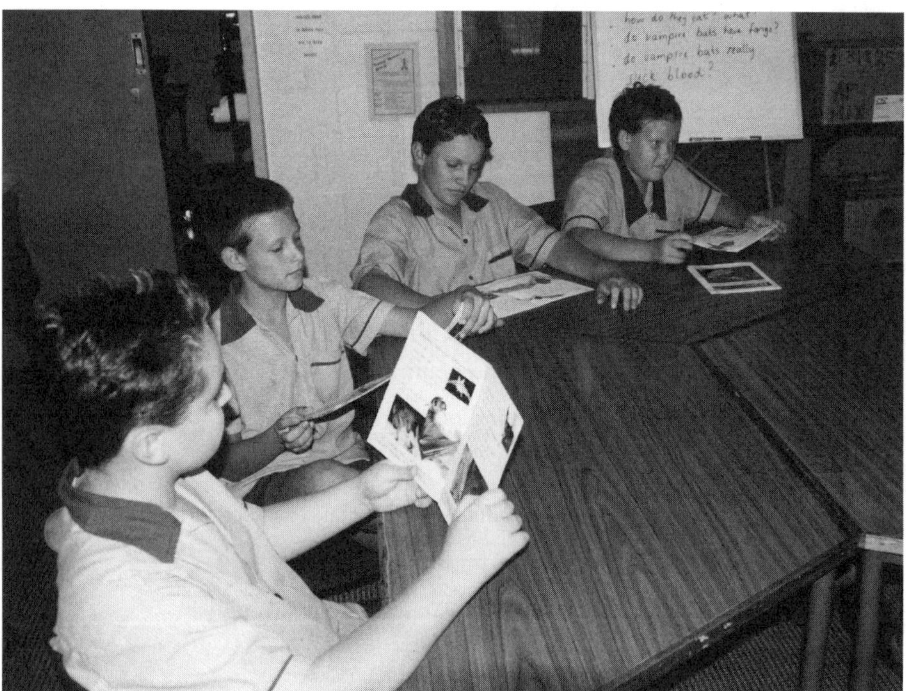

Students can work quietly as a group provided they understand the part they play in maintaining a positive classroom environment.

Ashman and Conway (1993) developed a model called Process-Based Instruction (PBI) in which teachers and students develop metacognitive skills through the structure of a plan (see Gillies, Chapter 8, this volume, for a more elaborate description of PBI). In PBI, a plan is a sequence of steps leading to the solution of the task, and contains four components: cueing, acting, monitoring, and verifying. The critical component for the student with a behaviour problem is monitoring, as the ability to use feedback to assess the effects of his or her own behaviour is a critical variable missing from the student's behaviour repertoire. It is also the critical variable missing from traditional behaviour management programs, in which the assessor and reinforcer of behaviour is the teacher.

Initially the plan is developed cooperatively by teacher and student while the student learns to take responsibility for his or her own behaviour. As the student is able to accept responsibility, the teacher takes on an advisory role, and the student adapts the existing behaviour plan or develops a new plan. It is important that teachers assist in the acquisition of skills, rather than assuming that the student has the skills to take responsibility. Inservice programs emphasise the importance of teachers being thoroughly conversant with the concepts before assisting the student.

Using general learning or counselling advice

Teachers have access to advice from within the school, and from external sources. Most education departments employ specialist resource teachers who assist schools to meet the needs of students with learning difficulties. Specialist resource teachers also often assist with associated behavioural difficulties, particularly when no specialist behaviour support teacher is available.

Assistance to teachers and students is also provided through school counselling services, either within the school or in clinics. School counsellors are a valuable resource in providing ongoing assessment of students with behaviour disorders, in supporting the regular class teacher, and in making referrals to government and non-government agencies.

The use of welfare committees and/or discipline committees in schools provides a further avenue of assistance for teachers. Although some school staff recognise the need to keep the operation of these two groups separate, they do serve a common purpose of meeting the needs of students. If they operate in isolation this can convey the impression that the discipline committee takes the tough decisions whereas the welfare committee is for the soft options. In reality, both should work to ensure that the safety net of student welfare services is implemented to provide social skills and coping strategies before the student is punished or suspended for failing to demonstrate these skills unassisted. The use of Year advisers as student counsellors, rather than relying solely on school counsellors and psychologists for formal counselling, has considerable support from high school staff and students.

Developing individualised behaviour plans

If the student has significant emotional and behavioural problems such that he or she cannot function within the class and school behaviour system, individualised behavioural instruction might be necessary. To develop a behaviour intervention plan, a functional behaviour assessment will have been completed. The plan comprises part of the total Individual Educational Plan (IEP) which provides the overall educational program for the student.

Research and classroom practice have shown that reactive programs following negative behaviour are ineffective in preventing a recurrence of the behaviour because such reactive programs fail to teach acceptable replacement behaviours. Similarly, implementing package programs that teach specific skills often fail to address the specific needs of each student and might never address the real reason for the student's initial misbehaviour. "Knowing what compels a student to engage in a particular behavior is integral to the development of effective, individualized positive behavioral intervention plans and supports" (CECP, 2000, p. 3).

The Behaviour Intervention Plan (BIP) is developed, implemented, and monitored through a four step procedure that continues on from the sixth step of the functional behavioural assessment (CECP, 2000). These steps are outlined below.

Develop and implement a behaviour intervention plan

The behaviour plan includes (where appropriate): strategies and supports; program modifications; and supplementary aids and services that might need to be provided. Within the American system there are forms that can be used to complete a behaviour intervention plan (see e.g., CECP, 2000). These might assist in the development of the plan and can be accessed through the CECP website (without copyright restrictions) at <www.air.org/cecp>.

When the plan is complete it provides strategies that:

(a) teach the student more appropriate ways to get what he or she wants;

(b) decrease further occurrences of the misbehaviour; and

(c) address any repeated episodes of the misbehaviour.

Hence, the final plan is really a series of interventions that addresses these three needs. As the plan consists of multiple intervention strategies, CECP suggests a number of techniques that might be useful. Rosenberg et al. (1997) is another good source of intervention strategies. The following strategies are suggested.

Children of all ages can benefit from a quiet time by themselves.

- Teach more acceptable replacement behaviours that serve the same function as the inappropriate behaviour, or use conflict resolution skills, or use alternative strategies such as self-management or coping.
- Teach how to deal with the physical location such as the layout of the classroom or places that are safe to play in the playground. Often this is referred to as changing the setting events.
- Manipulate the things that happen before the behaviour (antecedents), such as changing the teaching materials or teacher instructions.
- Manipulate what happens after the misbehaviour (consequences), such as how you react. Think about reinforcing an incompatible behaviour instead.
- Change the teaching–learning ecology of the classroom—what you teach, and how you teach it.

These strategies form the basis of the plan that is then tailored to meet the specific needs of the student.

If the behaviour difficulties are specific—such as attention-seeking behaviour, or escape-motivated behaviour—the behaviour intervention plan needs to address the specific needs of the student. The use of a chart can demonstrate which behaviours are

used by the student to obtain something, and which behaviours are used to avoid something. Remember, the behaviours of each student may be different for the same desired outcomes which is why each student who is causing a severe behavioural disruption in the class will need a specific behaviour assessment and intervention plan.

Monitor the faithfulness of implementation of the plan

The monitoring of the plan is a check on the consistency and accuracy of the its implementation. This can take the form of a checklist drawn up from the various components of the behaviour intervention plan. It is recommended that monitoring occurs regularly on a three to five-day cycle.

Evaluate the effectiveness of the plan

Using the baseline data collected during the functional behaviour assessment, and that collected during the intervention, it is possible to determine whether the intervention has achieved its aims. If there is no positive change,and a severe behaviour problem is very resistant to change, it might be necessary to reconsider the functional behavioural assessment.

Modify the behavioural intervention plan

The plan must be modified if the goals have been achieved. New goals need to be established if the intervention no longer addresses the current needs of the student, if there is a change in the placement of the student, or if the existing plan is not producing a positive behavioural change.

Behaviour assessment or intervention does not work effectively when the teacher and other support personnel need to look at whether the assessment has targeted the correct behaviours, whether the plan has been correctly constructed and implemented and whether the teacher is actively supporting the intervention appropriately.

Specialist behaviour services

Although students, support personnel, and executive staff expect that teachers will handle most of behaviour problems within the regular classroom by themselves, there are some students whose behaviour requires specialist assistance. If the student is causing problems in other classes or in other places (such as the playground) it might be appropriate to seek specialist assistance. Confident teachers are aware that additional assistance can be requested, and are willing to seek such assistance when needed. Working with behaviour support services can enhance the learning and social environment for all students in the class. Such assistance can be provided in the class, or through short-term intensive withdrawal.

Specialist assistance with behaviour disorders

The main focus of specialist behaviour services is the provision of assistance to teachers and students in managing behaviour disorders such that students can remain within the regular school. Each of the education departments in the various states and territories has different provisions for services, and even within states variations occur in the operation of a particular service.

In New South Wales, the Support Teacher (Behaviour), or ST-B, model is a good example of a specialist advisory service for teachers of students with behaviour disorders. Although it operates slightly differently in each education district in New South Wales, the ST-B model is designed to provide services to teachers of students who:

- present continuing behavioural and adjustment difficulties (e.g., they fail to respond to the usual range of management strategies employed by the regular school); and
- are likely to benefit by maintenance in their regular class with provision of specialist support to the classroom teacher(s).

The ST-B works in a role similar to the support teacher learning. Although the ST-B might provide individual or small group assistance in some circumstances, the role is essentially to consult and team-teach. Unlike the learning difficulties support model, referral to the ST-B follows a more formal sequence. Teacher referrals are usually made through the school counsellor, to a district behaviour team leader, with each ST-B serving a cluster of schools. Box 5.2 (page 214) provides a typical day in the life of an ST-B. Notice that the ST-B role involves considerable skill in balancing, at the same time, the needs of difficult students and their teachers across a number of schools.

An additional group of support teachers at this level in some states, are the itinerant teachers. These teachers provide support to students who are emotionally disturbed, but who are able to cope with full-time or part-time mainstream placements. Support is also provided to the teachers of these students. The students might have received early intervention support prior to school entry, or might have had a previous placement in a special school for the emotionally disturbed.

Teacher inservice training packages are used in some states and territories to supplement behaviour services or to provide teachers with additional information on behaviour strategies. In some cases specialist behaviour teachers provide staff inservices based on the available resources. A current example is the *Strategies for safer schools program* (NSW Department of School Education, 1995a). This three-part staff development package assists the school staff to develop discipline policies and practices that make schools into safer learning environments through an understanding of issues

Box 5.2 A day in the life of a Support Teacher Behaviour

8.30 am–8.55 am

Address primary staff meeting on management strategies for Attention Deficit Hyperactivity Disorder. Most of the staff members are receptive, finding that the ideas have relevance for all students. One vocal dissenter wonders why ADHD didn't exist 20 years ago. It is difficult to cover the topic in 25 minutes, but I'm aware that there are other topics on the staff meeting agenda. One teacher follows me outside to discuss the possibility that her son has ADHD symptoms and how she might get a professional assessment. It's not my role but I offer some quick suggestions anyway.

I slip a note in the pigeonhole of a Year 3 teacher to remind her of our meeting and her release from face-to-face teaching tomorrow.

Travel to a nearby high school.

9.40 am–10.20 am

Social skills group with four males in Years 7 and 8. Group arrives with surliness, physical hostility, and verbal reticence. I find it need to allow eight minutes debriefing at the beginning of the session for them to air their frustrations about school, certain teachers, boring lessons, and disciplinary consequences they are suffering. I encourage conformity, positive thinking, and commonsense. I run the session on the topic of peaceful resolution of conflict. They remain on-task and ask if they can stay for an extra period, but I give a friendly refusal. In the last five minutes, I attempt to make them less vocal, as teachers have complained that they are overconfident and outspoken when they return from my sessions.

Travel to a primary school two suburbs away.

10.55 am

Chat to the principal about a Year 5 student (C) who engages male teachers in verbal battles and power plays. I suggest that perhaps the teachers could be advised to model a calm, rational approach rather than escalating the conflict, as appears to be happening. The principal discloses frustration in previous attempts to implement this change in some staff members, despite providing training in Change Theory/Reality Therapy (CT/RT).

"They are angry at the system and all of the changes. It's hard enough keeping them on side as it is!"

I watch the student briefly during recess, noting positive and negative social skills.

11.25 am

Quick chat with the school counsellor to plan the content and approach for the ensuing meeting with C's parents.

11.30 am

Interview with the school counsellor and C's parents. The purpose is to encourage the parents to build C's self-esteem, modify the domestic emotional abuse that the student reports, and advise them of the behaviour management program we have implemented. Also suggest they visit a family counselling service and talk about the importance of ongoing check-ups for C's recurring glue ear (that caused hearing problems in infants' school and delayed acquisition of writing and speech).

I give quick feedback to the principal.

Travel to District Office and drink a few sips of mineral water from the Esky kept on the passenger seat.

12.15 pm

Arrive at District Office and hand in mail for posting. Touch base with the senior education oficer (SEO) about a submission for some teacher's aide time for some students. The SEO hands over four new applications for IST-B service. I pass the Aboriginal community liaison officer who advises me of the results of her intervention with the family of one of my cases.

Travel to my base, which is in the grounds of a school near the District Office. It is home to two school liaison officers (HSLOs), three support teachers (ST-B) and one substitute care teacher.

12.45 pm

Check the mail and clear the answering machine. A school counsellor wants me to fax him a program for dealing with teasing. A high school teacher wants to borrow our Bill Rogers video. A principal wants someone to ring him urgently. A Department of Community Services officer wants me to ring. One of my cases has had his first epileptic fit at the weekend and the teacher wants to know how this will affect the program we are running. I collect resource sheets for this afternoon's and tomorrow's sessions and do some photocopying. I discuss with a HSLO a student we have in common and the problems we are having with staff resistance in a certain high school.

1.20 pm

Travel to a secondary school three suburbs away. Eat lunch from the Esky. The departmental car is automatic and this makes eating lunch easier.

The aim of my visit to this school is to get feedback from the head teacher (student welfare), have a social skills lesson with a student, and have half an hour with an aide (to reassure her, give her some resources, and reinforce the program).

1.50 pm

I seek the head teacher (student welfare) for quick feedback on an outspoken, defiant, attention-seeking Year 7 student, but the head teacher is away. The student doesn't turn up for our period and I go to the office to check the roll, but the deputy principal sees me and says: "*Your* kid has been suspended."

It appears that the student has continued to abuse teachers and has put in a written complaint that teachers are harassing him for using the staff toilet. The aide is also not present.

2.10 pm

Now I have half an hour to spare! I decide to make a quick trip to the primary school across the road to monitor the progress of a Year 6 student who has had two suspensions for "running amok" and assaulting peers. He's on an anger-control program and has been referred to a psychologist. The teacher wants an urgent five-minute chat outside the classroom. She tells me that the student has spoken of a nice man friend who lets him use his spa, plays tickling games with him, and buys the student expensive gifts. The student has become withdrawn and is not making eye contact. I discuss the protective behaviours program with the teacher and remind her of the compulsory notification policy.

I pass the school counsellor who wants a quick chat about submitting a referral for a child from another school.

2.35 pm

I ring the Year 6 student's psychologist about our sessions, which have the same purpose. I inform him of the potential paedophile in case he wants to pursue the issue as well.

There is a message from the school secretary to ring the principal of another school urgently. I ring and he is having an "urgent" case conference tomorrow morning and wants an IST-B to attend. He also wants advice for the class teacher who has taken three days' stress leave because of this student.

I suggest that he contact the staff welfare officer.

I return to the problems of the Year 6 boy at the present school, and have a brief discussion with the principal about the boy's pleasing lack of violence recently.

3.25 pm

I go to the car, which also serves as an office, and complete the itinerary for the day. I jot down a summary of today's cases and put them in the relevant files (otherwise they slide around the car as I travel!). I insert the case conference into tomorrow's already crowded diary and make some adjustments to the plans for the day. I cross out the time that I had allotted for programming and updating of files on the computer, leave the RFF meeting in its time-slot and shift a planned in-class observation.

3.45 pm

No inservices or staff meetings today, so it's home to start on my own kids!

such as bullying, classroom management and conflict resolution. In addition, there are many commercial programs available that specialist behaviour teachers can use in assisting individual teachers and school staff.

Withdrawal behavioural services in the regular school

For the 1–7% of students with more severe behaviour problems that are beyond services that can be provided at the school and small-group level in the Effective Behaviour Support model (Lewis & Sugai, 1999), there is the possibility, in some educational systems, of limited short-term withdrawal by a specialist behaviour disorder teacher or integration teacher. In some states, large schools might have a special needs support unit within the school to meet a wide range of special needs, including behaviour disorders. Support units are able to provide a wider range of services than can supply individual resources and support teachers. Within regular schools, specialist teachers can conduct small-group withdrawal sessions on social skills training and can establish behavioural programs (see Box 5.2, page 214).

In some schools, funding has been provided to combat bullying or general anti-violence measures have been used to establish programs within schools. Often these are short-term because of the nature of the funding. In some cases schools might pool funds to run a program to meet local needs. Examples of these are discussed in the following section as they are specialist programs often operated in alternative settings such as police-citizens clubs. Lockhart and Hay (1995) provided an example of the work that can occur through short-term school-based programs. Their program was designed to meet the needs of a group of girls from a Brisbane high school who were at risk of suspension because of their classroom behaviour and their poor academic performance.

The program focused on the development of self-esteem and social skills through a cognitive-focused training program combined with a physical activity course. They demonstrated the importance of providing assistance at the school level to maintain enrolment, rather than using the discipline policy to remove the students and then have to look for alternative services. Students maintained their enrolment in the school following the conclusion of the training.

Specific behaviour problems in regular schools

There are some students who provide specific challenges to teachers and schools in general. These are those with Attention Deficit Hyperactivity Disorder (ADHD), those who bully, and those with Asperger's Syndrome. Each of these is discussed below, with specific strategies that might assist in meeting the behavioural needs of students with these diagnoses.

Attention Deficit Hyperactivity Disorder

Attention Deficit Hyperactivity Disorder (ADHD) was previously known as a group of behaviour problems, including disruption, inattention, impulsivity and hyperactivity (Carroll, 1994). All students display these behaviours at some time—they become behaviour problems only when they are more frequent or more severe than usual for that age. Today such behaviour is known as ADHD, with two main types: predominantly hyperactive and predominantly inattentive (Houghton et al., 1999). The specific behaviour patterns for each of the two subtypes are shown in Box 5.3 (page 219).

We know that there is a strong genetic component to ADHD. Students with ADHD might have trouble with:

- remaining seated;
- following instructions;
- concentrating on one task;
- taking turns;
- finishing work;
- understanding and following rules;
- organising tasks; and
- working and playing in groups.

Although the student is likely to have a formal diagnosis by a paediatrician and might be on medication, there is a number of strategies that can be implemented. The New South Wales Department of School Education's *Talk time teamwork* publication (NSW Department of School Education, 1995b) recommends several strategies. The document highlights that "medication does not replace the need for an effective teaching program" (p. 3). The recommendations include:

- a structured environment (home, class, playground) and uncluttered desk space;
- being taught how to organise time, work space, and work tasks;
- appropriate placement in the classroom and supportive peers;
- rules and expectations clearly communicated and reinforced and frequent feedback on progress;
- clear design and communication of academic tasks so students can see progress, including step-by-step instructions given orally and visually;
- interactive teaching strategies and an allowance for slow speed of response;
- increased frequency, greater immediacy, and use of more relevant consequences;
- use of positive statements rather than negative ones, and the teaching of new behaviours;

Box 5.3 Diagnostic criteria for Attention Deficit Hyperactivity Disorder

A. SIGNS AND SYMPTOMS

Either (1) or (2):

(1) Six or more signs and symptoms of *inattention* that have persisted for at least six months such that they are maladaptive and inconsistent with developmental level.

These signs and symptoms of *inattention* are:

- fails to attend to details or makes careless mistakes in school work or other activities
- has difficulty sustaining attention in activities
- does not seem to listen when spoken to directly
- does not follow instructions and fails to finish work or duties (not due to oppositional behaviour or failure to understand instructions)
- has difficulty organising tasks and activities
- avoids, dislikes, or is reluctant to engage in tasks that need sustained mental effort
- loses things needed for tasks or activities (e.g., school assignments, pencils, or tools)
- is easily distracted by external stimuli
- is forgetful

OR

(2) Six or more signs and symptoms of *hyperactivity-impulsivity* that have persisted for at least six months such that they are maladaptive and inconsistent with developmental level.

These signs and symptoms of *hyperactivity* are:

- fidgets or squirms in seat
- leaves seat when remaining in seat is expected
- runs about or climbs excessively when it is inappropriate (might be limited to subjective feelings of restlessness)
- has difficulty playing or engaging in leisure activities quietly
- is "on the go"; talks excessively

The signs and symptoms of *impulsivity* are:

- blurts out answers before questions have been completed
- has difficulty awaiting a turn
- interrupts or intrudes on others (e.g., butts into conversations)

B. HISTORY

Some hyperactive-impulsive or attention symptoms that caused a problem were present before age seven years.

C. TWO OR MORE SETTINGS

Some impairment from the symptoms is present in two or more settings.

D. IMPAIRMENT

There must be evidence of clinically significant impairment in social, academic, or occupational functioning.

E. NOT DUE TO OTHER CAUSE

The symptoms do not occur exclusively during the course of a Pervasive Developmental Disorder, Schizophrenia, or other psychotic disorder, and are not better accounted for by another mental disorder (e.g., Mood Disorder, Anxiety Disorder, Dissociative Disorder, or a personality disorder).

Source: Adapted from American Psychiatric Association (1994, pp. 83–85).

- consistency in instructional methods and structuring of workload into manageable sections or mini-assignments;
- consistent routines for transition between activities and lessons; and
- coordination between home and school.

There is also a need for the teacher to work with parents and medical personnel if the student is on medication, particularly if the teacher is involved in the administration of medication (Purdie, Hattie, & Carroll, 2001). School systems have set procedures for the management of medications in schools, including those for students with specific behavioural needs. Teachers are also able to provide medical personnel with information on the effects of the medication during school time.

Bullying

Many students are affected by bullying at some time during their schooling—as a bully, as a victim, or as an observer. In some cases students are involved in more than one role. Students who bully might themselves be bullied by others. Bullying in schools affects more than 15% of students (Rigby, 1996). Bullying can occur at any age, affects boys and girls of all cultures and socioeconomic groups, and is a major issue for many schools in Australasia. Two of the leading researchers on bullying, Rigby and Slee, are Australians, and they have conducted many studies in Australian schools.

Bullying has been defined as a power imbalance between, and exploitation of, people that is random and has the intent to injure (Slee, 1993). Bullying has many forms: verbal; physical; extortion; damage to property; isolation; gestures; and intimidation. Bullying frequently occurs out of teachers' sight, often in the playground. Although students do not like bullying they commonly do not expose bullies, and not to their teachers if they do. Hence, studies of bullying in schools often reveal levels of which school staff were unaware.

The consequences of bullying for the victim include physical injury, loss of confidence and self-esteem, school avoidance, and loss of friends (as they can be despised by others). Bullies can become more aggressive, more demanding, more brazen over time and can attract students who seek association with powerful students in the school.

Dealing with bullying requires a whole-school approach that includes teachers, students, and parents. Seven aspects of the school need to be addressed in a total approach: victim; bully; school environment; role modelling; administration; curriculum; and teaching. Before tackling the specific problems, the school needs to know the actual extent of bullying, the types of bullying, its frequency and severity, where it occurs, who is involved and why. This can occur through surveys of students, checks of the playground, record keeping and an examination of the school discipline and administrative procedures. Once the extent and nature of the problem are known, a policy can be put in place. To do this, all staff members, students and parents need to be involved in implementing and maintaining the policy of no bullying. Staff training and development ideas can be found in *Strategies for safer schools part 3* (NSW Department of School Education, 1995a), as well as in resources such as Rigby (1996).

Asperger's Syndrome

In broad terms, Asperger's Syndrome is a neurological disorder in which social relationships are impaired, difficult and not age-appropriate. Both verbal and non-verbal communication is affected. The student has restricted interests and repetitive behaviours are common (The University of Kansas Medical Center, 2000). It is important to realise that a student with Asperger's Syndrome does not have the same learning and behavioural profile as a student with classic autism (Attwood, 1998)

The specific behavioural criteria were developed as diagnostic criteria for Asperger's Syndrome (see Garnett & Atwood, 1994). They identified the following characteristics.

- Social impairment (extreme egocentricity) with at least two of the following dispositions: inability to interact with peers; lack of desire to interact with peers; lack of appreciation of social cues; socially and emotionally inappropriate behaviour.
- Narrow interest to the extent of at least one of the following: exclusion of other activities; repetitive adherence; more rote than meaning.
- Repetitive routines including at least one related to self or to others.
- Speech and language peculiarities displaying at least three of the following: delayed development; superficially perfect expressive language; formal pedantic language; odd prosody, peculiar voice characteristic; impairment of comprehension including misinterpretations of literal and implied meanings.

- Nonverbal communication problems with at least one of the following: limited use of gesture; clumsy or gauche body language; limited facial expression; inappropriate expression; peculiar stiff gaze.
- Motor clumsiness (poor performance on neuro-developmental examination).

The original diagnostic criteria were modified in the form of a school-aged screening questionnaire by Ehlers, Gillberg, and Wing (1999). There is also an *Australian Scale for Asperger's Syndrome* for primary school children that is now in its second edition (Garnett & Attwood, 1994). This version has the advantage of using a five-point Likert Scale (from rarely to frequently) rather than a checklist. It has been developed for primary children because the authors argue that this is when the unusual patterns of behaviours and abilities are most conspicuous (see Garnett & Attwood, 2000).

There are four emerging educational issues for students with Asperger's Syndrome: screening and assessment; placement; educational support; and social skills instruction. The first issue is addressed in the screening methods discussed above. The issue of educational placement and support is confused because the student is not acutely disturbed, and does not have an intellectual disability that is severe enough to warrant either specialist psychiatric or developmental disability services. Hence, the student is most often placed in the regular classroom. In many ways this provides the most appropriate placement as other students might provide models of appropriate social behaviour. In some regular schools, specialist assistance might be available. For example, in New South Wales there is specific training for specialist behaviour teachers to provide assistance to schools, and Queensland has specialist advisory visiting teachers to provide assistance.

Attwood (2000) identified a number of teacher characteristics that are important for assisting students with Asperger's Syndrome. He suggested that teachers need to have a calm disposition, be predictable in their emotional reactions, be flexible in teaching style and curriculum presentation to accommodate the child, and recognise his or her positive aspects. A sense of humour helps as the child can change from one emotional state to another within seconds.

As change is a critical issue for the student, a stable quiet classroom is important. A supportive, calm regular teacher in a small well-ordered room is preferable. Changes in school—particularly in the transition phases from early education to primary, and from primary to secondary—are critical times, and multiple orientation sessions are important. Having teacher and student buddies is also helpful. Secondary schools can be very difficult due to the academic structure of schooling, combined with the difficulties of adolescence. In these circumstances, the chance of negative social interactions increases dramatically as the stability of the primary school is replaced by constant change.

In secondary school, there is a risk that students with Asperger's Syndrome will develop an anxiety disorder, an obsessive–compulsive disorder, depression, or aggression in response to the attitudes of teachers and students. Some will end up being expelled as a result of their unusual behaviour patterns and parents might seek alternative placements for their children, often in specialist settings comprised of other students with the same needs.

Students with Asperger's Syndrome vary greatly in their performance from day to day. One day they concentrate, conform, socialise, and learn fairly well, wheras on other days the reverse is true. Attwood (2000) identified this as a series of internal waves or tides in the student that affects performance. On the positive tides, it is time to learn, whereas, on the off-tide revision is a better approach.

Social skills training has been identified as the fourth area of need. Attwood (2000) recommended that one-to-one training might be provided by either a specialist behaviour teacher or a trained teacher's aide. Specific aspects of support include:

- encouragement to be sociable, flexible, and cooperative when playing or working with other children;
- help for the child to recognise social cues and learn the codes of social conduct;
- provision of personal tuition on understanding and managing emotions;
- tuition and practice to improve friendship and teamwork skills;
- help for the student to develop special interests as a means of improving motivation, talent and knowledge;
- a program to improve gross and fine motor skills;
- encouragement to take perspectives of others; and
- encouragement to develop conversation skills.

Any social skills program needs to include cognitive, linguistic, and sensory abilities.

A summary of questions and possible solutions for the management of behaviour problems in the classroom is shown in Table 5.3 (page 224). These were drawn from Daniels (1998) and are given as a list of questions that teachers can ask themselves in relation to managing disruptive behaviour in the classroom. Note that the first question relates to a behaviour that is teacher-controlled: curriculum and teaching strategies. The questions and answers have been modified to fit Australian circumstances.

When reading through them, reconsider the two case studies at the beginning of this chapter and think about the teaching and management approaches used by the teachers, and the relevance of the choices to the students with behaviour problems and to other students in the class. Also think of the classroom situations you have experienced.

Table 5.3 Teaching hints—Questions to ask in managing disruptive behaviour in inclusive classrooms

Questions to ask	Possible actions
1. Could this misbehaviour be the result of inappropriate curriculum or teaching strategies?	Possibly the diverse needs of students are not being met. Identify the blockages to learning (curriculum content, resources, and equipment). Adapting teaching and learning can reduce the occurrence of student misbehaviour.
2. Could this misbehaviour be the result of the student's inability to understand the concepts being taught?	Use task analysis to check prerequisite skills, learning styles, and ability to determine the functional level of students and assist them in moving to mastery of relevant skills.
3. Could this misbehaviour be an underlying result of the student's disability?	A knowledge base of the disability and potential behaviour problems is useful (e.g., autism).
4. Could this misbehaviour be a result of other factors?	The ecology of the classroom is important beyond the instructional issues in question 1 above. This includes how students and teachers interact and respond to the included student.
5. Are these causes of misbehaviour that I can control?	The level and forms of feedback to the student are important.
6. How do I determine if the misbehaviour is classroom based?	Again the classroom ecology is important and conducting a functional assessment might be useful, including identifying events, variables, and circumstances that contribute to the problem.
7. How do I teach students to self-regulate or self-manage behaviour?	Teaching students to self-instruct, self-monitor and self-reinforce have been shown to be successful in reducing behaviour problems.
8. How do I determine what methods of control are appropriate without violating the rights of students with disabilities?	Under the Australian Commonwealth and state Disability Discrimination Acts, certain management procedures might be illegal. In addition, use of physical restraint might not be permitted in some educational services. Remember to be positive in feedback including the use of words, facial expressions, closeness, activities, and rewards.
9. How do I use reinforcement strategies to reduce disruptive behaviour?	Reinforcement needs to be continuous and systematic over time. Reinforcing alternative positive behaviours and incompatible behaviours have been found to be useful.

QUESTIONS TO ASK	POSSIBLE ACTIONS
10. Is it appropriate for me to use punishment?	Punishment does not have to be physical. It includes time out, loss of earned rewards (response cost), restitution, and overcorrection. Any punishment should be paired with reinforcement of positive behaviours. It should not be the first or prime management strategy.

Source: Adapted from Daniels (1998).

Services beyond the regular school

In considering educational options, the focus is on the provision of services rather than on specific programs. There are no formal curricula for students in special placements, and student attendance is not regarded as permanent. Most special placements follow one of two approaches. They are:

1. regular curricula with strong emphasis on social and personal development skills to assist the student to return to the regular class; or
2. alternative programs aimed at social skills development and preparation for post-school options such as employment or further job training programs.

Special behaviour disorder or emotionally disturbed classes and units

The level of specialist classes and units for students provides one of the largest and most diverse ranges of service for children and adolescents with behaviour problems. Full-time and part-time special classes and units are provided in all Australian states and in New Zealand, although the terminology, function, and operational definition of services differ within and among jurisdictions. In many Australian states and territories there is a distinction between behaviour disorder programs at the primary level and conduct disorder programs at the secondary level, although there are clear overlaps both in diagnosis and service provision.

One of the major difficulties confronting secondary conduct disorder units has been their objective to meet the needs of adolescents who were unable, or unwilling, to comply with the discipline and academic constraints of the secondary school. As an alternative environment, secondary conduct units have been able to act as a transition to the post-school world through the provision of work experience programs, access to job training courses and leisure activities. This has worked well for many students aged 14–15 years. However, the increasing number of referrals of students in the first year of high school, or even directly from primary schools, has placed competing demands

on these services because these younger students are ineligible for work experience placements. Consequently, the focus for this group is more commonly on academic skills with the aim of reintegration into mainstream secondary programs.

Another outcome of the failure of secondary schools to cater for students who have behaviour problems is the rapid expansion of specialist adolescent behaviour programs. As discussed above, many of these programs were developed by pooling resources across two or three schools to provide an alternative program for students. A major achievement of the locally based programs has been the satisfaction of specific local needs, particularly those of socially disadvantaged communities and minority communities.

There is no universal support for the development of separate programs. It has been argued that such centres are unlikely to change teacher behaviour and school environments that contribute to disruptive behaviours. Off-site centres might reduce the likelihood of regular schools attempting to alter their approach because they could send their troublesome students to another location. Not having access to off-site units places the responsibility for catering for students with disruptive behaviours back on regular classrooms and schools, and thus encourages the development of more effective whole school policies.

To overcome the problems of reintegrating students from special classes, many programs now operate either with half-day attendance at the class (with the remainder of the day in the student's regular class), or with four days at the special class and one day in the regular class. These models have distinct advantages for the students and special class teacher as they avoid the need for students to leave their home school and enable the special class teacher to integrate social and academic programs with those of the class in which the behaviour disorder was demonstrated. In addition, part-time placement avoids the need to arrange reintegration of students into schools in which the staff might otherwise have perceived that the problem student had been successfully removed. A potential disadvantage in part-time placement is the occasional need to separate the students from the home school environment. This allows the student, teachers, and peers relief from continued confrontation.

Following placement in the special class, some students might be more appropriately integrated into a neighbouring school than be reintegrated into, or continue enrolment in, the home school. This is most common when return to the home school would prejudice the gains made during special class placement.

In most Australian states, special classes for students with severe behaviour disorders (emotionally disturbed students) are provided in small units attached to regular primary and secondary schools. Students attending these units are usually assessed by Education Department personnel (such as school counsellors and regional guidance staff), and by Department of Health staff (such as psychiatric services personnel).

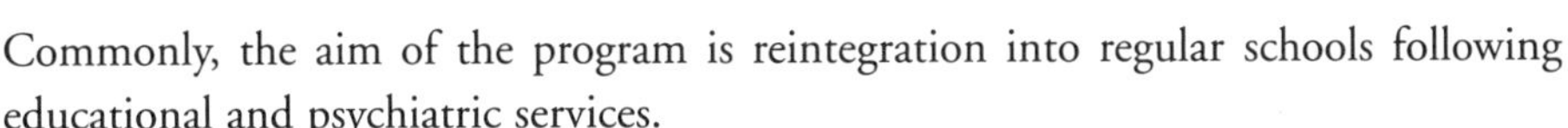

Commonly, the aim of the program is reintegration into regular schools following educational and psychiatric services.

Other students with emotional disturbance are educated in special schools. Another option is to have outreach teachers assist students (previously enrolled full-time in units or schools for those diagnosed as emotionally disturbed) integrate back into regular education settings either full-time or part-time.

An interesting trend in the United States is the establishment of an increasing number of private schools for students with behaviour problems, conduct disorders, or emotional disturbance, as well as a large growth industry in private juvenile correction facilities. Although levels of private schooling are very high in Australia, the development of private schools for students with emotional and behavioural problems has been very small. It is of interest that the reasons given by many parents for enrolling their children in private schools are avoidance of behaviour problems in government schools and avoidance of the perceived lack of discipline in the state school system.

Residential schools and shared facilities

Residential schools for students with behavioural disorders are provided:

- as specialist private schools; or
- as facilities operated by education departments on premises belonging to departments of health, community welfare, or juvenile justice.

The most common educational facilities at level 6 within the cascade model (Figure 5.1, page 195) are units within psychiatric facilities in regular hospitals, designated psychiatric hospitals, or within juvenile justice detention facilities.

In all Australian states and territories, and in New Zealand, residential facilities are provided for young offenders and educational services exist on-site for school-aged residents. Behavioural disorders of young offenders are a major concern because, while they are in detention, they cost taxpayers considerable amounts of money. There is also concern that adolescents from minority groups are disproportionately represented in the juvenile justice systems in Australia and New Zealand.

Because education staff members working in juvenile justice facilities are operating in a setting that typically belongs to juvenile justice, education staff can have difficulty gaining access to space. In addition, the movement of students and the daily management of inmates is controlled by youth workers. Educational programs, therefore, rely on the inmate being allowed to attend by juvenile justice staff. As the educational training and philosophies of teachers might differ from those of youth workers, conflict can arise when approaches to student management differ.

Educational services for students with emotional disturbance are also provided through residential psychiatric facilities in hospitals and clinics. The ownership of the

facility buildings by a hospital, with programs under the control of medical staff, can again be a problem for education staff who provide just one facet of the total program.

The issue of reintegration

One of the prime concerns of placements at all levels discussed in this chapter is the goal of reintegration of students with behaviour problems into regular school settings or the maintenance of such students in the regular classroom. Studies in Australian schools (Center, Ward, Ferguson, Conway, & Linfoot, 1991) have shown that students with behaviour problems are among the least acceptable of students with special needs for reintegration. In the case of adolescents with a history of prior behaviour problems, there is a strong reluctance on the part of secondary school staff to accept them back in their home schools, and even a reluctance to accept out-of-area placements (Conway, 1994). Hence, meeting the needs of these students not only involves providing the specialist programs, but also involves having students accepted back into the regular school. For many secondary students, the aim of specialist conduct disorder settings is not to reintegrate students but to look for alternative, non-school placements—such as technical and further education (TAFE) and employment—and assistance in acquiring personal and social skills for post-school settings.

One method of ensuring this is either to maintain the student part-time in the regular class throughout the specialist intervention, or to secure a post intervention placement prior to accepting the student. Where full-time withdrawal occurs, academic and social skill training in special classes and schools (in preparation for re-entry to mainstream education) must be accompanied by preparation in the regular class.

To enhance the placement of students with behaviour problems in regular classes, teachers and specialist staff need to focus on those skills that assist students to be absorbed into the regular classroom with minimum focus on their difficulties. As discussed earlier this requires both staff and students to develop specific and general skills that are mutually supportive.

SUMMARY

Behaviour disorders, perhaps more than most other special needs areas, challenge both regular and special needs educators. Students exhibiting severe behaviour disorders are among the first to be referred out of regular classes and are among the last to be socially integrated back into them. Such students are seen to threaten teacher discipline and to contribute to teacher stress.

The term *behaviour disorder* cannot be defined objectively because it applies to a constellation of influences that include people's perceptions and values, situational factors, the needs of educational systems, and differing perceptions of helping

professionals. The definition adopted in this chapter reflects the link between normal and disordered behaviour and is sufficiently broad to encompass the range of severity of behaviour disorders. From time to time we all demonstrate behaviours that could be considered disordered. What makes behaviours disordered is their exhibition in the wrong places, at the wrong time, in the presence of the wrong people, and to an inappropriate extent.

Allowing for the variety of definitions used nationally and by states, the prevalence figure for students with behaviour disorders in Australian schools is in the range 3.2 to 4.3%. Prevalence is not uniform, with higher incidence levels occurring in specific locations and in specific socioeconomic and cultural groups.

Behaviour disorders have been linked to biological, social, environmental, cultural, and psychological causes. From the perspective of educators, home, school and peers provide important contributing factors and these need to be addressed in the provision of assistance. Although the behavioural approach has been widely used in regular and specialist settings in the past, there is growing awareness of the need to consider other approaches, particularly ecological influences and the importance of social skills training and problem-solving. There is also an increased awareness of the contributions that other professions make, and the need to work in conjunction with the methods and approaches of other professions.

There is no one accepted measure of behaviour disorders, and classroom teachers, counsellors, and specialist behaviour disorders teachers must select from a wide range of checklists, rating scales, projective tests, interviews, and classroom observation schedules. Of these, classroom observations are perhaps the most effective, particularly if used in combination with other techniques that seek information from home and peers. For students with severe behaviour problems, the use of functional behavioural assessment provides a systematic and detailed basis for the development of an effective behavioural intervention plan.

Students with behaviour disorders display a range of behavioural characteristics. Those with mild behaviour disorders might demonstrate poor academic achievement, poor interpersonal relations and poor self-esteem. Students with severe behaviour disorders might demonstrate extreme and unprovoked aggression, and very poor interpersonal skills.

The lack of adequate definitions, assessment, and diagnostic techniques increases the difficulty of identifying students in need of additional services. Inappropriate identification often results in inappropriate intervention procedures in the regular school, including the widespread use of restrictive discipline procedures. Thus, students with severe behaviour disorders might be misidentified, leading to suspension or expulsion, rather than to appropriate educational services. Adolescents who are unable or unwilling to comply with regular secondary education need access

to alternative education programs during their school years in order to develop the social and behavioural skills needed in the post-school environment. Removal of funding for alternative adolescent programs increases the level of behaviour problems in the adult population and increases the cost to society.

In many states, there has been a deliberate policy of not expanding segregated special class services to students with behaviour disorders, preferring to focus on preventative whole-school approaches. If the focus includes appropriate classroom instruction and cooperative approaches to learning, supplemented by specialist itinerant services, students with mild to moderate behaviour disorders should be able to learn beside their peers. However, for students with severe behaviour disorders, special education placement continues to be needed on either a full-time or part-time basis.

Suggested reading

Books and journal articles

Ashman, A. F. & Conway, R. N. F. (1997). *Introduction to cognitive education: Theory and applications*. London: Routledge.

Barber, C. (1996). The integration of a very able pupil with Asperger's syndrome into a mainstream school. *British Journal of Special Education*, 23, 19–24.

Dodd, S. M. (1994). *Managing problem behaviour: A practical guide for parents and teachers of young children with special needs*. Sydney: MacLennan & Petty.

Kauffman, J. M. (1997). *Characteristics of emotional and behaviour disorders in children and youth* (6th ed.). Columbus, OH: Merrill Publishing Company.

Leone, P. E., Mayer, M. J., Malmgren, K., & Meisel, S. M. (2000). School violence and disruption: Rhetoric, reality and reasonable balance. *Focus on Exceptional Children, 33*, September.

Porter, L. (2000). *Student behaviour: Theory and practice for teachers* (2nd ed.). Sydney: Allen & Unwin.

Websites

Council for Exceptional Children, <www.cec.sped.org>.

Council for Children with Behaviour Disorders, <www.ccbd.net>.

Positive Behavioral Support, <www.pbis.org>.

Center for Effective Collaboration and Practice, <www.air.org/cecp>.

Journals

There are several journals that specialise in the study of students with behavioural and emotional disorders. These include:

Behavioral Disorders;

Beyond Behavior;

Journal of Emotional and Behavioral Disorders; and

Reaching Today's Youth.

General special education, adolescent and behavioural journals also have relevant articles.

Practical activities

1. Consider a regular education classroom at the early childhood, primary, or secondary level in which some students are misbehaving. List possible contributing factors to the behavioural problems in the room, using the headings:
   - the physical environment;
   - the teacher;
   - the curriculum and its teaching; and
   - the students.

   What changes can be made to each of these to reduce the likelihood of the behaviour problems continuing?
2. Go to a local school and obtain a copy of its discipline and welfare policy. Look through the policy and identify the discipline approach(es) used. Can you identify both positive rewards and punishers? What positive strategies are used to encourage students who are unable to comply with the policy? Is there a link between welfare practices and discipline practices?
3. Select a specific behaviour disorder—such as Attention Deficit Hyperactivity Disorder (ADHD), conduct disorder, or oppositional defiance disorder—and carry out a brief library search on the topic. What are the main recommendations for teaching strategies?
4. Does your region or state have a definition and assessment protocol for identifying students with behaviour disorders? How does it correspond or differ from those in this chapter?
5. Why do teachers prefer that students who have behaviour problems be taught in special settings? What are the advantages of segregated settings? What are the disadvantages?
6. Why has there been an increase in the number of children in early childhood settings referred for behavioural assistance?

References

Aboriginal and Torres Strait Islander Commission (ATSIC). (1999). *Submission to the Human Rights and Equal Opportunity Commission Enquiry into rural and remote education in Australia.* (Online 9/11/2000). <www.atsic.gov.au/default-ns.asp>.

Achenbach, T. M. (1991). *Integrative guide to the 1991 CBCL, YSR and TRF Profiles.* Burlington, VT: University of Vermont, Department of Psychiatry.

Alberto, P.A. & Troutman, A. C. (1999). *Applied behavior analysis for teachers* (5th ed.) Englewood Cliffs, NJ: Merrill/Prentice Hall.

American Psychiatric Association. (1994). *Diagnostic and Statistical Manual of Mental Disorders: DSMIV* (4th ed.). Washington, DC: Author.

Ashman, A. F. & Conway, R. N. F. (1993). *Using cognitive strategies in the classroom.* London: Routledge.

Ashman, A. F. & Conway, R. N. F. (1997). *Introduction to cognitive education: Theory and applications.* London: Routledge.

Attwood, T. (1998). *Asperger's Syndrome: A guide for parents and professionals.* London: Jessica Kingsley Publications.

Attwood, T. (2000). Appropriate educational placements for children with Asperger's Syndrome. <www.tonyattwood.com>.

Beaman, R. & Wheldall, K. (1997). Teacher perceptions of troublesome classroom behaviour: A review of recent research. *Special Education Perspectives, 6,* 49–56.

Bor, W., Presland, I., Lavery, B., Christie, R., & Watson, K. (1991). Teachers' perceptions of students' adjustment difficulties. In J. Elkins & J. Izard. (Eds) *Student behaviour problems: Context, initiatives and programs* (pp. 77–94). Melbourne: ACER.

Bradley, G. (1992). Increasing student retention. *Youth Studies Australia, 11*(2), 37–42.

Bradley, G. (1994). Identifying students at risk of early withdrawal from secondary school. *Australian Educational and Developmental Psychologist, 11*(1), 1–7.

Canter, L. & Canter, M. (1992). *Assertive discipline: Positive behavior management for today's classroom.* Seal Beach, CA: Canter & Associates.

Carroll, A. (1994). Current perspectives on attention deficit in hyperactivity disorder: A review of literature. *Australasian Journal of Special Education, 18,* 15–24.

Carroll, A., Bain, A., & Houghton, S. (1994). The effects of interactive video versus linear video on the levels of attention and comprehension of social behavior. *School Psychology Review, 23,* 29–43.

Carroll, A., Houghton, S., Hattie, J., & Durkin, K., (1999). Adolescent reputation enhancement: Differentiating delinquent and nondelinquent youths. *The Journal of Child Psychology and Psychiatry and Allied Disciplines, 40,* 593–606.

Carroll, A., Hattie, J., Houghton, S., & Durkin, K. (in press). Goal setting and reputation enhancement among delinquent, at-risk adolescents. *Legal and Criminological Psychology.*

Center for Effective Collaboration and Practice (CECP). (1998a). *Addressing student problem behavior B Part 1: An IEP team's introduction to functional behavioral assessment and behavior intervention plans.* Washington DC: Author.

Center for Effective Collaboration and Practice (CECP). (1998b). *Addressing student problem behavior B Part 2: Conducting a functional behavioral assessment* (3rd ed). Washington DC: Author.

Center for Effective Collaboration and Practice (CECP). (2000). Addressing student problem behavior B Part 3: Creating positive behavioral intervention plans and supports (2nd ed.). Washington DC: Author.

Center for Effective Collaboration and Practice (CECP). (2000). *Addressing student problem behavior—Part III; Creating positive behavioral intervention plans and supports* (2nd ed.). Washington DC: Author.

Conway, R. N. F. (1994). Meeting the needs of adolescents with conduct disorders. In M. Tainsh & J. Izard (Eds), *Widening horizons: New challenges, directions and achievements* (pp. 12–27). Melbourne: ACER.

Conway, R. N. F. (2001). Adapting curriculum, teaching and learning strategies. In P. Foreman (Ed.), *Integration and inclusion in action* (2nd ed., pp. 262–310). Sydney: Harcourt Brace.

Conway, R. N. F., Schofield, N. J., & Tierney, J. T. (1991). *The Fair Discipline Code: A review of the application of the Fair Discipline Code in NSW secondary schools*. Report to the NSW Department of School Education. Newcastle, NSW: University of Newcastle.

Conway, R. N. F., Tierney, J. T., & Schofield, N. J. (1990). Coping with behaviour problems in NSW high schools. In S. Richardson & J. Izard (Eds) *Practical approaches to resolving behaviour problems*. Melbourne: ACER.

Council for Children with Behavior Disorders. (1995). *Proposed definition for emotional and behavioral disorders*. CCBD.

Cunneen, C. (1999). *Zero tolerance policing: Implications for indigenous people*, Arlington, VA. (Cited online 9/11/2000). <www.atsic.gov.au/zero-tolerance/2ztp.htm>.

Daniels, V. I. (1998). How to manage disruptive behavior in inclusive classrooms. *Teaching Exceptional Children, Mar/Apr*, 26–31.

Dwyer, K., Osher, D., & Warger, C. (1998). *Early warning, timely response: A guide to safe schools*. Washington: United States Department of Education.

Ehlers, S., Gillberg, C., & Wing, L. (1999). A screening questionnaire for Asperger's Syndrome and other high functioning autism spectrum disorders in school age children. *Journal of Autism and Developmental Disorders, 29*, 129–141.

Elksnin, L. K., & Elksnin, N. (1998). Teaching social skills to students with learning and behavior problems. *Intervention in School and Clinic, 33*, 131–140.

Garnett, M. S., & Attwood, T. (1994). *Australian Scale for Asperger's Syndrome* (2nd ed.). <www.tonyattwood.com>.

Garnett, M. S., & Attwood, T. (2000). *The Australian Scale for Asperger's Syndrome*. <www.tonyattwood.com>.

Gordon, C., Arthur, M., & Butterfield, N. (1996). *Promoting positive behaviour*. Melbourne: Nelson.

Guetzloe, E. (2000, November). *On a positive note: The prerequisites for positive behavior support in the classroom: Conditions, curriculum and consequences*. Paper presented at 24th Annual Conference of TECBD, Scottsdale, AZ.

Hemphill, S. A. (1996). Characteristics of conduct-disordered children and their families: A review. *Australian Psychologist, 31*, 109–118.

Holden, E. & Dwyer, P. (1992). *Making the break: Leaving school early*. Working paper No. 8. Melbourne: University of Melbourne, Institute of Education, Youth Research Centre.

House of Representatives Standing Committee on Education, Employment and Training. (1996). *Truancy and exclusion from school: Report of the inquiry into truancy and exclusion of children and young people from school*. Canberra: Australian Government Printing Service.

Houghton, S. & Carroll, A. (1996). Enhancing reputations: The effective use of behavior management strategies by high school adolescent males. *Scientia Pedagogica Experimentalis, 33*, 227–244.

Human Rights and Equal Opportunity Commission. (1989). *Our homeless children: Report of the national inquiry into homeless children*. Canberra: Australian Government Publishing Service.

Ishii-Jordan, S. R. (2000). Behavioral interventions used with diverse students. *Behavioral Disorders, 25*, 299–309).

Karr, S. & Wright, J. (1995). Assessment: Proper use for persons with problem behaviours. In F. E. Obiakor & B. Algozzine (Eds). *Managing problem behaviours: Perspectives for general and special educators* (pp. 64–95). Dubuque, OH: Kendall/Hunt Publishing Co.

Kauffman, J. M. (1997). *Characteristics of emotional and behavioral disorders in children and youth* (6th ed.). Columbus, OH: Charles E. Merrill.

Kauffman, J. M., Hallahan, D. P., Mostert, M. P., Trent, S. C., & Nuttycombe, D. G. (1993). *Managing classroom behavior: A reflective case-based approach*. Boston: Allyn & Bacon.

Kauffman, J. M., Lloyd, J. W., Baker, J., & Riedel, T. M. (1995). Inclusion of all students with emotional or behavioral disorders? Let's think again. *Phi Delta Kappan, March*, 542–546.

Knight, B. A., Graham, L., & Hughes, D. (1995). Fostering the acceptance of students with learning disabilities in the regular classroom. *Australian Journal of Remedial Education, 27(3)*, 6–12.

Leone, P. E., Mayer, M. J., Malmgren, K., & Meisel, S. M. (2000). School violence and disruption: Rhetoric, reality and reasonable balance. *Focus on Exceptional Children, 33*, September.

Lewis, T. J. & Sugai, G. (1999). Effective behavior support: A systems approach to proactive schoolwide management. *Focus on Exceptional Children, 31*(6), 1–24.

Lockhart, J. & Hay, I. (1995). Enhancing the self-concept of at-risk adolescent girls using reflective thinking and a challenge-based program. *Journal of Cognitive Education, 5*, 55–70.

McGrath, H. (1997). *Dirty tricks: Classroom games for teaching social skills*. Melbourne: Longman Australia.

McGrath, H. & Edwards, H. (2000). *Difficult personalities: A practical guide to managing the hurtful behaviours of others (and maybe your own!)*. Marrickville, NSW: Choice Books.

McGrath, H. & Francey, S. (1991). *Friendly kids, friendly classrooms: Teaching social skills and confidence in the classroom*. Melbourne: Longman Cheshire.

McGrath, H. & Noble, T. (1993). *Different kids, same classroom*. Melbourne: Longman Cheshire.

Meadows, N. B., Neel, R. S., Scott, C. M., & Parker, G. (1994). Academic performance, social competence, and mainstream accommodation: A look at mainstreamed and nonmainstreamed students with serious behaviour disorders. *Behavioral Disorders, 19*, 170–180.

Munns, G. (1998). *"Let them be king pin out there on their own in the streets". How some Koori boys responded to their school and classroom*. Paper presented as part of the symposium, Boys and schooling: Shifting frames and masculinities. Annual meeting of the American Educational Research Association, San Diego. ED422140

NSW Department of School Education. (1995a). *Strategies for safer schools*. Sydney: Author.

NSW Department of School Education. (1995b). *Talk time teamwork: Collaborative management of students with ADHD.* Sydney: Author.

NSW Department of School Education. (1996). *The school discipline policy*. Sydney: Author.

Obiakor, F. E. & Schwenn, J.O. (1996). Assessment of culturally diverse students with behavior disorders. *Advances in Special Education, 10*, 37–57.

Oswald, M. (1995). Difficult to manage students: A survey of children who fail to respond to student discipline strategies in government schools. *Educational Studies, 21*, 265–276.

Pavuluri, M. N.& Luk, S. L. (1996). Pattern of preschool behaviour problems in New Zealand, using the behaviour checklist. *Journal of Paediatrics and Child Health, 32*, 132–137.

Porter, L. (2000). *Student behaviour: Theory and practice for teachers* (2nd ed.). Sydney: Allen & Unwin.

Purdie, N., Hattie, J., & Carroll, A. (2001). A review of the research on treatment of children with Attention Deficit Disorder: Which treatment works best? Submitted to *Review of Educational Research.*

Rigby, K. (1996). *Bullying in schools and what to do about it.* Melbourne: ACER.

Rosenberg, M. S., Wilson, R., Maheady, L., & Sindelar, P. T. (1977a). Standardised instruments for assessment and classification. In M. S. Rosenberg, R. Wilson, L. Maheady, & P. T. Sindelar (Eds). *Educating students with behavioural disorders* (2nd ed., pp. 122–137). Needham Heights MA: Allyn & Bacon.

Rosenberg, M. S., Wilson, R., Maheady, L., & Sindelar, P. T. (1977b). Direct and systematic observation. In M. S. Rosenberg, R. Wilson, L. Maheady, & P. T. Sindelar (Eds). *Educating students with behavioural disorders* (2nd ed.) (pp. 139–176). Needham Heights MA: Allyn & Bacon.

Ryan, C. A. & Lindgren, S. J. (1999). How to work effectively with girls: Promising practices in gender-specific interventions. *Reaching Today's Youth, 3*(3), 55–58.

Russell, D. (1999). The importance of identity in the retention and attainment of Aboriginal students at secondary school: Some research findings. *The Australian Journal of Indigenous Education, 27*(1), 10–19.

Schmid, R. E. & Evans, W. (1998). Functional assessment and support plans. In R. E. Schmid & W. Evans (Eds). *Curriculum and instructional practices for students with emotional/behavioral disorders*. Reston VA: CCBD.

Slee, P. T. (1993). Children stressful life events and school adjustment: An Australian study. *Educational Psychology, 13*(1), 3–10.

Stephenson, J., Linfoot, K., & Martin, A. (2000). Behaviors of concern to teachers in the early years of school. *International Journal of Disability, Development and Education, 47*, 225–235.

Stewart, J. (1999). The empowerment of Indigenous Australians in mainstream education. *The Australian Journal of Indigenous Education, 27*(2), 27–31.

Sugai, G. & Evans, D. (1997). Using teacher perceptions to screen for primary students with high risk behaviours. *Australasian Journal of Special Education*, *21*(1), 18–35.

Taffe, R. & Smith, I. D. (1994). Behavioural and cognitive approaches to social skills training. *Australasian Journal of Special Education, 18(1)*, 26–35.

Tasmanian Department of Education and the Arts. (1992). *Student behaviour of serious concern: A student services resource booklet*. Hobart: Author.

The University of Kansas Medical Center. (2000). *Asperger's Syndrome Research Project*. Paper presented at the 24th Annual TECBD National Conference, Scottsdale AZ.

Thompson, P. (1992). One, two, three, four: How do you stop the classroom war? Two, four, six, eight: It's easy, just negotiate. In G. Boomer, N. Lester, C. Onore, & J. Cook (Eds). *Negotiating for the 21st century* (pp. 232–252). London: Falmer Press.

Walker, H. M., Colvin, G., & Ramsey, E. (1995). *Antisocial behavior in school: Strategies and best practices*. Pacific Grove, CA: Brooks/Cole.

Williams, H. & Carmichael, A. (1991). Depression in mothers and behaviour problems with their preschool children. *Journal of Paediatric Child Health*, *27*, 76–82.

Wood, F. H. (1979). *Defining disturbing, disordered and disturbed behavior: Perspectives on the definition of problem behavior in educational settings*. Minneapolis, MN: Advanced Institute for Training Teachers for Seriously Emotionally Disturbed Children and Youth.

6

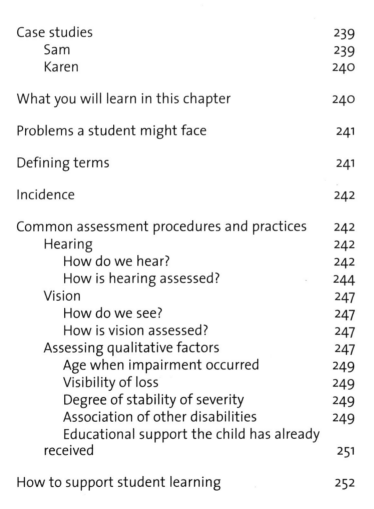

Using all the senses

PAUL PAGLIANO

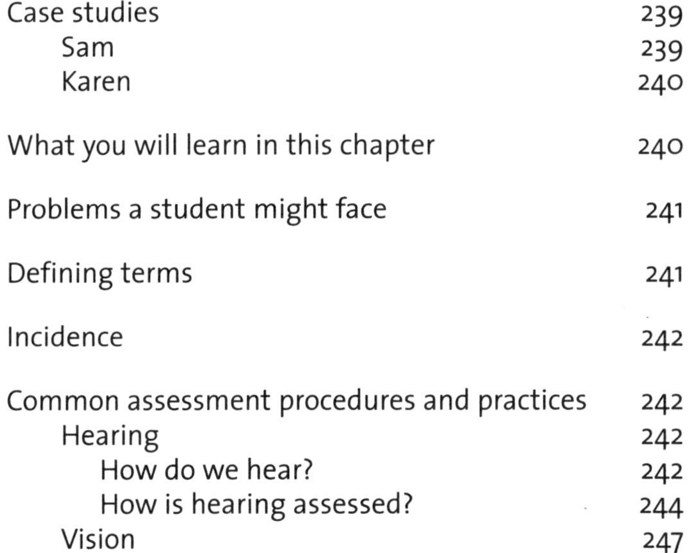

Case studies

When you read the first case study, think about how different it would have been if Deirdre had not received any warning that she was going to have Sam in her class. Also consider what it would have been like if Sam had not received any educational services before he started primary school.

Sam

Two weeks before the end of the school year the principal asks Deirdre, a Year 1 teacher, if she is willing to include Sam in her class—a six-year-old with a moderate hearing loss. Deirdre decides to spend time observing Sam in his preschool setting.

The two days that Deidre spends with Sam and the individualised education program team make quite a difference. She had no idea that including Sam would mean having to include other people as well. Still she knows they will be there to help. She just needs to brush up on her collaboration skills. She is used to having her classroom to herself so it is quite threatening to have so many other people observing her. The team meet regularly and everything is coordinated by Felicity, the advisory visiting teacher.

Resources accompany Sam from preschool, such as the frequency-modulation radio hearing-aid system. Hilary, his preschool teacher's aide, wants to continue working with him. Annette and Troy, Sam's parents, help Deidre to solve problems. They have a communication book in which they write every day. Kerry, the speech language pathologist helps Deidre to work on Sam's speech and language development, making certain that Sam picks up plurals and tense.

Sam has many strengths. He knows most of his basic concepts but needs a lot of help, particularly with communication. He becomes very frustrated sometimes. Sam's education had begun shortly after his hearing loss was diagnosed at six months of age. It must have been a big shock for his parents, but they got right in there and started working with Felicity straight away. Sam can hear better with his right ear, so it helps if he is seated at the front left-hand side of the classroom. From there he can see the whole class. Vision is enormously important for Sam's learning. The teacher must make absolutely certain Sam is looking before any activity can begin, with no obstructions and no distractions. As a class they need to reduce background noise so Sam can use his hearing as much as possible, and Deidre must consistently support his hearing with explicit visual cues and clear demonstrations. It will be lots of fun, a bit like play-acting, and good for the other children in the class. Deidre said that she was looking forward to the challenge.

As you read the following case study think about the most suitable educational program for Karen. Do you think she should have exactly the same program as her sighted peers, or do you think she needs to be taught other things that are not part of the regular curriculum?

Karen

Karen is a Year 12 student with no vision at all. All her learning is through nonvisual methods. Fortunately, Karen has very good braille reading skills because she loves to read. Actually, her parents think she reads too much, but Karen says that reading gives her a view of the world she can't get in any other way. Her favourite subjects are English, German, and history. She has had to work very hard to get into the top five in her class in these subjects. She wants to attend university but, like most other students her age, she is not really sure what she wants to do after that.

Karen finds that getting access to, organising, and storing information is very time-consuming. Six months beforehand her teachers listed all the resources she would require for Year 12. These were obtained from libraries, specially brailled, or put into audio format. Karen's German novel did not arrive until April, putting her a long way behind the rest of the class. Over the holidays her English teacher decided to change one of the plays, and this caused many problems.

Karen's braille books and equipment take up a lot of space. They are stored either in the special education unit at her school or at home. Karen allows an extra 30 minutes before and after school for personal organisation, which really bites into her social life but it's a sacrifice she has to make to keep on top of her studies. Karen's lightweight braille computer is a tremendous help and her collection of tactile maps, hand-prepared by a retired schoolteacher, has been an invaluable aid for history. Karen communicates with quite a few people by email. Some don't even know that she is blind.

Weekly orientation and mobility lessons mean that Karen can independently catch the bus to and from school and the city library, and that she can even catch trains and planes if necessary. At present she is learning how to get to university independently. Karen particularly enjoys mixing with other blind people. They understand what it's like being an outsider in a sighted world. She is a member of the VIPs. They have regular social get-togethers playing swish and blind cricket. Lately Karen has been taking lessons in self-advocacy.

She said, "When I go to university I'll need to be much more assertive and independent. I've been learning how to stand up for myself and how to let teachers know exactly what I need when I'm a student in their classes."

What you will learn in this chapter

As you work your way through this chapter, you will learn:

- about the four major categories of sense impairment: hard of hearing, deaf, low vision and blind;
- how we see and hear, how hearing and vision are assessed and how sense loss affects student learning;

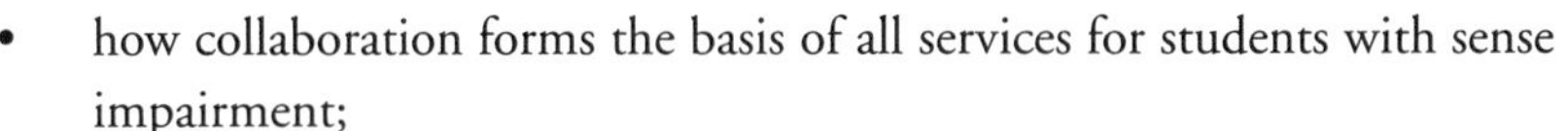

- how collaboration forms the basis of all services for students with sense impairment;
- how learning for students with sense impairment is supported through the use of an individualised family services plan, an individualised education plan and an individualised transition plan; and
- how to modify materials and methods to ensure that a student with sense impairment can participate fully in regular classroom activities.

Problems a student might face

Like many other young people with a hearing loss, Sam is going to find starting primary school a challenge because of his communication capabilities. He will find it difficult to hear instructions in class, especially when there is a lot of background noise. He is also going to find it difficult to answer questions and he will probably be reluctant to talk to the other students, so it will take time for him to make friends and feel comfortable. His teacher says that she feels positive about having him in her class, but this is the first time that she has actually taught a student who is hard of hearing. Deirdre needs to be sensitive to Sam's problems and to introduce quickly methods to help reduce his frustrations.

Similarly, other students with a vision impairment, like Karen, can ask themselves some very confronting questions. Karen, for example, wonders whether she has spent too much time doing academic work at the expense of other things. Was all that reading really necessary or was it a way of avoiding other things—like the fact that she does not have really close friends or that she cannot cook very well? Karen has started a list of potential problems she might face next year. Here's Karen's list.

- Am I able to look after myself? Can I shop, prepare my own food, care for my clothes, keep my house tidy, eat out at restaurants, do my banking, and go to the doctor?
- How am I going to make friends at university? What kinds of leisure activities would help me meet people?
- Do I know enough about my own feelings, especially as they relate to sexuality, boyfriends and being blind?
- What kind of career do I want to have? How will I find a job?

Defining terms

There are four major categories of sense impairment: deaf, hard of hearing, blind and low vision. Hearing and vision loss both exist on a continuum of severity from mild (common) to profound (rare). Educational definitions focus on how a sense impairment affects the child's learning. In the following categories the impairment is

significant enough to require support at school in addition to what is usually provided by the classroom teacher.

- *Educationally deaf* means that there is a total lack of functional hearing for learning.
- *Hard of hearing* means that after correction some functional hearing is available for learning.
- *Educationally blind* means that there is a total lack of functional vision for learning.
- *Low vision* means that after correction some functional vision is available for learning.

Incidence

The number of school children who are either deaf or hard of hearing is very small—about 0.4% (Moores, 1996). The number of school children who are blind or have low vision is even lower, approximately 0.2% (Hubner, 2000; Kelley, Gale, & Blatch, 1998). However, at least 50% of children with sense impairment have more than one disability (Silberman, 2000).

Common assessment procedures and practices

Providing the most appropriate support to students who have a sense impairment cannot occur unless the teacher knows exactly what problems the students are facing as a consequence of an impairment. Hence, some assessment must occur, but assessment is usually preceded by a recognition that a problem exists. This might be through astute observation, or through an active search by screening. The problem might be identified by medical examination, particularly in the immediate prenatal period or through parental and/or teacher observations. A useful screening tool is the hearing–vision checklist (see Box 6.1, page 243).

If items are positively identified on the checklist, then parents or caregivers should obtain a formal hearing or vision assessment by a health-care professional. The signs and symptoms in the checklist are suggestive but not diagnostic. Apart from assessing the degree of sensory loss, the health-care professional will also check the health of the sensory organ and investigate whether some form of correction is possible (e.g., medical and/or surgical treatment, hearing aids/low-vision devices).

Hearing

How do we hear?

The ear is divided into three parts and damage to any part can result in hearing loss. The air-filled outer ear collects sound waves from the environment, and the auricle funnels sound along the external auditory canal into the middle ear. The middle ear

Box 6.1 The hearing–vision checklist

Student:

Year:

Teacher:

Does the child have any of the following signs of a hearing problem? (Please tick the appropriate boxes.)

1. ☐ Answers questions inappropriately
2. ☐ Omits some speech sounds or substitutes others
3. ☐ Is overtly inattentive
4. ☐ Frowns or strains forward when listening
5. ☐ Closely watches speaker's face
6. ☐ Frequently asks for things to be repeated
7. ☐ Frequently not aware that someone is speaking, especially when there is background noise
8. ☐ Mispronounces words
9. ☐ Complains of noises in the ears
10. ☐ Has difficulty when asked to repeat the words of songs or rhymes
11. ☐ Watches other children following instructions before starting work
12. ☐ Has a particularly soft or loud voice
13. ☐ Often has trouble locating the source of a sound
14. ☐ Holds head in a peculiar position when listening to someone speak
15. ☐ Language is ungrammatical for the child's age
16. ☐ Has regular colds or sore throats or discharge from ears
17. ☐ Appears to have greater problems hearing especially after an illness

☐ None of the above

☐ Other

Comments:

[Although a tick in one or several boxes does not necessarily indicate a hearing problem, testing by an audiologist is recommended.]

Does the child have any of the following signs of a vision problem? (Please tick the appropriate box.)

1. ☐ Reddened eyes or lids
2. ☐ One eye sometimes turns in or out
3. ☐ Complains of headaches in forehead, especially after close work

4 ☐ Complains that the print blurs after reading for a short time

5. ☐ Holds the book too closely or puts the face too close to the desk when working

6 ☐ Covers or closes one eye when reading

7. ☐ Loses place often when reading

8. ☐ Cannot write on a straight line
9. ☐ Repeatedly omits small words when reading (e.g., "a", "the")
10. ☐ Complains that distance objects are blurry (e.g., as a reason to sit close to the television)
11. ☐ Reverses letters and/or words (e.g., "b—d", "was—saw")
12. ☐ Whispers to self when reading silently
13. ☐ Uses the hand or finger to keep place on the page
14. ☐ Tilts the head noticeably to one side when working at the desk
15. ☐ Has difficulty reading rows or columns of numbers
16. ☐ Has difficulty seeing in dim light
17. ☐ Misses details in illustrations

☐ None of the above

☐ Other

Comments:

[Although a tick in one or several boxes does not necessarily indicate a vision problem, testing by an optometrist is recommended.]

transports sound as vibrations via the ear drum and the ossicles to the oval window which leads into the inner ear. The middle ear is filled with air because it is connected to the nose via the Eustachian tube. The inner ear consists of the cochlea which is composed of hair cells and neural and supporting structures, and which is filled with lymphatic fluid. In the inner ear, sound vibrations become pressure waves, which deform the hair cells to emit a chain of neural impulses along the auditory nerve to the auditory area on the temporal lobe of the cortex of the brain where the message is perceived as sound (see Figure 6.1, page 245).

How is hearing assessed?

Evaluation of the degree of hearing loss is made by an audiologist before or after medical review. An audiologist is a non-medical practitioner who prescribes hearing aids. It is best if hearing loss is identified as early as possible. Babies can be tested either by using an auditory brain stem response test that measures brain waves or by using acoustic emmittance that measures the response that hair cells in the inner ear make to an external sound. Older children are given a behavioural audiological evaluation that involves the child acknowledging hearing a sound at a particular frequency and volume by pressing a record button or by raising a hand.

The hearing loss is then recorded on an audiogram, a grid system on which the x-axis represents the frequency of sound waves in hertz (Hz) and the logarithmic y-axis represents volume in decibels (dB). Separate records are kept for each ear, both

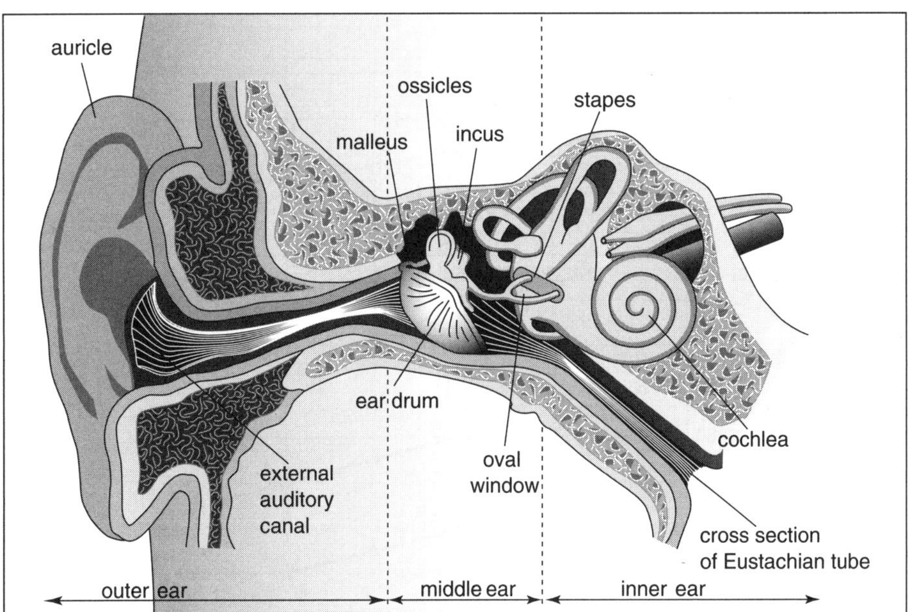

Figure 6.1 Human hearing mechanisms.
Illustrator: Nives Porcellato

unaided (e.g., O for right, X for left) and aided (A for right, * for left). Hearing loss can be unilateral (present in one ear only) or bilateral (present in both ears). Students who require special support at school generally have bilateral hearing loss. Information from the audiologist helps the educator to detail those sounds, particularly speech sounds that the individual can and cannot hear (see Figure 6.2, page 246). Speech ranges between 250 and 4000 Hz with vowels being relatively low in pitch and louder than consonants. The pain threshold for sound is about 120 dB, thus limiting any correction that can be achieved by simple volume adjustment.

The audiologist confirms the presence of hearing impairment, and profiles its severity. The pattern of hearing loss on the audiogram gives clues to the diagnosis. An otorhinolaryngologist is a surgeon who specialises in diagnosing and treating ear conditions.

Conductive hearing loss relates to problems in the outer and middle ear. Hearing in the inner ear is not impaired but a problem is created because the sound energy that reaches the inner ear has been muffled and distorted. One cause of conductive hearing loss is chronic otitis media, inflammation of the middle ear. Unfortunately, otitis media has become endemic in many indigenous populations particularly in more isolated parts of Northern Australia. This is because many children have extremely narrow Eustachian tubes. Infections result in blockages to the Eustachian tube thereby preventing air from circulating within the middle ear. In children for whom middle ear infections are common, preventative measures include practising and repeating

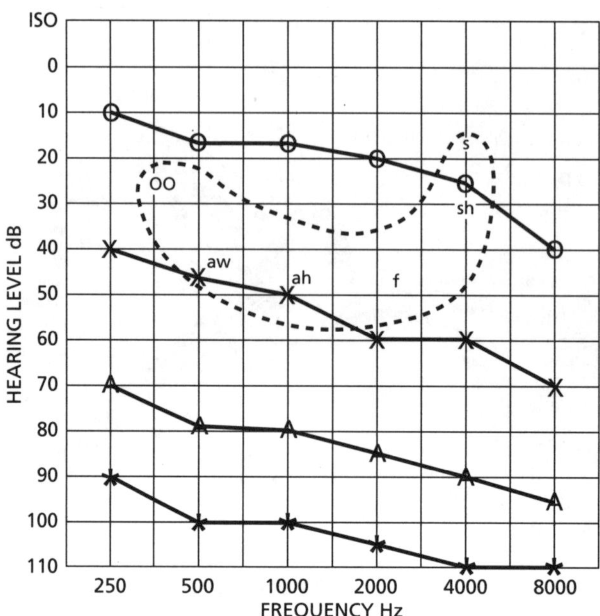

Figure 6.2 The speech sound banana superimposed on an audiogram showing mild (O), moderate (x), severe (A) and profound (*) hearing loss.

a cycle of "breathe, blow and wipe nose, jump up and down". Earache should be attended to promptly.

Chronic middle ear disease results in fluctuating conductive hearing loss. Adults can mistakenly believe that a child's hearing is fine, based on observations of the child's hearing on a good day during a quiet, one-to-one conversation. However, during times of high infection the child might have very little hearing and experience considerable difficulty with background noise. Worse still, because hearing comes and goes, the child might miss essential prerequisites for learning. This is particularly a problem during early childhood when language is developing. The child's resultant limited language skills can negatively affect all aspects of learning and development, especially if the child speaks English at school and a different language at home. The perception by some cultural groups that eye contact is disrespectful can be an additional complication by denying opportunity to speech read. The good news is that conductive hearing loss is often amenable to medical and surgical treatment, and usually responds well to amplification. Solutions can be culturally complex for rural Aboriginal children (Higgins, 1997).

Sensorineural hearing loss results from problems in the inner ear or nerve pathways. Damage to the cochlea or neural tissue is not usually surgically or medically treatable and, therefore greater emphasis must be placed on finding suitable hearing aids and providing appropriate educational support. Hearing loss involving both conductive and sensorineural impairment is called a mixed hearing loss. Damage to the high-level

neural pathways or to the auditory cortex of the brain results in central hearing loss. Hearing loss can range from difficulty in interpreting the auditory signal to having no appreciable hearing at all. Central hearing loss, although difficult to demonstrate unequivocally, is thought to be at least partly responsible for problems such as aphasia, by which children might hear speech but experience difficulties interpreting it. It can also lead to certain forms of learning difficulties, particularly those that relate to language delays and disorders.

Educational assessment of a deaf or hard-of-hearing student is usually compromised because the student has significantly delayed language development. This means that a test might reflect the student's limited language ability rather than the hearing component under examination. Most standardised tests reflect an underestimation of student ability and should be treated with scepticism. However, rewriting the test in language that the child can understand makes the standardisation invalid. Most assessment information will, therefore, be obtained informally using language samples and assessment tools that are teacher-made or curriculum-based. The most important assessment is a comprehensive communication assessment, particularly as it relates to competence in English, speech, and/or sign language. This assessment is made by a speech language pathologist (SLP), or by an advisory teacher in hearing impairment. Assessment needs to focus on the student's communicative competence in a range of natural settings including home, classroom, playground, and community. This assessment informs the educational plan that will direct the support needed by the student.

Vision

How do we see?

Seeing involves four steps. The first step, light energy transmission, begins when light enters the eye and is refracted (bent) by the transparent cornea and aqueous humour. The amount of light entering the inner eye is regulated by adjusting the size of the pupil and iris. Accommodation (focusing) is achieved by ciliary muscle action which changes the shape of the lens. The light then passes through the vitreous humour onto the retina, which is the light sensitive inner lining at the back of the eye. The second step involves the retina which has millions of specialised cells (including the peripheral rods for night vision and the central cones for colour vision) that convert light energy to electrical energy. The third step, electrical impulse transmission to the brain, involves retinal stimulation which is transmitted as neural energy along the optic nerve to the visual cortex of the brain. The fourth step occurs in the brain, with the interpretation of neural energy as the perception of sight.

As with hearing the whole process is incredibly rapid and streamlined. The extrinsic muscles around the eyeball control the movement of the eyeball in its socket. The brain coordinates these movements to enable both eyes to fix and maintain fixation on an object in the visual field. This ability is called convergence or, more correctly, fusional vergence. Accommodation and fusional vergence are important complementary visual skills. Visual skills are either monocular or binocular. If a visual skill can be achieved by each eye independently, it is monocular. Binocular skills depend upon brain integration so that the two eyes work together as a team. Vision impairment is usually defined as a reduction in one or more of the following: accommodation, binocular skill, visual field, central vision and colour vision (see Figure 6.3, page 249).

How is vision assessed?

Evaluation of vision is made by an optometrist (a non-medical practitioner who prescribes lenses or visual therapy) or by an ophthalmologist (a surgeon who specialises in diagnosing and treating eye conditions). The eyes are examined and tests are made of the full range of monocular and binocular functions. As with hearing impairment it is best if vision impairment is identified at as early an age as possible.

Most children with vision impairment have errors of refraction, that is, they are long-sighted or short-sighted, and vision can be corrected by wearing spectacles. Most conditions causing low vision or blindness in childhood cannot be medically or surgically treated.

If medical or surgical treatment is not possible, a child can be referred to a paediatric low-vision clinic for extra assessment to determine if the visual efficiency of the remaining eyesight can be increased. A range of low-vision aids can be prescribed.

An educational assessment of the impact of the vision impairment on education is made by the advisory teacher in vision impairment.

Once significant sense loss has been identified, an education team is established. The team collects information to help the members decide where best to send the child to school, and the amount and type of specialist support that is necessary. In particular, the team focuses on:

- how the sense loss is affecting the student's learning;
- what program modifications, adjustments, and accommodations are necessary;
- what the student can already do;
- what the student needs to learn; and
- how this will be taught, evaluated, and reviewed. The team makes ongoing regular critical assessments throughout the school years.

Assessing qualitative factors

Many factors modify the qualitative nature of the sense impairment and thereby influence its educational impact. These include the following.

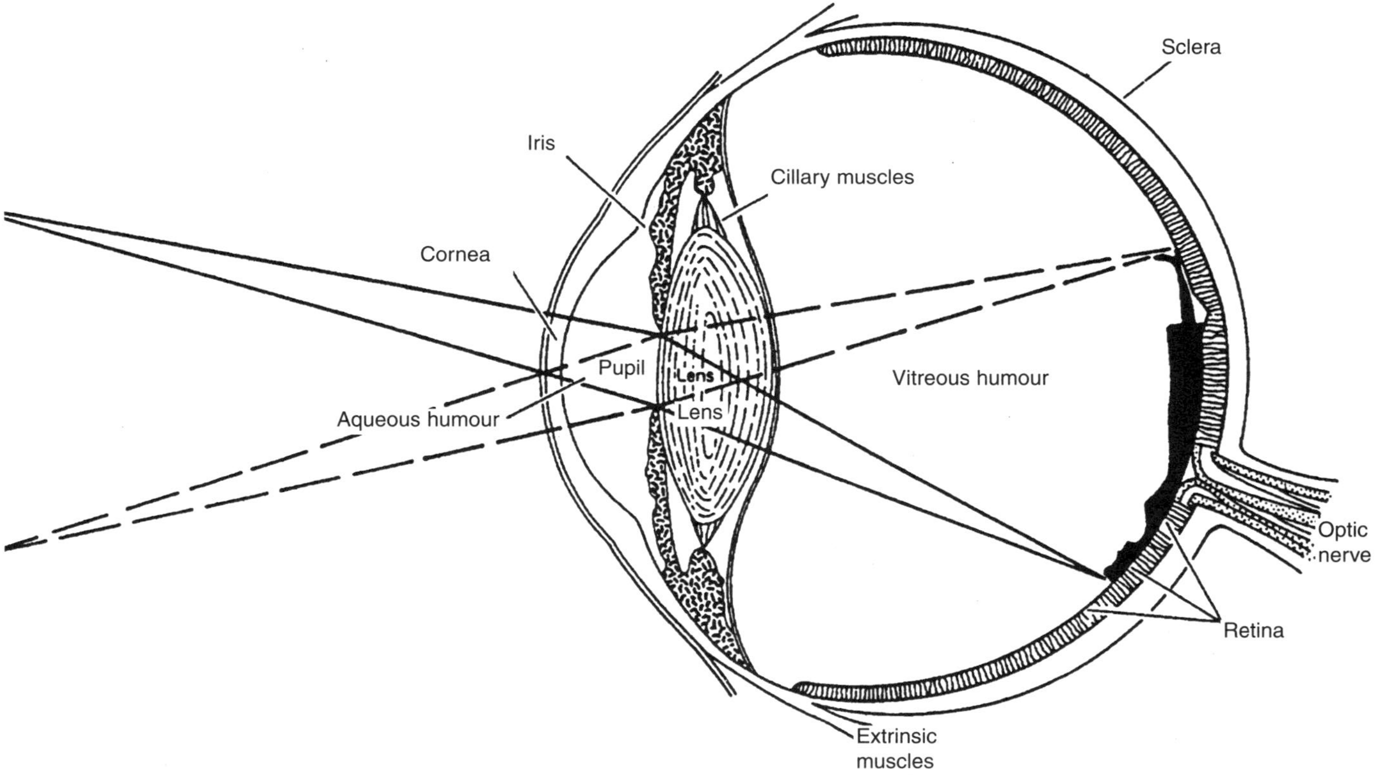

Figure 6.3 How the eye works.

Age when impairment occurred

Hearing and vision loss, although primarily associated with ageing, can occur at any age. Loss that is present at birth is called *congenital.* Identifying when hearing or vision loss first appeared lets the educator know what type of intervention is required. Onset of blindness can occur before or after spatial concept development. (Vision loss after the child has acquired a visual memory is called *adventitious.*) Learning spatial concepts through non-visual means is more challenging than learning them visually. Similarly, hearing loss occurring before the acquisition of a sound-based language (*prelingual deafness*) requires a much more specialised and intensive program than hearing loss that occurs after spoken language has been acquired (*postlingual deafness*).

Visibility of loss

Casual observers might not be able to tell that a person has a sense impairment, particularly when the loss is mild. Hearing loss is sometimes described as a hidden disability because limitations might become evident only when sound-based communication is required. Mild-to-moderate sense impairment can take time to identify. Delay in identification means that the child meanwhile misses out on important educational experiences. Severe vision loss poses its own problems. Parents can misread lack of eye contact as rejection whereas the most appropriate response is to learn non-visual ways to bond with a blind baby. Parents also should be explicitly taught to communicate with a deaf baby.

Degree of stability of severity

It is important to recognise that sense loss might not always be stable. It can deteriorate due to disease or can improve through the use of prosthetics or surgery. Sense loss might also fluctuate, depending on personal health, medication, and environmental factors such as acoustics or lighting.

Association of other disabilities

There might be one additional disability (called an *associated disability*) or more than two disabilities (termed *multiple disabilities*). Each of these disabilities can range from mild to profound. With each additional disability the challenges are substantially compounded. For example, dual sense disabilities (deaf-blind) pose serious challenges to both communication and literacy learning. Add an intellectual or physical disability, and the child has major challenges with learning in virtually all areas of development. The proportion of students with sense disabilities who have associated or multiple disabilities is increasing. This is because modern medicine is keeping many students with multiple disabilities alive for much longer than was the case in the past. Also technological improvements and sociological developments have meant that many more students with multiple disabilities are now having their sense loss formally tested and prosthetic devices prescribed and supplied.

Students with sense loss can also be gifted and talented. High-level intellectual functioning might enable students to develop compensating strategies that greatly help them reduce the difficulties posed by their sense loss.

Educational support the child has already received

Early effective intervention is the goal. Collaboration through teamwork is intended to optimise placement and program plans. Three important concepts for education defined by Barraga (1983) in relation to vision impairment also apply to hearing loss.

Visual or auditory perception

Visual or auditory perception refers to the ability to understand and interpret all visually or aurally received information. It is more related to learning capabilities than to the condition of the eyes (or ears) and, therefore, is still possible with low vision or hearing.

Visual or auditory functioning

Visual or auditory functioning refers to how people use whatever vision or hearing they might have. It is strongly influenced by personal "experiences, motivations, needs and expectations . . . in relation to whatever visual [auditory] capacity is available to satisfy curiosity and accomplish activities for personal satisfaction" (Barraga, 1983, p. 24).

Visual or auditory efficiency

Visual or auditory efficiency refers to the degree of ease, comfort, and minimum time that an individual needs to perform specific visual or auditory tasks. It is unique to each child. Even though visual and auditory efficiency is difficult to measure accurately or predict, it helps teachers to determine appropriate individualised educational methods, and is the most significant consideration.

Strongly encouraging sense perception, function, and efficiency in sense impairment is an important role for educators. Generally speaking, the following principles apply. The likelihood of the student attending a regular school is greater if the child has:

- a higher intelligence;
- fewer disabilities;
- disabilities that are mild;
- onset of disabilities occurring later in life; and
- disabilities that are less visible.

Although there is a steady ongoing push for the regular school system to accept students with more severe disabilities, the likelihood of the student attending a special school is greater if the child has:

- a severe to profound intellectual impairment;
- multiple disabilities;
- disabilities that are severe to profound;
- onset of these disabilities occurring early in life; and
- disabilities that are highly visible.

How to support student learning

Stories from ancient Greece and Rome indicate that deaf and blind citizens were largely separated from society through veneration or execution. With the spread of Christianity, deaf and blind individuals were pitied and protected. The first school for deaf children was established in Spain in the 1500s, and the first school for blind children started in Paris in 1784. Schools for children with sense impairments first appeared in Australia in the 1860s in both Sydney and Melbourne. In New Zealand, the first school for deaf students opened in 1880, and the first school for blind students (now Homai Vision Education Centre, Royal New Zealand Foundation for the Blind) was established in 1891. Until the 1970s the majority of students attended special schools. Since then, New Zealand and Australian education systems have tended to follow US trends and have moved toward inclusion. The result has been a steady increase in the number of students attending regular schools, initially as students enrolled in attached special education units and, more recently, as students who attend regular classes with specialist services provided in the regular classroom.

Identifying the most appropriate educational placement for students with sense impairments remains a hotly debated issue, especially for students with profound sensory loss. There are advantages and disadvantages in special school education. Critics of inclusion point out that decreased opportunities for students with similar sense impairments to congregate has eroded deaf and blind communities and increased the sense of individual isolation. Closure of special schools is being blamed for the worldwide shortage of educational experts in hearing and vision because teachers now find difficulty in gaining extensive experience.

> Placing a deaf child in a classroom in physical contiguity to hearing children does not automatically provide equal access to information. In fact, it can be isolating, both academically and socially. We should be past the point where we advocate one approach—in terms of placement, mode of instruction, or curricular content—for all children in a particular category. In this pluralistic society, we will have to be particularly sensitive to the need to open up educational opportunities to all children while addressing individual differences. (Moores, 1993, p. 251)

Equal access to information for students with significant sense impairment mandates the acquisition of specialist skills as a prerequisite to learning. These prerequisite skills take time to master and this time is not spent in the mainstream class. Inclusion is, therefore, not a linear or "either/or" argument.

In the post-inclusion era, the real challenge for the educational team is to entertain constantly the full range of disparate educational options, rather than just giving lip service to the alternatives. The education team must maintain a willingness to fine tune the balance between program appropriateness and a least restrictive environment throughout the school life of the student. Particular emphasis must be placed on educating the whole child including physical, emotional, and psychological wellbeing, as well as academic achievement. The focus is now on outcome rather than process.

Current education practices

To promote equal opportunity and a least restrictive environment, students with sense impairment should optimise their auditory or visual perception, functioning, and efficiency by acquiring and developing certain new skills and by using technology.

Hearing

Technical approaches

Hearing aids

Hard of hearing and deaf students receive a free diagnostic hearing aid fitting and maintenance service provided in Australia by the Australian Hearing Services (AHS) and in New Zealand by agencies related to both health and education. Two of the most commonly prescribed hearing aids are the behind-the-ear aid and the radio hearing aid.

Features of the typical modern behind-the-ear acoustic hearing aid (see Figure 6.4, page 254) are the controls for gain adjustment and volume. The aid is battery operated. Problems such as discomfort and the squeal of acoustic feedback can occur if ear moulds do not fit properly or if the aid is ill-adjusted. These hearing aids are easily damaged and need regular maintenance.

With simple acoustic aids, the teacher's voice must travel to the student. It must, therefore, compete with other environmental noises. With a radio, or FM, hearing aid, the teacher's voice is broadcast through a microphone worn by the teacher directly to the child's hearing aid. (This is the system Sam is using.) One disadvantage is that unless special provision is made, only the teacher's voice is amplified, so the student misses other classroom sounds, including his or her own voice. In situations in which children cannot wear hearing aids (e.g., because of ear infections) it is possible to build FM amplification systems for the whole classroom.

Cochlear implant

A cochlear implant can give a deaf individual access to otherwise unavailable auditory information. The implant relays information from a microphone worn by the deaf

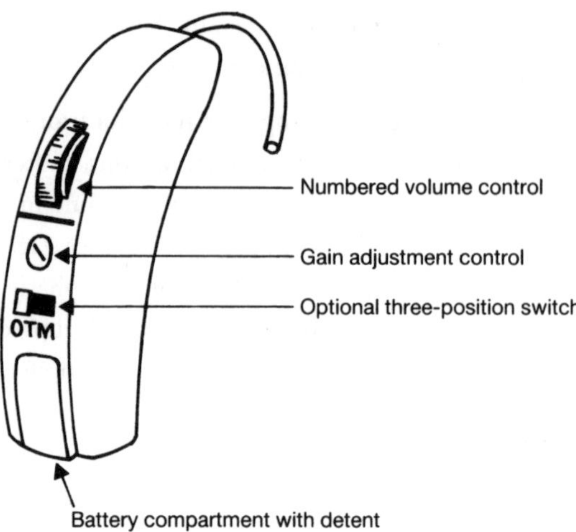

Figure 6.4 Typical modern behind-the-ear acoustic hearing-aid.

person directly to an electrode array surgically placed in the cochlea that stimulates the auditory nerve. The child must undergo extensive speech language therapy to learn how to use the new sense input effectively. Even so, the outcome is variable. In general, implants move the deaf person out of the profound loss category into the moderate to severe range. Cochlear implants do not rule out the use of sign. About 40% of students with cochlear implants currently use sign language interpreting services in the classroom (Johnson, 2000).

Sign language

Sign language is different from signed English (a direct translation of English into hand movements). Sign language has its own grammar, morphology, syntax, location, semantics, and pragmatics. Meaning is achieved through the combination of hand shape, location, movement pattern, and intensity, as well as through facial and bodily expression. In both Australia and New Zealand, the language of the deaf community is recognised as a legitimate national language. Sign languages used in Australasia are Australian Sign Language (Auslan) and New Zealand Sign Language. For a comprehensive description of Auslan, see Johnston's Auslan dictionary (1998a, b). Sign language is best taught to congenitally deaf children as early as possible. Young deaf children begin to produce their first signs from about five months of age. A recent development is the preparation of signs for specialised areas such as computer science (Parker & Schembri, 1996). This means that deaf people using sign language now have greater access to specialised positions in the work force.

Communication approaches

The three major approaches of teaching communication to deaf and hard-of-hearing students are oral communication, total communication, and bilingual-bicultural approaches. All require the acquisition of special skills.

Oral communication

In the oral approach, speech is the principal focus of communication. Emphasis is placed on student talk using amplification, speech reading, cued speech, auditory training, and state-of-the-art technological aids to assist with auditory, tactile, and visual information input. *Speech reading* is of use to those with a mild-to-moderate impairment. For those with a more severe loss, *cued speech* is a method of supplementing oral communication, consisting of hand signals near the chin. The signals do not have meaning, rather they are visual cues designed to help the child identify sounds not able to be distinguished through speech reading alone. *Auditory training* involves the teaching of listening skills and develops awareness of sounds. The child learns to listen more precisely and to make associations with noises. The teaching of speech skills should be based on "what the child can hear, and what features are important for effective speech communication" (Ching, 1994, p. v). Family involvement in the use of oral methods is strongly encouraged. The less severe the hearing loss the better the chances are that the child will learn to communicate effectively through speech. The more successful the child is at oral communication, the more likely he or she will be included in regular school.

Total communication

Since total, or simultaneous, communication first emerged in the 1960s it has overtaken the oral method to become the major instructional approach, because of its greater utility in those with more severe levels of hearing impairment. Total communication involves simultaneous presentation of speech (through speech reading and residual hearing) with manual communication providing a visual speech supplement (by signs and finger spelling). The emphasis is on the child having both an auditory (sound) and visual (sign) access to communication. *Finger spelling* is a manual version of the alphabet. In Australia and New Zealand, Victorian Finger Spelling, a two handed method, is used (see Figure 6.5, page 256).

In North America a one-handed finger spelling is used. This one-handed method of communicating enables the communicator to sign and do other things simultaneously—such as eating. Signs are invented or borrowed from signed English or sign language. Jeanes, Reynolds, and Coleman (1988) developed a dictionary which lists signs used to translate English into sign. Often signs are combined with finger spelling to reproduce the precise English translation (e.g., the sign for "girl" plus the sign for the letter "s" makes "girls"; the sign for "jump" plus letter signs for "e" and "d" make "jumped").

Bilingual–bicultural approaches

The bilingual–bicultural approach is based on the view that deafness is not primarily a disability, but is a cultural and linguistic difference. (Disability is mainly dependent on social milieu.) It is important to recognise that there are sociocultural definitions

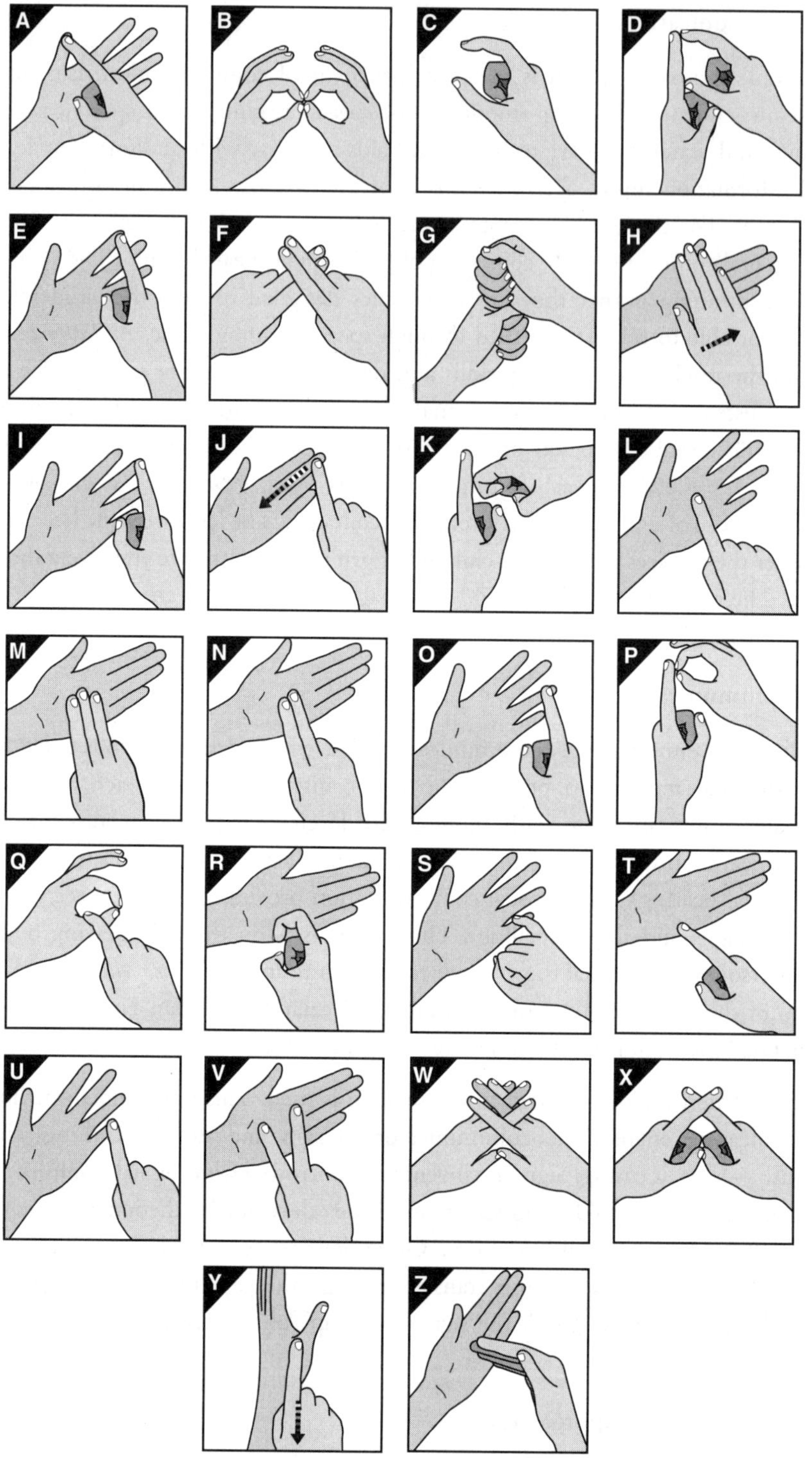

A B C D
E F G H
I J K L
M N O P
Q R S T
U V W X
Y Z

Figure 6.5 Finger spelling alphabet.
Source: <www.vicdeaf.com.au/aboutus/auslan/about_auslan.htm>

of hearing loss as well as medical and educational definitions. People who are Deaf (with a capital D) regard themselves as a separate group with their own culture and language, a de facto non-English speaking cultural minority (hence Deaf rather than deaf). Deaf culture is so strong that some Deaf people regard cochlear implants as cultural erosion. In Deaf culture in Australasia, Australian Sign Language (Auslan) or New Zealand Sign Language is the child's first language of instruction. Proponents of this approach argue that sign language provides a more natural, foundational support pathway toward linguistic competence. Deaf children of deaf parents acquire sign language in the same easy way that hearing children acquire spoken language from hearing parents. The bilingual-bicultural approach seeks to capitalise on the fact that deaf children can learn a language in a spontaneous and natural way, as long as they are provided with the opportunity to do so. Once the child is fluent in his or her native sign language, a sound-based language (e.g., English) is taught within the context of a bilingual–bicultural education. A sound-based language is necessary to be able to read because sign language has no written equivalent.

Vision

Low-vision devices

Low-vision devices (LVD) are prescribed aids to assist long-distance and short-distance vision. They include the following:

- Hand magnifiers, with or without a light and handle, are suitable for short working distance activities involving short inspection. The larger the lens the lower the magnification.
- Stand magnifiers contain one or two convex lenses (3.5x–15x) mounted in a fixed distance stand, with or without a light. They can be placed over a page of print or object to be viewed. They are suitable for short working distance activities involving prolonged tasks.
- Electronic magnifiers such as a closed circuit television (CCTV) can be used for short working distance activities involving prolonged tasks. The unit consists of a television camera focused for short-distance viewing, a light source, and a monitor with reverse contrast (white-on-black, black-on-white) and contrast enhancement capabilities.
- A monocular consists of a hand-held tube mounted with a lens at either end which can be focused for different distances (2x–10x). It is a single-eye distance aid. A pair of monoculars joined together is called a binocular. A less cosmetically attractive option is for the student to attach the short-distance or long-distance LVD to his or her glasses or to a head band.

Personal acceptance of the LVD is determined by the way in which the LVD is introduced, the amount of visual reward the student receives, and how comfortable he or she feels about using the device in public. Teachers can do much to create a supportive classroom environment.

Braille

A 19th-century blind Frenchman, Louis Braille, developed a tactual language system based on a cell of six potential raised dot positions, arranged in two columns and three rows. Various combinations of these six dots then form the basis for all braille symbols.

1• •4

2• •5

3• •6

The Australian and New Zealand braille codes are similar to those used in the United States and the United Kingdom. Grade I braille (see Figure 6.6, below) is a match with regular print, symbol for symbol. Grade II braille, Standard English braille, is a shorthand form that includes the braille alphabet, plus 189 contractions, abbreviations, and short-form words (see Kelley & Gale, 1998, pp. 326–7). Most sighted code systems, including mathematics, science, and music, have braille codes.

a	b	c	d	e	f	g	h	i	j
•-	•-	••	••	•-	••	••	•-	-•	-•
- -	•-	—-	-•	-•	•-	••	••	•-	••
- -	- -	—-	- -	-	- -	- -	- -	- -	- -

k	l	m	n	o	p	q	r	s	t
•-	•-	••	••	•-	••	••	•-	-•	-•
- -	•-	—	•-	•	•	••	••	•-	••

u	v	x	y	z	w	.	,	?	!
•-	•-	••	••	•-	-•	- -	—-	- -	—-
- -	•-	—-	-•	-•	••	••	•-	•-	••
••	••	••	••	••	-•	-•	—-	••	•-

#	+a(1)		#	3		#	5	6	0
-•	•-		-•	••		-•	•-	••	-•
-•	- -		-•	—-		-•	-•	•-	••
••	- -		••	- -		••	- -	- -	- -

Figure 6.6 Grade 1 braille.

A young boy reading braille.

Letters “a” to “j” are formed by dots in rows one and two. Letters “k” to “t” are formed by adding dot three. Letters “u” to “z” are formed by adding dots three and six. Notice that “w” is out of sequence because French does not have this letter. Punctuation signs do not have dots in the first row. Numbers are formed by placing the numeral sign in front of the first nine letters. Numeral sign “a” is added to make “1”, numeral sign “c” to make “3”, and numeral sign “efj” to make “560”.

Learning braille is more difficult than learning print. As with print reading, the emergent literacy approach is used to teach braille, but with modifications (Koenig & Holbrook, 2000a; Lamb, 1996; Mangold, 1994). It is essential that the early teaching of braille involve considerable input from a trained specialist (Gillon & Young, 2001). Some children with intellectual impairment and vision impairment are being taught Moon, a more simple tactile reading system (see Kelley & Gale, 1998, pp. 328–30; McCall, 1997).

In today’s classroom blind students have “braille’n’print/speak” attachments, which mean that braille, print, and audio translations are always close at hand. They help to ensure that the braille-using child is actively involved in all class activities, including those involving computers. Scanners can convert written text to braille and computers can be attached to braille or text printers.

Braille plays an important role in providing life chances for students with vision impairment. For many blind adults braille represents competence, independence, and equality. Braille will enable Karen to achieve her dream of university.

Orientation and mobility training

Knowing one's position in relation to other objects in space (orientation) and being able to safely, independently, and purposefully move about (mobility) are essential skills for physical and functional integration (Brannock & Golding, 2000; LaGrow, 1998). Orientation and mobility (O&M) training should begin early to overlap with development of body image and concept. Considerable attention must be given to motor development at preschool level by including a daily routine of structured movement training. Children are also taught about the nature of terrain, different surfaces (e.g., grass or concrete, level or sloping, straight or curved), and the special identifying sounds and odours of the environment (e.g., the road, a train, the bakery).

Listening, especially locating objects by reflected sound (echolocation) is valuable in O&M. Young children are taught to take advantage of the Doppler effect—to recognise that a movement toward a sound source results in the sound being heard at a lower pitch. Mobility can be aided by the use of human guides, guide dogs, a white cane, and various electronic devices. Human guides reduce independence. Guide dogs, although they are the answer for some, require extensive training and might not suit people who dislike dogs or live in an apartment. A cane, itself a symbol that the user is vision impaired, is a popular and helpful tool. It enables the user to detect obstacles and terrain changes. Many of the new electronic devices work on the principle of reflected sound to describe the environment, with pitch indicating distance, volume indicating size, and sound clarity indicating texture.

You will recall that O&M skills have been important for Karen in promoting her independence. This will be especially important when she begins to negotiate the new environment at university.

Use of remaining sight

Vision is enormously important in helping a child to obtain accurate and extensive information about the world. About 80% of learning is visual. Many concepts acquired effortlessly by children with vision will not be learnt by children with vision impairment unless they are explicitly taught.

Binocular control abilities have normally developed by the age of seven months, and are mostly refined by 36 months. Children with low vision need special help to take maximum advantage to the visual abilities they have, including visual or optical training, visual stimulation, and creating an optimal environment for visual development and learning.

Optical training exercises are designed to improve fixating, focusing, converging, and scanning. Appropriate visual stimulation encourages children with low vision to develop an awareness of visible objects, to foster the reception of visual information, and facilitate the organisation of the information so that visual development and

learning occurs. Optical training and visual stimulation functions are passive, although they are prerequisites for self-directed visual searching. To create an optimal environment for visual development and learning, important variables relevant to the classroom are colour, contrast, shape, spatial relationships, and the provision of enough time for looking.

Depending on the level of low vision, some children might need longer than usual reading readiness programs with extensive specialist teacher input.

Listening skills

Tuttle (1996, p. 173) defined literacy as "the recognition, interpretation, and assimilation of the ideas represented by symbolic material, whether it is displayed visually, tactually, or aurally". His definition includes listening as a literacy form. For individuals with visual impairment, good listening skills are very valuable in increasing their access to information. Audio-format resources are now more extensive than braille, require less storage space, and are cheaper, easier, and faster to produce. Students with low vision also use listening to supplement their knowledge if their reading of print is slow, inefficient, or cognitively demanding. The technology is advancing with an ever-increasing range of synthetic-voice and voice-recognition machines. Some materials do not reproduce well in audio format (e.g., charts, tables, maps, graphs) and writing using dictating equipment can be difficult.

Efficient listening skills, especially audio reading, must be taught systematically as a reading process, in the same way that print and braille are taught. Early introduction to listening skill training can support the development of print or braille reading skills. As the student progresses into higher grades, audio reading and good listening skills become increasingly more useful, and help to improve quality of life.

Changing the way we teach

When you have a student with a sense impairment in your class, the biggest change to the way you teach undoubtedly relates to the need for you to become part of an individual education plan (IEP) team. Instead of working by yourself, you find that you become an active member of a sophisticated network of highly coordinated experts, with you as the expert on regular education. This team becomes the central force that oversees the ongoing education of the student in your class. The team oversees student assessment to determine his or her needs and achievements, and uses this assessment to determine the level of support and the kind of educational programs the child requires. Membership of this team changes as the student's needs change.

Long-term members include the parents or caregivers and the advisory visiting teacher (hearing and/or vision). The advisory teacher in sense impairment helps inform team members on the unique needs of each student and advises how to develop appropriate ways to cater for these needs over time. The more traditional multidisciplinary and

interdisciplinary teams, in which members have rigid role boundaries and work in isolation from each other, are being replaced by more flexible, transdisciplinary teams in which roles are in a constant state of transition and in which planning is highly collaborative. Deirdre, the teacher in the case study at the beginning of this chapter, was finding the prospect exciting but daunting. Collaboration is the basis for all services for students with a sense impairment.

Support is not only educational and might include:

- helping parents accept their having a child with a disability;
- information about the range of available government services;
- information detailing the effects of sense loss on the child and his or her family throughout the family life cycle;
- assistance in learning how best to provide child care and learning experiences to stimulate optimum development;
- help from other parents who have an older child with sense loss; and
- help from adults who have sense loss.

All team members help each other by assuming roles that are supportive (caring), facilitative (promoting independent problem-solving), informative (providing direct assistance), and prescriptive (identifying specific paths of action) but often the advisory teacher in hearing or vision impairment takes on the pivotal role of primary programmer and communication facilitator (Topor, Holbrook, & Koenig, 2000).

Birth to school

For children from birth to three years of age, an individualised family services plan (IFSP) is used to ensure that all services being provided to the child are coordinated and organised to fit in with the needs of the whole family. Ideally, all major hearing and vision loss should be identified before three months of age so that expert early intervention can be introduced immediately.

For the infant with *hearing loss* these specific needs relate primarily to communication. It is important to distinguish among language (the code or system used for communication), speech (the oral production of a sound-based language) and sign (the visual production of a gestural-based language or a sound-based language). Hearing loss affects speech and sound-based language development. Deaf and hard-of-hearing children experience problems in learning speech and sound-based language, depending on the level of hearing loss and opportunities for learning. Problems with communication lead to flow-on problems, especially in social development and learning experiences. From birth to three years of age is regarded as a critical time, with early diagnosis, amplification, and early intervention being of paramount importance. Parents must make decisions about their child's communication and which teaching

method is best to use: oral communication, total communication, or bilingual–bicultural approaches or some combination of these. The early-intervention teacher works with the parents to help them learn to communicate with their child in the most natural (for both child and parents) and effective way.

For the infant with *vision loss*, specific needs relate to security, communication, exploration, and mobility. Early experiences shape the way in which the child constructs the world, and lay the foundation for future learning. Many factors at or around the child's birth can conspire to isolate the child. Parents and families are especially likely to be emotionally vulnerable at the time of diagnosis, not knowing how best to help their child. The family might need to be taught how to engage in and enjoy physical interactions. Parents can be taught to use talk and touch to make the child's world more predictable and secure, and to help interpret sounds and smells. During bathing, drying, or dressing, body parts can be named (e.g., "I'm washing your feet"). Lack of vision inhibits the development of the child's ability to act on his or her environment. There can be a "mismatch in the timing between when an infant is physically ready to reach (by about 5 months) and when his or her auditory processing ability can attach some meaning to sound (the last quarter of the first year)" (Bishop, 2000, p. 226), and this means that unless development is explicitly encouraged the child might not act on the environment until after the first year. From birth to three years of age is therefore a critical time for children with vision impairment, with early diagnosis, vision correction, and early intervention being very important.

The school years

Children with sense loss might start school at around three years of age. Attention should be given to the transition from home to school. School might begin with one or two half-day kindergarten sessions a week, gradually increasing to five full-day sessions by the age of five years, with up to half of these being spent at inclusive preschool programs. During these two to three years the teacher, along with the individualised education plan (IEP) team, will emphasise language and concept development, exploration, independence, play, and social skills. An IEP will be used throughout the school years. Much of this time will be spent preparing the child to begin primary school with his or her same-age peers. Particular attention must be given to ensuring that the child has a well-developed understanding of basic concepts that relate to one-to-one correspondence, size, shape, quantity, time, order, and direction because they are prerequisites for future work in primary school (Bishop, 2000).

Students with hearing loss typically acquire language in the same order as, but at a slower rate than, their hearing peers (Paul, 1998). Hearing loss causes students to miss many incidental opportunities to learn. This slows down speech and language acquisition. Deaf students typically have smaller vocabularies, use simpler sentence structure

(poorly arranged and incomplete), employ more rigid language composition, find difficulty in differentiating between questions and statements, and experience problems with plurals and tense. For hearing children, speech and language acquisition is largely spontaneous and natural. Hearing children arrive at school as already competent communicators. They also have much knowledge about what it means to read and write. Literacy (the decoding and producing of text to graphically represent a phonologically based language) is relatively easy for hearing children to learn, especially those with advanced speech and language skills. It is much more difficult for deaf and hard-of-hearing children (Power & Leigh, 1998). Many deaf and hard-of-hearing students complete their education, having achieved only a Year 4 or 5 reading level. This means that they progress about three months for each calendar year.

Sam has had an intensive early childhood program that has been strongly supported by his parents. He already knows most of his basic concepts and, even though he becomes frustrated, his oral language skills are only 12 to 18 months behind the other students. He has a smaller vocabulary and makes errors, especially with tense and plurals. Also his speech lacks precision—he misses some consonants and lacks modulation. He knows a lot about reading. He has had literally several hundred books read to him over the years. A lot of the books his teacher Deirdre will use in Year 1 will undoubtedly be old favourites for Sam, so hopefully this will give him a head start.

Low reading levels, together with gaps in the range, depth, and breadth of background knowledge, make learning more difficult in all academic areas. Despite slower oracy and literacy development, the student with hearing loss might well have the same intellectual ability as his or her peers. Even though the language might have to be simplified, the intellectual challenge of the material must not be compromised. Teachers achieve this by respecting the student's age and experience when choosing learning goals, and by encouraging the student to think more deeply about what he or she has been communicating. Teaching approaches in the past identified problem or deficit areas, and explicitly taught these skills in isolation. Nowadays the emphasis is on recognising and encouraging the student to use and expand his or her skill base. Holistic methods that actively involve the student in the learning process enable the student to learn to communicate through self-expression. The student communicates about issues that are important to him or her, to an audience that is important to him or her. Ongoing assessment is used to inform instruction by identifying the compensatory skills that the student needs to learn.

Difficulties with communication affect the child's social and emotional development negatively. Incomplete communication makes it difficult for the student to learn social norms, conversation rules, ways to respond appropriately, and even how to develop close relationships. Consequently, students who are deaf or hard of hearing experience higher levels of childhood depression, withdrawal, and isolation. Parents, peers, and teachers can all play valuable roles in promoting positive psychosocial and emotional development, especially in the development of a positive self-concept (van Gurp, 2001). Research indicates that deaf children of deaf parents who learn sign language arrive at school with more sophisticated language skills, attain higher levels of social maturity, exhibit greater levels of behavioural self-control, and seem better adjusted when it comes to accepting their own hearing loss.

Even though *students with vision impairment* follow the same core curriculum as sighted students and work toward the same high expectations, their core curriculum must also include an extended component. Many things that sighted students learn incidentally through vision must be systematically and sequentially taught to students with vision impairment. This extended curriculum includes compensatory academic skills, including large print, audio reading, and braille. For the student with vision impairment, the basis of independence is literacy. Other compensatory skills include O&M, social-interaction skills, recreation and leisure skills, career education, technology, and visual-efficiency skills.

Preparation to move to secondary school begins in primary school, with particular attention being given to the development of increasing independence and organisational skills. Secondary school is very different from primary school. In primary school there is a class teacher who is responsible for a single group of students. This group of students spends most of its time in the same classroom. In secondary school there are many different teachers, each responsible for a particular subject. They might teach upwards of 180 students a week, so they have less time to consider the needs of individual students. Students move from one classroom to another, so there are many different spaces to understand. No single staff member oversees student needs. This makes problem-solving and communication more complicated. There are pedagogical differences as well. Teachers in primary school use multisensory teaching approaches that enable them to offer flexible curricula. Secondary teaching approaches are more didactic and less flexible. Strategies that can help students in secondary school include dropping one subject or applying to replace one school subject with one expanded curriculum subject (e.g., O&M), taking three years to complete Years 11 and 12, and organising volunteers to help with reading and tutoring.

School to adulthood

The IEP changes as the student's needs change. As students mature, increased levels of responsibility are given to them. By secondary school, the student should be making a major contribution to the IEP himself or herself. A student does this by learning about personal needs and communicating these to teachers and parents. Learning self-advocacy skills is an essential part of the process. For students 14 years and older, an individualised transition plan (ITP) is also implemented. The ITP is developed to help students prepare for independent adult community living. To address these issues,

team members include non-educational representatives from the community, particularly those who will help the student plan in the areas of work, leisure and life skills.

Daily living skills are an important component and might have to be specifically taught (e.g., clothes care, house-cleaning, personal grooming, food preparation, shopping, identifying, and avoiding risky situations). Another area is sex education with

Box 6.2 A view from the classroom

The following is taken from Tony Smith's school report. Tony is eight years old. He and his 10-year-old sister, Tanya, attend Mango Creek Road State School. Tony is fully included in Ms Browne's Year 3 classroom and has weekly visits from an advisory teacher in vision impairment. Tony has low vision (6/60 in his better eye after correction). This means that he has to be six metres away to see what visually unimpaired children can see at 60 metres. At present Tony is reading N24 print (see the size of the school name on the report). Tony finds it easier to read print that does not have a serif, such as Helvetica.

Mango Creek Road State School

2001 Progress Report

Year 3 Semester 1

NAME: Tony Smith

CLASS: 3B

TEACHER: Ms Browne

The early years of childhood are the formative years when children rapidly grow and develop. It is a time when much learning takes place. All children are individuals. Each child is unique and will develop at his or her own pace. This report is a summary of your child's achievements in Year 3. The report highlights your child's particular strengths and identifies areas where ongoing support is still required.

The report is organised as a continuum of your child's progress from works with support (S) to starting to work independently (I). Works with support (S) means your child needs assistance to keep on task when learning required skills, processes and knowledge. Starting to

work independently (I) means your child is starting to show interest, motivation, and is demonstrating mastery of required skills, processes and knowledge.

Additional information is provided about your child's effort.

C = Commendable

S = Satisfactory

N = Inconsistent

ENGLISH

SPEAKING & LISTENING	Effort: C I S
Speaks audibly and clearly to an audience	<------X------------>
Expresses ideas clearly	<------X------------>
Listens attentively in class situations	<-X----------------->
Understands and follows directions	<----X-------------->

HANDWRITING	Effort: S
Writes neatly	<-----------------X->
Uses correct pencil grip	<-----------------X->
Correct formation of letters and numerals	<-----------------X->

WRITING	Effort: S
Use of sentence structure	<---------X--------->
Use of story structure	<---------X--------->
Use of proofreading and editing strategies	<-----------------X->
Application of strategies to assist spelling	<-----------------X->

READING	Effort: S
Use of reading strategies	<---------X--------->
Independent selection of appropriate books	<-----------------X->
Gains meaning from text	<---------X--------->

TEACHER COMMENT

English:

Tony works consistently in all areas of his school work. Tony speaks clearly and expresses himself well. He follows directions accurately and has very good listening skills (probably the best in

the class). Tony now holds his head up and faces the person he is speaking to. Also he has stopped swaying from side to side while he is talking. He is getting much better at being able to tell the mood of the conversation, whether the person is happy or sad, angry or relaxed. He needs to be congratulated for his progress in this area.

Handwriting continues to be the biggest challenge. Tony has to get so close to his work that he smudges it with his nose. This means it is often messy. Using a black felt-tip pen on thick ruled A3 paper has helped. We have increased the slope on his desk and added a desk lamp and these changes have also been beneficial. Tony's writing is more legible but he is still quite slow. This means he does not finish his work at the same time as the other students. With your support I would like Tony to do 15 minutes writing practice each week night for homework next semester. This will build up his confidence and speed. Tony responds well to goals so we could count the number of words he can write in a 15-minute period and give him a reward when he can double this number.

Tony has a clear understanding of sentence and story structure. His slowness at writing means he often does not get around to proofreading and editing, nor does he reflect on his spelling as much as I would like. His reading is continuing to develop. He likes reading and uses a range of strategies including looking closely at the illustrations. He has a reasonable understanding of the meaning. The fact that Tony has been reading largeprint books which have been provided by the advisory teacher means that he has not been going to the library with the other students to select his own reading material. This is a problem which we could focus on at the next IEP meeting. A CCTV would make a big difference.

attendant concepts of gender identity, privacy, and appropriate time and place. You will recall that issues such as these were preoccupying Karen during her last year at school.

Tertiary education institutions, such as technical and further education (TAFE) colleges and universities, have a high level of support to assist those with sense impairment in their studies. However, the workplace is usually another story. It is a sad fact that there are still widespread negative attitudes in the community about the capabilities of people with sense impairment. A much higher percentage of people with a sense impairment are unemployed than is the case with the non-disabled population, especially among women and minority groups. Schools can help to address this problem by explicitly teaching pre-employment skills, by promoting social interaction between those with sense disabilities and their peers, and by providing more on-location job training.

Individualising education

Individualising education for students with a sense impairment encompasses psychosocial aspects as well as teaching strategies. Table 6.1 (page 270) summarises ways to help students with sense impairments overcome psychosocial problems that they might encounter in school. The regular teacher has an important role.

Instructional strategies for deaf and hard-of-hearing students

Communication

Significant hearing loss causes delayed language development and speech problems, and thus has a major impact on the student's ability to communicate orally. Teachers must, therefore, pay particular attention to supporting student communication. Ensure that the student is aware that someone is about to talk. Make certain the student is watching the speaker's face. Monitor the student's ability to follow classroom talk by asking the student to repeat major points and rephrase instructions for the student by using simpler language. Provide written backups when oral communication is taking place. Encourage hearing peers to contribute by sharing lesson notes, and by signalling nonvisual changes. Promote home–school communication by maintaining a daily dialogue or record of student learning, to be completed by the student, the parents and the teacher.

Experiential learning

Because of difficulties with communication, deaf and hard-of-hearing students find lessons that are based on a lot of teacher talk very hard to follow. They respond much better to being actively engaged in activities that enable them actually to experience the concept that is being studied. Experiential learning means that the teacher makes certain that the student is thoroughly conversant with a concept at a practical level before that concept is studied at an abstract level. A teacher can introduce experiential learning in the classroom in various ways, including field trips, acting out a story, role plays and conducting experiments.

Build new learning on what is already known

Communication problems caused by hearing loss often result in gaps in learning. Therefore, the teacher needs to assess the student's knowledge before teaching begins. The teacher then scaffolds learning. This means that the teacher uses the student's knowledge to develop a sequence of instruction, with each new step being a logical extension of what the student already knows. With each step, the teacher provides opportunity for practice and practical application. As the student becomes more confident of his or her ability, the teacher gradually reduces the level of support until the student is able to function at an independent level.

Table 6.1 Ways to include students with sense impairments (SWSI)

Challenge	Peers	Low vision	Blind	Hard of Hearing	Deaf
Student to play games with other students in playground	Start a buddy system where volunteers identify ways to include student in game	Explicitly teach student skills that enable active participation in game	Adapt game in ways that enable or promote student involvement	Explicitly teach student rules of the game; practice these skills before student joins game	Interpreter starts game rolling by providing a communication bridge
Student to interact socially with other students	Increase student awareness of what having a sense impairment means (e.g., teach essential signs)	Ensure student is functionally independent; give student social tasks (e.g., hand out worksheets to class)	Work with parents to establish opportunities for social interactions with class peers outside school	Introduce peer tutoring by which a hearing student works with the HOH student on a set activity	Structure regular natural opportunities for social interaction with peers in class; involve interpreter
Student to participate in academic school work	Establish high expectations for *all* students; seat SWSI near hard-working students; reward engagement; help with transitions, beginnings; endings, starting new activities	Ensure low-vision aids are appropriate (felt pens, thick lined paper); check lighting, print size contrast; reduce visual clutter; reduce frustration; increase opportunities for success	Build lesson on experiences familiar to student; encourage child to learn by doing; use concrete materials; provide opportunities for over-learning; help child generalise from one setting to another	Ensure hearing aids are working; use FM system; place student in good viewing position; check room acoustics; reduce background noise; face student when talking; reduce movement around room	Ensure interpreting needs being met; motivate student by taking into account student's strengths, personal interests, learning style; increase predictability by providing consistent, explicit lesson structure

Student misses large chunks of classroom work	Roster students to become note takers; notes available for *all* students; teach from known to unknown; check for understanding; use differentiated curriculum	Allow student to move around class room so he or she can view visual material up close; enlarge visual aids; locate aids near child; allow extra time to complete work	Ensure all visual aids have been taped, brailled or translated into tactile format before class begins; describe visual components of lesson; attend to organisational needs	Pretest for foundation skills; explicitly teach missing concepts; provide ample opportunity for practice; constantly check for gaps in learning	Give interpreter lesson plan, highlighting key concepts, worksheets, proposed questions for deaf student before class; match task difficulty with student ability
Student to work independently	Provide ongoing opportunities for students to work independently; resist temptation to do work for student; have exciting enrichment tasks on hand; allow students who complete work early to self-correct and move onto new activity	Low-vision student might need extra time to complete activity independently; whole of class correction can result in student missing out on independent work activity; allow time for student to complete set activity independently	Student might be used to working in one-to-one situations and over-rely on adult guidance; make certain student knows what to do, and that student is capable of doing the task; identify time when no helpers are around, then allow time for student to complete task	Begin with task student can confidently complete within short time period; gradually increase task length or complexity; set aside weekly sessions in which student must complete set tasks within set time limit before being able to move onto new independent activity	Ensure interpreter, teacher's aide, deaf specialist, parent, and other students are *not* helping student complete independent task; emphasise importance of independent work; allow student to complete enrichment task in own time if he or she wishes
Student to participate in organisational decision-making	Establish a classroom or school culture in which *all* students are actively involved in organisational decision-making; liaise with parents, staff, school community	Involve low-vision student in the planning stages of activities by using brainstorming, home projects; research methods such as surveys, interviews; give students advance notice of a planning session	Adapt class responsibilities so blind student can actively participate in full range of student jobs, both within class and whole of school; consult with blind adults	Hold meetings in which students develop class rules; ensure HOH student involvement by holding formal voting using written preferential voting forms; involve student in vote counting	Invite Deaf adults to visit the school and participate in learning activities; invite Deaf adults to improve class room; start a file of Deaf heroes

Collaboration

As a member of the IEP team, the teacher is involved in ongoing collaboration with the parents, specialist teachers, therapists, and the interpreter. The deaf or hard-of-hearing student, and even other class members, can be involved. Apart from hearing students being assigned tasks such as note-taker or communication buddy, deaf and hard-of-hearing students can be actively involved in collaborative class learning activities such as peer tutoring and cooperative learning. In peer tutoring, students take turns at being tutor and tutee. Cooperative learning involves the formation of groups in which students of varying ability level each play a vital role in the learning activity and achieve at a level appropriate to them.

Visual learning

For deaf and hard-of-hearing students, the classroom must be highly visual. Every learning activity should be translated into a visual form. The student's problems with communication make it particularly important to rethink oral information in visual forms. A teacher might reinterpret ideas into a visual medium in various ways, including demonstrations, modelling, natural gestures, visual cues, preferential seating, pictures, illustrations, cartoons, semantic maps, graphic organisers, flow charts, videos (with captioning), printed lesson plans, charts, slides, and computer technology (Lewis & Jackson, 2001).

Environment

The teacher must be constantly aware of what it means to have hearing loss. It is a good idea to request a separate classroom that is removed from the rest of the school and noise sources such as roads. Instruct the groundsperson to mow at times other than lesson times. Redesign the classroom to minimise distraction and to maximise student participation. Reduce noise by adding carpets, rugs, and curtains, and create noise absorbers by strategically locating bulletin boards, partitions, and cork display boards. Ensure that fans, heaters, overhead projectors, and air conditioners run quietly. Involve other students by allocating equity roles (e.g., explicitly identifying a change of speaker), by helping the student follow a conversation, preparing a text copy of intercom or loudspeaker messages, and by visually representing the fire alarm or non-visual changes to routine. Allow any student who speech reads to sit close to speaker. Encourage deaf and hard-of-hearing students to feel free to move around the class when necessary. Invite deaf adults to visit your classroom to offer suggestions on how to make it even more deaf friendly.

Interpreter

Deaf students who sign might attend regular classes with an interpreter who acts as a communication bridge to hearing students and teachers. An interpreter can use either signed English or sign language. The interpreter might or might not be prepared to

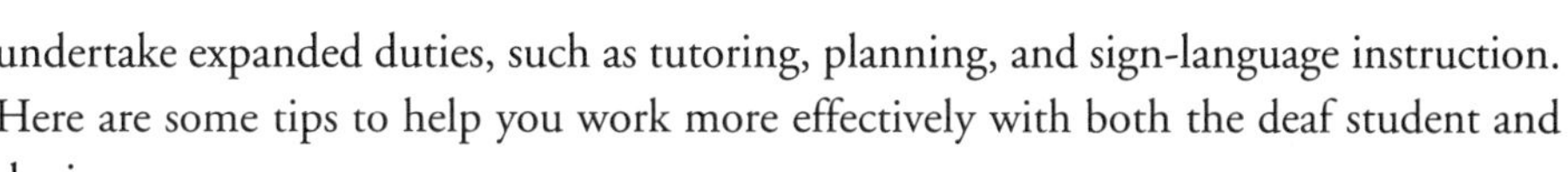

undertake expanded duties, such as tutoring, planning, and sign-language instruction. Here are some tips to help you work more effectively with both the deaf student and the interpreter.

Before the lesson

Give the student and the interpreter copies of your lesson plan, highlighting key vocabulary and concepts, and particular questions that you intend to ask the deaf student. Include copies of all worksheets that will be completed during the lesson, together with details of any student learning activities. Discuss how learning activities can be organised to promote student involvement (e.g., which students could be included in a cooperative learning group, and what the teacher and interpreter could do to help). Check deaf student's own planning for the lesson. Does the student have the required materials? Does the student have sufficient knowledge or skills to be able to participate in the lesson? Has homework been completed? If not, can these concepts be explicitly taught before the lesson? Identify ways to promote social interaction with other students during the lesson. Ensure that both the student and the interpreter understand you have high expectations regarding student participation, and that you expect to be informed immediately a problem arises during the lesson.

During the lesson

Ensure that the deaf student and the interpreter can clearly see you, your visual aids, and the other students. Keep movement around the class to a minimum. Face the student when you are talking. Do not talk while you are writing on the blackboard. Be careful not to obscure your face behind objects such as hair or reading material. Remember that it takes time for your message to get to the deaf student, so give the student advance warning that you are going to ask a question. Stick closely to your lesson plan. Allow time for the student to look at visual aids and to receive your message. Provide frequent, comprehensive checks to make certain that the student understands what was presented. Expect the deaf student to be actively involved in all aspects of the lesson, including class discussion and cooperative learning activities. Pay particular attention to reverse interpretation. Emphasise obtaining meaning from the communication. The student can use sign during group acting out situations, with the interpreter providing the voice-over.

After the lesson

Debrief. Check that the student has a clear understanding of homework and independent learning tasks. Does the interpreter have any comments? Keep a record of this communication in a diary. Use a diary to help plan the next lesson. Once routines have been established before and after the lesson, meetings will tend to be shorter and less frequent.

Table 6.2 Hearing loss as it relates to volume, ability to use speech in communication and classroom implications

Hearing in better ear (dB)	Degree of loss (support)	Student's ability to use speech in communication	Classroom implications
20–40	Mild (might benefit from preferential seating, speech language pathology (SLP), hearing aids, speech reading, auditory training)	Difficulty telling that you are being addressed; some difficulty in conversation—might miss unvoiced consonants ("s", "f"); mild language delay possible; some speech problems (articulation)	Teacher and peers use explicit method (tactile or visual) to inform student conversation is about to begin; frequently check student is following and understanding classroom communication (plurals, tense); create communication-rich supportive classroom environment; coordinate with SLP
40–65	Moderate (preferential seating, SLP, hearing aids, speech reading auditory training special education advisory teacher in hearing impairment + IEP)	Difficulty in conversation (hear only louder voiced sounds); difficulty hearing at a distance; difficulty hearing over background noise; some language delay likely; speech problems (articulation, modulation)	As above; require student to watch speaker; speaker's face and body in clear view; teacher must have clear enunciation for speech reading; seat student closer to conversation; reduce background noise (FM); improve classroom acoustics; explicitly teach key concepts; simplify language (match language difficulty to student ability); collaborate with IEP team, parents, advisory teacher in hearing impairment, SLP

65–95	Severe (as above; more substantial level of special education support required)	No speech sounds without amplification; some understanding of speech with amplification but normal conversation virtually impossible; language delay; flow-on learning difficulties	As above (increase level of support); total communication (simplify language for all classroom work, particularly reading and writing); increase visual cues; adjustments, modifications, accommodations to suit individual learning needs and learning style
95+	Profound (as above; more substantial level of special education support required, might benefit from cochlear implant)	No functional hearing; no speech or other sounds without amplification; normal conversation impossible; visually dependent; significant language delay; significant flow on learning difficulties	As above (increase level of support); use interpreter (Auslan, NZ sign language); visual classroom (all learning based on vision); support social and emotional development; fill in gaps in learning; compensate for reduced learning opportunities

Instructional strategies for low-vision and educationally blind students

Physical environment

Teachers must make an effort to provide a suitable vision-support environment that encourages and facilitates learning. Here are some suggestions.

Artwork displayed in windows can block natural light and overhead displays can be distracting. Glare is to be avoided. Students should not be seated facing a window and the teacher should not stand in front of a light source. Usually the student is positioned at the front of the class. The child should be encouraged to exercise control over his or her particular needs. In terms of lighting, most students benefit from additional lighting directed to the work surface. However, some students are light-sensitive and work better in dim light. If the student has stronger sight in one eye than the other he or she might prefer to sit on the opposite side of the classroom.

Plan how you want your room, then invite the student and his or her IEP team to help you redesign it. It is best to do this before school begins and to keep this design throughout the year. The student's desk might have an adjustable, sloping surface to prevent posture problems when doing close visual work, and raised edges to stop equipment accidentally falling off. The desk needs to be located close to power-points for additional lights, LVDs, tape recorder, and other technology. Preferential seating allows the student with vision impairment to sit close to the action (e.g., blackboard, demonstration, sit slightly to one side of the TV screen or computer monitor) and participate in class activities without interfering with the rest of the class. He or she might need to sit very close to the TV. A blind student might need extra shelf and cabinet storage because braille books and equipment take up a lot of space. Students will need to be taught how to organise and store information for fast retrieval.

Acoustics should be factored into the design. The less vision a student has, the more important listening becomes. Therefore, background noise must be kept to a minimum.

The student should already have a functional working knowledge of the classroom before classes begin. Orient the student to the room by introducing the whole first, and then fit in the various parts. For example:

- "We have a square wooden classroom that is six metres by six metres. Can you tell me how long a metre is on this ruler?"
- "The ceiling is two metres high. Let's see if we can touch it with the ruler."
- "The room has one door and ten windows. Let's walk from the door, and around the room, noting each window."

The student must be notified if there are going to be any changes. Minimise danger spots by keeping doors fully open or closed, and drawers closed. Ensure that sighted students do not leave things lying around. Appoint sighted monitors to check frequently that the environment is safe. Encourage the vision impaired student to feel free to move around the class when necessary. Invite blind adults to visit your classroom to offer suggestions on how to make it even more blind-friendly. Early dismissal provides the student with enough time to travel independently from one class to another.

Learning environment

Low expectations negatively affect the student's self-concept and motivation (self-fulfilling prophecy). Holbrook and Koenig (2000) recommend that students with vision impairment be held to the same academic and social standards as their sighted classmates, to prepare them for adult life. When working with students with vision impairment, teachers should follow a commonsense approach. This includes maintaining high but realistic expectations, acknowledging the limitations imposed by the sense loss, and recognising student achievements. Koenig and Holbrook (2000b) emphasised the need for three special methods.

Concrete experience

Concrete experiences are encounters that involve real objects. Knowledge of experiences can be expanded using scale models, explicit instruction, and enrichment activities. Concrete experiences provide students with a sense of reality that might otherwise be missed when students learn by listening alone.

Learning by doing

Learning by doing involves the student completing the task by himself or herself. If students cannot observe how an activity is done, they must learn how to do it by being led through the actions over and over again until independent mastery is achieved. If an adult does the task for the student, the student misses out on this opportunity to learn.

Unifying experiences

Unifying experiences involve the need for the student with vision impairment to be taught explicitly how to make connections between parts and the whole. They need help to make connections between what is learnt in the classroom and what one does in the real world. This is particularly important in the area of self-advocacy.

Auditory environment

By talking, teachers help students with vision impairment understand what is happening in the classroom. Teachers announce their presence and teach other class members to do the same. When moving from one cooperative learning group to

Table 6.3 Vision loss and classroom implications

Visual acuity (metres)	Degree of loss (support)	Student's ability to see	Classroom implications
<6/6 to 6/12 or field of vision <160 to 80 degrees	Mild (glasses, improved lighting)	After correction student will be able to see most things other students can see; might experience some problems seeing the blackboard, whiteboard, illustrations, charts, pictures, especially if the print is small; might experience problems in poorly lit classrooms	Allow student to move to see material; switch on overhead lighting if natural light dim
<6/12 to 6/18 or field of vision 80 to 40 degrees	Moderate (glasses, reduced glare, improved lighting, preferential seating, vision therapy)	Problems seeing the blackboard, whiteboard, illustrations, charts, pictures unless the print is large; might experience problems switching between blackboard to workbook (e.g., copying from the blackboard); might experience problems during overcast, rainy days, in poorly lit classrooms	As above; use curtains to minimise glare; use large print for blackboard, whiteboard, illustrations, charts, pictures, or else provide print copy of teaching material; check for visual fatigue
6/18 to 6/60 or field of vision 40 to 20 degrees	Low vision; severe (glasses, vision-training, reduced glare, improved lighting, preferential seating, low-vision devices, special education, advisory teacher in vision impairment +IEP)	Great difficulty seeing blackboard, whiteboard, OHT, illustrations, charts, pictures even up close; difficulty reading print (especially unusual or fancy print, with serifs, with background shading poor colour contrast); great difficulty switching between blackboard and workbook (e.g., copying from the blackboard) requiring low-vision aids; eyes will tire, especially after extended fine-vision work after lunch	Increase level of support; provide print copy of of teaching material; teacher works with student to ensure contrast, space (size, clutter), illumination, time and colour used to maximise visual efficiency; student given desk light, special equipment—desk, LVD; teacher acknowledges and respects student's

			preferences re using vision and/or other sources of sense information; organise fine-vision work in morning; allow student to use other senses—alternate activities (one usual, one auditory); describe visual component of lesson; collaborate with IEP team, parents, advisory teacher in vision impairment, O&M instructor
≤6/60 or field of vision ≤20 degrees	Legally blind to educationally blind; profound (as above, more substantial level of special education, core plus extended curriculum, braille, audio reading, O&M, daily living skills)	Vision might be sufficient to see only enlarged well-contrasted shapes; might be able to perceive only light; might not have any vision at all	As above (increase level of support); print and/or braille (print materials and illustrations transcribed into braille or audio format—requires advance planning); specialised braille or audio equipment; classroom design—ensure space, no changes; all learning non-visual = concrete experiences, learning by doing, unifying experiences; support social and emotional development; fill in gaps; compensate for reduced learning opportunities

another the teacher might say: "Hi, Mrs Smith here. May I join your group? Tell me about what you've been doing?" And, when leaving, the teacher might say: "Thanks guys. I'm going to check on another group now." Verbal instructions must be clear and unambiguous, and must avoid vague positional language (such as "here" and "there"). If visual information (such as a blackboard message) is not available as a handout, it must be read out. Demonstrations can be made more accessible through descriptions, repeated visual or hand-over-hand kinaesthetic re-enactments and peer tutoring.

Visual environment

Children with normal vision should keep their work knuckle-to-elbow length away from their eyes to maintain optimum fusional vergence and accommodation ability. However, it is necessary and acceptable for children with low vision to hold their reading material very close to their eyes in order to see the print. This technique is a natural and effective form of magnification. Copying involves changes of focus that can quickly induce visual fatigue. The student might need to rest the eye muscles and change task. General measures to improve visual efficiency are photo enlargements, improved lighting, increased contrast, and reduced visual clutter. Visual items can be reproduced so the student can understand what is required (e.g., use real objects, photo enlargements, colour, audio description).

Extra time

Plan early to ensure that backup braille, large print, and audio resources are available on the day of the lesson. Useful classroom resources include playdough, builder blocks, string, buttons, spur wheels, glue, sticky tape, staples, Blu-Tack (to anchor objects), Braillabel (adhesive plastic sheets for nametags), felt adhesive paper, felt-tip pens, bold lined paper, hats or visors to reduce glare, colour acetate to go over printed page, Crammer abacus (for use in mathematics), raised line paper, writing guides (for signatures), and special measurement tools (talking or braille clock, braille ruler).

When teaching, allow the student with vision impairment extra time to become familiarised, visually or tactually, before requiring the student to complete a set task. Allow extra time to complete a task at the same level of achievement as sighted peers. Make certain that classroom tests are accessible for students with vision impairment in their own primary medium (e.g., braille, large print, audio). Whenever possible tests should be given to students with vision impairment at the same time as other students are doing their test. Therefore tests should be prepared well in advance. Students with vision impairment are given extra time to complete examinations (for one hour, 20 minutes of extra time is needed for braille, and 15 minutes if the student has low vision).

Table 6.3 (page 278)relates the degree of vision loss to its educational implications. All teachers should be aware of the visual status of every student in their classes. The

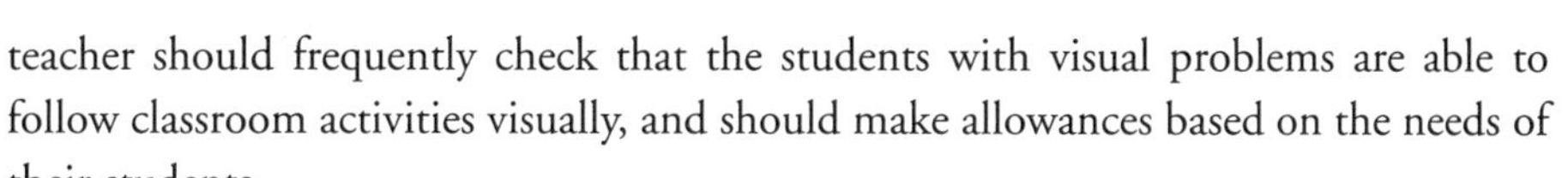
teacher should frequently check that the students with visual problems are able to follow classroom activities visually, and should make allowances based on the needs of their students.

SUMMARY

There are four major categories of sense impairment: deaf, hard of hearing, blind and low vision. Both hearing and vision loss exist on a continuum of severity from mild (high incidence) to profound (low incidence). Educational definitions of sense impairment focus on how the sense impairment affects the student's learning. In children, isolated sense impairments that are severe enough to require special education are rare.

Assessment follows on from identification by astute observation and/or screening. The teacher can use a screening checklist to help define suspicions. Medical referral is then made for diagnosis, treatment and/or the prescription of aids or prostheses. On confirmation of a sense impairment an educational plan team is established, which collaborates to organise educational service delivery. This is an ongoing process from the time of diagnosis throughout the school years.

Factors that modify the qualitative nature of the sense impairment are:

- age when the impairment occurred;
- visibility of loss;
- degree of stability of severity;
- association of other disabilities and abilities; and
- type and level of educational support that the child has already received.

An historic overview illustrates how the current position in the post-inclusion era has been reached, and that there is now a focus on educational service delivery outcome rather than process.

Promoting sense functioning and efficiency is an important role for educators. There are certain skills that need to be mastered. These are taught by specialists, such as advisory teachers and allied therapists. These skills include:

- learning how to use the aids and prostheses efficiently;
- sign language for the deaf;
- braille; and
- orientation and mobility training for the blind.

Technology includes hearing aids (behind-the-ear and radio/FM), cochlear implants, and low-vision devices.

Three communications strategies are presented and discussed. These are oral communication, total communication, and bilingual–bicultural approaches.

Strategies to promote information-gathering in the blind and those with low vision include maximising the use of any remaining sight and developing listening skills.

Hearing loss affects speech and sound-based language development. Problems with communication can lead to flow-on problems, especially social development and the range and depth of learning experiences. Vision loss considerably narrows the child's incidental experience of the world. Vision loss makes it more difficult for the individual to travel safely and independently. These are fundamental areas addressed by the individualised education plan (IEP). As the student moves up the school, the IEP expands its remit to emphasise work, leisure, and life skills.

Instructional strategies that work for students with a sense impairment were discussed in detail. For deaf and hard-of-hearing students, these strategies include facilitated communication, experiential learning, scaffolding, collaboration, visual learning, environmental manipulation, and working with an interpreter. Instructional strategies that work for blind and low-vision students include manipulation of the physical, visual, auditory, and learning environments, and the provision of extra time to get work completed.

Suggested reading

Texts

Gregory, S., Knight, P., McCracken, W., Powers, S., & Watson, L. (1998). *Issues in deaf education.* London: David Fulton Publishers.

Holbrook, M. C., & Koenig, A. J. (Eds). (2000). *Foundations of education (2nd ed.) volume I (volume II Koenig & Holbrook) Instructional strategies for teaching children and youths with visual impairments.* New York, NY: American Foundation for the Blind.

Kelley, P. & Gale, G. (Eds). (1998). *Toward excellence: Effective education for students with vision impairment.* Parramatta, Australia: North Rocks Press.

Luetke-Stahlman, B., & Luckner, J. (1991). *Effectively educating students with hearing impairments.* New York, NY: Longman.

Mason, H., McCall, S., Arter, C., McLinden. M., & Stone, J. (Eds). (1997). *Visual Impairment: Access to education for children and young people.* London: David Fulton Publishers.

Moores, D. F. (1996). *Educating the deaf: Psychology, principles, and practices* (4th ed.) Boston, MA: Houghton Mifflin.

Journals

Australian Journal of Education of the Deaf

American Annals of the Deaf

Journal of the South Pacific Educators in Vision Impairment

Journal of Visual Impairment and Blindness

Practical activities

1. Plan a 30-minute lesson for your school experience class (can be for early childhood, primary or secondary). Provide a full script of the lesson plus details of all learning activities. Rewrite the lesson to include:
   (a) a student with low vision;
   (b) a student who is blind;
   (c) a student who is hard of hearing; and
   (d) a student who is deaf.

   What kind of changes did you make to the lesson? How? Why?
2. Start a resource folder of assistive technology (both high technology devices such as voice synthesisers, and low technology devices such as white canes) that could be used by students who are blind or have low vision. In the description of each item include details of price, where available, areas where the device could be used (e.g., a white cane could be used for O&M), level of vision required, and the appropriate age of a student to be able to use it. Start a second resource folder of assistive technology for students who are deaf or hard of hearing, and provide the same details. How is the assistive technology different for students who are deaf and hard of hearing from those who are blind or have low vision?
3. Describe your bedroom to a friend. Remember to begin with the whole and then fit the details into the whole. List the problems you and your friend experience. How could you overcome these problems?
4. Prepare a seminar on Deaf culture. Is Deaf culture the same in Australia and New Zealand as it is in other countries?
5. Plan a route of travel from your home to a nearby facility. What important concepts (e.g., those related to time, distance, direction, environmental layout) would be required before a blind person could independently travel from your home to this facility? Make a list of important factors that need to be considered when students who are deaf or hard of hearing learn to travel independently.

References

Barraga, N. (1983). *Visual handicaps and learning* (rev. ed.). Austin, TX: Exceptional Resources.

Bishop, K. (2000). Early childhood. In A. J. Koenig & M. C. Holbrook (Eds). *Foundations of education (2nd ed.) volume II Instructional strategies for teaching children and youths with visual impairments* (pp. 225–263). New York, NY: American Foundation for the Blind.

Brannock, G. & Golding, L. (2000). *The 6-step method of teaching orientation and mobility.* Brisbane, Q: G. Brannock & L. Golding.

Ching, T. Y. C. (1994). *Speech perception in hearing-impaired children. Renwick College Monograph Number One.* Parramatta, NSW: North Rocks Press.

Gillon, G. & Young, A. (2001). *The phonological awareness skills of children who are blind.* Poster Session, 'FOCUS SPEVI—build the future, value the past', South Pacific Educators in Vision Impairment Biennial Conference, Auckland, New Zealand.

Higgins, A. (1997). *Addressing the health and educational consequences of otitis media among young rural school-aged children.* Townsville, Q: Australian Rural Education Research Association.

Holbrook, M. C. & Koenig, A. J. (2000). Basic techniques for modifying instruction. In A. J. Koenig & M. C. Holbrook (Eds). *Foundations of education (2nd ed.) volume II Instructional strategies for teaching children and youths with visual impairments* (pp. 173–195). New York, NY: American Foundation for the Blind.

Hubner, P. (2000). Visual impairment. In M. C. Holbrook & A. J. Koenig (Eds). *Foundations of education (2nd ed.) volume I History and theory of teaching children and youths with visual impairments* (pp. 55–76). New York, NY: American Foundation for the Blind Press.

Jeanes, R. C., Reynolds, B. E., & Coleman, B. (Eds). (1988). *Dictionary of Australasian signs for communication with the deaf* (2nd ed.). Melbourne: Victorian School for Deaf Children.

Johnson, R. C. (2000). Gallaudet forum addresses cochlear implant issues. *Research at Gallaudet, Spring,* 1, 5–10.

Johnston, T. (1998a). *Auslan dictionary—A dictionary of the sign language of the Australian Deaf Community* (2nd ed.). Parramatta, NSW: North Rocks Press.

Johnston, T. (1998b). *Signs of Australia—A new dictionary of Auslan (CD-ROM version)*. Parramatta, NSW: North Rocks Press.

Kelley, P. & Gale, G. (Eds). (1998). *Toward excellence: Effective education for students with vision impairment.* Parramatta, Australia: North Rocks Press.

Kelley, P., Gale, G., & Blatch, P. (1998). Theoretical framework. In P. Kelley & G, Gale (Eds). *Toward excellence: Effective education for students with vision impairment* (pp. 33–40). Parramatta, NSW: North Rocks Press.

Koenig, A. & Holbrook, M. C. (2000a). Literacy skills. In A. J. Koenig & M. C. Holbrook (Eds). *Foundations of education (2nd ed.) volume II Instructional strategies for teaching children and youths with visual impairments* (pp. 264–329). New York, NY: American Foundation for the Blind.

Koenig, A. J. & Holbrook, M. C. (2000b). Planning instruction in unique skills. In A. J. Koenig & M. C. Holbrook (Eds). *Foundations of education (2nd ed.) volume II Instructional strategies for teaching children and youths with visual impairments* (pp. 161–221). New York, NY: American Foundation for the Blind.

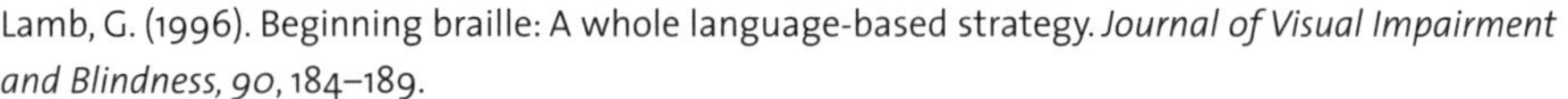

Lamb, G. (1996). Beginning braille: A whole language-based strategy. *Journal of Visual Impairment and Blindness, 90*, 184–189.

LaGrow, S. (1998). Orientation and mobility. In P. Kelley & G, Gale (Eds). *Toward excellence: Effective education for students with vision impairment* (pp. 193–207). Parramatta, NSW: North Rocks Press.

Lewis, M. S. J. & Jackson, D. W. (2001). Television literacy: Comprehension of program content using closed captions for the Deaf. *Journal of Deaf Studies and Deaf Education, 6*, 43–53.

McCall, S. (1997). The development of literacy through touch. In H. Mason & S. McCall with C. Arter, M. McLinden & J. Stone (Eds). *Visual Impairment: Access to education for children and young people.* London: David Fulton Publishers.

Mangold, S. (1994). *The Mangold developmental program of tactile perception and braille letter recognition.* Castro Valley, CA: Exceptional Teaching Aids.

Moores, D. F. (1993). Total inclusion/zero rejection models in general education: Implications for deaf children. *American Annals of the Deaf, 136*, 251.

Moores, D. F. (1996). *Educating the deaf: Psychology, principles, and practices* (4th ed.) Boston, MA: Houghton Mifflin.

Parker, D. & Schembri, A. (1996). *Technical signs for computer terms. A sign reference book for people in the computing field.* Parramatta, NSW: North Rocks Press.

Paul, P. V. (1998). *Literacy and deafness.* Boston, MA: Allyn & Bacon.

Power, D. & Leigh, G. (1998). Teaching reading and writing to deaf students: A brief history. *Australian Journal of Education of the Deaf, 4*, 16–19.

Silberman, R. K. (2000). Children and youths with visual impairments and other exceptionalities. In M. C. Holbrook & A. J. Koenig (Eds). *Foundations of education (2nd ed.) volume I History and theory of teaching children and youths with visual impairments* (pp. 173–196). New York, NY: American Foundation for the Blind Press.

Topor, I. L., Holbrook, M. C., & Koenig, A. J. (2000). Creating and nurturing effective educational teams. In A. J. Koenig & M. C. Holbrook (Eds). *Foundations of education (2nd ed.) volume II Instructional strategies for teaching children and youths with visual impairments* (pp. 3–26). New York, NY: American Foundation for the Blind.

Tuttle, D. (1996). Is listening literacy? *Journal of Visual Impairment and Blindness, 90*, 173–174.

van Gurp, S. (2001). Self-concept of Deaf secondary school students in different educational settings. *Journal of Deaf Studies and Deaf Education, 6*, 54–69.

7

Gifted and talented children and their education

EDDIE BRAGGETT

Case studies

When reading the following three case studies, you should ask yourself:

- What type of giftedness or talent did each of the students possess?
- Why was it difficult for some teachers to cope with each student's abilities?
- What particular teaching strategies were required to allow each student to excel?
- How did the teachers adapt the curriculum to each student's specific needs?
- What lessons can be learnt by all teachers when considering these three case studies?

Matthew

Matthew was a 6-year-old who caused considerable difficulty for his teacher and often reduced her to tears. He was an avid reader who had an exceptional vocabulary and spelling ability years in advance of his chronological age. Unfortunately, he knew that his spelling was extraordinarily advanced and taunted his teacher and other children to try to "catch me out"—something that they rarely did.

The teacher—in collaboration with his parents—devised weekly spelling lists for him based on those supplied by a local high school, but his success with these words simply increased the difficulty. After seeking further assistance, the teacher asked Matthew to underline in pencil in his latest reading books 50 words that he would like to learn to spell. He did this in three weeks, indicating such words as "disciplinarian", "homogeneous", "catastrophe", "manoeuvrable", and "boisterous". This prompted the teacher to require Matthew to devise his own spelling lists each week, an exercise that gradually expanded to planning his own reading with the aid of a local mentor who worked closely with the teacher.

After six weeks, Matthew was permitted to display some of his written work (together with other children) in the foyer of the neighbourhood bank and to read a story on a local FM radio station. As Matthew took increasing control of his learning and acquired additional skills, his arrogance quickly declined and he began to settle into normal group activities.

The regular curriculum was inappropriate for Matthew. A differentiated curriculum was essential.

Peta

Peta, 13 years of age and already in Year 9 at school, was an exceptionally bright student who had little difficulty in meeting all the school's requirements with a minimum of effort. Her parents and teachers were aware that she was capable of more challenging work but Peta resisted any attempt to increase her output or to undertake more demanding studies. She was quite happy to coast along academically and to spend time with her less-able peers in a range of healthy social activities. When told that she was underachieving, she readily agreed but was not the least concerned.

In the following year, Peta's parents moved house and Peta was enrolled in a different school in Year 10, one in which teachers grouped students in the classroom on interests, ability, and performance. Students worked in small groups and could accelerate the pace of their learning when necessary. Suddenly, Peta was challenged to work with students at her own level, a challenge that she gradually—and at first ruefully—accepted, but which over time, afforded her considerable satisfaction. She now acknowledges the advantages of working more closely to her potential while still enjoying friendships with others in a school that accepts and provides for different learning rates.

Ivan

Ivan was 14 years old, his family having emigrated to Australia when he was 11. He spoke with an accent and had problems expressing difficult concepts in English. His written work was understandably poor and his underdeveloped reading skills resulted in difficulties in most subjects. He liked physical activities and took a keen interest in sports.

One day in class, his English teacher found him inattentive and, upon enquiring, found him doodling in an exercise book. After the class had finished, the teacher asked if she might seek the book and Ivan reluctantly—and with embarrassment—gave it to her. She was so impressed by his sketches, his understanding of perspective, and his use of colour that she took the mildly protesting Ivan to the teacher of industrial arts who was likewise captivated by Ivan's ability. Gradually responding to the enthusiasm of the two teachers, Ivan brought some of his sketches to school and quickly won the praise of other staff. He was given assistance in graphic arts and referred to a commercial artist who lived near the school.

Within months, Ivan's creative potential showed up very strongly and he began to forge ahead in industrial arts, even assisting other students with their work. Although his English studies did not advance at the same rate, he acquired new confidence and zeal and made remarkable progress in his area of specialised interest.

What you will learn in this chapter

You will discover that:

- the concepts of giftedness and talent have changed considerably over the past 20 years or so;
- there are many different types and degrees of giftedness and talent;
- each teacher has a responsibility to identify students' gifts and talents through a curriculum-driven approach;
- modifications are required to classroom management techniques and to teaching strategies;

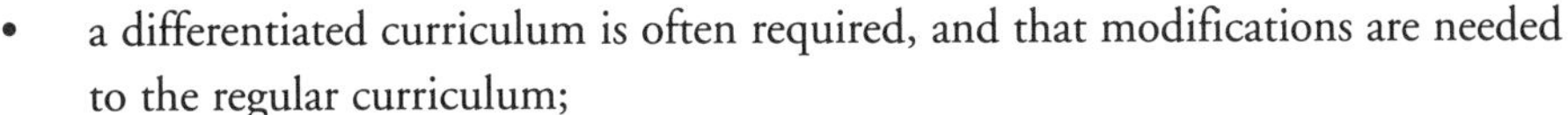

- a differentiated curriculum is often required, and that modifications are needed to the regular curriculum;
- many of the strategies used with gifted or talented students are applicable to all students in the classroom;
- a balance between inclusive approaches and separate provision is necessary; and
- the school and the home must be involved in a positive working relationship.

Problems that students might face

Students face a range of potential problems, depending upon the degree of giftedness they possess and the types of talent they have developed. In general, they might:

- realise that they are different from others and experience a sense of loneliness;
- be teased, even harassed, by other children;
- have fewer social contacts if their talents are individualistic;
- display increased sensitivity to social issues;
- experience boredom with simple learning tasks, revision exercises, and repetitive basic skills from an inappropriate curriculum;
- suffer from a lack of peer competition (challenge) in the regular classroom;
- underachieve and show decreased motivation for school-related learning; and
- suffer from ill-suited teaching methods.

Defining terms

There are several terms that constantly appear in the literature on gifted children, but they are often used very loosely and in quite different contexts. Moreover, some of these definitions have been modified over the years, reflecting a rapidly changing society, psychological advances, a concern for equity, and a heightened awareness of individual children and their needs We can trace the major changes in a brief overview.

Intelligence, creativity, and special abilities

Before the 1920s, gifted students were identified through the quality of their school performance and their ability to excel at school examinations. Others were conspicuous as prodigies who displayed precocious ability or skill at an early age. The advent of intelligence testing provided a more reliable method of assessing ability among larger numbers of children. One of the early advocates of intelligence testing, Louis Terman (1954), believed that giftedness could be measured by a single IQ score that reflected the child's ability to think logically and abstractly.

Accepting Terman's belief, educators in the 1920s and 1930s began to advocate separate classes for children who were identified as gifted on the basis of intelligence testing. They chose students who performed well at school and who fell within the top 2% of measured intelligence. By the 1940s it was widely believed that giftedness referred to higher mental processes as measured by intelligence tests (in thinking, reasoning, and making judgments). Talent was thought to be confined to those who were highly endowed with special talents (abilities) for inventive or creative production of which music and art were clear examples (Miles, 1946). Since that time, the constancy of the IQ has been disputed, and the predictive value of intelligence scores has been questioned. Today, it is widely accepted in Australasia that a child's measured intelligence needs to be considered with some caution and that other factors must be included when an educational decision is made.

Intelligence tests do not tap creativity and Guilford (1950) argued strongly for a range of primary abilities that were not included in the traditional view of intelligence. When he introduced the concepts of convergent and divergent abilities and spoke about flexibility, fluency, originality, spontaneity, and sensitivity to problems and improvisation, he questioned the older unitary view of giftedness (based on IQ alone) and advanced a multidimensional concept involving a range of factors. In doing so, he blurred the tenuous distinction between giftedness and talent. Then, when the USSR launched the first satellite, Sputnik, in 1957, further emphasis was given to specialised abilities—especially mathematics and science—and the school curriculum was strengthened in these areas. The importance of talent in technological courses was increasingly emphasised during the period from 1960 to 2000, and now forms an integral part of the curriculum in the 21st century.

A multidimensional concept

By the early 1980s, Australasian educators no longer viewed giftedness as a unitary concept based on measured intelligence, but as a multifaceted notion that included intelligence, creative thinking and production, and excellent school performance. Renzulli (1986) advocated a three-dimensional model involving above average intelligence, creativity, and task commitment, and Marland's (1972) multi-dimensional approach also received increasing recognition. He advocated that gifted and talented children are persons who, by virtue of outstanding abilities, are capable of high performance in the following areas, singly or in combination (Marland, 1972, p. 10):

- general intellectual ability;
- specific academic aptitude;
- creative or productive thinking;
- leadership ability;

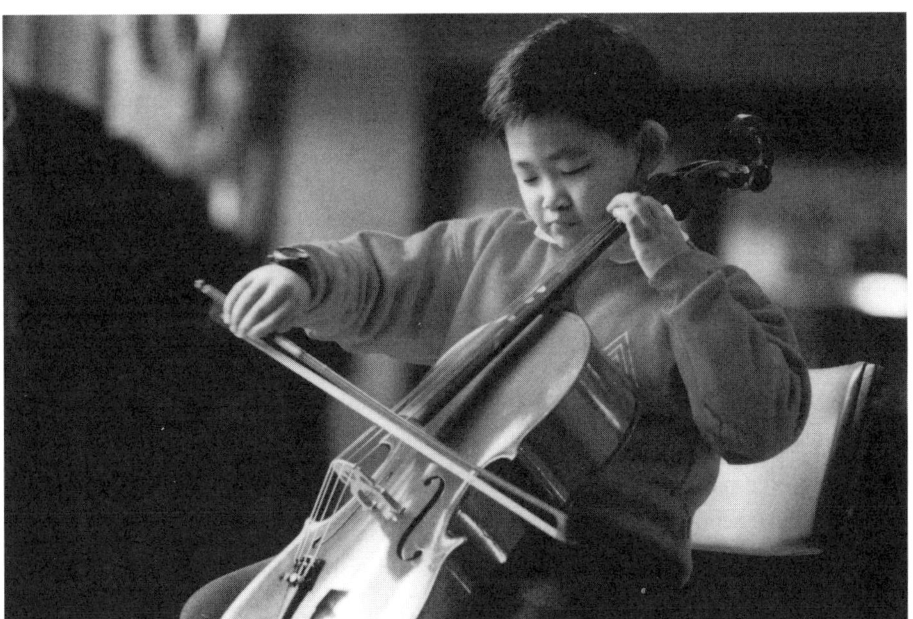

Musically gifted students may display their abilities at an early age and benefit from expert tuition.

- visual and performing arts; and
- psychomotor ability.

Even in the 1990s, a neo-Marland classification (e.g., Heller, Perieth, & Sierwald, 1990) continued to influence educators despite the lack of distinction between giftedness and talent, the continued acceptance of psychomotor abilities, and the inclusion of potential ability in the definition.

Issues of equity

From the mid-1980s, there was a growing concern with issues of equity that related to gifted students. Stemming from government initiatives, there was a move to consider indigenous populations (Australian Aborigines and Torres Strait Islanders, Maori, and Polynesians), students from non-English speaking backgrounds (NESB), girls, youngsters from educationally disadvantaged home backgrounds, students from country and remote areas, and those who had an impairment in some way. It was gradually accepted, and then emphasised, that gifted students were to be found in all these populations.

Numerous studies were conducted during the 1990s and into the 2000s in an effort to identify disadvantaged gifted and disabled gifted students, and to provide appropriate educational programs for them. These included provisions for Aboriginal students (Chaffey, 2000; Day, 1996; Gibson, 1992; Seletto & Diezmann, 2000); for

Maori and Polynesian students (Bevan-Brown, 1996); for children living in rural areas (Bisley, 1996; Dooley, 2000; Karvouni, 2000); and for girls (Kerr, 2000; Imison & Imison, 2000; Fitzgerald & Keown, 1996). Some attention was given to students with physical impairments and learning disabilities when the basis of medical classification helped to mask the talents of gifted students who have a disability (Leder, 1985; Savage, 1990), a problem accentuated by the reduced communication skills that characterise some forms of disability. There are, however, few up-to-date Australasian research findings on gifted children with a disability.

Gifts and talents

In their desire to be egalitarian, some educators adopt an ideological stance that emphasises the development of the gifts and talents of all students. It is argued that:

- all children have potential gifts and talents that need to be encouraged within the regular school; and
- the classroom teacher should be aware of, and provide for, these needs with resource assistance.

Although there are few teachers who would oppose the concept of maximising individual abilities (this being a general aim of Australian and New Zealand schools), this concept should not be confused with giftedness and its development. Gifts and talents, as used in this wider sense, can include any ability that a child possesses or any quality that might be further nurtured: the term refers to individual differences that should be developed to their potential no matter what that level might be. However, although all children can possess individual gifts and talents, not all children are gifted, and even fewer exhibit outstanding abilities. Because of teacher limitations or inadequate resources, there is a grave danger that students with exceptional potential will be overlooked or neglected if a policy of gifts and talents is adopted. Such a policy can ignore the starkly different needs that highly gifted students possess and can fail to recognise that all children are not gifted in comparison to their age-peers.

Multiple intelligences

In a separate development, but still within a multidimensional framework of giftedness, Gardner (Ramos-Ford & Gardner, 1997) challenged the notion of general intelligence and advocated multiple intelligences in its place. In the words of the authors: "we believe that human cognitive competence is better described as a set of abilities, talents, or mental skills that we have chosen to call 'intelligences'" (p. 55). According to Gardner, intelligence refers to an ability or abilities that "permit an individual to solve problems or fashion products that are of consequence in a particular cultural setting" (p. 56). Originally it was explained that there are seven intelligences, namely: linguistic, logical–mathematical, spatial, musical, bodily–kinaesthetic, interpersonal, and intrapersonal, with the chance that others might also

exist. Gardner (1996) has also accepted the existence of at least one more intelligence relating to natural abilities (abilities and experiences in natural surroundings, e.g., mountains, the skies, the earth, the beauty of nature).

Some teachers have been quick to accept Gardner's thesis of different intelligences because it seemingly explains students' specialised abilities in both primary and secondary schools. Moreover, some teachers plan their lessons to provide classroom activities to develop each of the intelligences. This approach might be based on a major misunderstanding of Gardner's position. Although the different intelligences can be conceived as separate, he still refers to the intelligences working "in consort with one another" and resulting in an individual profile for each student (Ramos-Ford & Gardner, 1997, p. 57). Teachers are wise to think of each child as possessing a unique blend of intelligences, requiring the need for differentiated curriculum provision.

A developmental concept

Today it is generally accepted that giftedness is a developmental concept and that a wide and complex range of factors impinges on its development over time. The conception of giftedness outlined below is influenced by the writings of Braggett (1997a; 1997b), Gagné (2000), Scheidner (2000), and Sternberg (2000).

Giftedness is not a single entity and does not consist of a single attribute, but is a complex set of variables that emerge as powerful combinations and show up in different ways in different people. Giftedness might be shown, for example, in:

- highly effective problem-solving behaviour;
- visionary leadership;
- imaginative planning ability;
- high capacity for evaluative or reflective thought;
- ability to integrate and synthesise ideas;
- power to visualise and plan spatially (visual imagery);
- beauty in forming and using language;
- abstract thought in mathematical-scientific-technological areas; and
- advanced musical composition and/or performance.

Box 7.1 (page 296) provides an overview of a general developmental approach within which giftedness can be conceived. It is helpful to examine this model under four headings.

Inherited abilities

All children are born with a range of innate abilities that are gradually revealed over time. We can group these abilities into major areas such as cognitive, creative, interpersonal, intrapersonal, kinaesthetic and academic.

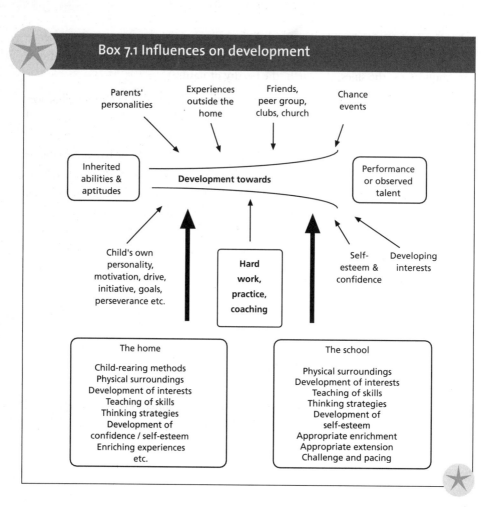

Box 7.1 Influences on development

Teachers and parents realise that some children display advanced ability in one or more of these areas far in excess of their age peers and often without assistance from others. Educators usually refer to an outstanding ability that shows up with little or no systematic development or training as giftedness because it:

- is an outstanding ability or aptitude in relation to one's age peers;
- seems to be inborn or innate; and
- can occur in one or more areas of a student's life (Braggett, 1997a; 1997b; Gagné, 2000).

Learning, practice and support

Although it is possible for children and adolescents to achieve at a high level without assistance or intervention, it is usual for them to achieve even higher levels of competence when they receive appropriate training, instruction, coaching, and support. As indicated in Box 7.1 (above), inherited abilities and aptitudes are developed over time, but effort is involved. Many gifted students combine natural ability with long hours

of practice, hard work, perseverance, and a desire to excel. They might be ardent readers, spend hours at the computer, train consistently for some sport, or have a passion for learning in some subject area or areas. It is not without sustained effort that their excellence is attained.

Contributing factors

Box 7.1 also indicates a range of influences that contribute to the expression of giftedness. Inherited abilities cannot be guaranteed to show up automatically. Nor can it be assumed that children will reach their potential level without input from parents, friends, and the general community. A stimulating home background, an enriched life, and an active involvement with the community all contribute to talented behaviour. These external factors interact with a person's own motivation, initiative, self-esteem, confidence and perseverance—that is, with a host of internal factors that are reflected in one's personality, attitudes and values about life, study, and work.

Developed performance

Finally, as a result of their own innate ability and the assistance they receive from others (what Gagné refers to as systematic development), some students reach an outstanding level of performance (or talent). Although this can be reflected in any area

Box 7.2 Giftedness and talent

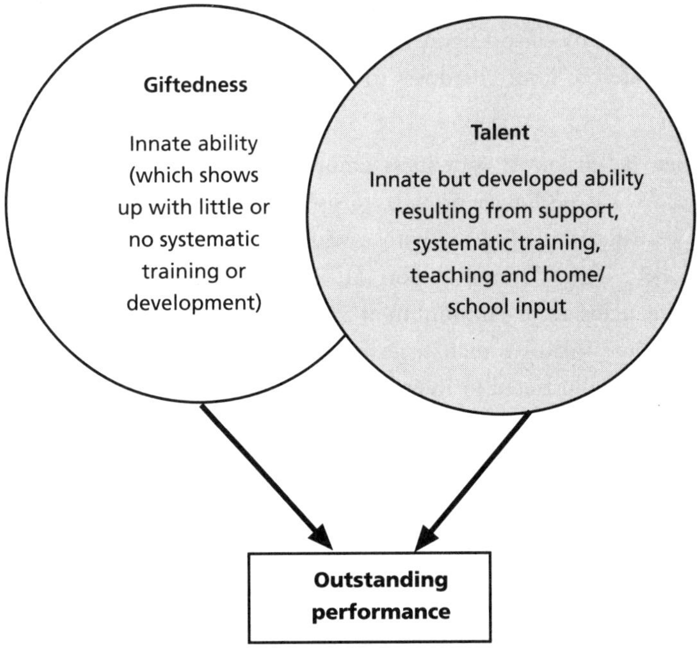

Giftedness

Innate ability (which shows up with little or no systematic training or development)

Talent

Innate but developed ability resulting from support, systematic training, teaching and home/ school input

Outstanding performance

of endeavour, it is more usually seen in some aspect of schoolwork that involves the ability to solve problems, to perform at an outstanding level, or to produce different or creative products.

Box 7.2 (page 297) shows the relationship between giftedness and talent, and reveals how both are related to outstanding performance. It must be stressed that innate giftedness does not automatically result in talented output: it must be nurtured and supported in most students over time. Teachers are well aware of those students who appear to have considerable natural ability but who are unmotivated or inconsistent in their work habits, resulting in underachievement, a lack of confidence, and little desire to excel. Teachers and parents have a critical role to play in the translation of innate giftedness into outstanding performance (talent).

Incidence and prevalence

Whichever definition of giftedness is accepted will determine the incidence of giftedness or talent in the population. When the cognitive or thinking aspects of giftedness are considered in relative isolation, one is reminded of Terman's (1925, 1954) approach. He equated giftedness with intelligence and initially set a lower limit of 140 IQ, although this was subsequently reduced to 135, corresponding to approximately 1% of the child population. Terman's standards were more stringent than they appeared, however, for he tested only those who were achieving at the top of their school classes; the rest were not included. Coy was the first to limit the term gifted to the top centile (or 1%) but, with the later development of paper-and-pencil tests, this figure was often lowered to IQ 130 or just over 2% of children (see Miles, 1946). Of course, any cut-off figure could have been set (e.g., 10% of the population) but it was decided to limit giftedness to the very best thinkers in terms of measured intelligence.

A broadened definition of giftedness embraces a larger percentage of the school population. As it is no longer prudent to use IQ or school examinations as the sole means of identification; students with a wider spectrum of abilities and talents are being included. The Marland Report (1972) widened the range of abilities and advocated the inclusion of a minimum of 3% to 5% of the school population. In their desire to be more inclusive than exclusive, educators sometimes set the figure even lower. This is best illustrated in Renzulli's revolving-door approach which encourages the selection of 15–20% of the school enrolment and the provision of programs on a rotating schedule for smaller groups drawn from this larger pool (Renzulli & Reis, 1986).

Although there are some educators who still wish to restrict the concept of giftedness to a small, confined group of students, there appears to be a growing acceptance of a more inclusive approach. Teachers in Australia and New Zealand often express agreement with Gagné's 1993 recommendations that are shown in Box 7.3 (page 299).

Box 7.3 Definitions of giftedness and talent

Giftedness corresponds to a level of competence in the *non-systematically developed* abilities of at least one aptitude domain that places subjects among the upper 15–20% of their age peers.
Talent corresponds to a level of performance in the *systematically developed* skills of at least one field of human activity that places subjects among the upper 15–20% of the same age members of the field (Gagné, 1993, p. 85).

Although the potential number of gifted children in the population is unlikely to increase unless we change our definitions substantially, there should be a steady increase in the number identified, as educators and researchers work with groups not previously included, and as a wider range of identification measures is developed. Moreover, it might be possible to identify an even larger group if educators can foster appropriate classroom conditions that help nurture specific forms of talent. In childhood and adolescence, talents are gradually emerging and educators are not sure of the proportion of students who will go on and actually create or who will exhibit very gifted behaviour as adults. It is wise, therefore, to be relatively liberal and to choose 15%, even 20%, of children, although we are well aware that a much smaller proportion—perhaps no more than 1 or 2 %—will actually turn out to be creators or produce outstanding intellectual output in later life. Realising that there are degrees of giftedness and talent among children, one is simply broadening the range by setting the figure at 15–20% and not restricting it to an unrealistic figure. A more liberal figure permits some margin for identification error as well.

Common assessment procedures and practices

There are two broad areas in which assessment procedures and practices are adopted. These are the identification and selection of gifted and/or talented students, and the cultivation of talented behaviour.

Selection of gifted and talented students

In regard to the selection of gifted and talented students, the assessment and/or identification usually occurs for one or more of the following reasons, to:

- meet a legal requirement that children should be tested for placement;
- screen large groups of children and to choose a group for more detailed assessment;
- select children for particular programs;
- check on learning or behaviour difficulties that might have arisen;

- confirm a teacher's (or parent's) hunch that a child might be gifted; or
- determine the degree of a child's giftedness on one or more assessment procedures.

In Australia and New Zealand there is no law that mandates the testing of all children in order to determine the degree of their giftedness, but there are numerous state (and private school) programs in Australia that require prior assessment before entry can be granted.

The identification and selection of gifted and talented students is not a simple matter because it can occur at two different but overlapping levels: the identification of innate abilities, aptitudes or potential; or the identification of high-performing students.

Innate abilities

Those who are interested in innate abilities, aptitudes, and/or intelligences are more likely to use standardised measuring instruments when identifying gifted students—the psychometric approach. Group tests of general ability might be administered as a screening device to children from around nine years of age, and might be followed by a more accurate and individually administered intelligence test.

The Australian and New Zealand Councils for Educational Research have developed, modified, and/or normed such screening tests as the Test of Scholastic Abilities and Test of Learning Abilities (TOLA 4 and 6). The Stanford Binet, Wechsler, or Slosson Intelligence Scales/Tests are employed if a more accurate assessment is required. The Raven Standard Progressive Matrices Test has been used with minority groups and with children with language difficulties as it is non-verbal and based on figures and patterns. We should remember, however, that tests do not operate in a cultural or social vacuum and that they tap the values of the dominant culture. For this purpose, they should be used with caution, or alternative methods used when minority groups are involved. When used appropriately, however, they are relatively objective, valid and reliable, and are useful in detecting some underachieving children. Alternatives to general abilities testing include specific aptitude testing (such as the Scholastic Aptitude Test—Mathematics) or the assistance of experts in areas of artistic ability. In some instances, knowledgeable teachers—particularly those who use checklists—might identify innate giftedness through their own observations.

High-performing students

Those who stress student performance are more likely to base their identification on competition results, examination scores, achievement test results, specialised evaluations, and high school or university entrance examinations, all of which are normative approaches—that is, they compare an individual's performance to that of others on outcomes. Some of these methods are described in Box 7.4 (page 301).

Box 7.4 Methods of assessing high-performing students

Achievement tests

It is often necessary to use standardised achievement tests in specific discipline areas such as modern languages, science, social sciences, language, music, and mathematics. Most take 30 to 40 minutes to administer and are applicable to primary and junior secondary grades. They indicate the level at which a child is achieving and usually tap a wider performance range than those set by classroom teachers. They reflect prior learning in nominated areas rather than the ability to learn and it is advisable to administer both a test of general abilities and an achievement test to gain maximum information.

Tests of creativity

Creativity is a very elusive concept (Urban, 2000). It might refer to a process (an aspect of creative thinking) or to a finished product (such as a work of art). Tests of creativity depend on the theoretical models accepted by the constructors of the tests. Guilford (1975) measured fluency (e.g., the flow of ideas), flexibility (the ability to change the direction of one's thoughts), originality (the ability to respond in a clever and unusual way), and elaboration (the ability to produce additional detail). These tests are not used widely in Australia or New Zealand, partly because of the time required to administer them. A new test, *Test for Creative Thinking—Drawing Production*, produced by Urban (2000) and described by Copley and Urban (2000), can be group administered and takes less time to score.

Aptitude tests

Aptitude tests can be used to identify primary or secondary school age students with abilities in particular areas. The mathematics segment of the Scholastic Aptitude Test (SAT-M) is used to discover high mathematical performance and potential (Benbow & Minor, 1990) and the verbal segment is used to discover precocity in literacy (Williams, 1984). These tests are usually administered to college entrants in the United States but are useful as long-range predictors with precocious children.

Teacher selection

Teachers can nominate students who are capable of gifted behaviour. Research evidence indicates, however, that teachers do not have a very impressive selection record as they are more likely to nominate conforming students who are well behaved. They do not always seek to determine the full range of learning or understanding, or to appraise each student's potential. Dutch research has concluded that teachers of secondary students are relatively proficient at identifying underachieving gifted students (Mönks et al., 1986) but there are conflicting findings resulting from different definitions of giftedness and the inclusion or exclusion of underachieving children.

Despite these problems, teacher identification remains important. The insight and ability of teachers can be enhanced if they have well-devised checklists that sensitise and refine their awareness of characteristics that should be observed (Kanevsky, 2000). Numerous checklists are available in many curriculum areas and include Meeker's (1969) Rating Scale which ranges over cognition (understanding), memory, evaluation, convergent, and divergent production; special skills; social, attitudinal, and emotional growth; and motivation and interest.

The Renzulli-Hartman Scale for Rating Behavioral Characteristics of Superior Students is a well-known checklist that has four sections, each containing eight to ten questions about learning, motivation, creativity, and leadership (Renzulli, 1983). Some sample questions from the checklist are given below.

Learning characteristics

- Has unusually advanced vocabulary for age or grade level; uses terms in a meaningful way; has verbal behaviour characterised by "richness" of expression, elaboration and fluency.
- Is a keen and alert observer; usually "sees more" or "gets more" out of a story or film than others.

Motivational characteristics

- Is bored with routine tasks.
- Is quite concerned with right and wrong, good and bad; often evaluates and passes judgment on events, people, and things.

Creativity characteristics

- Generates a large number of ideas or solutions to problems and questions; often offers unusual, unique, clever responses.
- Is sensitive to beauty; attends to aesthetic characteristics of things.

Leadership characteristics

- Seems to be well liked by classmates.
- Adapts readily to new situations; is flexible in thought and action and does not seem disturbed when the normal routine is changed.

The teacher rates each child on each question on a scale of 1 (seldom or never) to 4 (almost always).

Parent nomination

Parents might contribute to the identification of giftedness because of their intimate knowledge of their children's development. Although they can underestimate or overestimate their children's abilities, and might not even be aware that they are gifted, parents can complete checklists and answer questions about physical, social, and intellectual development, including language, reading, writing, and specific interests. Davis and Rimm (1994) suggest that parents be asked to provide the following information: the

child's special interests and hobbies; recent books that he or she has enjoyed or read; special interests other than reading; unusual accomplishments, past or present; special talents; special opportunities that the child has had; preferred activities when alone; relationships with others; and special problems and/or needs

When younger children are involved, it is suggested that a teacher–parent interview might probe the child's fluency of speech, memory, reading, imagination, hobbies and interests, and independent learning (Freeman, 2000; Perleth & Schatz, 2000). When added to other data, the parent information can be most informative.

Peer nomination

It is possible to use peer nomination as a form of identification if the situation is sufficiently specific. When the child is given the opportunity to choose a co-worker in a task that is particularly demanding (one that requires detailed knowledge and understanding), it is usually found that another child with high ability is chosen. In the early 1980s, the Gifted Children Task Force in Victoria devised a form in which children are asked to answer such questions as:

- To whom would you go for help if the teacher was not present?
- If you cannot do something that you planned, who in your class is likely to come up with another plan or idea?
- Who in the class is aware of, and enjoys, beautiful things?
- Who is the most curious about many things?
- Who should thank a guest speaker? (Comerford & Creed, 1983, p. 26).

Pupil self-nomination

It is prudent to allow children to nominate themselves for particular programs if they believe they qualify for selection. The process might range from a simple question or statement ("Please see me later if you are interested in science-fiction novels") to student evaluation scales requiring all students to respond to specific questions such as: "How often do you read a magazine, article or book about a topic that is of interest to you?"

Cultivation of talented behaviour

You will recall from the previous section on the selection of gifted and talented students (page 299) that those identified or selected are either (a) already performing at a high level and are considered to be achievers, or (b) deemed to have the potential for high achievement. This is because they have scored highly on some standardised test or selection procedure. This raises the issue of underachievement among students, especially among those who have high potential ability but who perform at a mediocre

level only and appear unchallenged by school learning. Teachers frequently comment on such underachievement that may be associated with:

- an unwillingness to stand out or excel in front of others;
- an overwhelming desire to conform to the standards of the peer group;
- a lack of challenge presented by the teacher;
- the low expectations of the school (inappropriate curriculum or teaching strategies);
- a school emphasis on language-, maths- and science-related subjects without a corresponding emphasis on other intelligences; and
- lack of motivation in the home.

When Renzulli (1986) originally devised a model to explain giftedness, he included task commitment as one of the three ingredients of giftedness. By this he meant the desire to do well, to persevere, and to excel—we might term it high motivation. It is evident, however, that some students mask their abilities and underachieve to such an extent that some—perhaps many—are not even aware of their own potential.

In addition, we must understand that giftedness can manifest itself in different ways and at different stages of a person's life. For example, there are some who will not excel in leadership or in financial management, for example, until they have left school and entered the world of commerce. As indicated in Box 7.1 (page 296), the context (or environment) plays an important role in the expression of giftedness, providing challenges, experiences, and opportunities. A developmental concept of giftedness might account for later development of talent, one that is not evident at school.

These two issues, underachievement and the importance of the immediate environment, should make us cautious when discussing the identification of gifted and talented students. There are some potentially gifted students who might not show up in our identification process and there will be others who are developing only slowly toward talented behaviour. Their abilities are not immediately apparent to parents, teachers, vocational guidance personnel, or counsellors.

Hence, the identification of gifted and talented students must go well beyond the selection process outlined in the previous section and must extend to the *cultivation* of giftedness or talent. We need to ask how can we design and implement regular classroom programs to assist another group of unidentified students to develop their potential to the point that they also show up (be identified) as gifted and talented students?

When you read the story described in Box 7.5 (page 305), you will discover how one teacher was able to use the regular curriculum to discover and cultivate the abilities of Josh and Mike, to increase their enthusiasm, and to provide them with basic training in skills and strategies. The boys' abilities were not identified through standardised

Box 7.5 Cultivating abilities

Josh was a student in Year 7 where he was well liked and had a wide range of friends who spent a great deal of time together, in and out of school. His teachers suspected that he had considerable ability and that he might perform at an exceptionally high level in his academic studies if he desired to do so. Josh, however, was more interested in sport and social activities. He did the minimum amount of study and showed little motivation to excel in his class work. In desperation, one of his teachers suggested that Josh and one of his friends (Mike) produce a class newspaper on sport. The two responded positively and set to work with gusto, but they soon found that they lacked a number of required skills.

When working with a mentor, they had to refine their computing skills and learn how to produce graphics and how to format in a tabloid form. Moreover, they were deficient in basic interviewing skills when they met local sports people, and were oblivious to the need for planning their approach and for developing checklists. It was a steep learning curve for the two but, through perseverance, they learnt how to set realistic goals, improve their computing skills, and gradually refine their writing ability. By the end of nine months, they were performing at a creditable level and had improved so much that the principal asked them to edit sections of the school's newspaper in the following year. Their enthusiasm gradually carried over into some other subjects and gradually influenced others in the class.

tests but through one teacher's willingness to discover the boys' interests, to vary the curriculum, and to provide assistance in a venture that had real meaning for the young adolescents.

When teachers set out to cultivate unknown talents (and thereby identify them as they develop), they are being proactive. Swimming coaches often adopt a similar approach with large groups of children when they:

- allow all children to enjoy themselves in the pool;
- teach them the fundamental techniques of swimming;
- involve all children in two or three weeks of intensive coaching;
- teach additional skills and strategies to those who advance most quickly; and
- identify those who improve most or who appear to have the most potential.

In other words, the most able are identified through the regular program that provides training for all.

When applied to classroom teaching, this proactive approach demands that teachers permit, encourage, and actively train students to:

- proceed at their own pace and not to be restricted to the average speed of classroom learning;
- develop such process skills and strategies as critical thinking, problem-solving, and metacognitive thinking (i.e., the ability to plan, check, and evaluate their own thinking and performance);
- explore interests at considerable depth and over extended periods of time (time management skills);
- develop other skills that permit autonomous learning (e.g., the ability to use a library or database; computer skills; reporting skills; interviewing skills); and
- interact with others of similar ability or interest in order to provide a challenge for each other.

This form of curriculum-driven identification is based on sound educational practices that assist all students while simultaneously permitting gifted students to forge ahead. Because the regular classroom teacher is involved, it is the preferred method of identifying gifted and talented students across Australia. Moreover, within the New Zealand context of providing for children with special abilities, it meets McAlpine's criteria of being unobtrusive, continuous, and a means to an end. As McAlpine (1996) says: "It is counterproductive to spend months and months on identifying the 'right' children at the expense of time spent in designing appropriate and challenging educational programmes" (p. 67).

Hence, the identification and selection of gifted and talented students should not be confined to those who are already achieving at a high level and who score highly on standardised tests. It needs to be extended to regular classroom activities that—when planned and manoeuvred—help to discover and cultivate each student's potential. In this way, it is possible to identify an even greater percentage of gifted and talented students over time.

Ways of supporting students' learning

During the 20th century (particularly after 1975) and stretching into the 21st century, a number of strategies were developed to assist educators to meet the needs of gifted and talented students at primary and secondary school levels. The following discussion analyses the major strategies under three headings:

(a) beyond the school;

(b) reorganising the school; and

(c) a total school approach.

Beyond the school

Some strategies involve state departments of education, diocesan authorities, enrichment and extension activities outside the school, competitions, associations and mentors—all of which operate beyond the bounds of the individual school.

State policies

Between 1978 and 2000, the departments or ministries of education in all Australian states and territories issued formal policy statements on gifted and talented children and on the educational provisions that might be made for them. Although they did not dictate any particular approach, they encouraged state schools to make specific provision for gifted students and outlined a range of options that might be adopted, such as enrichment activities, accelerated progression through the grades, cluster groups, and/or withdrawal groups inside the school.

Many of the departments provided professional development for teachers and administrators, and some developed and issued kits and other resources for classroom use. The Victorian Ministry went so far as to develop a range of Internet-based programs for primary and secondary students. Such events led some Catholic diocesan schools and other independent schools to formulate their own formal policies.

Enrichment schools and camps

Educational authorities often organise camps for talented students to nurture and develop specific abilities. Each camp is usually confined to one talent area (such as computing, creative writing, art or music) and provides for students who have already demonstrated commitment and ability. Such camps are provided in all states and territories and often form an integral aspect of the provision for talent development of a school, a district, or a region.

Enrichment schools or enrichment weekends add a variation to camps in that they are often organised by non-school authorities (e.g., universities, Commonwealth education centres, state associations for the gifted and talented) and seek to provide for a range of talents. Students usually attend on a fee-paying basis and have a choice of themes or subject areas from which they may choose. The Northern Territory Department of Education, in conjunction with the University of the Northern Territory, organises vacation camps at Dharra and Gurrung schools for Years 6/7 and Years 10/11.

Mentor programs

Mentor programs permit a gifted or talented student to be tutored by an expert, usually from outside the school system. Individual students are placed in touch with adult tutors who meet with them or correspond regularly (often by the Internet), and assist with content, style and skills. Mentor programs have been organised in most

states and by individual regions and schools, and have been found to be most useful when highly able students are involved and enthusiastic mentors are available.

Competitions

Students can be encouraged to enter regional, state or national competitions in such areas as mathematics, computing, history, environmental studies, and literacy (creative writing, poetry). These competitions might be organised or sponsored by industry, banks, universities, or associations, and some are annual events that have become well known over time.

Other competitions require group entries, often on a school basis. Tournament of Minds, for example, has proved to be most popular since its introduction in Victoria in 1987 and has spread to all Australian states and New Zealand. It allows schools to enter teams of students who compete against each other on a regional basis in problem-solving situations involving mathematics and engineering, language and literature, and the humanities. The Future Problem Solving Program is a year-long venture that promotes critical, creative, and futuristic thinking among students of all ages.

State associations

Associations for Gifted and Talented Children exist in all states and territories of Australia and in New Zealand and are support groups for parents and teachers who need assistance in meeting the needs of gifted children and young adolescents. Some provide an array of courses for preschool, infants and primary school children and occasionally organise advanced courses for students in the junior secondary school. Most associations distribute a newsletter or magazine to members, thereby extending services to families outside cities or towns. Over time, the associations have proved most valuable for parents who have faced crisis situations and for teachers who have looked for alternative methods when teaching gifted children. The Australian Association for the Education of the Gifted and Talented (AAEGT) has assumed a major role in organising conferences, disseminating conference papers, and in combining with state associations on state or regional issues.

Reorganising the school

Individual schools have likewise sought to cope with the educational needs of all students by modifying the traditional school organisation to provide for more homogeneous groups or for individual student needs Six organisational forms that have improved the educational opportunities for gifted and talented students can be considered.

Special secondary schools or streams

Believing that gifted and talented students benefit when they are educated with others of like ability or performance, some school systems have created special schools for

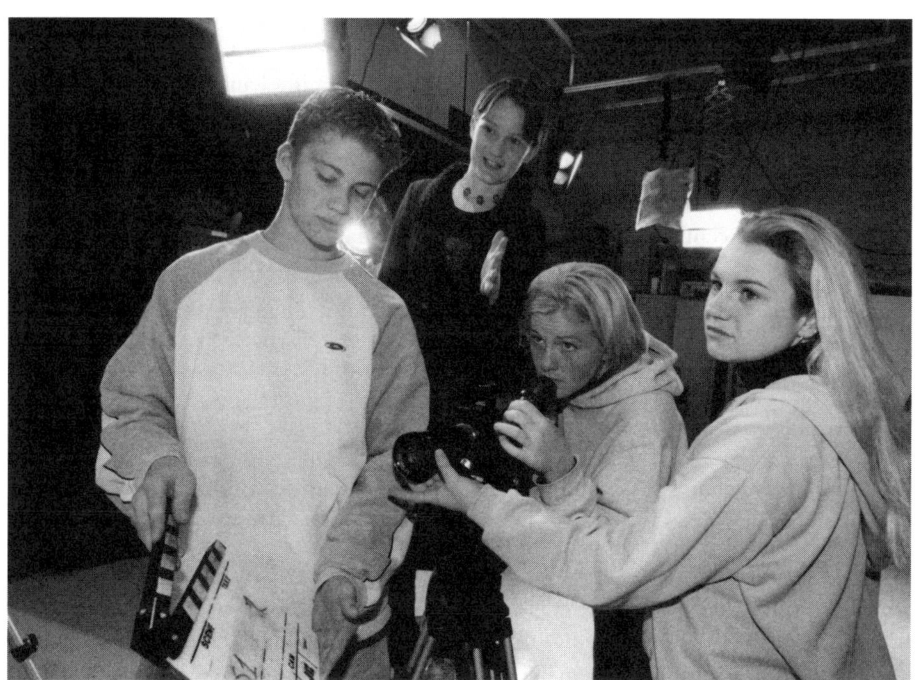

Talented students in the performing arts choreograph and film a scene from a play.

secondary school students. Most of these are located in New South Wales and are designated as selective or agricultural high schools. They require students to sit for state-controlled examinations and to reach a required academic level before gaining entry. Popular with many parents who seek an academic education for their adolescents, these selective schools provide an alternative education for some students who would otherwise attend independent schools. The schools have a high reputation and are among the most academic in the state, and their pupils achieve outstanding results in university-entrance examinations each year (Flood, 2000).

Other secondary schools have specialised streams that also require high entry standards for admission. Western Australia has special streams in language, music, dance and drama, art, foreign languages, and academic studies; South Australia in music, agriculture and languages; and New South Wales in music (Conservatorium High School) and performing arts. Some states, such as South Australia and Queensland, have schools that are lighthouse in nature (i.e., they provide examples of excellent practice for others to emulate); and Victoria has specially designated schools in which students can accelerate their progress and complete their secondary education in less than usual time. In addition, Tasmania, the Australian Capital Territory, and Victoria have senior colleges for students in Years 11 and 12 (and sometimes Year 10).

Special primary classes

Most Australian states do not provide special classes for gifted and talented students at primary school level, but New South Wales, with its OC classes (Opportunity C classes) and the Northern Territory are exceptions. Students are selected on the bases of general ability, school performance, student and parent nomination, and counsellor or psychologist recommendation. The students usually attend classes during the last two years of primary education, undertaking an enriched and extended curriculum that often involves increased community participation. There are more than 120 OC classes in New South Wales.

Cluster groups

Because most schools have limited resources and cannot afford a wide range of additional programs or extra staff to assist the most able students, groups of schools in close proximity might provide a common program for selected students from all schools. A specialised computer class (usually at a high school) for three hours each week for ten weeks, for example, might involve 25 children, five from each of five participating schools. This arrangement is much cheaper and more efficient than if each school were to provide a course for a small number of pupils. Cluster groups have been successfully developed in all states and might include students from different systems—state, Catholic, and other independent schools.

Western Australia, for example, has developed cluster groups as an integral part of the state's provision for gifted students. Known as Primary Extension and Challenge (PEAC), the program provides enrichment and extension opportunities for children in Years 5 to 7. Those students who are nominated and selected are able to attend PEAC courses in specified subjects at special centres throughout the state, most involving withdrawal for one half-day a week for 6 to 10 weeks. Children not in the pool of selected students are also permitted to attend individual courses if they demonstrate high ability in the specified area.

Most Australian cluster groups are not part of a formal statewide system, however, and rely on regional or school initiatives if they are to succeed. In many parts of Australia they involve only two or three schools working in cooperation, with little financial assistance, and supported by teachers, parents and community helpers. Cluster group activities might be restricted to children who exhibit the most gifted behaviours or might be widened to a larger group with a broader range of interests and talents. Box 7.6 (page 311) outlines the diversity of themes around which cluster groups have developed programs in a number of Australian states and illustrates the different levels at which enrichment can occur.

Box 7.6 Diversity of cluster group themes

The following examples illustrate the range of cluster group themes that might be developed while emphasising the potentially different levels at which the activities might be pitched:

- **astronomy, chemistry, literature, drama, geology, ancient history**
- **geography, advanced mathematics, statistics, physiology, archaeology**
- **music, painting, drama, ceramics, foreign languages (e.g., Italian)**
- **famous people, newspapers, local history, Japanese culture, media**
- **advertising, wetlands, time, money, propaganda, maths in society**
- **cheese-making, golf, athletics, bushwalking, "Tournament of Minds"**
- **problem-solving abilities, independent research, design**

Graded classes

When there are sufficient numbers of students to form two or more classes in the same grade, classes might be formed so that those with higher measured ability or higher performance are placed together in one class. If grading is introduced in primary classes, the grading is usually based on performance in English and mathematics (science and social studies are sometimes added). At secondary level, the grading is usually on a subject basis. The current practice in many Australian schools is to avoid grading in primary and junior secondary classes and to have heterogeneous or representative groups in each class (a spread of abilities or performances in each class). High school mathematics classes, nevertheless, are frequently graded in the junior secondary grades. An alternative secondary approach is to create two or three classes of higher performers, two or three of lower performers, and one class of students at risk.

Grading is a contentious issue, sometimes dividing a school staff when they consider the benefits and disadvantages of its implementation. Although it might advantage students in the top classes, and assist teachers who have to provide for a smaller ability range, it might increase problems in lower-performing classes, especially if anti-academic attitudes are also prevalent. The work of Gross (1999), however, indicates clearly that gifted students need to spend time with intellectual peers and to be challenged by like-minded students if they are to achieve consistently near their potential. Although there might be strong opposition to grading is some educational circles (see Gillies, Chapter 8, this volume), an appropriate alternative must be found to prevent academic underachievement among gifted and talented students: rarely are ungraded classes sufficient unless the curriculum is differentiated for very able students.

Withdrawal (pullout) groups

During the late 1970s and into the 1990s, a strategy often employed was to select a group of students who excelled in a particular subject (or group of subjects) at either primary or secondary level, and to provide a special program for them outside the regular classroom. At a specified time each week, these students withdrew to another room for a special program, often characterised by enriching or broadening activities. The strategy is still employed, although less frequently because of the disruption caused to the regular program, the lack of resources to employ additional staff, the provision of elective subjects in the high school, and the growing desire to differentiate the regular classroom curriculum for gifted and talented students.

Acceleration

Acceleration is "the adjustment of learning time to meet the individual capacities of students [and usually involves] higher levels of abstraction, more creative thinking and more difficult content" (Fox, 1979, p. 106). There are different meanings that can be applied to acceleration in the Australasian context:

- Young children may be permitted to enter the first school year at an earlier age than normal. A few may enter when four years of age under a policy not surprisingly termed Early Entry.
- Students might be advanced or accelerated by grade skipping in all subjects. It might be decided, for example, that a student finishing Year 3 will be placed in Year 5 after the summer vacation. If this occurs at the secondary level, it is more likely in the junior secondary years.
- Students might be advanced by grade skipping in one or more (but not all) subjects. In such an instance, two Year 8 students might remain in the Year 8 class for most of their subjects but work in a Year 9 class for mathematics.
- Acceleration might not imply grade skipping at all but refer instead to the *accelerated learning* of which the student is capable. Two students in Year 5, for example, might remain with their age peers but study Year 6 work in all subjects with the teacher's assistance.
- Acceleration may be permitted within a policy of flexible progression. Under this policy, all students work at their own pace and depth, and progress through their studies on an individual basis. This permits a student to study seven subjects, for example, and to be at seven different levels (e.g., English might be at Year 10 level; Mathematics might be at a mid-Year 9 level) regardless of age. This occurs, for example, at Sanderson High School in Darwin.
- Acceleration might occur through differentiated programs in which another replaces the regular curriculum (in one or more subjects), sometimes after negotiation with the student.

In the last two sections, you will notice that the regular classroom teacher is not usually involved in the strategy unless in a graded class or through acceleration. Provision for gifted students has often been viewed as an addition: it has occurred when the regular program has been completed, or it has been implemented outside the regular class. Throughout the 1990s, however, there was a growing reaction in some educational circles to this type of extra or special provision, and an increasing desire to cater for the gifted within the normal classroom and by the regular teacher. Nevertheless, this trend raised problems for many teachers who found it difficult—or impossible—to cope with the extension required by gifted students. These teachers found that lack of time, physical resources and/or expertise prevented their providing adequately for the most outstanding students in the classroom.

It is essential to pose four questions about the two issues of classroom provision and separate provision.

- Under what conditions should gifted and talented students be educated in special schools, special classes, or in separate programs?
- When is it desirable for gifted and talented students to be educated within the regular classroom?
- If gifted and talented students are educated in regular classrooms, what different provisions should be made for them in terms of school organisation, classroom management, teaching strategies, and/or differentiated curriculums?
- Is the regular classroom teacher capable of providing for gifted and talented students in a heterogeneous class consisting of a wide range of intellectual skills and abilities?

These issues are pursued further below.

A total school approach

Selective schools or classes are not usually available to the majority of Australian school students and most parents are forced to send their children to a local comprehensive primary or secondary school (state or Catholic). These schools have limited resources and can rarely afford staff to set up additional classes for gifted and talented students, especially when there are competing priorities to provide educational resources to a wide range of students. Although schools might be able to implement some of the strategies outlined in the previous two sections, it is usually left to regular classroom teachers to identify gifted students, provide appropriately for them, and be largely responsible for their welfare.

This is not an easy task. A teacher in a primary school with a class of 25 to 30 children (with a wide spectrum of abilities) and teaching a wide range of subjects, has only limited time to provide for students with special abilities and different learning styles, while also meeting changing curriculum requirements. The teacher has to consider those who are at-risk, who are poor readers, who have low self-esteem, who come from non-English speaking backgrounds, who are physically or emotionally abused at home, and those who display signs of disturbed behaviour. Is it too much to ask regular teachers in the primary or secondary schools to negotiate activities with gifted students, to differentiate the curriculum for them, and to give them the time they rightly deserve?

It is apparent that provision for gifted and talented students is a large issue and challenges many teachers. In reality, it is a matter for the entire school community (teachers, administrators, support staff, parents, students and the wider community) just as provision for students with impairments and learning difficulties is a wider issue. Although individual teachers can do so much, it is necessary to have a total school plan that incorporates the entire staff and all students.

Box 7.7 A total school approach

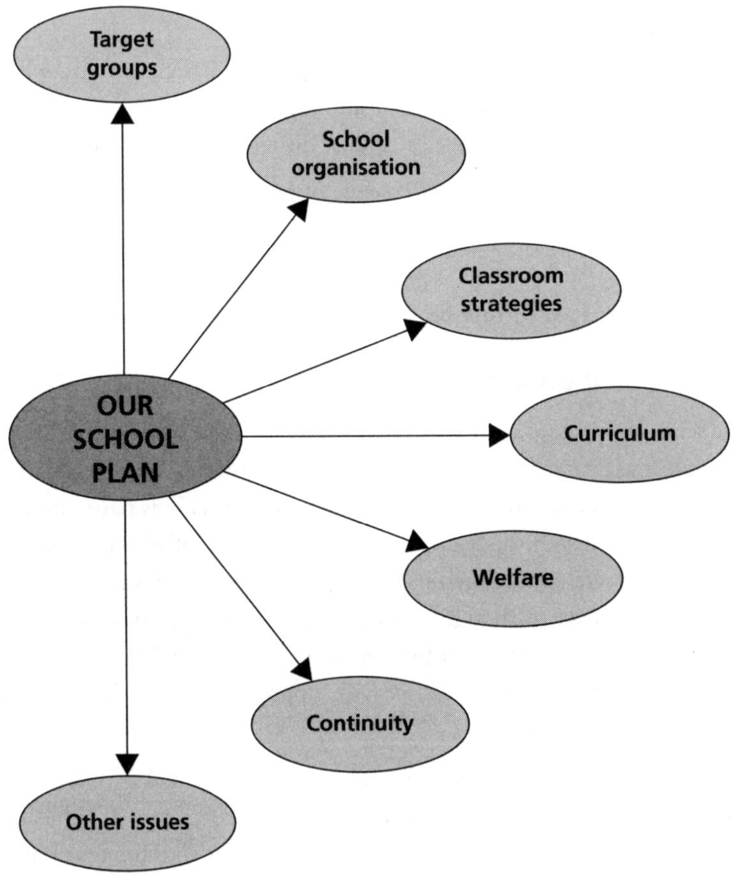

Box 7.7 provides the basis for such a plan and specifies seven broad areas for detailed consideration. You will notice that these include the student groups to be targeted, the school organisation, the teacher's classroom management and teaching strategies, the planned learning experiences (curriculum), the school's total welfare policy, continuity among the grades and from primary to secondary school, and a range of other issues discussed below. The following sections elaborate these areas in some detail.

Changing the way we teach and individualising instruction

Target groups

If one is to develop a total school approach to enhance the educational opportunities for all students, it is essential to know which group or groups will be targeted. If only a small group of children is chosen, we can be sure that some students will be overlooked and that a charge of elitism (founded or unfounded) will be brought against the school. Moreover, as indicated earlier, we are not even sure of some students' individual gifts and talents that might be developed into outstanding performance over time. For this reason, we specify the objectives relating to seven different (but overlapping) target groups (see Box 7.8, below).

Because students come from varied cultural and family backgrounds, the school has the task of broadening each person's experiences—a form of cultural enrichment. It introduces them to different ways of life and to different patterns of thinking, to a range of cultural and art forms (e.g., drama, music, painting, dance, film), to other cultures, religions and philosophies, and to values that might differ from their own. In Australasia, this is usually accomplished within a multicultural framework and, it is to

Box 7.8 Objectives relating to seven target groups

1. To enrich the lives of *all* students through experiences not gained at home (broadening and enriching).
2. To discover the individual gifts of *all* students and to cultivate them.
3. To develop and satisfy the abilities of students with *high specialised abilities*.
4. To develop further the abilities of *high performers* (the all-rounders).
5. To work closely with the *parents, guardians* and *mentors* as students' talents are developed.
6. To assist *teachers* to develop their own talents.
7. To develop a *school culture* that prizes high-level performance (an attitude of excellence).

be hoped, without recourse to stereotypes. Hence, the cultural enrichment of all students is a major aim of the school plan and one that is a fundamental component of the gifted and talented policy.

In a similar fashion, teachers should allow *all* students to outline their individual interests, express their own talents, demonstrate their own skills, and improve them with assistance. In many instances, the individual talents will be poorly developed, and students will need encouragement to express them. Not all will impress with developed ability, and even fewer will reach an outstanding level, but all can be encouraged and assisted to achieve satisfaction from genuine attempts to demonstrate their abilities. Those who improve or exhibit high performance can be tutored or referred to others for assistance.

Many students have a specialised talent in a specific area of competence. Whereas the school places emphasis on linguistic (language) activities and on mathematics, science, and technological subjects, it might unwittingly downplay—or even ignore—other talent areas. Perhaps there are some students who can display leadership ability. They work best in small groups as they interact with others. They are reflective thinkers who enjoy the chance to mull over issues, think more clearly when they see diagrams or other spatial representations, can sketch or draw with ease, or express themselves better through movement (physical action) than in writing. Teachers need to contemplate these different abilities and provide scope for students to demonstrate and cultivate them throughout the year.

A small number of students in the regular class might achieve at a high level in most of their work. They might be termed the "all-rounders" who enjoy schoolwork and gain satisfaction when achieving at a high standard. Sometimes they might be assisted by working closely with another person, from placement in a high-achieving group in the class, or by having a mentor to assist them. They certainly need to be extended and provided with skills and strategies to work alone or in small groups.

It is essential for parents and guardians to be apprised of each student's talents and for the school and the home to work closely together. Some talents come with a cost when musical instruments, sporting equipment, artist supplies, transport, or community involvement are required. Moreover, it is only courteous for parents to know about their child's progress at school, particularly if some talents spread over to out-of-school activities.

Teachers also have interests and talents that might not normally be apparent to their teaching colleagues or to their students. Indeed, it is not unusual for a school staff to possess collectively a wide range of talents that can be useful in the classroom, for cooperative or team teaching purposes, and for tutoring special-interest groups and extra-curricular activities. Some teachers have little opportunity to develop their talents in the humdrum of everyday teaching and lesson preparation.

Finally, it is crucial to develop a school culture that accepts and prizes excellence. There are some Australian schools where this is achieved in sporting programs without a corresponding acceptance of academic and artistic pursuits. Friday awards are often granted to those who have achieved at sport but less frequently for poetry reading, mathematics achievement, or social studies research. Although the motto, *Striving for Excellence*, is adopted by many schools, it is not always translated into practice in many strands of school life. A school culture of excellence takes time to develop and requires all staff, parents, and students to be involved in a long-term, concerted effort.

Hence, the school plan for students who have special gifts and talents is not elitist in direction: it involves all teachers and all students, and it also involves those with a range of abilities not yet developed and awaiting cultivation. The implementation of a total school plan can be an exciting venture when approached in this inclusive manner.

School organisation revisited

There are some forms of school organisation that need to be reconsidered and discussed by the staff when gifted and talented students are involved. Some of these aspects have already been discussed earlier under the heading, "Reorganising the school" (page 308), and include:

- graded or heterogeneous classes (at least for some students);
- largely ungraded classes but with one full-time or part-time class for high achievers;
- cluster groups;
- withdrawal (pullout) programs;
- accelerated progression;
- multi-age classes; and
- individual progression.

Multi-age groups (e.g., a class comprising children from two or more grades) have become more popular during the past decade or so as teachers believe that they have both social and academic benefits. If implemented in a positive fashion, they allow children to perform at different levels (not just one grade level) and permit gifted students to move ahead at their own pace. It is probably easier for teachers to break away from a grade-centred approach when working in multi-age groups and to accept, instead, broad levels as outlined in curriculum framework or standards documents.

Although benefits might accrue from reorganising the school, there are potential dangers. Some schools have the mistaken belief that a change in school organisation (e.g., introducing multi-age classes) will automatically produce better results for all students, including the gifted and talented, but school reorganisation, by itself, is not

necessarily the answer. It is possible for teachers to continue their traditional teaching patterns even when a new form of organisation is introduced. Changes to the curriculum and to teaching strategies are far more important when coping with students' individual differences; school organisational changes simply assist sound modifications to curriculum and teaching practices.

Classroom strategies

The way that teachers organise their classrooms and the instructional strategies that they employ are strong indicators of their approach to student learning and to the way they see their own role. This is particularly so when gifted and talented students are involved.

It is interesting to observe teachers who enter a classroom for the first time. They often change the arrangement of students' desks, place their own table in a different position, make more space for student movement, and—if possible—develop areas where small groups can meet. This reflects the way they wish to interact with the class.

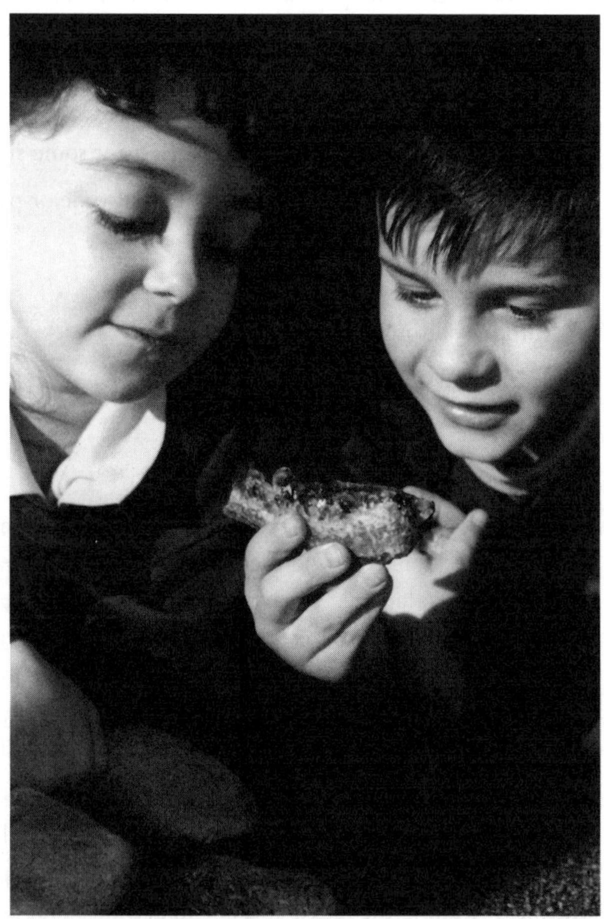

Working in pairs, children classify gems and rocks in a geology extension class.

Other teachers are more traditional and have students facing the teacher, allowing a minimum of movement and student-to-student interaction. In view of such differences, one has to ask whether there are most effective classroom strategies for gifted and talented students.

In one sense the gifted and talented display the same range of learning characteristics and styles as others, but some of their needs are more specific, allowing us to outline a few general principles on which teaching can be based. If we single out the intellectually gifted, we discover that generally they:

- are able to learn quickly with less practice and repetition and with reduced need for revision in areas that interest them;
- learn earlier than others in logical and abstract pursuits including school-related basic skills (Davis & Rimm, 1994);
- are able to employ deductive rather than inductive thinking, allowing them to understand a general rule and then to seek examples rather than to study many examples and gradually develop a general concept (Braggett, 1997b);
- have needs that cross cognitive, affective, social, and aesthetic areas of curriculum experiences; they enjoy integrated studies (VanTassel Baska, 1997, p. 126);
- have relatively strong interests that they pursue with vigour and enthusiasm; they enjoy developing their own interests and skills (Renzulli & Reis, 2000).
- are highly motivated to learn, persevere and excel in areas of personal interest (Renzulli & Reis, 2000);
- accept large-group tuition when factual information or principles are enumerated but have a preference to work in smaller groups, in pairs, or alone when engrossed in their own studies (Davis & Rimm, 1994);
- develop their own learning styles in which intuition might be an important element; they sometimes feel a solution rather than being able to explain it in detail (Hall, 2001); they prefer independence in learning rather than didactic instruction and desire to control their own learning; and
- can become bored and restless, lose motivation, and underachieve if they are not challenged, if the curriculum is not properly paced or is not at an appropriate level, or if teaching strategies are too rigid (VanTassel Baska, 2000).

Based on these findings and the reports of teachers of gifted and talented students, we can outline five general classroom strategies that must be considered when teaching such students.

Grouping

Not all students learn at the same pace or in the same way and, hence, it is imperative to group students for those learning experiences where ability or performance is involved. At primary and secondary levels, the division of the class into two, three, or four smaller groups permits students to work at different levels, to proceed at different speeds, and to be involved in a wide range of activities. In reading comprehension or mathematics, there might be three groups with seven or eight children in each; whereas, in social studies, two children might work together on a problem while the rest are engaged in a teacher-directed exercise. It is not proposed that group work should be the only form of teaching: it is completely unproductive, for example, to repeat the same information or instruction many times when all might benefit from a common activity. In the basic skills, however, and in those studies where learning differences are apparent, grouping of students can be most productive.

In schools where heterogeneous classes are formed and grading is avoided, it might still be necessary for the most able students from two or three classes to be grouped together for some learning tasks. The research evidence is quite emphatic that gifted students are challenged and motivated when they study and learn together.

Grouping patterns might sometimes be formed on the basis of interests rather than on actual ability. Just as students form groups themselves outside the classroom based on their sports, hobbies, or social interests, this form of interest can also be promoted in the classroom. When studying ancient Egyptian civilisation, for instance, one self-chosen group might wish to study the pyramids, another to construct a shadoof for irrigation (a pole on a pivot with a bucket on one end and weight on another), and yet another to explore the construction of ancient temples. Perhaps there will be some who wish to work individually. It is often found that gifted students elect to study integrated themes that cut across subject boundaries and involve abstract concepts (e.g., the influence of religious thinking on everyday life in Egypt and Greece). Integrated studies will be further explored in the section on curriculum (page 328).

Classroom layout

Grouping naturally affects the layout of the classroom. The tables and chairs must be arranged in appropriate configurations and these patterns can change during the day as different activities are undertaken. This is more difficult in the secondary school where non-specialist rooms are involved and where different teachers have special needs, but it can usually be accomplished when students become accustomed to group work and assume greater responsibility for their own learning conditions.

Although many classrooms are not designed for excessive movement, it is highly desirable to have interest centres around the room to which individuals or small groups can move when they require. The wide-scale use of information technology (IT) requires that some part or parts of the room be devoted to computers, printers,

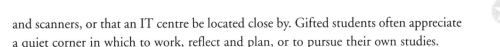

and scanners, or that an IT centre be located close by. Gifted students often appreciate a quiet corner in which to work, reflect and plan, or to pursue their own studies.

In older buildings—originally designed for a different educational era—it might be necessary to use wider corridors, spaces under stairs, or general-purpose areas if students are to work in groups or to undertake individual study. Some primary schools are fortunate in having withdrawal rooms or walk-in storage spaces that allow greater flexibility. Of course, there are increased difficulties of student control when groups are dispersed and not under the immediate supervision of the teacher, but the problems are minimised when gifted students are taught to negotiate their own learning tasks and to control their own learning.

Communication and displays

All students require a sense of direction and an outline of the activities for the day or week. In highly structured classes, this is provided by the daily timetable but, even in more flexible settings, it is most desirable for students to have a general list of tasks to be accomplished during the day, especially when high-use specialised facilities need to be rostered. This might simply amount to a chalkboard statement that indicates: "By the end of the day, you should aim to accomplish the following five tasks . . ."

When a student's work is assessed in an authentic fashion (i.e., work that is useful and purposeful, and which has been negotiated between the student and the teacher), there is merit in displaying the final product in a meaningful way. You will remember from Matthew's experience (case study, page 289) that his work was displayed in a local bank and his story read on local FM radio. Students appreciate the exhibition of work (not just teacher-directed exercises) from which they have gained satisfaction. These might be presented in book form, reproduced on Christmas or birthday cards, displayed on a website, exhibited in the entry foyer to the administration block, or presented in a display case or on the class notice board.

Teaching strategies

Basic skills

Intellectually gifted and talented students are able to learn quickly with less practice and repetition, and with reduced need for revision than is typical for their same-age peers. This does not imply that they do not need to learn the basic skills or perfect them to a high degree. Indeed, it is imperative that skills be learnt to avoid later problems. Some skills can be learnt in a considerably shorter time, through a process of *compaction*, thereby avoiding needless repetition, boredom, and even negative attitudes to classroom learning. The same is true in areas of specialised talent—such as gymnastics, wood-turning, ceramics, or debating—in which basic skills can be mastered quickly because of inherent giftedness, allowing students to advance quickly and reach high standards.

Assessment

If students are to advance more quickly, then teachers, parents and students themselves require some guarantee that basic skills (and basic information) have been learnt and understood. Teachers frequently use pretesting for this purpose—a check that there are no gaps in learning. Assume, for example, that a teacher intends to introduce a unit in mathematics on three-dimensional figures. She sets out the content and the skills to be mastered in the unit but, as a precaution, devises two or three exercises that she will set at the end of three weeks to check whether the students have learnt the concepts. Instead of waiting until the end, the teacher sets these few examples for the class at the commencement of the unit and is surprised when two students answer them correctly. While the rest of the class start on the unit, she again checks with the two youngsters and finds that they have already mastered the planned work. The simple pretest has shown the futility of requiring the two students to study the work with the rest of the class; hence the teacher finds a meaningful alternative for the students to pursue for three weeks in mathematics (or another aspect of their studies). This is a favourite strategy used by teachers to ensure that basic skills have been mastered and to determine which students might accelerate their learning or negotiate alternative work.

Another problem arises very frequently when teachers assess the progress of students on a traditional Friday test or at the conclusion of a unit of work. Having set the criteria that they wish students to meet, teachers devise a set of exercises or an assignment to determine whether the students have mastered the work. If they have, they are given a score (9 out of 10, or even a perfect 10) and allowed to pass on to the next stage of the syllabus. In this way, teachers fail to tap the extent of each student's learning. As an alternative, they need to raise the ceiling of the test so that more advanced students can indicate their real ability, or need to set open-ended questions that allow more competent students to indicate the depth of their understanding. This form of assessment is much more authentic for teachers and students alike as it helps determine the direction of future studies.

Inductive or deductive reasoning

Many teachers in primary and junior secondary schools base their teaching on inductive reasoning whereby they provide students with many examples—graded from easy to difficult—and gradually lead them to a general principle or rule. In doing so, teachers accept that a generalised concept stems from repeated and varied examples over time. This time-honoured approach seeks to build up a store of knowledge and develop networks or patterns in the thinking of students, moving from the concrete to the abstract, and from the particular to the general. Intellectually gifted students, however, have advanced thinking abilities, frequently reaching logical and abstract

thought before their age peers. With an advanced and relatively large thinking network (i.e., being able to integrate many aspects of thought), they often have the ability to grasp extended concepts with a minimum of examples and sometimes without props at all. A mathematical or scientific formula might be all that is required to solve individual examples.

Deductive thinking is frequently involved in integrated studies that embrace broad themes that transcend subject boundaries. Topics such as *Preserving the Ecology* and *The Ethics of Medical Research* require students to think analytically and divergently, consult different databases for information, and synthesise their reasoning, often in a highly creative fashion. Although some gifted students are capable of deductive reasoning from an early age, others require the assistance of parents and teachers for it to become an established way of thinking. Inductive or deductive reasoning is also an enabling skill but, because of its importance it has been examined separately. Other skills are outlined in the following section.

Enabling skills

Because talent can be developed over time, a positive school environment is vital in fostering, nourishing and training those enabling skills that influence the development of abilities. *Strategies* (plans and methods of acting) and *skills* (habitual behaviours) not only influence the expression of giftedness but are also amenable to learning and are collectively termed enabling skills (Braggett, 1994).

There are enabling skills in practically every field of human endeavour and they are certainly too numerous to detail here. However, Box 7.9 (page 324) provides a sample of the areas in which they are important in the classroom. In the following discussion, two are examined in some detail.

Critical thinking skills

An important aspect of teaching concerns the development of thinking skills, and teachers are often exhorted to emphasise the higher-order thinking skills as they are believed to underlie a critical approach. Rarely will you find a list of these higher skills, although it is commonly assumed that they include analysis, synthesis, evaluation, judgment, and aspects of metacognitive thinking (i.e., being aware of how you think and how effectively you do so).

A list of critical thinking skills and strategies is outlined in Box 7.10 (page 324), drawn chiefly from Reid (1993), Bellanca and Fogarty (1991), Fogarty and Bellanca (1991), and Braggett, Kay, and Lowrie (1998). As you can see, the list is quite long, referring to the skills to be targeted and to some of the strategies that might be employed. A list such as this can appear deceptively simple as the example of

Box 7.9 A sample of enabling skills

Acquiring information
exploring
specialising
encoding information
investigation or research

Interpersonal or communication
self-awareness
social roles
cooperative learning
conflict resolution

Psychomotor performance
fine motor skills
gross motor skills
coordination
enhancing performance
specialised skills

Decision-making
independence
self-confidence
responsibility
motivation
moral strength

Problem-solving
problem definition
creativity
higher-order thinking
metacognition

Emotional responsibility
awareness of emotions
techniques of control
avoiding prejudice or bias
avoiding some conflicts

Box 7.10 Teaching or instructional strategies

Enabling skills
CRITICAL OR LOGICAL THINKING
classification
comparison
patterning
sequencing
cause and effect
labelling
devising webs
Bloom's taxonomy
Krathwohl's taxonomy
how to plan
The scientific method
CoRT especially. PMI and CAF (see text for a description of these programs)
inferences
forecasting
narrowing options (decision-making)
inductive reasoning
deductive reasoning
evaluation
future problem-solving

Creative thinking
fluency
originality
elaboration
brainstorming
modification (e.g., SCAMPER)
imagery
associative thinking
creative problem-solving (Parnes)
relationships
metaphorical thinking

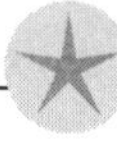

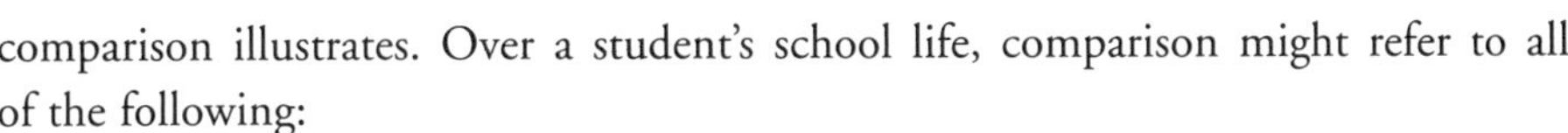

comparison illustrates. Over a student's school life, comparison might refer to all of the following:

- comparing the length of two sticks or rods;
- comparing the areas of two-dimensional drawings and the volumes of three-dimensional models;
- comparing behaviours and deciding which are desirable and which are not;
- comparing and deciding between the morality of two different situations; and
- making decisions among two or more different ethical considerations.

Bloom's Taxonomy (see Table 7.1, below) provides a relatively well-known approach used in many schools. Teachers and students are encouraged to extend thinking activities beyond the levels of *knowledge*, *comprehension*, and *application* and to tap higher levels of *analysis*, *synthesis*, and *evaluation*.

Two items drawn from the CoRT program (devised by deBono in 1975 to teach complex thinking skills) are often used in the classroom. These are:

- when contemplating ideas, consider the PMI (pluses, minuses, and interesting aspects); and
- when making a decision, use CAF (consider all factors).

The skills of *forecasting* are vital because they entail "What if . . ." considerations.

Creative thinking skills

Creative thinking (see Box 7.10, page 324) is involved when students can synthesise ideas (put them together in a particular way) and come up with original solutions. Although there are numerous strategies that might be employed to develop creative thought, Parnes' Creative Problem Solving (CPS) model is widely known.

Table 7.1 Bloom's (1956) Taxonomy explained

1. Knowledge	**2. Comprehension**	**3. Application**
tell, list, find, locate, describe, relate, name	explain, outline, discuss, translate, compare, restate, discuss, predict	solve, show, illustrate, calculate, construct, complete, classify
4. Analysis	**5. Synthesis**	**6. Evaluation**
identify, analyse, explain, investigate, contrast, explain	create, invent, compose, plan, design, construct, devise, formulate, predict, propose	judge, decide, assess, recommend, prioritise, verify, justify, decide, argue, rate

The CPS model encourages groups of students to approach and solve problems using five steps:

- Fact finding: collect information about the problem. Observe the problem as objectively as possible.
- Problem-solving: examine the parts of the problem to isolate the major part. State the problem in an open way.
- Idea-finding: generate ideas about the problem (brainstorming).
- Solution-finding: choose the most appropriate solution. Develop and select criteria to evaluate the alternative solutions.
- Acceptance-finding: create a plan of action.

In an actual example, a group of students was asked to consider the problem of factory pollution in a part of the city and to come up with a solution. You will see their ideas for Step 3 (Idea-finding) across the top of the grid and targeted Effect areas down the left-hand side (Education Department of Western Australia, 1995). See Table 7.2, (below).

Table 7.2 CPS model

	Creative ideas				
Evaluation criteria	**Close down factories**	**Find other ways of making products**	**Place restrictions on factories**	**Eradicate the technology**	**Package waste and send to another**
Cost-effective?					
Time involved?					
Effect on workers?					
Long-term effects?					
Ease of doing?					

5 points = excellent idea; 4 = good; 3 = average; 2 = below average; 1 = poor

The SCAMPER technique can also be used by individual students to change any plan or suggestion by these methods. The acronym SCAMPER stands for the following (Eberle, 1987):

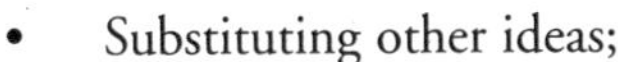

- Substituting other ideas;
- Combining ideas;
- Adopting new suggestions;
- Modifying-magnifying-minifying some ideas;
- Putting ideas to other uses;
- Eliminating some parts; and
- Reversing–rearranging ideas.

Research skills

Another crucial set of enabling skills relates to the ability to work independently, to locate information, and to conduct research. Some of the these skills are detailed in Box 7.11 (below). Like many skills, their development is continuous, cumulative, and long-term, one on which parents and successive teachers build over years. The development of IT and easy access to worldwide databases have highlighted the need to develop skills during the primary school years and to achieve a degree of expertise during adolescence. Research skills are important not only for modern living but also to allow students to progress through school at their own pace without continual assistance from teachers.

Negotiation

One of the basic teaching strategies that works well with gifted and talented students is the negotiation of aspects of the curriculum with an individual or with small groups of students collectively. Negotiation is a courteous acceptance by the teacher that students have their own interests, time schedules, learning styles and other needs, and that much more is achieved when the student and teacher agree (negotiate) on the work to be undertaken and/or the type of assessment to be made. There are some aspects of the curriculum that are not open to negotiation, of course, especially when state authorities set the curriculum and when the demands of external examinations

Box 7.11 Research skills

- setting goals
- library use
- book skills (table of contents, index)
- dictionaries, thesauruses, encyclopaedia, etc.
- keyboard skills
- accessing and employing databases
- email; Internet (obtaining and sending information)
- writing reports, assignments, research papers

are a reality. When there are alternatives or options, however, negotiation is entirely possible, especially when different modes of learning and reporting are available. The same findings might sometimes be presented in prose, graphical, or diagrammatic form; as a tape recording or small video; through a diorama, model, or sketch to scale; through a poem, play, ballet, or dance (especially if choreographed by a student); or by any other form of representation. Allowing students the chance to negotiate aspects of their studies can be a rewarding exercise and lead to heightened effort, increased motivation, and outstanding production. This issue if further amplified in the following section.

Curriculum

Together with teaching strategies, the curriculum is the most crucial element for the teacher to consider when gifted and talented students are involved. According to Maker's (1982) original analysis, it is necessary to modify the curriculum in terms of abstractness, complexity, variety, organisation and economy, the study of people, and the methods of inquiry.

Her criteria have been amended and amplified by VanTassel Baska (2000) and others, but there is complete agreement that, unless the regular-class curriculum is modified, it can prove to be unchallenging, even deadening, for outstanding students. If we heed this advice and change aspects of the curriculum to suit the identified needs of gifted students, the result is termed a differentiated curriculum. Actually, differentiation entails three interrelated steps.

- Step 1: Determine the specific needs of an individual student or a group of students.
- Step 2: Determine how to change the curriculum to meet these specific needs
- Step 3: Negotiate the learning experiences and curriculum modifications with the student or students.

Curriculum differentiation

There are seven broad areas to which curriculum differentiation may be directed and these are outlined in Box 7.12 (page 329).

Enrichment and extension

An area of differentiation referred to above is enrichment and extension, one of the most favoured methods of differentiating the curriculum in Australian and New Zealand schools. Although one is impressed with the number of teachers who seek to implement enrichment activities or programs in their classrooms, it is clear that not all teachers understand the concept or its importance. Students who finish their work earlier than others are sometimes given activities to pursue while others catch up:

Box 7.12 Types of curriculum differentiation

Appropriate speed

Many gifted students can work at a faster pace than their age peers because of their deeper level of understanding. Consequently, they need less time on revision, consolidation, routine work, and repetitive study. It is vital to pretest students when a major unit of work is introduced to determine those with advanced knowledge or understanding of the topic. These students should not be required to study the same work with the rest of the class, but should have the chance to negotiate substitute study, enrichment, and/or extension activities.

Cognitive processes

Much greater emphasis might be placed on the development of cognitive processes and higher-order thinking skills, including:

- comparison, application, sequence, analysis, composition, creation, synthesis, evaluation and justification;
- critical thinking (e.g., definition, clarification, judgment, inference, analysis of assumptions);
- creative, flexible thinking; and
- creative problem-solving including the sequencing of problem-solving steps (see Creative thinking skills, this box, below).

Enrichment and extension

Enrichment, as discussed below, is appropriate if it is negotiated with the student and extends or stretches the student's knowledge, skills, abilities, performance and/or interests (Braggett, 1994). Integrated studies and individualised education plans might be required.

Personal experience or autonomy

In this form of differentiation, stress is placed on self-directed learning in which students negotiate an aspect of their own studies or their own learning style and are trained in the skills required. Independent or small group work is often involved, activities are usually open-ended in nature, time-management skills need to be cultivated, and students are frequently involved in evaluating their own products.

Multiple intelligences

Work on multiple intelligences points to the range of areas in which abilities can develop and warns against the tendency to concentrate only on academic excellence. It must be reiterated, however, that each student has a blend of intelligences and it is unwise to concentrate on only one ability for each student.

Deductive thinking

In this form of differentiated approach, students might seek to grapple with general ideas or principles (e.g., propaganda and the forms it takes in society)

and to explore such ideas across a range of discipline areas. It is a reversal of the more usual inductive approach in which many concrete examples gradually lead to a general principle.

Social change

Some believe that the school should be an agent of social change and that gifted students should take an active part in the process of change. Hence, students study real social problems and take part in actual projects (e.g., opinion polls, publicity drives, reports on social issues such as noise pollution, newspaper articles, speeches and videos). They are taught the skills to participate in these problem-solving activities. The students who pondered factory pollution and sought a community solution (page 326) were certainly involved in social change activities.

Career and vocational education

Finally, the secondary school might differentiate the curriculum by providing a bridge between the school and the world of work. Students might be involved in work programs, internships, career counselling and/or mentor programs. Students might visit post-school institutions and explore the expectations of colleges and universities.

Many differentiated activities involve a number of the above areas combined.

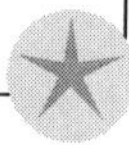

in the early years, they might colour-in or read a book, whereas, in later grades, they might undertake supplementary exercises. However, to consider these as enrichment activities is to demean the concept altogether.

Enrichment is:

> . . . any activity or program designed to broaden or develop a student's knowledge, understanding, application, processes, skills or interests beyond the basic (core) program and at a level that is appropriate to the developmental abilities and interests (intellectual, social etc.) of the student. (Braggett, 1994, p. 75)

To complicate the nature of enrichment, one must understand that it can be implemented at different levels and for different purposes (Braggett, 2000). This is apparent when you study the different types outlined below.

Type 1

In this type of program, students are introduced to a range of activities designed to develop interests. In the primary school, for example, it might include ceramics, bookbinding, photography, rock collections, batik, tie-dyeing, macrame, candle-

making, paper-making, and puppetry. In the secondary school, it might include hobbies and interest groups or extracurricular activities, often involving physical activities (e.g., sports, canoeing, bushwalking, abseiling) or visits to cultural institutions (galleries, studios, displays). These activities are not designed specifically for gifted children and each might last for only a few weeks, but it is hoped that *all* students will find enjoyment exploring new activities and discovering new interests which might be taken up on a leisure-time basis. It would be wrong, however, to consider that such activities provide adequately for gifted students; they are designed for all (as outlined in target group 1, Box 7.8, page 315). Programs for gifted students must have other characteristics as well.

Type 2

Another type of enrichment program aims to determine and build on emerging or existing interests and to develop them further (target group 2, Box 7.8, page 315). Students who have already developed some expertise in such areas as electronics, theatre, religion, video production, painting, or garment-making are encouraged to pursue their interests and are provided with assistance to do so. This often means the timetabling of elective lessons and the support of parents and members of the community. The depth of the interests is more pronounced and permits specialisation over an extended period of time.

Type 3

A third type of enrichment—sometimes called horizontal enrichment—allows students who finish their work at a faster pace than others to study an additional subject, unit or theme, during the time saved. They are permitted to negotiate the work, which might be a formal subject (e.g., archaeology, Japanese language, or legal studies) or a thematic unit (e.g., a study of wetlands). The student chooses the work to be studied. It is often apparent in senior high school where some students study additional subjects in the final two years of school (see target group 4, Box 7.8, page 315).

Type 4

Another type of enrichment program encourages students to study a section of the curriculum in much greater depth over an extended period of time. Some students are avid readers and might be introduced to a wider range of literature as a form of enrichment, whereas others might find pleasure in a deeper knowledge of history, physics mathematics, or environmental studies. Senior secondary school usually permits students to pursue some of their subjects at a deeper level (e.g., advanced mathematics or advanced English literature). Such enrichment is characterised by a qualitative depth of knowledge and understanding in a specialised area (see target group 3, Box 7.8, page 315).

Type 5

This type of enrichment program places emphasis on processes and seeks to develop further the thinking and/or performance skills of gifted students to a higher level. Students' skills are trained and developed through negotiated programs that are aimed at analysis, synthesis, application, justification, evaluation, prediction, inference, and cause and effect. Other programs provide opportunities to create and develop each student's own uniqueness. The development of metacognitive abilities might be a major goal (Sternberg, 2000). These programs might be commercially produced or can be negotiated with individual students.

Type 6

A sixth type of program is based on interdisciplinary studies and permits students to study issues from a variety of approaches. The theme of social justice and injustice, for example, might be studied through an examination of pertinent literature, an analysis of art, a study of the law, an investigation of political writers, a comparison of different sociopolitical ideologies, an analysis of religious philosophies, and a judgment about the effectiveness of modern welfare agencies and services. Knowledge and understanding are demanded, and students are required to think in systems, the highest form of conceptualisation. These programs are usually negotiated and take the form of an individual education plan.

These examples indicate the range of approaches to enrichment and highlight the difficulties that can emerge if teachers are not sure of their objectives. Many Australasian teachers are misguided when implementing programs for gifted and talented students. They have heard that enrichment is a suitable method of providing for able students and, without understanding the issues involved, design low-level activities similar only to those outlined in the type 1 program above. It can be quite dangerous to mistake the level of the program required: low-level work amounts to little more than filling-in-time, or busy work, and can lead to poor work attitudes and slovenly habits. Relevant enrichment activities are designed to meet the needs of individual students and, in the case of the gifted, require rigour, depth and long-term goals.

Renzulli's schoolwide enrichment model

The approach of Renzulli and Reis (2000) is an example of a scheme for primary and secondary schools, involving all students in a pyramid-type organisation. All students are included in first-level activities, but this number tapers to a smaller percentage as more demanding and complex projects are demanded at the third level.

In Renzulli type 1 programs the school provides a wide array of enrichment experiences that allow students to explore a range of interests that are either extensions to the existing curriculum or departures from it. These include:

Table 7.3 Three types of enrichment in history

TYPE 1	TYPE 2	TYPE 3
Type 1 activities seek to enrich generally and are useful with all students.	**Type 2 pursuits are designed to develop such specific research and**	**Type 3 activities use research methods of enquiry in real-problem**
Teacher-led discussions.	Locating information sources.	Report on an historical walking tour of the city.
Exciting speakers (including older folk in the community).	Interviewing skills.	Oral history interviews with past mayors and other civic dignitaries.
Simulating past events.	Affective training in dealing with controversial historical issues.	Development of a simulation war game.
Excursions (original sites, museums, art galleries, homes of older residents).	Advanced research and reference skills.	A media presentation of the music of the 1940s.
Presentation of old pictures and historical memorabilia (including family archives).	Organisation, cataloguing, and preparation of materials.	Oral history interviews recording a factory's influence on the community.
Presentation of old newspapers, letters, and books.	Advanced writing and editing; summarising skills.	A book summarising local folklore.
Panel discussions.	Evaluation of primary versus secondary sources; determining credibility of sources.	A study of some ethnic group in society.
Films and videos (especially archival material).	Textbook stereotyping and bias in portraying history.	A family tree: a study of genealogy.

Source: Adapted from Renzulli and Reis (2000).

- *resource persons:* speakers, mini-courses, demonstrations, artistic performances, panel discussions/debates;
- *media:* films, slides, audiotapes and records, videotapes, television programs, newspaper and magazine articles; and
- *other resources:* interest development centres, displays, excursions, museum programs, learning centres.

Although any child can attend enrichment sessions in elective times or at the instigation of the classroom teacher, up to 20% who exhibit high performance and who are selected for a pool are permitted to attend on the basis of:

(a) an assessment of their interests;

(b) their preferred learning styles (e.g., for projects, drill and recitation, peer teaching, discussion, teaching games, independent study, programmed instruction, lecture, or simulation); and

(c) time saved in the regular class by compacting or accelerating their learning of the normal program. Enrichment activities in the primary school might be thematic, but in the secondary school they are usually discipline-based.

Renzulli type 2 enrichment consists of process-orientated teaching activities that are designed to develop specific skills involved in creative thinking, problem-solving, self-directed and independent study skills, and research and reference skills, together with other skills related to processes rather than to content or product. This type of training seeks to nurture independent learners who are capable of individual or small group work with a minimum of supervision. Renzulli type 3 enrichment then follows as students from the talent pool class become involved in real problems and use research methods of enquiry that are appropriate to the actual discipline being studied. Table 7.3 shows the progression of type 1, type 2, and type 3 enrichment activities for students in a talent pool class in history.

Individual project: Australian studies

Renzulli's type 3 enrichment activities need not entail a whole class, but can also apply to an individual or to a few students who work together. Box 7.13 overviews a type 3 project devised by a 15-year-old student who is interested in the increasing problem of algae in Australian waterways. The student selects the topic because of its interest and challenge, and develops a plan in consultation with the teacher and with the assistance of community members.

A school-based program of the Renzulli type has appeal because it caters for the top 15–20% of selected students. As a bonus, the activities in types 1 and 2 are relevant to all the students. In Renzulli's plan, students who are not chosen in the talent pool but who show sustained interest or improved performance, are afforded the chance to pursue type 3 extension and enrichment activities with the talent pool students.

Welfare

Schools are responsible for the general welfare of all students and they usually develop a student welfare policy that outlines the school's responsibilities and the measures it will adopt to ensure its implementation. In most respects, the welfare of gifted and talented students is the same as for all students but there are some areas that need to be highlighted so that no students are forgotten or neglected.

- In collaboration with the Policy on Gifted and Talented Students, it is important for the intellectual, affective, social, and moral characteristics of gifted and talented students to be clearly delineated to remind teachers of the particular needs of these students. Two issues stand out. The first concerns the students' advanced thinking skills which require curriculum differentiation and the modification of classroom instructional strategies to avoid the development of poor attitudes to education. The second refers to the loneliness that some

Box 7.15 Topic: Water pollution—blue-green algae in local waterways

Problems I would like to answer

1. What is blue-green algae?
2. What causes it? Is it natural or a result of human intervention?
3. Where and why does it occur in the local area and throughout the state?
4. Solutions to help control and combat blue-green algae.

General resources

- CSIRO department
- University department
- Local and school libraries
- Nature and science magazines
- Recent Australian encyclopaedias
- Australian Water Resources Commission

Specific resources

So far, I have found the following resources useful:

- Burton, J. (1974) *Man and his world: Resources.* London: Blackie & Son.
- Australian Association of Adult and Community Education Inc. and the Murray–Darling (1994). *Blooming blue-green algae* (Kit). Study kit with video.
- Murray–Darling Basin Commission (1994). *Blue-green algae*: *The story so fa.* (Kit). Contains one video with brochure, 18 slides and four booklets.
- *Australian Journal of Marine and Freshwater Research.*
- Blue-Green Algae Task Force (NSW).

Product

I would like to produce:

- material for other students to use as a reference in the school library;
- a display, with slide presentation, on the causes and effects of blue-green algae;
- a report on preventative methods for blue-green algae (i.e., what the local community and farmers can do); and
- a map of the state showing where blue-green algae is occurring.

Target audience

- Local community and farmers
- Other school students
- Parents and teachers
- CSIRO
- Local newspaper

My skills

To conduct this work, I will need skills in:

- letterwriting;
- reporting and collating information;
- using the Internet and CD-Rom; and
- researching books, articles, papers, and kits.

Timeline

- I will submit my plan after three weeks.
- I will finish the project in 12 weeks.

My plan (after three weeks)

After initial research I have come up with the following questions that I would like to answer in my presentation.

- What is blue-green algae?
- How long has it occurred in my area?
- Where in my state is it to be found?
- What causes it? Under what conditions does it flourish?
- What can be done to control its spread? (e.g., what alternative farming methods can be used?)
- Is there a naturally occurring substance that can control or kill it?
- How does it affect the waterways?
- Does it harm humans, other animals, or fish?
- What can the local community and farmers do to prevent its further spread or to destroy it?

Note: This unit was developed by Megan Rudd.

gifted students experience when they are placed in ungraded classes with few others who think at their own level. It is particularly revealing (and often quite sad) to hear the comments of gifted students in regular classes who enrol in enrichment weekends for talented students. They frequently express relief and appreciation for the chance to be with like-minded peers and for the opportunity to perform at a high level without feelings of negative sensitivity or guilt. Teachers rarely understand the loneliness that can result when gifted students' needs are not recognised or heeded.

- A small committee of two or three staff members is often set up in primary school to monitor the needs of children considered to be at risk (e.g., emotionally disturbed, disabled, sick, achieving poor results), to follow their progress, and to recommend any changes required. This is more likely to occur at the faculty level in secondary school. Some schools extend this principle to gifted and talented students, reporting very positive results for teachers and students alike.

- Students who have a physical or sensory impairment or who experience communication disabilities, and who are also gifted (intellectually or in specialised areas) need particular assistance as their physical or sensory limitation might be considered by teachers at the expense of their potential talent (Yewchuk & Lupart, 2000).
- An adequate counselling service is required for all students and for the specialised needs of the gifted and talented. Apart from the loneliness that some experience in particular classes, they might also be more sensitive to social problems, injustices, and the prejudices experienced by minority groups in society. They can worry excessively about problems that cause little concern for others and be anxious over personal and family issues, often criticising or blaming themselves unjustifiably (Colangelo, 1997; Colangelo & Assouline, 2000).
- Perrone (1997) commented on the multipotentiality of many gifted students who have the ability to enter a wide range of career paths and who require vocational guidance so that they do not shut off their options too early. They need to be aware of professional opportunities open to them, the entry requirements of many courses, the availability of joint courses (e.g., university joint degrees) that enhance their options, and opportunities to savour the professional world through work experience programs, vacation programs, and personal contacts.

In short, the intellectual and affective characteristics of giftedness often expose gifted young people to a range of potential problems that might not even be visible to teachers and parents unless they are made aware of the issues. It is crucial, therefore, that the school's welfare policy be attuned to these needs, and that special measures be adopted to monitor the progress of the gifted and talented and to provide appropriately for them.

Continuity

Although there has been considerable concern with the education of gifted and talented students in general, there has been only muted attention in Australia to the disorganisation and disruption that can occur as children progress from grade to grade—in particular, as they make the transition from primary school to secondary school or college. Curriculum documents refer to the ideal of a seamless curriculum in which gaps and disruptions do not occur but, for the majority of gifted students, this is not a reality.

Primary school

It is pleasing to note that there are many examples of primary staff members planning their teaching in concert and of students passing from grade to grade without interruption to their academic or social progress. In these instances, the teachers plan together, know what their colleagues have achieved in the lower grades, and are aware of the progress made by each student. When students are promoted at the beginning of the year, the new teachers are able to provide genuine continuity of curriculum experiences, simply building on each child's detailed record.

This is not always the case, however, and it is not uncommon for new teachers to plan their teaching in advance, revising earlier work whether students require it or not, and teaching to a predetermined level for the entire class. There is nothing more disconcerting for students (whatever their academic level) than to revise large sections of the program and to work additional examples when they have already mastered the content. The lack of continuity for some students is a more complex problem than many primary teachers realise.

Secondary school

The transition to secondary school proves to be extremely difficult for many students and even more so for a proportion of the gifted. Not only do the youngsters have to negotiate new buildings, different routines, a range of teachers, different instructional strategies, and new expectations, but also they meet compartmentalised teachers who are skilled in one or two subject areas and who work in faculty groups (Braggett, 1997c). Some gifted students respond very positively to this faculty structure and appreciate the specialisation permitted.

A serious problem, however, is the curriculum discontinuity that usually prevails between primary and secondary schools. Secondary schools enrol students from a range of primary departments with different expectations and with variable academic standards. Consequently, much of the teaching over the first few months of the year—sometimes longer—is devoted to what is termed consolidation. By this the secondary school means reteaching, revising, and checking on concepts encountered earlier in primary school. For average and below-average performers this is most important and it is likewise useful for those students who have gaps in their understanding. For gifted performers, however, it can prove to be a depressing experience and one that quickly leads to boredom and dismay. For outstanding students it is a waste of time.

Many secondary schools respond that they have neither the resources nor the time to house and read all the primary school records on individual students and that such records are not always useful because of the different expectations of some smaller primary schools (Braggett Morris & Day, 1999).

The criticism of discontinuity is sometimes more trenchant from students who complete two years in a special primary class for gifted students (e.g., an OC class in New South Wales) and who then graduate to a secondary school (state, Catholic or independent) in which one program is provided for all students in the class. The lack

of curriculum continuity is particularly obvious and disconcerting and even extends to the division between the preparatory and secondary departments of the same independent school.

It is apparent that the lack of continuity between classes, and especially in the transition from primary to secondary education, is a major difficulty for many students and particularly for gifted and talented youngsters who perform extremely well in one or more subject areas. In order to reduce the problem, major changes are required.

- Where the primary schools that feed into a secondary school are relatively stable from year to year, there is a need for a closer liaison between the two to ensure less curriculum discontinuity when students make the transition.
- Secondary teachers should ensure that the needs of gifted and talented students are quickly discovered. It is too late to wait for half-yearly examination results to discover the high performers.
- Secondary school teachers need to provide differentiated programs based on individual student needs from the start of the academic year when the new student intake arrives.

Other issues

When planning a total school approach, teachers and school administrators must consider a range of other divergent, but equally important issues, that bear on gifted and talented education.

Resources

If teachers are to provide for students with a wide range of abilities in their classrooms, to differentiate the curriculum according to student needs and to group students for different activities, it is imperative that they have access to an up-to-date supply of resources. These should include:

- books for teachers (including teaching manuals) that provide a wealth of ideas on grouping practices, classroom management, the characteristics of gifted students, teaching strategies, and ways of differentiating the curriculum;
- a range of reading materials and reference books for students, either in a class library or central library;
- kits for teachers and students to use;
- a range of textbooks for use in the classroom so that outstanding students are not restricted to one textbook or to one approach;
- access to the Internet and to email facilities;
- access to databases and/or encyclopaedias on disk; and

- the names of mentors whom teachers might approach to provide assistance for students (local or through the Internet).

Readily available books to assist teachers are listed at the end of this chapter.

Budgeting

It is surprising to note that many schools indicate a genuine concern for gifted and talented students but do not budget funds for the purchase of appropriate resources on a regular basis. As well as budgeting for hardware and software, it is necessary to budget well in advance for the professional development of teachers, especially when experts are available to conduct professional development days (or workshops) or when teachers wish to attend special courses that will assist the school.

Outside assistance

A great deal of assistance is freely obtainable from departments or ministries of education. Kits, books, and other resources are available from these sources in most states, sometimes for a nominal charge. States such as Victoria have a range of videos available on gifted and talented education, as well as ongoing programs for students through art galleries, zoological gardens, tertiary institutions, and overseas contacts. Many retired citizens have a wealth of expertise (e.g., history, geography, writing, computing, and engineering) and are willing to afford assistance to gifted students if their parents grant written permission.

Home–school relations

Finally, it should be remembered that the school and the home need to work closely together and this is equally true when the education of gifted and talented students is involved. Parents have a great store of knowledge about their own young children and this can prove invaluable when the home and the school liaise during the early primary and later primary years. Teachers often recommend books, kits, excursions, enrichment camps and weekends, specialised resources, sport coaching schools, and a range of other specialised activities, all of which involve costs. It is imperative that the home and the school agree on these before any recommendation leads to financial, social, cultural, or religious embarrassment. If a student's learning is profoundly advanced and if accelerated school progression is recommended, parents (and the student) must have the final decision. Healthy home–school relations need to underpin the education of gifted and talented students, even during the high school years when young adolescents do not always wish their parents to be seen on the school grounds.

SUMMARY

The concepts of giftedness and talent have changed over time. Originally based on high academic performance, giftedness was later associated with high measured intelligence, and talent with special abilities such as music and art. Guilford's work on creativity and the increasing emphasis on mathematical, scientific and technological abilities broadened the concept of giftedness and blurred the distinction between giftedness and talent. By the 1980s, giftedness was no longer conceived as a unitary concept (based on intelligence alone) but as a multidimensional notion with various manifestations.

In the period from 1980 to 2000, issues of equity extended the concept of giftedness to a wider range of populations and cultures. Educators emphasised the need to cater for the gifts and talents of all students; and Gardner's theory of Multiple Intelligences became popularised.

Although some writers wish to restrict giftedness to a small percentage of the population (e.g., 1% or 2%), schools are now more likely to specify up to 15% (or even more).

Common assessment procedures and practices include: (a) the assessment of so-called innate abilities through psychometric methods (testing); and (b) the identification of high achievement or potential high achievement through achievement tests, tests of creativity, aptitude tests, teacher selection, parent nomination, peer nomination and/or pupil self nomination. More recently it has been realised that sympathetic and well-designed teaching approaches might also cultivate and develop the special abilities of children and help to identify other students with outstanding potential.

To support the learning of gifted and talented students, a number of strategies have been developed beyond the school: state policies, enrichment schols and camps, mentor programs, competitions, and state associations that operate as support groups for parents and teachers. Within the educational system itself, six broad approaches have been developed: special secondary schools or streams, special primary classes, cluster groups of schools working together, graded classes, withdrawal (or pullout) groups, and student accelerated progress in its many forms.

Because most of these approaches take the emphasis off the regular classroom teacher, a total school approach is required if a developmental concept of giftedness and talent is to be implemented in its entirety. A model was outlined that embraced seven areas for the consideration of each school. Then, a section concentrated on these seven areas and analysed them in some depth as indicated below.

The school needs to target the cultural enrichment of all students; the development of emerging talents; the development of highly specialised abilities; the extension of students with high all-round abilities; the creation of a close liaison between home and school; the development of teachers' talents; and the cultivation of a culture of excellence within the school.

School organisation needs to be scrutinised so that it enhances and supports the education of gifted students. In addition to normal organisational patterns, multi-age groups and individual student progression should be closely considered.

Classroom strategies include grouping practices, the importance of the classroom layout, and the need for communication and for open displays of students' work. Teaching strategies were explored through the compaction of basic skills; assessment procedures that emphasise pretesting and the setting of tests and quizzes with high ceilings or open-ended questions; the importance of deductive teaching methods; the deliberate and sustained teaching of advanced skills and strategies (particularly in the areas of critical thinking, creative thinking, and research skills); and the need to negotiate the curriculum and teaching methods with students.

The curriculum should be differentiated to suit the specific needs of gifted and talented students. Differentiation can occur if the curriculum is paced at an appropriate speed; cognitive processes are emphasised and taught; appropriate enrichment and extension programs are devised; personal experience and autonomy are developed; multiple intelligences are heeded and nurtured; deductive thinking is accepted and encouraged; the possibility of social change is allowed into the curriculum; and career and vocational education are afforded a rightful place in secondary school. Enrichment and extension programs require close attention as they are often inappropriate and pitched at a low level that does not assist outstanding students. Six different types of enrichment programs were explored and an example of a Renzulli-type 3 approach for a group of students was provided.

Student welfare of gifted and talented students is an issue that requires closer attention in many schools, especially relating to the loneliness of gifted students in regular classrooms, the needs of gifted disabled students, the counselling of those with individual problems, and the multipotentiality of career possibilities that exist.

The continuity of curriculum experiences as students progress from grade to grade, or pass from primary school to secondary school is a much-neglected area in the education of gifted and talented students. Consolidation or revision work upon entering a higher grade can be a deadening experience for outstanding students.

Other issues were explored under the headings: resources, school budgeting, the assistance of outside agencies, and the importance of continued home-school relations.

Suggested reading

Research-orientated texts

For those who wish academic and research-orientated texts, the two most obvious are:

Heller, K. A., Mönks, F. J., Sternberg, R. J. & Subotnik, R. F. (Eds). (2000). *International handbook of giftedness and talent* (2nd ed.). Oxford: Pergamon.

Colangelo, N. & Davis, G. A. (Eds) (1997). *Handbook of gifted education* (2nd ed.). Boston: Allyn & Bacon.

(The first includes a chapter on Australian and New Zealand provisions for gifted and talented students by E. Braggett and R. Moltzen.)

Classroom approaches

Teachers and parents who seek information on classroom approaches might consult:

Braggett, E. J. (1997a). *Differentiated programs for primary schools: Units of work for gifted and talented students*. Melbourne: Hawker Brownlow Education.

Braggett, E. J. (1997b). *Differentiated programs for secondary schools: Units of work*. Melbourne: Hawker Brownlow Education.

Lazear, D. (1998). *Eight ways of teaching [Multiple Intelligences]*. Melbourne: Hawker Brownlow Education.

Reid, L. (1993). *Thinking skills resource book*. Melbourne: Hawker Brownlow Education.

Wilks, S. (1995). *Critical and creative thinking: Strategies for classroom inquiry*. Melbourne: Eleanor Curtin Publishing.

Teaching kits

There are two useful teaching kits issued by the Education Department of Western Australia issued in 1995 and 1996:

Teaching TAGS [Talented and Gifted Students]—Primary (grades K–7)

Teaching TAGS [Talented and Gifted Students]—Secondary.

The Ministry of Education, Melbourne, Victoria, has a range of videos on gifted students and their education.

Practical activities

1. Invite a successful talented person (e.g., a local businessperson or a sportsperson) to speak about his or her work and talent. Ask the person about motivation, hours

of practice or preparation, hard work, attitudes to work, and community reactions. What advantages and disadvantages are highlighted?

2. Ask two friends or acquaintances to outline their interests, hobbies, reading habits, TV preferences, and study patterns for you. What patterns emerge?
3. Ask six people to detail their preferred styles of learning. Question them on which of the following they prefer: reading to learn, watching visual presentations, active physical learning, group discussions, classroom lectures, or individual study. What are the implications for the classroom teacher?
4. Find a student who is very talented in some aspect of the visual or performing arts (e.g., painting, ceramics, drama, or ballet) and observe the person closely when he or she is engrossed in this interest. Then talk to the person about his or her work, interests and motivation. What characteristics appear to be important?
5. Find a teacher who has had experience, at some time, in teaching both highly gifted students and students of average ability. Enquire about the differences of the two groups in terms of skills, knowledge, attitudes to study, specialised interests, and curiosity. What are the implications for teachers?

References

Bellanca, J. & Fogarty, R. (1991). *Catch them thinking.* Melbourne: Hawker Brownlow Education.

Benbow, C. P. & Minor, L. L. (1990). Cognitive profiles of verbally and mathematically precocious students: Implications for identification of the gifted. *Gifted Child Quarterly, 34,* 21–26.

Bevan-Brown, J. (1996). Special abilities: A Maori perspective. In D. McAlpine & R. Moltzen (Eds), *Gifted and talented: New Zealand perspectives* (pp. 91–110). Palmerston North, NZ: ERDC Press, Massey University.

Bisley, B. (1996). Giftedness in isolation. In A. Jacob & G. Barnsley (Eds), *Gifted children: The challenge continues* (pp. 267–270). Sydney: NSW Association for Gifted and Talented Children.

Bloom, B. S., Englehart, M. D., Furst, E. J., Hill, W. H., & Krathwohl, D. R. (1956). *A taxonomy of educational objectives: Handbook 1 Cognitive domain.* New York: David McKay.

Bloom, B. S. (1974). *Taxonomy of educational objectives.* New York: McKay.

Braggett, E. J. (1994). *Developing programs for gifted students: A total school approach.* Melbourne: Hawker Brownlow Education.

Braggett, E. J. (1997a). *Differentiated programs for primary schools.* Melbourne: Hawker Brownlow Education.

Braggett, E. J. (1997b). *Differentiated programs for secondary schools.* Melbourne: Hawker Brownlow Education.

Braggett, E. J. (1997c). *The middle years of schooling: An Australian perspective.* Melbourne: Hawker Brownlow Education.

Braggett, E. J. (2000). Gifted education: A total school approach involving all teachers. In K. Maitra (Ed.), *Toward excellence: Developing and nurturing giftedness and talent* (pp. 35–47). New Delhi: Mosaic Books.

Braggett, E. J., Kay, R. & Lowrie, T. (1998). *Thinking skills and their development in young children.* ARC-funded project, Charles Sturt University, NSW.

Braggett, E. J. & Moltzen, R. I. (2000). Programs and practices for identifying and nurturing giftedness and talent in Australia and New Zealand. In K. A. Heller, F. J. Mönks, R. J. Sternberg & R. F. Subotnik (Eds), *International handbook of giftedness and talent* (2nd ed., pp. 779–797). Oxford: Elsevier.

Braggett, E. J., Morris, G. & Day, A. (1999). *Reforming the middle years of schooling.* Melbourne: Hawker Brownlow Education.

Chaffey, G. (2000). *Finding hidden gold: An exploration of a dynamic process to determine high academic potential in Aboriginal children.* Paper presented at the 8th National Conference of the Australian Association for the Education of the Gifted and Talented, Brisbane, July.

Colangelo, N. (1997). Counseling gifted students: Issues and practices. In N. Colangelo & G. A. Davis (Eds), *Handbook of gifted education* (2nd ed.) (pp. 353–365). Boston: Allyn & Bacon.

Colangelo, N. & Assouline, S. G. (2000). Counseling gifted students. In K. A. Heller, F. J. Mönks, R. J. Sternberg & R. F. Subotnik (Eds), *International handbook of giftedness and talent* (2nd ed., pp. 595–607). Oxford: Elsevier.

Comerford, T. & Creed, K. (1983). *Gifted and talented children: A teacher's guide.* Melbourne: Education Department of Victoria, Gifted Children Task Force.

Copley, A. J. & Urban, K. K. (2000). In K. A. Heller, F. J. Mönks, R. J. Sternberg & R. F. Subotnik (Eds), *International handbook of giftedness and talent* (2nd ed., pp. 485–498). Oxford: Elsevier.

Davis, G. A. & Rimm, S. B. (1994). *Education of the gifted and talented* (3rd ed.). Englewood Cliffs, NJ: Prentice Hall.

Day, A. (1996). Development of the talents of Indigenous Australians. *Australasian Journal of Gifted Education, 5*(1), 26–29.

deBono, E. (1975). *CoRT thinking, CoRT.* Teacher notes. Elmsford NY: Pergamon.

Dooley, P. M. (2000). *The Internet: An accessible resource for the mathematically gifted.* Paper presented at the 8th National Conference of the Australian Association for the Education of the Gifted and Talented. Brisbane, July.

Eberle, B. (1987). *Scamper games for imagination development.* Melbourne: Hawker Brownlow Education.

Education Department of Western Australia (1995). *Teaching TAGS* [Kit]. Perth: Education Department of Western Australia.

Fitzgerald, J. & Keown, R. (1996). Gifted and talented females. In D. McAlpine & R. Moltzen (Eds), *Gifted and talented: New Zealand perspectives* (pp. 427–442). Palmerston North, NZ: ERDC Press, Massey University.

Flood, A. (2000). *Student, family and peer-related factors in high academic achievement in the NSW Higher School Certificate.* Paper presented at the 8th National Conference of the Australian Association for the Education of the Gifted and Talented, Brisbane, July.

Fogarty, R. & Bellanca, J. (1991). *Teach them thinking.* Melbourne: Hawker Brownlow Education.

Fox, L. H. (1979). Programs for the gifted and talented: An overview. In A. H. Passow (Ed.), *The gifted and talented: Their education and development* (78th Yearbook of the National Society for the Study of Education, Pt. 1, pp. 104–126). Chicago: NSSE.

Freeman, J. (2000). Families: The essential context for gifts and talents. In K. A. Heller, F. J. Mönks, R. J. Sternberg & R. F. Subotnik (Eds), *International handbook of giftedness and talent* (2nd ed., pp. 573–585). Oxford: Elsevier.

Gagné, F. (1993). Constructs and models pertaining to exceptional human abilities. In K. A. Heller, F. J.Mönk & A. H. Passow (Eds), *International handbook of research and development of giftedness and talent* (pp. 69–87). Oxford: Pergamon.

Gagné, F. (2000). Understanding the complex choreography of talent development through DMGT-based analysis. In K. A. Heller, F. J. Mönks, R. J. Sternberg & R. F. Subotnik (Eds), *International handbook of giftedness and talent* (2nd ed., pp. 67–79). Oxford: Elsevier.

Gardner, H. (1996). Personal communication to E. Braggett, Melbourne, 1996.

Gibson, K. L. (1992). Ensuring identification of disadvantaged and culturally diverse gifted students in Queensland. *Australasian Journal of Gifted Education, 1*(2), 27–30.

Gross, M. U. M. (1999). Gerric Centre, University of New South Wales. Personal communication, August 1999.

Guilford, J. P. (1950). Creativity. *American Psychologist. 5*, 444–454.

Guilford, J. P. (1975). Varieties of creative giftedness: Their measurement and development. *Gifted Child Quarterly, 19*, 107–121.

Hall, M, (2001). *Learning styles of gifted and talented adolescents: Student needs and school provision.* Unpublished PhD thesis, Charles Sturt University, NSW.

Heller, K. A., Perieth, C. & Sierwald, W. (1990). The Munich longitudinal study of giftedness. In S. Bailey, E. Braggett & M. Robinson (Eds), *The challenge of excellence: A vision splendid* (pp. 37–47). Sydney: Australian Association for the Education of the Gifted and Talented.

Imison, K. & Imison, A. (2000). *The 'mind-fields' of gender differences in gifted students.* Paper presented at the 8th National Conference of the Australian Association for the Education of the Gifted and Talented. Brisbane, July.

Kanevsky, L. (2000). Dynamic assessment of gifted students. In K. A. Heller, F. J. Mönks, R. J. Sternberg & R. F. Subotnik (Eds), *International handbook of giftedness and talent* (2nd ed., pp. 283–295). Oxford: Elsevier.

Karvouni, A. (2000). *Interactive technology programs for isolated gifted students.* Paper presented at the 8th National Conference of the Australian Association for the Education of the Gifted and Talented. Brisbane, July.

Kerr, B. (2000). Guiding gifted girls and young women. In K. A. Heller, F. J. Mönks, R. J. Sternberg & R. F. Subotnik (Eds), *International handbook of giftedness and talent* (2nd ed., pp. 649–657). Oxford: Elsevier.

Leder, G. (1985). Challenges provided by the gifted disabled. In E. J. Braggett (Ed.), *Education of gifted and talented children from populations with special needs: Discussion documents* (pp. 61–54). Canberra: Commonwealth Schools Commission.

Maker, C. J. (1982). *Curriculum development for the gifted.* Rockville, MD: Aspen Systems.

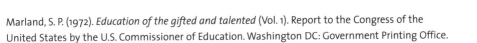

Marland, S. P. (1972). *Education of the gifted and talented* (Vol. 1). Report to the Congress of the United States by the U.S. Commissioner of Education. Washington DC: Government Printing Office.

McAlpine, D. (1996). The identification of children with special abilities. In D. McAlpine & R. Moltzen (Eds), *Gifted and talented: New Zealand perspectives* (pp. 63–89). Palmerston North, NZ: ERDC Press, Massey University.

Meeker, M. N. (1969). Understanding the evaluation of gifted: A new method. *Gifted Child Quarterly, 13*, 230–236.

Miles, C. C. (1946). Gifted children. In L. Carmichael (Ed.), *Manual of child psychology* (pp. 886–953). New York: John Wiley.

Mönks, F. J., Van Boxtel, H. W., Roelefs, J. J. & Sanders, M. P. (1986). The identification of gifted children in secondary education and a description of their situation in Holland. In K. A. Heller & J. F. Feldhusen (Eds), *Identifying and nurturing the gifted: An international perspective* (pp. 39–65). Toronto: Hans Huber Publishers.

Perleth, C. & Schatz, T. (2000). Early identification of high ability. In K. A. Heller, F. J. Mönks, R. J. Sternberg & R. F. Subotnik (Eds), *International handbook of giftedness and talent* (2nd ed., pp. 297–316). Oxford: Elsevier.

Perrone, P. A. (1997). Gifted individuals' career development. In N. Colangelo & G. A. Davis (Eds), *Handbook of gifted education* (2nd ed., pp. 398–407). Boston: Allyn & Bacon.

Ramos-Ford, V. & Gardner, H. (1997). Giftedness from a multiple intelligences perspective. In N. Colangelo & G. A. Davis (Eds), *Handbook of gifted education* (2nd ed., pp. 54–66). Boston: Allyn & Bacon.

Reid, L. (1993). *Thinking skills resource book*. Melbourne: Hawker Brownlow Education.

Renzulli, J. S. (1983). Rating of the behavioral characteristics of superior students. *Gifted/Creative/Talented. Sept–Oct.*, 30–35.

Renzulli, J. S. (1986). The three-ringed conception of giftedness: A developmental model for creative productivity. In R. J. Sternberg & J. E. Davidson (Eds), *Conceptions of giftedness* (pp. 53–92). New York: Cambridge University Press.

Renzulli, J. S. & Reis, S. M. (1986). The enrichment triad/revolving door model: A schoolwide plan for the development of creative productivity. In J. S. Renzulli (Ed.), *Systems and models for developing programs for the gifted and talented* (pp. 218–266). Mansfield Center, CN: Creative Learning Inc.

Renzulli, J. S. & Reis, S. M. (2000). The schoolwide enrichment model. In K. A. Heller, F. J. Mönks, R. J. Sternberg & R. F. Subotnik (Eds), *International handbook of giftedness and talent* (2nd ed., pp. 367–382). Oxford: Elsevier.

Savage, L. B. (1990). Where do gifted children with learning disabilities belong? In S. Bailey, E. Braggett & M. Robinson (Eds), *The challenge of excellence: A vision splendid* (pp. 166–169). Sydney: Australian Association for the Education of the Gifted and Talented.

Schneider, W. (2000). Giftedness, expertise, and (exceptional) performance: A developmental perspective. In K. A. Heller, F. J. Mönks, R. J. Sternberg & R. F. Subotnik (Eds), *International handbook of giftedness and talent* (2nd ed., pp. 165–177). Oxford: Elsevier.

Seletto, R. & Diezmann, C. (2000). *Supporting gifted Aboriginal students.* Paper presented at the 8th National Conference of the Australian Association for the Education of the Gifted and Talented, Brisbane, July.

Sternberg, R. J. (2000). Intelligence as developing expertise. In K. A. Heller, F. J. Mönks, R. J. Sternberg & R. F. Subotnik (Eds), *International handbook of giftedness and talent* (2nd ed., pp. 55–66). Oxford: Elsevier.

Terman, L. M. (1925). *Mental and physical traits of a thousand gifted children.* Stanford CA: Stanford University Press.

Terman, L. M. (1954). The discovery and encouragement of exceptional talent. *American Psychologist, 9,* 221–230.

Urban, K. K. (2000). *Responsible creativity – competence for the future.* Paper delivered at the 6th Asia–Pacific Conference on Giftedness. Beijing, August.

VanTassel Baska, J. (1997). What matters in curriculum for gifted learners: Reflections on theory, research and practice. In N. Colangelo & G. A. Davis (Eds), *Handbook of gifted education* (2nd ed., pp. 126–135). Boston: Allyn & Bacon.

VanTassel Baska, J. (2000). *Twelve lessons in curriculum development for the gifted.* Paper presented at the 8th National Conference of the Australian Association for the Education of the Gifted and Talented, Brisbane, July.

WA Ministry of Education, (1988). *Exceptionally able children—Guidelines for early childhood years.* Perth: Ministry of Education, Western Australia (Academic Extension).

Williams, J. (1984). Identification of intellectually gifted students. In *First national conference on the education of gifted and talented children (1983),* (pp. 450–466). Canberra: Commonwealth Schools Commission.

Yewchuk, C. & Lupart, J. (2000). Inclusive education for gifted students with disabilities. In K. A. Heller, F. J. Mönks, R. J. Sternberg & R. F. Subotnik (Eds), *International handbook of giftedness and talent* (2nd ed., pp. 659–670). Oxford: Elsevier.

8

Programs that support inclusive education

Robyn M. Gillies

Case studies

Michael

Michael was very affectionate and loved to sit at his Year 1 teacher's feet while she read stories or explained the day's activities to the class. He'd cuddle up to her legs and stroke and pat them, almost as a way of stroking himself. These sessions on the mat were among the few times during the school day when Michael was calm and settled.

Michael was one of 52 children in a double-teaching, open-area space with two class teachers. The teachers worked together in tandem or separately, depending on the activity.

Although Michael was five-and-a-half years old when he started school, he was small for his age. His preschool teacher had expressed concerns about his readiness for school because he was very active and impulsive, he experienced difficulty in concentrating, his expressive language skills were delayed, and he was often unable to follow instructions unless he was prompted. In addition, he experienced difficulty using scissors and pencil or crayon. In short, Michael was regarded as being immature for his age and not ready to begin formal schooling.

Michael's teachers in Year 1 soon realised that, although he was probably of average ability, he was very immature, that he was not ready to deal with a structured school day, and that he would require high support. This support was intensive and ongoing, with Michael receiving special assistance not only from his teachers but also from a specialist learning support teacher and a speech therapist. In addition, a teacher's aide worked with him on specific learning activities on a daily basis. However, in spite of these difficulties and the frustrations he encountered with learning, Michael liked school and he took great interest in what the other children in his class were doing.

His teachers noticed that he liked to be involved with his peers and they decided to pair him with a more capable student to work on a number of small cutting and pasting tasks. This went quite well with the more capable peer adopting the role of the tutor and providing Michael with the cues and prompts to complete each task. Michael enjoyed the attention of this student and eagerly sought to respond to the tutor's assistance by completing the tasks with her.

During these tutoring sessions, Michael was more settled and willing to complete the different tasks he was asked to do than when he was in the larger class group. His teachers noticed that he chatted openly with his tutor whereas, in the larger class group, he was less likely to talk unless he was specifically asked a question, and then his answer was often a simple "yes" or "no". In this small tutoring arrangement, Michael seemed to be less inhibited and more likely to try new ways of doing things or learning information. His teachers realised that Michael benefited from these tutoring sessions and regularly used this strategy to help him adjust to the formal demands of the classroom.

Gary

Gary is in his second year of high school and he appears to have adjusted well to his school routine. However, this wasn't always the case. When he first arrived, he was clearly overwhelmed. The continual movement after each period from room to room, and from building to building, was very stressful for Gary who had trouble understanding his timetable and reading the school map which showed where the different buildings were located. Gary had an intellectual disability and, although he could participate in most activities, he had difficulties organising the books he needed for each period and understanding instructions. It was not long before his teachers realised that unless they did something, he would always be late for lessons and become the butt of peer ridicule.

Providing Gary with some additional prompts to avoid making his difficulties obvious was the first step. He was assigned a buddy who had the responsibility of making sure that Gary arrived for his next lesson on time. Although only one student was initially assigned this task, others in Gary's class often took it upon themselves to help him arrive at the right room with the correct materials.

Gary was very sociable and well liked by his peers. His teachers decided to build on this attribute by setting up small, cooperative learning groups in different subject areas to enable him to participate in a wide range of subject activities. The opportunity of working closely with others enabled Gary to take risks with his learning that he would have found intimidating in the larger classroom. The group members were very supportive and they actively encouraged Gary.

The opportunity to contribute in a meaningful way improved Gary's status among his class peers, and this contributed to Gary's sense of purpose, achievement, and self-confidence. Gary is now enjoying school. While he is working on an adjusted program he is fully included in his classes.

What you will learn in this chapter

The general goal of this chapter is to describe how children can help each other to learn and how the interpersonal relationships that result can be used to promote inclusion of children with diverse needs in mainstream classrooms. When you have finished this chapter you will know:

- the academic, social, and adjustment benefits that can be attained by children helping each other learn;
- how to structure cooperative learning experiences in mixed-gender and mixed-ability groups to promote learning, adjustment and inclusion;

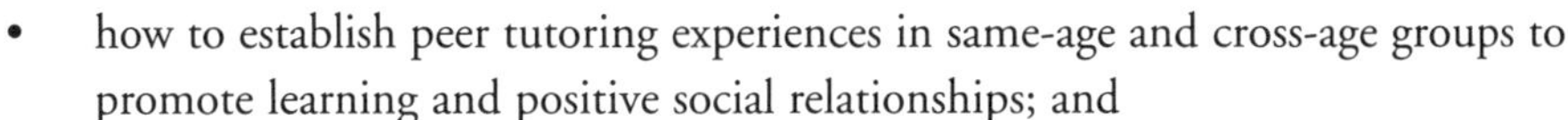

- how to establish peer tutoring experiences in same-age and cross-age groups to promote learning and positive social relationships; and
- how to use different learning and teaching strategies within small groups to promote thinking skills and learning.

Problems a student might face

In today's schools, many teachers work with a wide range of children with diverse learning and adjustment needs, such as those of the children described above. Although many children arrive at school well equipped with the pre-academic and social skills that will enable them to adjust to the requirements placed on them, others are less able and experience more difficulties with the demands of school. These children are of particular concern to their teachers because they have to develop individual programs for them based on their specific needs These often include difficulties in the following areas:

- speech and language;
- social interactions;
- following instructions;
- understanding and responding to social cues;
- gross motor skills (e.g., problems with balance and walking up stairs);
- using a pencil and scissors;
- behaviour (e.g., inattentive and impulsive behaviour);
- maturity (e.g., emotional immaturity); and
- personal hygiene (e.g., problems using the toilet).

Defining terms

To be consistent with current practices in Australia, the term *learning difficulties* has been used rather than *learning disabilities* (except when referring to specific research from the United States where learning disabilities is used). This is the result of a report of a Select Committee of the Australian House of Representatives that investigated the problems of children and adults who experienced trouble with literacy or numeracy. The committee chose the term *learning difficulties*, arguing that most of the children who experienced problems in school were not demonstrably impaired or disabled (Cadman, 1976). See van Kraayenoord, this volume, for an elaborated discussion of this issue.

Cooperative learning involves students working together in small groups (usually of 4 to 6 members) to accomplish a common goal or to complete a shared task. Groups truly cooperate only when each member works to complete his or her part of the goal or task while ensuring that others do likewise.

Peer tutoring involves a more capable student helping a less able student learn specific skills or information.

Scaffolding is a way of supporting and providing assistance (e.g., by use of prompts, cues and feedback) until students can perform the task independently.

Cooperative learning

Cooperative learning has been used successfully in schools over the past 30 years or so to promote academic achievement, more positive attitudes toward school and learning, a positive self-concept in students, and greater acceptance of students with disabilities. It also influences the development of positive student attitudes toward other group members and, because it encourages students to accept more autonomy over their own learning, promotes motivation to learn. In effect, cooperative learning enhances the prospect of achieving a range of cognitive and affective goals (Stevens & Slavin, 1995a, 1995b).

Cooperative learning involves children working together in small groups to accomplish shared goals. In cooperative learning, each student is not only required to complete a task, but is also required to ensure that others do likewise (Johnson & Johnson, 1999a). The technical term for this dual responsibility is *positive interdependence* and it is the most important element in cooperative learning (Deutsch, 1949).

Positive interdependence exists when students perceive that they cannot succeed unless others do and that they must coordinate and synchronise their efforts to complete the task. When individuals are in a situation in which they have clear, interdependent goals, and in which there is an expectation that they will cooperate, they see themselves as having interdependent goals. As a consequence, if one individual attempts to achieve his or her goal, the others will do likewise. In this way, members influence each other and contribute to the group effort.

Although positive interdependence is the most important element in cooperative learning, there are four other important elements:

- promotive interaction;
- individual accountability;
- interpersonal and small-group skills; and
- group processing.

Promotive interaction

Promotive interaction involves individuals encouraging and facilitating each other's efforts to complete the task and achieve the group's goals. Promotive interaction involves students:

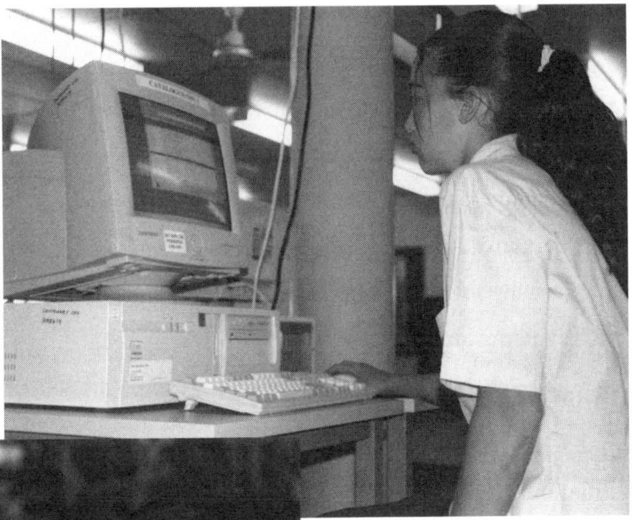

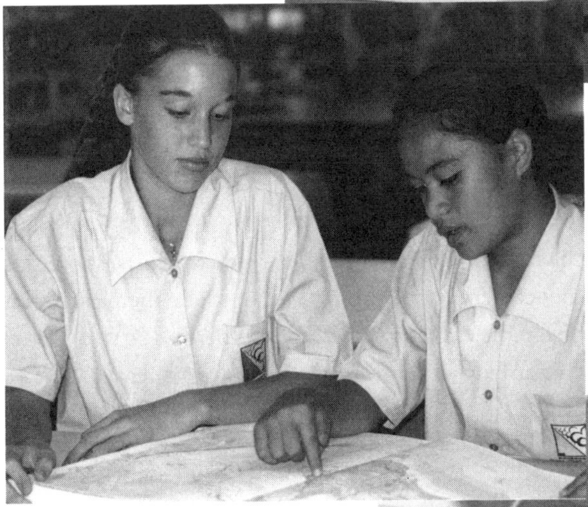

Two students work independently to collect information for a project and then compile their findings to achieve their goal.

- providing help to each other;
- sharing resources;
- providing constructive feedback to each other to improve task performance;
- challenging conclusions to develop greater insights into problems;
- encouraging each other's efforts;
- demonstrating goodwill toward each other;
- striving for mutual benefits; and
- avoiding anxiety and stress.

Individual accountability

Individual accountability involves group members accepting responsibility for their contributions to the group's goal and facilitating the work of others. It has been suggested that the stronger the positive interdependence structured within a group, the more group members will feel personally responsible for contributing to the collective effort (Johnson & Johnson, 1999a). This means doing as much as one can to achieve the group's goal.

One way in which students can be helped to be accountable for their efforts is to assign them different roles at the commencement of the project and to rotate them each time the group works together. For example, as adapted from McInerney & McInerney (1998), roles that the children might play in cooperative group work are:

- *Motivator:* helps to get the group moving with the task;
- *Contributor:* makes an active contribution to the group task and encourages others to do likewise;
- *Summariser:* recaps on points raised in the group;
- *Writer:* jots down the main points for the group;
- *Reporter:* reports on the group's progress to the wider class group; and
- *Timer:* keeps track of the time for the group.

The class teacher adjusts the roles of the children to ensure that no child is asked to perform a role that he or she finds difficult. Provided this is managed sensitively, most children accept their roles and participate accordingly.

Interpersonal and small-group skills

Interpersonal and small-group skills need to be systematically taught if students are to use them effectively. Placing students in groups and telling them to cooperate does not ensure that they will use the interpersonal and small-group skills required to facilitate communication and to capitalise on the opportunities presented by a cooperative learning experience.

In a study that examined the effect of training in interpersonal and small-group skills on children's behavioural interactions and achievement during small-group work, Gillies and Ashman (1996) found that the children in the trained groups were more cooperative and helpful to each other, used language which was more inclusive, and gave explanations to assist each other more often as they worked together, than did children in the untrained groups. Furthermore, the children in the trained groups exercised more autonomy in their learning and obtained higher learning outcomes.

The interpersonal skills that facilitated communication included:

- listening actively to each member of the group as he or she spoke;
- trying to understand the other person's perspective;
- stating ideas freely without fear of a 'put down' by another group member;
- accepting responsibility for one's own behaviour; and
- providing constructive feedback on ideas that were presented.

In addition, there was a number of small-group skills that facilitated participation in the group. These included:

- taking turns so that each group member had the opportunity to present ideas or share resources;
- sharing tasks so that everyone had a smaller task to complete as part of the larger group task;
- clarifying differences of opinion; and
- democratic decision-making so that everyone was involved in the group decision.

To be motivated to use these skills to achieve mutual goals, group members need to get to know each other, and must learn to trust one another, communicate accurately, accept and support each other, and resolve conflicts positively (see Johnson & Johnson, 1999a).

Group processing

Group processing has two aspects. First, it involves group members reflecting on what the group achieved and, in particular, on recognising which actions were helpful and which were unhelpful. Second, it involves making decisions about what actions to continue or change. Questions such as "What have we done well?" "What could we have done better?" and "What do we still need to do?", are examples of what group members need to ask. Johnson and Johnson (1999b) draw attention to the importance of group processing for the psychological health of the group because it enables members to:

- maintain good working relationships;
- develop cooperative learning skills;
- receive feedback on their participation;
- think on the metacognitive as well as the cognitive level; and
- celebrate the success of the group and reward positive behaviours of group members.

Cooperative learning is a relatively common practice in primary classes, but it is not often used in secondary schools because of the emphasis on content learning and the frequent mixing of students across subject areas. Nevertheless, in a study that examined the effects of group processing among high-ability senior high school students and beginning college students, Johnson, Johnson, Stanne, and Garibaldi (1990) found that cooperative conditions assisted students to perform more effectively in problem-solving activities than when they worked individually. The best problem-solving occurred in the groups in which the teacher and the students gave feedback on the group's performance. Hence, time needs to be allowed at the end of each group session for feedback and group members need to frame their responses so they provide specific, positive feedback to each other.

How to enhance classroom cooperation

Establishing a cooperative environment was not easy for Gary's teachers (case study, page 352) because they had to plan together how the work groups would operate, what their tasks would be, and who would be included. These issues are important because teachers often mistakenly assume that students will cooperate and work together as expected. Gary's teachers had to consider group size, composition (ability and gender), and type and duration of activity to be undertaken.

Size

Setting the optimal group size is important. If groups are too large, some students will be overlooked while others coast along at the expense of the workers. Groups of three or four members are best because they are too small for any member to opt out of the activity, or loaf at others' expense. A small group ensures that all members are visible and involved.

Group composition

The ability and gender composition of work groups have an effect on the interactions among members and, ultimately, on achievement. For example, in mixed-ability groups, high-ability students give more help to their peers than they do in uniform-ability groups. Both high-ability and low-ability students are quite active in teacher–learner relationships whereas medium-ability students tend to be ignored. In contrast, in uniform high-ability groups, students often assume that others know how

to solve the problem and make little effort to explain the material. In uniform low-ability groups, few students understand the problem well enough to explain it to others. However, medium-ability students work well with students of similar ability

In different gender compositions, the achievement of males and females is nearly identical in gender-balanced groups, whereas in majority male or majority female groups, males outperform the females. When groups are gender-balanced, males and females are equally interactive, whereas in majority female or male groups, the interactions of females are often detrimental to achievement because they direct most of their questions and help to the male, to the neglect of others in the group. In majority male groups, females are largely ignored (Lou et al., 1996; Webb, 1995).

In contrast, Gillies and Ashman (1995) found that Year 6 students who worked in different mixed-ability and mixed-gender cooperative learning groups did not differ much in behaviours or interactions, possibly because positive interdependence had been established and the children had been trained in the interpersonal and small group skills needed to facilitate group interactions. It appeared that the group task created the momentum to cooperate so that as the groups had more time to work together they became more responsive to the needs of each other and gave more explanations to assist each other's learning.

In a recent study of group ability composition of students in Years 7 and 8 who worked collaboratively, Webb, Nemer, Chizhik, and Sugrue (1998) found that all students who participated in mixed-ability groups gave higher-quality explanations to assist understanding than did students in uniform-ability groups. This contributed more to their achievement test scores than did their own ability scores, particularly for children with low ability and low-to-medium ability.

Group task

The tasks that students undertake in their groups also affect the discussions that occur. Cohen (1994) argued that in well-structured tasks such as mathematical and computational tasks (e.g., 26 x 57), there is little need for discussion because there is a right answer. In these tasks that require low levels of cooperation, achievement is consistently related to giving detailed explanations to each other on how to solve the problem. In contrast, in ill-structured tasks (such as open-ended and discovery tasks in which there are no standard answers or procedures to follow) discussion among the members is vital to creative solutions or to the discovery of underlying principles. An example of a less-structured task of this type might be the question: "What would be the social and political implications of the greenhouse effect?" Achievement gains depend on task-related interaction.

When students are assigned to either of these types of group tasks (i.e., well-structured or ill-structured), teachers should make sure that students understand what type of assistance will be more helpful as they work together. For example, being ignored, not

receiving an explanation in response to a request for help, or being given only the right answer with no explanation, are all negatively related to achievement. Teachers must be mindful of the different forms of help that students require, and should ensure that group members are trained to provide that help.

Structuring interactions in groups

Group tasks can be designed in a number of ways to ensure participants' interactions. For example, if young children are required to discuss and summarise the main points from the teacher's lesson—so others in their group can understand the concepts taught—they perform better on follow-up achievement tests than do those who only discuss the lesson or those who work by themselves.

Similarly, when children are taught to use a specific, *guided questioning strategy*—designed to help them make links between their own knowledge and the new information they are learning—they outperform their peers who do not use this strategy. The guided questioning strategy teaches children to ask more strategic questions and to give more detailed explanations. This strategy promotes problem-solving success by teaching children how to ask for, and how to provide, appropriate detailed help and explanations during small group activities.

Some teachers script interactions among children as they work in cooperative groups so that they talk about task content. This generally helps the children to learn and develop better cognitive awareness than do students who work cooperatively but do not use this scripted interaction approach. Structuring interactions in small groups promotes achievement among students in elementary grades.

In summary, cooperative learning is enhanced when the following guidelines for forming groups are used:

- restricting groups to three to four members;
- ensuring gender balance;
- ensuring ability mix (high-, medium-, and low-ability);
- providing well-defined tasks (e.g., specific steps to follow, or open and discovery-based tasks); and
- providing training in asking for and giving help (e.g., guided questioning, scripted interactions).

Changing the way we teach

Promoting inclusion through cooperation

With the current emphasis on including children with a range of learning and adjustment needs in mainstream classes, creating classrooms in which students support and encourage each other to learn can have wide-ranging positive effects.

The benefits of cooperative learning for children with social and academic needs were first outlined in the 1980s by Robert Slavin (1984) and by David and Roger Johnson (1986). Slavin summarised research on a mathematics program that encouraged cooperative learning among mainstreamed students with mild academic disability and their non-disabled peers. He found that a cooperative environment led to improvements in social and academic behaviour and to increases in mathematics achievement. In both studies, non-disabled students gained markedly in mathematics achievement. This outcome is important because teachers can be reluctant to promote cooperation if they believe that non-disabled students are unlikely to benefit. Positive effects on the behaviour and attitude of non-disabled peers was also found, with these children being more inclusive and more accepting of their less-able peers.

The results reported above have been confirmed by many studies of cooperative learning that show academic and social benefits accruing to children with learning difficulties in mainstream settings. These benefits include increased friendships and positive relationships between students with learning difficulties and their non-disabled peers, improved achievement, and increased motivation to learn (Pomplun, 1996; Putnam et al., 1996). However, if students with learning difficulties are to be effectively integrated into cooperative group activities, there are a number of guidelines to be followed. These are shown in Box 8.1 (page 362).

Including children with severe disabilities

Many studies using cooperative learning as a strategy to promote inclusion have focused on children with mild disabilities, whereas children with greater support needs have been ignored. There have been two significant exceptions.

One was a study conducted by Putman, Rynders, Johnson, and Johnson (1989) who examined the effects of cooperative skill training on interactions between children with severe disabilities (IQ 35–55) who had never participated in mainstream classes and their non-disabled peers as they worked on group-based science activities over three weeks. The children were trained in sharing materials and ideas, encouraging everyone to participate, saying at least one nice thing to everyone in the group, and checking to see if everyone understood and agreed with the answers. The teachers of the cooperative groups identified the skills to be practised and provided descriptions and examples of each skill. The teacher then checked for understanding and the children were then asked to use the skills during their group activities. The results showed that non-disabled children interacted more with their peers with a severe disability—by looking at them, talking with them, and working cooperatively with them—than did the children in the untrained groups. Furthermore, there were no instances of negative comments being directed at or about the children with a severe disability. The results led Putnam et al. to conclude that:

> . . . the fear that moderately and severely handicapped students will be openly ridiculed and rejected by nonhandicapped peers, a fear sometimes expressed by those who oppose social integration of mentally handicapped students, may not be well founded, especially for those situations in which interaction procedures are structured properly (Putnam et al., 1989, p. 554).

In a later study, Hunt, Staub, Alwell, and Goetz (1994) investigated the extent to which three second grade children with multiple severe disabilities could acquire basic communication and motor objectives within cooperative learning activities conducted in their general education classrooms. The groups were established so that the

Box 8.1 Guidelines for included students with learning difficulties in group activities

Carefully explain the procedures the cooperative group will follow.

Train non-disabled children in helping, tutoring, teaching, and sharing skills. The use of prompts and praise are easily taught and will encourage students with learning difficulties to remain engaged with the task.

Make the academic requirements for the children with disabilities reasonable. Requirements for different tasks can be adapted so the students with different achievement levels can participate in the same cooperative group through:

- the use of different criteria for success for each group member;
- varying the amount each group member is expected to master;
- giving group members different subtasks to complete and then using the average percentage worked correctly as the group's score; and
- using improvement scores as a measure of success, especially for students with learning difficulties.

Pretrain the children with learning difficulties in the academic skills that they will need to complete the group's work. Try to give these children a source of expertise that the group will need.

Pretrain the children with learning difficulties in collaboration skills. Use a special education teacher or aide to teach these skills to the children with learning difficulties.

Give the children with learning difficulties a role that they are able to manage in the group (e.g., if they cannot read, they might be able to facilitate the group's work by organising materials, and by offering encouragement to other members).

Give bonus points to groups that have students with disabilities. This will create a situation in which the non-disabled students will want to work with their less-able peers to receive bonus points.

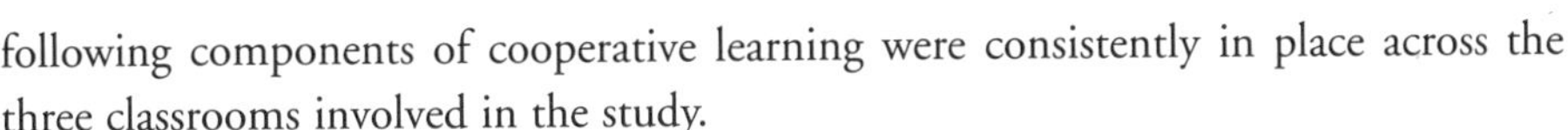

following components of cooperative learning were consistently in place across the three classrooms involved in the study.

- The activities required interdependent participation to achieve a common goal.
- Achievement of the goal required coordination among members of the group and successful contributions from all members.
- The goals included both academic and social skill development.
- There was both individual and group accountability.

In addition, the groups containing a child with a disability were trained to provide the cues and prompts to that student to enable him or her to generate the targeted communication and motor responses. The children were also taught to provide positive feedback to the students when these behaviours were attempted. The children worked in their groups on a series of maths activities, once a day for 8–10 weeks. The results showed that each of the students with severe disabilities was producing, independently, the targeted communication and motor responses during the cooperative learning activities. The students without disabilities in the cooperative learning groups consistently and accurately provided cues, prompts, and consequences to facilitate learning by the member with disabilities. Furthermore, follow-up maths achievement tests demonstrated that group members without disabilities achieved as well as did their peers in groups without a child with disabilities. In other words, the facilitative interactions by group members without disabilities did not negatively affect their achievement.

Both of the studies described above—Putnam et al. (1989) and Hunt et al. (1994)—demonstrate that children with severe disabilities can be successfully included in cooperative groups to achieve specific targeted objectives. Furthermore, provided that the non-disabled group members are trained in the specific help they are to provide, they will willingly interact with their disabled peers to help them achieve. Both studies show clearly that the children with disabilities are not rejected and, in fact, that their peers will actively praise, facilitate, and encourage their efforts. In a survey of more than a thousand middle-school and high-school students, Hendrickson et al. (1996) found that students were very willing to form friendships with students with severe disabilities and to include them in learning situations. Students perceived themselves, teachers, and youth organisations as primarily responsible for facilitating these friendships. The specific strategies that students suggested would facilitate friendship and inclusion included:

- students working together in cooperative groups;
- teachers presenting information on disabilities to students, other teachers, and parents; and
- teachers and parents arranging social events for all students.

Although teachers acknowledge the benefits that accrue from students working together, they often express concern about how they can adapt the curriculum to enable students with disabilities to experience success in cooperative groups. Nevin (1993) proposed that the following adaptations could be considered:

- changing response modes so that students can demonstrate in different ways how they have learnt the material (e.g., writing an answer rather than having to report it verbally to the class, using sign language to summarise a story, talking about a topic rather than writing about it, or creating an object such as a diorama to demonstrate knowledge and understanding of a particular topic);
- developing functional equivalents such that one student might be required to complete a mathematics worksheet with 90% accuracy, whereas another might be required to determine that he or she has received the correct change when purchasing items; and
- allowing for different amounts of work and completion rates for different students.

In Box 8.2 (page 365), you will find a brief report by a guidance officer who observed three young students with high support needs in a primary school classroom. As you read, notice what the teachers were doing to include the children in normal classroom activities.

The importance of training in cooperative behaviours

The importance of training children to work cooperatively has already been mentioned. What does this involve? In a study that investigated the effects of cooperative learning on students with learning difficulties, Gillies and Ashman (2000) trained children in the small-group and interpersonal behaviours believed to facilitate cooperation. The small-group behaviours included:

- breaking each activity into smaller parts with members accepting responsibility for completing their parts;
- encouraging group involvement; and
- sharing resources and information.

The teachers discussed these behaviours with the children and then role-played them so the children could see and understand what the behaviour looked like.

In a similar way, the interpersonal behaviours needed for successful group cooperation were identified and practised. They included:

- listening to each other;
- providing constructive feedback on ideas and issues discussed;
- sharing tasks fairly;

Box 8.2 Room 1B—a guidance officer's first impression

I'll never forget the first time I saw cooperation in a learning task in action. I was a guidance counsellor and responsible for monitoring three children who had a developmental disability, and who had been placed in a double teaching classroom in Year 1. The school had no previous experience with children who required high levels of support in the areas of speech and language, fine and gross motor development, and personal self-management. It must have been quite overwhelming for these children after having attended a special preschool where there was a higher ratio of adults to children and an environment that had been specially modified to accommodate their specific needs (e.g., toilets adjacent to the teaching area for children with mobility difficulties). Their present classroom was staffed by two very experienced teachers who worked hard to ensure that they optimised each child's potential to learn and develop and what they did with the three new children was no exception.

One afternoon early in first term I went to observe the children and discuss their progress. One of the teachers had just finished reading a story to the class and was giving the children instructions on the picture they were to draw about the animal characters they had encountered. The children were divided into groups of three and were given a sheet of paper and a set of paints and they were to draw a farmyard picture of the animals. One was to draw the duck and the pond, someone else the barn and the tree, and someone else the farmer and his dog. The three tasks were explicitly identified and the children had to decide who would complete each part. Completing the picture could not be achieved until each child had completed his or her part.

The children very quickly worked out who would do what. Each child took turns to paint his or her part of the picture while the other two in the group offered advice, pointed out what could be done, and shared the resources. The children talked, laughed, and giggled with each other. Both teachers moved around the groups ensuring that the children had the required resources and providing encouragement for their efforts. The three children with high support needs were in different groups and I was very impressed with the ease with which they participated in the task. They all contributed to their group's efforts, including the presentation of their picture to the whole class, pointing out parts that they had completed, and telling the children what everyone had done.

Follow-up discussions with the teachers indicated that they frequently used cooperative tasks because they believed that it was one way of promoting inclusion. By working together, the children were in situations where they had to discuss ideas, listen to others, share materials and reach a consensus on what they needed to do to complete the task.

- resolving differences democratically and fairly; and
- trying to understand the other person's point of view.

This training was crucial for establishing how the children with learning difficulties could work in their groups and the help they could provide. In the untrained groups, the children with learning difficulties exhibited significantly more off-task behaviour than their trained peers, possibly because they felt less involved with their groups. Certainly, their class teachers noted that they were only tacitly involved. Remarks such as: "He wasn't disruptive, but he just sat there and didn't say much" and "She participated but more by just sitting" were typical of the comments made by teachers. In essence, the children passively watched what others did and followed their lead.

In contrast, in the trained groups, the children with learning difficulties appeared to be actively involved. They gave more helping directions to other group members. For example, "Have you seen this book? It's got some things [pictures] we can use"; "No, this is what we got" [meaning an alternative answer to the problem]; "Look at him. He's got it" [meaning the answer] were typical of the helping directions the children provided. It was this willingness to help others that led their teachers to comment on the children's explicit involvement in their groups. For example, "He was certainly keen to point out what the group needed to see"[a book needed for the activity], and "He is so keen he stumbles over his words trying to tell his group what he wants to tell them".

It appeared that when the children with learning difficulties provided helping directions they initiated interactions that often led to further exchanges of information and ideas with other group members, and it is these interactions that contributed to an increase in their direct involvement in the learning process. Through discussion, these children learnt how to construct solutions to problems they would probably never have been able to complete alone. Certainly, the learning outcomes attained by the children in the trained groups demonstrated that they were making better links between the different problem-solving activities they undertook in their groups and were applying that information to novel situations.

Peer tutoring

From a very young age, children learn from their peers, and teachers have used this approach to learning as a way of providing additional help to children experiencing difficulties in a specific area of the curriculum. Peer tutoring usually involves a more capable child (tutor) helping a less able peer (tutee) master specific information or skills. It is assumed that the tutor has greater competence and, through the peer tutoring process, can transmit this expertise to the tutee. The tutor acts as a surrogate teacher with control over the information and the instructional process. In this sense,

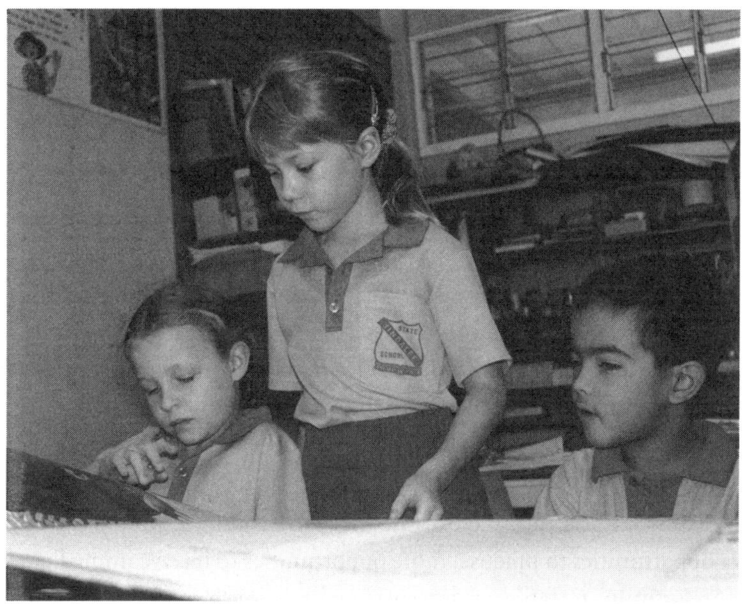

Three students help each other by directing attention to important information and asking probing questions.

the relationship is not equal because the tutor is perceived as the expert whose role is to instruct the novice. Despite this lack of equality, there are mutual benefits that can be derived by the tutor and the tutee.

Michael (case study, page 351) is typical of a number of children who start school and are expected to cope with the academic demands of a Year 1 classroom when they are not mature enough to do so. This immaturity is often seen in such ways as:

- a lack of concentration;
- impulsive behaviour;
- poor expressive language skills;
- difficulties following directions; and
- difficulties with fine motor skills (e.g., cutting and using a pencil).

If Michael's teachers had not intervened, he would have experienced great difficulties with the more formal academic requirements of school that would, over time, have adversely affected his self-confidence. To their credit, his teachers quickly recognised the difficulties that he was having and set in place special assistance (e.g., specialist teachers and aide) to help him. They also recognised that Michael was intensely interested in school and liked to be involved with the other students, so they capitalised on this interest and involved him in a number activities with a more capable peer. In effect, they set up a peer tutoring arrangement where the more capable child helped Michael with these tasks.

Some of the behaviours his teachers saw that assured them that this peer tutoring arrangement was beneficial for Michael were his willingness to:

- work with his tutor;
- ask his tutor for help when it was needed;
- listen to the directions his tutor provided; and
- stay on task during the tutoring activity.

Michael's confidence grew as he realised that he could complete the tasks his teachers had set for him to do with his tutor. He developed a very positive relationship with his tutor and this extended to activities outside the classroom where he was often seen participating in games in the playground with other children, including his tutor.

Benefits

Tutees benefit from peer tutoring because they have additional one-to-one instruction and extra opportunities to practise, more opportunities to receive immediate feedback, and the opportunity to build an interpersonal relationship with a high-status tutor. This last benefit can often provide the additional self-confidence and momentum for the tutee to remain on task.

Tutors also benefit from the tutoring experience because they have to explain the task clearly. This forces them to restructure mentally the material to be taught and, in so doing, they often learn the material better than before. Topping (1992) referred to this process as learning by teaching. It seems that when children adopt the role of the tutor they display behaviours that are consistent with that role so that, just as teachers are expected to teach and present information in an uncomplicated way so it can be understood, similar expectations apply to peer tutors. Thus, in organising material and explaining it in simple terms they develop a better understanding of it.

Cross-age and same-age tutoring

Peer tutoring can involve cross-age or same-age children working in pairs on specific tasks. Cross-age tutoring usually involves an older child working with a younger child, whereas same-age tutoring involves a more capable tutor working with a less capable tutee. In both cases, if peer tutoring is organised properly so the tutors know what to teach and how to teach, benefits can accrue to both children.

Tutor training

In a study that examined the effects of training versus no training in-peer tutoring on students' interactions in pairs, Fuchs, Fuchs, Bentz, Phillips, and Hamlett (1994) found that tutors who had been trained provided more explanations that incorporated sounder instructional principles than the untrained tutors. Training tutors is essential if peer tutoring is to be successful.

In a follow-up study that investigated how students' helping behaviour could be enhanced during peer tutoring in mathematical tasks, Fuchs et al. (1997) examined the differences in achievement for students who were taught how to mediate each other's learning by providing elaborated help, and contrasted these groups with a comparison group of children who did not participate in peer tutoring. The results showed that the tutors who had been trained to give help that included specific conceptual material asked more participatory, procedural questions and provided more explanations than did the tutors who had been trained to provide elaborated help only. Moreover, the achievement of students given conceptual help was higher than the achievement of the students in the other groups.

Training that works most effectively involves two processes. First, the students in the peer-mediated learning groups learn to use the following procedure in helping each other master the material.

- The tutor models and gradually fades the directions about the steps needed to complete the task (this is a form of scaffolding).
- The tutor provides step-by-step feedback to confirm and praise correct responses and explains and models strategic behaviour when answers are incorrect.
- Both the children engage in regular written interactions together on the problem.
- Both the tutor and tutee reverse roles during each session.

Once the students learn these steps, the second part of the training is undertaken. This involves teaching students how to seek elaborated help in conjunction with conceptual understanding. Elaborated help includes such behaviours as asking for help and maintaining the request for help until understanding is attained. Offering elaborated help includes listening to one's partner and giving detailed help if required, and not just giving the answer. Conceptual understanding is enhanced when students have the opportunity to:

- relate material being learnt with real-life examples that are easy to imagine;
- use visual marks or pictures to represent specific facts;
- use materials that can be manipulated by both partners to represent information being learnt;
- discuss the problem and how to solve it; and
- ask questions that began with "what," "where," "when," "how," and "why."

Reciprocal teaching

Many of the ideas used in peer-mediated learning are adapted from Annemarie Palincsar and Ann Brown's (1988) reciprocal teaching approach to learning. The

purpose of reciprocal teaching is to help students develop specific strategies to assist their comprehension of written text. Because reciprocal teaching is conducted in the context of a collaborative learning environment in which students work together to understand the curriculum, leadership in the group is rotated so each member accepts responsibility for employing the specific strategies of *predicting*, *questioning*, *summarising*, and *clarifying* to direct the discussion.

As each section of text is discussed, the leader generates a question to which the group members respond. The participants then formulate additional questions while reading the material. The leader then attempts to summarise the main issues in the text with the group members having the opportunity to talk about the summary. Word meanings and confusing text are clarified before the students predict what might happen in the next paragraph. This process is repeated as each new paragraph is read.

The purpose of reciprocal teaching is to have children mimic the strategies used by successful readers. In essence, strategic readers hypothesise and anticipate what might happen. They rephrase information and seek relationships between key ideas, story-lines, and characters, and they are alert to breakdowns in their understanding of what they are reading.

During the initial stage of reciprocal teaching, the teacher models the process with the children. The children then practise the strategies and the teacher provides feedback, coaching, modelling, and additional help to use the strategies successfully. This process is repeated until the children can use the strategies competently in their interactions with each other. The teacher then increases the demands, requiring the children to participate at a more challenging level.

Reciprocal teaching was designed as a small-group instructional activity in which the participants work together as a community of learners to construct meaning from the text they are reading. Students learn because the group help to scaffold their learning. In this sense, reciprocal teaching is a form of cooperative learning that has been used widely with children at risk of academic failure. Palincsar and Brown (1988) reported teaching reciprocal teaching strategies to junior high school students in remedial classes whose reading comprehension was two to five years below their grade level. After initial training in the reciprocal teaching and 20 days of using these strategies in their reading groups, the students' comprehension levels improved markedly, and the strategies learnt were generalised to other classes and tasks distinctly different from the original training task.

Reciprocal teaching has also been used successfully in regular classrooms and with students with learning difficulties (e.g., Johnson, 2000, King & Johnson, 1999; Lederer, 2000). In a slightly older study designed to enhance the mathematics of primary school children who were at risk of academic failure, a reciprocal teaching strategy was used with low-achievers in mathematics. Fantuzzo, King, and Heller

(1992) found that the children who were taught reciprocal teaching strategies were more accurate in comprehension than were children who were not taught this strategy. Furthermore, when reciprocal teaching was coupled with rewards, the children also showed improved self-control over their behaviours.

Parent tutoring and reciprocal teaching

In a follow-up study that examined the effects of a home-based parent involvement and reciprocal teaching on the self-concept and mathematics achievement of academically at-risk school children, Fantuzzo, Davis, and Ginsberg (1995) found that participating students were better at computations and had higher self-concept than children who worked only with a parent on mathematics or had no intervention at all. Both studies showed that low-achievers can learn very explicit strategies to monitor their own performances and improve their mathematics achievement scores and that, as a consequence, they can improve their relationship with peers.

Cognitive apprenticeships

Apprenticeships, in which a novice learner works with a master trainer, have long been accepted as a way of training young people in specific skills and knowledge for different trades, arts, and sporting activities. By working with a more competent trainer, the apprentice is provided with an opportunity to observe how the task is managed and to try it out for themselves, with guidance and feedback that allows them to correct any errors readily, and to improve their performance. As the apprentice becomes more competent, the trainer teaches more difficult and complex skills while continuing to provide the support and scaffolding needed to assist learning. Success with this type of training depends not only on the competence of the trainer to teach the required skills but also on their ability to establish a personal bond with the novice learner that is supportive and motivating.

Cognitive apprenticeships are based on similar principles to general apprenticeship training—that is, a novice learner works with a more competent individual (usually the teacher) to learn how to approach and manage a complex, problem-solving task. Although there are different cognitive apprenticeship models, Woolfolk (1998) proposed that they all share the following features:

- students observe an expert model the task;
- students' performances are monitored and prompts, feedback, and models are provided to help them complete the task;
- conceptual scaffolding is provided initially and is then faded as the student becomes more proficient with the task;
- students verbalise their understanding of the processes and content that they are learning;

- students evaluate their progress and performances; and
- students try to apply their learning to novel situations.

Schools can provide cognitive apprenticeship experiences to students by using more able students, parents, or community volunteers to model specific processes while simultaneously providing feedback and support to students trying to learn new skills. Reciprocal teaching (discussed earlier) is a form of cognitive apprenticeship in which students learn to use a specific questioning technique to help develop a better understanding of the material they are reading. In essence, cognitive apprenticeships are a form of peer tutoring that provides assistance to students seeking to master new skills.

Ways of supporting students' learning

Peer tutoring, reciprocal teaching, and cognitive apprenticeships are three programs that have been shown to work effectively in regular classrooms to increase cooperation between students. The research literature points to benefits accruing to all students who are involved—those who are progressing normally through school and those who need support because of a learning difficulty. Although peer tutoring, reciprocal teaching, and cognitive apprenticeships are distinct, coherent programs, each relies on training children in specific techniques to make them effective helpers. Peer support models have a number of general characteristics that are summarised in Box 8.3 (page 373).

In a review of the characteristics of effective helpers, Meichenbaum and Biemiller (1998) proposed that the characteristics include being able to:

- offer detailed help and cues without specifically providing the answer;
- ask well-designed questions to assess understanding;
- relate the current problem to something familiar to the other child (e.g., previous background experience or knowledge);
- demonstrate how to use self-cueing techniques (e.g., prompt cards, self-questioning strategies);
- monitor progress; and
- encourage and praise effort.

Using children with learning disabilities to support each other

There have been numerous studies conducted over the last two decades or so that show that children with learning disabilities benefit academically and socially from tutoring, and that this is true whether they function as tutors or tutees, or both (Scruggs, Mastropieri, & Sullivan, 1994). Academic gains have been recorded in reading, spelling, and mathematics, and social gains have included improved attitudes toward

Box 8.3 Characteristics of peer support models

One clear goal is the promotion of positive self-concept and attitudes.
Students work in pairs or very small groups.
Children work in situations that are typical of the class composition (e.g., same-age or cross-age groupings; same-ability or cross-ability groupings).
Each student has a specific role (e.g., expert tutor or novice).
The activity is of short duration (usually only a few weeks).
Skills-based activities are used in which students learn a explicit teaching strategy to assist learning (e.g., reciprocal teaching).
Positive social interactions are encouraged among students.
Interpersonal skills are taught and learnt, thereby assisting to reduce classroom behaviour problems.
Practice time is provided.
There are mutual benefits that accrue to all participants.

learning, school, and other students. Overall, however, tutoring can be expected to benefit tutors and tutees academically and socially only if students are appropriately selected and trained in their roles, if the content of the tutoring is appropriate to both the tutor and tutee, and if progress toward specified goals is continuously monitored (Scruggs & Mastropieri, 1998).

To optimise the benefits to be derived from tutoring, Scruggs and Mastropieri (1998, pp. 167–168) have suggested the following guidelines for establishing tutoring behaviour in tutors and tutees:

- be nice to your partner and sit facing each other;
- decide who will be the tutor first, then take turns asking and answering questions in an orderly fashion, and reverse roles when all questions have been answered correctly;
- speak in a pleasant tone when answering questions or responding;
- encourage your partner by using statements such as "great job, good answer" or "not quite, can you think of something else?";
- record the correct and incorrect responses; and
- review any incorrect question several times.

Process-Based instruction

Another way of supporting students' learning is through Process-Based Instruction (PBI). PBI was developed by Ashman and Conway (1993) and is based on the premise that students need to be taught to be responsible for their own learning behaviours,

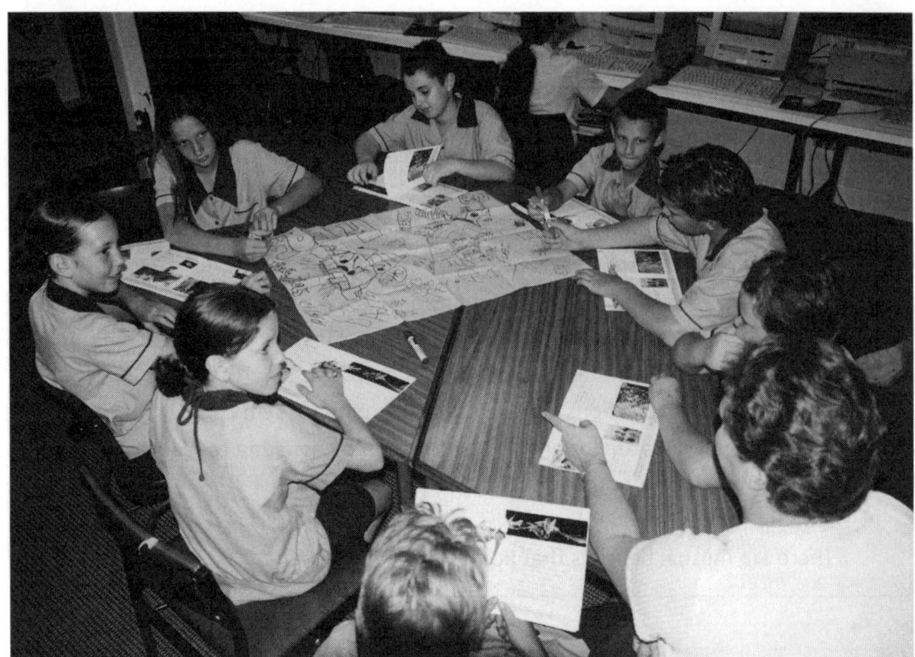

Students working together on a group project with a well-defined task to complete.

and that this can be achieved by actively involving them in the teaching–learning process.

PBI is not a collaborative process like peer tutoring or collaborative learning, but is student-centred, promotes positive interactions between students, and emphasises their participation in the teaching–learning process. PBI is linked to other collaborative teaching methods because the emphasis on the planning and decision-making process is equally appropriate in group settings or one-to-one or individual learning situations. Specifically, PBI:

- helps students to play an active role in the teaching–learning process;
- provides a way for students to work at their own pace without the need for constant attention from the teacher;
- enables students to achieve the lesson goals by planning the process and the outcome;
- encourages students to gain individual help from the teacher and other students, thereby promoting cooperation; and
- provides a way of learning about the process of planning and problem-solving.

PBI differs from collaborative learning in its non-reliance on the key elements of positive interdependence, promotive interaction, individual accountability, and small-group skills.

PBI integrates two lines of research on how students learn—the development of thinking skills and an understanding of the conditions under which students learn—with established classroom practices that are used by effective teachers. The emphasis on thinking skills is based on research on metacognition, planning, and problem-solving, whereas understanding the conditions under which students learn evolved from research on classroom climate and instructional techniques (such as cooperative learning). PBI provides a model for classroom teaching and learning that enables teachers to present information in a manner that facilitates effective learning. It has been designed to:

- integrate learning processes and curriculum content;
- increase student activity in the teaching and learning process;
- build effective links among the learner, the teacher, the setting, and the curriculum to enhance learning;
- teach students to generalise learning strategies to other content areas; and
- build a success identity with learning.

Integral to PBI are two key concepts: plans and planning. A plan involves a sequence of steps designed to enable students to negotiate a task, whereas planning involves the process of putting the plan into action (i.e., actually carrying it out).

Plans consist of four basic components:

- cueing (where do I look?);
- acting (what do I do?);
- monitoring (is it working?); and
- verifying (is it correct?).

Children are taught to ask themselves the above questions consciously as a way of helping them to become effective planners. In essence, they are taught to think about what they are doing, to evaluate their progress, and to make changes to their plans when they realise they are needed.

PBI plans are designed to be taught in conjunction with different curriculum tasks. However, they need to be introduced systematically so that students learn how to develop, use, consolidate, and generalise their plans across different curricular tasks and activities. Box 8.4 (page 376) is an example of a plan to construct a bar graph provided by Ashman and Conway (1997, p. 175).

Although the class teacher initially teaches the students to develop plans in different curricular areas, the students are expected, eventually, to develop their own plans and to monitor their implementation without ongoing scrutiny by the teacher. In this way, students are taught to become active in their own learning so they can be autonomous and independent learners.

Box 8.4 An example of a PBI plan for drawing a bar graph

1. **What should a bar graph look like?**
2. **What information and equipment do I need?**
3. **Draw axes and decide scale.**
4. **Check scale and spacing against information.**
5. **Label graph (axes, bars).**
6. **Draw bars.**
7. **Check all information.**
8. **Verify with a friend.**

The importance of integrating cognitive teaching and learning approaches within different curricular areas has been consistently reported in studies in which students have been helped to develop better reading comprehension skills, improved information-processing skills, and better understanding in mathematics. PBI is one way in which students are taught to play a more active role in their own learning by becoming strategic learners who consciously plan, monitor, and evaluate their own learning.

The outcomes mentioned above have been shown in a several PBI studies. Hay (2000), for example, introduced PBI in a secondary school in which students were taught by their art teacher to use PBI plans in a photography project. Students learnt to prepare and modify plans over a five-week period, and their performance was compared with a matched group who did not receive PBI instruction. Teacher ratings were collected on the students' performances and those in the PBI condition showed a significant gain when compared to their peers in the contrast experimental condition. The students were also asked to evaluate the strategies used by their classroom teachers. Those in the PBI group commented that the strategies helped them to clarify the task to be learnt, and to establish the teacher's expectations. Hay reported that the PBI group was actively involved in developing, checking, and reviewing plans, and were enthusiastic about its own learning.

In another study, Conway and Hopton (2000) compared the performance of primary school students in PBI and non-PBI classes lessons. The researchers reported significant gains in performance of mathematics and spelling, students' perceptions of their ability, and on two measures of planning.

There are numerous programs reported in the professional literature related to teaching–learning approaches that adopt methods that support cooperative strategies and mediated learning activities. Ashman and Conway (1997) provide an extensive review of these programs.

SUMMARY

Cooperation between students, and between students and teacher, provides a climate in which children's learning and problem-solving can be advanced (Johnson & Johnson, 2000). This view is reiterated by most authors in this book.

Cooperative learning involves children working together in groups to accomplish a shared goal. The five essential elements of cooperation are: positive interdependence, promotive interaction, individual accountability, interpersonal and small-group skills, and group processing.

- Positive interdependence exists when students perceive that they are linked together in such a way that no one can succeed unless they all do, and that they must coordinate their efforts to help each other complete the group's task.
- Promotive interaction involves students' encouraging and facilitating each other's efforts by providing help to each other, by sharing resources, and by providing positive and constructive feedback on each other's efforts.
- Individual accountability involves each group member accepting responsibility for completing his or her share of the task and facilitating the work of other group members.
- Interpersonal and small-group skills include the skills of actively listening to each other, trying to understand the other person's perspective, stating ideas freely and clarifying differences, accepting responsibility for one's own behaviour, taking turns, sharing resources, and making democratic decisions.
- Group processing involves the members reflecting on the group's progress and determining what still needs to be done for the group's goal to be achieved.

Issues that teachers must consider when establishing cooperative learning groups are their size and composition, and the task that the group is to undertake. Research indicates that the optimum group size is three or four members. In this way, everyone is visible in the group and there is little opportunity for members to free-load at the expense of others. If there is a balance of boys and girls and a mixture of abilities, members are more likely to be included in the group, and more likely to offer better explanations to each other. Group discussion is also likely to be influenced by the type of task undertaken. Mathematics and computational tasks often require little discussion because the procedure for solving them is quite straightforward, whereas open-ended and discovery-based tasks often generate more discussion because there are no standard answers or procedures to follow.

Cooperative learning has been used successfully to promote the inclusion of children with diverse learning needs in mainstream classrooms. Strategies that have been employed include carefully explaining the procedures for group work, teaching the skills

needed to collaborate, ensuring that children with learning difficulties have a role they can manage, and making sure that non-disabled children are trained to help and encourage children with learning difficulties. If children with severe disabilities are included, group members need training in the prompts and praise needed to encourage and maintain their efforts.

The curriculum might also need to be adapted to ensure that children with learning difficulties can be successful in cooperative groups. Adaptations might include allowing these children to use different response modes to demonstrate their success in learning the material, using functional equivalents, and allowing different amounts of work and completion rates for different students.

In peer tutoring, a more capable peer (tutor) works with a less able student (tutee) to master specific skills or information. Peer tutoring can involve cross-age or same-age children working together on a specific task. Cross-age tutoring usually involves an older child tutoring a younger child on a specific task in reading, spelling, or mathematics. This approach to learning has been used effectively—particularly when the older child has similar difficulties—because it enables the older child to learn by teaching while the younger child has the advantage of having additional opportunities to engage with the task.

Benefits also accrue to same-age tutors and tutees. However, before the tutors are able to help the tutees, they must first reorganise the information in their own minds. In so doing, they often learn it better than before. Tutees benefit from the tutoring experience because of the additional practice they receive, and the opportunities that exist to receive immediate feedback on their progress.

Researchers have shown that for tutoring to be effective, tutors need to be appropriately selected and trained, the content needs to be appropriate to both the tutor and tutee, and progress toward specific goals needs to be monitored. Effective tutors need to learn how to offer detailed help without giving the answer, use effective questioning skills to assess the tutee's understanding of how to do the task, help link the current problem to something more familiar to the tutee, help the tutee use strategies such as cue cards to anticipate problems and ways of overcoming them, monitor the tutee's progress and discuss it with him or her, and praise and encourage the tutee. Other researchers have used many of these ideas to help tutors learn specific strategies, such as the questions used in reciprocal teaching (predicting, questioning, summarising, and clarifying) to enhance reading comprehension (Palinscar & Brown, 1988) and techniques to improve mathematics performance for low-achieving students working on basic computational tasks (Fantuzzo et al., 1992; Fantuzzo et al., 1995).

Reciprocal teaching is a type of cognitive apprenticeship in which students take responsibility for modelling aspects of the task, asking key questions that help to cue, prompt, and scaffold the task for others to learn, and providing feedback on progress and

performances. In essence, both reciprocal teaching and cognitive apprenticeships are designed to encourage students to accept responsibility for their own learning processes.

Another strategy that encourages students to be responsible for their own learning is process-based instruction. PBI is designed to teach students to develop plans on how they can negotiate tasks, including the processes involved in putting their plan into operation. As students become more proficient at developing plans, they learn to generalise the planning process to other curricular tasks and areas.

Cooperative learning, peer tutoring, reciprocal teaching, cognitive apprenticeships, and PBI are some of the programs that teachers can use to assist children's learning and social adjustment, including children with learning difficulties. However, the strategies they teach work effectively only if teachers take the time needed to identify the participants and establish the group (i.e., dyads or small groups), train the participants, and structure the group activity (i.e., identify specific task or goal to be achieved). This requires good planning and a time commitment but, when it is done correctly, the benefits are evident in the learning and socialisation that occurs, and the support that the children provide to each other as they work together.

 Suggested reading

Ashman, A. F. & Conway, R. N. F. (1997). *An introduction to cognitive education: Theory and applications*. London: Routledge.

Johnson, D. W. & Johnson, F. P. (2000). *Joining together: Group theory and group skills* (7th ed.). Boston: Allyn and Bacon.

Putnam, J. (Ed.) (1993). *Cooperative learning and strategies for inclusion: Celebrating diversity in the classroom*. Baltimore: Paul H. Brookes.

<www.google.com/search?sourceid=navclient&q=cooperative+learning>
(This website provides access to other key cooperative learning websites.)

 Practical activities

1. Arrange to have some of your friends or student colleagues work together in small groups (of three to four members) to construct the highest geometric shape they can make that will stand unsupported for one minute. Give each group a bundle of 30 plastic straws and some Blu-Tack and tell them that they have five minutes to

complete their construction. Stand back and observe. How did the group members decide what they would do? Was everyone involved? How did they support each other's efforts while they were constructing the geometric shape? How did the group members react to the task? What have you learnt from this activity that you could apply to other group activities?

2. Visit a local primary or high school and ask to see students working in peer tutoring dyads or small cooperative groups. Make a note of the following: age of the students, numbers in the group, type of activity the students are working on together, and time spent on the activity. Watch for student involvement in the group, the type of help provided (e.g., sharing materials, sharing information, explaining difficult ideas).
3. Identify a child with learning difficulties. Watch to see how he or she is included in the group activities. Is the task explained clearly so this child can understand what he or she has to do? How do the other children provide help (e.g., point to the answer, explain how to do it)? Does this child have a meaningful role in the group? How is this help provided (e.g., explanations, or prompts and cues, or through "put-downs")?
4. At the completion of the group activity, ask the students about the activity they were doing. You might like to use the following questions as a guide to exploring the activity with them:
   - What were you doing?
   - What sort of help were you providing?
   - Tell me what you think of small group work (such as peer tutoring or cooperative learning).
   - What have you learnt about each other from working together?
5. Ask a class teacher who has had experience using peer tutoring and/or cooperative learning what they think of these strategies for helping students to learn. Frame your questions so you can obtain information on how frequently they use these approaches, the type of activity students are required to do, the behaviour of the students during small group activities, the levels of student motivation they have observed, and how they monitor the activity.

References

Ashman, A. F. & Conway, R. N. F. (1993). Teaching students to use process-based learning and problem solving strategies in mainstream class. *Learning and Instruction*, 3, 73–92.

Ashman, A. F. & Conway, R. N. F. (1997). *An introduction to cognitive education: Theory and applications*. London: Routledge.

Cadman, A. G. (Chairman). (1976). Learning difficulties in children and adults (Report to the House of Representatives Select Committee on Specific Learning Difficulties). Canberra, Australia: Australian Government Publishing Service.

Cohen, E. (1994). Restructuring the classroom: Conditions for productive small groups. *Review of Educational Research, 64*, 1–35.

Conway, R. N. F. & Hopton, L. (2000). Application of a school-wide metacognitive training model: Effects on academic and planning performance. *Journal of Cognitive Education and Psychology, 1*, 140–153.

Deutsch, M. (1948). An experimental study of the effects of cooperation and competition upon group process. *Human Relations, 11*, 199–231.

Fantuzzo, J., King, J., & Heller, L. (1992). Effects of reciprocal peer tutoring on mathematics and school adjustment: A component analysis. *Journal of Educational Psychology, 84*, 331–339.

Fantuzzo, J., Davis, G., & Ginsburg, M. (1995). Effects of parent involvement in isolation or combination with peer tutoring on student self-concept and mathematics achievement. *Journal of Educational Psychology, 87*, 272–281.

Fuchs, L., Fuchs, D., Bentz, J., Phillips, N., & Hamlett, C. (1994). The nature of student interactions during peer tutoring with and without prior training and experience. *American Educational Research Journal, 31*, 75–101.

Fuchs, L., Fuchs, D., Hamlett, C., Phillips, N., Karns, K., & Dutka, S. (1997). Enhancing students' helping behavior during peer-mediated instruction with conceptual mathematical explanations. *The Elementary School Journal, 97*, 223–249.

Gillies, R. & Ashman, A. (1995). The effects of gender and ability on students' behaviours and interactions in classroom-based work groups. *British Journal of Educational Psychology, 65*, 211–225.

Gillies, R. M. & Ashman, A.F. (1996). Teaching collaborative skills to primary school children in classroom-based work groups. *Learning and Instruction, 6*, 187–199.

Gillies, R. M. & Ashman, A.F. (2000). The effects of cooperative learning on children with learning difficulties in the lower elementary school. *The Journal of Special Education, 34*, 19–27.

Hay, I. (2000). Cognitive strategies in the secondary school: Investigating Process-Based Instruction and students' perceptions of effective teaching strategies. *Journal of Cognitive Education and Psychology, 1*, 164–176.

Hendrickson, J., Shokoohi, M., Hamre-Nietupski, S., & Gable, R. (1996). Middle and high school students' perceptions of being friends with peers with severe disabilities. *Exceptional Children, 63*, 19–28.

Hunt, P., Staub, D., Alwell, M. & Goetz, L. (1994). Achievement by all students within the context of cooperative learning groups. *JASH, 19*, 290-301.

Johnson, D. W. & Johnson, R. T. (1986). Mainstreaming and cooperative learning strategies. *Exceptional Children, 52*, 553–561.

Johnson, D. W. & Johnson, R. (1999a). Making cooperative learning work. *Theory into Practice, 38(2)*, 67–73.

Johnson, D. W. & Johnson, R. (1999b). *Learning together and alone: Cooperative, competitive, and individualistic learning* (5th ed.). Boston: Allyn & Bacon.

Johnson, D. W. & Johnson, F. P. (2000). *Joining together: Group theory and group skills* (7th ed.). Boston: Allyn and Bacon.

Johnson, D., Johnson, R., Stanne, M., & Garibaldi, A. (1990). Impact of group processing on achievement in cooperative groups. *Journal of Social Psychology, 130*, 507–516.

King, C. M & Johnson, L. M. P. (1999). Constructing meaning via reciprocal teaching. *Reading Research and Instruction, 38*, 169–186.

Lederer, J. M. (2000). Reciprocal teaching of social studies in inclusive elementary classrooms. *Journal of Learning Disabilities, 33*, 91–106.

Lou, Y., Abrami, P., Spence, J., Poulsen, C., Chambers, B., & d'Apollonia, S. (1996). Within-class grouping: A meta-analysis. *Review of Educational Research, 66*, 423–458.

McInerney, D. & McInerney, V. (1998). *Educational psychology: Constructing learning* (2nd ed.). Sydney: Prentice Hall.

Meichenbaum, D. & Biemiller, A. (1998). *Nurturing independent learners*. Cambridge, Massachusetts: Bookline Books.

Nevin, A. (1993). Curricular and instructional adaptations for including students with disabilities in cooperative groups. In J. Putnam (Ed.). *Cooperative learning and strategies for inclusion: Celebrating diversity in the classroom* (pp. 41–56). Baltimore: Paul H. Brookes.

Palinscar, A. & Brown, A. (1988). Teaching and practising thinking skills to promote comprehension in the context of group problem solving. *Remedial and Special Education, 9*, 53–59.

Pomplun, M. (1996). Cooperative groups: Alternative assessment for students with disabilities. *The Journal of Special Education, 30*, 1–17.

Putnam, J., Markovchick, K., Johnson, D., & Johnson, R. (1996). Cooperative learning and peer acceptance of students with learning disabilities. *Journal of Social Psychology, 136*, 741–752.

Putnam, J., Rynders, J., Johnson, R., & Johnson, D. (1989). Collaborative skill instruction for promoting positive interactions between mentally handicapped and nonhandicapped children. *Exceptional Children, 55*, 550–557.

Scruggs, T. & Mastropieri, M. (1998). Tutoring and students with special needs In K. Topping and S. Ehly (Eds). *Peer assisted learning* (pp. 165–182). London: Lawrence Erlbaum.

Scruggs, T. Mastropieri, M., & Sullivan, G. (1994). Promoting relational thinking skills: Elaborative interrogation for mildly handicapped students. *Exceptional Children, 60*, 450–457.

Slavin, R. (1984). Team assisted individualization: Cooperative learning and individualized instruction in the mainstream classroom. *Remedial and Special Education, 5*, 33–42.

Stevens, R. & Slavin, R. (1995a). The cooperative elementary school. *American Educational Research Journal, 32*, 321–351.

Stevens, R. & Slavin, R. (1995b). Effects of a cooperative learning approach in reading and writing on academically handicapped and nonhandicapped students. *The Elementary School Journal, 95*, 241–262.

Topping, K. (1992). Cooperative learning and peer tutoring: An overview. *The Psychologist, 5*, 151–157.

Webb, N. (1995). Group collaboration in assessment: Multiple objectives, processes, and outcomes. *Educational Evaluation and Policy, 17*, 239–261.

Webb, N., Nemer, K., Chizhik, A., & Sugrue, B. (1998). Equity issues in collaborative group assessment: Group composition and performance. *American Educational Research Journal, 35*, 607–651.

Woolfolk, A. (1998). *Educational psychology* (7th ed.). Boston: Allyn and Bacon.

Section 3

Adapting curriculum and instruction

Sometimes we sit and reflect on our school experiences. They are amazingly different. So different that we wonder how the paths of our life brought us to roughly the same place at the same time. One of us was a very naughty boy who achieved a personal childhood goal of expulsion from high school with its entire attendant stresses and family complications. The other was the son of a technical and further education (TAFE) principal. This boy loved just about everything that school could offer and his vocational objective was set from a relatively early age, to go on to tertiary education, although he too experienced corporal punishment.

The reason for mentioning our personal histories is to emphasise the hugely different education demands we presented as children and young adults. It is more important, however, to emphasise that neither of us was located at the furthest limits of the continuum of students' skills and abilities that classroom teachers face today.

Given the current policy of including students with very widely varying needs in regular schools, the authors of the various chapters of this book have endeavoured to present a framework for understanding how to accommodate difference, rather than emphasising the students' problems. Nevertheless, the authors are still cognisant of the impact that some conditions have on students and on those working with them. In the third section of this book we deal with an area that is conceivably the most challenging for teachers at all levels of education—adapting the curriculum to enable all students to participate as fully as possible in the ongoing activities of the classroom and school.

In previous editions of this book we have not included separate chapters on literacy, numeracy, or information and communication technology. Certainly, these three areas were addressed by authors but, in most cases, only as examples of problem areas and, in the case of technology, as emerging resources and learning tools.

Literacy and numeracy are fundamental to our ability to operate effectively within society. That you can read this book means that you are extremely fortunate. More

than two billion people in the world cannot read at all—equivalent to the combined populations of China and India, or more than seven times the population of the United States, or 110 times Australia's population. Those who live in Australia and New Zealand who cannot read, or who have great difficulty in reading, face immense challenges in their lives because so much of what is required of them as participating members of our community is compromised by a print handicap. Books and many magazines are out of reach. The capacity to understand employment advertisements, the ability to exercise voting rights, the capacity to read legal documents (such as a will, rental, or mortgage document), and even the comprehension of uncommon road signs are beyond people with significant print handicaps.

Numeracy is equally important now that financial institutions have moved very quickly toward the virtual bank. And there are still many people within our society who have extremely modest arithmetical skills. Some cannot tell the difference in value between a two-dollar coin and a twenty-cent coin and, when asked which can buy more ice-cream, might point to the twenty-cent coin because it is larger. There are those who do not know if they are given the correct change after purchasing some small item at a corner store or supermarket. And, there are still quite a few of us who stare wide-eyed at the mystery called our bank statement, never truly understanding how we managed to be overdrawn yet again.

Making words and numbers accessible to all members of our community is one of the goals of education and is a persisting item on the agenda of state and federal governments. It is false to think that the development of these skills is an issue for primary schools only. There are many students who enter secondary school without achieving the relevant skill levels. This is calamitous because so much of the curriculum at that level is based upon the ability the read and cipher, and not just in English and mathematics.

In each of the following four chapters, the authors deal with general teaching and learning principles that address what should be taught and how. At the fundamental level it is important that all students acquire the building blocks of acquisition and problem-solving. In the early school years, students learn facts through didactic (chalk-and-talk) teaching, discovery, and from informal learning experiences that occur outside school. At the secondary school level, facts are often presented in a structured way through systematic curricula or syllabi. But learning facts is only one aspect of understanding because we must also learn how to be strategic. This means learning about the use and effectiveness of strategies that help organise information (e.g., memory strategies), the importance of setting priorities, planning, monitoring and regulating thinking. These building blocks of thinking (or cognition) are the same for an intellectually gifted child and one who has a serious disability. Of course, how these skills are taught is not the same and this will become clear as you work your way through Chapters 9, 10, and 11.

The last chapter reflects developments in the information superhighways that have opened in recent years. Computers are so powerful now that they can store, handle, exchange, and modify data at breathtaking speed, and with an efficiency never imagined by the creators of the original computers. Computers can link us as easily to friends on the other side of the world as they can to our next-door neighbours. But technology is not just about computers. It also encompasses remarkable developments in aids and prosthetics that have occurred with the invention of synthetic materials and micro-electronics—as was evident from many reports in the media during the recent Paralympic Games. Technology is about access—access to information, space, and time.

In these four chapters, the authors make no assertions that they are covering all of the territory, or dealing with the needs of every child who attends a preschool, primary school, or secondary school. There is also recognition that—at this time—there is still a need for special schools, special classes, and support services operating in parallel with regular schools. In these teaching–learning contexts, staff are accustomed to, and skilled in, working with a constellation of teaching–learning factors that might address the educational demands of students with very high support needs However, more than ever before, there is need for professional development that expands skills and encourages changes in attitude—to accommodate all students, regardless of their learning histories and needs

We must not conclude this introduction to Section 3 without making links between the chapters of this section and those of earlier sections. For example, there is evidence that students with intellectual disability can gain much from working with more skilled peers in cooperative learning situations. Information and communication technology has been an important part of teaching students with sense impairments since Louis Braille invented his six-dot system of reading and writing in 1825. And, as you can read in Chapter 12, computers are opening up many opportunities for all students from preschool to tertiary education to learn in creative and compelling ways. As you work toward the end of this book, many of the connections between chapters will become obvious.

9

Focus on literacy

CHRISTINA E. VAN KRAAYENOORD

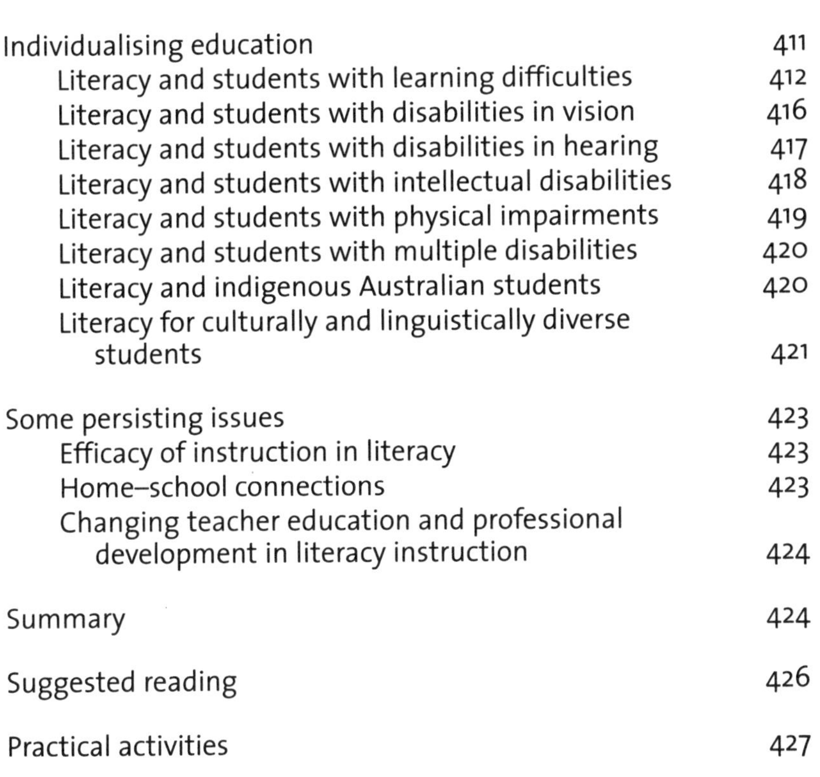

Case studies

Amanda

Amanda is eight years old and in Year 3. She lives with her European-Australian mother in a middle-income suburb of a large coastal town. She has a severe vision impairment that is related to a congenital condition that was diagnosed when she was three years old and results in blurred distance vision and short-sightedness in one eye. She wears corrective glasses but still must sit close to any visual source. Amanda has an individual educational plan that has been negotiated between staff at her school and her mother. The plan identifies such issues as the management of her glasses, seating position in class, extra time for activities, enlarged copies and extra time for formal or high-stakes tests, and the use of well-contrasted materials by the teacher.

Amanda's teacher uses the outcomes in the key learning areas as stated in the state syllabi to determine her goals for instruction. These include cross-curricular goals in literacy that are consistent with those of the other pupils in her class. Amanda is involved in the same literacy activities as her peers, with the teacher using the same teaching approaches. Adaptations are made in her program in that she is encouraged to use a computer to produce work rather than writing by hand. She must have her seat adjusted to ensure she is very close to the screen. Lighting must be such that there is no (or very little) glare on print materials or screens.

When Amanda writes she uses exercise books with dark lines and a dark pen or soft black pencil. Her teacher uses only white chalk on the blackboard. If the whiteboard is used it is positioned so that there is no glare on its surface. Work that is presented on an overhead projector screen must be duplicated for Amanda, as a print hardcopy.

Amanda's teacher also uses a variety of assessment strategies, and reports to the girl's mother in writing at the end of each term. Students in Amanda's class create a portfolio that is used at the twice-yearly, parent-teacher conferences as an adjunct to reporting. To date Amanda's achievement in literacy is little different from that of her peers.

Joseph

Joseph is 14 years old and in Year 8. His father is a Yugoslavian migrant and his mother is an Anglo-Australian. Joseph has had difficulty with reading since early primary school and repeated Year 1 when it was evident from his assessments that he had difficulty with language and emergent literacy.

In Year 2 he was assessed and was put on the Reading Recovery program. A visiting speech pathologist assessed his language in Year 3 but he did not receive any language support. Typically, only students with speech difficulties received support from the speech pathologist and it appeared that Joseph's problems were in the area of language, and not speech.

Intermittently, during his primary schooling, Joseph has received assistance in reading (both decoding and comprehension) and writing (especially spelling) in withdrawal settings or in-class support from a parent-helper or support teacher. On entry to high school Joseph was identified as a student who would struggle with all aspects of literacy in his subjects. As a consequence school staff suggested that he take a subject called "Modified English" which uses a commercial package called Accelerated Reader to teach reading using drill and practice on a computer. Although the subject focuses more on reading than the other literacy strands, the subject's goals also refer to teaching a range of genres (text types) used in everyday life. There are no explicit goals in listening, speaking or viewing, the strands of literacy in which Joseph has some strengths. The nature of the Accelerated Reader package means there is little teacher involvement in Joseph's reading development, except as a monitor.

When teaching writing, the teacher uses strategies consistent with current theories and practices, such as modelling, joint construction of text, and guided practice. Because Joseph also struggles with literacy in his other subjects, he and his teacher are supported by a teacher's aide from time to time. However, this support is not systematic or evaluated. In order to accommodate his learning needs, subject assessment is adapted through the use of modified assessment tasks, as well as time extensions. He uses the school's after-school homework centre to help him complete his assignments. His achievement is reported to his parents twice-yearly via a school report card. His parents do not come to teacher–parent interviews that are held in the evenings because his father feels that his English is a barrier and because his mother has shift work at that time. His parents are concerned about Joseph's difficulties and poor grades because he has expressed negative comments about his being in an alternative program, about his struggles in his other subjects, and his lack of confidence. He would like to leave school as soon as possible.

What you will learn in this chapter

The main purpose of this chapter is to introduce you to the domain of literacy. The title of this chapter refers to the importance of literacy in the lives of all students in Australia's classrooms and the need for teachers to make literacy teaching and learning a core business of instruction. The case studies describe some aspects of the literacy learning of two students in Australian classrooms. You will notice that although students might have learning difficulties or disabilities, they might not have difficulties in literacy. Amanda is an example of such a student. However, there are many other students who do have difficulties and, therefore, the chapter will examine some of the features of students with literacy difficulties. The reasons for these difficulties will be discussed. Reference will also be made to how literacy can be assessed.

The use of the word "focus" also reflects the emphasis that has been given to literacy in recent government policies at federal and state levels in Australia. Specifically, the *National literacy and numeracy plan for schools* (Department of Employment, Education, Training and Youth Affairs, 1998) calls for literacy for all, and the *Adelaide declaration on national goals of schooling in the twenty-first century* states that "students should have attained the skills of numeracy and English literacy; such that, every student should be numerate, able to read, write, spell, and communicate at an appropriate level" (Ministerial Council on Education, Employment Training and Youth Affairs, 1999, p. 2). For such goals to be achieved, attention must be given to the ways in which students are taught literacy in regular classrooms. In this chapter, an account is provided of both the historical and current practices in teaching literacy. Reference is made to inclusive approaches, characteristics of successful instruction, use of media and materials and the role of technology, and the organisation and management of instruction.

Due to the individual needs of students, literacy instruction also must be individualised or differentiated. In this chapter, attention is given to both the literacy-related characteristics of particular groups of students and the teaching approaches commonly used with them. The groups discussed in this chapter are students with learning difficulties, vision impairment, hearing impairment, intellectual disabilities, physical impairments, and multiple disabilities, as well as indigenous Australian students, and students from culturally and linguistically diverse backgrounds.

The following questions can be used as a framework to guide the reading of the chapter, and as a review device.

- What is/are literacy/literacies?
- What are some of the difficulties in literacy ?
- What might be the reasons for students' literacy problems?
- How is literacy assessed?
- What is meant by the term inclusive approaches to literacy instruction?
- What is meant by the phrases "individualising literacy instruction" and "differentiating literacy instruction"?
- What elements of media and materials should teachers pay attention to when teaching?
- What is the relationship between literacy and technology for all students, and what role does adaptive technology play in literacy learning for particular groups of students?
- What might be the consequences of selecting particular patterns of organisation and management for literacy instruction?
- What issues in the field of literacy require new solutions? Are there others?

Literacy

Literacy can be understood in a number of ways. However, the most recent conceptualisations view it as a set of situated, social cultural practices involving symbols (e.g., letters, words, pictures, graphs, braille) (Gee, 1996; Green, 1999; The New London Group, 1996). Such conceptualisations suggest that literacy is developed through interactions with others and is a consequence of engaging in a series of practices prescribed by the symbols themselves, the cultural contexts, social situations, and factors such as gender, age, and disability. Literacy learning is developmental and changes over time.

Several authors (Gee, 1996; Green, 1999; Lankshear, 1997) use the term literacies in contrast to literacy because the latter tends to connote print literacy. The plural, literacies, has been adopted to indicate the multiple ways in which people are literate. They refer to the processes used when engaging with all media of communication: print, oral, and multimedia. With reference to print, people use the processes of reading and writing. With reference to oral communication they use speaking and listening, and with respect to multimedia communication they use all of these processes plus viewing. Reading, writing, speaking, listening, and viewing are, therefore, referred to as literacies, or as the strands of literacy.

A model of literacy that embraces this notion of literacy and literacies and that is becoming increasingly widespread in Australian classrooms is the Four Resources Model (Freebody & Luke, 1990; Luke & Freebody, 1997, 1999). This Model suggests that there is an array (repertoire) of practices in which individuals engage when interacting with print, oral language, or multimedia. The practices are related to four roles:

- code-breaker (how do I crack this text?);
- text-participant (what does this mean?);
- text-user (what do I do with this text?); and
- text-analyst (what is this text trying to do to me?).

It should be noted that the word text does not refer only to the written word, but to any activity. That is, a game of soccer, a conversation, and a film clip are all examples of text.

The practices used in code-breaker and text-participant focus on the traditional decoding and meaning-making aspects of literacy. Text-user refers to establishing a purpose for the text and thinking about other possible purposes, whereas text-analyst involves thinking analytically about the contents of the text and considering the underlying and implicit assumptions in the text. The latter involves examining how the reader, listener, or viewer is positioned by the text and the degree to which the individual accepts or challenges that position. Freebody and Luke (1990) did not

regard these four practices as organised hierarchically by age or ability. Rather, they argued that all four are necessary and are typically employed in a flexible manner with a range of expertise according to the nature of the text and the task.

The model that one has of literacy will determine how literacy difficulties are viewed. If literacy is seen from a Four Resources Model perspective, literacy difficulties will be understood as problems, with these practices in interaction with the text and the task. Certainly, how one conceptualises and defines literacy influences the prevalence of literacy difficulties. An examination of the research into literacy difficulties that appears in this chapter reveals that most of the investigations have examined literacy from within a framework of code-breaking and meaning-making. As broader conceptualisations of literacy emerge, researchers will begin to examine what other practices individuals use and how effectively they are employed. In turn, these will be investigated and reported.

Prevalence

Establishing prevalence is extremely difficult as it is determined to a great extent by definition, how this definition is operationalised, what measurement tools are used, and the different methods of reporting. In the case of establishing prevalence for literacy difficulties, it is important to recognise not only that literacy can be understood in many ways, but also that the groups of students about whom literacy is to be reported can be poorly described, and that the membership can vary from state to state. In Australia, for example, disability itself is variously defined, and the naming of groups of students with disabilities also varies greatly. In Australia, students with disabilities are often defined and provided with support solely on the basis of their eligibility for funding (Colbert & van Kraayenoord, 2000).

In a large national study of literacy and students with disabilities (van Kraayenoord et al., 2000) it was noted that little is known about the achievement levels in literacy of students with disabilities. The most common outcomes data (usually reported as levels against a reporting framework) are provided by the state school sector to state and Commonwealth governments at Years 3, 5, and 7, although some states also collect data at other year levels (e.g., Queensland in Year 2) or in all year levels. Colbert and van Kraayenoord (2000) noted that few states were able to provide literacy achievement level data for students with disabilities because many of these students are exempted from state-mandated tests. In a number of other cases, students with disabilities take part in the tests but under conditions of special consideration or provision (known as test accommodations). These include alternative formats, additional time, use of assistive devices or scribes, or modifications to the environment. In statewide testing in Australia these conditions are seldom recorded.

With respect to the literacy achievement of students with learning difficulties, Louden et al. (2000) have pointed to the range of definitions used across Australia. Educational authorities do not differentiate learning difficulties in literacy from difficulties in numeracy. Thus, establishing the prevalence of literacy difficulties in those with learning difficulties is problematic. After discussing the range of estimates from government and non-government providers, and from surveys and case studies, Louden (2000) concluded that 16% of children nationally experience learning difficulties, with private providers' estimating 10%, and the school sectors and systems commonly estimating 20%.

However, students are more likely to be identified as having a learning difficulty in literacy than in other domains. Louden (2000) suggested that this might be due to the priority given to literacy in schools in recent years.

Australia appears to have a good record of literacy achievement for older people. In a study of the prose literacy (ability to understand and use information from texts such as newspapers) and document literacy (ability to locate and use information in materials such as tables and graphs) Australians aged 15 to 65 had skills similar to that of Canada and New Zealand. More than 55% of Australians in the survey were at level 3 or higher (level 1 is very poor skills, level 5 is very good skills) for prose literacy and document literacy (Australian Bureau of Statistics, 1999).

Features of students with literacy difficulties

Within the classroom, difficulties that students have in literacy result from a complex interaction of variables related to the learner, teacher, text, and environment. Other variables that also influence literacy learning include policies related to provision of literacy instruction and/or intervention, and access to human and material resources and support. Finally, the nature of a student's disabilities or learning difficulties (e.g., its severity) plays an important role in literacy learning.

The elements in Box 9.1 (page 396) appear to be the most common in which students might experience literacy difficulties. The list is not exhaustive but is provided to allow teachers and others to identify areas for assessment and instruction. It should be noted that students often have problems in more than one of the elements. Finally, other elements—for example, language background and motivation (specifically self-concept, locus of control, and attributes of success and failure)—are not included, although they play a salient role in literacy learning. It should also be noted that not all elements are the same for all students nor are they necessary to be a competent literacy learner. For example, for blind students and those with vision impairment, the knowledge and use of colour can be different from that of sighted students; and handwriting can be redundant for students with a physical impairment who use computers for word-processing.

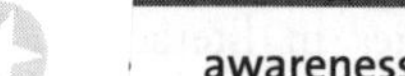

Box 9.1 Elements of literacy

- awareness of environmental media
- prior knowledge
- vocabulary, including subject-specific vocabulary
- letter knowledge
- concepts about print
- phonemic awareness
- the alphabetic principle
- word recognition and identification
- decoding
- automaticity and fluency of reading
- handwriting
- automaticity in handwriting
- spelling conventions
- comprehension
- metacognitive knowledge
- knowledge of the writing process and skills necessary for its execution (e.g., planning, drafting, editing, revising)
- writing conventions
- strategies, especially in reading and writing
- knowledge and understanding of a variety of genres (including the purposes and textual features of the genres) in written, visual, and spoken forms
- awareness of audience and purpose in written, visual, and spoken forms
- composition of written, visual, and spoken text
- knowledge of use of words, colour images, sound, and video
- communicative intent and skills
- generation, organisation, elaboration, integration, and analysis of ideas
- keyboard skills
- awareness of context and history and its influence on text, creator, and user
- awareness of social organisation and power relations on text, creator, and user
- evaluation of sources and evidence
- developing an analytic and critical perspective
- creating and designing information
- transforming information

Why do students have difficulties in literacy?

It is most unlikely that students have difficulties with literacy for a single reason. Indeed, because the strands of literacy are complex, there are likely to be multiple causes.

Most difficulties in reading (one of the literacy strands) have a language basis and support for a relationship between language abilities and reading achievement is well documented (Catts, Fey, Zhang, & Tomblin, 1999). Many authors have suggested that the main difficulty of poor readers is phonological processing. Of particular significance is the link between phonemic awareness (an aspect of phonological processing comprising the ability to blend, segment and sequence sounds in words) and word recognition and identification (Byrne & Fielding-Barnsley, 1995). Failure to recognise words automatically (i.e., individual differences in the accuracy and speed of single-word reading) is often a characteristic of poor phonological processing that also affect students' reading (Grigorenko, 2001). The relationship between phonemic awareness and word recognition has implications for spelling too. Specifically, that spoken words can be analysed into component parts, and the sounds matched to combinations of letters, is crucial for spelling words (Templeton & Morris, 2000; Reason, 1998). If students are not aware of this connection they often have difficulties with spelling.

Another cause of reading difficulties is found in the link between decoding (ability to use knowledge of the relationships between sounds and letters to say unknown words) and comprehension (Shankweiler et al., 1999). However, for some students this is often a pervasive difficulty and difficulties with comprehension that are a result of a lack of phonemic awareness or decoding skills have been found in older students and adult readers (Shankweiler et al., 1999). Indeed, Stanovich (1986) coined the term the Matthew Effect to describe the spiralling negative consequences of the failure to learn to decode. The Matthew Effect proposes that students who are unable to decode read less and take up fewer and fewer opportunities to read which, in turn, leads to poor reading achievement.

Recent studies of brain structure and function involving autopsy, structural magnetic resonance imaging techniques, and electrophysiological techniques (i.e., electro-encephalograph) in normal and dyslexic readers have shown several differences. For example, there is evidence that phonological processing is rooted in the temporal gyrus and that the patterns of activity vary for dyslexic and normal readers (Grigorenko, 2001). Similarly, there are now several studies that have examined the hereditary and familial probability of reading difficulties, including genetic studies in which chromosomes might be associated with reading difficulties (see Grigorenko, 2001, for a review). However, although many studies break new scientific ground and might be helpful in understanding the possible causes of difficulties, there are many writers

(including Grigorenko) who have argued that environmental factors (i.e., social and educational factors) should not be overlooked in the search for causes of reading difficulties.

Indeed, many researchers and teachers who have sought deficiencies within the students themselves (or their families) have been criticised for holding this deficit view (Gadsen, 2000; Luke & Freebody, 2000). The deficit view is rapidly being challenged as teachers and researchers recognise that most difficulties are caused by a mismatch between the individual's learning needs (e.g., lack of prior knowledge, difficulties with phonemic awareness and phonological decoding, and/or lack of strategies for comprehension) and classroom factors under teacher control (such as the curriculum and resources) (Maglen, 1999).

In an interview, Michael Pressley, a noted researcher in cognitive and educational psychology, suggested that poor-quality literature, boring content material, and poor classroom instruction (especially in the upper-primary and secondary school levels) contributed to the difficulties of struggling readers (Brownwell & Walther-Thomas, 2000). For example, with respect to the content material, Pressley singled out poor organisation, lack of interesting topics, and inclusion of information that was irrelevant to students' lives as common problems. Inconsiderate content (i.e., material that does not provide readers' with sufficient background information) also causes difficulties because students are unable to make links between what they know and the text, leading to poor comprehension. According to Pressley, worksheets (which do little to promote literacy) become more prevalent as students move through the grade levels, and many activities (e.g., memorising vocabulary, or answering lower-order questions) require only low-level cognitive skills. Such activities constitute teaching that does little to engage students or challenge them to become active and self-regulating learners.

Students will quickly become disenagaged if classroom teaching does not connect with their lives, and if it does not engage them as learners with topics and issues that have interest and meaning for them. The development of students as analytic and critical literacy learners means that teachers must teach in ways that allow students to investigate, share, and discuss the multiple media with which they are interacting, and to affirm or challenge the stances that they are being positioned to adopt. Thus, the onus is on the teacher to ensure that curricula, pedagogy, and assessment practices are responsive to the students and their situations.

Common assessment practices

Assessment involves the collection of information about a student. Assessment is used to pinpoint the exact difficulties of a student and leads to an identification of the literacy difficulties. It is important to assess all the literacy strands and focus on a broad understanding of achievement within these strands.

The administration of specially designed, often normed, standardised tests can be one element of assessment. It is very important that teachers are sure that the use of any test is guided by certain principles. As adapted from Wood (1998/1999), these principles are that:

- tests must be tailored to a specific purpose;
- tests should be reliable, valid and fair;
- tests should be age-appropriate in terms of content and collection of information;
- tests should be linguistically appropriate, recognising to some extent that all assessments are measures of language;
- tests should be culturally appropriate; and
- test information should be used in ways that are appropriate.

However, most teachers find it more helpful to obtain information from assessment tools that examine a student's abilities and skills in terms of individual progress and not through the use of tests that examine performance in relation to the achievement of other children. As an information gathering process, assessment might involve observations, interviews, examination of school records and past results, the use of checklists, obtaining samples of work and performance, tests of various kinds, and the use of measures to examine attitudes, interests, and aspects of motivation. Whatever assessment tools are used, their selection and use should be tailored to the students themselves and their classroom context.

When assessment practices are connected to classroom practices, the information gathered by assessment is likely to have greater relevance and validity. For the teacher, the primary purpose of collecting assessment information about literacy is to inform instruction and, therefore, the teacher will want to ensure that what is collected links with the instructional context. See Box 9.2 (page 400) for a list of assessment practices in literacy.

A number of people might be involved in collecting literacy assessment information. They include the classroom teacher, support teacher, educational adviser (for students with particular disabilities), guidance officer, or educational psychologist. Sometimes a speech pathologist or occupational therapist might also be involved. Given the range of people involved a team approach is often taken in which members work in a collaborative and consultative manner to collect information and provide a synthesis of the information. This synthesis is often called a "literacy profile" and provides a coherent picture of a student's literacy strengths and needs In order for this profile to be revisited, assessment should not be a one-off occurrence but should occur over time. This means often that the classroom teacher and other professionals are responsible for the ongoing collection of assessment information so that changes in

Box 9.2 Literacy assessment practices

- observational techniques including: anecdotal records, checklists, rating scales
- interviews, which might include interviews with the parents as well as the student
- testing, including standardised tests, and criterion-referenced tests
- direct assessment, including curriculum-based assessment (CBA)
- dynamic assessment
- outcomes-based assessment
- miscue analysis
- reading and/or writing logs
- journals and diaries
- writing samples and the use of assessment matrices and rubrics
- self-assessment, including self-observation and self-report
- informal prose inventories
- retellings
- teacher-made cloze and maze tests
- error analyses
- portfolio assessment

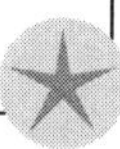

literacy achievement and attitudes can be monitored, and decisions about instruction and support altered if necessary.

Assessment information should be shared with the students and with the parents. Often it is used as part of the process of identification of services or support, including intervention, and for changing instruction in the classroom context. Thus, it is important that whoever collects the data (or a spokesperson for the assessment team) conveys the outcomes to the student and parents and provides an indication of the changes to instruction that will be made based on the student's literacy profile. Teacher or professional staff–parent conferences are necessary for the sharing of such information. Student attendance and active participation in these conferences can also be very helpful as these allow the student to be part of the information sharing and goal setting.

Louden (2000) noted that across Australian educational systems and sectors very similar assessment instruments are used. Clay's Observational Survey (Clay, 1993) and the First Steps Developmental Continua (Education Department of Western Australia, 1994) were often used in the first years of schooling. The case studies in Louden et al. (2000) also highlighted the use of these and several other measures of reading, word recognition, phonemic awareness, oral retelling, and expressive and receptive language. The national survey of schools undertaken as part of the L et al. study also revealed that, in addition to the above elements, schools a students' reading comprehension and spelling. The most commonly used t reading comprehension were the Tests of Reading Comprehension (TO Mossenson, Hill, & Masters, 1987) and the Neale Analysis of Reading Ab..., Revised (Neale, 1988). Some schools also assessed students' intelligence. What is significant about the findings is the almost singular attention to the assessment of reading and the comparative lack of assessment in the other literacy strands. This reflects attention to reading in government priorities, teacher comfort with assessing it, and the predominance of reading measures.

Of interest in the Louden et al. (2000) report was the finding—repeated in the case studies, national school survey, and survey of private providers—of the use made of a range of professionals other than classroom teachers to identify students' literacy difficulties. These professionals included specialist teachers (such as support teacher–learning difficulties, school psychologists or guidance officers, speech pathologists, and speech therapists). Many of these professionals used more formal assessment measures (such as standardised tests) than the classroom teachers, although the researchers also detected an increase in the use of formal tests by classroom teachers in recent years.

In the study of literacy and students with disabilities by van Kraayenoord et al. (2000), it was noted that a range of assessment techniques was used to assess literacy performance. Like Louden's (2000) findings, many of the assessment measures were similar to those 400 used with nondisabled peers (see Box 9.2, page 400). However, in the case of students with disabilities, many of the assessment measures were adapted or modified in terms of the tasks, texts, instructions, conditions, and environments in which the assessments occurred. Notable again was the emphasis on assessment of reading, and in particular phonemic awareness, word recognition, and oral reading fluency. The researchers also admitted surprise at the number of commercial, published reading tests, although it is not known if these were used under standardised conditions or with adaptations and, in the latter case, if they were used only diagnostically. The two reports also commented on the use of tests of reading, writing, and spelling in Years 3, 5, and 7 that are part of state-mandated testing for reporting to state school and government authorities.

Accommodations in the assessment of literacy

For students with learning difficulties and disabilities there is often a need to make accommodations in the assessment of literacy. They include:

- time and scheduling accommodations (e.g., multiple assessment sessions, extended time to complete assessments, untimed sessions);

- setting accommodations (e.g., individual assessment or assessment in a small group in a separate location, with special acoustics or lighting, with adaptive or special furniture, in a location with minimal distractions such as a carrel);
- presentation accommodations (e.g., large print or braille editions, directions and/or items read out by the assessment administrator, directions given in simplified language, the use of practice items, size, space or location for answers altered, prompts (such as arrows or stop signs), directions and assessment items signed by an interpreter); and
- response accommodations (e.g., student uses large spaced paper, student dictates answers, student signs or points as alternative responses, student audiotapes responses, word processor used, spell-check device used, scribe is used).

It should be noted the choice of accommodation(s) is based on individual student needs As Australian students with learning difficulties and disabilities are increasingly required to participate in regular classroom instruction and assessment, and in statewide mandated testing (in the United States the latter is a requirement under legislation), teachers will have to come to terms with providing these accommodations. If the student has the accommodation for daily functioning in literacy activities in the classroom then he or she should also be provided with this accommodation in classroom assessment and in any externally mandated testing.

Ways of supporting students' learning literacy

Historical overview

Students with literacy difficulties have been assisted in ways that reflect the dominant theoretical understandings about literacy and learning at the time. Whichever field of study or group of learners is examined, one notices changing and often competing perspectives about how students should be supported through instruction. For example, in the field of learning difficulties, teaching approaches have often been selected based on the teachers' beliefs about the underlying basis for the reading problem. Crudely described, there have been two dominant views about the most effective way of teaching reading. Educators can view reading problems of students with learning difficulties in reading as based on difficulties with phonological awareness or the ability to decode words. They have argued for the use of highly structured, explicit instruction in these areas. Other educators view reading as a meaning-based activity, which primarily requires abilities to use the context of language. They have argued for more holistic approaches emphasising meaning and purpose with these students (see Adams & Bruck, 1993; Foorman, 1994; Pressley & Rankin, 1994; Stacey & Wheldall, 1999 for reviews). Alongside these, in the 1990s there was a focus on the teaching of metacognitive knowledge and strategies for reading (and writing). Thus, many educators incorporated aspects of metacognition

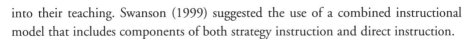

into their teaching. Swanson (1999) suggested the use of a combined instructional model that includes components of both strategy instruction and direct instruction.

A second example related to students with intellectual disabilities is also illustrative of the evolution in instructional approaches across time as expectations changed about what could be achieved by students with intellectual disabilities. Some of these changes were associated with changes in belief and practice related to the location of schooling, namely integrated or segregated settings (Bochner, Outhred, & Pieterse, 2001). With respect to instruction of students with Down syndrome, literacy teaching in the 1960s and 1970s was dominated by behaviourist approaches that emphasised teaching functional reading using behavioural techniques. In the 1980s there was a transition to more holistic approaches with less of a focus on purely functional reading skills and, more recently, some authors have advocated the use of social–cultural approaches for the literacy learning of students with intellectual disabilities (see van Kraayenoord, Moni, Jobling, & Ziebarth, in press). As a consequence of broader conceptualisations of literacy and altered expectations related to the literacy learning of students with Down syndrome, better understandings of their needs and how they can be met are also being developed.

Current practices

There are numerous programs for the development and/or the intervention of literacy. Many programs were identified in Louden et al. (2000) and van Kraayenoord et al. (2000). Most of these programs are limited to the early years of schooling on which the Australian government has placed significant attention. Typically, they focus on reading and/or writing, and increasingly they represent commercial programs. Many programs lack formal evaluation within Australia using rigorous research designs.

A recent trend is to categorise programs in terms of first wave, second wave, and third wave teaching (Hill, 1997; Louden et al., 2000). First wave teaching refers to early years classroom-based teaching with the focus on preventing literacy problems. Second wave teaching refers to early intervention programs, and third wave teaching refers to subsequent interventions typically involving older primary school students. Rohl (2000) has referred to the Early Years Literacy Program, Schoolwide Early Language and Literacy (SWELL), First Steps, Teaching Handwriting Reading and Spelling Skills (THRASS), Letterland, and school-developed programs as examples of first wave teaching. Two of these programs will be discussed.

Schoolwide Early Language and Literacy program (SWELL)

SWELL was developed in New South Wales (Center & Freeman, 1997). Based on the US program, Success for All (Slavin et al. 1994), it is a highly structured program that uses explicit teaching of sequenced skills, in particular phonemic awareness and phonological skills. Lessons involve modelling and talk about the task, structured

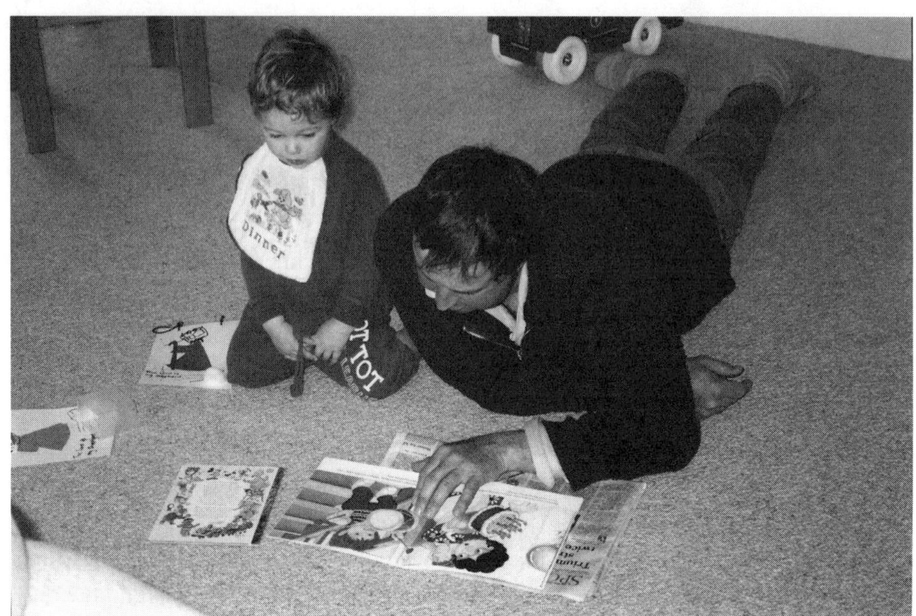

This father is developing his son's interest in reading and is providing a model for the boy's future development.

group work, whole class teaching and review. The activities involve reading, writing, speaking and listening. Research undertaken by the developers indicated that the approach holds considerable promise (Center & Freeman, 1997).

Early Years Literacy program

The Early Years Literacy program is a whole school literacy program developed in Victoria that has spread throughout Australia. It is based on the work of Crevola and Hill (1998) and Hill and Crevola (1998) and has several essential features, namely a daily focused two-hour literacy session, planned home–school liaison, an early years school coordinator, and a whole school commitment. During the literacy session, activities include reading to, and writing with, students, language experience, shared reading and writing, guided reading and writing, and independent reading. Following a three-step process these activities move from whole-class teaching to small group work with a teacher or independently, and then back to whole-class sharing of what has been learnt.

With respect to second wave teaching, early intervention programs identified by Rohl (2000) include Reading Recovery and teacher-developed teaching.

Reading Recovery

Reading Recovery is aimed at children who have the poorest performance in reading after one year of instruction. The program provides accelerated learning so that

students can catch up with their peers who are performing at the average of their
Typically this takes 12 to 20 weeks. If students do not achieve satisfactorily in t
program they are removed and offered alternative support. The program is intensive with short lessons of 30 minutes daily. Extensive evaluation of Reading Recovery has been undertaken, although little of it has occurred in Australia. Opinions on its efficacy are strongly polarised and the results of the studies are ambiguous (Chapman, Tunmer, & Prochnow, 2001; Fletcher-Flinn, White, & Nicholson, 1998; Hiebert, 1994; Shanahan & Barr, 1995; Slavin & Fashola, 1998). In one of the studies, Elbaum, Vaughn, Tejero-Hughes, and Watson-Moody (2000) concluded that there was little to support the claim of superiority of Reading Recovery over other one-to-one programs. Typically, approximately 30% of students who began the program did not complete it and did not perform significantly better than children in control groups. To deliver greater efficacy, some researchers (Fletcher-Flinn, White & Nicholson, 1998; Iversen & Tunmer, 1993; Tunmer & Chapman, 2001) have called for the explicit instruction to develop phonological skills within Reading Recovery. Noting the ambiguity of the Reading Recovery research findings, Luke and Freebody (2000, p. 27) raised the following concerns that relate to its use as a program given state education funding: "Is the standard for successful completion of RR equitable? Does RR raise overall achievement levels? . . . Does RR reduce the need for other compensatory reading services? Are alternative interventions more effective than RR?"

Many individuals and reports on literacy have pointed to the importance of early intervention to counteract difficulties becoming persistent, and to prevent long-term literacy problems (Snow, Burns, & Griffin, 1998). Early intervention programs such as Reading Recovery have been especially evident in the area of reading, although there are also many other initiatives throughout the world (e.g., Torgesen, Wagner, & Rashotte, 1997). One criticism of many of these programs is that they involve the withdrawal of children from the regular classroom environment. Infrequently are students reintegrated into the regular literacy curriculum and classroom instructional program.

The task of developing effective interventions in reading for older students, or third wave teaching, has been more difficult. Many authors have argued that these students (still) need to have intensive, explicit, and systematic instruction in phonemic awareness, sight word recognition and phonemic decoding (e.g., Foorman, Francis, Fletcher, Schatschneider, & Mehta, 1998; Torgesen & Burgess, 1998). A study by Torgesen et al. (2001) demonstrated that instructional interventions that focused on these skills and that used teaching procedures—such as explicit teaching, error correction routines, and many opportunities to practise with appropriate materials—were highly effective in helping older students.

In assisting students with difficulties in reading comprehension, Mastropieri and Scruggs (1997) and Swanson (1999) have also demonstrated that systematic instruction

e gains for students. It should be noted, however, that researchers
antly used standardised comprehension measures that suggest there is
or correct meaning associated with text. Other conceptualisations of
s the Four Resources Model [Freebody & Luke, 1990]) are based on
there are multiple meanings of text and that students have their own
hich might differ from those of the author or other readers. Such
ews of reading comprehension mean that the usefulness of standardised tests of comprehension is limited. Nevertheless, the development of comprehension skills and strategies is one of the most important areas of instruction, especially for older students.

In Australia a wide variety of literacy programs is used to support older students. Rohl (2000) found that some of these programs focused on the explicit teaching of word level skills whereas others concentrated on comprehension, or both word level skills and comprehension. Many were designed by teachers or were collections of elements from various programs. Several schools used commercial programs such as Accelerated Reader, and Teaching Handwriting Reading and Spelling Skills (THRASS). The efficacy of most of these programs for older students is unknown.

Many of the first, second, and third wave programs for students with learning difficulties have been listed by state education departments for students with disabilities. In practice, however, it appears more typical for teachers of students with disabilities to use the curriculum frameworks or syllabus to identify outcomes and to teach these using a variety of approaches that is not specifically bound to a particular program. Interestingly, most of the teaching approaches used to teach literacy to students with disabilities were similar to those used with regular students.

Changing the way we teach

The major characteristic of the teaching used with students with literacy difficulties is the use of inclusive approaches that cater for students' individual needs Inclusive approaches are those typically used by regular classroom teachers to ensure that students acquire, maintain, and generalise the knowledge and skills of literacy. Such approaches are often regarded as effective teaching. An inclusive classroom is one in which all learners move along a developmental continuum in literacy development and in which instruction matches this continuum (Munro, 1999). In a classroom in which this supportive environment has been created, modelling and demonstration occurs during teaching, and students are engaged in both guided and independent practice. Feedback is given frequently and is based on performance.

Inclusive practices involve the use of relevant tasks that encourage students to talk about literacy learning and about the strategies they use to engage with task and the text. Technology is integrated into the instructional practices for all the students. For example, an audiorecording of text might be used alongside the reading of print. Adaptive technologies are also used as appropriate for students with learning

Box 9.3 Inclusive effective teaching of literacy

- Explicitly tell students the purpose and goals of the lesson.
- Provide an outline or overview of what will be taught in a lesson.
- Make connections between what is to be learnt and students' interests, motivation, and everyday life.
- Create a media-rich environment and use the artefacts around the classroom during teaching, and encourage students to use the artefacts when they are working in groups or independently.
- Provide information orally, in print and through multimedia.
- Provide examples (e.g., genres to be taught) and annotate them to identify the features that require attention.
- Focus on the process of learning.
- Teach strategies explicitly, through modelling, demonstration, and thinking aloud.
- Ensure that there are frequent opportunities for students to respond.
- When working in groups make sure students are aware of the purpose of the group.
- Actively monitor progress.
- Provide individual instructional support when necessary.
- Provide explicit feedback that focuses on achievement and motivation.
- Allow for alternative or supplementary formats for the presentation of work.

difficulties or disabilities. For example, a speech synthesiser might be used to accompany material appearing on a computer screen. See Box 9.3 for some suggestions for making literacy teaching inclusive and effective.

In referring to students with learning difficulties in Australia, Rohl (2000) identified several characteristics of successful teaching. With respect to first wave teaching, they included: explicit instruction, a strong oral language focus, an emphasis on letter-sound correspondences, systematic and plentiful practice in reading and writing connected text, instructional texts at students' individual reading and writing levels, and a combination of shared and individual reading and writing activities. In the second wave, important components were: a variety of literacy activities (with an emphasis on listening to stories), explicit teaching of letter–sound decoding (combined with reading and writing connected text), and intervention programs for children outside the classroom. Effective third wave teaching had an emphasis on self-regulation, metacognition and self-esteem, explicit instruction (including modelling), and practice in the application of taught strategies. In addition, during third wave

teaching, reference was made to focusing on both learning to read and reading to learn.

With respect to students with disabilities, Colbert and van Kraayenoord (2000) found most literacy practices were similar to those used with students with learning difficulties.

Media and materials

Teachers must ensure that students have access to materials that meet their needs They should also use a variety of narrative (e.g., novels) and non-narrative print texts (e.g, reports), and other media materials (including computer programs, videos, and models). The use of a range of media and materials not only provides students with choice, which is motivating, but also is likely to develop knowledge and skills across all the strands of literacy.

Technology

Traditionally, technology has been seen as an add-on to literacy. However, more recently, with the concept of multiliteracies, authors have made reference to new technologies and l(IT)eracy (Durrant & Green, 2000). Although most investigators who have examined technology and literacy have referred to computers (and then mainly with reference to word processing), the use of the Internet, e-books, audio players, digital cameras, modems, laser disk players, video players, and CD-Roms is part of more recent conceptulations of l(IT)eracy and multiliteracies.

Computer technology has often been used to develop the literacy skills of students with learning difficulties in reading and/or writing. One review of 17 studies designed to evaluate the use of computer-assisted instruction in reading found that most of the programs made use of drill and practice routines, followed by strategy instruction and then simulation (Hall, Hughes, & Filbert, 2000). These authors found that the programs focused predominantly on either word recognition or reading comprehension. The results of these evaluations suggested that most of these 17 programs were successful. Their success, the authors suggested, was due to significant program design features, including the integration of systematic instruction and effective correction procedures.

In another review, MacArthur, Feretti, Okolo, and Cavalier (2001) examined the use of computer technology in word identification, written text comprehension, and writing (and spelling) as applied to students with mild disabilities (i.e., students with learning disabilities, reading disabilities and mild cognitive disabilities). They noted that there was "qualified support" for the use of technology-based interventions for assisting students with difficulties in phonological awareness and word identification. Programs that make use of digitised (recorded) or synthesised speech feedback are

sometimes used to assist in the development of reading words in isolation or connected text. Referring to the research of Wise, Olson, Ring and Johnson (1998), these reviewers noted that to date there was strong evidence that synthesised speech was helpful, when it was coupled with intensive training in phonological awareness.

With respect to the effects of computer assisted instruction on text comprehension, most programs add enhancements to the text. These include speech synthesis, definitions, graphics, and supplementary text. MacArthur et al. (2001) stated that the results of the research involving the effects of speech synthesis in association with screen text (i.e., the simultaneous auditory and visual presentation of words) on comprehension were equivocal. There was also a lack of consensus on the efficacy of specific enhancements on comprehension.

In the domain of writing, there is now quite substantial evidence that technology (especially word processing) does help students with difficulties in the area of writing. However, it is not sufficient merely to provide a word processor to students. Instructional support must also be built into the program and/or be provided by the teacher alongside the program. The review of MacArthur et al. (2001) indicated that text revision and the overall quality of students' work can be improved with the use of word processors. The use of spell-checkers and the use of word prediction programs can also assist poor spellers. However, spell-checkers and word prediction programs do require additional attentional resources from students and thus they might not be effective unless the issues of attention are addressed by the other instructional support. The reviewers noted that some of the writing programs can remove one burden but introduce another (e.g., a student's difficulty with handwriting might be removed, but he or she might then need to pay attention to typing, and this might slow production unless the student learns to type.) Thus there was a need for instruction to be linked to the use of word processors and spell-checkers.

Indeed, there appear to be several elements that are necessary before computer technology has any positive outcomes on the literacy achievement of students with learning difficulties. These include well-designed programs (e.g., incorporating correction procedures) and additional instruction (including assisting students to cope with new attentional demands). In addition, many authors (e.g., Wong, 2001) have called for a match between the specific skill difficulties of the student and the particular focus of the computer programs. Unless such a match is achieved, the optimism that surrounds the use of computers for improving the literacy learning of students with learning difficulties might be misplaced.

Computers have been used effectively with students with disabilities to develop their reading and writing (Erickson & Koppenhaver, 1998; Lahm, 1996; Sturm & Koppenhaver, 2000). Research evidence shows that computers heighten motivation and lead to higher quality work. In turn, this increases the chance of literacy success. It is

of interest that the Ministerial Advisory Committee: Students with Disabilities, South Australia (1998) documented three research projects that involved technology to teach written expression to students with disabilities. The projects indicated the successful use of technology, but highlighted several issues related to integrating technology with curriculum, teaching procedures, and assessment, together with the need for ongoing technological support and staff expertise. Another innovative Australian project involving the use of computers with older individuals with intellectual disabilities is Literacy and Technology—Hands On (LATCH-ON) (Moni & Jobling, 2000). This project develops the literacy of young adults with Down syndrome through the use of text production software, the Internet, email, and the traditional practice of word identification and sentence reading.

In addition, Brown (2000) suggested that, to bring about equitable access to technology, the selected software must be matched to the students' needs and the goals of curriculum. To ensure that instruction involving technology is effective, teachers must plan for its use, develop ways in which it can be integrated into everyday classroom practices, design activities that involve all the literacy strands, consider its use vis-à-vis classroom organisation and management, and evaluate its effects.

Organisation and management of instruction

There are many ways in which teaching is organised in regular classrooms. Whole class teaching, the use of homogeneous or heterogeneous groups, teaching through peer tutoring, or one-to-one instruction with a teacher, support teacher, teacher's aide, paraprofessional, or other volunteers are all common. Teachers typically use most of these organisational arrangements. Rankin-Erickson and Pressley (2000) found that special education teachers working with students with reading disabilities used homogeneous grouping for about half of their lesson time. In another study, Schumm, Moody, and Vaughn (2000) undertook interviews and classroom observations of Year 3 teachers' grouping practices, and then examined the impact of the reported practices on academic progress and attitudes to reading. They found that teachers in their study predominantly used whole class teaching and heterogeneous grouping practices. However, the students' performance suggested that such practices might not be effective for all, especially those with learning difficulties. The authors argued that the one-size-fits-all approach to classroom organisation might not be appropriate. They argued that students with learning difficulties need more intensive and explicit instruction to meet students' specific reading needs Thus, teachers need to be flexible in adopting organisational structures tailored to individual students.

Similarly, in Australian research, Fields (1999) drew attention to the impact of heterogeneity in the classroom. He argued that teachers feel less effective and are less responsive to students with learning disabilities as diversity increases in the classroom. Some educators might believe that such findings suggest that these students need

greater in-class support from teachers or need to be withdrawn from regular classroom instruction, but this is not the case. Fields argued that the claim of greater support to teachers can be applied to many groups and individuals in classrooms and was not supportive of segregation. Indeed, with respect to the efficacy of withdrawal, a study by Allington, Guice, Michelson, Baker, and Li (1996) indicated that there is little congruency or consistency between practices adopted in withdrawal settings and in the regular classroom and little transfer from one setting to another. Fields suggested that the nature of instruction in the regular classroom must be examined and changed. How teachers view students as learners, how they approach instruction, their instructional repertoire, their use of flexible and various organisational patterns within the classroom, and how they respond and adapt to students' needs are at the core of managing instruction.

Individualising education

Individualising does not mean one-to-one instruction. It means using curricula, teaching, and the assessment of individual students and their needs This has sometimes been referred to as differentiation (Deschenes, Ebeling & Sprague, 1999;

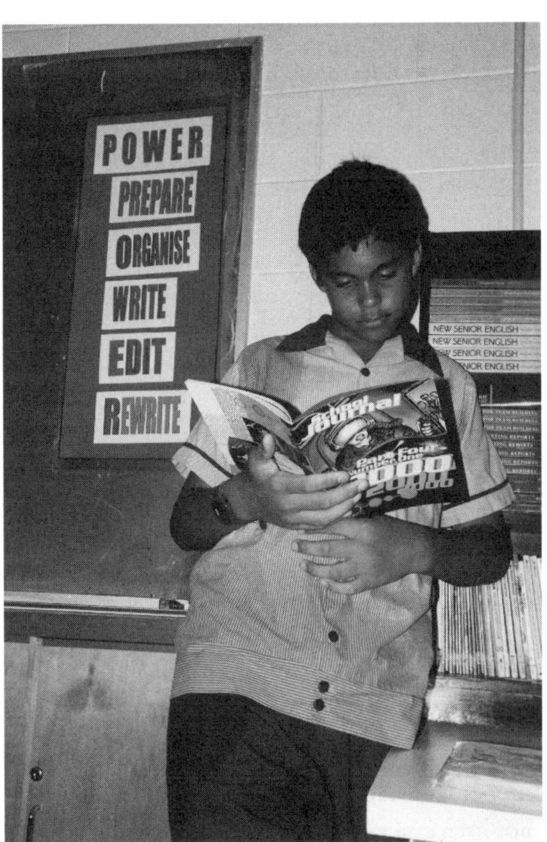

This student uses his free time to extend his reading skills.

Hart, 1996; Tomlinson, 1996; Westwood, 1997). It is based on the premise that teachers understand the students and that this leads to knowledge of the students in interaction with curricula, during teaching, and in assessment (Kliewer & Landis, 1999). As a result of such matching, modifications must occur. Sometimes modifications are documented in an individual education plan (IEP) alongside the students' characteristics and the teaching and learning goals. However, the presence or absence of an IEP depends on the policy requirements of the education system or sector in the state or territory in which a student resides. Students with low incidence disabilities (such as those with vision impairment) are more likely to have IEPs than students with learning difficulties.

In this section, the literacy needs of students with certain characteristics are identified. Although it must be recognised that the literacy knowledge and skills of students in each section below are varied, there are some commonalities that will be described before making reference to the teaching approaches that are frequently used with them. It should also be noted that many of the teaching methods and procedures discussed below are frequently used with other groups (see Keel, Dangel, & Owens, 1999; Mifsud, Evans, & Dowson, 1999).

Literacy and students with learning difficulties

Students with learning difficulties make up the largest student group in schools who have difficulties with literacy. Often the literacy difficulties these students experience are identified early in their schooling and continue throughout their lives. Problems with oral language affect the literacy development of many of these students and are often linked with problems in processing phonological information (e.g., metalinguistic abilities, syntactic awareness) and with phonological processing skills (e.g., phonological coding). These students also often display difficulties with word recognition and processing spoken and printed words (e.g., vocabulary knowledge, listening comprehension, and metacognition). Thus, their difficulties can touch on all the literacy strands.

Most typically, students with learning difficulties in the early years of schooling are supported through programs such as Reading Recovery or other school-developed, education department-developed, or commercial programs implemented by a support teacher (learning difficulties), parent helper, or volunteer. Two programs that use trained parent helpers or volunteers are being trialled in some Australian states to provide additional help to beginning readers. These include Support-a-Reader (Education Queensland, 1991) and Support-a-Writer (Education Queensland, 1996). These are one-to-one interventions. The steps involved in Support-a-Reader include introducing the book, reading the book for the first time, reading the book again, supported reading, and independent reading. The effectiveness of these programs has not been evaluated in carefully designed, controlled studies.

Despite initiatives to intervene in the learning difficulties of students in the early years of schooling, most interventions appear to be insufficient to reverse early difficulties in literacy. Torgesen (2000) has spoken of students who fail to respond to early intervention as treatment resisters. He argued that researchers and educators do not understand the conditions necessary for all children to become adequate readers through early intervention. Thus, many students with problems in the early years continue to have difficulties beyond Year 3. Indeed, studies in the United States have revealed that fewer than one student in eight who is failing to read by the end of Grade 1 ever achieves grade-level performance (Juel, 1988; Torgesen & Burgess, 1998).

In the upper primary grades, many of the problems of students with learning difficulties continue. Difficulties with reading fluency and accurate word recognition often persist but, as students are expected to engage with and understand extended text and to read to learn, other difficulties emerge that are often related to comprehension. Problems with vocabulary, a lack of prior knowledge, and difficulties with the skills and strategies for understanding text are prevalent.

Chan (2000) has suggested that there are three dominant forms of assistance for students with difficulties in comprehension. The first is basic skills training which focuses on developing fluency, vocabulary, and prior knowledge. The second is assisting students to use text enhancements to highlight or organise information and improve understanding of it. Using visual representations (e.g., graphs, charts) and adjunct aids (e.g., study guides) has been suggested. The third form of support is through metacognitve approaches. Among metacognitive approaches, strategy instruction—including teaching awareness of task demands and strategies such as prediction, monitoring and correction procedures—is the key. Strategy instruction involves techniques that include modelling, guided practice and feedback, and student self-regulation. One of the most often cited metacognitive approaches in reading is Reciprocal Teaching (Palincsar, 1986) which focuses on using four strategies (predicting, questioning, summarising, and clarifying) to comprehend text. Teachers and students are involved in discussing how and when these strategies can be used during reading.

Areas of difficulty for students with learning difficulties in writing include idea generation, text organisation, and metacognitive knowledge. Fundamental to intervention in writing has been a focus on the cognitive activities underlying the writing process. In Chan and Dally's (2000) review of the literature she commented that the research has suggested two prominent approaches. The first focuses on the process of writing by emphasising the communicative purpose and an understanding of the recursive processes of planning, drafting, editing, and revising. This approach stresses a supportive classroom with frequent opportunities to write, student-selection of topics for writing, group-sharing and peer-editing, direct experience with planning, drafting and the like, and feedback through writing conferences. The second approach

is known as strategy instruction and involves the provision of information about the use and significance of a strategy, mastery of the target strategy, and development of self-regulation of the strategy on like tasks and in generalised contexts. Two programs that use strategy instruction and have considerable research support are Englert and Raphael's (1988) Cognitive Strategy Instruction in Writing (CSIW) and Graham and Harris' (1989) Self-Regulated Strategy Development (SRSD).

CSIW focuses on teaching writing strategies through the use of teacher modelling and think-aloud procedures in which the steps of various strategies are verbalised by the teacher. Task-specific (e.g., brainstorming considering audience and purpose) and metacognitive strategies are taught together. Students are provided with think sheets that contain self questions or self-instructional statements that assist the students use the strategies until they are internalised. The acronym POWER (plan, organise, write, edit, revise) is used to learn the processes of writing.

SRSD also explicitly teaches strategies for writing using overt modelling. The goals and significance of the strategies are explained to the students. Students then implement the strategies while verbalising the instructions. Like CSIW, teacher support and verbalisations are slowly faded until the student can implement the strategies independently. Students are taught a three-step strategy for writing essays using Think, Plan, and Write.

One element of writing with which students with learning difficulties have considerable difficulty is spelling. Again Chan and Dally (2000) indicated that the main techniques that show promise for these students are:

- error correction with modelling and feedback;
- limiting the use of word lists to reduce cognitive overload;
- explicit teacher-directed training in strategy use; and
- encouraging self-directed study and self-monitoring.

Chan also noted that computer programs and peer support can assist the development of spelling by acting as instructional agents.

Despite a host of suggestions for intervention in different areas (such as those referred to above) many students continue to have difficulties in reading and learning from text into middle school and high school. Multiple reasons for continuing problems have been provided, including poor instruction (Greene, 1998; Williams, Brown, Silverstein, & de Cani, 1994). Coupled with their ongoing difficulties in developing literacy, there is evidence in Australia that as students with learning difficulties progress through the levels of primary school much of the support they receive in literacy fades away (Ashman, van Kraayenoord, & Elkins, 1995).

By the time that the students with learning difficulties reach high school, many of them receive no (or very little) ongoing support. If students with learning difficulties

do receive assistance, this is often in the form of alternative programs (e.g., Modified English). In a recent study, van Kraayenoord and Farrell (1998) listed the types of knowledge and skills associated with reading that were taught in the alternative programs. These included:

- vocabulary and concept development;
- oral reading accuracy and fluency;
- comprehension skills; and
- higher level thinking skills.

For writing, the focus was on:

- assisting students to generate ideas;
- extending previous ideas;
- elaborating and organising ideas;
- teaching the writing process (planning, drafting, editing, and revising); and
- teaching skills of spelling, grammar, punctuation, and dictionary and thesaurus use.

Research skills and computer skills also often featured as part of students' learning.

Techniques suggested in the literature for teaching students with learning difficulties in literacy in secondary schools include:

- modelling or demonstration, and think alouds (Wong, 1997);
- explicit procedure-based instruction (Englert, 1992);
- using Directed Reading Thinking Activity (Santa, 1988);
- K-W-L (Ogle, 1986);
- genre-specific instruction (Graham & Harris, 1993);
- strategy instruction in reading, writing and listening (Alley & Deshler, 1979; Englert, Raphael, & Mariage, 1994; Graham & Harris, 1994);
- peer tutoring and collaboration (Slavin et al., 1992); and
- story planners (Martin & Manno, 1995).

See also Morretta & Ambrosini (2000), Blair-Laresen & Vallance (1999), Dymock & Nicholson (1999), and Lebzelter & Nowacek, (1999) for other suggestions for teaching comprehension, especially for students in the middle and secondary levels of schooling.

Teachers in the van Kraayenoord and Farrell (1998) study used a number of these teaching techniques and incorporated other elements into their lessons. These included explaining what would be learnt and what was expected in a lesson, and/or providing a summary of the previous day's lesson, clarifying key terms and concepts, and walking

through what was required to complete a task. Teachers also reported modifying activities such as using large-print formats, oral reading, written comprehension questions, and simplifying tasks through more structure, less reading, less writing, highlighting key vocabulary, sentences and phrases, and indicating relevant page numbers. Scaffolded worksheets (which use prompts and cues) and assessment tasks were also employed. Some teachers also used checklists on which students recorded their progress through the steps of a task.

When teaching by support teachers (learning difficulties) was investigated, there were several similarities to the approaches used by regular classroom teachers. However, as might be expected, there was greater use of teacher-directed, systematic teaching involving extensive teacher explanation. The use of reteaching was also an important element as this was often needed by the students.

Although speaking, listening, and viewing skills are used to support the accomplishment of reading and writing tasks, these skills are often strengths of these students and, therefore, could be exploited more in teaching. In addition, it appeared that reading and writing in alternative literacy programs were taught through English and particularly through the use of narrative texts (e.g., novels, short stories). Students rarely used non-narrative text (e.g., reports), especially from other curriculum areas.

Notable in this study was the pervasiveness of the difficulties for these students with learning difficulties at the secondary school level, and the need for ongoing and comprehensive support for these students, something which was not always forthcoming.

There is some debate about the importance of handwriting as a skill. Some authors such as Jones (1997) and Einhorn (1999) suggest that students need to be fluent handwriters. They have suggested teaching strategies to assist students in practising letter formation and developing legibility. Although there can be some advantages from assisting young children to acquire handwriting skills as an aid to the recognition of letters and words, for older students difficulties with handwriting can be a source of frustration and negative self-beliefs. For older students who have difficulties with handwriting, alternative means of recording their thoughts and other material might be used. Tape recorders, word processors, and scribes can be used to ensure that students can communicate successfully in written form (Smith, Carroll, & Elkins, 2000).

Literacy and students with disabilities in vision

The key to assisting with the difficulties of students with vision impairment is an assesment of the nature and severity of their impairment and environmental factors. These determine the degree of adaptation and the nature of modifications to tasks that are needed. However, Palmer (2000) pointed out that impaired vision does not mean impaired ability and, therefore, many students with vision impairment achieve literacy

skills that are commensurate with their sighted peers. Palmer noted, however, that early identification and intervention, support for families, and appropriate teaching programs, are essential to ensure that students do not miss out on the incidental literacy learning that is accessible to their sighted peers.

According to Palmer (2000), the following are central in teaching literacy to students with visual impairment:

- carefully selected textbooks;
- appropriately adapted reading materials;
- the correct choice of medium (e.g., braille, large print, tapes);
- an environment that pays attention to appropriate illumination, seating position, and the blackboard or whiteboard;
- appropriate special equipment (e.g., magnifiers, computers, other technology with voice output); and
- considerations such as extra time.

Modifications vary depending on whether the student has a vision impairment or is braille-dependent. Teaching strategies often require modification through an increased use of a variety of concrete experiences and the sequencing of learning into small steps. Palmer (2000) reviewed the debate related to various teaching approaches for this group of students and has called for a balanced approach involving elements of whole language and explicitly taught, skills-based (phonics) approaches.

There is a great deal of optimism expressed in the literature about the literacy achievement of students with vision impairment and those who are blind. If teachers ensure that special measures are put into place to enable these students to access the curriculum, then these students can achieve well in literacy.

Literacy and students with disabilities in hearing

The literacy learning of students with hearing impairment, like those with visual impairment, is affected by the severity of their hearing loss and environmental factors. Students who are deaf might not have spoken language, although some do and might also use sign language. Students who have a hearing impairment and students who are deaf can acquire literacy to the same extent as their nondisabled peers, although those who are deaf might vary more widely in their ability than the population of hearing children. In addition, many (but not all) students who are deaf are less likely to do as well in reading as do other students with hearing impairments (Bortoli, Furlonger, & Rickards, 2000). One of the main reasons for their difficulties in reading is their delayed development in speech and language, thus leading to difficulties with phonological processing, which is a prerequisite for reading.

Again, the keys to the acquisition of literacy and to the maintenance of literacy

learning are early identification, early intervention, an optimal acoustic environment, family support, and appropriate teaching programs (Bortoli, Furlonger, & Rickards, 2000). With respect to access to spoken communication, which is fundamental to literacy learning for these students, auditory amplification or assistive learning devices (e.g., hearing aids) and/or visual devices (e.g., subtitled videos) are essential. There is also a need for appropriate management of the assistive devices.

With regard to instruction, regular classroom teachers must adopt strategies and teaching practices similar to those used for nondisabled students, but must also give attention to ways of accommodating the students' speech and language development, which can be delayed. Bortoli, Furlonger, and Rickards (2000) reviewed the literature relating to two main literacy approaches that have influenced the teaching of students with hearing impairment and students who are deaf. As with the field of vision impairment, there has been ongoing debate about a holistic view of literacy learning versus a skills-based or code-oriented view. This debate remains unresolved. There is also considerable controversy surrounding two approaches used with this group of students, namely the aural–oral approach and the bilingual–bicultural approach. The aural–oral method stresses the use of spoken language, whereas the bilingual approach refers to the combined use of a manual language (sign language) and English in written form. Again, the research is equivocal in terms of the efficacy of these approaches for teaching these students. Further longitudinal research in classroom settings is required.

Many students with a hearing impairment are also assisted in the classroom by notetakers and interpreters who use sign language (usually Auslan) which means that teachers need to be skilled at working collaboratively with other professionals to support their students with hearing impairment or students who are deaf.

Literacy and students with intellectual disabilities

Students with intellectual disabilities display a wide range of achievement in literacy that is related to their cognitive capacity. They will have difficulties in literacy learning and some might not attain the same outcomes as other students. However, these appear to be related strongly to the expectations of parents, teachers, and others. van Kraayenoord (2000) noted that the majority of students with intellectual disabilities can learn to read, and that many learn to write. Even students with profound intellectual disabilities can be taught to use symbol systems to communicate.

Although there is considerable heterogeneity among these students, there are also many similarities in the development of literacy that is consistent with that of their non-disabled peers. Indeed, several authors have argued that the way in which students with intellectual disabilities acquire literacy is consistent with that of their peers. For example, many of the principles related to emergent literacy have influenced the ways in which students with intellectual disabilities have been taught. Instructional techniques that have been used with students with intellectual disabilities include

explicit teaching, peer tutoring, reciprocal teaching, shared reading, cloze activities, modelling, and think aloud. Interventions such as the Bridge program, which uses icons or visual pictures for words, has been used in Australia, sometimes coupled with Makaton, a sign system (van Kraayenoord, 2000). During their literacy lessons, teachers of students with intellectual disabilities report using authentic and integrated activities, brainstorming prior to a reading or writing activity, shared or guided reading, discussion of pictures, the language experience approach with pupil dictated text, the use of flash cards, and computer software.

Literacy and students with physical impairments

Some students with physical impairments are affected by mobility only, but others have cognitive or neurological difficulties that influence their ability to learn literacy. McKenzie's (2000) synthesis of the literature and information from case studies has indicated that some students need special technologies to interact with print and symbols, and that others have more complex needs such as difficulties with written and spoken communication. They can find skills such as handwriting difficult or impossible.

As with all the groups of students reported on in this section, the literacy development of students with physical impairments can be severely hindered unless attention is given to the their individual needs, and unless appropriate support is provided. Alternative or augmentative communication systems are important for many students' development in literacy. The use of computer technology in particular has meant that many of these students can gain access to various media, and can communicate themselves (McKenzie, 2000).

However, alternative or augmentative communication systems should be used alongside effective teaching methods. Although there is some discussion in the literature related to the theoretical orientations to teaching these students, activities based on the idea that literacy is acquired socially have been advocated over teacher-directed activities (Erickson & Koppenhaver, 1995). The literature calls for a balanced approach involving explicit teaching, hands-on activities, and problem-solving in everyday-type activities. In line with this position, many of the recently adopted approaches used by classroom teachers to teach literacy with nondisabled students are appropriate for this group, provided that they have been carefully selected to take into account matters such as the student's mobility, gross and fine motor skills, communication, stamina, and motivation. Issues such as seating, posture, and multiple opportunities to interact with nondisabled peers are also important. Comments related to the use of alternative or augmentative communication systems indicate that there is a need for time and deliberate teaching of the symbols or the method of communication itself (McKenzie, 2000).

High expectations of other people, access to all media through the use of technology,

and adaptation of curricula and teaching to meet individual needs, suggest that many students with physical impairments can achieve good literacy outcomes.

Literacy and students with multiple disabilities

The limitations of students with multiple disabilities arise from impairments in neuromuscular, neurological, and/or orthopaedic systems that affect posture, movement, and communication. Posture, mobility, and communication all affect students' abilities to learn literacy. Problems with motivation can also influence these students' literacy achievement. In most cases their literacy achievement does not match that of their nondisabled peers.

Bortoli and Preston (2000) have indicated that several sources of support will influence literacy achievement. Typically, these supports will be identified on the student's individual educational plan and will range from the use of prosthetic devices, augmentative communication systems (e.g., electronic speech devices), technology (e.g., computers and computer peripherals such as braille-to-print conversion), appropriately adapted texts, simplified tasks and additional time to complete tasks, and significant alterations to curricula and teaching. Some students might require alternative curricula. Teaching approaches for these students need to be both creative and flexible. In some cases intensive intervention will be required.

Literacy and indigenous Australian students

Indigenous Australian students comprise one of the most disadvantaged groups in our school systems. They are also most likely to be underachieving in literacy (Masters & Forster, 1997). In a comparison of performance in reading comprehension among junior secondary students between 1975 to 1995, Aboriginal students and Torres Strait Islander students made no gains when compared with the other groups involved in the study (Marks & Ainley, 1997). The authors of this report have suggested, however, that socioeconomic and other differences contribute to poor performance. Thus a number of interacting factors influence the literacy achievement of indigenous Australian students, the most important of which is poverty. The incidence of health conditions among these students is another salient factor contributing to poor literacy achievement. Middle ear disease is a particular problem and leads to hearing disabilities that affect students' abilities to hear and perceive speech.

Many students from Aboriginal and Torres Strait Islander communities do not have English as their first language and, therefore, do not have the English language experiences on which they can draw for English literacy activities in schools. As a consequence, some communities have developed bilingual programs and others have introduced literacy programs in the language of the community. Some researchers and educators have developed approaches closely aligned with recent literacy and learning models. For example, Rose, Gray, and Cowey (1999) developed the Scaffolding

Literacy Approach that uses an integrated literacy development sequence. It begins with an orientation to books involving the elements of the Four Resources Model and includes discussions using preformulation (drawing students' attention to aspects of text), focus questions, and reformulations (accepting students' responses and expanding on them). Students then undertake independent reading before moving to a sequence for writing. The approach has been used with indigenous students in central Australia and is one of the best-recognised endeavours to assist indigenous students in Australia.

A number of literacy achievement initiatives was documented in the Commonwealth government's *Indigenous Education Strategic Initiatives Program* (Commonwealth Department of Education, Training and Youth Affairs, 2000). This report argued for the development of culturally appropriate materials for indigenous students and for literacy skills across contexts. With respect to the first-mentioned aim the report stated:

> It has seemed particularly important that Aboriginal students have culturally relevant learning materials that affirm their identity, respect their past and verify the lineage of their people. (Commonwealth Department of Education, Training and Youth Affairs, 2000, p. 54)

With regard to the second aim, the report called for:

> A curriculum which starts from what the students bring to the classroom, allows students to negotiate learning plans and outcomes, deliberately scaffolds literacy learning, monitors student progress, makes explicit the words of the dominant cultures, and celebrates and affirms the individual cultures the students bring to the classroom. Teaching methodology which includes sharing and negotiation, that makes literacies (Indigenous, Standard Australian English) explicit and that makes links across cultures. (Commonwealth Department of Education, Training and Youth Affairs, 2000, p. 62)

Literacy for culturally and linguistically diverse students

Our classrooms are also heterogeneous sites in terms of culture and linguistic backgrounds. Although some preschool children from non-English speaking backgrounds who come to Australia as migrants enter school and develop English literacy along with their peers, many other (often older) students on arrival in the Australian school system are likely to be fluent speakers and to be developing literacy in their mother tongue. According to Hammond (1999), when these older students start school they make substantial progress in English language but require special support (rather than remediation) for a number of years. However, Hammond reported that that when these students are assessed on statewide tests designed for students whose mother tongue is English and their achievement is reported against national benchmarks their

These students are developing their critical thinking skills in a special literacy setting.

performance is often perceived as poor. She argued, however, that " . . . it would be inaccurate to suggest that these students are 'failing' in literacy development. It would also be inaccurate to portray the needs of such students as 'problems'" (p. 127).

The increasing cultural and linguistic diversity of students in Australia's schools means that teachers must acknowledge and use the linguistic and cultural knowledge that students bring with them to school. Teachers must provide experiences and materials that reflect the cultural and linguistic skills and backgrounds of their students. In the same way as it is important for indigenous Australian students, students from migrant backgrounds need teachers to supply activities and materials that help students to understand the importance of their backgrounds, and that lead them to an awareness that their backgrounds are valued. In this way too, the classroom materials connect with students' lives.

We also know that literacy is used by people for particular purposes. Teachers should, therefore, develop students' literacy competencies such that these competencies allow students to recognise positions or perspectives being taken by the creators of materials. Moreover, these literacy competencies can allow students to see how these materials are used to position the creators of them. In acquiring analytical skills as part of their literacy learning, students are also being shown how such positions can be accepted or resisted.

It is important for educators to realise that it is insufficient to have books of Aboriginal myths, legends, and characters, or multicultural videos, in the classroom. This is simply placing instructional media that refer to other cultures alongside those from a main Eurocentric culture. Rather, students need to develop literacy competencies that allow them to recognise different perspectives in and around the materials with which they interact, and to understand that these perspectives are based on particular historical and social assumptions or experiences. Through analysis and evaluation these perspectives can be affirmed or challenged.

Although it is important that teachers do not stereotype students, and do not over-generalise about different linguistic and cultural backgrounds, there are some teaching strategies that might be especially helpful in literacy instruction for culturally diverse students. These include:

- making use of the reading and writing abilities that students already have (in their mother tongue) to acquire skills in English;
- providing authentic and meaningful tasks based on students' linguistic strengths and interests;
- using real-life or lifelike examples;
- creating opportunities to use multimedia;
- using demonstration and hands-on activities; and
- involving members of the students' communities as teachers and support staff.

Some persisting issues

Efficacy of instruction in literacy

The proliferation of instructional approaches in literacy, especially the use of commercial packages and kits for both first wave teaching and intervention in schools means that teachers need to be especially vigilant and careful in making their selections. Evaluations of efficacy, appropriateness, and usefulness are essential. The use of experimental analysis might be appropriate if teachers are investigating the use of a particular approach for an individual student (e.g., Eckert, Ardoin, Daisey, & Scarola, 2000).

Home–school connections

The key to success in developing literacy learners is the development of positive relationships between home and school. School staff are wise to take into account the resources and experiences that students bring with them from their homes. This can be especially important in communities in which English is not the first language, or in schools that are located in areas of poverty. Although these communities might not have school-like resources, they do have other significant resources that can be used in

school settings. It is also important for the acquisition and development of literacy that parents see themselves as partners with schools in the educational enterprise. Support can be fostered by informing parents about the purposes and applications of school-related literacies that are being learnt. In terms of intervention, many authors have stressed the importance of school staff and parents working as partners or as a team (Bhat, Rapport, & Griffin, 2000; Cairney & Munsie, 1995; Leslie & Allen, 1999). Partnerships and teamwork have been advocated for planning (especially where students have individual education plans), for developing an understanding about the approaches to teaching used in the intervention, and for examining the outcomes of intervention. It has also been suggested that teachers should assist parents so that they can support their children at home (Leslie & Allen, 1999).

Changing teacher education and professional development in literacy instruction

The implementation of literacy instruction based on research-based practices in classrooms is more likely to occur if practices that are known to be effective are adopted in teacher education and professional development. Therefore providers of inservice programs need to be aware that change in teacher practice is based on planned and realistic approaches. Following on the work of various authors (Bryant et al., 2000; Fuchs & Fuchs, 1999; Gersten, Chard & Baker, 2000), approaches that target the following are required:

- specific useable instructional practices;
- time for observation;
- feedback and reflection;
- a close fit with local curricula, standards, and students' needs;
- the use of systems to enhance teacher efficacy (e.g., professional communities, peer networks, knowledgeable peer coaching);
- discussions about classroom-based issues;
- explicit connections between reform and student outcomes; and
- programs that are intensive and ongoing.

SUMMARY

This chapter began with the premise that literacy is a part of government policy, and an important area of learning in Australian schools. Schools have many diverse students and, as our case studies of Amanda and Joseph suggested, their literacy achievement and needs are varied. However, in order to appreciate the diverse abilities and needs of students it is important to understand the concept of literacy. This chapter suggests that literacy is a situated social cultural practice that involves the strands of reading, writing,

speaking, listening and viewing. Some people refer to literacy in the plural to acknowledge the multiple ways in which people are literate. Literacies are an accepted part of the Four Resources Model (Freebody & Luke, 1990) that has been widely adopted in Australia.

The view that one holds about literacy determines, to a large extent, the prevalence of difficulties in literacy. There have been two key studies that have examined the question of prevalence in Australian schools in recent years, namely Louden et al. (2000) with regard to students with learning difficulties and van Kraayenoord et al. (2000) with regard to students with disabilities. Louden et al. found that an estimated 10–20% of students had literacy learning difficulties, whereas van Kraayenoord et al. reported that it was impossible to give accurate prevalence figures because many students with disabilities were exempted from statewide achievement tests. A study of older Australians reported by the Australian Bureau of Statistics (1999) indicated that Australian performance in literacy is similar to that of like countries, such as Canada.

Difficulties with literacy might be in one or several areas. The chapter provides a list of the most common areas in which problems might be experienced. Teachers should undertake assessments and provide instruction in these areas. It is important to note that any such list is not exhaustive and that each of the elements on the list can change as a result of interactions among the learner, teacher, text, and environment.

There are many reasons for students' literacy problems. However, central to many of the reasons for a difficulty in reading is the relationship between language abilities and reading achievement. Specifically, difficulties with phonological processing appear to be one of the main causes of problems, especially in young learners. Poor instruction and poor quality materials are other reasons that have been suggested for poor literacy achievement. These appear to be particularly salient at the upper levels of primary school and in secondary school.

The detection of such difficulties requires assessment. This is a very controversial topic in the area of literacy. In particular, there have been concerns about the appropriateness of using standardised tests to measure reading achievement, especially for students with learning difficulties and disabilities. The studies by Louden et al. and van Kraayenoord et al. showed that students in Australia are assessed using a range of measures, and that these measures are administered by a range of people. The chapter identifies many of the literacy assessment practices that can be observed in Australian classrooms. Teachers often make accommodations for students with learning difficulties and disabilities in the assessment of literacy.

If the outcome of assessment has determined that a student has problems in literacy, instructional support or intervention is required. First, an historical account is given of some of the ways in which two groups of students—those with learning difficulties and those with intellectual disabilities—have been supported in Australian classrooms. Then follows a discussion of current practices for students with learning difficulties and

students with disabilities. Attention has predominantly been given to the intervention of students in the first three years of schooling in Australia. However, increasingly, programs are being developed for older students.

One of the main thrusts of teaching students with literacy difficulties in recent years has been the use of inclusive approaches to literacy instruction. Such approaches use effective teaching techniques that cater for students' individual needs The chapter provides numerous examples of inclusive literacy teaching. In addition to the use of these approaches it is important that teachers select media and materials that meet the students' needs, and organise and manage instruction (e.g., groups, one-to-one instruction) in ways that match the purposes of learning. Attention is given in the chapter to issues such as the use of withdrawal for the intervention of students, a practice that might have negative consequences for students. The use of technology of various types is also seen as a component of inclusive teaching. Such technology appears to have many positive benefits for learners.

Individualising or differentiating literacy instruction refers to matching what is known about the students' knowledge and abilities to the curricula, instruction, and assessment in the classroom. In this part of the chapter the literacy characteristics of several groups of learners are described and the ways in which teachers can differentiate instruction is explained. The groups that are discussed are students with learning difficulties, with disabilities in vision, in hearing, with intellectual disabilities, with multiple disabilities, indigenous Australian students, and culturally and linguistically diverse students. In reviewing the literacy-related teaching characteristics of these groups it is interesting to note the commonalities among the groups, as well as the unique features of each. The chapter emphasises that teachers can assist these students to become better literacy learners through the use of a variety of teaching approaches that are adapted to meet the students' needs

Finally, the chapter raises some persisting issues. These are the efficacy of literacy instruction, home-school connections, and teacher education and professional development in literacy instruction. These issues warrant further research or new initiatives.

Suggested reading

Casteel, C. P. (2000). Creating confident and competent readers: Transactional strategies instruction. *Intervention in School and Clinic, 36*(2), 67–74.

Grainger, T. & Tod, J. (2000). *Inclusive educational practice: Literacy*. London: David Fulton Publishers.

Jones, D. (1997). *Handwriting: A fundamental skill in written language: Effective learning and teaching strategies to develop handwriting and written language skills (P–10)*. Brisbane: The State of Queensland (Education Queensland).

Department for Employment, Education and Training. (1995). *Now you're talking*. Canberra: Commonwealth of Australia: Author. (Video and booklet).

Queensland University of Technology for the Association of Independent Schools of Queensland Inc., Education Queensland and Queensland Catholic Education Commission. (2000). *Teachers @work:Supporting Years 8–10 literacy and numeracy—Professional development and teaching resource*. Canberra: Commonwealth of Australia, Department of Education, Training and Youth Affairs. (CD-Rom)

Richards, J. C. & Gipe, J. P. (2000). *Elementary literacy lessons: Cases and commentaries from the field*. Mahwah, NJ: Lawrence Erlbaum Associates, Publishers. (CD-Rom)

State of Queensland (Department of Education), Queensland Catholic Education Commission and the Association of Independent Schools of Queensland Inc. (2000). *Spelling: Improving learning outcomes*. Brisbane: Authors. (CD-Rom)

Practical activities

1. Ask your parents how you learnt to read and write. What does this tell you about the views of literacy held by them and those who taught you? Are these views consistent with how *you* think you learnt to read and write? How do these views differ from those of others and those suggested in this chapter?
2. Visit a classroom during a literacy lesson. Undertake an observation of what occurs. Focus on a particular student. Following your observation, respond to the following questions:
   - What do you think was the purpose of the lesson with respect to the development of literacy?
   - Were all the literacy strands addressed, and if so how?
   - In what ways did the student respond to the lesson?
   - Was it consistent with the purpose and do you think the purpose was achieved for this student?
   - What seemed to work well in the lesson?
   - What would you want to improve to further the student's literacy development?

   Consider your responses in light of your reading of this chapter.
3. Obtain a copy of the policy or guidelines of your education department or school on the use of accommodations in classroom assessment and/or in statewide tests.

What statements does the policy make about accommodations? What are the underlying beliefs about individual needs suggested by the policy or guidelines?

4. Speak to a family who has a child who is a confident and independent reader and writer. What do family members believe contributed to their child's success in literacy? What type of support did they provide for their child at home? In what ways did the school contribute? In what ways did other significant people contribute?

5. Gain access to the Internet. Find a website for teachers related to literacy teaching. What current issues (hot topics) appear there? Select one of these issues (e.g., explicit teaching of phonemic awareness). Create an activity for the classroom that addresses this issue.

   A suitable website for this activity might be:

   <www.educate.org.uk/teacher_zone/classroom/literacy>

References

Adams, M. J. & Bruck, M. (1993). Word recognition: The interface of educational policies and scientific research. *Reading and Writing: An Interdisciplinary Journal, 5*, 113–139.

Alley, G. & Deshler, D. (1979). *Teaching the learning disabled adolescent: Strategies and methods.* Denver: Love.

Allington, R., Guice, S., Michelson, N., Baker, K., & Li, S. (1996). Literature-based curricula in high poverty schools. In M. M.Graves, P. van den Broek & B. M. Taylor (Eds), *The first R: Every child's right to read* (pp. 73–95). Newark, NJ: International Reading Association.

Ashman, A. F., van Kraayenoord, C. E., & Elkins, J. (1995, April). *How successful are we in meeting the needs of children with learning difficulties? Data on primary school children from a longitudinal study.* Paper presented at the International Special Education Conference, Birmingham, England.

Australian Bureau of Statistics. (1999). *Education and training. Special Article—Australians' literacy skills: How do they rate internationally? (Year Book Australia, 1999).* <www.abs.gov.au/Ausstats/ABS%40.nsf>

Bhat, P., Rapport, M. J. K., & Griffin, C. C. (2000). A legal perspective on the use of specific reading methods for students with learning disabilities. *Learning Disability Quarterly, 23*, 283–297.

Blair-Laresen S. M., & Vallance, K. M. (1999). Comprehension instruction in a balanced reading classroom. In S. M. Blair-Larsen & K. A. Williams (Eds), *The balanced reading program: Helping all students achieve success* (pp. 37–52). Newark, DE: International Reading Association.

Bochner, S., Outhred, L., & Pieterse, M. (2001). A study of functional literacy skills in young adults with Down syndrome. *International Journal of Disability, Development and Education, 48*, 67–90.

Bortoli, A., Furlonger, B.E. & Rickards, F. (2000). Chapter 3A: Literacy and deafness. In C. E. van Kraayenoord, J. Elkins, C. Palmer, F. Rickards, & P. Colbert. *Literacy, numeracy and students with disabilities, Vol. 2* (pp. 175–191). Canberra: DETYA.

Bortoli, A. & Preston, G. (2000). Chapter 6A: Literacy, numeracy and students with multiple disabilities. In C. E. van Kraayenoord, J. Elkins, C. Palmer, F. Rickards, & P. Colbert. *Literacy, numeracy and students with disabilities, Vol. 2* (pp. 333–339). Canberra: DETYA.

Brown, M. R. (2000). Access, instruction, and barriers Technology issues facing students at risk. *Remedial and Special Education, 213*, 182–192.

Brownwell, M. T. & Walther-Thomas, C. (2000). An interview with Dr Michael Pressley. *Intervention in School and Clinic, 36*(2), 105–108.

Bryant, D. P., Vaughn, S., Linan-Thompson, S., Ugel, N., Hamff, A., & Hougen, M. (2000). Reading outcomes for students with and without reading disabilities in general education middle-school content area classes. *Learning Disability Quarterly, 23*, 238–252.

Byrne, B. & Fielding-Barnsley, R. (1995). Evaluation of a program to teach phonemic awareness to young children: A 2- and 3-year follow-up and a new preschool trial. *Journal of Educational Psychology, 85*, 1–5.

Cairney, T. H. & Munsie, L. (1995). Parent participation in literacy learning. *Reading Teacher, 48*, 392–403.

Catts, H. W., Fey, M. E., Zhang, X., & Tomblin, J. B. (1999). Language basis of reading and reading disabilities: Evidence from a longitudinal investigation. *Scientific Studies of Reading, 3*, 331–361.

Center, Y. & Freeman L. (1997). A trial evaluation of SWELL (Schoolwide Early Language and Literacy): A whole class early literacy program for at-risk and disadvantaged children. *International Journal of Disability, Development and Education, 44*, 21–40

Chan, L. K. S. & Dally, K. (2000). Review of literature. In W. Louden, L. K. S. Chan, J. Elkins, D. Greaves, H. House, M. Milton, S. Nichols, M. Rohl, J. Rivalland, C. van Kraayenoord, *Mapping the territory. Primary students with learning difficulties: Literacy & numeracy*, Vol. 2 (pp. 161–331). Canberra: DETYA.

Chapman, J. W., Tunmer, W. E., & Prochnow, J. E. (2001). Does success in the Reading Recovery program depend on developing proficiency in phonological skills? A longitudinal study in a whole language context. *Scientific Studies of Reading, 5*, 141–176.

Clay, M. (1993). *Reading Recovery: A guide book for teachers in training.* Portsmouth, NH: Heinnemann.

Colbert, P. & van Kraayenoord, C. E. (2000). Mapping of provision: States, systems and sectors. In C. E. van Kraayenoord, J. Elkins, C. Palmer, F. Rickards, & P. Colbert. *Literacy, numeracy and students with disabilities, Vol. 2* (pp. 3–88). Canberra: DETYA.

Commonwealth Department of Education, Training and Youth Affairs. (2000). *National Indigenous English Literacy Strategy, 2000–2004*. Canberra: Author.

Crevola, C. A. & Hill, P. W. (1998). Evaluation of a whole-school approach to prevention and intervention in early literacy. *Journal of Education for Students Placed at Risk, 3*, 133–157.

Department of Employment, Education, Training and Youth Affairs. (1998). *Literacy for all: The challenge for Australian schools*. Canberra, ACT: Author.

Deschenes, C., Ebeling, D., & Sprague, J. (1999). *Adapting curriculum and instruction in inclusive classrooms.* New York: National Professional Resources Inc.

Durrant, C. & Green, B. (2000). Literacy and the new technologies in school education: Meeting the l(IT)eracy challenge? *The Australian Journal of Language and Literacy, 23*, 89–109.

Dymock, S. & Nicholson, T. (1999). *Reading comprehension: What is it? Why do you teach it?*. Wellington, New Zealand: New Zealand Council for Educational Research.

Eckert, T. L., Ardoin, S. P., Daisey, D. M., & Scarola, M. D. (2000). Empirically evaluating the effectiveness of reading interventions: The use of brief experimental analysis and single case designs. *Psychology in the Schools, 37*(5), 463–473.

Education Department of Western Australia. (1994). *First Steps reading resource book*. Melbourne: Longman.

Education Queensland. (1991). *Support-a-Reader Program* (video and booklets). Brisbane: Author.

Education Queensland. (1996). *Support-a-Writer Program* (video and booklets). Brisbane: Author.

Einhorn, K. (1999). Handwriting success for all. *Instructor, 110*, 35–39.

Elbaum, B., Vaughn, S., Tejero-Hughes, M., & Watson-Moody, S. (2000). How effective are one-to-one tutoring programs in reading for elementary students at risk for reading failure? A meta-analysis of the intervention research. *Journal of Educational Psychology, 92*, 605–619.

Englert, C. S. (1992). Writing instruction from a socio-cultural perspective: A holistic dialogic and social enterprise of writing. *Journal of Learning Disabilities, 25*, 153–172.

Englert, C. S. & Raphael, T. E. (1988). Constructing well-formed prose: Process, structure, and metacognitive knowledge. *Exceptional Children, 54*, 513–520.

Englert, C. S., Raphael, T., & Mariage, T. V. (1994). Developing a school based discourse for literacy learning: A principled search for understanding. *Learning Disability Quarterly, 17*, 2–32.

Erickson, K. A. & Koppenhaver, D. A. (1995). Developing a literacy program for children with severe disabilities. *The Reading Teacher, 48*, 676–684.

Erickson, K. A. & Koppenhaver, D. A. (1998). Using the "Write Talknology" with Patrik. *Teaching Exceptional Children, 31*(1), 58–64.

Fields, B. A. (1999). The impact of class heterogeneity on students with learning disabilities. *Australian Journal of Learning Disabilities, 4*, 11–16.

Fletcher-Flinn, C. M. White, C., & Nicholson, T. (1998). Does Reading Recovery improve phonological skills? *Queensland Journal of Educational Research, 14*, 4–28.

Foorman, B. R. (1994). The relevance of a connectionist model of reading for "the great debate". *Educational Psychology Review, 6*, 25–45.

Foorman, B. R., Francis, D. J., Fletcher, J. M., Schatschneider, C., & Mehta, P. (1998). The role of instruction in learning to read: Preventing reading failure in at-risk children. *Journal of Educational Psychology, 90*, 37–55.

Freebody, P. & Luke, A. (1990). Literacies programs: Debates and demands in cultural context. *Prospect, 5*, 7–15.

Fuchs, D. & Fuchs, L. S. (1999). Researchers and teachers working together to adapt instruction for diverse learners. *Learning Disabilities Research and Practice, 13*, 126–137.

Gadsen, V. L. (2000). Intergenerational literacy within families. In M. L. Kamil, P. B. Mosenthal, P. D. Pearson, & R. Barr, (Eds), *Handbook of reading research III* (pp. 871–888). Mahwah, NJ: Lawrence Erlbaum Associates, Inc., Publishers.

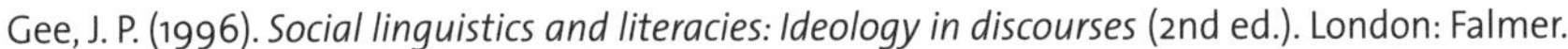

Gee, J. P. (1996). *Social linguistics and literacies: Ideology in discourses* (2nd ed.). London: Falmer.

Gersten, R., Chard, D., & Baker, S. (2000). Factors enhancing sustained use of research-based instructional practices. *Journal of Learning Disabilities, 33*(5), 445–457.

Graham, S. & Harris K. R. (1989). Improving learning disabled students' skills at composing essays: Self-instructional training. *Exceptional Children 56*, 201–214.

Graham S. & Harris, K. R. (1993). Teaching writing strategies to students with learning disabilities: Issues and recommendations. In L. J. Meltzer (Ed.), *Strategy assessment and instruction for students with learning disabilities: From theory to practices* (pp. 271–292). Austin, TX: Pro-Ed.

Graham S. & Harris, K. R. (1994). The role and development of self-regulation in the writing process. In D. H. Schunk & B. J. Zimmerman (Eds), *Self-regulation of learning and performance: Issues and educational applications* (pp. 203–228). Hillsdale, NJ: Lawrence Erlbaum.

Green, B. (1999). The New Literacy challenge? *Literacy Learning: Secondary Thoughts, 7*, 36–46.

Greene, J. F. (1998). Another chance. *American Educator, 22*, 74–79.

Grigorenko, E. L. (2001). Developmental dyslexia: An update on genes, brains, and environments. *Journal of Psychology and Psychiatry, 42*, 91–125.

Hall, T. E., Hughes, C. H. & Filbert, M. (2000). Computer assisted instruction in reading for students with learning disabilities: A research synthesis. *Education and Treatment of Children, 23*, 173–193.

Hammond, J. (1999). Literacy crisis and ESL education. *The Australian Journal of Language and Literacy, 22*, 120–134.

Hart, S. (1996). *Differentiation and the secondary curriculum: Debates and dilemmas.* London: Routledge.

Hiebert, E. (1994). Reading Recovery in the United States: What difference does it make to an age cohort? *Educational Researcher, 2*, 15–25.

Hill, P. W. (1997, October). The literacy challenge in Australian primary schools. Paper presented at the APPA/ACPPA National Conference, Sydney.

Hill, P. & Crevola, C. (1998). Characteristics of an effective literacy strategy. *Unicorn, 24*, 74–85.

Iversen, S. & Tunmer, W. (1993) Phonological processing skills and the Reading Recovery program. *Journal of Educational Psychology, 85*, 112–126.

Jones, D. (1997). *Handwriting: A fundamental skill in written language: Effective learning and teaching strategies to develop handwriting and written language skills (P–10).* Brisbane: The State of Queensland (Education Queensland).

Juel, C. (1988). Learning to read and write: A longitudinal study of 54 children from first through fourth grades. *Journal of Educational Psychology, 80*, 437–447.

Keel, M. C., Dangel, H. L., & Owens, S. H. (1999). Selecting instructional interventions for students with mild disabilities in inclusive classrooms. *Focus on Exceptional Children, 31*(8), 1–16.

Kliewer, C. & Landis, D. (1999). Individualising literacy instruction for young children with moderate to severe disabilities. *Exceptional Children, 66*, 85–100.

Lahm, E. A. (1996). Software that engages young children with disabilities: A study of design features. *Focus of Autism and Other Developmental Disabilities, 11*, 115–124.

Lankshear, C. (1997). *Changing literacies*. Buckingham and Philadelphia: Open University Press.

Lebzelter, S. & Nowacek, E. J. (1999). Reading strategies for secondary students with mild disabilities. *Intervention in School and Clinic, 34*, 212.

Leslie, L. & Allen, L. (1999). Factors that predict success in an early literacy intervention project. *Reading Research Quarterly, 34*, 404–424.

Louden, W. (2000). Mapping the territory: In W. Louden, L. K. S. Chan, J. Elkins, D. Greaves, H. House, M. Milton, S. Nichols, M. Rohl, J. Rivalland, C. van Kraayenoord (Eds) *Mapping the territory—Primary students with learning difficulties: Literacy and numeracy*, Vol. 1 (pp. 1–27). Canberra: DETYA.

Louden, W., Chan, L. K. S., Elkins, J., Greaves, D., House, H., Milton, M., Nichols, S., Rohl, M., Rivalland, J., & van Kraayenoord, C. (2000). *Mapping the territory—Primary students with learning difficulties: Literacy and numeracy* (Vols. 1–3). Canberra: Commonwealth of Australia, Department of Education, Training and Youth Affairs. <www.gu.edu.au/school/cls/cler>

Luke, A. & Freebody, P. (1997). Shaping the social practices of reading. In S. Muspratt, A. Luke & P. Freebody (Eds) *Constructing critical literacies: Teaching and learning textual practice* (pp. 185–226). Cresskill, NJ: Hampton Press Inc.

Luke, A. & Freebody, P. (1999). A map of possible practices: Further notes on the Four Resources Model. *Practically Primary, 4*(2) pp. 5–8.

Luke, A. & Freebody, P. (2000). *Literate futures: Report of the literacy review for Queensland state schools*. Brisbane: The State of Queensland (Department of Education). <http://education.qld.gov.au/tal/kla/lri/html/report.html>

MacArthur, C. A., Feretti, R. P., Okolo, C. M. & Cavalier, A. R. (2001). Technology applications for students with literacy problems: A review. *The Elementary School Journal, 101*, 273–301.

Maglen, F. (1999). Tackling literacy problems with adolescents and young people. *Australian Journal of Learning Disabilities, 4*, 17–22.

Marks, G. N. & Ainley, J. (1997). *Reading comprehension and numeracy among junior secondary students in Australia*. Melbourne: Australian Council for Educational Research.

Martin, K. F. & Manno, C. (1995). Use of a check-off system to improve middle school students' story compositions. *Journal of Learning Disabilities, 28*, 139–149.

Masters, G. N. & Forster, M. (1997). *Mapping literacy achievement: Results of the 1996 National School English Literacy Survey*. Canberra: Department of Education, Training and Youth Affairs.

Mastropieri, M. M. & Scruggs, T. T. (1997). Best practices in promoting comprehension in students with learning disabilities 1976–1996. *Remedial and Special Education, 18*, 197–213.

McKenzie, S. (2000). Chapter 5A: Literacy and students with physical disabilities. In C. E. van Kraayenoord, J. Elkins, C. Palmer, F. Rickards, & P. Colbert. *Literacy, numeracy and students with disabilities, Vol. 2* (pp. 293–308). Canberra: DETYA.

Mifsud, S., Evans, D., & Dowson, M. (1999). A strategic approach to teaching reading to students with diverse education needs *Special Education Perspectives, 8*, 32–43.

Ministerial Advisory Committee Students with Disabilities, South Australia. (1998). *Action research projects: Children and students with disabilities using technology*. Adelaide, SA: Author.

Ministerial Council on Education, Employment Training and Youth Affairs. (1999). *The Adelaide declaration*. Carlton South, VIC: Author.

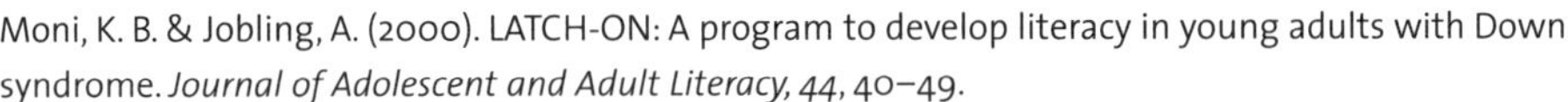

Moni, K. B. & Jobling, A. (2000). LATCH-ON: A program to develop literacy in young adults with Down syndrome. *Journal of Adolescent and Adult Literacy, 44*, 40–49.

Moretta, T. & Ambrosini, M. (2000). *Practical approaches to teaching reading and writing in middle schools.* Newark, D.E: International Reading Association.

Mossenson, L., Hill, P. & Masters, G. (1987). *Tests of Reading Comprehension* (TORCH). Hawthorn, VIC: Australian Council for Educational Research Ltd.

Munro, J. (1999). Epilogue: A gear shift in literacy support. *Australian Journal of Learning Disabilities, 4*, 39.

Neale, M. D. (1988). *Neale Analysis of Reading Ability-Revised*. Hawthorn, VIC: Australian Council for Educational Research Ltd.

Ogle, D. (1986). K-W-L: A teaching model that develops active reading from expository text. *The Reading Teacher, 39*, 771–777.

Palincsar, A. S. (1986). Metacognitive strategy instruction. *Exceptional Children, 53*, 118–124.

Palmer, C. (2000). Chapter 4: Disabilities in vision. In C. E. van Kraayenoord, J. Elkins, C. Palmer, F. Rickards, & P. Colbert (Eds) *Literacy, numeracy and students with disabilities, Vol. 1* (pp. 47–66). Canberra: DETYA.

Pressley, M. & Rankin, J. (1994). More about whole language methods of reading instruction for students at risk for early reading failure. *Learning Disabilities Research and Practice, 9*, 157–168.

Rankin-Erickson, J. L. & Pressley, M. (2000). A survey of instructional practices of special education teachers nominated as effective teachers of literacy. *Learning Disabilities Research and Practice, 15*, 206–225.

Reason, R. (1998). Effective academic interventions in the United Kingdom: Does the "specific" in specific learning difficulties (disabilities) now make a difference to the way we teach? *School Psychology Review, 27*, 57–65.

Rohl, M. (2000). Patterns of support: What do schools do to support children with difficulties in learning literacy. In W. Louden, L. K. S. Chan, J. Elkins, D. Greaves, H. House, M. Milton, S. Nichols, M. Rohl, J. Rivalland, C. van Kraayenoor (Eds) *Mapping the territory. Primary students with learning difficulties: Literacy and numeracy*, Vol. 1 (pp. 67–107). Canberra: DETYA.

Rose, D., Gray, B.& Cowey, W. (1999). Scaffolding reading and writing for indigenous children in school. In P. Wignell (Ed.), *Double power: English literacy and indigenous education* (pp. 23–60). Melbourne: Language Australia.

Santa, C. M. (1988). *Content reading including study systems*. Dubuque, IA: Kendall Hunt.

Schumm, J. S., Moody, S. W., and Vaughn, S. (2000). Grouping for reading instruction: Does one size fit all? *Journal of Learning Disabilities, 33*, 477–488.

Shanahan, T. & Barr, R. (1995). Reading Recovery: An independent evaluation of the effects of an early instructional intervention for at-risk learners. *Reading Research Quarterly, 30*, 958–996.

Shankweiler, D., Lundquist, E., Katz, L., Stuebing, K. K., Fletcher, J. M., Brady, S., Fowler, A., Dreyer, L. G., Marchione, K. E., Shaywitz, S. E., & Shaywitz, B. A. (1999). Comprehension and decoding: Patterns of association in children with reading difficulties. *Scientific Studies of Reading, 31*, 69–94.

Slavin, R. E. & Fashola, R. S. (1998). *Show me the evidence! Proven and promising programs for America's school.* Thousand Oaks, CA: Corwin.

Slavin, R. E., Madden, N. A., Karweit, N. L., Dolan, L. J., & Wasik, B. A. (1992). *Success for All: A relentless approach to prevention and early intervention in elementary schools* (Research Monograph). Arlington, VA: Educational Research Service. (ERIC Document Reproduction Service No. ED373 863)

Slavin, R. E., Karweit, N. L., Wasik, B. A., Madden, N. A., & Dolan, L. J. (1994). Success for All: A comprehensive approach to prevention and early intervention. In R. E. Slavin, N. L. Karweit, & B. A. Wasik (Eds), *Preventing early school failure* (pp. 175–205). Boston: Allyn and Bacon.

Smith, S., Carroll, A., & Elkins, J. (2000). Outreach and support for Australian university students with learning disabilities. *Australian Journal of Learning Disabilities, 5*, 23–31.

Snow, C., Burns, M. S., & Griffin, P. (Eds). (1998). *Preventing reading difficulties in young children.* Washington, DC: National Academy Press.

Stacey, S. & Wheldall, K. (1999). Essential constituents of effective reading instruction for low progress readers. *Special Education Perspectives, 8*, 45–58.

Stanovich, K. E. (1986). Matthew effects in reading: Some consequences of individual differences in the acquisition of literacy. *Reading Research Quarterly, 19*, 278–303.

Sturm, J. & Koppenhaver, D. A. (2000). Supporting writing developments in adolescents with developmental disabilities. *Topics in Language Disorders, 20*, 73–91.

Swanson, H. L. (1999). Reading research for students with LD: A meta-analysis of intervention outcomes. *Journal of Learning Disabilities, 32*, 504–532.

Templeton, S. & Morris, D. (2000). Spelling. In M. L. Kamil, P. B. Mosenthal, P. D. Pearson, & R. Barr, (Eds), *Handbook of reading research, III* (pp. 525–544). Mahwah, NJ: Lawrence Erlbaum Associates, Inc., Publishers.

The New London Group. (1996). A pedagogy of multi-literacies: Designing social futures. *Harvard Education Review, 66*, 60–92.

Tomlinson, C. A. (1996). *Differentiating instruction for mixed-ability classrooms.* Alexandria, VA: Association for Supervision and Curriculum.

Torgesen, J. K. (2000). Individual differences in response to early interventions in reading: The lingering problem of treatment resisters. *Learning Disabilities Research and Practice, 15*(1), 55–64.

Torgesen, J. K., Alexander, A. W., Wagner, R. K., Rashotte, C. A., Voeller, K. K. S. & Conway, T. (2001). Intensive remedial instruction for children with severe reading disabilities: Immediate and long-term outcomes from two instructional approaches. *Journal of Learning Disabilities, 341*, 33–58,78.

Torgesen, J. K. & Burgess, S. R. (1998). Consistency of reading-related phonological processes throughout early childhood: Evidence from longitudinal–correlational and instructional studies. In J. Metsa & L. Ehri (Eds), *Word recognition in beginning reading* (pp. 161–188). Hillsdale, NJ: Lawrence Erlbaum.

Torgesen, J. K., Wagner, R. K., & Rashotte, C. A. (1997). Prevention and remediation of severe reading disabilities: Keeping the end in mind. *Scientific Studies of Reading, 1*, 217–234.

Tunmer, W. & Chapman, J. (2001). The case for a Reading Recovery review. *New Zealand Educational Review, March 9*, 8.

van Kraayenoord, C. E. (2000). Chapter 6: Intellectual Disabilities. In C. E. van Kraayenoord, J. Elkins, C. Palmer, F. Rickards, & P. Colbert (Eds). *Literacy, numeracy and students with disabilities, Vol. 1* (pp. 77–98). Canberra: DETYA.

van Kraayenoord, C. E. & Farrell, M. E. (1998). *Responding to students with severe and persistent literacy difficulties in secondary schools*. Brisbane: Fred and Eleanor Schonell Special Education Research Centre, The University of Queensland. <http://education.qld.gov.au> and follow prompt to support articles.

van Kraayenoord, C., Elkins, J., Palmer, C., Rickards, F. & Colbert, P. (2000). *Literacy, numeracy and students with disabilities* (Vols. 1–4). Canberra. Commonwealth of Australia, Department of Education, Training and Youth Affairs. <www.gu.edu.au/school/cls/cler>

van Kraayenoord, C. E., Moni, K. B., Jobling, A., & Ziebarth, K. (in press). Broadening approaches to literacy education for young adults with Down syndrome. In M. Cuskelly , A. Jobling & S. Buckley (Eds), *Down syndrome across the life span* (pp. 81–92). London Whurr Publications.

Westwood, P. (1997). *Commonsense methods for children with special needs* (3rd ed.). London: Routledge.

Williams, J. P., Brown, L. G., Silverstein, A. K., & de Cani, J. S. (1994). An instructional program in comprehension of narrative themes for adolescents with learning disabilities. *Learning Disability Quarterly, 17*, 205–221.

Wise, B. W., Olson, R. K., Ring, J., & Johnson, M. (1998). Interactive computer support for improving phonological skills. In J. L. Metsala & L. C. Ehri (Eds), *Word recognition in beginning literacy* (pp. 189–208). Mahwah, NJ: Erlbaum.

Wong, B. Y. L. (1997). Research on genre-specific strategies for enhancing writing in adolescents with learning disabilities. *Learning Disability Quarterly, 20*, 140–159.

Wong, B. Y. L. (2001). Commentary: Pointers for literacy instruction from educational technology and research on writing instruction. *The Elementary School Journal, 101*, 359–369.

Wood, J. K. (1998/1999). Principles and recommendations for early childhood assessments. *Childhood Education, 75*, 119.

10

Numeracy

Case studies

Mary

Mary is in Year 4 and managing most of the topics that her teacher introduces, but she finds arithmetic very difficult. She makes many simple or careless errors, and she has developed some dislike of mathematics lessons. Indeed, she has begun to think of herself as a hopeless student in mathematics, especially when she needs to ask her teacher for help or when she is trying to complete her homework assignments.

Mary's parents and teacher have discussed whether she should use a calculator and she has started doing so to check her homework. As she is an average reader, she does not find the reading of word problems difficult. However, she often finds it difficult to work out the relevant mathematical aspects so she can write down number sentences and then proceed to obtain a solution.

Mary wishes that she did not have to study mathematics at school. She does not enjoy it or find the work relevant to her.

"After all," she complains, "when I go to the supermarket, the machine does the adding and calculating of the change."

Even doing maths games on a computer becomes boring after a while. Mary might not receive special help with mathematics since support teachers give priority to students who have literacy difficulties. Her parents and teacher wonder what mathematical tasks she will need if she is to live effectively after she finishes her schooling. What will numeracy be for Mary in the coming decades of this century?

Aaron

Aaron is 11 years old and enrolled in a special class at his local primary school. He participates in many activities with other students of his age, apart from language, literacy and mathematics. He is part of a group of ten students who are working well below age expectancy. Aaron is working at about Year 3 level.

Aaron can do some mental arithmetic, although his progress is slow. When he uses concrete objects, such as Multibase Arithmetic Blocks, Aaron can work out many computations, although this method is slow and sometimes laborious. For example, to compute 7 x 6, he needs to form an array of seven sets of six blocks and then count them. Recently he has learnt to rearrange them as sets of ten with some left over (i.e., 4 tens and 2 units).

Another activity that Aaron finds helpful is to use the centimetre marks on his ruler to serve as a number line. Although limited to combinations less than 30, this method can be extended using a measuring tape, although it soon becomes cumbersome.

The mathematics incorporated in Aaron's IEP is numeracy and includes measurement of length, area and weight, telling the time and some extensions, such as the time of arrival after a trip, and estimation. His parents and teacher hope that, on leaving school, he will be able to manage everyday situations requiring mathematical knowledge and be able to manage the mathematical demands of a future job.

Not only does Aaron find concrete objects helpful, but also he is better able to work out solutions if he tackles tasks in context. His teacher uses real life activities as a framework by taking the class to situations such as shopping, or by using classroom simulations, such as setting up a small shop.

Although Aaron's progress in mental arithmetic has been slow, his teacher is giving him practice at memorising basic addition and multiplication facts using computer programs. The first target was the doubles 2 + 2, 4 + 4, and so on, with the relationship to counting by twos, and multiplying by 2 being used to strengthen these bonds.

What you will learn in this chapter

In this chapter you will learn:

- the difference between mathematics and numeracy;
- that numeracy is a crucial aspect of curriculum for students of all kinds;
- the prevalence of difficulties in numeracy;
- how to assess numeracy and diagnose the nature of students' difficulties;
- the characteristics of numeracy learning in students with disabilities and learning difficulties; and
- ways of helping students acquire useful mathematical skills and knowledge.

In recent years the Australian federal government has paid increasing attention to numeracy as well as to literacy since these have been recognised as important goals of Australian education for all students, irrespective of ability. In an excellent guide to numeracy for students with learning difficulties, Westwood (2000, p. vii) reinforced the point that numeracy means something more than elementary arithmetic.

It also embraces the notion of being able to communicate effectively with others through the basic language of mathematics, to interpret everyday quantitative information, and to have a repertoire of strategies and "number sense" to deal with problems that may arise.

It is also clear that what is taught in mathematics and how it is taught has changed over past decades. Classrooms today are likely to reflect constructivist approaches to learning. This means that there is a conceptual rather than a procedural emphasis, with students being encouraged to invent strategies and find innovative solutions to problems. For some students, difficulties in learning occur in these constructivist classrooms if due attention is not paid to ensuring that students build a sound foundation of basic mathematical skills such as the four processes (+, −, ×, /) and

place value. With the present constructivist emphasis, "there is a real danger that the educational pendulum will swing so far in the opposite direction that teachers will feel that they must abandon all forms of direct teaching" (Westwood, 2000, p. vii).

To understand students with difficulties in learning numeracy, it can be helpful to appreciate factors that might be especially important in the new millennium. One of these is certainly the rise of constructivist approaches (Dengate,1998). Constructivism involves:

- posing problems and open tasks, and encouraging reflection involves high-level language and logical thinking;
- staging situations that evoke, sustain, and modify elegant mathematical thinking to replace the routine practice questions that fill mathematics textbooks (and which are inadequate);
- emphasing independent but interactive mathematical activity that enables students to choose to work together at certain times;
- adopting a facilitative role that empowers teachers to ask key questions to guide students as they try to solve problems; and
- promoting discussions in the classroom about mathematical problems.

Numeracy has become a term for those aspects of mathematics that are related to functioning in society. It is often paired with literacy and recent government initiatives in Australia have emphasised this pairing (e.g., Louden et al., 2000; van Kraayenoord et al., 2000). However, in this book we have kept them separate, as advocated in the report *Numeracy = everyone's business* (Australian Association of Mathematics Teachers, 1997). Numeracy encompasses more than number sense and involves data, spatial and formula sense. It is also cross-curricular and can be found in the sciences, geography, art, and industrial arts. Even in English, there are opportunities to teach numeracy, as Baker and Baker (1991) pointed out in their entertaining book *Raps & rhymes & maths*. Rowbotham and van Kraayenoord (2000) noted that, although numeracy was proposed as a parallel term to literacy, it now comprises a facility with mathematics for the purposes of daily living. Thus, it varies with cultural contexts and among individuals.

The requirements to be numerate increase with age. Thus, for a student starting school, the main attribute of numeracy might be a positive attitude to number and space, whereas for a child in the upper primary school, numeracy includes interpreting data, using time, representing space, using money, mental computation, and a range of mathematical skills and knowledge. By the end of the compulsory school years, young adults should be able to use their numeracy out of school in a wide range of contexts, including organising their leisure and engaging in part-time work. With this goal in mind, however, Ellerton, Clarkson, and Clements (in press) argued that there is some uncertainty among mathematics educators as to just what mathematical knowledge is required for citizenship in Australia.

A conference organised by the Australian Association of Mathematics Teachers (1997) took thinking about numeracy in Australia to new levels of interest with its theme that it was everyone's business. By introducing sociocultural theory based on the ideas of Vygotsky, Renshaw (1996) helped to bring a new theoretical framework—mathematics in everyday contexts—to thinking about numeracy. In the United Kingdom there has been increased emphasis on numeracy recently through the National Numeracy Strategy as part of the Labor government's education policy (Brown et al., 2000). It emphasised mental calculation, including estimation, daily mental arithmetic, interactive teaching and review, detailed curriculum guidance, and a systematic training program for teachers and aides. The rhetoric surrounding this policy spoke of future workforce needs, but promoted old-fashioned methods that work. There are signs of the same logic in Australia, although thus far numeracy has been neglected in comparison to literacy.

Affective aspects

There is little doubt that, for many children, mathematics is the subject they least like. Apart from diminished achievement, this aversion to things mathematical also produces anxiety while mathematics remains a required part of the curriculum in primary and lower secondary school. It is also true that among primary school teachers a genuine liking for mathematics and a command of the subject matter are less frequently found than is true for literacy. So, students are less likely to receive skilled support from the teacher, while support staff are also more likely to prefer to help students with literacy than numeracy. Although current approaches to teaching mathematics might make the subject more exciting for those who can handle the ideas presented, they might not be effective for those who have despaired at ever being able to get the right answer. Successful teaching of students who have failed in mathematics relies as much on building self-confidence as on the teaching techniques used.

The role of anxiety is somewhat contradictory. On the one hand, some anxiety can be beneficial within a context that, on the whole, is supportive. Students need to guess and try various options. This is particularly true of problem-solving situations. But because mathematics provokes anxiety in most students, teachers should treat students gently if they venture an answer that is wrong. It is also very helpful if teachers occasionally use the Socratic method in which they avoid telling students they are wrong and, instead, ask another question that will lead them to recognise that their earlier attempts were wrong and where their reasoning was faulty.

There are several features of schools that contribute to failure and lack of motivation in secondary school students. According to Larcombe (1985, p. 13), these include:

- choice of work that does not match the mathematical level of the pupil;
- teaching style that does not match the individual needs of the pupil;
- incorrect assumptions about the strengths and weaknesses of individual pupils;
- choice of current and subsequent pieces of work that does not relate to past success or failure;
- teaching materials that are not suited to the needs of the pupil; and
- school assessments that are in conflict with a teaching model based upon meeting needs of pupils.

Prevalence

American researchers suggest that about 6% of students experience marked difficulties in learning mathematics (Rourke & Conway, 1997). Although earlier Australian prevalence data based on teacher judgments appear to be have been similar (Andrews et al., 1979), recent Australian data collected by Rohl, Milton, and Brady (2000) have suggested a much higher prevalence. Unfortunately, many schools do not systematically assess children for numeracy so current Australian data are very shaky estimates.

It seems that many students experience difficulties in numeracy for the same reasons that they do in literacy. Thus, a substantial proportion of students with literacy difficulties also have problems in numeracy, particularly in computation, word problems, mathematical language, and reasoning.

A recent study of numeracy in Australian secondary schools by Marks and Ainley (1997) revealed that overall performance of 14 year olds had improved slightly between 1975 and 1995. However, "performance declined marginally on computational items but improved on conceptual items" (p. iii). Overall it was judged that 15 to 20% of junior secondary students had not attained a mastery level on the tests. This is a disquieting result as no school or education system appears to offer support to such a high percentage of students. Instead, some secondary schools stream students into two or three levels according to achievement, thereby denying the low achievers access to a rich curriculum. However, such streaming might improve students' chances of acquiring the numeracy they will need as citizens.

Most of the research discussed in this chapter has been conducted in relation to the school subject *mathematics* rather than to *numeracy*. This reflects the fact that most (although not all) aspects of numeracy are to be found in mathematics curricula and that research on numeracy itself is very young.

Features of students with numeracy difficulties

Computation requires speed and accuracy in basic fact retrieval since these enable cognitive resources to be allocated to more complex tasks. Geary (1993) described how students who have problems with numeracy make slow progress in replacing physical counting strategies (using fingers or objects to count) with verbal counting and, in turn, with accurate and quick retrieval from memory. Later, Cumming and Elkins (1996) emphasised that students can be at different levels of proficiency for different basic facts. For example, a student might be able to retrieve doubles up to 9 plus 9 from memory, add one by verbal counting on, and yet need to manipulate blocks for 8 plus 4. Although students might understand mathematics problems such as adding two 2-digit numbers, they lose confidence if they obtain incorrect solutions because of a weakness in underlying skills such as mental addition.

Although occasional errors can be due to inattention, most are systematic and offer teachers insight into the student's problems (Cumming & Elkins, 1994). It is often difficult to reconstruct students' errors unless the teacher can ask a student how he or she obtained an answer. Teachers who make time to interview those students whose performance on class tests is weak can obtain useful diagnostic information. Nevertheless, teachers must be cautious in interpreting errors and it is valuable to present students with further examples to check that there is a consistent pattern of errors for each type of problem.

Word problems are sometimes difficult because students are unfamiliar with the situation described. It can be helpful to involve students in real situations requiring numeracy, such as purchasing goods or calculating quantities needed for some practical task. Students can be shown how to express such problems in words. This can help them to understand the sorts of word problems they find in textbooks although, if they have underlying reading problems, they might require complementary reading support. A common error is incorrect choice of mathematical operation. It is difficult to determine the cause of this type of error and it can be valuable to give students practice in translating word problems into mathematical sentences. It is also useful to incorporate redundant information into word problems and to teach students how to select only the relevant information. This skill is especially important if the teacher is focusing on numeracy since, in authentic situations, there is usually much redundant data. Students might find that diagrams assist in representing real world situations, and in developing skills of paraphrasing, visualising, and hypothesising (Montague & Applegate, 1993a, 1993b).

Multimedia tools can also be used to help students think through a complex problem before expressing it in words or calculating component parts. For example, Bruer (1993) described a tool at Vanderbilt University. After viewing a video that provides contextual information, students were set a challenge such as: Can the boat skipper

return to the dock before nightfall? Students learn how to identify constraints such as fuel left, time before sunset and maximum boat speed. Multimedia teaching aids like these—or the use of actual situations—help students to write their own word problems. Because they have a deeper understanding, they are more likely to recognise which operation is needed to compute the solution.

Another aspect of word problems has been highlighted by Carey, Fennema, Carpenter and Franke (1995) who showed that there were different ways of tackling the same problem according to how it was worded. For example, "You have some marbles and Tom gives you 8 more. Now you have 12 marbles. How many did you have to start with?" is more difficult than "You have 12 beads and give 4 to Tom. How many do you have left?"

Some of the difficulty experienced with word problems can be due to students having insufficient real world knowledge of mathematical situations. A valuable insight into how school mathematics differs from numeracy can be seen in the work of Nunes, Schleimann, and Carraher (1993) with Brazilian children who sell goods in the street. They observed that, working aloud, such children were able to compute costs of several items and the change to be given yet, in school mathematics, their performance was substantially less impressive. One feature was their failure to refer to numbers in an abstract way. Instead, they used tens and hundreds, relying on the concrete model provided by the currency to exchange quantities. Thus, mathematics used by these Brazilian children is part of social practice, which is another way of defining numeracy. It is not difficult for teachers to create worthwhile mathematical situations in the classroom or school. By participating in such activities students can gain skills and confidence in recognising the mathematical aspects of situations.

Young children can find the language of mathematics to be a stumbling block, as teachers might assume that concepts such as more, less, more than, less than, first, next, or last are familiar to students. Later, students can have trouble in remembering the meaning of specifically mathematical words or symbols. It is useful to teach mathematical symbol-reading explicitly. Also, in English the number words between 11 and 19 represent their magnitude less clearly than larger numbers do (21, 22, and so on). Students can therefore have difficulty recognising the structure of numbers from 11 to 19 if these are expressed only in words.

A broader language issue is the verbal interaction that occurs in mathematics classrooms (Bartolini Bussi, 1998). In a traditional classroom, the teacher asks the questions and knows the answers. If questions are repeated, this signals to students that they have not supplied the right answer. In contrast, it is possible to use language as a scaffold for learning about mathematics. Borasi and Siegel (2000), for example, discussed how an expanded role for reading can go beyond issues of handling word problems or maths textbooks to develop a rich context for language in mathematics learning.

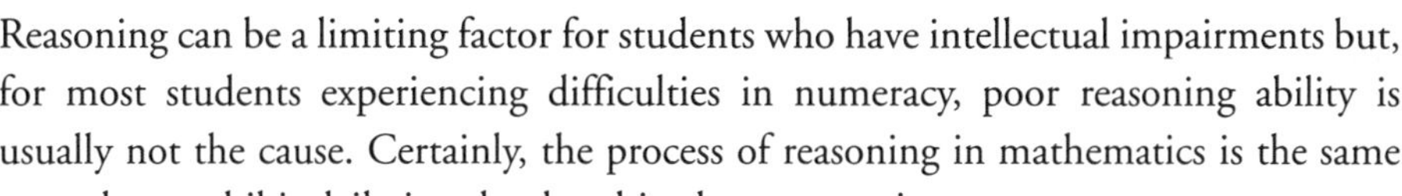

Reasoning can be a limiting factor for students who have intellectual impairments but, for most students experiencing difficulties in numeracy, poor reasoning ability is usually not the cause. Certainly, the process of reasoning in mathematics is the same as students exhibit daily in school and in the community.

Why do students have difficulties in numeracy?

One issue about which there is little evidence is whether severe difficulties in learning arithmetic or other aspects of numeracy can be traced to a constitutional abnormality. Miles and Miles (1992) reviewed the available literature. On the one hand, they concluded that most students with severe reading problems will have some degree of difficulty in numeracy, but most of these students respond to specific assistance in those aspects of numeracy in which they need help. In other words, their mathematical difficulties are more tractable than their literacy problems. On the other hand, the idea that there is a separate group of students who find severe difficulty with learning mathematics is well established. These students are sometimes referred to as having dyscalculia although this term has the disadvantages associated with the term dyslexia. There is little solid evidence as to why some students find learning mathematical ideas difficult.

One field that has been studied extensively is affect (the emotional response to success and failure) which includes motivation to learn mathematics, and self-concept. For example, Chinn (1992) examined the influence of cognitive style—whether students are procedural (inchworms) or inventive (grasshoppers). Table 10.1 (page 446) delineates the major characteristics of these two cognitive styles.

Teachers might prefer one or other of these cognitive styles, and it is valuable to identify, through observation, whether students are in tune with the instruction provided. It is likely that success in numeracy relies upon the use of both approaches, and teachers should encourage students to try the non-preferred approach if their usual method is unsuccessful. For example, in learning multiplication facts, some students (and teachers) might rely exclusively upon memorising times tables. Another approach, using the array of all 121 facts from 0 x 0 to 10 x 10, seeks to capitalise on relationships between pairs of facts, for example, that 6 times tables are twice the 3 times facts. Part of the art of good teaching is to observe how students approach learning and decide when to help them develop more flexible strategies.

As has been shown by many researchers (e.g., Cumming & Elkins, 1996), students who have problems with mathematics frequently have problems learning the basic number facts. The memorisation aspect is most acute for multiplication since it is too laborious and error-ridden to attempt to work out the answer by repeated addition. For addition facts, strategies such as counting on are feasible, although not optimal. Furthermore, if we consider what competent students do, we find that they frequently minimise the memorisation load by using patterns. Thus 8 + 9 is tackled as 2 x 8 + 1,

Table 10.1 The cognitive characteristics of inchworms and grasshoppers

TASK	INCHWORMS	GRASSHOPPERS
Analysis and problems	Focuses on parts; attends to detail; separates	Seeks out wholes, forms concept and puts things together
	Seeks out facts to determine a useful formula	Looks at facts to determine an estimate of answers or range of restrictions
Problem solution	Uses a formula; recipe	Controlled exploration
	Constrained focusing using one method or sequential steps along one pathway, generally forwards	Flexible focusing using several methods or pathways; generally works back from an answer and tries new routes
	Uses numbers exactly as given	Adjusts, breaks down and builds up numbers to make an easier calculation
	Tends to add and multiply; resists subtraction and division	Tends to subtract
	Tends to use paper and pencil to compute	Tends to compute mentally
Verification	Unlikely; but if done, uses the same procedure or method	Likely to verify; often uses alternative procedures or methods

Source: Adapted from Chinn (1992).

and products with 9 are checked by noting whether the sum of the digits in the product is 9. For example, as Chinn and Ashcroft (1992) pointed out, there is no substitute for accurate knowledge of basic addition and multiplication facts and, where possible, of the inverse results to bring subtraction and division facts to the same level of automaticity or fluency. But it is also important to help students use this knowledge flexibly. Figure 10.1 (page 447) portrays the way in which counting and the four arithmetic processes are related.

Chinn and Ashcroft (1992) have strongly advocated teaching activities that stress patterns among numbers, believing that patterns are of great assistance to students who find learning difficult. Another advantage of using patterns is that learning

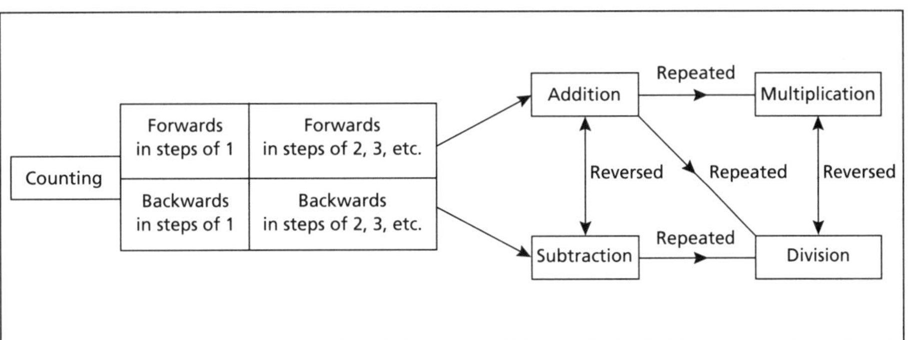

Figure 10.1 The numeracy continuum.
Source: Chinn, S. J. & Ashcroft, J. R. (1992).

becomes more enjoyable, a view that is supported by Benjamin and Shermer (1991) in their book for parents of children learning elementary mathematics.

Number sense

It has been suggested that number sense (feeling at ease with numbers and counting) is the foundation of early numeracy. For example, Gersten and Chard (1999) claimed that understanding what numbers mean, and some ability to handle numbers mentally, are essential for numeracy. Although most students develop number sense through everyday experiences, others need opportunities to develop it in school. It is likely that attempts to teach formal mathematics can be hindered if students do not have adequate number sense. It is well known that some students start school already familiar with print concepts and a well-developed phonemic awareness, whereas others need to be taught these fundamentals at school. Similar differences exist for mathematical ideas such as number and spatial concepts (length, area and shape).

Teachers working with students who experience difficulties might need to strengthen number sense to place students' procedural knowledge on a firm foundation. Number sense forms the basis of being able to compute mentally, which is an essential aspect of numeracy, and also enables the use of approximations to check that paper and pencil or calculator answers are right.

Mochon and Roman (1998) also gave examples of operations that might be handled mentally. First there are the basic facts for the four operations (e.g., 7 plus 8, 45 divided by 9). Next are basic facts with numbers involving place value (e.g., 125 – 20). More demanding are the sorts of operations met in daily life, such as 16 x 4 or 145 + 17 (although some students might be able to handle even more demanding computations such as 819 divided by 7 without recourse to paper and pencil or a calculator). The goal of numeracy ought to include these three types.

Some teachers have paid little attention to mental computation in their desire to have students develop strategies for computation based on firm understanding. Compensating adjustment is a common strategy. For example, 28 + 34 is handled by adding 30 to 34 to get 64 and adjusting by subtracting 2.

Teaching principles

Teachers need to combine systematic instruction with careful observation and questioning of students to catch faulty mathematical thinking before it becomes established. One approach often used is to teach students to recognise problem types and then to provide a series of steps that should enable each type of problem to be solved. However, as students move through the grades, the number of steps required could be daunting and difficult to use unless the student has sufficient understanding of the mathematical operations needed.

The use of cognitive strategies with adolescents has been advocated by a number of writers. Montague (1997), for example, reported studies in which a checklist was used (e.g., Read, Paraphrase, Visualise, Hypothesise, Estimate, Compute, Check) to help students to improve their performance. Metacognitive strategies such as self-questioning, self-instruction, and self-monitoring should also be taught. As an example of what can be done, Miller et al. (1998) studied how students with learning difficulties were able to learn as members of regular classes. Six teachers were prepared to teach multiplication to 81 students over 21 lessons. To a large degree students with learning difficulties performed as well as other students. The authors explained their success as being due to the use of research-based methods and careful preparation of the class teachers. Techniques used included modelling and feedback—moving from concrete to representational to abstract levels—problem-solving using manipulatives, cognitive and mnemonic strategies, continuous monitoring, and graduated word problems.

An ongoing instructional issue is whether to teach students strategies for computation directly, or to seek greater conceptual understanding through students inventing their own methods (Carroll, 1999). In general, students using taught standard algorithms (i.e., routines to obtain solutions) seem to perform at similar levels to students who have invented their own routines. However, the former group tends to make errors involving faulty sub-computations, whereas the latter group fails to follow the steps in the strategies that have been taught. This suggests that diagnosis of learning problems in mathematics might require some knowledge of the past curricular emphases in the classroom.

Assessment of numeracy

Because numeracy is a relatively new concept, most tests appear to have been designed to reflect school mathematics curricula, rather than reflecting the knowledge and skills that comprise numeracy. Also, there are more assessment procedures for early years than for high school or adult use. However, some tests can be applied across a wide age range and these can be helpful to a teacher who is trying to establish the extent of a new student's mastery of mathematical concepts and skills.

One important idea in the assessment of numeracy is that the student can provide the teacher with valuable information if the teacher approaches assessment with a good theoretical understanding of numeracy and an encoding stance. Thus, students should be encouraged to offer their insights into the difficulties they experience. Another useful idea is to approach assessment through individual teaching. As Skinner and Schock (1995) have pointed out, older students might feel affronted if, as a result of identifying them as performing many grades below their class placement, they are given work that is clearly identified as juvenile. It might be much better to work back from age appropriate content in a diagnostic fashion as weaknesses are identified. It is not unusual to find that students have insecure understanding well back into primary school, as shown in Box 10.1 (page 450).

One well-established Australian instrument is the Booker Profiles in Mathematics (Booker, 1995). This is an extensive individual assessment tool that covers numeration and computation. As its name suggests, the instrument enables a profile to be built, rather than produce a normative score. For numeration an array is compiled in which the magnitude of numbers handled can be seen for each aspect of numeration. Similarly, the computation component leads to an array of aspects (concept, basic facts, algorithm, problem-solving) for each of the four operations. Valuable aspects of the Booker Profiles are the many examples of common difficulties that students experience, and the suggestions for overcoming them.

The errors that are likely to be observed in students' work have been well documented by Wong (1996). Partial completion of a problem often signifies that the student is unsure about the algorithm. Errors resulting from regrouping are common in addition and subtraction, whereas the multiplication and division algorithms require careful attention to placing digits in the correct places. Other errors that sometimes appear involve the student using an incorrect operation, such as adding instead of subtracting. Wong noted that zero sometimes constitutes a stumbling block. Research by Thompson (2000) also suggested another problem. He stated that place value might not be established in students who can use numbers up to 20. He argued that teaching place value too early might be unwise, as students might think of double-digit numbers as being single-digit numbers. As a check it can be useful to ask students to explain the 7 and then the 1 in 17.

Teachers can approach diagnosis of arithmetic difficulties using specific diagnostic instruments, or by careful analysis of student work in class. If students are required to unpack the meaning of word problems, they can find it difficult to keep all of the

Box 10.1 Jason's math problems

Jason was in Year 11 and intent on entering a mechanical trade course at a technical and further education (TAFE) college. However, his performance in mathematics was jeopardising his chances of gaining entry to the course. When his teacher sat with him after school, she quickly noted that he could handle the conceptual aspects of calculus, but when he needed to perform algebraic manipulations involving associative and distributive laws, he was slow and uncertain. Jason responded well to reteaching of the mathematical ideas involved but he was hesitant when he had to practise examples from his textbook.

On closer examination it was clear that he was hesitant with a few basic addition facts such as 7 + 6 and 8 + 7, as well as with quite a few multiplication facts. By sharing these insights with Jason, his teacher was able to establish a reteaching plan that Jason agreed would help him, and he readily agreed to practise those number facts about which he was insecure. In time Jason came to see that he needed to gain mastery of mathematical content that he had not mastered in earlier grades and, now well motivated, made good progress. This was helped by his teacher preparing a chart of goals he should meet each week and plotting his progress on those goals. Although there was extra work for the teacher, she willingly made the effort as she could see what a difference the individual program could make to Jason.

variables and operations in mind, resulting in either abandoning the task or failing to incorporate all necessary information. A comprehensive example of a full assessment is given in Box 10.2 (see page 451).

Understanding mathematics

Visualisation

Numeracy requires an understanding of the way in which mathematics is related to real life situations. Booth and Thomas (1999) have found that students aged 11 to 14 years who have visualisation problems are likely to experience problems interpreting diagrams and pictures with which they are presented in mathematics classes. Such students need to have extensive support, such as verbal explanations of the concepts represented pictorially. Teachers should not assume that students find the interpretation of illustrations to be straightforward. Lowrie (2000) reported on an able student who was reluctant to use pictorial imagery when solving mathematical problems. The student appeared to regard mathematics as a subject to be approached analytically. In general, being able to visualise situations is a valuable component of

Box 10.2 An example of an assessment procedure

Hannah was 13 years old when she was referred for a comprehensive mathematics assessment by her paediatrician because an initial assessment had suggested that she had specific learning difficulties in mathematics and spelling. Her Year 7 teacher had noticed that Hannah had good learning abilities in some areas, which seemed inconsistent with her very pronounced difficulties in mastering mathematics. The teacher had recommended a detailed psychometric assessment to clarify Hannah's abilities, strengths, and weaknesses. The results suggested that Hannah had overall abilities in the average range for her age with good verbal and analytical skills. On the Differential Ability Scales (DAS) she scored at the 88th percentile on the verbal cluster. However, she also showed significant weaknesses in processing speed (4th percentile) and pattern construction (8th percentile) that might have been affecting her ability to note number and spelling patterns since her early years of schooling.

Hannah had a history of difficulty in learning mathematics and expressed a strong dislike for the subject. She was very aware that she was slow in her responses to computing even basic additions, in which she used her fingers for larger combinations (e.g., 8 + 9), and she equated her slowness with being dumb at mathematics. Hannah could remember that she did not feel part of the class oral activities in mathematics in Year 2 and Year 3, saying: "I didn't participate much; I used to look out the window." Even at this early stage in her learning, it seems that Hannah felt left behind.

"The teacher used to go too fast. The really smart people—the real brains—would call out the answers."

At the time of the assessment, Hannah was in the lowest maths group in her class and she received extra help from the learning support teacher. Hannah spoke positively about the support teacher who showed the group strategies such as turning around a sum when the smaller digit comes first (e.g., "3 + 8" becomes "8 + 3" so the student can count-on "9, 10, 11"), but she expressed some concern that this might be cheating.

"When you get really smart, you can work out ways to cheat; well, it's not really cheating."

Hannah was appreciative that the support teacher taking her group taught more slowly and it was clear that, at times, she could not understand her regular class teacher's explanations. Hannah said class mental arithmetic tests were "just like a bunch of numbers. I sometimes miss all of them". Although she knows a few of her times tables, Hannah said "I never get any of the divides". It seemed that the class teacher had suggested using the relevant times table, but Hannah's limited store of multiplication facts meant she was not able to benefit from these drills.

Hannah's mathematical knowledge and understanding were explored using a combination of standardised and diagnostic tools, and measures of processing speed. On a standardised test of mathematics achievement, the Wide Range Achievement Test, Third Edition (WRAT-3)—Arithmetic test, Hannah performed at a very low level for her age, at the 1st percentile or about Year 2 level.

Although the WRAT-3 uses American norms and, therefore, might not be as accurate as we would like, Hannah's results were consistent with her results on the DAS Arithmetic test (also 1st percentile). As well as making two errors through mistaking or overlooking operator signs, Hannah's low scores were brought about because she was confident to attempt only addition, subtraction, and single-digit multiplication. It appeared from Hannah's answer to a two-digit by one-digit multiplication that she had misunderstood the operation

$$\begin{array}{r} 23 \\ \underline{x3} \\ 56 \end{array}$$

Hannah could carry out two-column addition and two-column subtraction with and without regrouping correctly, but she was slow in computing larger addition and subtraction facts. On multiplication items Hannah knew the answer to 3 x 4 but had devised an interesting and elaborate strategy to compute 7 x 6. She used the joints of two fingers to count up to 6 and continued to use these fingers to count up to 42 by ones (i.e., repeating the process 7 times). When Hannah saw the division problem 6 divided by 2, she said she could not do division and would not attempt any further questions, convinced she would not be able to.

Royer, Cisero, and Carlo's (1993) Computer-based Academic Assessment (CAAS) tasks were then administered to measure Hannah's processing speed on both numerical and non-numerical tasks. Hannah's reaction times were measured on a simple processing task (naming stars or plusses), and on tests of number recognition (single-digit and multi-digit), letter recognition, and addition.

Hannah's average reaction time on the number-naming tasks was consistent on two occasions (her mean reaction time being 0.71 seconds). This reaction time was a little slower than her letter-recognition time of 0.62 seconds. It took longer for Hannah to process the star and plus symbols (1.17 and 1.00 seconds respectively), and this might point to an issue in relation to processing operator signs.

On the triple-addition task, Hannah noted that she was reliant on counting to feel secure in her answers. After giving the answer "9" to 5 + 2 + 2, she commented: "I knew it, but I kept counting."

The Booker Profiles were given to Hannah. When she was first asked to name the number of blocks on the table (six blocks in a horizontal row) she named "8". When asked to have another look, she moved the blocks into groups of two (in a 3 x 2 array), saying it was easier when they were together. She tended to count in twos to identify other groups (e.g., a row of eight cups). Hannah was confident in choosing a plate of nine biscuits quickly from three examples, explaining that "9" was "more" and that she could tell "5" just by looking. Hannah was able to identify the value of tens in place value questions, but faced considerable difficulty when asked to add or subtract tens mentally. When asked to compute "10 less than 25", she counted back on her fingers but gave the answer "17". Her backwards counting was not efficient.

Hannah frequently used a counting-on strategy for larger digit additions and became exasperated with the difficulty of keeping track when doing multicolumn additions with pencil and paper. Hannah was quite fast on her small single-digit subtractions, with the exception of "8 take away 3". However, as soon as she was asked a multidigit subtraction involving regrouping, she made a consistent smaller-from-larger error (e.g., 13 – 9 = 16).

Norms are available only up to 11 years of age on the Westwood (2000) One Minute Basic Facts Test, but the addition and subtraction tests were administered as an alternative to the oral presentation of facts on the Booker profiles. Hannah was able to complete 14 addition facts and 17 subtraction facts in one minute (normal range for the 11-year-old age group is 20–27 addition facts, and 14 facts is considered a critically low score at this age level). Hannah's performance was slowed down considerably by her counting-on to solve the larger facts from 4 + 9. Her subtraction speed was closer to the normally expected rate (17–25 facts at the age of 11 years), but this included only single-digit subtractions with sums less than 10.

Hannah sees herself as very slow at maths in comparison with her peers, and she appears to feel comfortable with being put into the lowest maths group this year following school-based assessment at the commencement of Year 8. Feedback from this assessment included the information that Hannah's group could use calculators regularly to assist in completing problems and computations.

On a computer task (CAAS) designed to measure reaction times for processing symbols and numbers, as well as more complex mathematical tasks, Hannah showed that she processed numbers quite quickly and at a consistent speed. Although Hannah can add and subtract small single-digit numbers quite readily, her capacity to add digits that have a sum greater than 10 is limited to very slow counting strategies. This was evident in her reaction times on the CAAS addition tasks as well as on other tasks throughout the assessment. During an early session, when describing an addition fact sheet she had completed for homework, Hannah said she got only one wrong (4 + 2 = 5). She identified 8 + 8 and 9 + 9 as hard ones which she had to count, clearly not knowing them automatically as doubles facts. Hannah herself recalled that she was able to learn her addition facts up to what she thought was Year 4 level, and she pointed to the intersection of column 6 and row 5 on a 9 x 9 addition table as containing the facts she knew by heart.

With multiplication, Hannah said that she can remember only her two and five times tables. As described earlier, when answering 7 times 6 on the WRAT-3, Hannah had explained that she used the three joints on two of her fingers to count up to 3 twice, to make 6, and she used this structure to help her keep track while continuing to count by ones up to 42.

Hannah tended to use a concatenated single-digit conceptual structure for multi-unit numbers. This might be interfering with her ability to form multi-digit conceptual structures that would allow her to understand and apply the base-ten structure of our number system, and to develop more fully the concept of place value. It might also be a constraining factor in limiting Hannah's ability to develop flexible and adaptive strategies for basic addition and subtraction, and in limiting her desire to explore multiplicative and divisive number relations.

Note: This case study is based on information provided by Maureen Finnane, an experienced child psychologist.

numeracy. Sometimes students feel that school mathematics is to be approached only analytically. However, in being able to use mathematical knowledge to deal with the everyday world, visualisation is an important strategy.

Fractions

If a student is able to tell the teacher that a numerator is the top number in a fraction, is this evidence that the student has a clear concept about fractions? Boulet (1998) suggested that the conceptual issues go far beyond correct labelling of vinculum, numerator, and denominator. A fraction involves a part–whole relationship, its quantification as a ratio, and conventions for its representation. Boulet argued that difficulties can arise in the concept and procedure of forming equal parts. (Is the whole discrete like a cake, or is it a collection of items?) Children may find difficulty in dividing a circle into odd-numbered equal parts. If they are asked to share a collection of objects equally among a smaller number of persons, they can be confused as to what to do with a remainder. Their decision might be based on whether they assume that the objects left over are themselves divisible. Other mathematical ideas that arise as students learn to deal with fractions include the reversibility of the process of partitioning, and the notion that $1/m < 1/n$ where $m > n$.

Boulet (1998) argued that students need much more experience with partitioning and recombining than many presently receive. She emphasises the need for the teacher to use real situations in which students can experience fractions, rather than typical textbook cake cutting exercises. It is important also to ensure that students' attention is drawn to the relevant perceptual elements. If this is not done they might well become confused because a large fraction of a small object can appear smaller than a small fraction of a large object (or collection).

Fluency

Although it might be thought that there are few parallels between learning literacy and numeracy, they share two goals: fluency and accuracy. With regard to reading, Bussis, Chittenden, Amarel, and Klausner (1985) have presented a theoretical model in which novice readers strive for meaning while keeping fluency and accuracy in balance. If either of these two factors is neglected, then the process of reading is unlikely to lead to understanding. With mathematics, the learner faces a similar challenge. For their mathematical knowledge to be useful, students need to be able to calculate components of a complex task both accurately and quickly, so that they are able to devote the majority of their cognitive resources to the analysis of the task.

Language

Where young students are having difficulties in both literacy and numeracy, it might be helpful to plan intervention in parallel. Older students can be asked to write about mathematical ideas or situations in which numeracy plays a role. This helps the students to think better about mathematical ideas, and also offers a window that teachers can use to understand better the students' thinking (Bickmore-Brand, 1990).

Gender

It was once thought that girls were more likely to experience problems in school mathematics although, in recent years, any differences between the achievement of the genders seem trivial. It is worthwhile observing to see if students—particularly girls—appear indifferent to, or have negative attitudes toward, school mathematics. Boaler (1997) explored differences between boys and girls in mathematics and concluded that it was the way in which school mathematics often becomes competitive that was responsible for girls feeling apprehensive, since teachers seemed to value being correct more than they valued understanding. It would appear that presenting mathematics as social practice might enable both girls and boys to acquire the numeracy that society expects.

Culture

Where students are from non-English speaking backgrounds or other cultures it is possible that parents and other community members have different views about mathematics. For example, some Asian people believe (with justification) that the abacus is a very good tool for computation. Hatano (1997) explained very clearly how to learn to use an abacus, noting that it improves written computation skills, but not the place value concept. Nelson, Joseph, and Williams (1993) have given many

examples of how teachers can introduce mathematical ideas which were developed in other parts of the world. Nelson (1993) showed how common curriculum elements such as percentages, measurement and proportion have been handled by other cultures. For example, Vedic multiplication is shown below:

$$\begin{array}{r} 57 \\ \times\ 24 \\ \hline 1368 \\ \hline 32 \end{array}$$

This has the following steps:

4 x 7 = 28, write 8, carry 2

5 x 4 + 2 x 7 + 2 = 36, write 6, carry 3

5 x 2 + 3 = 13, write 13

Perhaps this is easier than the usual long multiplication algorithm that is taught today.

Joseph (1993) described an ancient way of avoiding having to learn the multiplication facts above 5 x 5. For 8 x 7, we write the digits in a column, with their tens complement beside each digit, thus:

8 2

7 3

Either diagonal subtraction gives 5 for the tens position and multiplying the two numbers in the right hand column gives the unit digit of 6.

Numeracy in students with special needs

Very little is known about the extent of numeracy in students with disabilities. Despite the recent emphasis on system-wide testing, the data for students with special needs are either unidentified within the results, or these students have been excluded from the testing program. Colbert and van Kraayenoord (2000) noted that for some students with disabilities to be included in mandated testing, alternative means of presenting the tests would be needed. The simplest alternative forms of testing are to allow extra time to read the test to students or to provide an amanuensis (someone to write at the student's dictation). However, for some students alternative media—such as Braille—might be required.

It is expected that in future more attention will be paid to assessing the numeracy of students with particular impairments, and schools will have to provide evidence of the effectiveness of their instructional programs in numeracy for all students.

In Queensland there is some information about students' numeracy from the Year 2 Diagnostic Net <www.education.qld.gov.au/tal/y2dn>. First, a small proportion of students with disabilities are exempt (e.g., those with intellectual impairment). Among others who were assessed using the Queensland Year 2 Diagnostic Net, performance was distinctly lower for students with intellectual impairment, and somewhat lower for students with other impairments. Data from a statewide test of number, measurement, and space at Year 6 (in 1977) indicated that all categories of students with disabilities performed below the state average.

Students with a vision impairment

Students with vision impairments can be taught to achieve similar outcomes as students of similar abilities who do not have impaired vision (Palmer, 2000). Success can require substantial effort on the part of teachers since adaptations to materials and methods might involve extensive preparation. Palmer also pointed out that some studies have indicated that vision is very important in developing spatial concepts, so teachers might need to provide enriched opportunities for students to develop mathematical concepts. However, some students with impaired vision are able to perform at superior levels in mathematics. Recently a student graduated with first class honours in mathematics from the University of Queensland, showing that it is possible to attain excellence despite impaired vision.

Palmer (2000) also pointed out that several aspects of mathematical knowledge—such as measurement, space, and statistics—rely on visual concepts and information. Also, because numeracy is concerned with daily activities, having impaired vision can result in a lack of understanding of the practical contexts in which numeracy is needed. In some cases this might mean that a student with vision impairment needs more time to carry out exploration of mathematical applications such as in measurement, money, or graphing. Clamp (1997) claimed that young students with vision impairments might have particular difficulty in perceiving whole things, and might need extensive experience in constructing the idea of whole objects from their parts. There are usually greater problems facing students who are congenitally blind than those who lose their sight during their school years and those with partial vision. All might, to some degree, experience difficulties due to their thinking being more concrete than that of their sighted peers (MacCluskie, Tunick, Dial, & Paul, 1998), and because extensive practical experience with the real world contexts that give rise to mathematical ideas is vital. Also, Donaldson (1998) found that it is more difficult for students with vision impairments to keep up with the curriculum when the mathematical ideas extend beyond number and elementary geometry.

One reason why students with vision impairments may find it difficult to keep pace with the curriculum is that they have also to learn many extra things, including braille, or the use of vision aids, mobility in new contexts and working with teacher's aides and

teachers. However, if specialised support is provided to students and their teachers, many students with vision impairments are able to succeed in school, although they might need to make greater efforts than their peers.

A supportive placement in a regular class is likely to provide the best conditions for students to become numerate. It is important to consider the safety and accessibility of the school and classroom. Students with low vision need lighting appropriate to their individual needs A specialist teacher might be needed to provide appropriate advice but, in many cases, the regular teacher is able to include such students with relatively little difficulty.

Students with a hearing impairment

There has been relatively little research on numeracy among students with hearing impairments and this contrasts sharply with the considerable attention to their literacy. Obviously, problems with language affect learning in other areas. This includes numeracy—which has a complex language that requires precise interpretation (Christopherson, 1997). Students who are deaf or have a hearing impairment often have limited metacognitive awareness that can limit their problem-solving ability.

Numeracy for indigenous students

One of the early major studies of numeracy in remote Aboriginal students was completed by Harris (1991). She took an approach that fits well with the concept of numeracy, and her chapter on money is a valuable explanation of the differences between a traditional Aboriginal economy and a money economy. Recent research has identified some differences between school mathematics and the use of mathematics by indigenous students in their communities. For example, Rudder (1999, p. 40) described Aboriginal mathematics like this:

> Aboriginal mathematics is about people and things. It is about how things relate together. It is about "how big" things are or "how many" or "how much" of something there is. It is also about sorting and size and time and space and directions just the same as the mathematics we use at school. In a special way it does this almost completely without numbers, and without money. It uses relationships instead.

Traditional Aboriginal people in north-east Arnhem Land use relationships instead of counting. These are lone, pair, full set, group, and rule. Rudder explained that if a family collected turtle eggs they put them in piles of four eggs with one egg on top, and each person would be allotted an appropriate set of piles. This apportioning was carried out without counting.

Time was identified by co-occurrence of events in the environment. It was expected that the cycle of seasons would repeat and there was no value in counting days,

months, or years. Space was identified and named by events that occurred at particular places, rather than by measuring areas of land.

Intellectual disabilities

For students with a mild intellectual disability who are likely to be included in regular classes, it is often possible to use the standard curriculum, with modification, on an individual basis. It is important not to oversimplify content as this might deny these students the opportunity to become familiar with important aspects of numeracy. Efforts should be made to have these students acquire fluency with addition and multiplication facts so that they can apply these in real life tasks such as measurement and understanding data.

For those with more severe intellectual disability, Rowbotham and van Kraayenoord (2000) argued that three approaches have been recommended. These are:

(a) a developmental curriculum that prescribes content suitable for much younger nondisabled peers;

(b) a basic academic skills approach that is closer to age-appropriate content, but lacks functionality; and

(c) a functional curriculum that is consistent with numeracy.

The COACH model developed by Giangreco, Edelman, Dennis, and Cloniger (1995) involves skills for both school and vocational purposes. Rowbotham and van Kraayenoord listed useful instructional techniques for developing the numeracy of students with intellectual impairments. These are:

- direct instruction;
- cooperative learning groups;
- peer tutoring;
- modelling;
- corrective feedback;
- teaching mathematical words and concepts;
- game activities;
- concrete–abstract–representational learning sequences;
- mnemonic devices;
- guided practice;
- independent practice;
- computer-assisted instruction; and
- problem-solving models.

A broad appreciation of numeracy can provide useful guidance for teachers trying to establish IEPs for students with intellectual impairments. It is also valuable to use numeracy across the curriculum.

Students with learning difficulties

Numeracy in students with learning difficulties has been studied extensively. In a survey of learning difficulties in Australia, Louden et al. (2000) found that, in primary schools, numeracy received much less attention than did literacy. In addition, in reviewing relevant literature, Chan and Dally (2000) found that the volume of research on mathematics difficulties was much less than for literacy, although it is increasing. They describe numeracy problems that are experienced by some students with learning difficulties as "both persistent and pervasive" (p. 166). The causes can lie within the student, but are also to be found in teaching inadequacies, inappropriate curricula, lack of appropriate strategies, and low motivation. Most commonly, difficulties in computation are identified but areas such as reading mathematical text, the language of mathematics, and logical reasoning are also involved. Mathematics requires accuracy at all steps and, thus, can be more difficult than literacy since there is usually some redundancy in language.

Where the problems appear to stem from slow or inaccurate computation, intervention might require a detailed examination of what strategies are used. It is not unusual to find that doubles are retrieved from memory, whereas facts such as 8 + 6 are tackled by a counting-on strategy subvocally, aloud, or with the aid of fingers. Thus, understanding is always a priority, although at some point it will be necessary to increase students' speed of use of strategies or the use of recall from memory.

If problems with applying mathematical reasoning are found, students should use both cognitive and metacognitive strategies, just as is true for reading comprehension (see Chapter 9).

Adults

When we consider adults who need to learn relevant mathematics we can easily understand the importance of numeracy in their lives. As Fitzsimons, Jungwirth, Maasz, and Schloeglmann (1997) have stressed, adult numeracy is influenced by societal socioeconomic and technological changes. It should not be assumed that having a high school mathematics education automatically brings numeracy. It has been shown that some adults use methods other than those taught in school. For example, tradespersons might measure by direct comparison rather than by using a tape, and an office worker might use a pocket calculator and not the algorithm taught in school.

State initiatives

In several states it has been recognised that increased emphasis should be given not only to literacy, but also to numeracy. In New South Wales, under the leadership of Robert Wright (Wright, 1991; Wright, Martland, & Stafford, 2000), a series of projects was carried out during the 1990s under the general title of Mathematics Recovery. Wright, Martland, & Stafford (2000) provided a detailed account of how young children can be assessed and helped in early number knowledge.

According to Wright et al. (2000, pp. 2–3), some key features of Mathematics Recovery are:

- intensive, individualised teaching of low-attaining 6- to 8-year-old children by specialist teachers for teaching cycles of 10–15 weeks in length;
- an extensive professional development course to prepare the specialist teachers, and ongoing collegial and leader support for these teachers;
- use of a strong underpinning theory of young children's mathematical learning;
- use of a learning framework to guide assessment and teaching; and
- use of an especially developed instructional approach, and distinctive instructional activities and assessment procedures.

Assessment is interview-based, and seeks both student knowledge and strategies used. The assessment can be profiled over time, and linked to teaching via the Learning Framework in Number. The approach to instruction conforms to Vygotsky's zone of proximal development (Moll, 1990). Mathematics Recovery has led to an inservice program in New South Wales called Count Me In Too.

In Queensland, a screening device known as the Year 2 Diagnostic Net operates for both literacy and numeracy (www.education.qld.gov.au/tal/y2dn). The goals are to identify Year 2 students who require support and to provide such support. In most cases this consists of a tutor who has been trained to use Support a Maths Learner: Number, which is an early intervention resource

> . . . comprising training workshops for use by program coordinators and learning–teaching materials for use by trained teacher aides, parents/carers and volunteers when working with children experiencing difficulties in aspects of early number-counting, patterning and number representations. (http://education.qld.gov.au/learning_ent/ldf/schools/maths/html/intro.html)

This program requires that volunteer tutors and teacher aides undertake a series of workshops to learn how to implement the program. There is considerable detail on the program on the website at <www.education.qld.gov.au/tal/y2dn>. In Victoria there has been considerable interest in the Early Numeracy Research project (Clarke & Cheeseman, 2000). This was a large-scale study of 70 schools involving "the development

of a framework of growth points of early numeracy learning and a task-based interview designed for one-to-one use by classroom teachers" (p. 6). Teachers reported many positive changes in their teaching practices as a result of their involvement in the research project. Benefits to students included:

- better explanations of their thinking;
- more enjoyment of mathematics;
- greater willingness to experiment and persist; and
- greater awareness of mathematical thinking processes.

It is likely that more emphasis will be placed on numeracy in all systems and sectors of Australian education in the future, as can be seen from the research projects funded by the Commonwealth government. These include:

- Middle Years Numeracy Project (ACT);
- Enhancing Numeracy Outcomes Project (ACT);
- Counting On (NSW);
- Count Me into Measurement (NSW);
- Count Me into Space (NSW);
- Secondary Numeracy Assessment Program (NSW);
- Supporting Literacy and Numeracy in Queensland Schools (Qld);
- Support a Maths Learner: Number (Qld);
- Junior Secondary Numeracy Project (SA);
- Thinking and Working Mathematically (Tas.);
- Early Numeracy Research Project (Vic.);
- Middle Years Numeracy Research Project (Vic.);
- First Steps in Mathematics (WA); and
- Numeracy across the Curriculum (WA).

You should try to find out about the projects that are being conducted in your state or territory.

Teaching ideas

As with other areas of the curriculum, peer-tutoring can be effective in assisting students to learn basic number facts. Many students need assistance in attaining fluency and they feel defeated having persisted in trying unsuccessfully to learn to do mathematics over several years. What Johnson and Layng (1992) call generative instruction can build fluency, confidence, and problem-solving ability. The Morningside Model can be used with up to 15 students. Its components include precision placement testing, a 15-minute session of interactive instruction, and the monitoring

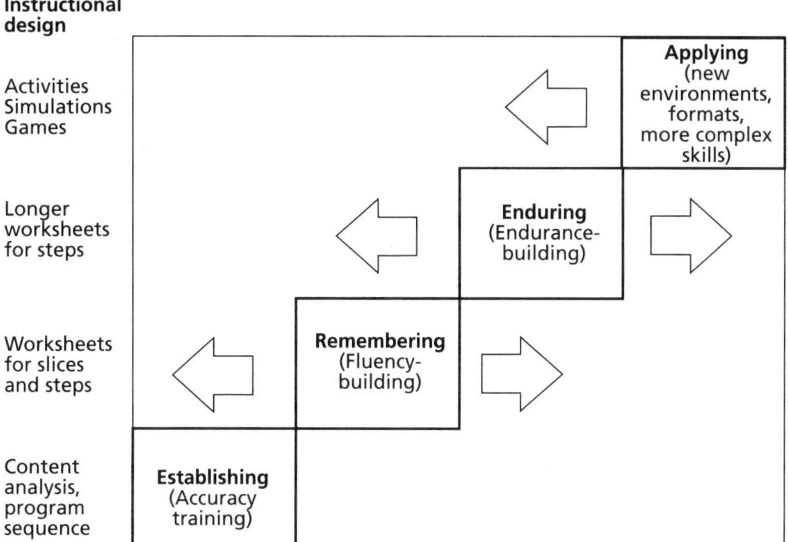

Figure 5.2 The Morningside Model of Generative Instruction.
Note: The large arrows indicate that steps can move horizontally to provide overlapping learning phases. True mastery is the product of the steps.
Source: Johnson, K. R., & Layng, T. V. J. (1992). Copyright © 1992 by the American Psychological Association. Reprinted with permission.

of fluency against the goal of constant growth in each type of problem. Johnson and Layng claimed that when fluency of component tasks is established and if fluency can can be demonstrated weeks after the last targeted instruction, "new and complex repertoires then emerge with little or no instruction, producing *curriculum leaps* that allow students to make rapid academic achievement" (p. 1475) (emphasis in original text).

For secondary students, direct instruction by the teacher, clarifying confusions, strategy instruction (both cognitive and metacognitive), and improving students' understanding of the context of word problems are among the instructional approaches for which there is research support (Maccini & Hughes, 1997). Van Luit and Naglieri (1999) tested a remedial program that involved the teacher discussing strategy choices, but that allowed students to choose which strategy they would use in basic multiplication and division. This approach requires children both to identify strategies and to decide which strategies are the best.

Sleeman (1985) found that 14-year-old students had many misunderstandings of algebra. Strategies used included substituting values and following a rule (such as collecting all numbers on one side of the equals sign). He found that students could solve problems such as:

$2x + 4 = 16$

but not:

$2x + 3x = 14$.

Overall, Sleeman concluded that students often began by being unpredictable in their attempts to solve algebraic equations (they applied mal-rules consistently), but finally came to the consistent use of the correct algebra. He also commended the use of diagnostic interviews to understand students' reasoning.

SUMMARY

It is not surprising that learning the mathematical ideas needed for numeracy is difficult for some students. First, not all teachers feel secure in their own understanding of mathematics or of the rationale for changing emphases in teaching methods, such as the introduction of constructivist principles. Second, becoming numerate requires that students understand the everyday contexts in which they apply their sense of number, space, and measurement. Third, various groups of students have been found to have particular difficulties in acquiring numeracy. These include students with disabilities and some students from low socioeconomic backgrounds. Last, there are students who, through apparent confusion in the early years, become apprehensive about mathematics and avoid it as soon as they are able.

Yet there are several ways in which students can be helped to learn the mathematics they need for numeracy. One is that they should be given sufficient practice with basic mathematical terminology, fundamental number facts, and learning to approximate. It is important that this be done as mental arithmetic as well as in paper and pencil tasks. Another is that students need to be encouraged to respond quickly, rather than relying on slow strategies or concrete aids. Teachers also must create an enjoyable atmosphere for mathematics lessons and ensure that all students are appropriately rewarded, intrinsically or extrinsically, for their mastery of successive components.

Good teaching depends upon careful observation of students at work, not relying upon correcting the finished products of mathematics tasks. Careful observation as students work on tasks designed to have diagnostic value, as well as interviews with them about their reasoning, can help teachers decide when and how to re-teach certain topics. More recent research that measures the time taken to respond to arithmetical tasks is proving to have great utility, although few teachers yet have access to convenient computer programs for diagnosis or practice. It is anticipated that the the future will see greater attention paid to numeracy by education authorities, and that this will reduce the number of students experiencing difficulties.

Suggested reading

Books

Fleishner, J. (1994). Diagnosis and assessment of mathematics learning disabilities. In G. Lyon (Ed.), *Frames of reference for the assessment of children with learning disabilities* (pp. 444–458*)*. Baltimore: Paul H. Brookes.

MacNeal, E. (1994). *Mathsemantics: Making numbers talk sense.* New York: Viking.

Paulos, J. A. (1988). *Numeracy: Mathematical illiteracy and its consequences.* New York: Hill & Wang.

Thornton, C. A. & Bley, N. S. (Eds) (1994). *Windows of opportunity:Mathematics for students with special needs* Reston, VA: National Council of Teachers of Mathematics.

Westwood, P. (2000). *Numeracy and learning difficulties: Approaches to learning and development.* Camberwell, Vic: Australian Council for Educational Research.

Journals

Focus on Learning Problems in Mathematics

Equals: Mathematics and Special Education Needs

Journal of Learning Disabilities

Australian Journal of Learning Disabilities

Practical activities

1. Observe a student who is finding it difficult to understand mathematical ideas. Try to formulate hypotheses about the knowledge or skills that seem to be the cause of the student's difficulties. Develop a set of mathematical tasks that will enable you to test your hunches. You might need to use several activities involving the same concept to obtain reliable information.
2. Study a job situation considered suitable for a 16-year-old student with mild intellectual impairment and try to identify the key aspects of numeracy required for success in the position. Then check curriculum guidelines to see whether the required knowledge should have been covered.
3. Select one of the major disability categories and search for references that give you useful information about numeracy instruction for these students. You might start with Volume 2 of the report *Literacy and Numeracy and Students with Disabilities* by van Kraayenord et al. (2000). Also use the World Wide Web to extend your information.

References

Andrews, R., Elkins, J., Berry, P. B., & Burge, J. (1979). *A survey of special education in Australia:Provisions, needs and priorities in the education of children with handicaps and learning difficulties*. St. Lucia: Fred and Eleanor Schonell Educational Research Centre.

Baker, A. & Baker, J. (1991). *Raps & rhymes & maths*. Armadale,Vic: Eleanor Curtain.

Bartolini Bussi, M. G. (1998). Joint acivity in mathematics clasrooms: A Vygotskyian analysis (pp. 13–49). In F.Seeger, J. Voigt, & U. Waschescio (Eds), *The culture of the mathematics classroom*. Cambridge: Cambridge University Press.

Benjamin, A. & Shermer, M. B. (1991). *Teach your child math*. Los Angeles: Lowell Press.

Boaler, J. (1997). *Experiencing school mathematics*. Buckingham: Open University Press.

Booker, G. (1995). *Booker profiles in mathematics: Numeration and computation*. Camberwell, Vic: Australian Council for Educational Research.

Booth, R. D. L. & Thomas, M. O. J. (1999). Visualization in mathematics learning: Arithmetic problem-solving and student difficulties. *Journal of Mathematical Behavior, 18*, 160–190.

Borasi, R. & Siegel, M. (2000) *Reading counts: Expanding the role of reading in mathematics classrooms*. New York: Teachers College Press.

Boutet, G. (1998). Didactical implications of children's difficulties in learning the fraction concept. *Focus on learning problems in mathematics, 20*, 19–34.

Brickmore-Brand, J. (Ed.) (1990). *Language in mathematics*. Carlton South, Vic: Australian Reading Association.

Brown, M., Millett, A., Bibby, T., & Johnson, D. C. (2000). Turning our attention from the what to the how: The national numeracy strategy. *British Educational Research Journal, 26*, 457–471.

Bruer, J. T. (1993). *Schools for thought*. Cambridge, MA: MIT Press.

Bussis, A. M., Chittenden, E. A., Amarel, M., & Klausner, E. (1985). *Inquiry into meaning: An investigation of learning to read*. Hillsdale, NJ: Erlbaum Associates.

Carey, D. A., Fennema, E., Carpenter, T. P., & Franke, M. L. (1995). Equity and mathematics education. In W. G. Secada, E. Fennema, & L. B. Adajian (Eds), *New directions for equity in mathematics education* (pp. 93–125). New York: Cambridge University Press.

Carroll, W. M. (1999). Invented computational procedures of students in a standards-based curriculum. *Journal of Mathematical Behavior, 18*, 111–121.

Chan, L. K. S. & Dally, K. (2000). *Review of literature*. In W. Louden, L. K. S. Chan, J. Elkins, D. Greaves, H. House, M. Milton, S. Nichols, M. Rohl, J. Rivalland, C. van Kraayenoord. *Mapping the territory: Primary students with learning difficulties: Literacy and numeracy*. Vol 2, (pp. 161– 331). Canberra, ACT: Department of Education, Training, and Youth Affairs.

Chinn, S. J. (1992). Individual diagnosis and cognitive style. In T. R. Miles & E. Miles (Eds), *Dyslexia and mathematics* (pp. 23–41). London: Routledge

Chinn, S. J. & Ashcroft, J. R. (1992). The use of patterns. In T. R. Miles & E. Miles (Eds), *Dyslexia and mathematics* (pp. 98–118). London: Routledge.

Christopherson, S. (1997). Math, new teaching for an old challenge. *Perspectives in Education and Deafness, 15*(3), 4–6.

Clamp, S. (1997). *Mathematics*. In H. Mason & S. McCall (Eds), *Visual impairment: Access & education and young people*. London: David Fulton.

Clark, D. & Cheeseman, J. (2000). Some insights from the first year of the Early Literacy Research Project. Proceedings of the ACER Research Conference, 2000 (pp. 6–10).

Colbert, P. & van Kraayenoord, C. (2000). Mapping of provisions: States, systems and sectors. In C. van Krayenoord, J. Elkins, C. Palmer, F., Rickards, P. Colbert et al. *Literary, numeracy and students with disabilities* (pp. 3–88). Canberra: Department of Education, Training and Youth Affairs.

Cumming, J. J. & Elkins, J. (1994). Are any errors careless? *Focus on Learning problems in Mathematics, 16*(4), 21–30.

Cumming, J. J. & Elkins, J. (1996). Stability of strategy use for addition facts: A training study and implications for instruction. *Journal of Cognitive Education, 5*, 101–116.

Dengate, B. (1998). Constructivism and the mathematics classroom. In N. Ellerton (Ed.), Issues in mathematics education: A contemporary perspective (pp. 199–213). Perth: MASTEC, Mathematics, Science and Technology Education Centre, Edith Cowan University.

Department of Employment, Education, Training and Youth Affairs (1997). *Numeracy = everyone's business*. Report of the Numeracy Education Strategy Development Conference, May 1997, Canberra: Author.

Donaldson, N. (1998). Teaching "visual" subjects to visually impaired teenagers. *ANZAEVH Newsletter, 32*(2), 21–26.

Ellerton, N. F., Clarkson, P., & Clements, P. A. (in press). Language factors in mathematics teaching and learning. In Mathematics Research Group of Australasia. *Four yearly review of mathematics education research*. Waikato, NZ: Author.

Fitzsimons, G. E., Jungwirth, H., Maasz, J. & Schloeglmann, W. (1997). Adults and mathematics. In A.J. Bishop, K. Clements, C. Keitel, J. Kilpatrick & C. Laborde (Eds), *International Handbook of Mathematics education Part 2* (pp. 755–784). Dordrecht: Kluwer.

Geary, D. C. (1993). Mathematical disabilities: Cognitive, neuropsychological and genetic components. *Psychological Bulletin, 114*, 345–362.

Gersten, R. & Chard, D. (1999). Number sense: Rethinking arithmetic instruction for students with mathematical disabilities. *Journal of Special Education, 33*, 18–28.

Giangreco, M. F., Edelman, S., Dennis, R., & Cloniger, C. J. (1995). Use and impact of COACH with students who are deaf–blind. Jou*rnal of Association for Persons with Severe Handicap, 20*, 121–135.

Harris, P. (1991). *Mathematics in a cultural context: Aboriginal perspectives on space, time and money*. Geelong, Vic.: Deakin University Press.

Hatano, G. (1997). Learning arithmetic with an abacus. In T. Nunes & P. Bryant (Eds), *Learning and teaching mathematics: An international perspective* (pp. 209–232). Hove, UK: Psychology Press.

Johnson, K. R., & Layng, T. V. J. (1992). Breaking the structuralist barrier: Literacy and numeracy with fluency. *American Psychologist, 47*, 1475–1490.

Joseph, G. G. (1993). Multiplication algorithms. In Nelson, D., Joseph, G. G., & Williams, J. (Eds), *Multicultural mathematics: Teaching mathematics from a global perspective* (pp. 85–125). Oxford: Oxford University Press.

Larcombe, T. (1985). *Mathematical learning difficulties in the secondary school: Pupil needs and teacher roles.* Milton Keynes: Open University Press.

Louden, W., Chan, L. K. S., Elkins, J. Greaves, D., House, H., Milton, M., Nichols, S., Rohl, M., Rivalland, J., & van Kraayenoord, C. (2000). *Mapping the territory: Primary students with learning difficulties: Literacy and numeracy*. Canberra, ACT: Department of Education, Training and Youth Affairs.

Lowrie, T. (2000). A case of an individual's reluctance to visualize. *Focus on learning problems in mathematics, 22*, 17–26.

MacCluskie, K. C., Tunick, R. H., Dial, J. G., & Paul, D. S. (1998). The role of vision in the development of abstraction ability. *Journal of Visual Impairment and Blindness*, 92, 189–199.

Marks, G. N. & Ainley, J. (1997). *Reading comprehension and numeracy among junior secondary school students in Australia*. Melbourne: Australian Council for Educational Research.

Miles, T. R. & Miles, E. (Eds) (1992). *Dyslexia and mathematics*. London: Routledge.

Miller, S. P., Harris, C.A., Strawser, S. Jones, W. P., & Mercer, C. D. (1998). Teaching multiplication to second graders in inclusive settings. *Focus on Learning Problems in Mathematics, 20*(4), 50–70.

Mochon, S. & Roman, J. V. (1998). Strategies of mental computation used by elementary and secondary school children. *Focus on Learning Problems in Mathematics, 20*(4), 35–49.

Moll, L. C. (Ed.) (1990). *Vygotsky and education: Instructional implications and applications of sociohistorical psychology*. Cambridge: Cambridge University Press.

Montague, M. (1997). Cognitive strategy instruction in mathematics for students with learning disabilities. *Journal of Learning Disabilities, 30*, 164–177.

Montague, M. & Applegate, B. (1993a). Middle school students' mathematical problem solving: An analysis of think-aloud protocols. *Learning Disability Quarterly, 16*, 19–32.

Montague, M. & Applegate, B. (1993b). Mathematical problem-solving characteristics of middle school students with learning disabilities. *The Journal of Special Education, 27*, 175–201.

Nelson, D. (1993). Ten key areas of the curriculum. In Nelson, D., Joseph, G. G., & Williams, J. (Eds), *Multicultural mathematics: Teaching mathematics from a global perspective* (pp. 42–84). Oxford: Oxford University Press.

Nunes, T., Schleimann, A. L., & Carraher, D. (1993). *Street mathematics and school mathematics*. New York: Cambridge University Press.

Palmer, C. (2000). Disabilities in vision. In C. van Kraayenoord, J. Elkins, C. Palmer, F. W. Rickards, P. Colbert. *Literacy, numeracy and students with disabilities*. (Vol. 1, pp. 47–66). Canberra: Department of Education, Training and Youth Affairs.

Renshaw, P. (1996). A sociocultural view of the mathematics education of young children. In H. Mansfield, N. Pateman, & N. Bednarz (Eds) *Mathematics for tomorrows' children: International perspectives on curriculum* (pp. 59–78). Dordrecht: Kluwer.

Rohl, M., Milton, M. & Brady, D. (2000). Survey of schools. In W. Louden, L. K. S. Chan, J. Elkins, D. Greaves, H. House, M. Milton, S. Nichols, M. Rohl, J. Rivalland, & C. van Kraayenoord. *Mapping the territory*. (Vol. 2, pp. 7–46). Canberra, ACT: Department of Education, Training, and Youth Affairs.

Rourke, B. P. & Conway, J.A. (1997). Disabilities of arithmetic and mathematical reasoning: Perspectives from neurology and neuropsychology. *Journal of Learning Disabilities, 30*, 34–46.

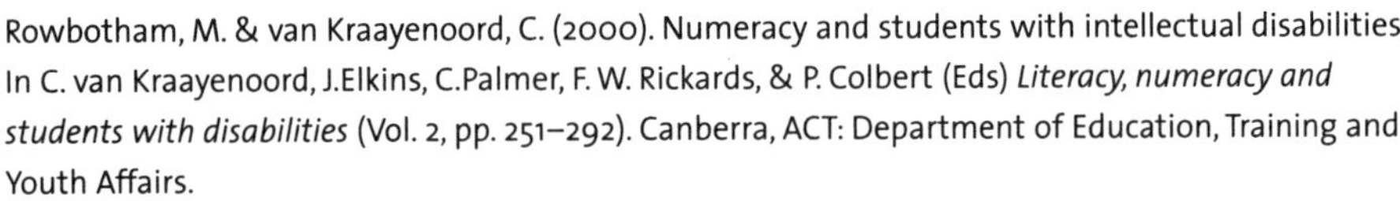

Rowbotham, M. & van Kraayenoord, C. (2000). Numeracy and students with intellectual disabilities, In C. van Kraayenoord, J.Elkins, C.Palmer, F. W. Rickards, & P. Colbert (Eds) *Literacy, numeracy and students with disabilities* (Vol. 2, pp. 251–292). Canberra, ACT: Department of Education, Training and Youth Affairs.

Royer, J. M, Cisero, C. A, & Carlo, M.S. (1993). Techniques and procedures for assessing cognitive skills. *Review of Educational Research,63*, 201-243.

Skinner, C. H. & Schock, H. H. (1995). Best practices in assessing mathematics skills. In A. Thomas & J.Grimes (Eds), *Best practices in School psychology III* (pp. 731–740). Washington, D.C.: The National Association of School Psychologists.

Sleeman, D. (1985). Basic algebra revisited: A study with 14 year olds. *International Journal of Man-Machine Studies, 22*, 127–149.

Thompson, I. (2000). Teaching place value in the UK: Time for a reappraisal? *Education Review, 52*, 291–298.

van Kraayenoord, C., Elkins, J., Palmer, C., Rickards, F., Colbert, P., et al (2000). *Literacy, numeracy and students with disabilities*. Canberra: Department of Education, Training and Youth Affairs.

Westwood, P. (2000). *Numeracy and learning difficulties: Approaches to learning and development*. Camberwell, Vic: Australian Council for Educational Research.

Wong, B. (1996). *The ABCs of learning disabilities*. San Diego: Academic Press.

Wright, R. J. (1991). What number knowledge is possessed by children entering the kindergarten year of school? *Mathematics Education Research Journal, 3*, 1–16.

Wright, R. J., Martland, J. & Stafford, A. K. (2000). *Early numeracy: Assessment for teaching and intervention*. London: Paul Chapman.

11

Educating students with high support needs

JEFF SIGAFOOS AND MICHAEL ARTHUR

Case studies

The term *high support* conjures up images of students with a variety of special educational needs that are intensive, extensive, and pervasive. The following case studies describe two students with high support needs You will notice some similarities and differences between Rita and Evan. Both could be described as having high support needs but each is also, of course, a unique individual with many distinct characteristics. It is hoped that these brief descriptions will give you an understanding and appreciation of the characteristics of students who are considered to have high support needs

As you read each case, ask yourself:

- What type of educational program do Rita and Evan need?
- How could other students in a regular classroom help in Rita and Evan's education?
- How is the type of program related to their age and unique learning and behavioural characteristics?
- More specifically, what assessment information could assist you in developing this program?
- What types of educational goals might be included in the child's individualised education plan (IEP)?
- How would you set out to teach these goals? And what adaptations might better enable the child to achieve these goals?

Rita

Everything seemed fine when Rita was born six years ago. She was a lovely girl with a passive temperament and she thrived during her first few months of life. But near her first birthday, her parents noticed that she seemed much more irritable and grizzly. Instead of the happy content child they had known, she started to cry and scream much more often and for no apparent reason. Equally disturbing was the fact that she also stopped using the few single words that she had previously mastered. As if these changes were not worrying enough, she also seemed to be having a lot of trouble just moving around and was especially clumsy when she used her hand to reach for and grasp something.

Shortly after these initial signs appeared, a curious hand mannerism was noticed. Now it seemed that all Rita wanted to do was rub her hands together as if she were continually washing them. At this time, Rita was seen at a paediatric clinic and was suspected of having Rett syndrome. This initial and tentative diagnosis was later confirmed by a genetic test.

As with most girls with Rett syndrome, at six years of age Rita is unable to walk or talk, and unable to use her hands very well for any real functional activity. But she retains a number of informal gestures, such as facial expressions and body movements, that seem to be her way of communicating. When she likes something (music, for example), she smiles, vocalises, and wiggles excitedly. When she does not like something, she lets you know by looking away and tensing her arms.

Rita attends a special education classroom with four other children with high support needs associated with a combination of developmental and physical disabilities. The classroom is staffed by a teacher and teaching assistant. A large portion of the school day is spent with eating and self-care tasks. When instructional activities are implemented, Rita does not show much active participation, mainly because of her physical limitations. Although she is sometimes very alert and responsive to surroundings, these times are increasingly interspersed with longer and longer periods in which she seems completely unresponsive to her surroundings. Rita essentially functions in the profound range of intellectual disability although it has been very difficult to get a good estimate of her cognitive ability. It is certain that she requires complete assistance with most daily living tasks, such as dressing, toileting, eating, and washing.

Evan

Evan is 17 years old and has autism. He does not speak but often vocalises and has learnt to use a few manual signs to request preferred objects such as food, drinks, and help. However, he does not use his signs to communicate unless he is prompted to do so by the teacher. Instead, he often lets people know what he wants by guiding their hands to an object, such as guiding his mother's hand to the refrigerator when he wants a drink. He often shows an intense interest in an object or activity for a few weeks and then moves on to some other interest. Currently, for example, he seeks out magazines about automobiles but last month he was more interested in pocket calculators.

Evan lives at home and attends a regular classroom where there is a full-time teaching assistant to facilitate his inclusion. Both his parents and teachers find it hard to keep him occupied unless he is directly engaged in whatever activity is of interest to him at the time. Otherwise, he does not seem interested in doing anything else and lacks the skills needed to participate in other age-appropriate leisure activities. In addition, his behaviour is often inappropriate. For example, when given a turn at basketball he might simply hold the ball or drop it and walk away. Because he does not have any job skills, Evan's parents are very concerned about what will happen when he leaves school.

When Evan is given an activity at school, he tends to remain on task for only two to three minutes at most. After this he tends to wander around the room inappropriately grabbing people and objects. He is also highly distractible and it is difficult to ensure that he does not wander off. At times, Evan appears completely oblivious to his surroundings. For example, if someone enters the room or talks to him, he often fails to show any overt response or even a hint of recognition. At other times, however, even the slightest noise drives him to a highly agitated state.

One of the most disturbing aspects of Evan's behaviour is self-injury. This behaviour is sometimes precipitated by a state of agitation and a tantrum that includes yelling and dropping to the ground. This might then escalate into slapping and hitting himself in the face and head. This has been an ongoing problem since early childhood and it has made his parents and teachers reluctant to take him out or make him do things he does not want to do, in case he becomes upset and starts hitting himself. Even minor changes to his daily routine can make him highly agitated and can set off a major tantrum.

Reflecting on Rita and Evan

Now that you have been introduced to Rita and Evan, you will understand that some students described as having high support needs face considerable problems at school. We hope that you also generated some responses to the questions posed earlier about designing an educational program for students with high support needs

Let us take a moment to reflect on what might be included in an educational program for Rita. From the brief description, you might have thought it important to focus on maintaining her existing skills and trying to get something going in the area of communication. Do you think there could be anything done to increase her levels of alertness? Might it be important to assess her preferences and teach choice-making? What might be done to promote peer interaction, and to increase her participation in everyday home, school, and community-based activities?

Now Evan. Would you agree that he needs to improve his skills and behaviours? What specific adaptive skills might be priorities? Should it be social skills, communication skills, or perhaps leisure skills? Why not all three? What about planning for his transition from school to work? What is he going to do after school? You probably also noted a need for positive behavioural support to address his tantrums and self-injury.

What you will learn in this chapter

The overall aim of the chapter is to help you gain a basic understanding of the unique characteristics of students with high support needs There are numerous issues that arise in designing and implementing educational programs for these students. One of the more specific aims of this chapter, therefore, is to assist you in better understanding these educational issues. In addition, after having read this chapter, we hope that you would be able to:

- describe the range of conditions associated with the term *high support needs*;
- list the learning and behavioural characteristics of students with high support needs;
- distinguish among the various curriculum models and content that would be appropriate for students with high support needs;
- demonstrate a general understanding of techniques for assessing students with high support needs;

- outline the types of educational goals relevant for students with high support needs;
- show an understanding of the basic instructional principles that have proven effective in teaching students with high support needs;
- discuss the role of integrative and inclusive practices that facilitate the participation, socialisation, and independence of students with high support needs; and
- delineate the process for developing positive behavioural interventions to support individuals with high support needs and challenging behaviours.

In the next section, we begin with a comprehensive definition of the term *high support needs* Following this we provide a description of some of the learning and behavioural characteristics that are common among children with high support needs These descriptions are meant to illustrate the range of characteristics and the many and varied issues associated with teaching students with high support needs

Defining high support needs

The term *high support* needs has only recently become commonly used in Australia. One of the great benefits of using this term is that it focuses on what is needed to enable the student to participate in daily life. In contrast, other terms that have been used, such as students with severe, *multiple*, or *profound* disabilities, focus on the type and degree of disability that the child experiences rather than on what an educational program might need to provide. This is an important distinction because the level of support required varies within a group of children. Even within a classroom of children who have similar types of multiple disabilities, children are unlikely to have exactly the same educational needs.

Still, the students considered in this chapter share some characteristics. The following definition identifies many of the characteristics of students with high support needs:

> Students considered to have the most severe disabilities are students with combinations of a wide range of multiple impairments. The seriousness of these impairments, always in combination with a severe intellectual impairment, causes a profound loss of functioning. Many of these students have various orthopaedic and sensory disabilities and may have little or no voluntary control over their movements. Many are medically at risk, chronically ill, or medically dependent, while others have extremely severe behavior disorders. These students often do not demonstrate any obvious choices or preferences, may show no signs of anticipation, or show very little affect. Their self-injurious or assaultive behavior may be so severe that they are restricted from participation in many environments. (Sailor, Gee, Goetz, & Graham, 1988, p. 89)

As you might gather from this quotation, there are some common general characteristics, but there is also much individual variability. That is, each child has varying combinations of needs, although all have severe intellectual disabilities and other impairments. This complexity makes the task of pinpointing elements of best practice for this population an engaging one for researchers and teachers alike.

Describing students with high support needs

Because of the complexity of the matters with which we are dealing, you will appreciate why is it helpful to have a more complete description of the learning and behavioural characteristics of children with high support needs Along these lines, Thompson and Guess (1989) conducted interviews with teachers of students with high support needs From these interviews they learnt that students with high support needs demonstrate several common characteristics. These included limited levels of awareness and responsiveness to the environment, medical complications, and limited communication ability. Let us take a closer look at some of these learning and behavioural characteristics.

Numerous and complex conditions

Students with high support needs can have numerous and complex conditions arising from a combination of developmental and physical disabilities, sensory impairments, and health or medical problems (such as seizure disorders). Developmental disability includes severe to profound intellectual disability and/or severe autism. Physical disabilities can be caused by cerebral palsy, brain injury, muscular dystrophy, and a number of other genetic disorders, such as Rett syndrome (Batshaw, 1997). Several of these terms are defined in the Glossary. The interaction of developmental, intellectual, physical, sensory, and health or medical issues can certainly complicate the educational process. The needs of the students not only are complicated, but also change over time as developmental processes and medical conditions necessitate. For example, the special health needs of students might include the need for non-oral (tube) feeding procedures, catheterisation, management of a tracheostomy or shunt, and perhaps administration of medication to control epilepsy (Orelove & Sobsey, 1996).

In addition, specific genetic conditions and syndromes can be associated with specific learning and behavioural characteristics (Dykens, Hodapp, & Finucane, 2000). Rett syndrome, for example, is associated with the stereotyped hand mannerisms that were described in the case study of Rita. Autism, in contrast, is often associated with ritualistic behaviours and obsessive routines. If the routine is disrupted, as in the description of Evan, autism can lead to emotional outbursts. Teachers do not necessarily have to become experts in syndromes—because every child is an individual, even if they have the same genetic syndrome—but it is important that teachers understand the educational implications of these associations between syndromes and behaviour.

Need for adaptations

As mentioned above, students with high support needs often experience difficulties with hearing, vision, motor control, and mobility. Vision and hearing acuity, and limb and muscle control, are challenges for students. Accordingly, the identification of ways to maximise student participation and independence is a high priority. Examples of adaptations and equipment include wheelchairs and other adapted seating and positioning devices, magnifying glasses to assist vision, hearing aids, adapted utensils for eating and drinking, adapted fasteners for clothing, and architectural modifications (such as wider doorways and toilets for children in wheelchairs). Additional assistive technology includes voice-output communication aids and switch operated toys and appliances (Flippo, Inge, & Barcus, 1995). Therefore, teachers should know something about adapting materials and teaching children to use assistive technology.

Lack of responsiveness and lack of motivation

Some students with high support needs seem unresponsive to environmental stimulation. For example, it might be difficult to gain and maintain the child's attention, they might be easily distracted, and they might appear to look through, rather than look at, you. In addition to a general unresponsiveness, it can be extremely difficult to motivate students to participate in classroom and educational activities. This might indicate that the task itself is less than functional or boring and needs to be reconsidered. It might also reflect the fact that some children with high support needs have not yet learnt to value the usual types of social reinforcers, such as praise, doing a task well (referred to as intrinsic motivation), or gaining new knowledge in a topic. They might also be uninterested in some tangible rewards (such as gold stickers or special privileges).

One important task for the teacher is, therefore, to teach functional or useful skills in the context of relevant activities (e.g., feeding, dressing, shopping, playing, and swimming). If possible, it is also helpful to select tasks that are related to the child's interests.

A teacher also needs to identify potential reinforcers that can be used to motivate students to learn, and this often requires undertaking a systematic preference assessment (Lohrmann-O'Rourke & Browder, 1998). Teachers must be aware that many environmental and/or constitutional factors can account for a lack of responsiveness or motivation, and fluctuating behavioural states.

Fluctuating behavioural states

Behavioural states refer to the child's levels of alertness. The child's level of alertness can fluctuate widely in students with high support needs A child's state can change

from active and alert at one moment to inactive and sleepy the next. Over the day, the observed states of a child might include being awake, drowsy, dazed, or completely asleep. Studies have investigated the nature of behaviour states in individuals with high support needs (e.g., Ault, Guy, Guess, Bashinski, & Roberts, 1995). Their results suggest that students with high support needs spend a considerable amount of time in behaviour states that appear less than optimal for learning. Imagine trying to teach a child who is drowsy, dazed, or sleeping. In addition, various contextual factors (such as the type of activity, amount and type of social interaction, and even the child's diet), might influence these behavioural states. The implication here is that teachers should try to assist the movement of a student into a behavioural state that is better suited for teaching—such as by arranging conditions to increase the child's level of alertness—if learning is to occur.

Challenging behaviour

As with any child, children with high support needs might occasionally have episodes of inappropriate, unacceptable, or disruptive behaviour. It does appear, however, that individuals with developmental disabilities are more likely to have frequent and severe behaviour problems (Thompson & Grey, 1994). Common types of problem behaviours in children with high support needs include:

(a) tantrums (screaming, crying);

(b) aggression (hitting, kicking, biting);

(c) stereotyped movements (body rocking, head weaving, mouthing fingers);

(d) self-injury (biting, hitting, and scratching self); and

(e) a number of other problems, (food refusal, eating inedible objects, and excessive spitting).

When these problems are frequent and severe they are called *challenging behaviours*. Challenging behaviours cause harm and damage and interfere with teaching and learning. Assessment and treatment is a major educational priority for children with challenging behaviours. The aim of intervention is to replace the problem behaviour with socially acceptable alternatives.

Since the early 1980s, a steady stream of evidence has been accumulating on the causes of challenging behaviour among individuals with developmental disabilities, including students with high support needs (Schroeder, Tessel, Loupe, & Stodgell, 1997). This evidence strongly suggests that in some cases challenging behaviours can be influenced by a poor environment, such as one that is devoid of meaningful activities or, worse yet, can be influenced by neglect and abuse. Challenging behaviours can also be exacerbated by medical and psychiatric problems, such as illness, infection, pain, and depression or related mood disorders. In addition, it now appears certain that in many cases, perhaps even in the majority of cases, problem behaviours in persons with

developmental disabilities represent learnt behaviours that might serve one or more of the following functions or purposes:

- *attention:* problem behaviour is used as a means to gain and maintain the attention of another person;
- *escape:* problem behaviour is used as a means to escape and avoid nonpreferred activities (such as academic tasks or even unwanted social interaction);
- *tangible:* problem behaviour is used as a means to gain and maintain access to preferred objects and activities (such as preferred foods, drinks, and toys); or
- *sensory stimulation:* problem behaviour occurs because it automatically provides the individual with reinforcing sensory consequences (such as tactile, visual, or vestibular stimulation).

The discovery that challenging behaviour is often learnt and serves one of more of these functions has led to major changes in the way these behaviours are managed. Instead of focusing on suppressing problem behaviour, interventions today are more focused on the provision of comprehensive support programs. This more constructive approach is known as *positive behavioural support* (Koegel, Koegel, & Dunlap, 1996). In addition to investigating and improving general environmental factors, successful intervention for challenging behaviours requires attention to medical and psychiatric matters. In addition, behavioural interventions have become more positive and educational. The aim of behavioural intervention is to replace problem behaviours by teaching alternative and more appropriate skills (Scotti & Meyer, 1999). The key to success when using this more educative approach is to teach alternative skills that serve the same function or purpose as the problem behaviour. Some examples of alternative skills that might be taught to replace problem behaviours for each of the functions listed before are shown in Table 11.1.

Incidence, prevalence, and epidemiology

How many children are born with high support needs (incidence) and, at any given time, how many children have high support needs (prevalence)? Epidemiology is also concerned with the range of conditions that lead to high support needs

It appears that the incidence is actually increasing in some countries because of improved neonatal care. This has, in turn, meant an increase in prevalence, meaning that schools must be prepared for the task of educating more students with high support needs In terms of epidemiology, there is a number of biological, genetic, and environmental factors that can result in a child having high support needs For example, there are hundreds of genetic syndromes associated with developmental and physical disability (Batshaw, 1997). In addition, brain damage prior to, during, or shortly after birth can result in injuries that result in the child having high support

Table 11.1 Examples of skills to replace attention, escape, tangible, and sensory-related problem behaviour

IF THE PROBLEM BEHAVIOUR IS USED TO ACHIEVE:	TEACH THE CHILD:
Attention	a better way to gain attention such as by using a voice-output device
Escape	to request help with difficult tasks or indicate "no" in a more appropriate manner
Tangible	to request objects and activities using augmentative communication
Sensory stimulation	to play with toys that provide an alternative source of stimulation

needs Exposure to toxins or injuries from physical assault can also cause severe disability.

According to the Australian Bureau of Statistics (1998a, 1998b), 19% of the Australian population has a disability of one type or another (3.6 million people). Only about 3% of the population (or roughly 598,200 individuals) are described as having severe disability, and a similar number (537,700) are said to have disabilities resulting in profound levels of restriction in core activities of daily life (such as feeding, dressing, mobility, and communication). These data suggest perhaps up to 1 million Australians—across all ages—might be considered to have high support needs

Turning now to schools, in 2000 the New South Wales Department of Education and Training (2000) estimated how many students with severe intellectual or physical disability were expected to be attending government schools in 2001. The department also described the type of school the children were expected to attend. These estimates suggested that 26 students with severe intellectual disability were expected to attend regular classes in regular schools in 2001. That is, 26 students were expected to be fully included. In contrast, 220 students with severe physical disabilities were to be fully included in regular classes in 2001. A large number with severe intellectual disability (1,064) was to be placed in support classes in regular schools, and another 1,707 in special schools. It is not possible to determine from these data exactly how many students were described as having high support needs The best guess is that there are now thousands of children with high support needs in schools in New South Wales alone, and obviously thousands more across Australia. It appears that a small percentage of these children are educated in regular classrooms, although there is a trend to include them in support classes in regular schools in which there are

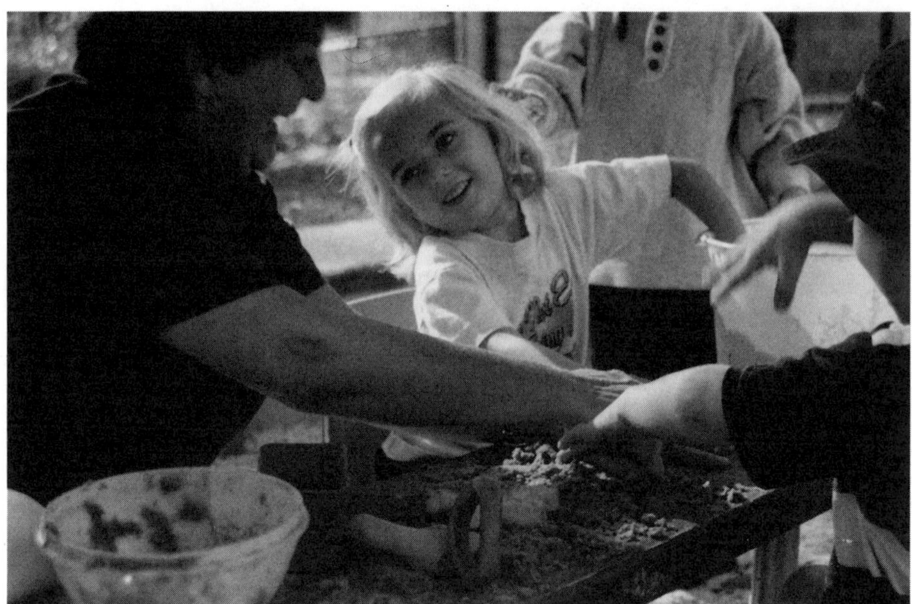

This young girl is learning social, intellectual, and aesthetic skills in this play activity.

opportunities for interaction with typical students. A considerable number, perhaps the majority of children with high support needs, are educated in special schools in which, of course, there is less opportunity for incidental contact with non-disabled peers.

Individualised instruction

For students with one or more of these characteristics, there is clearly the need for a comprehensive and individualised educational program that provides an alternative to the academically oriented curriculum designed for the majority of school-aged students. Although students with high support needs should not be excluded from the potential benefits of academic instruction or from contact with peers in regular classrooms, they must also have opportunities to learn self-care, social skills, communication skills, daily living skills, and leisure skills. Additional instruction in everyday domestic, community, and vocational settings might also be required to ensure the generalisation and maintenance of these functional skills.

Because some students might have a combination of complex conditions, teachers of students with high support needs often require input from a variety of other professionals. Children with high support needs are candidates for communication intervention, physiotherapy, and occupational therapy, and might also require specialist social work services to address communication access. Others might need psychological and psychiatric services to address challenging behaviours, treatment for psychopathology, or medical interventions to be undertaken in the classroom (such as tube feeding, catheterisation, and administration of seizure-controlling medication) that might require frequent consultations with nurses and doctors. Siblings and peers also play an integral role in the educational process and should be included when planning educational programs.

Coordinating this variety of input often rests with the teacher, but current state-of-the-art practice suggests that this process is facilitated when teachers work as part of a collaborative team working in a partnership with parents (Giangreco, Whiteford, Whiteford, & Doyle, 1998). Collaboration in assessment, program design, and strategy implementation are defining characteristics of the transdisciplinary team model (Orelove & Sobsey, 1996). Within the transdisciplinary team model, educators and therapists not only provide a hands-on service (such as direct physiotherapy to the student), but also provide indirect services in their roles as consultants to parents and teachers (Lamorey & Ryan, 1998). The range of both direct and indirect services constitutes the student's individual education plan (IEP).

Integration and inclusion

Integration is the process of moving individuals with disabilities from more restrictive to less restrictive situations, and enhancing their participation and autonomy in these environments. Inclusion usually means the involvement of these individuals within the regular class and school that they would normally attend if they did not have a disability. Inclusive practices are the means by which inclusion is achieved and include (but are not limited to) the modification and adaptation of curriculum materials, peer networking and individualised instruction (see Box 11.1, page 482).

The data that we considered for New South Wales students enrolling in 2001 were broadly consistent with the findings of Dempsey and Foreman (1997) who analysed trends in the placement of students with various disabilities in New South Wales between 1986 and 1994. They found evidence of a movement of students with moderate or severe intellectual disability from special schools to support classes in regular schools, although there was no significant change in the number of students moving on to regular classes. In addition, they concluded that the overall proportion of students with disabilities in special schools or support classes was stable during this period.

Nevertheless, as part of the process of integration and inclusion, regular teachers are often considered to be the key partners in the design of educational programs for students with high support needs in the regular school. How can we prepare for the involvement of a student with complex needs in our classroom, in such a way that academic and social learning goals for all students are attained? In Box 11.2 (page 483), a regular teacher reflects on the enrolment and participation of Joshua, a student with a range of needs, in her Year 5 class. When you have read this, consider the tips for promoting inclusion that are provided, in light of this case study. As you

Box 11.1 Teacher tips to promote inclusion

Before inclusion

- Find out about the specific needs of your student, including assessment and programming information from the previous school.
- Identify the support resources available to you.
- Establish a peer committee in your class to welcome all new students.
- Define team processes for planning an individual education plan (IEP).

During inclusion

- Use teacher support information in syllabus materials, such as the Literacy and Communication documents for English K–6 produced by the NSW Board of Studies (1997a, 1997b), in order to individualise learning goals and relevant teaching approaches.
- Foster social networks and learning activities that aim to encourage interaction and participation by all students. Examples of teaching strategies include peer tutoring and cooperative learning.
- Monitor progress and conduct IEP review meetings.

After inclusion

- Plan a transition program.
- Liaise with new host teacher.

read them, consider your present skills, knowledge, attitudes, and teaching practices and try to identify other areas that you could address in order to involve a student with high support needs in your classroom.

As we turn now to assessment and curriculum issues, keep in mind how a child's classroom and school placement might dictate their educational experiences. For example, is a teacher in a special school likely to focus on interaction with non-disabled peers? Probably not, as there would be limited opportunities for this to occur in a special school. Does this mean that peer interaction is unimportant for students with high support needs?

Assessment, curriculum development, and intervention

Assessment, curriculum development, and intervention are sometimes viewed as distinct enterprises in special education. For students with high support needs, however, assessment, curriculum development, and intervention are intimately linked. The educational team undertakes assessments to formulate goals, which become the basis of the child's individualised curriculum as reflected in the IEP. Interventions are then designed and implemented to teach these goals.

Box 11.2 Reflections on the inclusion of Joshua in my Year 5 class

It was the week before Easter and my Year 5 class and I were madly preparing gifts as well as finalising assessments of learning outcomes in two Key Learning Areas. At lunch, my principal asked for a quick chat and told me that the school was enrolling a young boy, Joshua, who had a range of fairly complex support needs She indicated that my class was the logical choice, given Joshua's age. In addition, the fact that we were such a small school meant that I had the only Year 5 class.

Joshua had moved to our town from a larger city where he had attended a special school for all of his schooling. He needed to be moved around in a wheelchair for most of the day and also required tube feeding twice a day. Over the years, Joshua had learnt to use a synthetic speech output device that he activated using a specially designed switch and pointer.

My first reaction was to panic. How could I meet the needs of Joshua while maximising the learning of the 28 other students in my class? Certainly, I had taught many classes with a diversity of student ability levels and so I was no stranger to the use of small and large group work and a focus on individual learning outcomes. However, I felt sure that the type of curriculum that Joshua would need and the level of instructional support that was needed to effectively teach him in such a large group were beyond me.

As I write, it is 10 December and Christmas is upon us. There is no fairytale ending. It has been a busy but, I believe, very successful year for all of the students in my class, for me, the families of my students, and the additional people who work in this program. After I calmed down, I discovered that there were quite a few resources that were available to support the participation of Joshua and to ensure that the learning experiences of each and every student were maximised. These resources included an occupational therapist, Vi, who worked with Joshua and me at mealtimes, a physiotherapist, Ray, who assisted me when it came to moving and positioning Joshua and a teacher's aide, Lois, who provided invaluable support for the whole class for three days each week. Oh, and I forgot to mention the special education support teacher, Brian, who worked alongside me on a daily basis and assisted me as we prepared for our review meetings each term.

In retrospect, I can identify three specific reasons for the success of the program so far.

First, the sense of teamwork and commitment that has emerged among Joshua and his family, staff, as well as his peers in the class and the wider school community. This seems to have emerged through the many and varied opportunities that have arisen for Joshua to network and interact across places, activities, people, and times.

Second, the emphasis we have placed on what Joshua can do rather than what he is challenged by or is physically unable to achieve. This idea of partial participation has seen the students in the class involving Joshua in activities in the most positive manner, and has been helped by Joshua's own exuberance and perseverance. In terms of learning outcomes, I have tried to find ways for Joshua to engage with his peers and experience curriculum in a way that is dignifying, interesting, and relevant to Joshua. While not always easy, this task was less daunting when I started to look at recent syllabus documents in which adapted materials and teaching considerations for diverse classrooms had been included. I was always able to identify learning outcomes in key learning areas that were meaningful for Joshua and linked to the work that the rest of the class was doing.

Finally, I believe that my positive role modeling has led to a greater acceptance of Joshua and a wealth of social activities involving Joshua, all of which have been affirming of his inclusion and involvement in the school and class communities. I am especially aware of the way in which I speak with Joshua, allowing him time to respond and providing him with choices and the selection of preferred activities, just as I would with my other students. All in all, this year has been a journey of discovery for Joshua and those with whom he interacts. After a Christmas break, I will be keen to watch Joshua thrive in Year 6 next year.

Source: Valerie Nugent.

To follow up these suggestions, you might like to read the work of Bauer and Shea (1999), Foreman (2001), Salend (1998), and Stainback and Stainback (1996).

During instruction, the child's progress is assessed on a regular basis. If the child is making good progress and achieves the initial goals, variations might be added to promote generalisation and maintenance of the newly acquired skills. At this point, new skills might also be added to the IEP, and the necessary strategies to teach them would be introduced. If progress is slow during intervention, modifications are made to the materials, contexts, or teaching procedures to promote better learning. Here, the teacher attempts to troubleshoot the floundering intervention program based on observations of the problems that the child (or teacher) is having.

The idea is to find another way of teaching the skill, and this might include making adaptations to the materials and/or instructional strategies. Along these lines, changes might be made to the way in which the child is taught, or to how the teacher implements the strategies. Changes might also be made to the IEP goals themselves. If, for example, a goal appears too complicated, it might be broken down into smaller teachable objectives, or it might be replaced with an easier goal. In short, effective educational programs for students with high support needs are those that link

assessment to curriculum development and to intervention as illustrated in Figure 11.1 (below).

Traditionally, assessment in special education focused on the use of standardised measures of intelligence, or on related measures of ability and achievement. The classification of a child as having a mild, moderate, severe, or profound disability was often guided, in large part, by the results of one or more such tests. Placement decisions, into a remedial program, a support classroom, or a special school, were then often based on this classification.

Today, these decisions are still made, but they are now more often based on a range of information that might still include the results of formal standardised psychological assessments. This change in practice reflects the fact that the assessment process is used for a variety of additional purposes beyond screening, diagnosis, classification, and placement. These other purposes include the use of assessment data to assist educational teams in, among other things, formulating educational goals for inclusion in the IEP, and for evaluating the intervention strategies that are used to teach these goals.

It is important to remember that standardised tests can also provide useful information about a child's perceptual and cognitive strengths and weaknesses that has considerable implications for designing educational programs. For example, if a test shows that the child has considerable difficulty with processing auditory stimuli, the teacher would provide supplementary visual cues and use clear and precise language during instruction. On the whole, such tests are less useful for designing educational programs for students with high support needs In addition to formal measures of

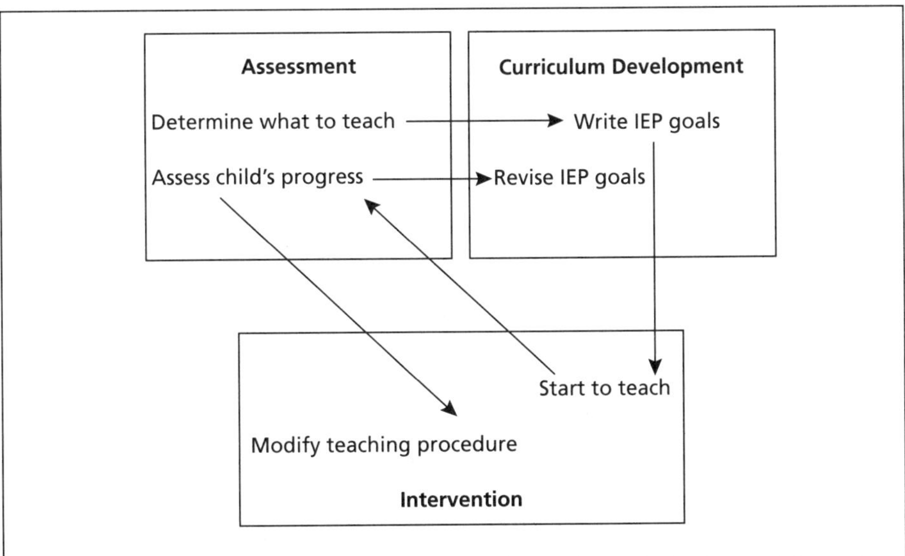

Figure 11.1 Association between assessment, curriculum development, and intervention.

intelligence, achievement, and ability, a variety of additional assessment approaches are used to assist teachers in formulating educational goals and selecting intervention strategies.

Formulating educational goals

One of the major concerns in planning an educational program for students with high support needs is deciding just what to teach these students who, by definition, have a lot of needs Where does one start? What should be the educational priorities? How does one go about formulating the educational goals that will be included in the IEP and thereby become priorities for instruction?

Formulating educational goals for students with high support needs involves consultations with parents and professional colleagues to identify the demands of the settings that the child goes to (home, school, community) and the various sub-environments within these settings (kitchen, bathroom, classroom, playground). A teacher should record where the child goes and what he or she needs to do in these settings to participate more fully. Formulating educational goals depends upon obtaining an accurate description of what is expected of the child in the course of a typical daily routine, and of the child's current skills and abilities in relation to those expectations.

Consider Evan, who was described at the beginning of this chapter (page 472). Evan is expected to accompany his parents to the shopping mall. Therefore, he needs to learn how to act appropriately in this setting and its sub-environments (department stores, cafés). Using the shopping mall includes:

(a) staying with his parents and not wandering away;

(b) purchasing items that he needs; and

(c) ordering a meal in the mall café.

So, what does Evan need to be taught? The answer depends on what he currently knows how to do. If he already knows how to order a meal at the café, but not how to make a purchase in a department store, making a purchase would be a good instructional priority. One of the major aims of instruction is to teach the child new skills that will enable him to participate more fully in the activities of daily life.

As another example, Rita's parents would like her to participate in self-care tasks and learn to do some independent leisure activities. They also want to work on teaching Rita to communicate using augmentative communication because they are aware that she is unlikely to learn how to speak. Therefore, it is important to find out what Rita can do by way of self-care and leisure tasks, in addition to what she might be able to accomplish with assistance. That is, she might never become completely independent in eating, dressing, or playing with toys, but she might still learn skills that will enable her to participate at least partially in these types of activities. She might, for example,

learn to choose the clothing that she wants to wear, make a choice from a variety of food and drink, and use a switch to operate a CD player so that she can listen to her favourite music. It is important first to find out how Rita currently communicates various functions, such as what she wants or does not want. In addition, it is helpful to know whether Rita's motor skills indicate that she could learn to use manual signs or whether she would be better suited to a switch-operated communication aid.

In line with the parents' priorities, Rita's teacher arranges to collaborate with the school's speech pathologist to assess how Rita currently indicates when she wants something. This information is then used to develop a beginning communication intervention for Rita. To give you an idea of the assessment and intervention process, we include the actual reports prepared for Rita's parents. The first report (Box 11.3, below) describes the assessment, and the second report (Box 11.4, page 489) describes the initial intervention outcomes.

Box 11.3 Teacher report: communication assessment for Rita Samson

Dear Mr and Mrs Samson,

Thank you for your patience. I have now had a chance to summarise the results of Rita's communication assessment that the speech pathologist and I conducted in the classroom earlier this month. Enclosed please find a graph that summarises the results. I believe that this information will help us in developing a more effective communication intervention program for your daughter.

Let me now try to give you an overview of the results of the assessment. The graph that I have included below is a summary of the results.

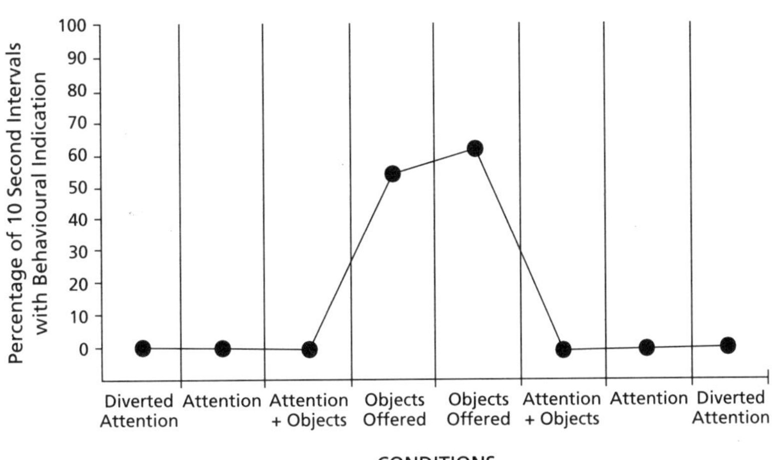

For this assessment, we observed Rita during a number of conditions, each of which lasted three minutes. The conditions were:

(1) Diverted Attention—when we were near, but did not interact with Rita;

(2) Attention—when Rita received undivided attention;

(3) Attention + Objects—when Rita received undivided attention plus there were several preferred objects present; and

(4) Choice-making—when we gave Rita the opportunity to make choices for preferred items.

The purpose of these conditions was to see how Rita might try to (a) gain and maintain our attention, and (b) gain and maintain access to preferred items.

From the videotape, we recorded how often Rita showed any of the actions that we call behavioural indicators of communication. These include actions such as reaching for or touching an item or person. Young children often use these types of behaviours to gain attention or to gain and maintain access to preferred objects.

As you can see from the graph, Rita had a lot of reaching and touching during the choice-making condition when she was offered objects, such as toys and a drink. During the assessment, Rita also showed a considerable amount of social responsiveness by making eye contact and frequently vocalising. All of this indicates to us that she could, indeed, be motivated to participate in social-communicative exchanges. This is a good sign in terms of the likely success of any communication intervention program. Another good sign is that Rita very clearly showed increased reaching and touching when objects were offered to her.

Overall, the findings suggest to me that Rita is a good candidate for an intervention to establish the use of an augmentative communication system. She has what I consider to be the necessary prerequisites for moving forward. These are: (a) a high degree of social responsiveness; (b) definite preferences and (c) a reliable way of indicating when she wants something by reaching for or touching an offered item. With these prerequisites fulfilled, communication intervention can begin by teaching the child to request preferred items.

Therefore, I suggest that we begin by teaching Rita to reach out and touch a switch on an electronic communication device as a way of requesting access to preferred items.

We can start the teaching process next week. The results from this teaching phase will enable me to provide you with guidance on how to expand her communication skills to indicate other wants and needs I will provide another report, in about a month or so, on the results of our initial teaching efforts to let you know how things are going.

Sincerely,

Ms Teri Komparis

Special Education Teacher

Middle Ridge Special School

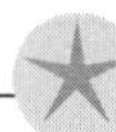

The second report describes progress during the communication program. As you will see in Box 11.4 (below), Rita made very rapid progress. It is significant that Rita was willing to continue her contact in situations beyond the lesson in which the communication program was introduced.

Note that the teacher based her evaluation on collected data, and not just on a feeling that the program was working. Data-driven interventions are extremely important when working with students with high support needs Also note that the teacher's description is very instructive for Rita's parents.

Box 11.4 Teacher report: communication intervention for Rita Samson

Dear Mr and Mrs Samson,

Although it has only been a few weeks since my last report, I wanted to write to give you some great news. We are all very excited because Rita has been making very good progress in her communication program. Not only does she seem to like the program, but also she has shown rapid progress, as you can see from the results on the graph below.

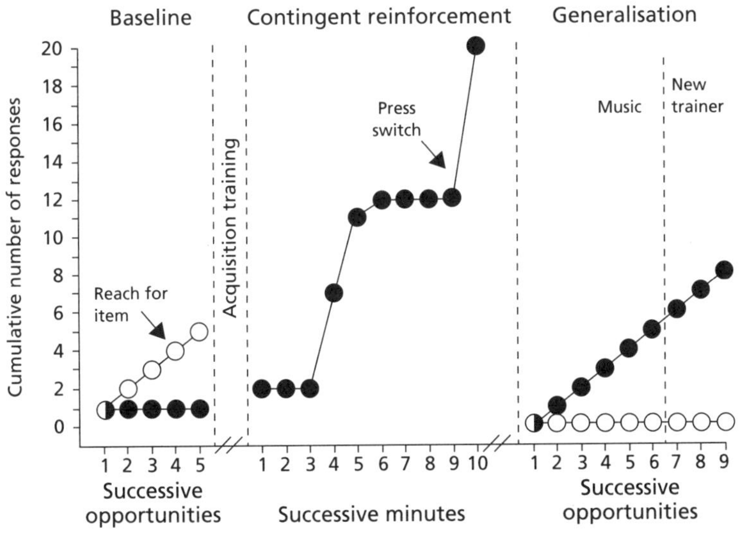

The graph shows the frequency of two behaviours (i.e., reaching versus using an augmentative and alternative communication device—we call this an AAC device). Initially, during the Baseline phase, Rita reliably reached for the preferred items that were made available. She did this on five out of five opportunities, and she did not press the BigMack switch at any time during Baseline.

Next, we implemented some strategies to teach Rita to use the AAC device as a way of communicating a request. This teaching phase involved waiting for

Rita to reach for the preferred item and then guiding her hand to press the switch. When she pressed the switch, she was given the requested item. We also included some verbal prompts during this Acquisition Training.

After this brief teaching phase, which lasted about 20 minutes, we simply waited for Rita to make a request, before giving her the preferred item. This is called the Contingent Reinforcement phase. As you can see, this phase was associated with a high rate of requesting. In the final two phases, Rita also used the switch to request music, even when my teaching assistant, Mrs Roberts, was the trainer. This result suggests that Rita had generalised the skill, and was able to request other objects from other people.

Overall, the results of the intervention are very positive and show very clearly that Rita learnt to use the AAC device to request preferred items. Given these promising results, Rita is probably a good candidate for an expanded communication system involving the use of a picture-based AAC device with digitised (recorded) speech. If you are happy for us to continue with this voice-output communication device, I would like to keep working on expanding these initial skills as part of her IEP goal to improve her communication ability.

You might also be interested in following up on some of this at home. In case you do, I have included the communication symbols that might be relevant to Rita at home.

Of course, it is one thing to provide some symbols, but it is another to ensure that Rita uses these for meaningful communication. Rita should be able to learn to use some of these symbols to request access to preferred objects (e.g., sandwich, drink, music). To teach this, you could follow these steps:

- Offer the item.
- Wait for Rita to reach for the item.
- As she reaches, guide her to touch the symbol for that item.
- Give her the requested item as soon as she points to the correct symbol.
- Over time, provide less and less guidance so that Rita independently points to symbols to request things she wants and needs
- It will help to make sure that you do not always offer the item, so that she learns to make requests more spontaneously.

I hope some of this information is useful. As I said, we will continue to work on this program and I will keep you posted on Rita's progress. In the meantime, feel free to contact me if you want to talk about any aspect of Rita's education.

Sincerely,

Ms Teri Komparis

Special Education Teacher

Middle Ridge Special School

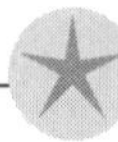

Descriptions such as these can be obtained by using a combination of formal ratings and informal observations. Formal measures are typically obtained by asking parents or teachers to complete a rating of adaptive behaviour using a standardised rating scale. Commonly used adaptive behaviour rating scales include the Adaptive Behavior Scales of the American Association on Mental Retardation (Nihira, Leland, & Lambert, 1993) and the Vineland Adaptive Behavior Scales (Sparrow, Balla, & Cicchetti, 1984). These devices ask questions about a child's skills across a number of domains, such as communication, daily living skills, socialisation, motor skills, and maladaptive behaviour. For specific items, such as "Feed self with spoon", the informant gives a rating of whether or not the child can do the skill. Scoring options might be yes, sometimes or partially, no. Ratings of adaptive behaviour highlight the child's existing skills as well as areas of skill deficit that might then be targeted for instruction.

The reliability and validity of results from adaptive behaviour scales depend upon who completes the form and how he or she interprets the questions and the scoring system. As a result, it will often be helpful for teachers to observe the child in normal daily settings. The teacher might, for example, observe the child at mealtime to determine whether the child can use a spoon and, if not, what level and type of assistance might be required to enable the child to gain this skill. This information might also be used to formulate goals. For example, if the child can grasp the spoon but has difficulty getting it to her mouth, the education team might decide to work on increasing her fluency in using a spoon. It is natural to work on this goal during meals at home, at school, and in restaurants.

To illustrate the process outlined above, Table 11.2 (page 492) includes the initial educational priorities that were formulated for a 7-year-old boy with high support needs Kurt has profound intellectual disability, visual impairment, and cerebral palsy which makes it difficult for him to use his left hand. He does not speak and is unable to feed, dress, wash, or toilet himself. These limitation in adaptive skills are so significant that he requires physical assistance to complete tasks that most of us take for granted. This is his second year in a special education classroom that is located in a regular primary school. His parents completed the Vineland Adaptive Behavior Scales at the beginning of the school year, and in the first few weeks of Term 1 the teacher collected additional assessment data using informal observations in the classroom.

After this, in consultation with the parents, speech pathologist and occupational therapist, the team wrote the three goals listed in Table 11.2. These were the instructional priorities for Terms 1 and 2. As you examine Table 11.2, consider the fact that—on the Vineland—Kurt could indicate his preferences, when offered a choice, by reaching for his preferred item. As a result the teacher and speech pathologist thought it was good to take this a step further and teach Kurt to point to a picture of the item he wanted. This was considered of long-term benefit as it would provide him

Table 11.2 Instructional priorities for Kurt during Terms 1 and 2

Domain	Goal statement
Communication	If preferred items are offered, and if Kurt is provided with the communication book, he will point to the picture of the item he wants within 10 seconds, and he will then take the item that corresponds to the picture he pointed to. For example, if offered a choice of milk or juice, and if he points to the picture of juice, he should then take the juice. Instruction will continue until Kurt is 80–100% correct. At this point, we will work on teaching Kurt to be more spontaneous in his use of the communication book, as well as introducing additional picture symbols to request other preferred items.
Daily living	If Kurt needs to use the toilet he will approach the parent (at home) or the teacher (at school) and tug on his nappy. Instruction will continue until Kurt has gone for two weeks without a toileting accident.
Socialisation	During play times at home and school, or if given the opportunity to play, Kurt will learn to choose a toy and play with it appropriately and independently for at least 10 minutes. If he becomes bored with one toy, he will learn to use his communication book to request access to another toy. Instruction will continue until Kurt chooses toys and plays appropriately for at least 10 minutes across 20 successive opportunities. This represents about two weeks worth of opportunities. After this, we will introduce additional and more complicated play routines including peer and group play.

with a more symbolic way of communicating. The need for teaching this skill was indicated by the teacher's baseline observations, which showed that Kurt did not yet know how to use pictures to make choices.

The second goal was related to toilet training. Data from the Vineland and observations showed that Kurt could not indicate when he needed to use the toilet, but that he would tug on his nappy when he needed it changed. This was a major concern to the parents and so toilet training became a major goal. The first step was to teach Kurt to indicate, by tugging on his nappy, when he needed to go to the toilet, rather than after the fact.

The third goal was selected because the formal and informal assessment data showed that Kurt did not play with toys. Most seven-year-old children spend a great deal of

time playing, and so all agreed that Kurt needed to learn how to play. It was natural, it was age-appropriate, and it was also likely to be something that he would enjoy.

Notice that Table 11.2 does not specify how the teacher is to go about teaching these skills. It is one thing to formulate goals, but it is another to write instructional strategies for teaching them.

Selecting intervention strategies

From our experience, formulating goals is relatively easy when compared to selecting and implementing instructional strategies that are effective in achieving the goals. Once a set of goals has been formulated, teachers need to decide how to go about teaching the child so that he or she is likely to achieve these goals. To teach effectively, educators should be familiar with the instructional strategies that research has shown to be effective. Too often teachers rely on unproven methods or simply make up something, try it out for a few days, and then try something else if it does not seem to work. Their decisions are based on intuition rather than on reliable and valid evidence, which could be why the students do not seem to make much progress.

Fortunately, teachers can now turn to a large body of evidence that evaluates which strategies work and which do not. Strategies that good research has shown to be effective are known as *empirically validated strategies*. For example, if you wanted to teach a child to request preferred objects using a picture-based augmentative and alternative communication system, there are a number of studies that you could read to find out how to do this. A similarly large database exists for teaching any number of communication, daily living, and socialisation skills. The list of resources at the end of this chapter is a good place to start your search for empirically validated strategies.

As you delve into the research literature you will be amazed—and perhaps a little overwhelmed—by the volume of information that can be used to guide interventions for children with high support needs Indeed, there are well over 200 studies on how to teach individuals with developmental disabilities to make requests using augmentative and alternative communication systems. Which strategies are best suited to the individual student?

There is no easy answer to this question as there are many ways to support student learning. A strategy that seems appropriate, and that has been shown to be effective with students with similar needs, might not necessarily work when you use it in the classroom.

However, success in teaching students with high support needs requires more than empirically validated strategies. Success also requires an understanding of the basic principles of learning upon which these strategies are based. A full description of the basic learning principles that underlie empirically validated instructional strategies is beyond the scope of this chapter, but these can be found in several excellent textbooks,

such as Cipani and Spooner (1994), Westling and Fox (2000) and Snell and Brown (2000). The basic principles that these books describe remain as the bases for today's most effective instructional strategies. We also urge you to study Table 11.3 (below) carefully as these teaching tips are based on some of the most important learning principles.

Table 11.3 Tips for teaching students with high support needs

Find out what the student likes	This is important for several reasons. First, when you know what a child likes and dislikes, you can add these to the environment. This enriches the environment and improves the child's quality of life. Second, the use of preferred materials and activities during instruction might motivate the child to participate. Third, access to preferred objects and activities can be used as reinforcement for appropriate and correct responses during instruction, which is vital to the learning process. You can assess students' preferences by what they do frequently and willingly, or by offering the child a choice of items and noting which they select most often.
Take what the child gives you	The best place to begin a teaching program is to start with what the child is already doing. The child might reach for a toy, but not request it using manual signs. The child might open his or her mouth when you offer a cup of juice, but not hold the cup. These existing behaviours suggest that the child is motivated and these are therefore optimal times for teaching. If the child reaches for the toy, you assist him or her to produce the manual sign for "toy". If you offer juice, and the child opens his or her mouth, you assist the child to hold the cup before giving him or her a drink. Over time the amount of assistance provided by the teacher is reduced so as to promote greater independence.
Increase the number of opportunities for learning and practice	To promote the acquisition of new skills it is often helpful to ensure that the child receives an increased number of learning opportunities. This can be done by providing repeated experiences to learn during a single activity, as well as in a range of activities. Once the new skill has been learnt it is important to continue to provide opportunities for the child to practise the skill in a range of contexts to ensure generalisation and maintenance.
Think of every learning opportunity as a cycle	The cycle consists of four points. First, present the cue that you want the child to respond to. Ideally, this is the natural cue that sets the occasion for the response in the real world. For example, the natural cue for putting on sunglasses is going outside into the sun. Second, wait for the child to make the response. After going out the door, for example, you might wait ten seconds for the

child to put on his or her sunglasses. Third, if the child does not respond, or starts to make an incorrect response, provide a prompt that will lead to the desired behaviour. The prompt might consist of telling the child what to do, showing the child what to do, or physically guiding the child to do what is expected. Over time the amount and type of prompting is faded. Fourth, provide reinforcement as soon as the child completes the desired behaviour. Ideally, the reinforcement is the natural consequence of completing the task, such as avoiding the sun's glare, but initially you have to use contrived reinforcement, such as praise or tangibles (food, drink). Over time, the contrived reinforcers are faded by giving the contrived reinforcer only every second time, every third time, every fourth, and so on.

SUMMARY

The term *high support needs* covers students with severe and multiple disabilities. Their multiple and complex conditions are associated with a range of learning and behavioural characteristics that have numerous implications for educational programming. Given this range of needs, students with high support needs require a highly individualised education developed in collaboration with parents and professionals from other disciplines. Students with high support needs also require an alternative and more functional curriculum.

Formulating educational goals for students with high support needs involves collaborations between parents and professionals to identify the demands of the settings that the child goes to (home, school, community) and the various sub-environments within these settings (kitchen, bathroom, classroom, playground).

For these students, assessment, curriculum development, and intervention are intimately linked. The educational team undertakes assessments to formulate goals that become the bases of the child's individualised curriculum as reflected in the IEP. Interventions are then designed and implemented to teach these goals.

A functional curriculum is focused on increasing the child's current and future participation in the typical, age-appropriate activities of daily life that occur in regular home, school, community, and vocational settings. To increase participation in inclusive settings and activities, educators not only need to focus on developing effective communication, daily living, and socialisation skills, but also they might need to make adaptations and provide systems for ongoing support. Teaching these skills and providing the necessary adaptations and supports is what education is all about for children with high support needs

Formulating goals is relatively easy when compared to selecting and implementing instructional strategies that are effective in achieving these goals. Once a set of goals has been formulated, teachers decide how to go about teaching the child so that he or she is likely to achieve these goals.

To teach effectively, educators should be familiar with the instructional strategies that research has shown to be effective. Teaching decisions should not be based on intuition, but on reliable and valid evidence.

Suggested reading

Books

Batshaw, M. L. (Ed.). (1997). *Children with disabilities* (4th ed.). Baltimore: Paul H. Brookes Publishing Co.

Orelove, F. P. & Sobsey, D. (1996). *Educating children with multiple disabilities: A transdisciplinary approach* (3rd ed.). Baltimore: Paul H. Brookes Publishing Co.

Snell, M. E. & Brown, F. (2000). *Instruction of students with severe disabilities* (5th ed.). New Jersey: Merrill.

Westling, D. L. & Fox, L. (2000). *Teaching students with severe disabilities* (2nd ed.). New Jersey: Merrill.

Journals

American Journal on Mental Retardation

Augmentative and Alternative Communication

Australasian Journal of Special Education

Behavioral Intervention

Developmental Disabilities Bulletin

Focus on Autism and Other Developmental Disabilities

Journal of Applied Behavior Analysis

Journal of Applied Research in Intellectual Disabilities

Journal of the Association for Persons with Severe Handicaps (JASH)

Journal of Autism and Developmental Disorders

Journal of Behavioral Education

Journal of Developmental and Physical Disabilities

Journal of Intellectual and Developmental Disability

Journal of Intellectual Disability Research

Journal of Positive Behavior Interventions

Research in Developmental Disabilities

Websites

Australian Society for the Study of Intellectual Disability:

<www.rmit.edu.au/departments/ps/assid>

The Association for Behavior Analysis:

<www.wmich.edu/aba>

The Autism Society of America:

<www.autism-society.org>

International Society for Augmentative and Alternative Communication:

<www.isaac-online.org/isaac/index.html>

TASH—Disability Advocacy Worldwide:

<www.tash.org>

Practical activities

1. You have just learnt that, next year, a student with Lesch-Nyham syndrome will be in your classroom. You know nothing about this syndrome. Your task is to use the Internet to track down reliable journal articles so that you can create a resource kit about this syndrome.
2. There are various methods to assess the function of challenging behaviours including interviews, questionnaires, naturalistic observations, and experimental or functional analyses. You job is to compare and contrast these various methods, and to list the advantages and disadvantages of each. Which method would you use to assess the function of Evan's self-injury? Why? To help you in this activity, we suggest you consult Koegel, Koegel, and Dunlap (1996); Scotti and Meyer (1999); and Thompson and Grey (1994).
3. Evan seems unmotivated to participate in instructional activities. What strategies could you use to assess his preferences and to identify reinforcers for Evan? How would you use this information to motivate Evan? The article by Lohrmann-O'Rourke and Browder (1998) can help you with this activity.
4. How would you go about teaching self-feeding skills to a child with high support needs? How successful are these strategies? What are the basic learning principles

underlying the strategy? How might you adapt this strategy for a child who is unable to grasp a spoon or cup? The textbooks by Cipani and Spooner (1994) and Snell and Brown (2000) are good resources for this activity.

5. The mother of one of the children in your classroom has heard about a highly controversial technique called Facilitated Communication. She wants your advice about the merits of this procedure. After consulting the research literature, what is your opinion of Facilitated Communication? What do you tell the child's mother?

References

Ault, M. M., Guy, B., Guess, D., Bashinski, S., & Roberts, S. (1995). Analyzing behavior state and learning environments: Application in instructional settings. *Mental Retardation*, *33*, 304–316.

Australian Bureau of Statistics. (1998a). *Disability, ageing and carers: Summary of findings*. Canberra: Commonwealth of Australia.

Australian Bureau of Statistics. (1998b). *Disability, ageing and carers: User guide*. Canberra: Commonwealth of Australia.

Batshaw, M. L. (Ed.) (1997). *Children with disabilities* (4th ed.). Baltimore: Paul H. Brookes Publishing Co.

Bauer, A. M. & Shea, T. M. (1999). *Inclusion 101: How to teach all learners*. Baltimore: Paul H. Brookes Publishing Co.

Cipani, E. C. & Spooner, F. (1994). *Curricular and instructional approaches for persons with severe disabilities*. Boston: Allyn and Bacon.

Dempsey, I. & Foreman, P. (1997). Trends in the educational placement of students with disabilities in New South Wales. *International Journal of Disability, Development and Education*, *44*, 207–16.

Dykens, E. M., Hodapp, R. M., & Finucane, B. M. (2000). *Genetics and mental retardation syndromes*. Baltimore: Paul H. Brookes Publishing Co.

Flippo, K. F., Inge, K. J., & Barcus, J. M. (1995). *Assistive technology: A resource for school, work, and community*. Baltimore: Paul H. Brookes Publishing Co.

Foreman, P. (Ed.) (2001). *Integration and inclusion in action* (2nd ed.). Sydney: Harcourt.

Giangreco, M. F., Whiteford, T., Whiteford, L., & Doyle, M. B. (1998). Planning for Andrew: The use of COACH and VISTA in an inclusive preschool program. *International Journal of Disability, Development & Education*, *45*, 375–396.

Koegel, L. K., Koegel, R. L., & Dunlap, G. (1996). *Positive behavioral support*. Baltimore: Paul H. Brookes Publishing Co.

Lamorey, S., & Ryan, S. (1998). From contention to implementation: A comparison of team practices and recommended practices across service delivery models. *Infant–Toddler Intervention*, *8*, 309–331.

Lohrmann-O'Rourke, S. & Browder, D. M. (1998). Empirically based methods to assess the preferences of individuals with severe disabilities. *American Journal on Mental Retardation*, *103*, 146–161.

New South Wales Board of Studies (1997a). *English key learning area interim support document: Communication*. Sydney: Author.

New South Wales Board of Studies (1997b). *English key learning area interim support document: Literacy*. Sydney: Author.

NSW Department of Education and Training (2000). *Student services and equity data*. Sydney: Author.

Nihira, K., Leland, H., & Lambert, N. (1993). Adaptive Behavior Scales—Residential and Community Edition (2nd ed.). Washington, DC: American Association on Mental Retardation.

Orelove, F. P. & Sobsey, D. (1996). *Educating children with multiple disabilities: A transdisciplinary approach* (3rd ed.). Baltimore: Paul H. Brookes Publishing Co.

Sailor, W., Gee, K., Goetz, L., & Graham, N. (1988). Progress in educating children with the most severe disabilities: Is there any? *Journal of the Association for Persons with Severe Handicaps, 13*, 287–299.

Salend, S. J. (1998). *Effective mainstreaming: Creating inclusive classrooms* (3rd ed.). New Jersey: Merrill.

Schroeder, S. R., Tessel, R. E., Loupe, P. S., & Stodgell, C. J. (1997). Severe behavior problems among people with developmental disabilities. In W. E. McAllen, Jr. (Ed.), *Ellis handbook of mental deficiency, psychological theory, and research* (3rd ed.) (pp. 439–464). Hillsdale, NJ: Lawrence Erlbaum.

Scotti, J. R., & Meyer, L. H. (1999). *Behavioral intervention*. Baltimore: Paul H. Brookes Publishing Co.

Snell, M. E., & Brown, F. (2000). *Instruction of students with severe disabilities* (5th ed.). New Jersey: Merrill.

Sparrow, S. S., Balla, D. A., & Cicchetti, D. V. (1984). *Vineland Adaptive Behavior Scales*. Circle Pines, MN: American Guidance Service.

Stainback, S. & Stainback, W. (Eds), (1996). *Inclusion: A guide for educators*. Baltimore: Paul H. Brookes Publishing Co.

Thompson, T. & Grey, D. B. (Eds). (1994). *Destructive behavior in developmental disabilities*. Thousand Oaks, CA: Sage.

Thompson., B. & Guess, D. (1989). Students who experience the most profound disabilities: Teacher perspectives. In F. Brown & D. H. Lehr (Eds), *Persons with profound disabilities: Issues and practices* (pp. 3–41). Baltimore: Paul H. Brookes Publishing Co.

Westling, D. L. & Fox, L. (2000). *Teaching students with severe disabilities* (2nd ed.). New Jersey: Merrill.

12

Learning partnerships through information and communication technology

KEN RYBA, JOANNA CURZON, AND LINDA SELBY

Case studies

As you read each case study, ask yourself:

- How does technology help Stephen and Sherie?
- How are they empowered by the technology to achieve educational goals in ways that are personally beneficial?
- How has the technology been matched to the individual needs of these students?

Stephen

At six years of age, Stephen has been diagnosed with Autistic Spectrum Disorder (ASD), and is buffeted by the demands of everyday interactions. He takes refuge in persistent repetitive activities such as flicking all the light switches on and off, and is fascinated by running water. He makes no eye contact and utters few words. He rarely communicates even basic needs, preferring to help himself to what he wants. Stephen is hypersensitive to touch, and recoils from many textures. He does not scribble, draw, or paint.

Stephen is introduced to a computer with a touch screen and a simple drawing program. He watches the support person, Jenny, create patterns by dragging her finger across the screen, selecting different colours from a palette, and then using an erase tool to remove the lines. After several minutes, Stephen pushes past the support person and carefully draws all round the screen, keeping close to the edge. He rubs out the resulting lines with equal care. This sequence is repeated over several sessions with Stephen following the same order each time and choosing the same black colour.

Jenny starts one session by drawing a red circle in the middle of the screen, and then offers Stephen a turn. Stephen embarks on his usual routine. Jenny gently reaches beside him, explaining that "it is my turn". Stephen carries on, covering over her lines.

Over many weeks, this parallel activity gradually evolves into a shared creative exploration. Stephen moves his drawings into the centre of the screen, and recognisable images begin to emerge—taps, water—and he introduces new colours. He tolerates Jenny's contributions and responds to turn-taking cues.

After six months, Stephen becomes more and more confident and begins to use a variety of media (clay, paint, and pencil). He matches pictures to line drawings which, in turn, he uses to indicate his needs He works alongside other students on the computer, and can wait for his turn, most of the time.

Sherie

Sherie is 17 years old and has recently been placed in a community living situation after years at a residential training school. She can recognise some letters and reads at about a 7-year-old level. Despite severe paralysis in one hand her keyboarding skills have improved from two words per minute (with 40% accuracy) to seven words per minute (with 60% accuracy).

At the outset, Sherie was judged by her tutors to be unlikely to operate the mouse because of motor coordination difficulties. But, having observed the tutor print out her work, she goes on to do it by herself. This requires a complex series of selections from the menu and control of the mouse, as well as understanding clicking and dragging. When she finishes, she is so pleased and excited that she nearly falls out of her wheelchair.

The tutors learn a good lesson here about not making assumptions about the capabilities of students with disabilities.

What you will learn in this chapter

This chapter will provide you with an introduction to information and communication technology (ICT) with a particular focus on assistive technology. The main emphasis is upon creating student–technology partnerships for learning. Throughout the chapter, information is provided on how to establish student-centred learning environments. The self-system concept is presented to explain how technology can be used as a learning tool for enhancing motivation, cognition, and metacognition.

This chapter will explain:

- how adaptations enable access to technology by persons with disabilities;
- how assistive technology is used to overcome or significantly reduce the impact of disability;
- the teacher's role in designing effective learning environments and gaining access to resources needed to enhance student learning with technology;
- the special considerations for students with disabilities, learning difficulties, or other special education needs when using assistive technology and information and communication technologies;
- the best and most effective approaches for teaching and learning with technology; and
- where to find additional information on assistive technology and information and communication technology.

The importance of communication

The stories about Stephen and Sherie show that technology can be truly empowering in that it depends on students acting in a purposeful way to perform a task. They are compelled to reflect on their thinking to get a computer to work for them. For example, to start the printer, Sherie had to listen, watch, remember, and then accurately perform the task. Likewise, Stephen had to watch the support worker and process the sequence of steps needed to draw and erase lines. Both students were relative newcomers to technology. However, after a few weeks they came to see

themselves as capable learners and could demonstrate their abilities to teachers, fellow students, and families. Parents were proud and supportive of their new capabilities. For the first time in their lives, some of the parents reported positive learning achievements. As a result of learning with technology, Stephen and Sherie could demonstrate their intellectual skills and, most importantly, were free to communicate ideas in ways that had not been possible before.

Humans are compulsive communicators. We are social and sociable. We are fascinating to ourselves and we are curious about others. Are we like them? Are they like us? Do we interpret information in the same way and, if not, who is right? How do we exert control over our own lives, make choices for ourselves, and influence others?

Information and communication technology (ICT) can assist us to become better communicators. Although computers usually come to mind when we think of ICT, it is not, in fact, confined to electronic gadgets or machines. Chalkboards, papyrus scrolls, stone tablets, and even cave drawings are types of information and communication technology. ICT can also include an environment or system of acquiring, storing, retrieving, manipulating, and interchanging data (Brown, 1997).

Computers are powerful information and communication machines. They can store, handle, exchange, and modify data with breathtaking speed and efficiency. Computers linked to one another through telecommunication technologies (phone, radio) equate to immensely powerful tools. Link these tools with the human compulsion to interact, and you have a powerful communication partnership. The phenomenal rise in popularity of email and the Internet are proof of the allure of ICT.

Education is a process of sharing information and communicating. Students link external information—such as data, facts, and accounts of other people's experiences—with their internal knowledge to expand their understanding of the world and everything in it. Computers are powerful partners in this process. With computers, students can explore information from different perspectives, test ideas, manipulate sequences of actions, and take on different roles. No longer does the physical environment of the classroom bind these activities. Students can now work collegially with peers on the other side of the world as readily as they can with those in the next town or next seat, thereby opening up many opportunities for learning experiences. Computers can take care of much of the drudgery of information processing leaving students with more energy to focus on communicating with one another.

Overcoming barriers to participation

Although all students need removal of the barriers to participating in learning , those with disabilities, learning difficulties, or other education needs usually find it more difficult to achieve full inclusion in their communities. As you will recall from Chapter 2, the World Health Organization identified three aspects to disability. The first,

impairment, is at the anatomical or physiological level (e.g., the loss of a limb or reduced vision). The second is *activity*, which describes the nature and extent of function (e.g., communicating with peer or writing an assignment). The third is *participation*, which describes the person's involvement in life situations (e.g., being employed, having friends).

Wise use of computers and other assistive technologies can overcome or significantly reduce the impact of disability at all three levels. For example, an adapted keyboard can provide full access for a person with one arm, whereas enlarged text combined with audible feedback will compensate for low vision (overcoming *impairment*). A Year 1 student without speech or fine motor control can use a switch-activated communication device with recorded messages to contribute to the refrain during shared story reading. A secondary school student with laboured, illegible letter formation can use a lightweight electronic notetaker to take notes (overcoming barriers to *activity*).

Opportunities for students to use the Internet have expanded greatly. The Net can now be used to take courses of study, to communicate with family and friends via email, and to take part in online discussions and web-based forums. These have helped to minimise the barriers of participation for students with special needs, regardless of whether they are gifted or talented, or whether they experience one of a number of learning difficulties. Distance technologies also confer anonymity and equality. An email message might have been written by a blind person or by someone painstakingly selecting letters from a switch-activated scanning array. The end result is indistinguishable from a message written by a non-disabled person.

It is important to remember that many of the barriers to participation are imposed from outside the person, by society or the environment. Low expectations, prejudice, lack of understanding, and inaccessible buildings all present formidable barriers to participation.

Defining terms

Assistive technology

Assistive technology is the term most often used to describe a wide range of helping machines. The US *Individuals with Disabilities Education Act* amendments of 1997 define assistive technology as "an item, piece of equipment, or product used to increase, maintain or improve functional capabilities of individuals with disabilities" (see US Department of Education, 2000).

Lewis (1993) distinguished two uses of assistive technologies by people with special needs One is to augment a student's strengths, so counterbalancing the effects of disabilities. The other is to compensate for, or circumvent, the effects of disabilities. In a later article, Lewis (1998) grouped different types of barriers, identified some teaching strategies to overcome these barriers, and provided a research commentary on

effectiveness and conditions for success. Later in this chapter, attention is given to making adaptations to teaching and learning that overcome these barriers.

Universal access and control of ICT

Universal access is the ultimate goal for all people. All buildings should be accessible to everyone and there should be no need for specially adapted wheelchair toilets or afterthought ramps. All students should be ergonomically seated in height-adjustable work areas, and all information and communication technologies should be accessible to everyone. Major software developers already incorporate some special accessibility features into their programs. For example, both Macintosh computers and PCs using Windows 95™ or later versions include options for enlarged icons and pointers, and almost every model of computer allows for keyboard responses to be tailored to individual needs Internet websites can be designed to ensure accessibility by everyone including individuals who have a vision impairment.

Despite the advances that have been made, the conventional means of communicating with a computer (keyboard, screen) present major barriers to many people with disabilities. Fortunately, as the following section shows, there are many alternative forms of access.

Switches

The technology of electronics has greatly increased the communication, play, and learning opportunities for students with extremely limited motor control. Battery operated toys, computers, communications devices, home appliances, and wheelchairs can be adapted for use with single switches. New interface systems permit a person to have total control over a computer by using a single switch. With only an eye blink, toe wiggle, or finger movement, a person with a severe disability can access the same computer-based activities as a non-disabled person.

Other people often control events in the life of a student who has severe physical disabilities and/or multiple disabilities. The effect of this is passivity, a lack of learning of new behaviours or skills, and learnt helplessness in which the individual learns over time that he or she is incapable of controlling events in the environment. Accordingly, the student must learn how to stimulate events in his or her environment. A switch interface provides a channel of communication with the outside world. A number of skills (present or emerging) is required to use a switch interface successfully. According to Goossens and Sapp Crain (1992), these include the following skills:

- *Motor:* the student must initiate, release and/or maintain contact with the switch to control output of the device (e.g., adapted toy, computer).
- *Sense:* the student must be able to attend visually to an activity and switch his or her gaze from the switch to the activity, or use auditory feedback.
- *Cognitive:* the student must understand the concept of cause and effect.

- *Social:* the student must show some interaction (awareness) with others in his or her environment.

Matching the right switch to a student involves three steps:

- identification of a reliable, repeatable *movement* that does not make use of reflex muscle activity and does not cause undue fatigue;
- identification of the best *position* for the switch; and
- selection of the best *switch* for that action and site.

There is an enormous range of switches available, including those controlled by movements of the eyes, tongue, lips, head, limbs, and whole body. The switch might be activated by touch (e.g., pushing the switch with the knee), proximity (e.g., holding the hand near the switch), movement (e.g., passing the hand through an infrared beam), or air pressure (e.g., puffing and sipping on a tube). Switches are usually connected to a computer via an interface system and can be used for *direct selection* or for *scanning*.

Direct selection

In *direct selection*, the user activates the switch and something happens (cause and effect, sometimes referred to as stimulus and response). There is a range of simple software that has been designed to respond to direct selection. Although most programs cater for an early developmental stage and age, some age-appropriate designs are now available for older students who need to exert simple control over their environment.

Scanning

Scanning is a much more sophisticated interaction with a computer. Specialised scanning software is used to present a sequence of choices known as a scanning array. Choices can be identified by sound (e.g., a beep), by highlighting, or by framing. The switch user activates the switch when the desired choice is identified. A simple example is an array of words on a communication board. The cursor moves from one word to the next, and the student selects a word by activating the switch when the target word is highlighted.

The skills required for successful scanning are more complex than those needed for direct selection. The resources required are also more complex—such as Clicker 4™ which incorporates scanning options with a dedicated word processor, onscreen keyboard, and symbol-to-text capability. Alternatively, specialised scanning software (e.g., Clickit!™) is used to layer scanning capability onto regular software.

Rotary scanner

A *rotary scanner* is an invaluable low-tech scanning device that consists of a free-standing board and a switch-controlled pointer, rather like a clock face. Pictures,

small objects, and words can be attached to the face. The switch-user controls the movement of the pointer and makes the choice. A New Zealand model, the Fundial™, is a versatile classroom resource—particularly for students who are beginning to use scanners.

Alternative keyboards

Some students need special keyboard layouts to accommodate specific physical or cognitive challenges. For example, a one-handed user might need a chordic keyboard such as the BAT™. By holding down several keys together, the student can activate many functions that would otherwise be difficult to perform with one hand. A student reliant on graphics or photo representations might need an overlay keyboard such as Intellikeys™. A student with very weak muscles and limited reach might need a miniature keyboard such as that from TASH™. Good keyboard design includes consideration of ergonomics. For some people this might necessitate a completely different keyboard layout from the traditional Qwerty design.

Alternatives to a mouse

Controlling a mouse is cognitively quite challenging. Most of us can probably remember some embarrassment and frustration when we first encountered this pesky little device. For many students it is hard to understand the link between moving the mouse beside the computer and the antics of the pointer on the screen. A trackball is a much more accessible device than a mouse, cognitively and physically. A trackball can be propped up so that it is just below the screen, demonstrating a clear link between the movement of the ball and the movement of the onscreen pointer. People with early signs of occupational overuse syndrome often gain relief from their symptoms when they switch from a mouse to a trackball. Again, there is a large range of trackballs, some of which come with software enabling different actions to be programmed to different buttons.

Touchpads and fingertip controllers are popular with some users. Both require very little strength or range of movement.

Other means of controlling the pointer are:

- *Touch monitor:* The surface of the screen is responsive to touch. This is useful for younger students who are gaining an understanding of control over their environment, because there is an immediate response.
- *Ultrasound beam:* The user wears a headset that exchanges ultrasound beams with a receiver mounted on top of the monitor. Movements of the head (and so the beam) control the movement of the onscreen pointer. An example of an ultrasound beam device is the Headmaster™.

- *Infrared beam:* The user wears a light-reflective dot on a cap, spectacles, or forehead that intercepts an infrared beam from a small device mounted on the computer, and thus controls the pointer. An example is the Headmouse™.

The last two devices are usually paired with a switch in order to achieve the equivalent of the mouse click. As an alternative, some software can be programmed to interpret a defined dwell time on an icon or text as the select command.

Speech-to-text and text-to-speech

Software is available that can be taught to recognise the student's voice and convert the spoken word into text or computer commands. Speech recognition software has increased in power and ease of use while decreasing in price over the past decade or so. However, reasonable clarity and articulation of speech is required, together with at least senior primary reading ability and good understanding of the computer operating environment. Speech recognition is often recommended for people suffering from occupational overuse syndrome. However, worrying evidence is emerging that people who rely exclusively on voice input might develop occupational overuse of their vocal cords.

The facility to convert text to speech, and vice versa, is very useful for all people, especially for those with a vision impairment or learning disability. Recently, voice-activated mobile phones and other electronic devices have become a popular alternative to traditional text input. Information that is typed into a computer can be transformed into synthesised (computer-generated) speech, or recordings of the student's voice can be digitised and played back when certain actions are performed. Multimedia provides an excellent context for creating learning programs that contain speech.

Other specialised conversions

Devices such as the Mountbatten Brailler™ mean that typed text can be rapidly printed, embossed in braille, or spoken. Other devices convert text to refreshable braille. Braille can also be converted to speech through a portable braille-input and speech-output system such as the Braille Lite™ that contains a number of facilities (e.g., word processor, calculator, database, and diary).

Specialised assessors will provide advice and often have access to a loan pool from which a number of devices can be borrowed to try in the student's learning environment.

Software

All of the input and output devices described above allow students to operate a range of software, both regular off-the-shelf and specialised packages. It is interesting to note

that well-designed software has wide appeal. During a workshop on making simple multimedia resources and using an overlay keyboard, a teacher from a regular class said: "This is such fun and such good learning that *all* my students would want to use it."

The focus of specialised software is now on bridging the gap between software that is of general interest and that for special requirements (e.g., scanning and word prediction). With the relative ease of creating tailored resources now being within the grasp of anyone with a digital camera, multimedia software, patience and ingenuity, the demand for new commercial specialised packages appears to be declining.

Ways of supporting students' learning

ICT as educational tools

Early computers were promoted as teaching machines, providing patiently repetitive drill and practice sessions designed to promote mastery of specific facts (e.g., word reading and arithmetic operations). Sophisticated forms of computer-based drill and practice teaching are now available as integrated learning systems (ILS) of which, perhaps, Successmaker™ is one of the best known. This type of software presents information to students in carefully graded steps, clearly lays out the rules for success, and provides feedback on progress and there is evidence that many students enjoy using such software packages and some make good progress (BeCTA, 1998). However, there are also many concerns about the transfer of skills to other contexts. For example, a student might learn to add coin values to $10 whereas checking change at the supermarket can remain a mystery.

The clue to successful use of drill software appears to be the extent to which it is supplemented by functional daily opportunities, to integrate and transfer skills to other familiar settings in which these are required. Recent developments with multimedia applications make it possible to provide more realistic learning opportunities in which students can actively participate in relevant problem-solving contexts.

ICT as a learning partner

Many students with physical disabilities or learning difficulties have to work harder and longer than their typical classmates to complete their learning tasks. The extra effort leads to fatigue and the extra time taken may rob them of the satisfaction of completing an activity. A computer can be used as a working partner, taking some of the drudgery out of the task and making it possible for the student to keep up with classmates, especially if the student has limited manual dexterity.

For many students, writing is hard work. They might have an extensive spoken vocabulary but their written output is stilted and brief. Of course, it is important for students to learn how to form letters and how to assemble them into words. However,

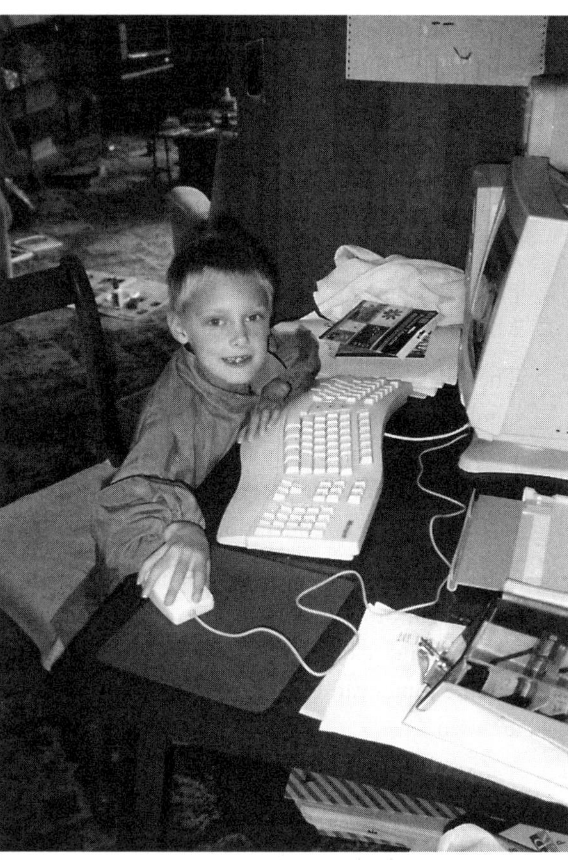

This boy is using computer skills he has learnt at school and in the home to gain access to information on the World Wide Web.

barriers to writing—such as pain, muscle weakness, muscle spasm, visual-perceptual confusion, or sequencing and planning difficulties—imprison many students. Their written output is impoverished and does not do justice to their rich inner language. A range of alternative information and communication technologies can come to the rescue. Based on the premise that it is easier to recognise than to recreate, word lists, word banks, or word prediction can tempt a struggling writer into selecting words which they would have balked at creating from scratch (Zhang, Brooks, Frields, & Redelfs, 1995). A number of solutions are available, ranging from effective low-tech approaches to highly sophisticated interventions. Knowledge of students' preferred styles of learning and their specific requirements guides the selection of the most appropriate resource. The following are some examples.

- Electronic spell-checkers generate word lists.
- Write Outloud™ is a talking word processor that offers pop-up lists of suggested alternative words when a word is misspelled. Click on a word to hear it (robotic speech, but very understandable). Is that what I wanted to say? Or is it this word? For many students this auditory feedback is extremely powerful.

- Concept Universal™ and Intellikeys™ are overlay keyboards that have banks of high-interest or high-frequency words, or both. Used in parallel with a regular computer keyboard, these boards consist of a grid of touch-sensitive cells. Simple software allows pictures, letters, words, or whole phrases and sentences to be assigned to these cells. Load up word processor software, press a cell, and the contents (e.g., picture, word, phrase) are transmitted to the word processor. Increase in quality and quantity of written output and increased collaboration have been noted during classroom use of overlay keyboards (Drew, Harrison, Millar, Stewart, & Wedde, 1998; Murray 1994).
- The Clicker™ series uses onscreen grids of pictures, symbols, words or combinations. Like an onscreen overlay keyboard, the user clicks on a cell to hear the contents. Select a cell and the contents appear in the word-processor. Instant graphics link to text. This is very simple to use and easy to modify. This is an important consideration in busy classrooms.
- With Penfriend™, start to type and a list of possible words pops up. Typing "ba" might bring up bag, bat, ball, or balloon. Again, click for spoken preview, and select to drop the word into the word processor. Word lists on specific topics can be created and the program learns new words as they are used.
- TextHelp™ is a powerful program designed to support students with specific learning difficulties. It includes word prediction and converts any word processor software into a talking package. This was recently replaced by WordSmith™ with even more features.
- CoWriter™ and KeyRep™ are also very powerful talking word prediction packages that are particularly useful to reduce keystroke load. The preceding sentence required 121 keystrokes. With smart prediction, this can be reduced to 20. Next likely word prediction is based not only on initial letter but also on patterns of usage, so that typing "I went" brings up the suggestion of "to" and "the".

These computer applications are examples of a range of available software and hardware options. For guidance in making the most appropriate purchase according to student needs, readers are encouraged to check out the information sources listed at the end of this chapter and to consult with experts in the field.

Changing the way we teach

The presence of new education technologies has given rise to some dramatic rethinking about the teaching and learning process in regular classrooms and especially in those in which there are students with specific education needs Early ideas of computer assisted instruction have given way to thinking about the social construction

of knowledge in which individuals learn through interaction with one another rather than being taught by a computer. An exciting feature of this shift in thinking is the recognition that technology offers a context not only for enhancing individual performance but also for creating communities of highly capable learners. This is evident in the widespread use of technology in educational settings as a basis for collaborative learning and enterprising new projects at all educational levels (Ryba, 1996).

Contrary to early concerns about the dehumanising effects of learning with technology, computers have provided sites for bringing students together. There is vast evidence of the benefits to be derived from interactive teaching methods, such as cooperative learning, in which students and teachers work side by side (see Frazer, Moltzen, & Ryba, 2000). Increasingly, recognition has been given to the fact that collaboration and ability to relate to others is a vital aspect of effectiveness as a learner. A major effect of assistive technology and new educational technology has been the willingness of teachers to think again about how people learn and what they are capable of achieving. This was evident in a project carried out with adults with an intellectual disability that learnt a simple version of the LOGO computer language. These adults became so proficient at using LOGO graphics that they were asked to teach it to students at a nearby school. This was successful and, as a result, LOGO became very popular at that school.

An interesting point about this early project was the young adults' ability to act as tutors. Not only did they teach school students, but also they demonstrated how to use new software to university students doing a computer education course. It is of interest that before becoming computer tutors, these trainees were assigned to mundane repetitive jobs such as packing dog biscuits and rolling newspapers into fire logs. The technology provided a situation in which people could see their capabilities and celebrate their learning achievements. It is important that we do not underestimate students' abilities. What we discovered using the technology is the capability of all students to learn and how easy it is to make technology educationally and personally relevant so that it creates better conditions for learning.

The effectiveness of the computer environment for all students depends upon the ability of the teacher to facilitate the teaching and learning process. In a definitive work in the area, Seymour Papert (1980) pointed out that computers have the potential to transform the way students learn. Papert also had some important things to say about the role of the teacher as an anthropologist whose job it is to study how to facilitate students' learning through providing them with the resources they need to build their intellectual structures. By studying the surrounding culture, teachers can guide student participation in the learning process and enable them to make effective use of the intellectual tools through networking with others.

Supporting social relationships and partnerships

Effective use of technology (with appropriate and well-designed software) has been shown repeatedly to foster social interaction and communication. Numerous studies across age groups lead to the same conclusions (Brett, 1994; Clements, Nastasi, & Swaminathan, 1993; Frampton, 1989; Howard, Greyrose, & Kehr, 1996; Mastrangelo 1996; Wizer, 1995). Despite early concerns that computers might isolate and control students, it is clear now that ICT offers excellent opportunities for students to learn together.

The promotion of interpersonal skills within the technology environment is important not only for social development but also because it provides a basis for intellectual growth (Ryba & Selby, 1993). The main themes in this research have been the creation of learner-centred environments and the development of positive interactions among students.

As early as 1988, Mary Male provided a good description of how social development of students with special learning needs can be enhanced in the computer environment through the use of cooperative learning strategies. She suggested three important questions that need to be considered (Male 1988):

- How can we use the computer to create positive interactions among students?
- How do we ensure that computer experiences enhance self-esteem of students?
- How should classroom use of computers be organised so those students develop interdependence, good work habits, and a sense of their own competence?

Social development is not a separate mission for computer use but one that can be linked directly to authentic curriculum-based activities. For example, ICT naturally lends itself to the the sorts of cooperative learning approaches discussed in Chapter 8. Cooperative learning is based upon the concept of interdependence, in which students learn and depend in a positive way on one another. Bryant and Bryant (1998) reported the effects of cooperative learning using information and communication technologies to assist students with disabilities.

Many students with disabilities and learning difficulties lack opportunities to engage in reflective learning and to demonstrate the learning steps they have taken. A window into this process can be opened through the discussions that accompany small group work around a computer. Students also often talk to the computer, thus providing further insights into their world. It is quite common for students to ascribe human-like emotions and intentions to the computer ("It doesn't like it when I click there") or talk to it ("Give me back my story!").

The technology provides an accepting, non-critical microworld in which to explore ideas and consequences. Many students who are overwhelmed by social interactions can find a safe and motivating environment in technology. The clear boundaries of the

Box 12.1 Promoting interpersonal communication and social skills

Twelve-year-old Jack has been diagnosed with Autistic Spectrum Disorders (ASD). He used just one simple picture-building program on the classroom computer and resisted all attempts to expand his choices. He appeared fascinated by numbers. When presented with complex 8-digit sums and a range of possible answers on a whiteboard, he unerringly selected the correct answer by rubbing it out. He appeared to merely glance at the figures on the board.

Jack showed no interest in people and did not talk to anyone. If he could not get what he wanted by himself, he occasionally grabbed someone's hand and used it as an extension of himself. He became very distressed at any changes in routine, and attempts to prepare him for events were unsuccessful. Jack and his support team urgently needed a reliable communication system.

Jack enjoyed weekly sessions with the local Riding for the Disabled Group. His specialist teacher used a digital camera to photograph Jack when he was riding. These images were compiled into an electronic scrapbook using Book Spinner™ software and the printed pictures were assembled into a simple book. Jack was shown the pictures during the riding session but did not take any interest in them. He was then introduced to the electronic story immediately after the riding session. He quickly engaged in turning the pages, responding readily to hand-over-hand guidance. Jack's teacher put the printed photo collection in a copyholder beside the computer and frequently pointed out the links between the two, encouraging him to turn the actual pages as well as the electronic ones.

Over successive weeks, Jack's team assembled more photos into the scrapbook that showed him engaged in a number of activities around school and home. All were linked with the printed photos.

Before a riding session, Jack's teacher got out the relevant photo book, showed him the pictures, and then put one in his hand as he went out of the classroom. After many weeks, Jack spontaneously got out the riding book when told that it was time to get ready. This was the start of a communication system whereby Jack was able to associate images with events.

screen, predictable responses, and lack of time constraints might be factors. The case study in Box 12.1 (above) illustrates the potential of technology as a means of promoting interpersonal communication and social skills.

Online communities of practice for professional development

With increasing access to the Internet, teachers are discovering new and exciting ways of using online resources to support school curriculum activities for all students regardless of age or capability, as well as for their own professional development

purposes. The Internet consists of intersecting communities of people who communicate using computer networks. These networks enable teachers, parents, siblings, special service providers, and students to meet, communicate, with others, and learn together. The community of practice framework represents a dynamic new way of understanding how to develop human potential through collaborative online communications.

The idea behind the online community of practice model is the provision of a basis for promoting change through a process of scaffolding and guided participation of students and teachers (Lave & Wenger, 1991). Scaffolded learning involves the teacher in providing guidance and structure for learning which is then faded away as the student takes more responsibility for his or her own performance.

Becoming a member of a sustained community of practice occurs through social relations in which individuals take on certain beliefs and practices that are embodied in the community. At the outset, newcomers begin their journey at the periphery of this community and progress toward the centre as they become more active and engaged within the organisational culture. They move from being a newcomer or novice toward assuming the role of expert or old-timer. Learning that is situated within the community is usually not directly taught, but is unintentional, occurring through active participation in working together with other people. These ideas are what Lave and Wenger (1991) referred to as the process of legitimate peripheral participation. Such participation is socially interactive in nature, and involves an apprenticeship and guided participation between newcomers and old-timers within the professional community.

The value of using a community building model is the development of active collaboration and personal ownership of the process by students and teachers alike. Unlike prescribed models, the community formulates its own principles and practices through general agreement that serves to guide the growth of the community. Although based on an established set of principles and expectations concerning the quality of services to be provided, each community is free to establish itself in ways that are in keeping with its own culture, understandings, and relationships among the members.

The communities of practice framework stresses a sense of identity as a community member and becoming knowledgeable and skilful are both parts of the same process. Self-identity is crucial for motivating, shaping, and giving meaning to the development of skills. As students are guided in their participation to become increasingly self-sufficient, they gain a sense of identity and a sense of effectiveness as learners. This personal development process is illustrated through the description of an online educational community in Box 12.2 (page 517).

Analysis of projects such as Global InfoLinks indicates that there are some important underlying principles for the creation of viable and sustainable communities of

Box 12.2 Global InfoLinks: An online educational community for Queensland students and their teachers

Since the 1980s, Australian schools have been searching for ways to make effective use of computers in the classroom to support the teaching and learning of students. Despite a series of initiatives over the past decade or so, the use of computers in classrooms is inconsistent and sometimes non-existent. Likewise, teacher use of computers outside the classrooms is relatively unsophisticated (Williams, McKeown, Masselos, Stubbs, & Potter, 1998). Although much time, energy, and money have been spent connecting buildings and local computer networks to the Internet, some of the most promising developments are those that have concentrated on connecting teachers to other teachers. For example, the Global InfoLinks (GIL) Project is a series of professional development initiatives throughout Queensland that have adopted a teachers-first approach in supporting teachers in their use of communication technology. The GIL Project showed that an investment in teachers can lead to quality educational and professional activity (Williams, 1995).

The GIL Project is based on the notion that the best forms of support for teachers are their colleagues. In a community of peers, teachers were able to find help for the everyday problems of using technology in educational environments, as well as being able to discuss together what it means to be an educator in an increasingly complex world. These peer support communities were based on Lave and Wenger's (1991) concept of communities of practice. These provided ways for newcomers and old-timers to share the knowledge and practices of the profession, and to share experiences and solve problems about educational issues relating to the use of the Internet. Many teachers were isolated from colleagues and learning opportunities by the fact that they spend the majority of their time working alone in classrooms.

The Ipswich City Council provided all schools in the city with access to the Internet at the beginning of 1995. The key principles on which the educational module of GIL was founded included:

- making decisions that focused on teachers and how teachers would be involved in the project;
- encouraging teachers to become immersed in the Internet for themselves so they would experience firsthand the impact of this new technology on their lives before they would have to think about the use of this technology in classrooms;
- reducing barriers to teacher participation by providing hardware and Internet access for teachers; and
- building a community of participating teachers that had a say in shaping the directions of the GIL Project.

One of the teachers on the GIL Project became involved in training and supporting other teachers as they became involved in using the Internet for

personal, professional, and curriculum purposes. Her story of "Koala Chris" the travel buddy, provided a good example of how teachers can work together to connect themselves and their students to a global community. Koala Chris was a toy bear that was sent around the world as an ambassador of the classroom. Every day that he was away, Koala Chris sent email messages home and kept a diary of his experiences with children overseas. One of the highlights was when Koala Chris visited NASA and generated so much interest that children tapped into NASA's database of pre-media pictures from the Hubble Space Telescope during the Shoemaker Levy Comet collision with Jupiter. Teachers and students had a chance to take a leadership role by hosting many information sessions and tours to share their experiences with the local community of teachers. Through this online collaboration, teachers began to understand how they could move from the periphery of activities to become skilled contributors to the professional development of teachers in the projects (Blackwell & McKeown, 1995).

By means of data collected from interviews and email of teachers participating in professional development programs online, a shift was noted in the teachers' definitions of the Internet and their attitudes toward it. This was evident in the following comment from a special education teacher:

"After only a few short weeks, I know that my Internet access has changed my perceptions of teaching and learning. The biggest change is my understanding that the Internet provides an opportunity for closer links between professionals. I hope that connections between special education teachers and other teachers in this way will result in truly inclusive curriculum and practices. I am convinced that students and teachers alike will benefit from the real-life information exchanges and communication experiences unique to email and the Internet."

Source: Williams and McKeown (1996).

practice that can enhance cognition and assist with the development of identity and professional knowledge. These principles are discussed below.

Active participation

Teachers and students should be active in observing and gathering information, and in practising skills, as they engage in their professional development activities. By being active learners, newcomers gain confidence and motivation to move from the periphery to the centre of community activities. Newcomers to an online community might at first simply observe and read messages, but there should be a way to encourage their active involvement. This can be facilitated by using a buddy system so that teachers and students have a point of contact within the community.

Guided learning opportunities

Participants in a community of practice should be provided with guided opportunities to enable them to become immersed in the community. By placing students with skilled people, they have an opportunity to carry out cognitive processes jointly that are more advanced than they could manage independently. This joint problem-solving process places the learner in their zone of proximal development (ZPD). This zone occurs when students who are ready to progress to the next stage in learning, participate in shared problem-solving to gain understanding and skills that will prepare them to perform tasks independently (Vygotsky, 1987).

Intellectual collective

Learning through collaboration with others can have synergistic effects in that the intelligence of the entire community can be raised through shared cognitions and problem-solving. The community forms what could be called an intellectual collective in which there is the potential for all members to advance their knowledge and skills. The joint problem-solving activities serve as the basis for subsequent independent efforts of participants.

Identity construction

Socialisation into a community of practice not only promotes skill development but also assists in the formation of self-identity as a capable practitioner. This inclusive process of generating identities is both a result of, and a motivation for, participation (Lave, 1988). This is evident with students and teachers alike who develop a sense of personal effectiveness through computer-based learning and online projects.

Building cognitive structures

Guided participation occurs in the process of individuals interacting informally with one another. Through the process of working with their social partners, participants build bridges from their current understanding to reach new understandings through processes inherent in the communications.

Shared decision-making

Individuals are more likely to be active participants and take responsibility for maintaining a community when their opinions are highly valued and are taken into consideration when making important decisions about the community's future. Leaders must be willing to unleash the initiative of the participants.

Altruism

Successful communities have strong norms for helping others. Participants have a positive reciprocity with one another. Individuals believe that helping peers enriches

the experience of peers, and increases the likelihood that the individual also will receive assistance.

Psychological safety

Professional growth occurs when individuals take risks and try new approaches to solving old problems. This risk-taking is most likely to occur in communities in which the participants have a sense of security that they will not be attacked or belittled because of inexperience or ignorance.

The communities of practice framework provides an encompassing theory for understanding how cultural processes and identity construct and shape one another. The use of the apprenticeship metaphor is relevant in explaining how guided participation enables newcomers to develop in their learning through communication and involvement with relatively more skilled old-timers.

In summary, guided participation within a community of practice ensures the formation of a collective in which all participants have an opportunity to gain knowledge and skills through active participation with capable peers. Such a view requires some rethinking about the process of learning, treating it as an emerging property of the whole person's legitimate peripheral participation in communities of practice. This framework fits well with the goals of inclusive education to create learning communities in which students and teachers have a sense of belonging and an opportunity to enhance their functioning level through partnerships with others.

Individualising education

Encouraging and supporting creativity and playfulness

As systematic education has emerged from the legacy of the Industrial Age and into the Information Age, different qualities have been valued. In the Industrial Age, workers were expected to be punctual, accurate, and inured to repetitive tasks. In the Information Age, the ability to construct new knowledge, to blend ideas in new combinations, and to fuse values with skills are considered desirable attributes. Rote learning, didactic teaching styles, and unquestioning obedience characterised the Victorian schoolroom. Student-centred learning, facilitative teaching styles, and reflective questioning characterise effective learning environments in the 21st century. The process of learning includes generating ideas, testing them against evidence and the comments of others, forming opinions, and gaining new insights. Arguably these processes are at least as important as coming to a right answer (the product). From this perspective, problem-solving can be a highly creative and enjoyable process with many opportunities for student-centred exploration and experimentation.

There are innumerable simple teaching adaptations that can provide an opportunity for students to be creative and playful. They can also provide a context for celebrating diversity, encouraging collaboration, and fostering inclusion of all learners in shared, creative classroom activities. Captions for cartoons, one-word-at-a-time shared story-writing, designing novel inventions, and constructing a futuristic model home are just some examples of successful learning activities that are commonly used in effective classrooms. All contributions are valued. Playfulness and participation are the only requirements.

For some teachers working with students with diverse abilities, this open invitation approach can feel uncomfortable. Observations and anecdotal evidence suggest that uncomfortable teachers can fall back on more-structured traditional teaching approaches when working with students who have certain disabilities (e.g., students with a serious learning difficulty). Unfortunately, many individualised learning programs and accompanying comments frequently emphasise task completion and achievement of the correct answer. Drill-and-practice computer programs foster the same responses and a typical commentary says: "Put the blue box on the table. You have put the blue box on the chair. Put the blue box on the table." The straightjacket of compliance and getting it right can seriously restrict students' learning and mask their true abilities by reducing their motivation to learn. These students are rarely encouraged to indulge in nonsense, fantasy, or make-believe activities and are thus denied powerful opportunities to learn and to express their thoughts and feelings.

As the example in Box 12.3 (below) shows, ICT can provide a playful context for students to reveal a hitherto unknown sense of humour.

Open and invitational software can springboard students into further rewarding educational, vocational, and recreational possibilities. For example, Josie could go on to a higher education short design course. She could work (perhaps work experience at first) in a copy shop and become involved in design and desktop publishing tasks.

Box 12.3 Expressing a sense of humour

Josie, a young lady with severe brain injury and no understandable speech, was experimenting with a talking word-processor. This particular package contained a range of voices: child, adult, fantasy, male, and female. Usually clients were helped to choose a voice similar to one of their own. Josie was having none of that! As her voice, she chose the deepest, sexiest male option! Josie then explored a painting program, and revealed her ability to express herself using bold colours and sweeping strokes. The results were stunning, and revealed hidden skills.

Moving from the concrete to the abstract

A hierarchy of symbolic representation, based on Piagetian concepts, identifies the following levels of abstraction:

- real object;
- toy or model;
- colour photographic image;
- black-and-white photograph;
- coloured drawing;
- black-and-white drawing;
- stylised line-drawing;
- formal symbol; and
- text and figures.

For people with some cognitive and behaviour disorders (e.g., Autistic Spectrum Disorder—ASD), it appears that this hierarchy can be disrupted. Rather than proceeding from concrete to symbolic, people with ASD can find abstract representations accessible but have difficulty in linking these abstractions to real-life events. In Box 12.1 (page 515), for example, Jack was able to perform complex abstract calculations but needed structured support to make the association between a concrete activity (riding) and an image of the activity.

Multimedia software, digital cameras, and high-quality sound recording take much of the drudgery out of creating curriculum adaptations. At the same time, these tools allow for authentic, personally relevant links to events and people of importance in the student's life.

Developing a positive self-system

A recurring theme of the case studies presented in this chapter is the developing sense of personal effectiveness as a learner (self-efficacy) that emerges through the use of technology. Personal effectiveness occurs when students perceive that they are capable problem-solvers who can experience success in learning. Experiencing success can enhance academic achievement and motivation which, in turn, helps to create a success cycle. The development of a positive self-system is important for all students but especially those who have experienced failure in learning. The interactions among metacognition, motivation, and achievement are reciprocally beneficial and culminate in the development of a positive self-system (Ryba, 1999). The self-system is portrayed in Figure 12.1 (page 523) as a triangle to show the interactions among these three components.

This developing sense of self can be the single most important factor in learning with technology. If students see themselves as capable learners, they are much more motivated to develop the skills and knowledge that they need to succeed in life (Ryba, 1996). The self-system appears to help determine the quality of academic achievement through activating the self-regulating executive skills necessary for strategy selection, implementation and monitoring.

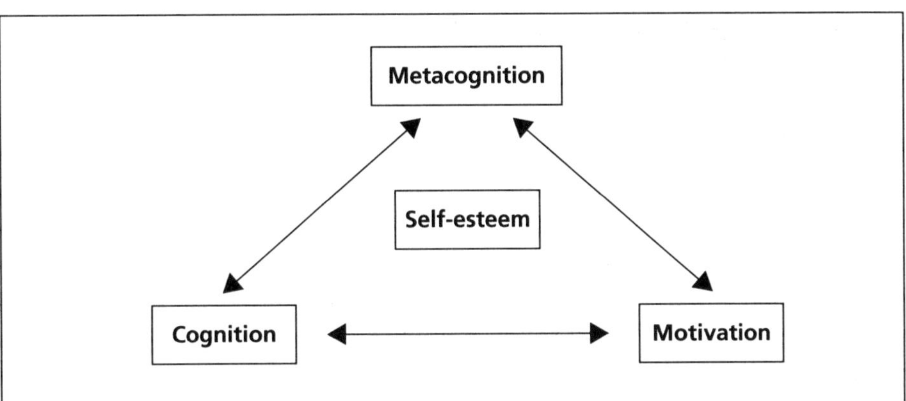

Figure 12.1 Positive self-system.

A brief description of the three main components of the self-system follows. These components have been mentioned in earlier chapters, but it is useful to review the concept in relation to learning with technology.

Metacognition

The ability to be aware of one's own thinking processes is referred to as metacognition. This awareness of oneself as an active agent in the process of knowing is important for becoming an effective learner. Some examples of metacognitive skills include:

- defining the problem in a personally relevant way;
- reflecting upon what needs to be known to arrive at a solution to a problem;
- devising a plan for attacking a problem; and
- checking or monitoring progress.

Research over two decades or so has shown that many students with learning difficulties have poorly developed metacognitive skills. They do not have a good understanding of how to go about learning, how to attend and what to attend to, how to remember, how to check on progress in learning or problem-solving, and how to use the knowledge they already have to learn new things (Chapman, 1992).

Computers and other forms of technology provide an ideal context for teaching these reflective thinking skills. This is because they encourage students to be aware of their thinking. Self-awareness is crucial for developing active involvement and a sense of internal control over learning. All students can benefit from reflective thinking because it transfers responsibility for monitoring learning from teachers to students themselves and promotes positive self-perceptions, affect, and motivation among students.

Cognition

Cognition refers to the mental processes that are involved in attending to, collecting, remembering, and interpreting information. It is concerned with the transformation

of information into knowledge and how the student represents this so that it can be recalled and acted upon. ICT offers valuable scaffolding that helps students to organise and represent knowledge in various ways. For example, a database is used to systematically organise, store, and recall information and the World Wide Web offers an enormous range of resources (images, music, text) that can then be stored or retrieved.

There is a huge body of literature on every aspect of cognition, too vast to summarise in this chapter. In recent times, there has been a growing interest in the use of ICT to overcome certain information processing difficulties. For example, research on attention shows that many students have difficulties in three main areas:

- coming to attention or focusing attention on a task;
- making decisions or thinking about all of the information in a problem; and
- maintaining attention or staying on-task for reasonable periods of time.

The intrinsic appeal of computers has been shown to play a major role in overcoming some aspects of attention problems.

In the area of language, students with learning difficulties often experience problems with syntax (meaning), comprehension, phonological awareness (sounds in words), and narrative knowledge (understanding how a story unfolds). They might experience difficulties with memory and require assistance in the form of learning strategies that can help them to remember (Chapman, 1992; Tunmer, Greaney, & Chapman, 1999).

In these areas also, the use of computers can be valuable in developing both cognitive and metacognitive skills. This is because the technology has facilities to store information in many ways and enables the development of a knowledge system that enables access to the information. For example, information that is stored in a multimedia database can be retrieved alphabetically or by the use of categories or key words.

Motivation

Motivation plays a crucial role in learning inside and outside the classroom (see Chapter 1). Motivational problems can be experienced by all students and can have an adverse effect on their achievement. There are many factors contributing to success and failure, many of which have a motivational aspect. These include self-concept, expectations, beliefs, and attitudes and ideas about what causes success and failure (attributions). Many of the problems of children with learning and behaviour difficulties arise from negative attitudes about themselves that accumulate through experiences of failure.

Many students with behaviour and learning difficulties start school work with negative expectations. They lack a sense of effectiveness as learners and do not think that they have the ability or means to succeed. Facing repeated failure, students become less motivated and increasingly passive and switched off. They eventually get to the point

where they see no reason to plan, organise, monitor, check, persist, or use thinking skills and learning strategies. Poor achievement is perpetuated and, along with the student, many teachers and parents tend to give up trying to encourage or coerce these children (Chapman, 1992). This failure cycle culminates in the formation of a negative self-system. The implications of this failure cycle are well summarised in a comment by Spear-Swerling and Sternberg (1994). They suggested that once children have entered the swamp of negative expectations, lowered motivation, and limited practice, getting them back on the road to success becomes increasingly difficult.

The concept of the positive self-system has led to an increasing awareness of the importance of promoting social and cognitive interactions in a technological environment. Increasing emphasis is being placed on the use of technology as a context for student-centred learning and the development of thinking skills and learning strategies. Teacher and students often work as partners in this environment with the result that they complement one another and adapt the teaching and learning processes to meet the individual needs of students.

The formation of effective learning partnerships requires that teachers gain a sound understanding of the teaching and learning process. This understanding must be based not only on curriculum content, but also on methods aimed at developing capable thinkers and learners.

SUMMARY

Assistive technology has evolved to the point where virtually all students can gain access to, and use, technology in personally relevant ways to enhance their communication and learning. In addition, technology can provide the context for the development of a student-centred learning environment in which the locus of control remains firmly with the student who can act purposefully to achieve his or her desired goal.

Technological developments have stimulated much rethinking about the teaching and learning process. Increasing recognition is being given to the design of socially interactive and reflective learning environments in which students can actively participate and construct their own knowledge and understanding. In the process of learning with technology, students can demonstrate their intellectual capabilities and, most importantly, are free to communicate their ideas in ways that have not been possible before.

With increasing access to the Internet, teachers are discovering new ways to use this online resource to support school curriculum activities, as well as for their own professional development.

The community of practice framework represents a dynamic new way of understanding how to develop human potential through collaborative online communications. There are

innumerable simple teaching adaptations that can provide an opportunity for students to be creative and playful. They can also provide a context for celebrating diversity, encouraging collaboration, and fostering inclusion of all learners in shared, creative classroom activities.

Multimedia software, digital cameras, and high-quality sound recording take much of the drudgery out of creating curriculum adaptation, and lead to authentic, personally relevant links to events and people of importance in the student's life.

Finally, technology provides a powerful context in which students can develop a positive self-system. Teaching them to reflect and regulate their own thinking enables them to experience success in learning.

Online reading and resources

A wealth of online information is now available on assistive technology specifically for individuals with special support needs The sites listed below are given as a starting point only, through which you can gain access to a vast number of other contacts in Australia and globally.

Australian Rehabilitation & Assistive Technology Association (ARATA)

ARATA is an association that serves as a forum for issues in rehabilitation and assistive technology. Membership is open to anyone with an interest in the use of assistive technology for people with disabilities:

<http://members.iinet.au/~sharono/arata>

Special Needs Apple Education Australia

Apple Education Australia has a long-standing commitment to helping people with special needs attain independence through assistive technology and computer adaptations. This site provides information on the Apple range of hardware, software, and adaptive technology:

<www.apple.com.au/edu/specialneeds/homepage.html>

rehabtool.com

This site offers a variety of high-tech assistive and adaptive technology products, augmentative and alternative communication devices, computer access equipment, multilingual speech synthesis and voice recognition software. The site owners specialise in building adaptations and custom software solutions for people with disabilities.

<www.rehabtool.com>

Special education sites

This site was developed by the Kenosha Unified School District in the USA as a resource for teachers to gain information on assistive technology. It contains a large collection of links to sites concerning specific disabilities, assistive technology, speech, language, and hearing, and information about inclusive education:

<www.kusd.edu/favorite/bookmarks/special_ed.html>

Special education resources management

This is a well-developed university site with a vast number of links to special education and rehabilitation organisations. It provides access to a range of information on general disabilities, medicine and health, national organisations, and parent resources. There are links also to products and technology for people with a disability, special education discussion groups, and mailing lists:

<www.wuacc.edu/mabee/special.html>

Special Education and Disabilities Network (SPED/NET)

This is a resource for individuals or organisations seeking information on the Internet. The project provides an interactive network of people working together to find solutions to questions about disabilities. This includes links to sites on assistive technology, parent, medical, and educational resources, and special education support:

<www.fortbragg.k12.ca.us/REDWD/spednet.html>

Practical activities

1. Check out the websites above and create your own bookmarks of sites that you consider to be most useful and relevant.
2. Visit a setting where assistive technology is being used so you can see firsthand how learners are using the adaptations described in this chapter. You will need to be creative to locate the site. Brainstorm ideas with some of your friends or study pals.
3. Obtain a copy of your national, state, or regional education statement on the uses of technology in the classroom. All of these are specific documents that relate to students with diverse abilities. Make sure you consider children who are gifted and talented, and those with the highest support needs
4. Attend a short course on using assistive technology so that you gain a working knowledge of the available hardware and software options. Again, you will need to be creative in your search.

5. Identify some educational settings where the theories and principles outlined in this chapter appear to be put into practice. Consult with teachers and students in those settings to learn about good educational practices for learning with technology.
6. Join an online community in a particular education field of interest to you. This could be a discussion group, newsgroup, or listserv to which you can actively contribute and obtain information.

References

BeCTA. (1998). *The UK Integrated Learning Systems (ILS) Evaluations: Final report*. Coventry, UK: The British Educational Communications and Technology Agency.

Blackwell, A. & McKeown, L. (1995). Pack your bags with travel buddies. *Classroom (Australia)*, December, 10–13.

Brett, A. (1994). Computers and social development of young children. *Dimensions of Early Childhood*, Autumn issue, 10–13.

Brown, M. (1997). Information and communication technology—more than just computers! In J. Burns (Ed.) *Technology in the New Zealand curriculum: Perspectives on practice* (pp. 248–265). Palmerston North: Dunmore Press.

Bryant, D. & Bryant, B. (1998) Using assistive technology adaptations to include students with learning disabilities in co-operative learning activities. *Journal of Learning Disabilities, 3*, 4–12.

Chapman, J. W. (1992). *Understanding learning difficulties: A guide for parents and teachers*. Palmerston North: Massey University Educational Research and Development Centre.

Clements, D., Nastasi, B., & Swaminathan, S. (1993). Young children and computers: Crossroads and directions from research. *Young Children, 3*, 56–64.

Drew, C., Harrison, P., Millar, M., Stewart, J., & Wedde, R. (1998). Overlay keyboards in inclusive education. Unpublished presentation to Specialist Education Services Conference, Auckland, New Zealand, September.

Frampton, A. (1989). An integrated approach to using computers in the classroom. *Computers in New Zealand Schools, 1(1)*, 5–7.

Frazer, D., Moltzen, R., & Ryba, K. (2000). *Learners with special needs in Aotearoa New Zealand*. Palmerston North: Dunmore.

Goossens, C. & Sapp Crain, S. (1992). *Utilising Switch interface with children who are severely physically challenged.* Austin TX: PRO-ED.

Howard, J., Greyrose, E., & Kehr, K. (1996). Teacher-facilitated microcomputer activities: Enhancing social play and affect in young children with disabilities. *Journal of Special Education Technology, 13*, 36–47.

Lave, J. (1988). *Cognition in practice: Mind, mathematics, and culture in everyday life*. Cambridge, England: Cambridge University Press.

Lave, J. & Wenger, E. (1991). *Situated learning: Legitimate peripheral participation*. Cambridge, England: Cambridge University Press.

Lewis, R. B. (1993). *Special education technology: Classroom applications.* Pacific Grove, CA: Brookes/Cole.

Lewis, R. (1998). Assistive technology and learning disabilities: Today's realities and tomorrow's promises. *Journal of Learning Disabilities, 31,* 16–26.

Male, M. (1988). *Special Magic: Computers, Classroom Strategies and Exceptional Students.* Mountain View, CA: Mayfield.

Mastrangelo, S. (1996). *Computers in special education.* Available online: <www.edu.york.ca/~tcs/~smastrangelo/specialed.html>

Murray, J. (1994) Early literacy: The benefits of using a concept keyboard. *Computers in New Zealand Schools, 6,* 21–28.

Papert, S. (1980). *Mindstorms: Children, computers and powerful ideas.* New York: Basic.

Ryba, K. (1996). Viewing students as capable learners. *Computers in New Zealand Schools, 8 (2),* 3–6.

Ryba, K. (1999). Dynamic learning strategies assessment. Conference Proceedings, School Psychologists Association, Fremantle, Western Australia.

Ryba, K. & Selby, L. (1993). Computers as empowering tools for students with intellectual disabilities. *Network,* 2, 8–15.

Spear-Swirling, L. & Sternberg, R. J. (1994). The road not taken: An integrative theoretical model for reading disability. *Journal of Learning Disabilities, 27,* 103–122.

Tunmer, W. E., Greaney, K. T. & Chapman, J. W. (1999). Orthographic analogy training as an intervention strategy for children with severe reading difficulties. In D. Greaves & P. Jeffery (Eds), *Strategies for intervention with special needs students* (pp. 1–26). Coldstream, Vic., Australia: Australian Resource Educators' Association.

Vygotsky, L. S. (1987). Thinking and speech (N. Minick, Trans.). In R. W. Rieber & A. S. Carton (Eds), *The collected works of L. S. Vygotsky* (pp. 37–285). New York: Plenum.

Williams, M. (1995). Case study of a professional development program conducted in distance education mode using communications technologies. Unpublished masters thesis, Deakin University, Melbourne.

Williams, M., McKeown, L., Masselos, P., Stubbs, J., & Potter, D. (1998). *Global InfoLinks: The story of building an online educational community for Queensland students and their teachers.* Available online:
<http://owl.qut.edu.au/qsite/qsite.html>

Williams, M. & McKeown, L. (1996). *Professional development model for implementing Internet projects at your school.* Queensland Society for Information Technology in Education Conference CD. Brisbane: Queensland Society for Information Technology in Education.

Wizer, D. R. (1995). Small group instruction using microcomputers: Focus on group behaviours. *Journal of Research on Computing in Education. 28,* 10–12.

Zhang, Y., Brooks, D., Frields, T., & Redelfs, M. (1995). Quality of writing by elementary students with learning disabilities. *Journal of Research on Computing in Education,* 27, 483–499.

Glossary

AAC See augmentative and alternative communication.

ability The power to perform a physical or mental act, whether innate or acquired by training or practice.

accommodation The ability of the eyes to maintain focus at near range. This also involves rapid and accurate change of focus from distance to near.

Adaptive Behavior Scale (ABS) This is a checklist that measures a person's ability to cope with the demands of independent living in a socially acceptable way. It was prepared under the auspices of the American Association on Mental Deficiency (now the American Association on Mental Retardation). The ABS is intended for use with children and adults across 24 skill areas.

adaptive behaviour This term relates to the ability of an individual to cope with the demands of independent living in a socially acceptable way. The adaptiveness of behaviour is varies according to the age of the individual.

Adaptive Functioning Index One of a number of measures of adaptive behaviour.

adventitious Refers to onset of blindness after the child has acquired a visual memory.

advocate A person who acts for, on behalf of, a person with a disability.

analytic touch The method of touch exploration in which the person mentally links separate part impressions together to gain a concept of the whole.

aphasia A language disorder in the presence of a neurological lesion; variable in type and severity, mostly caused by strokes and head injuries.

aphonia Lack of voice (see also dysphonia)

apraxia The inability to plan and carry out a motor task. Apraxic children may appear clumsy, but the problem is more with planning and understanding the movement rather than with muscles or coordination.

aptitude The capacity or potential to perform an unlearned task or act (see also skill).

articulation The movements of the organs involved in speech; the points of closest contact during the production of speech sounds.

ASD See autistic spectrum disorder.

ascertainment The process of determining the most suitable educational placement for a student with a disability or impairment

assistive technology Any item, piece of equipment, or product system that is used to increase, maintain or improve functional capabilities of individuals with disabilities.

associated disability Is a second disability as well as a primary disability (e.g., a student may have a mild hearing impairment associated with educational blindness).

ataxia Difficulty with performance of smooth coordinated movements. A person with ataxia moves in a jerky and uncontrolled manner, making grasp, balance, and walking difficult.

athetosis A writhing pattern of movement caused by variations in a persons muscle tone. Also excessive movements are seen.

at-risk This refers to children who have been identified by school personnel as being vulnerable to an educational or learning difficulty. The cause may be social, behavioural, intellectual or medical.

attention Process of focusing on particular stimuli in an environment. See also selective attention.

attribution retraining A form of intervention therapy the purpose of which is to alter or modify the explanations given by people for their successes and failures, particularly changing 'ability' attributions to 'effort' attributions. See also causal attributions.

audiogram Is a grid system for the recording of hearing loss, where the x-axis represents the frequency of sound waves in hertz (Hz) and the logarithmic y-axis represents volume in decibels (dB).

audiologist Is a non-medical practitioner who evaluates the degree of hearing loss and prescribes hearing aids.

audiometer Electronic device used to measure aspects of hearing.

audiometric zero At various frequencies, the average softest sound that can be heard by the human ear. It is the same as the threshold of hearing for normal ears. Sometimes called clinical zero.

auditory discrimination Ability to differentiate between sounds (e.g., "pad" or "pat").

auditory training Is the teaching of listening skills. The child learns to use residual hearing to listen more precisely and to make associations with noises.

augmentative and alternative communication (AAC) This involves the use of non-speech communication systems such as manual signs or picture-based communication boards.

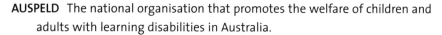

Auslan See Australian Sign Language

AUSPELD The national organisation that promotes the welfare of children and adults with learning disabilities in Australia.

Australian sign language (Auslan) Is the language of the Australian Deaf community.

autism See autistic spectrum disorder.

autistic behaviour Characteristic of a child classified as autistic. Behaviours include detachment from the environment, severe communication difficulties, development of relationship with inanimate objects rather than people, ritualistic and compulsive behaviour.

Autistic Spectrum Disorder (ASD) The symptoms and characteristics of autism can present themselves in a wide variety of combinations, from mild to severe. Although autism is defined by a certain set of behaviors, children and adults can exhibit any combination of the behaviors in any degree of severity. This is characterised by impairments in social interaction, communication, and stereotyped behaviors, interests and activities.

behaviour state assessment A variety of methods for assessing the individual's level of alertness. These assessment techniques are used to better understand the levels of alertness and involvement demonstrated by students in a range of settings.

behaviour disorders Although there is no agreed definition of behaviour disorders, most educators agree that behaviours that disrupt other students and teachers to a marked degree are disordered. Students with severe behaviour disorders have often been called emotionally disturbed.

behaviour modification A form of therapy or intervention used to promote a behavioural change in the target person or group. Behaviour modification is based on the learning theory proposed by B. F. Skinner (called operant conditioning) which asserts the need to establish a link between a response and a reinforcing stimulus. Terms commonly encountered include positive and negative reinforcement, extraction, shaping, time out and schedules of reinforcement.

Better Ear Average (BEA) A single number index of the threshold of hearing at various frequencies with the human speech range.

Binet scale A test of intelligence originally prepared by Alfred Binet in France in the late 1800s. Binet's test was translated into English and later adapted by Louis Terman into the Stanford-Binet Scale of Intelligence. The 4th edition of Binet was released in 1987 and varies markedly from earlier editions.

binocular vision The vision obtained when the two eyes work together as a team, simultaneously fusing and focusing two images to give an accurate three-dimensional interpretation.

Braille Is a tactual language system based on a cell of six potential raised dot positions, arranged in two columns and three rows. Various combinations of these six dots then form the basis for all braille symbols.

calliper A form of steel brace used to aid standing or walking.

cascade model A concept, introduced by Deno, that ranked educational placements form least to most integrated. Also referred to as a continuum of services from least to most restrictive.

categorical education A view of education that focuses upon dealing with, or overcoming, the problems associated with the disability or impairment as the primary goal of instruction.

causal attributions Explanations given by people for their successes and failures. See also attribution retraining.

central hearing loss Relates to damage to the high level neural pathways or to the auditory cortex of the brain.

cerebral cortex The outer layer of brain tissue (the grey matter) arranged in folds. The cerebral cortex is largely responsible for the coordination of higher mental activities (i.e., complex thought).

chromosome One of the microscopic sized bodies in cells that carry the hereditary characteristics. Chromosomes may be stubby, rod-, j-, or v-shaped and consist of protein and deoxyribonucleic acid (DNA).

clinical zero The same as audiometric zero.

cochlea The organ of hearing, situated inside the skull.

cochlear implant An electronic device that directly stimulates the remaining hair cells of the cochlea to produce a sensation of sound.

cognition The process of thinking, that is, knowing, perceiving, reasoning and problem solving.

cognitive behaviour modification A form of behaviour modification in which emphasis is given to establishing in the target individual an awareness of the link between a set of circumstances, desirable or appropriate behaviour and the reinforcing event.

cognitive curriculum The hierarchically structured content of an education program which incorporates not only the information to be learned but also instruction in learning and problem solving strategies.

cognitive modelling Providing both action and language that shows how a task is

to be completed and describes the accompanying thought processes so that the task may be learned.

coherence Smooth flow of spoken or written ideas, with logical connections and appropriate information. Not to be confused with fluency.

communicative competence The ability of a person to coordinate all aspects of the communication system adequately to meet all communicative needs and requirements.

communicative intent The assumption of motivation in behaviour interpreted as being communicative (see speech acts).

COMPICS Computer generated pictographs for communication. They are simple line drawings used for communication when speech is difficult to understand or cannot be obtained.

complex sentences Sentences containing more than one clause. An element of "syntax."

conceptual model These address the reason why certain behaviours occur, how thy can be identified and how they should be treated. Hence, they attempt to provide a unified approach to identification and treatment of a behaviour disorder.

conductive hearing loss Relates to problems in the outer and middle ear.

congenital Refers to the presence of a disability at birth.

consultant A specialist who advises teachers how to meet specific needs of children.

contract A behavioural technique involving an agreement between an individual and teacher or therapist that specifies behaviours and consequences.

convergence (near point of) The ability to point or aim both eyes exactly at the same near object at the same time.

convergent Relates to convergent thinking or production which is restricted to one form of response or product.

creativity A process in which a person creates a new idea (thinking) or a new product (outcome), or changes existing ideas or outcomes which result in something new for the individual.

cretinism A condition resulting from a problem with the production of thyroxin in the thyroid gland which may result in an intellectual disability. Also called hypothyroidism.

criterion-referenced assessment Assessment of student performance in relation to set standards, not in comparison to the performance of others (see norm-referenced assessment).

cued speech Is a method of supplementing oral communication, consisting of hand

signals near the chin. The signals do not have meaning, rather they are visual cues designed to help the child identify sounds not able to be distinguished through speech reading alone.

cultural-familial intellectual disability An intellectual disability which results from no known biological or organic cause. It is perceived to be a result of the interaction between heredity and environment and normally associated with people living in educationally disadvantaged or low socio-economic status conditions.

curriculum Structured content of schooling, often used to include all planned experiences of students.

Deaf culture Is the culture of the Deaf community. It is characterised by its own language (sign language) and its own pattern of beliefs, values, customs, arts, institutions, social forms and knowledges.

decibe A unit of measurement of the intensity of sound (perceived as the loudness of the sound). It is one-tenth of a Bel (named after Alexander Graham Bell) Usually abbreviated db.

decontextualised language The use of language to refer to past or future events, to abstract matters, or to things outside of the speakers' immediate context.

deinstitutionalisation The policy and practice of moving people with a disability out of large residential facilities into small homes in the community which cater for four or five people only.

descriptive linguistics Grammar based on normal usage (see prescriptive linguistics).

desegregation The process of returning children to regular school (see integration).

developmental disabilities Disabilities which arise or are manifested early in a person's life and which persist (most often refers to an intellectual disability)

diplegia Paralysis (loss of muscle control) of similar parts on both sides of the body (e.g., the legs).

direct care staff Staff of facilities who supervise, or care for, people with a disability.

direct instruction A teaching method used to teach reading and mathematics emphasising structured sequences. Lessons sometimes have scripted responses and solution strategies.

Disability Services Act Australian legislation introduced in 1986 to replace the Handicapped Persons Assistance Act. It has a strong emphasis upon consumer outcomes rather than the needs of service organisations.

discourse Units of language above single sentences. Includes conversation and story telling (narrative).

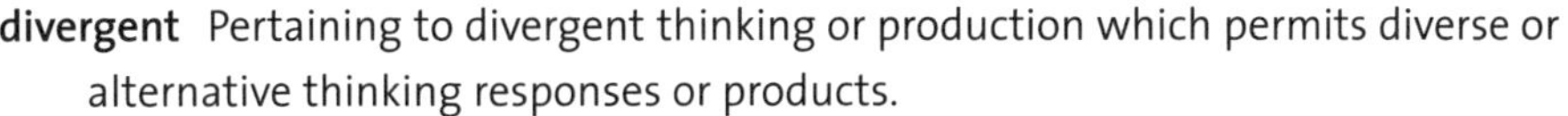

divergent Pertaining to divergent thinking or production which permits diverse or alternative thinking responses or products.

Down Syndrome A condition resulting from a chromosomal abnormality. There are three types, Trisomy 21, mosaicism and translocation.

dysarthria A speech disorder of neurological origin affecting the muscles of speech.

dyslexia An impairment of the ability to read. This is a controversial term more often used by medical practitioners.

dysphonia Problematic voice quality.

dyspraxia A speech disorder of neurological origin where coordination of speech musculature is affected.

early intervention A program provided for young children with a disability or impairment to optimise their chances for enrolment in regular education programs. Typically early interventions focus on management of bodily functions and on preacademic skills, such as concept development.

echolalia Imitation of the previous utterance (immediate echolalia) or previously heard utterances (delayed echolalia). May be partial or changed slightly (mitigated echolalia). Normal in children under the single-word stage, but very characteristic of disorder otherwise.

echolocation Locating objects by listening to and identifying the direction of reflected sound.

Education of All Handicapped Children Act (PL 94-142) This is the US legislation which prescribes education for all children. The legislation contains a mandatory provision which states that school systems must provide free, public education for every child between three and 21 years of age, regardless of disability, unless state laws do not provide for education between ages three and five years, or over 18 years. A supplementary law (PL 99-457) extended PL 94-142 to remove the exception a clause (for children aged 3-5 years) and to encourage early intervention incentives.

educationally blind Means there is a total lack of functional vision for learning.

educationally deaf Means there is a total lack of functional hearing for learning.

efficiency (visual or auditory) Is the degree of ease, comfort and minimum time which an individual needs to perform specific visual (auditory) tasks. It is unique to each child.

embedding A form of complex clause structure (see "complex sentences").

emotional disorder/disturbance A condition where emotional reactions are inappropriate or deficient. Emotional disturbance has often referred to extreme

acting out or withdrawn behaviour. It is now being replaced by the term severe behaviour disorders.

encephalitis An acute inflammation of the brain or its covering tissue caused by one of a number of viruses, some of which may cause neurological changes which continue after the inflammation has ceased. Symptoms typically include lethargy, varying degrees of stupor and coma, headaches and paralysis.

enclaves Work groups of persons with disabilities within regular industry.

Enrolment Support Group In Victoria, Australia, an essential part of the placement of a child with a disability in a regular school.

ethnographic research A qualitative method based on anthropological techniques of participant observation. Also known as naturalistic, observational research.

executive process Cognitive processes which are involved in the integration of information. These include planning, decision making, and an awareness of these intellectual activities (see also metacognition).

expressive language Relates to the production of language usually through speech or writing (e.g., correct pronunciation and grammar, letter formation and handwriting).

extensors Muscles which open the angle at a joint.

figure-ground The ability to recognise, "pick out" and attend to an item or items against a background of other objects (e.g., picking out a red pencil from a pencil box, finding a name in a telephone directory or hearing your name in a noisy environment).

fine motor skills Complex movement of especially the hands and fingers that require a high degree of coordination (e.g., manipulating a pencil to form letters, typing, fastening buttons and clasps).

Finger spelling Is a manual version of the alphabet. In Australia and New Zealand, Victorian Finger Spelling, a two handed method, is used (see Figure 6.5). In North America a one-handed finger spelling is used. This one handed method of communicating enables the communicator to simultaneously sign and do other things, like eat.

flexors Muscles which reduce the angle at a joint.

fluency Normally smooth delivery of speech. The opposite of fluency is stuttering (or stammering). Not to be confused with "coherence."

FM hearing aid A hearing aid which uses FM radio waves to broadcast directly to a hearing aid from a miniature transmitter worn by a teacher. Also known as a radio aid.

Fragile X syndrome A form of intellectual disability linked with an apparent weak,

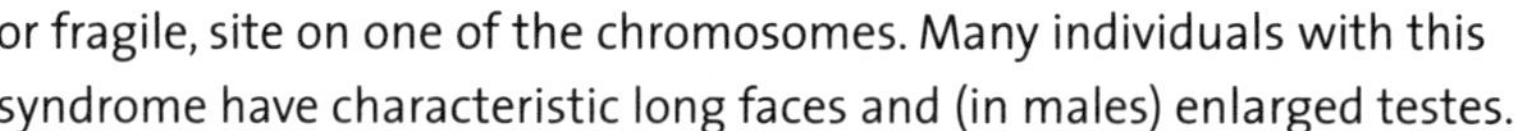

or fragile, site on one of the chromosomes. Many individuals with this syndrome have characteristic long faces and (in males) enlarged testes.

frequency The physical aspects of sound which is perceived as pitch (measures in Hertz, usually abbreviated *Hz*).

functional assessment Identifying the purpose(s) of behaviour by analysing the situations in which it occurs, including the antecedents, behavioural indicators and consequences which influence it.

functional academics Skills which allow a person with an intellectual disability to live with some degree of independence in the community. These skills include money handling, sign recognition, arithmetic operations, basic reading, writing, interpersonal and communication skills.

functional disorder (of speech, language, or voice) Used to indicate disorder with no known organic cause.

Functioning (visual or auditory) Is how people use whatever vision (hearing) they might have. It is strongly influenced by personal "experiences, motivations, needs and expectations . . . in relation to whatever visual [auditory] capacity is available to satisfy curiosity and accomplish activities for personal satisfaction" (Barraga, 1983, p. 24).

generic services Services in a specific field designed to be provided to the whole of the community (e.g., public transport, health services).

gifted/giftedness Giftedness corresponds to a level of competence in the non-systematically developed abilities of at least one aptitude domain that places subjects among the upper 15–20% of their age peers.

gifts and talents A concept that recognises that all people has some ability or abilities that may be developed. It implies that parents and teachers should seek to determine these abilities and to develop them to the level of their potential.

gross motor skills Those skills associated with the use of large muscles (e.g., arms, legs, trunk).

hard of hearing Means that after correction some functional hearing is available for learning.

hemiplegia Paralysis on only one side of the body.

hertz The unit of measurement of frequency. The human hearing range falls between about 350 and 20,000 Hertz in normally hearing young people.

human rights A convention prescribing opportunities for all individuals to gain access to the social, educational, vocational, legal and political structures of the society. In Australia there is no legal basis to guarantee human rights or access to the services provided in the community.

hyperactivity Excessive motor activity and restlessness. Frequently associated with poor attention and chronic distractability.

hypernasality Speech where there is too much nasal resonance or airflow through the nose.

hypertonia Abnormally high muscle tone. The muscles of a child with hypertonia seem tense or tight at rest and resistance to movement is greater than normal.

inactive learners Learners who fail to take an active role in learning by not using adaptive strategies as well as lacking an intent to learn.

incidence The relative frequency of an occurrence given as a number per 1,000 or a percentage (e.g., the occurrence of Down syndrome per 1,000 live births).

individual differences The various personal qualities (intellectual, personality, social-emotional) which constitute the differences between individuals.

individual education program (IEP) A written document which is intended to aid in the provision of educational programs for students with special needs. It includes a statement of the student's present performance, instructional objectives and goals (sometimes called the individual education plan), services required by the student and evaluation procedures to be used, Originally the concept was one generated from PL 94-142 called individualised education programs (IEPs).

information and communication technology Refers to the range of technologies that are being integrated into school environments as part of the infrastructure for learning. This definition encompasses the broad range of technologies used for accessing, gathering, manipulation, and presentation or communication of information.

integration The process of moving children from special education settings into regular classrooms where they undertake most, if not all, of their schooling. Also called desegregation.

Integration in Victorian Education, 1984 A landmark report to the Victorian Minister for Education affirming the right of children with disabilities to be placed in regular schools.

intelligence A general term related to the ability to learn and solve problems. There is no consensus on one definition of intelligence and, to a large extent, the term has ceased to be a useful one for describing the way in which thinking, learning and problem solving occurs. (See also IQ)

intensity The physical aspect of sound which is perceived as loudness (measured in decibels).

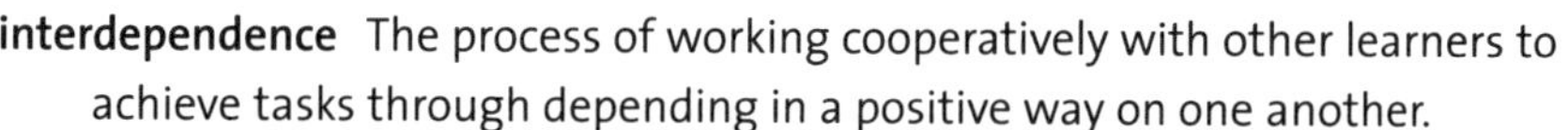
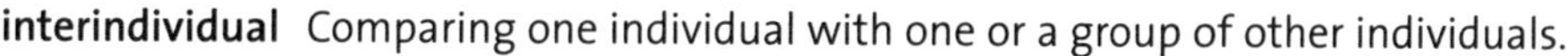

interdependence The process of working cooperatively with other learners to achieve tasks through depending in a positive way on one another.

interindividual Comparing one individual with one or a group of other individuals.

intonation The rising and falling tones of the voice over an utterance. For example, rising tone at the end of an utterance may be the only indicator of a question ("intonation question").

intraindividual Comparing characteristics within an individual.

IEP See Individual Education Program

IQ Is a figure determined as a results of the administration of one of the many tests of intelligence. The IQ represents the relative position of a person to others of similar age on the same test. An IQ of 100 is the convention which represents the average score of those taking the test. If an individual is given two different tests of intelligence, two different IQs are likely to result.

itinerant services Educational or therapeutic services provided by a professional person who travels from centre to centre to work with students in regular or special class who have a specific need (e.g., physiotherapy for a student with a mobility problem, speech therapy for a child with a hearing impairment).

jargon Pre-speech production of strings of sounds that sound like normal language but aren't.

kinaesthesia The sense of position and body movements as perceived through muscles, tendons and joints (as in kinaesthetic memory, kinaesthetic method).

labelling The practice of categorising children and adults according to a type of disability or impairment.

learned helplessness Beliefs held by individuals that they have no control over the outcome of events.

learning difficulties Term used in Australia and New Zealand to describe individuals who experience marked difficulties with achieving in school. These problems, however, may continue in adolescence and adulthood.

learning disabilities Term used in the US and Canada to describe children with difficulties in language and communication skills generally, but excluding those whose learning problems are primarily due to hearing, vision or motor impairment, emotional difficulties, cultural disadvantage or intellectual disability.

least restrictive environment The educational setting in which a child with a disability or impairment can succeed and which is as close as possible to the regular classroom (which is considered to the be the ideal).

lexical Word meaning level.

lexicon The store of words in semantic memory.

lipreading See speechreading.

Low vision Means that after correction some functional vision is available for learning.

maindumping A term suggesting that children with special needs are being integrated into regular classes without adequate support.

mainstream A US term that refers to the general education stream in which students with special needs may be placed. Mainstreaming is the US term for integration of students with special needs into the ordinary education system.

Makaton This is an augmentative communication system which involves oral and sign language. It was originally based upon British Sign Language and has been widely introduced into facilities catering for people with severe forms of intellectual disability. The word, Makaton, is derived from the names of its originators (see sign language).

marker variables Characteristics that may be used to identify subtypes of individuals with learning difficulties.

mediation deficiency This is said to occur when a person is unable to use a suitable information processing strategy (e.g., rehearsal) on a certain task when given instructions to do so.

metacognition The awareness of how one uses information processing strategies, learns and problem solves most effectively.

metalinguistics The use of language to comment on language and specific awareness of the nature of communication mechanisms.

minimal brain dysfunction A term once used synonymously with that of learning disabilities to describe children with no clinical (neurological) signs of brain damage. Also known as minimal brain damage and minimal cerebral dysfunction.

Mixed hearing loss Involves both conductive and sensorineural impairment.

modelling Providing a behavioural example of how a task is to be undertaken so that another can learn by imitation.

monocular vision The vision obtained from one eye working in isolation from the second eye.

morphology The study of the meaningful units that make up words (e.g., black/bird/s = 3 morphemes).

morphology The study of word formation, in particular how the addition and deletion of parts of words changes their meaning.

mosaicism A form of genetic abnormality which occurs when at least two cell lines

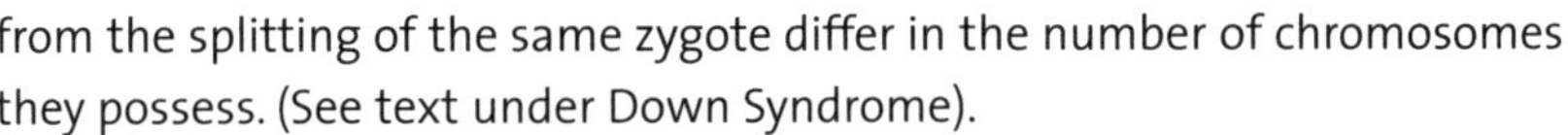

from the splitting of the same zygote differ in the number of chromosomes they possess. (See text under Down Syndrome).

multiple disabilities Usually refers to more than two disabilities.

narrative A monologue, either fictitious or recounting of real events (see also discourse).

national curriculum and achievement testing Movements within the United Kingdom and Australian seeking to standardise curricula and monitor student progress using achievement tests.

naturalistic, observational research See ethnographic research.

New Zealand sign language Is the sign language of the New Zealand Deaf community.

normal curve This is a symmetrical bell-shaped curve which is said to describe the distribution of many physical and psychological variables.

normalisation A belief that people with a disability or impairment should enjoy the same rights, privileges, opportunities and access to services and facilities as those who do not have a disability or impairment.

norm-referenced assessment Assessment of student performance in comparison to the performance of others, such as pupils in same grade or of the same age (see also criterion-referenced assessment).

occupational overuse syndrome Occupational overuse syndrome, also known as repetition strain injury (RSI), is a collective term for a range of conditions, characterised by discomfort or persistent pain in muscles, tendons and other soft tissues, with or without physical manifestations. Occupational overuse syndrome is usually caused or aggravated by work, and is associated with repetitive movement, sustained or constrained postures and/or forceful movements.

occupational therapy This refers to a paramedical service or rehabilitation program designed to improve the patient's muscular control, often through the use of handicrafts or other creative art activities. Occupational therapists are most commonly employed in hospitals and facilities for aged people and for those with an intellectual disability.

ophthalmologist Is a surgeon who specialises in diagnosing and treating eye conditions.

optometrist Is a non-medical practitioner who evaluates vision, prescribes lenses and/or visual therapy.

oral communication Is a method to teach deaf children where the emphasis is placed on student talk using amplification, speech reading, cued speech, auditory training, and state of the art technological aids to assist with auditory, tactile and visual information input.

orientation and mobility (O&M) Knowing one's position in relation to other objects in space (orientation) and being able to safely, independently, and purposefully move about (mobility) are important skills for individuals with vision impairment.

orthosis An apparatus or device which is used to replace a function which can no longer be performed by a person (e.g., a brace which holds a child's wrist stiff so that a pencil may be held).

ossicles The three small bones in the middle ear which transmit the vibration of sounds from the ear drum to the cochlea.

otitis media This is an inflammation of the middle ear and one cause of conductive hearing loss.

otorhinolaryngologist Is a surgeon who specialises in diagnosing and treating ear conditions.

parochial Parish-based Catholic schooling.

partially sighted After correction, some, but significantly reduced, functional vision is available for learning. Sometimes referred to as low vision.

PASS (Program Evaluation of Service Systems) An evaluation tool for adult disability services based upon the principle of normalisation.

peer tutoring A method of teaching whereby one individual takes on the role of the teacher while the other individual in a pair is the learner.

perception (visual or auditory) Is the ability to understand and interpret all visually/auditorially received information. It is more related to learning capabilities than to the condition of the eyes (or ears) and therefore is still possible with low vision/hearing.

phenylketonuria (PKU) A genetic disorder associated with the physical and chemical reactions that occur within the individual, in this case, related to the lack of an enzyme necessary for the oxidation of the chemical phenylalanine. Intellectual disability will occur if the disorder is undetected soon after birth and/or is untreated.

phonetics The study of sounds used in speech based on measurable characteristics (e.g., acoustic, articulatory or perceptual phonetics).

phonological processes or rules the ways sound patterns of a language are simplified. Can apply in normal development, in language changes over time, and in disordered phonology.

phonology The study of the way languages pattern their sound systems.

physiotherapy The treatment of physical disabilities through massage, systematic exercise, manipulation, or the use of heat, light, or water treatments.

PKU See phenylketonuria

postlingual deafness Refers to deafness that occurs after a sound based language has been acquired.

pragmatics The study of the uses to which communication is put.

preacademic skills Prerequisite skills for the development of academic skills such as reading and mathematics. Preacademic skills include attending and maintaining attention, discriminating between sounds and shapes, following direction or instructions, responding to questions, holding a pen or pencil, scribbling or copying, rote counting and sequencing.

precision teaching A system of monitoring performance based on individual objectives, records of daily progress, the use of tests or probes indicating where techniques need to be changed.

prelingual deafness Refers to deafness that occurs before a sound based language has been acquired.

prescriptive linguistics The grammar based on rules of correct usage (see descriptive linguistics).

presupposition Information that has already been signalled or can be assumed. eg. to refer to "she" can only be done if "she" has already been identified. An element of pragmatics.

prevalence The number of cases existing within the population at any given time (e.g., the percentage of the total school population having a learning difficulty).

prevocational training The development of prerequisite skills for training for certain jobs or work tasks. These skills include attending, remaining on-task or at a work station, responding immediately when given direction, developing gross and fine motor coordination, sorting, using appropriate language and/or communication skills. Prevocational training may occur informally and naturally at school for students with physical impairments, but specific attention may be needed to develop these basic skills in students with an intellectual disability.

primitive reflex A reflex present at birth which normally disappears within the first few months of life.

process training Teaching techniques used to train psychological processes involved in learning (e.g., linguistic, perceptual).

Process-Based Instruction (PBI) A systematic approach to classroom instruction that is designed to enhance students' independent learning and problem solving skills. PBI is based upon the development and presentation of teacher-made plans which students learn to amend to suit their individual needs. Later, students learn to develop their own plans individually.

production deficiency Involves the failure of the individual to produce or employ a strategy when the capability to do so is possessed.

proprioception The sense whereby we are aware of the position of our body parts without using vision.

prosthesis A mechanical, electronic or sometimes inert artificial replacement for a body part (e.g., an artificial limb).

psycholinguistic training Remediation focusing on inadequate psycholinguistic skills of reception, association and expression with the aim of improving academic skills.

quality-of-life The real or perceived status of the life experiences of an individual which satisfy the various levels of need including shelter, nutrition, friendships, emotional support, purpose and reason for existence.

Reading Recovery Developed in New Zealand by Professor Marie Clay this program selects the children at age six years who have the poorest performance in reading and writing and tries to bring them to average levels of performance. Tuition is individualised and lasts about 12–20 weeks.

receptive language Relates to the receiving and understanding of information (e.g., word recognition, auditory discrimination).

reciprocal teaching An instructional procedure taking the form of a discussion structured around the strategies of questioning, summarising, clarifying and predicting.

recruitment A condition in which a given increase in intensity of sound results in a greater than normal increase in perceived loudness. It limits the amount of amplification that a recruiting impaired ear can tolerate.

register (speech) The relative formality or type of language used.

Regular Education Initiative This is an education policy proposal in the US requiring services to people with a mild disability (e.g., a mild intellectual disability, learning disability, emotional disturbance) to be delivered in regular education classes. While this is in line with current legislation in the US, the REI proposes that special education will no longer be funded separately from regular education.

repair The requesting and providing of clarification when communication is inadequate in some way. An important aspect of communicative competence, and an element in pragmatics. Also called communicative repair.

Rhesus (Rh) factor An inherited factor in the blood to do with its ability to stick or adhere (agglutinate). The Rh factor was named after the rhesus monkey in whom it was first identified. When introduced into an organism who does not have the factor (i.e., being Rh negative) it causes jaundice, convulsions and paralysis.

rhotacism Unusual production of the "r" sound.

scaffolding A term which refers to the gradual withdrawal of teacher support given during an educational intervention as the learner become more capable and is, thus, able to work independently. In language development, scaffolding refers to the way a competent communicator builds conversation using the less adequate utterances of a partner.

Schonell Centre Short for the Fred and Eleanor Schonell Special Education Research Centre that was founded in 1951 by the late Professor Sir Fred Schonell. Schonell later became Vice Chancellor of The University of Queensland. The Centre began providing a clinic with teaching and research emphases. Clinical activities were phased out by 1971 and the focus narrowed to research and teaching. Professor Betty Watts was appointed to the first Chair in Special Education in 1974 which she held until retirement in 1982.

selective attention Involves selecting relevant from irrelevant stimuli. See also attention.

self-advocacy Organisations composed of persons with a disability which are dedicated to improving the opportunities for people to demand the privileges, opportunities and access to services which are considered to be their rights as members of society. Also, a person asserting the demand for human rights.

self-concept The perception or image that people have of themselves.

self-correcting materials Instructional materials that allow individuals to check their answers without reference to another human or material source.

self-efficacy The developing sense of personal effectiveness as a learner, enhanced awareness of one's own capacity to learn and perform tasks.

self-esteem The value which people place on the data of their self-concept. It refers to the positive and negative judgements of the characteristics people attribute to themselves.

self-fulfilling prophecy The belief that performance reflects what is expected.

self-help skills These are independent living skill such as dressing, grooming and using transport.

self-injury The infliction of a physical injury upon one's self (e.g., head banging, hair pulling, eye gouging). This is a characteristic of some people with severe and profound intellectual disabilities or of those exhibiting autistic behaviour.

self-instructional training A type of cognitive behaviour modification technique which incorporates talking aloud and later talking to one self in order to accomplish a task.

self-stimulation Stereotypic and repetitive behaviours (e.g., rocking, verbal repetition, hand-flicking) which acts as a compensation for sensory deprivation.

self-system The dynamic interaction between self awareness and regulation (metacognition), intellectual and academic performance (cognition) and a positive feeling state about learning (motivation).

semantics The study of meaning in language.

sensorineural hearing loss Results from problems in the inner ear or nerve pathways.

sensory impairments The loss or degradation or absence of a sense organ (e.g., vision, hearing) which leads to a learning problem.

sequential processing A cognitive process which enables information to be received, stored and retrieved unit by unit in a sequence-dependent manner (e.g., hearing a telephone number given orally).

service delivery The provision of a educational, training, therapeutic, medical, vocational or other program or treatment to an individual, group or organisation.

shaping A term commonly used in behaviour management programs which refers to the guiding of an individual toward a desired goal through successive approximations. Shaping allows the individual to receive reinforcement for responses which ultimately lead to the goal.

sheltered workshops Work setting for persons with disabilities in which low productivity and low wages predominate.

Sign language is a language in its own right. It has its own grammar, morphology, syntax, location, semantics and pragmatics. Meaning is achieved through the combination of hand shape, location, movement pattern and intensity as well as facial and bodily expression. In both Australia and New Zealand, the language of the deaf community is recognised as a legitimate national language.

Signed English Is a direct translation of English into sign. Signed English is not a sign language.

simultaneous processing A cognitive process which enables information to be received, stored and retrieved as a whole unit of information (e.g., recognising a best friend's face in a portrait photograph).

skill An acquired aptitude or learned act (e.g., reading, riding a bicycle).

slow learners A term formerly used for individuals with learning difficulties.

social role valorisation A re-formulation of the normalisation principle.

social skills Skills that relate to human interactions (e.g., waiting for a turn, asking questions politely, responding when spoken to, shaking hands when appropriate).

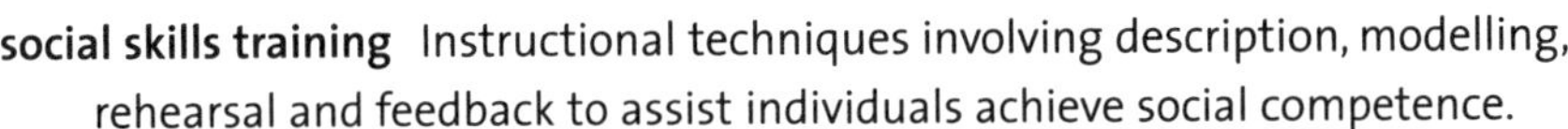

social skills training Instructional techniques involving description, modelling, rehearsal and feedback to assist individuals achieve social competence.

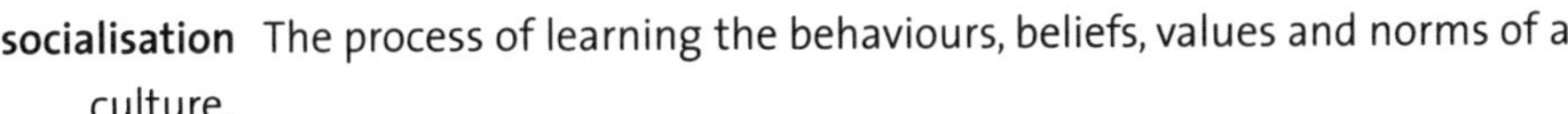

socialisation The process of learning the behaviours, beliefs, values and norms of a culture.

socio-economic status (SES) An individual's standing in society generally related to occupation. High SES is generally attributed to professional occupations, with low SES being attributed to semi- and unskilled jobs.

sound pressure level (SPL) The "absolute" scale of sound intensity measurement. Zero db SPL is the point at which no sound can be said to be occurring. It is below the threshold of normal human hearing.

spasm A sudden powerful involuntary contraction of a muscle.

spastic This term is used to describe one form of cerebral palsy characterised by increased muscle tone and difficulty in initiating movements.

spatial perception Ability to perceive the relationship of objects in space.

speech acts Categorisation of utterances by their function in the conversation (e.g., request for action; acknowledgment; disagreement) (also called conversational acts).

speech reading Is the use of all visual signs associated with speech including lip shapes and movements, facial expressions and body language to assist the person to understand what is being said.

speech therapy The diagnosis and treatment of speech and language problems by a trained professional. Speech therapists work in schools, hospitals and other settings where children and adults may attend or be referred.

speechreading The use of any non-auditory cues to understand speech. Its major component is lipreading but other cues such as gesture, facial expression and general context may also be used to aid in the interpretation of speech.

SPELD (Specific Learning Difficulties) The Federation for Specific Learning Disabilities (SPELD) is New Zealand's national body of groups concerned with individuals with learning difficulties. Also used for state groups in Australia (see AUSPELD).

spina bifida A group of congenital defects in which one or a number of spinal vertebrae do not fuse leaving a gap. In some instances, the spinal cord or its surrounding membrane may protrude through the gap.

standard deviation A statistical term referring to an index of variability of a distribution.

strategies Information processing techniques which are learned over time to assist in the organisation and intake of information received from the environment.

These include rehearsal, chunking, categorical clustering, visualisation and verbal elaboration.

subnormal A term which is not in common use in Australia or New Zealand which refers generally to an intellectual disability.

symptom An event, behavioural response or sign which is indicative of a disease or disorder.

syndrome A cluster or group of symptoms which is recognised as an entity (e.g., Down Syndrome is identified by the occurrence of a number of symptoms).

syntax The structures of language, sometimes synonymous with grammar. Terms such as clause and phrase belong here.

tactile dignity Meaning is able to be obtained through the tactual sense and, therefore, the meaning is not dependent upon the visual component.

tactile window The maximum data-gathering tactile input area to be covered and effectively processed at any one particular time.

TAFE Term for Colleges of Technical and Further Education in Australia. The New Zealand equivalent are the Polytechnic Colleges and Community Colleges.

talent/talented Talent corresponds to a level of performance in the systematically developed skills of at least one field of human activity that places subjects among the upper 15–20% of the same age members of the field.

teaching strategies Any of the numerous ways in which a teacher can present curriculum content or information to students.

token economies An element of behaviour modification where behaviour is managed by token reinforcement. Tokens are given as a reward for appropriate behaviour and later can be exchanged for material objects or privileges.

total communication Involves simultaneous presentation of speech (through speech reading and residual hearing) with manual communication providing a visual speech supplement (by signs and finger spelling). The emphasis is on the child having both an auditory (sound) and visual (sign) access to communication.

training centres A term common in the 1960s and 1970s for special schools for students with moderate to severe intellectual disabilities.

transition In an educational context, transition refers to the movement of a student from one learning context to another (e.g., from high school to employment, from a special class to an integrated, regular class setting).

translocation The rearrangement of genetic material within a chromosome or the attachment of a chromosome, or part of it, to another. (See text under Down syndrome)

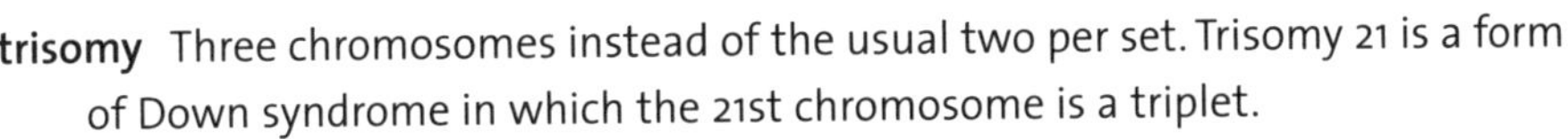

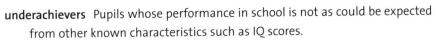

trisomy Three chromosomes instead of the usual two per set. Trisomy 21 is a form of Down syndrome in which the 21st chromosome is a triplet.

underachievers Pupils whose performance in school is not as could be expected from other known characteristics such as IQ scores.

verbal self-instruction A form of cognitive behaviour modification developed by Meichenbaum and his colleagues. This approach is based upon the premise that a teacher can instruct students to work through a series of self-instruction steps to facilitate learning and problem solving.

verbalisms Verbal unreality, or an inappropriate use of language which is outside the experience of the speaker.

vision impairment An umbrella term embracing all three categories educationally blind, partially sighted/low vision and visually limited.

visual efficiency A term used by Barraga (1983) to describe the degree of ease, comfort and minimum time which an individual needs to perform specific visual tasks.

visual functioning How people use whatever vision they might have.

vocalisation Any sound produced by the vocal cords whether this is speech or noise.

vocational training A program designed to teach the knowledge, skills and attitudes required for success on a particular employment position or a specific work task. Vocational training for students with an intellectual disability commonly occurs after leaving school. There are two philosophies in vocational training: one prescribes training before placing the individual in a work setting; the other prescribes placing the individual and training on the job for the specific job.

voluntary organisation Community groups, often started by parents, which provide services to, and advocate for, children and adults with disabilities.

Warnock Report Based on an inquiry in 1978 into special educational needs in the United Kingdom. It recommended the abolition of medical categories of handicap. The Education Act 1981 incorporated many of its recommendations.

Wechsler scale One of several tests of intelligence developed by David Wechsler. These include the Wechsler Adult Intelligence Scale—Revised (WAIS-R), the Wechsler Intelligence Scale for Children—Revised (WISC-R), and the Wechsler Preschool and Primary Scale of Intelligence—Revised (WPPSI-R).

zone of proximal development (ZPD) The point at which an individual is ready to progress to the next stage in learning through scaffolding and interactions with more capable peers. Participation in shared problem-solving within the ZPD can lead to a gain in understanding and skills that will prepare the learner to perform tasks independently.

Index